Ford Consul and Granada Owners Workshop Manual

by J H Haynes
Member of the Guild of Motoring Writers
and Ian Coomber

Models covered:

Consul and Granada, Saloon, Coupe and Estate,
2.0 litre, 2.5 litre and 3.0 litre, 1972 to August 1977

Covers manual and automatic transmission versions

ISBN 0 85696 371 2

© Haynes Publishing Group 1979

ABCDE 371
FGHIJ
KLMNO
PQR

All rights reserved. No part of this book may be reproduced or transmitted in any form or by any means, electronic or mechanical, including photocopying, recording or by any information storage or retrieval system, without permission in writing from the copyright holder.

Printed in England

**HAYNES PUBLISHING GROUP
SPARKFORD YEOVIL SOMERSET ENGLAND**
distributed in the USA by
**HAYNES PUBLICATIONS INC
861 LAWRENCE DRIVE
NEWBURY PARK
CALIFORNIA 91320
USA**

Acknowledgements

Thanks are due to the Ford Motor Company for the supply of technical information and certain illustrations. Castrol Limited provided lubrication data, and the Champion Sparking Plug Company supplied the illustrations showing the various spark plug conditions. The bodywork repair photographs used in this manual were provided by Lloyds Industries Limited who supply 'Turtle Wax', 'Dupli-color Holts', and other Holts range products.

Lastly, thanks are due to all of those people at Sparkford who helped in the production of this manual. Particularly Brian Horsfall and Les Brazier, who carried out the mechanical work and took the photographs respectively, John Austin and David Neilson who edited the text, and Stanley Randolph who planned the layout of each page.

About this manual

Its aim

The aim of this manual is to help you get the best value from your car. It can do so in several ways. It can help you decide what work must be done (even should you choose to get it done by a garage), provide information on routine maintenance and servicing, and give a logical course of action and diagnosis when random faults occur. However, it is hoped that you will make full use of the manual by tackling the work yourself. On simpler jobs it may even be quicker than booking the car into a garage, and having to go there twice, to leave and collect it. Perhaps most important, a lot of money can be saved by avoiding the costs the garage must charge to cover its labour and overheads.

The manual has drawings and descriptions to show the function of the various components so that their layout can be understood. Then the tasks are described and photographed in a step-by-step sequence so that even a novice can do the work.

Its arrangement

The manual is divided into twelve Chapters, each covering a logical sub-division of the vehicle. The Chapters are each divided into consecutively numbered Sections and the Sections into paragraphs (or sub-sections), with decimal numbers following on from the Section they are in, eg 5.1, 5.2, 5.3 etc.

It is freely illustrated, especially in those parts where there is a detailed sequence of operations to be carried out. There are two forms of illustration: figures and photographs. The figures are numbered in sequence with decimal numbers, according to their position in the Chapter: eg, Fig 6.4 is the 4th drawing/illustration in Chapter 6. Photographs are numbered (either individually or in related groups) the same as the Section or sub-section of the text where the operation they show is described.

There is an alphabetical index at the back of the manual as well as a contents list at the front.

Reference to the 'left' or 'right' of the vehicle are in the sense of a person in the driver's seat facing forwards.

Whilst every care is taken to ensure that the information in this manual is correct, no liability can be accepted by the authors or publishers for loss, damage or injury caused by any errors in, or omissions, from , the information given.

Contents

	Page
Introduction to the Ford Consul and Granada	4
Buying spare parts and vehicle identification numbers	5
Routine maintenance	8
Jacking and towing	10
Tools and working facilities	11
Chapter 1 Part A V4 and V6 engines	15
Chapter 1 Part B Four cylinder in-line engine	55
Chapter 2 Cooling system	86
Chapter 3 Carburation, fuel and exhaust systems	96
Chapter 4 Ignition system	115
Chapter 5 Clutch	124
Chapter 6 Manual gearbox and automatic transmission	128
Chapter 7 Propeller shaft	151
Chapter 8 Rear axle	155
Chapter 9 Braking system	163
Chapter 10 Electrical system	178
Chapter 11 Suspension and steering	218
Chapter 12 Bodywork and fittings	238
Chapter 13 Supplement	256
Metric conversion tables	262
Index	264

Introduction to the Ford Consul and Granada

Both the Consul and Granada were first introduced in March 1972. Sharing the same bodyshell, they were available with 2.5 or 3.0 litre V6 engines, with the option for the Consul only of a 2.0 litre V4 engine. The standard transmission is a 4-speed, fully synchromesh gearbox, with automatic transmission offered as an option. The Granada is the luxury model of the two and generally boasts several refinements over the Consul.

In October 1972 an Estate Car version of both models became available. April 1973 and January 1974 saw several minor improvements to trim, heating controls, etc.

In April 1974 the Granada Ghia was introduced to the range. This is a fully-equipped top-of-the-range version with automatic transmission and all other luxury options fitted as standard.

In September 1974 the Consul 2000 and 2000L saloons were fitted with a new 2.0 litre overhead camshaft (ohc) in-line engine in place of the earlier V4 engine. In April 1975 this new engine was made available on the Granada XL and GXL models. An estate car version of the Consul 2000L was also available and all models had suspension modifications.

October 1975 saw the discontinuation of the Consul range, and as a replacement, the Granada became available in 2000L and 2500L forms. The Granada 3000S replaced the Consul GT, and the Granada 2000/3000 GL versions replaced the Granada XL model.

In January 1976 the Ghia 2000 version became available and February of that year saw the Ford 'sonic idle' carburettor available on 2.0 litre engines. This is claimed to reduce fuel consumption by up to some 15%.

In August 1977 the range covered by this manual was discontinued, to be replaced by a new design range utilizing German-built engines.

Buying spare parts and vehicle identification numbers

Buying spare parts

Spare parts are available from many sources, for example: Ford garages, other garages and accessory shops, and motor factors. Our advice regarding spare part sources is as follows:

Officially appointed Ford garages - This is the best source of parts which are peculiar to your car and are otherwise not generally available (eg. complete cylinder heads, internal gearbox components, badges, interior trim etc). It is also the only place at which you should buy parts if your car is still under warranty - non-Ford components may invalidate the warranty. To be sure of obtaining the correct parts it will always be necessary to give the storeman your car's vehicle identification number, and if possible, to take the 'old' part along for positive identification. Remember that many parts are available on a factory exchange scheme - any parts returned should always be clean! It obviously makes good sense to go straight to the specialists on your car for this type of part for they are best equipped to supply them

Other garages and accessory shops - These are often very good places to buy materials and components needed for the maintenance of your car (eg, oil filters, spark plugs, bulbs, fan belts, oils and greases, touch-up paint, filler paste etc). They also sell general accessories, usually have convenient opening hours, charge lower prices and can often be found not far from home.

Motor factors - Good factors will stock all of the more important components which wear out relatively quickly (eg, clutch components, pistons, valves, exhaust systems, brake cylinders/pipes/hoses/seals/shoes and pads etc). Motor factors will often provide new or reconditioned components on a part exchange basis - this can save a considerable amount of money.

Vehicle identification numbers

Although many individual parts, and in some cases sub-assemblies, fit a number of different models, it is dangerous to assume that just because they look the same, they are the same. Differences are not always easy to detect except by serial numbers., Make sure, therefore, that the appropriate identity number for the model or sub-assembly is known and quoted when a spare part is ordered.

The vehicle identification plate is mounted on the left-hand side of the front body panel and may be seen once the bonnet is open.

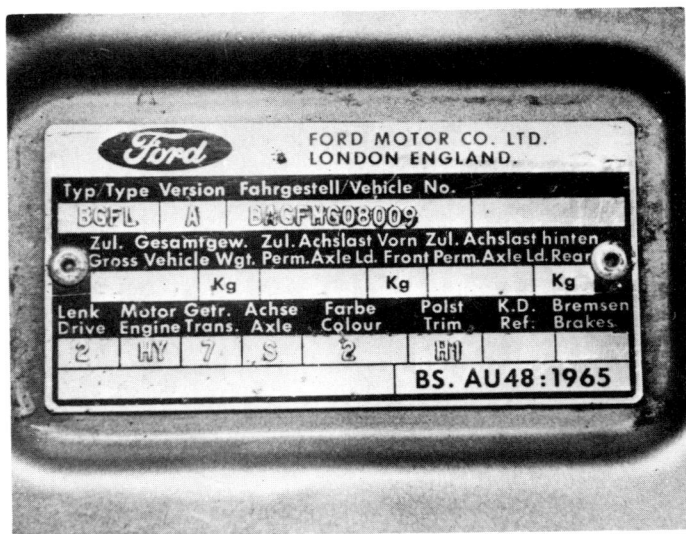

Vehicle identification plate

Check the engine oil level

Ford Granada Estate

Ford Consul Saloon

Routine maintenance

Maintenance is essential for ensuring safety, and desirable for the purpose of getting the best in terms of performance and economy from your car. Over the years the need for periodic lubrication - oiling, greasing and so on - has been drastically reduced, if not totally eliminated. This has unfortunately tended to lead some owners to think that because no such action is required, components either no longer exist, or will last forever. This is a serious delusion. It follows therefore that the largest initial element of maintenance is visual examination and a general sense of awareness. This may lead to repairs or renewals, but should help to avoid roadside breakdowns. Other neglect results in unreliability, increased running costs, more rapid wear and depreciation of the vehicle in general.

The maintenance instructions listed are those recommended by the manufacturer. They are supplemented by additional maintenance tasks proven to be necessary.

The additional tasks are indicated by an asterisk and are primarily of a preventive nature in that they will assist in eliminating the unexpected failure of a component (due to fair wear and tear).

Maintenance instructions are repeated in certain chapters where they form part of the repair and servicing procedures.

Weekly, before a long journey, or every 250 miles (400 km)

1 Remove the dipstick and check the engine oil level which should be up to the MAX mark. Top up the engine oil if necessary. On no account allow the oil to fall below the MIN mark on the dipstick (photos).
2 Check the tyre pressures with an accurate gauge and adjust as necessary. Make sure that the tyre walls and treads are free from damage. Remember that the tyre tread should have at least the minimum allowable depth specified by law (photo).
3 Check the battery electrolyte level and top up as necessary with distilled water. Make sure that the top of the battery is always kept clean and free from moisture (photo).
4 Refill the windscreen washer bottle with soft water. Add a special antifreeze sachet or methylated spirits in cold weather to prevent freezing (do *not* use ordinary coolant antifreeze). Check that the jets operate correctly (photo).
5 Remove the wheel trims and check all wheel nuts for tightness, but take care not to overtighten.
6 Check the level of coolant in the radiator when cold and top up if necessary with soft water. When antifreeze solution is being used top up with diluted antifreeze and not plain water (photo).
7 Check the level of hydraulic fluid in the brake master cylinder reservoir and top up if necessary. Take care not to spill any hydraulic fluid on the paintwork as it acts as a solvent (photo).
8 Systematically check the operation of all lights and indicators. Clean the light lenses and the windows.

Every 6000 miles (10 000 km) or 6 months

Complete the service items in the weekly service check plus:
1 Run the engine until it is hot and then place a container of at least 10 pints (5.58 litres) capacity under the engine sump drain plug. Unscrew and remove the drain plug and allow the oil to drain out for 10 minutes. Whilst this is being done change the oil filter as described in the next service operation. Clean the oil filler cap in petrol and shake dry. Refill the engine with the specified quantity of engine oil and clean off any oil which may have been spilt over the engine or its components. Run the engine and check the oil level. The interval between oil changes should be reduced in very hot or dusty conditions or during cool weather with much slow or stop/start driving. **Note**: *The engine sump drain plug washer should be renewed every time the plug is removed in order to avoid oil leaks.*
2 Unscrew the oil filter canister and discard it. Wipe the area around the filter location on the side of the cylinder block. Smear a little engine oil on the rubber O-ring located on the face of the new oil filter canister and screw on until it is hand-tight. Do not overtighten (photo).
3 Remove the spark plugs and inspect and clean them as described in Chapter 4.
4 Spring back the two clips and remove the distributor cap. Clean and adjust the distributor contact breaker points as described in Chapter 4 (photo).
5 Lift off the rotor arm. Apply a smear of grease to the cam surface. Apply a few drops of oil to the felt pad. Remove any excess oil or grease with a clean rag. Apply a few drops of oil through the hole in the contact breaker baseplate to lubricate the automatic timing control.
6 Check the ignition timing as described in Chapter 4. Wipe the distributor cap HT leads and top of the coil with a clean rag to remove traces of dust or oil.
7 Refer to Chapter 3 and check the carburettor idling and mixture settings.
8 If an emission control valve is fitted towards the rear of the carburettor, detach the hose and pull the valve out of its grommet. Dismantle the valve by removing the circlip and withdrawing the valve seal, valve and spring from the valve body. Thoroughly wash the components in petrol to remove any sludge. Reassemble the valve and refit the circlip. Push the valve back into its grommet and reconnect the hose.
9 Refer to Chapter 1 and adjust the valve clearances if necessary (photo).
10 The fan belt must be tight enough to drive the alternator without overloading the bearings, including the water pump and fan hub bearings. The method of adjusting the fan belt is described in Chapter 2. At the same time check the tightness of the alternator mountings (photo).
11 Refer to Chapter 10 and check the specific gravity of the electrolyte.
12 Wipe the top of the battery free from dust and moisture. Clean off any corrosion round battery terminals and clamps, and lightly smear such areas with a trace of petroleum jelly. Check that the earth connection is firm.
13 Generally inspect the radiator and heater hoses for signs of perishing and, if evident, fit new hoses. Check the tightness of all hose clips.
14 Lubricate the accelerator pedal pivot and linkage with a little engine oil.
15 Refer to Chapter 3 and clean the fuel pump filter.
16 Generally check the engine for signs of oil and water leaks and rectify as necessary.
17 *Manual gearbox only:* Wipe the area around the manual gearbox combined filler and level plug. Undo and remove the plug and check the oil level which, when correct, should be at the bottom of the threaded hole. Top up if necessary.
18 *Automatic transmission only:* With the car on a level surface and the transmission unit at normal operating temperature move the selector to the 'P' position and allow the engine to idle for two minutes. With the engine still idling in the 'P' position withdraw the dipstick, wipe it clean and refit it. Quickly withdraw it again and if necessary top up with the specified automatic transmission fluid. The difference between the LOW and FULL marks on the dipstick is 1 pint (0.59 litres) (photo).
19 Wipe the area around the rear axle combined filler and level plug.

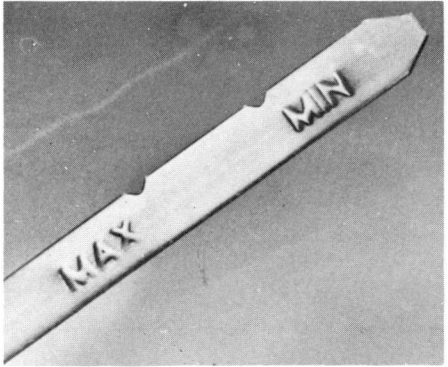
The dipstick showing max/min marks

Check the battery electrolyte level

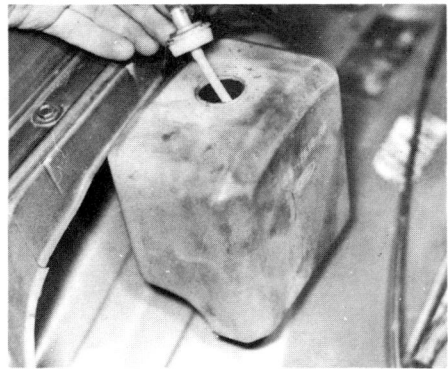
Check the windscreen washer bottle

Check the radiator coolant level

Check the hydraulic fluid level

Change the oil filter

Check the distributor contact breaker points clearance

Check the valve clearances

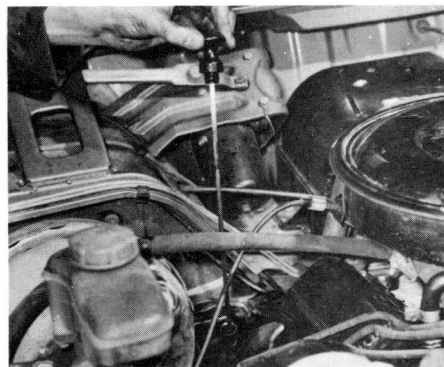
Check the transmission oil level

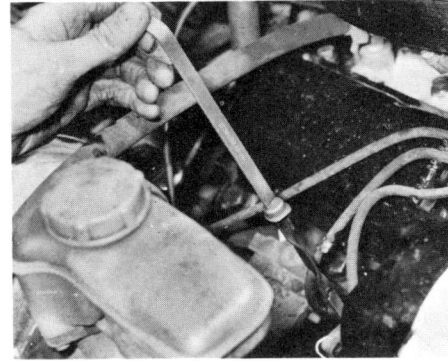
Check the engine oil level

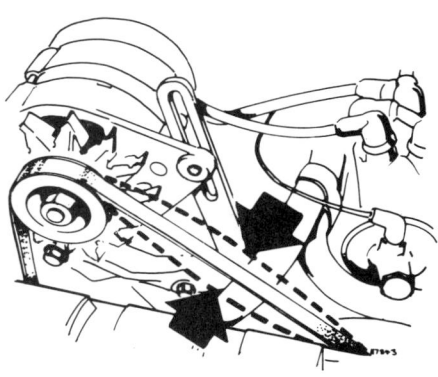
Fan belt adjustment

Check tyre pressures

Routine maintenance

Undo and remove the plug and check the oil level which, when correct, should be up to the bottom of the threaded hole. Top up if necessary (photo).
20 Refer to Chapter 9 and check the thickness of the front disc brake pads and rear drum brake shoe linings. Make sure that the adjusting mechanism is functioning correctly. Remove traces of dust from each brake unit.
21 Generally check all brake lines and flexible hoses for signs of leaks. Also inspect the calipers and wheel cylinders for signs of leaks. Rectify as necessary.
22 Inspect the exhaust system for signs of blowing or excessive rusting. Renew defective components as necessary. Check the tightness of exhaust manifold to downpipe securing nuts.
23 Generally check all suspension and steering linkages for signs of wear or accident damage. Rectify if necessary as described in Chapter 11.
24 Refer to Chapter 5 and check the adjustment of the clutch cable.
25 Check the operation of all controls, lights and instruments and rectify any fault found.
26 Lubricate all door locks, lock cylinders, bonnet safety catch pivot, door striker wedges, door check straps, hinges etc.
27 Refer to Chapter 9 and check the handbrake adjustment. Lubricate the handbrake linkage.
28 Check the seat belt webbing for signs of damage or wear and the anchorages for security
29 *Power assisted steering*: Check (where fitted) reservoir hydraulic fluid level and top up if necessary (photo).

The rear axle oil level/filler plug

Every 18 000 miles (30 000 km) or 18 months

Complete the service items in the 6000 mile service plus:
1 Refer to Chapter 3 and renew the air cleaner element.
2 *Power assisted steering*: Refer to Chapter 11 and apply grease to the power steering cylinder.
3 Systematically check all suspension and steering attachments for security.
*4 Wash the bodywork and chromium fittings and clean out the interior of the car. Wax polish the bodywork including all chromium and bright metal trim. Force wax polish into any joints in the bodywork to prevent rust formation.
*5 Check all fuel lines and union joints for leaks. Rectify any leaks found.
*6 If it is wished, change over the tyres to equalise wear.
*7 Lubricate the washer around the wiper spindles with several drops of glycerine. Fit new windscreen wiper blades.
*8 Steam clean the underside of the body and clean the engine and gearbox exterior as well as the whole of the front compartment.

Every 36 000 miles (60 000 km) or 3 years

1 Refer to Chapter 11 and clean and repack the front wheel bearings.
2 Completely drain the brake hydraulic fluid from the system. All seals and flexible hoses throughout the braking system should be examined and preferably renewed. The working surfaces of the master

Check power steering hydraulic fluid level

cylinder, wheel cylinders and caliper pistons should be inspected for signs of wear or scoring and new parts fitted as considered necessary. Refill the hydraulic system with fresh hydraulic fluid.

Jacking and towing

The jack supplied with the car was designed solely for wheel changing in the event of a puncture or roadside emergency.
If underbody repairs are to be carried out use a hydraulic, screw or trolley jack positioned under the body side, crossmember or suspension wishbones. Always supplement the jack with axle stands or at least solid blocks.
If the car is to be towed in an emergency, and it is fitted with automatic transmission, the following points should be observed. Select 'N', keep the speed down to a maximum of 30 mph (48 kph), and restrict the towing distance to 15 miles (24 km). If the automatic transmission is at fault, disconnect the driveshaft before towing.
In all cases ensure that the steering lock is not engaged before towing!

Tools and working facilities

Introduction

A selection of good tools is a fundamental requirement for anyone contemplating the maintenance and repair of a motor vehicle. For the owner who does not possess any, their purchase will prove a considerable expense, offsetting some of the savings made by doing-it-yourself. However, provided that the tools purchased are of good quality, they will last for many years and prove an extremely worthwhile investment.

To help the average owner to decide which tools are needed to carry out the various tasks detailed in this manual, we have compiled three lists of tools under the following headings: *Maintenance and minor repair*, *Repair and overhaul*, and *Special*. The newcomer to practical mechanics should start off with the *Maintenance and minor repair* tool kit and confine himself to the simpler jobs around the vehicle. Then, as his confidence and experience grows, he can undertake more difficult tasks, buying extra tools as, and when, they are needed. In this way, a *Maintenance and minor repair* tool kit can be built-up into a *Repair and overhaul* tool kit over a considerable period of time without any major cash outlays. The experienced do-it-yourselfer will have a tool kit good enough for most repair and overhaul procedures and will add tools from the *Special* category when he feels the expense is justified by the amount of use to which these tools will be put.

It is obviously not possible to cover the subject of tools fully here. For those who wish to learn more about tools and their use there is a book entitled *How to Choose and Use Car Tools* available from the publishers of this manual.

Maintenance and minor repair tool kit

The tools given in this list should be considered as a minimum requirement if routine maintenance, servicing and minor repair operations are to be undertaken. We recommend the purchase of combination spanners (ring one end, open-ended the other); although more expensive than open-ended ones, they do give the advantages of both types of spanner.

Combination spanners - $\frac{7}{16}$, $\frac{1}{2}$, $\frac{9}{16}$, $\frac{5}{8}$, $\frac{11}{16}$, $\frac{3}{4}$, $\frac{13}{16}$, $\frac{15}{16}$ in AF
Combination spanners - 5, 6, 7, 8, 9, 10, 11, & 12 mm
Adjustable spanner - 9 inch
Engine sump/gearbox/rear axle drain plug key (where applicable)
Spark plug spanner (with rubber insert)
Spark plug gap adjustment tool
Set of feeler gauges
Brake adjuster spanner (where applicable)
Brake bleed nipple spanner
Screwdriver - 4 in long x $\frac{1}{4}$ in dia (flat blade)
Screwdriver - 4 in long x $\frac{1}{4}$ in dia (cross blade)
Combination pliers - 6 inch
Hacksaw, junior
Tyre pump
Tyre pressure gauge
Grease gun (where applicable)
Oil can
Fine emery cloth (1 sheet)
Wire brush (small)
Funnel (medium size)

Repair and overhaul tool kit

These tools are virtually essential for anyone undertaking any major repairs to a motor vehicle, and are additional to those given in the *Maintenance and minor repair* list. Included in this list is a comprehensive set of sockets. Although these are expensive they will be found invaluable as they are so versatile - particularly if various drives are included in the set. We recommend the $\frac{1}{2}$ in square-drive type, as this can be used with most proprietary torque wrenches. If you cannot afford a socket set, even bought piecemeal, then inexpensive tubular box spanners are a useful alternative.

The tools in this list will occasionally need to be supplemented by tools from the *Special* list.

Sockets (or box spanners) to cover range in previous list
Reversible ratchet drive (for use with sockets)
Extension piece, 10 inch (for use with sockets)
Universal joint (for use with sockets)
Torque wrench (for use with sockets)
'Mole' wrench - 8 inch
Ball pein hammer
Soft-faced hammer, plastic or rubber
Screwdriver - 6 in long x $\frac{5}{16}$ in dia (flat blade)
Screwdriver - 2 in long x $\frac{5}{16}$ in square (flat blade)
Screwdriver - 1$\frac{1}{2}$ in long x $\frac{1}{4}$ in dia (cross blade)
Screwdriver - 3 in long x $\frac{1}{8}$ in dia (electricians)
Pliers - electricians side cutters
Pliers - needle nosed
Pliers - circlip (internal and external)
Cold chisel - $\frac{1}{2}$ inch
Scriber (this can be made by grinding the end of a broken hacksaw blade)
Scraper (this can be made by flattening and sharpening one end of a piece of copper pipe)
Centre punch
Pin punch
Hacksaw
Valve grinding tool
Steel rule/straight edge
Allen keys
Selection of files
Wire brush (large)
Axle stands
Jack (strong scissor or hydraulic type)

Special tools

The tools in this list are those which are not used regularly, are expensive to buy, or which need to be used in accordance with their manufacturer's instructions. Unless relatively difficult mechanical jobs are undertaken frequently, it will not be economic to buy many of these tools. Where this is the case, you could consider clubbing together with friends (or a motorists club) to make a joint purchase, or borrowing the tools against a deposit from a local garage or tool hire specialist.

The following list contains only those tools and instruments freely available to the public, and not those special tools produced by the

Tools and working facilities

vehicle manufacturer specifically for its dealer network. You will find occasional references to these manufacturer's special tools in the text of this manual. Generally, an alternative method of doing the job without the vehicle manufacturer's special tool is given. However, sometimes, there is no alternative to using them. Where this is the case and the relevant tool cannot be bought or borrowed you will have to entrust the work to a franchised garage

Valve spring compressor
Piston ring compressor
Balljoint separator
Universal hub/bearing puller
Impact screwdriver
Micrometer and/or vernier gauge
Carburettor flow balancing device (where applicable)
Dial gauge
Stroboscopic timing light
Dwell angle meter/tachometer
Universal electrical multi-meter
Cylinder compression gauge
Lifting tackle
Trolley jack
Light with extension lead

Last but not least always keep a supply of old newspapers and clean, lint-free rags available and try to keep any working areas as clean as possible.

Buying tools

For practically all tools, a tool factor is the best source since he will have a very comprehensive range compared with the average garage or accessory shop. Having said that, accessory shops often offer excellent quality tools at discount prices, so it pays to shop around.

Remember, you don't have to buy the most expensive items on the shelf, but it is always advisable to steer clear of the very cheap tools. There are plenty of good tools around at reasonable prices, so ask the proprietor or manager of the shop for advice before making a purchase.

Care and maintenance of tools

Having purchased a reasonable tool kit, it is necessary to keep the tools in a clean serviceable condition. After use, always wipe off any dirt, grease and metal particles using a clean, dry cloth, before putting the tools away. Never leave them lying around after they have been used. A simple tool rack on the garage or workshop wall, for items such as screwdrivers and pliers is a good idea. Store all normal spanners and sockets in a metal box. Any measuring instruments, gauges, meters, etc., must be carefully stored where they cannot be damaged or become rusty.

Take a little care when tools are used. Hammer heads inevitably become marked and screwdrivers lose the keen edge on their blades from time-to-time. A little timely attention with emery cloth or a file will soon restore items like this to a good serviceable finish.

Use of tools

Throughout this book various phrases describing techniques are used, such as:
'Drive out the bearing.'
'Undo the flange bolts evenly and diagonally.'

When two parts are held together by a number of bolts round their edge, these must be tightened to draw the parts down together flat. They must be slackened evenly to prevent the component warping. Initially the bolts should be put in finger-tight only. Then they should be tightened gradually, at first only a turn each; and diagonally, doing the one opposite that tightened first, then one to a side, followed by another opposite that, and so on. The second time each bolt is tightened only half a turn should be given. The third time round, only a quarter of a turn is given to each, and this is kept up till tight. The reverse sequence is used to slacken them.

If any part has to be driven, such as a ball bearing out of its housing, without a proper press, it can be done with a hammer provided a few rules for use of a hammer are remembered. Always keep the component being driven straight so it will not jam. Shield whatever is being hit from damage by the hammer. Soft headed hammers are available. A drift can be used, or if the item being hit is soft, use wood. Aluminium is very easily damaged. Steel is a bit better. Hard steel, such as a bearing race, is very strong. Something threaded at the end must be protected by fitting a nut. But do not hammer the nut: the threads will tear.

If levering items with a makeshift arrangement, such as a screwdriver, irretrievable damage can be done. Be sure the lever rests either on something that does not matter, or put in padding. Burrs can be filed off afterwards. But indentations are there for good, and can cause leaks.

When holding something in a vice, the jaws must go on a part that is strong. If the indentation from the jaw teeth will matter, then lead or fibre jaw protectors must be used. Hollow sections are liable to be crushed.

Nuts that will not undo will sometimes move if the spanner handle is extended with another. But only extend a ring spanner, not an open jaw one. A hammer blow either to the spanner, or the bolt, may jump it out of its contact: the bolt locally welds itself in place. In extreme cases the nut will undo if driven off with drift and hammer. When reassembling such bolts, tighten them normally, not by the method needed to undo them.

For pressing things, such as a sleeve bearing into its housing, a vice or an electric drill stand makes a good press. Pressing tools to hold each component can be arranged by using such things as socket spanners, or short lengths of steel water pipe. Long bolts with washers can be used to draw things into place rather than pressing them.

There are often several ways of doing something. If stuck, stop and think. Special tools can readily be made out of odd bits of scrap. Accordingly, at the same time as building up a tool kit, collect useful bits of steel.

Normally all nuts or bolts have some locking arrangement. The most common is a spring washer. There are tab washers that are bent up. Castellated nuts have split pins. Self-locking nuts have special crowns that resist shaking loose. Self-locking nuts should not be re-used, as the self-locking action is weakened as soon as they have been loosened at all. Tab washers should only be re-used when they can be bent over in a new place. If you find a nut without any locking arrangement, check what it is meant to have.

Working facilities

Not to be forgotten when discussing tools, is the workshop itself. If anything more than routine maintenance is to be carried out, some form of suitable working area becomes essential.

It is appreciated that many an owner mechanic is forced by circumstances to remove an engine or similar item, without the benefit of a garage or workshop. Having done this, any repairs should always be done under the cover of a roof.

Wherever possible, any dismantling should be done on a clean flat workbench or table at a suitable working height.

Any workbench needs a vice: one with a jaw opening of 4 in (100 mm) is suitable for most jobs. As mentioned previously, some clean dry storage space is also required for tools, as well as the lubricants, cleaning fluids, touch-up paints and so on which become necessary.

Another item which may be required, and which has a much more general usage, is an electric drill with a chuck capacity of at least $\frac{5}{16}$ in (8 mm). This, together with a good range of twist drills, is virtually essential for fitting accessories such as wing mirrors and reversing lights.

Spanner jaw gap comparison table

Jaw gap (in.)	Spanner size
0.250	$\frac{1}{4}$ in AF
0.275	7 mm AF
0.312	$\frac{5}{16}$ in AF
0.315	8 mm AF
0.340	11/32 in AF; $\frac{1}{8}$ in Whitworth
0.354	9 mm AF
0.375	$\frac{3}{8}$ in AF
0.393	10 mm AF
0.433	11 mm AF
0.437	$\frac{7}{16}$ in AF
0.445	$\frac{3}{16}$ in Whitworth; $\frac{1}{4}$ in BSF
0.472	12 mm AF
0.500	$\frac{1}{2}$ in AF
0.512	13 mm AF
0.525	$\frac{1}{4}$ in Whitworth; $\frac{5}{16}$ in BSF

Jaw gap (in.)	Spanner size	Jaw gap (in.)	Spanner size
0.551	14 mm AF	1.181	30 mm AF
0.562	$\frac{9}{16}$ in AF	1.200	$\frac{11}{16}$ in Whitworth; $\frac{3}{4}$ in BSF
0.590	15 mm AF	1.250	$1\frac{1}{4}$ in AF
0.600	$\frac{5}{16}$ in Whitworth; $\frac{3}{8}$ in BSF	1.259	32 mm AF
0.625	$\frac{5}{8}$ in AF	1.300	$\frac{3}{4}$ in Whitworth; $\frac{7}{8}$ in BSF
0.629	16 mm AF	1.312	$1\frac{5}{16}$ in AF
0.669	17 mm AF	1.390	$\frac{13}{16}$ in Whitworth; $\frac{15}{16}$ in BSF
0.687	$\frac{11}{16}$ in AF	1.417	36 mm AF
0.708	18 mm AF	1.437	$1\frac{7}{16}$ in AF
0.710	$\frac{3}{8}$ in Whitworth; $\frac{7}{16}$ in BSF	1.480	$\frac{7}{8}$ in Whitworth; 1 in BSF
0.748	19 mm AF	1.500	$1\frac{1}{2}$ in AF
0.750	$\frac{3}{4}$ in AF	1.574	40 mm AF; $\frac{15}{16}$ in Whitworth
0.812	$\frac{13}{16}$ in AF	1.614	41 mm AF
0.820	$\frac{7}{16}$ in Whitworth; $\frac{1}{2}$ in BSF	1.625	$1\frac{5}{8}$ in AF
0.866	22 mm AF	1.670	1 in Whitworth; $1\frac{1}{8}$ in BSF
0.875	$\frac{7}{8}$ in AF	1.687	$1\frac{11}{16}$ in AF
0.920	$\frac{1}{2}$ in Whitworth; $\frac{9}{16}$ in BSF	1.811	46 mm AF
0.937	$\frac{15}{16}$ in AF	1.812	$1\frac{13}{16}$ in AF
0.944	24 mm AF	1.860	$1\frac{1}{8}$ in Whitworth; $1\frac{1}{4}$ in BSF
1.000	1 in AF	1.875	$1\frac{7}{8}$ in AF
1.010	$\frac{9}{16}$ in Whitworth; $\frac{5}{8}$ in BSF	1.968	50 mm AF
1.023	26 mm AF	2.000	2 in AF
1.062	$1\frac{1}{16}$ in AF; 27 mm AF	2.050	$1\frac{1}{4}$ in Whitworth; $1\frac{3}{8}$ in BSF
1.100	$\frac{5}{8}$ in Whitworth; $\frac{11}{16}$ in BSF	2.165	55 mm AF
1.125	$1\frac{1}{8}$ in AF	2.362	60 mm AF

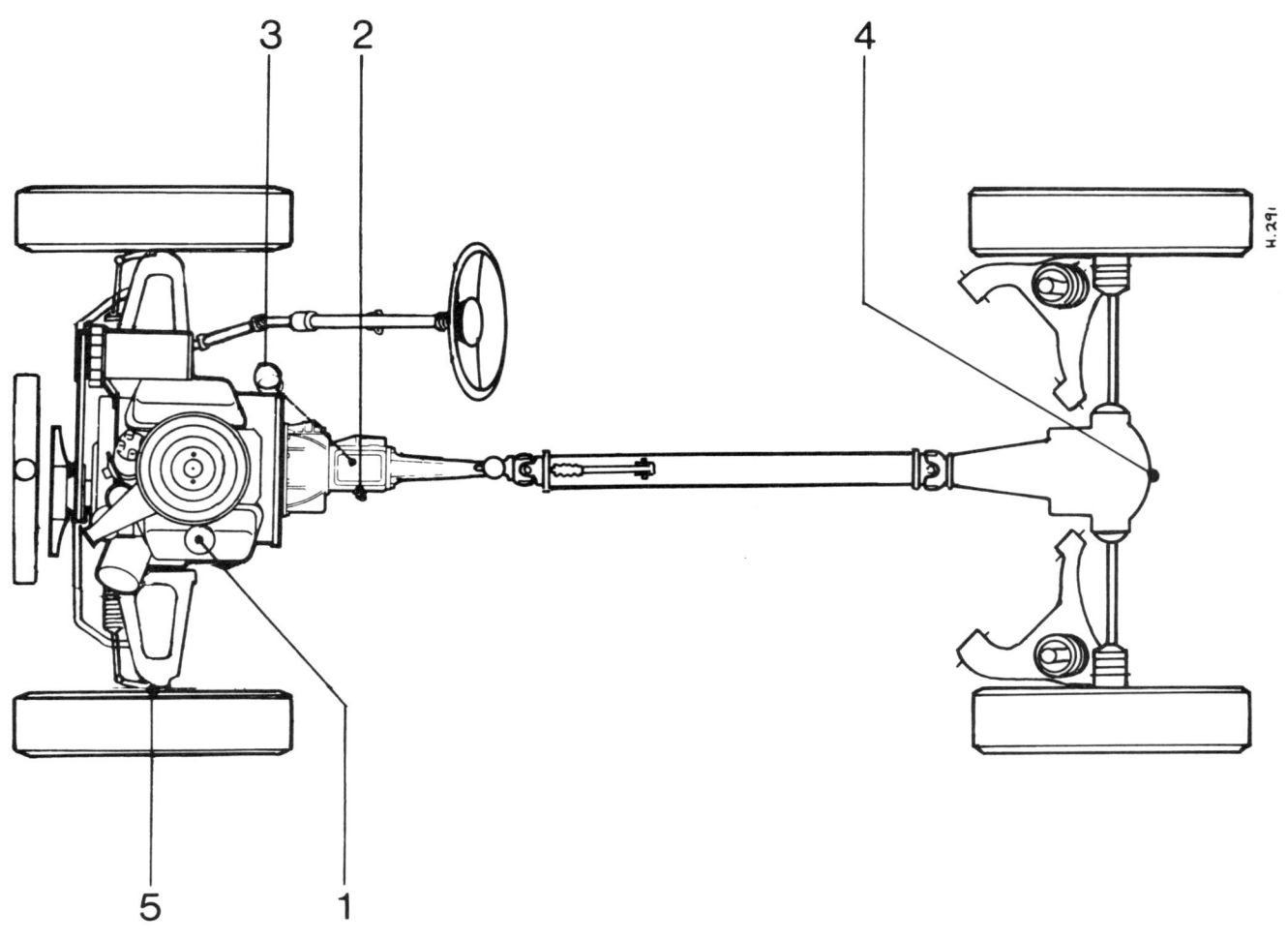

Recommended lubricants and fluids

Component	Type of lubricant or fluid	Castrol product
Engine sump (1)	Multigrade engine oil	**GTX**
Manual gearbox (2)	SAE 80EP oil	**Castrol Hypoy Light**
Automatic transmission (3)	Fluid to Ford Specification M2C33F	**Castrol TQF**
Rear axle (4)	SAE 90EP oil	**Castrol Hypoy**
Front wheel hub bearings (5)	Lithium based grease	**Castrol LM grease**
Distributor contact breaker cam and battery terminals	Petroleum jelly	
Brake fluid reservoir	Hydraulic fluid (SAE J1703C) to Ford specification ESEA–1001A	**Castrol Girling Universal Brake and Clutch Fluid**
Power steering fluid reservoir	Hydraulic fluid to Ford specification SQ–M2C–9007–AA or ESWM–2C33–F	
Antifreeze	Fluid to Ford specification M97B18–C	**Castrol antifreeze**
Locks, hinges, pivots etc	General purpose light oil	**Castrol Everyman**

The above are general recommendations only. Lubrication requirements vary from territory to territory and depend on vehicle usage. If in doubt consult the operator's handbook supplied with the vehicle, or your nearest Ford dealer.

Chapter 1 Part A V4 and V6 engines

Contents

Balance shaft (V4) – removal	26
Camshaft and camshaft bearings – examination and renovation	37
Camshaft – removal	18
Connecting rods and gudgeon pins – examination and renovation	36
Crankcase ventilation system – routine maintenance	28
Crankshaft – examination and renovation	32
Crankshaft (main) bearings and connecting rod (big-end) bearings – examination and renovation	33
Crankshaft pulley wheel – removal	13
Crankshaft rear oil seal – removal	23
Cylinder bores – examination and renovation	34
Cylinder heads and piston crowns – examination and renovation	12
Cylinder heads – dismantling of rocker gear valves and springs	11
Cylinder heads – removal with engine in car	10
Cylinder heads – removal with engine out of car	9
Engine components – examination for wear	31
Engine dismantling – general	8
Engine – initial start-up after overhaul or major repair	58
Engine reassembly – final ancillary components	55
Engine reassembly – general	44
Engine reassembly (V4) – balance shaft, camshaft, crankshaft and oil pump	45
Engine reassembly (V4) – pistons, piston rings, connecting rods, big-end bearings, end plates, timing gear and front cover	46
Engine reassembly (V4) – rear plate, crankshaft pulley wheel, sump and flywheel	47
Engine reassembly (V4) – valve gear, cylinder heads and inlet manifold	48
Engine reassembly (V6) – crankshaft oil seals, oil pump, camshaft, timing gears, end plate, front and rear cover and crankshaft pulley	51
Engine reassembly(V6) – crankshaft, pistons, piston rings, connecting rods and big-end bearings	50
Engine reassembly (V6) – sump and flywheel	52
Engine reassembly (V6) – valve gear, cylinder heads and inlet manifold	53
Engine – refitting without transmission	56
Engine – refitting with transmission	57
Engine removal – automatic transmission models	7
Engine – removal with manual gearbox	6
Engine – removal without transmission	5
Fault diagnosis – engine	59
Flywheel or intermediate plate (automatic transmission) – removal	14
Flywheel ring gear – examination and renovation	41
General description	1
Gudgeon pins – removal	22
Lubrication and crankcase ventilation system – description	27
Main bearings and crankshaft (V4) – removal	24
Main bearings and crankshaft (V6) – removal	25
Major operations with engine in place	2
Major operations with engine removed	3
Methods of engine removal	4
Oil filter – removal and refitting	30
Oil pump – overhaul	29
Oil pump – removal	19
Pistons and piston rings – examination and renovation	35
Pistons, connecting rods and big-end bearings – removal	20
Piston rings – removal	21
Rocker gear – examination and renovation	43
Sump – removal	15
Tappets – examination and renovation	38
Tappets – removal	12
Timing gear and cover (V4) – removal	16
Timing gear and cover (V6) – removal	17
Timing gears – examination and renovation	40
Valves and valve seats – examination and renovation	39
Valve rocker clearances (V4) – adjustment	49
Valve rocker clearances (V6) – adjustment	54

Specifications

General
Type:
- 2 litre .... 4 cylinder, OHV, 60° 'V'
- 2.5 and 3 litre .... 6 cylinder, OHV, 60° 'V'

Bore .... 3.6878 in (93.670 mm)

Stroke:
- 2.5 litre .... 2.376 in (60.35 mm)
- 2 and 3 litre .... 2.851 in (72.42 mm)

Cubic capacity:
- 2 litre .... 121.8 cu in (1996 cc)
- 2.5 litre .... 152.2 cu in (2495 cc)
- 3 litre .... 182.7 cu in (2994 cc)

Compression ratio:
- 2 and 3 litre - High .... 8.9 : 1
- 2.5 litre - High .... 9.1 : 1
- All - Low .... 7.7 : 1

Compression pressures:
- Low compression .... 140 to 160 lb/in² (9.843 – 11.25 kg/cm²) at cranking speed
- High compression .... 160 to 180 lb/in² (11.25 – 12.66 kg/cm²) at cranking speed

Chapter 1 Part A V4 and V6 engines

Maximum brake horsepower (gross)
    2 litre .... 94 at 5200 rpm (HC)
    2.5 litre .... 137 at 5500 rpm (HC)
    3 litre .... 157 at 5200 rpm (HC)
Idling speed .... See Specifications in Chapter 3
Firing order:
    2 litre .... 1(R), 3(L), 4(L), 2(R)
    2.5 and 3 litre .... 1(R), 4(L), 2(R), 5(L), 3(R), 6(L)
Location of No. 1 cylinder .... Right-hand bank next to radiator

Balance shaft

Material .... Special Ford cast iron alloy
Drive .... Gear
Bearing type .... Steel back, white metal bushes
Journal diameter:
    Front .... 2.6250–2.6258 in (66.675–66.695 mm)
    Rear .... 2.2500–2.2508 in (57.150–57.170 mm)
Bearing inside diameter:
    Front .... 2.6276–2.6283 in (66.741–66.759 mm)
    Rear .... 2.2526–2.2533 in (57.216–57.235 mm)
Bearing clearance .... 0.0018–0.0033 in (0.046–0.084 mm)
Endfloat .... 0.005–0.010 in (0.13–0.25 mm)
Thrust plate thickness .... 0.180–0.182 in (4.57–4.623 mm)

Camshaft

Material .... Special Ford cast iron alloy
Drive .... Gear
Bearing type .... Steel back, white metal bushes
Journal diameter:
    2 Litre:
        Front .... 1.8737–1.8745 in (47.59–47.67 mm)
        Centre .... 1.8137–1.8145 in (46.07–46.15 mm)
        Rear .... 1.7537–1.7545 in (44.54–44.56 mm)
    2.5 and 3 litre:
        Front .... 1.8737–1.8745 in (47.59–47.67 mm)
        No.2 Intermediate .... 1.8137–1.8145 in (46.07–46.15 mm)
        No.3 Intermediate .... 1.7537–1.7545 in (44.54–44.56 mm)
        Rear .... 1.7387–1.7395 in (44.16–44.18 mm)
Bearing inside diameter:
    2 litre:
        Front .... 1.8753–1.8763 in (47.63–47.66 mm)
        Intermediate .... 1.8153–1.8163 in (46.36–46.39 mm)
        Rear .... 1.7553–1.7563 in (44.58–44.60 mm)
    2.5 and 3 litre:
        Front .... 1.8753–18763 in (47.63–47.66 mm)
        No. 2 Intermediate .... 1.8153–1.8163 in (46.36–46.39 mm)
        No. 3 Intermediate .... 1.7553–1.7563 in (44.58–44.60 mm)
        Rear .... 1.7403–1.7413 in (44.22–44.24 mm)
Bearing length:
    Front and Rear .... 0.88 in (22.4 mm)
    Centre or Intermediate .... 1.1 in (27.9mm)
Bearing clearance .... 0.0008–0.0026 in (0.023–0.066 mm)
Endfloat .... 0.003–0.007 in (0.076–0.178 mm)
Thrust plate thickness .... 0.210–0.212 in (5.33–5.38 mm)
Cam lift:
    Inlet .... 0.25465 in (6.4681 mm)
    Exhaust .... 0.26065 in (6.6205 mm)
Cam heel to toe dimension:
    Inlet .... 1.3372–1.3462 in (33.96–34.19 mm)
    Exhaust .... 1.3432–1.3522 in (34.12–34.35 mm)

Connecting rods and big-end bearings

Type .... H-section steel forging
Weight .... 706 to 714 grams
Length between centres .... 5.641–5.643 in (143.28–143.32 mm)
Big-end bearings .... Steel back copper/lead liners
Big-end diameter .... 2.5210–2.5215 in (64.033–64.047 mm)
Bearing liner wall thickness .... 0.07145–0.0717 in (1.8149–1.8212 mm)
Undersize bearings available .... 0.002 in (0.051 mm), 0.010 in (0.254 mm), 0.020 in (0.508 mm)
                                                        0.030 in (0.76 mm), 0.040 in (1.02 mm) on ID
Crankpin to bearing clearance .... 0.0012–0.003 in (0.030–0.08 mm)
Endfloat on crankpin .... 0.004–0.010 in (0.102–0.254 mm)
Small end diameter .... 0.9358–0.9362 (23.769–23.779 mm)

Crankshaft and main bearings
Material .... Nodular Graphite Cast Iron
Main bearing journal diameter:
    Blue .... 2.5006–2.5010 in (63.515–63.525 mm)
    Red .... 2.5010–2.5014 in (63.525–63.536 mm)
    Green .... 2.4906–2.4910 in (63.261–63.271 mm)
    Yellow .... 2.4910–2.4914 in (63.271–63.282 mm)
Regrind diameters:

Undersizes	Block Grade	Journal Diameter
0.010 in (0.25 mm)	Red	2.4902–2.4906 in (63.251–63.261 mm)
	Blue	2.4906–2.4910 in (63.261–63.271 mm)
0.020 in (0.51 mm)	Red or Yellow	2.4802–2.4806 in (62.997–63.007 mm)
	Blue or Green	2.4806–2.4810 (63.007–63.017 mm)
0.030 in (0.76 mm)	Red or Yellow	2.4702–2.4706 in (62.743–62.753 mm)
	Blue or Green	2.4706–2.4710 (62.753–62.763 mm)
0.040 in (1.02 mm)	Red	2.4602–2.4606 in (62.489–62.499 mm)
	Blue	2.4606–2.4610 in (62.499–62.509 mm)

Main journal length:
  2 litre:
    Front .... 1.00–0.95 in (25.40–24.13 mm)
    Centre .... 1.061–1.059 in (26.95–26.90 mm)
    Rear .... 1.09–1.06 in (27.7–26.9 mm)
  2.5 and 3 litre:
    Front .... 1.00–0.95 in (25.40–24.13 mm)
    No. 2 Intermediate .... 1.061–1.059 in (26.95–26.90 mm)
    No. 3 Intermediate .... 1.07–1.05 in (27.18–26.67 mm)
    Rear .... 1.09–1.06 in (27.7–26.9 mm)
Main bearings .... Steel back copper/lead
Main bearing liner wall thickness:
    Red .... 0.08155–0.08180 in (2.0714–2.0777 mm)
    Blue .... 0.08195–0.08220 in (2.0816–2.0879 mm)
    Yellow .... 0.09405–0.09430 in (2.3889–2.3952 mm)
    Green .... 0.09445–0.09470 in (2.3991–2.4054 mm)
Main bearing clearance .... 0.0005–0.0018 in (0.013–0.046 mm)
Undersize bearing clearance:
    Std OD .... 0.010 in (0.25 mm)
                                      0.020 in (0.51 mm)
                                      0.030 in (0.76 mm)
                                      0.040 in (1.02 mm)
    0.015 in (0.381 mm) o/s on OD .... Std ID } Graded
                                      0.010 in (0.25 mm) }
                                      0.020 in (0.51 mm)
                                      0.030 in (0.76 mm)
Crankpin journal diameter .... 2.3756–2.3764 in (60.340–60.361 mm)
Crankpin journal length .... 0.838–0.842 in (2.128–2.139 mm)
Crankpin journal fillet radius .... 0.080–0.094 in (2.03–2.39 mm)
Crankshaft endfloat .... 0.003–0.011 in (0.008–0.28 mm)
Thrust washers .... Steel back copper/lead or aluminium/tin split washers
Thrust washer thickness .... 0.091–0.093 in (2.31–2.36 mm)
Oversize thrust washers available .... 0.0025 in (0.064 mm), 0.005 in (0.13 mm), 0.0075 in (0.191 mm), 0.010 in (0.25 mm)
Spigot bearing bore .... 1.3766–1.3778 in (34.966–34.996 mm)

Cylinder block
Type .... Cylinder cast integral with top half of crankcase
Material .... Ford cast alloy iron
Angle of 'V' .... 60°
Standard cylinder bore diameter .... Graded
  Grade:
    1 .... 3.6869–3.6872 in (93.647–93.655 mm)
    2 .... 3.6872–3.6875 in (93.655–93.663 mm)
    3 .... 3.6875–3.6878 in (93.663–93.670 mm)
    4 .... 3.6878–3.6881 in (93.670–93.678 mm)
    5 .... 3.6881–3.6884 in (93.678–93.686 mm)
    6 .... 3.6884–3.6887 in (93.686–93.693 mm)
Grading point .... $1\frac{7}{8}$ in (47.63 mm) from block face on thrust plate
Cylinder liners available .... Std and 0.020 in (0.51 mm) o/s on OD
Cylinder liner:
    ID .... 3.652–3.657 in (92.761–92.888 mm)
    OD .... 3.8345–3.8355 in (97.396–97.412 mm) Std
Bore for cylinder liners .... 3.8315–3.8325 in (97.320–97.340 mm) Std
Bore for balance shaft bushes:
    Front .... 2.8125–2.8137 in (71.438–71.468 mm)
    Rear .... 2.4375–2.4387 in (61.913–61.943 mm)

Bore for camshaft bushes:
  2 litre:
    Front ... 2.0400–2.0416 in (51.816–51.857 mm)
    Centre ... 1.9800–1.9816 in (50.292–50.333 mm)
    Rear ... 1.9200–1.9216 in (48.768–48.809 mm)
  2.5 and 3 litre:
    Front ... 2.0400–2.0416 in (51.816–51.857 mm)
    No. 2 Intermediate ... 1.9800–1.9816 in (50.292–50.333 mm)
    No. 3 Intermediate ... 1.9200–1.9216 in (48.768–48.908 mm)
    Rear ... 1.9050–1.9066 in (47.890–47.430 mm)
Bore for main bearing liners:
  Red ... 2.6654–2.6658 in (67.701–67.711 mm)
  Blue ... 2.6658–2.6662 in (67.711–67.721 mm)
  Yellow ... 2.6804–2.6808 in (68.082–68.092 mm)
  Green ... 2.6808–2.6812 in (68.092–68.102 mm)

Cylinder head

Type ... Cast iron with vertical valves. Separate inlet and exhaust ports
Combustion recess depth ... 0.10–0.11 in (2.54–2.794 mm)
Combustion recess volume ... 7.00–10.45 cc (HC)
                              13.72–17.28 cc (LC)
Valve guides ... Machined directly in the head but guide bushes are available
Bore for guide bushes ... 0.4383–0.4391 in (11.133–11.153 mm)
Valve guide inside diameter ... 0.3115–0.3125 in (7.907–7.938 mm)
Valve seat angle ... 44° 30'–45° inlet and exhaust
Valve seat width:
  Inlet ... 0.055 in (1.40 mm)
  Exhaust ... 0.076 in (1.93 mm)
Valve seat Inserts:

Insert	Valve	ID of recess in head	Depth of recess in head
Standard	Inlet	1.6400/1.6405 in (41.656/37.668 mm)	0.324/0.326 in (8.23/8.28 mm)
	Exhaust	1.4900/1.4905 (37.846/37.859 mm)	
0.010 in (0.254 mm)	Inlet	1.6500/1.6505 in (41.910/41.923 mm)	0.324/0.326 in (8.23/8.28 mm)
o/s dia, std depth	Exhaust	1.5000/1.5005 in (38.100/38.113 mm)	
0.010 in (0.254 mm)	Inlet	1.6500/1.6505 in (41.910/41.923 mm)	0.334/0.336 in (8.48/8.53 mm)
o/s dia and depth	Exhaust	1.5000/1.5005 in (38.100/38.113 mm)	
0.020 in (0.508 mm)	Inlet	1.6600/1.6605 in (42.164/42.177 mm)	0.324/0.326 in (8.23/8.28 mm)
o/s dia, std depth	Exhaust	1.5100/1.5105 in (38.354/38.367 mm)	
0.020 in (0.508 mm)	Inlet	1.6600/1.6605 in (42.164/42.177 mm)	0.344/0.346 in (8.74/8.79 mm)
o/s dia and depth	Exhaust	1.5100/1.5105 in (38.354/38.367 mm)	

Bore for rocker stud (std) ... 0.3685–0.3695 in (9.360–9.385 mm)

Flywheel and ring gear

Type ... Ring gear shrunk on
Number of teeth on ring gear ... 121
Maximum run-out ... 0.007 in (0.18 mm) at 3¾ in (95.25 mm) radius
Retaining bolt length:
  flywheel ... 29/32 in (23.0 mm)
  drive plate ... 21/32 in (16.7 mm)
Clutch pilot spigot bearing ... Sealed ball race in crankshaft
Spigot bearing outside diameter ... 1.3776–1.3780 in (34.991–35.001 mm)
Spigot bearing inside diameter ... 0.5903–0.5906 in (14.994–15.001 mm)

Lubrication system

Main, camshaft, balance shaft and connecting rod big-end
bearings and tappets ... Pressure fed
Gudgeon pin and cylinder wall lubrication ... Splash, and from oil squirts in connecting rods
Timing gear lubrication ... Metered jet of oil
Rocker lubrication ... Controlled feed through pushrods from tappets
Oil pump ... Eccentric bi-rotor or sliding vane types
Eccentric bi-rotor type pump:
  Capacity ... 10 Imp galls (12 US galls, 45.425 litres)/min at 2500 rpm
  Pump body bore diameter ... 0.500–0.501 in (12.700–12.725 mm)
  Driveshaft diameter ... 0.4980–0.4985 in (12.649–12.662 mm)
  Driveshaft to body clearance ... 0.0015–0.003 in (0.038–0.076 mm)
  Inner and outer rotor clearance ... 0.006 in (0.152 mm) maximum
  Outer rotor and housing clearance ... 0.010 in (0.254 mm) maximum
  Inner and outer rotor endfloat ... 0.005 in (0.127 mm) maximum
Sliding vane type pump:
  Capacity ... 10 Imp galls (12 US galls, 45.425 litres)/min at 2500 rpm
  Pump body bore diameter ... 0.500–0.501 in (12.700–12.725 mm)
  Driveshaft diameter ... 0.498–0.4985 in (12.639–12.662 mm)
  Driveshaft to body clearance ... 0.0015–0.003 in (0.038–0.076 mm)
  Rotor to pump body clearance ... 0.005 in (0.127 mm) maximum
  Vane clearance in rotor ... 0.005 in (0.127 mm) maximum

Chapter 1 Part A V4 and V6 engines

Rotor and vane endfloat	0.005 in (0.127 mm) maximum
Vane to body clearance	0.011 in (0.279 mm) maximum
Oil pressure	45 to 50 lb/in² (3.16–3.51 kg/cm²)
Oil filter type	External full flow pressure relief type
Sump capacity:	
2 litre	6 Imp pints (7.2 US pints, 3.4 litres)
2.5 and 3 litre	8 Imp pints (9.6 US pints. 4.54 litres)
Oil filter capacity	1.5 Imp pints (1.8 US pints, 0.85 litres)

Pistons

Type	Cut-away skirt with combustion chamber in crown
Material	Aluminium alloy tin plated
Weight:	
2.5 litre	608.0–612.0 grams
2 and 3 litre	563.0–567.0 grams
Number of rings	Two compression, one oil control
Width of ring grooves:	
Compression rings	0.080–0.081 in (2.032–2.057 mm)
Oil control ring	0.1885–0.1875 in (4.787–4.762 mm)
Gudgeon pin bore diameter	Graded
Grade:	
Red	0.9374–0.9375 in (23.810–23.813 mm)
Yellow	0.9375–0.9376 in (23.813–23.815 mm)
Blue	0.9376–0.9377 in (23.815–23.818 mm)
Gudgeon pin bore offset	0.06 in (1.5 mm) towards thrust face
Piston clearance in cylinder bore	0.002–0.0026 in (0.051–0.066 mm)
Effective piston diameter	Graded
Grade:	
1	3.6846–3.6849 in (93.616–93.624 mm)
2	3.6849–3.6852 in (93.624–93.631 mm)
3	3.6852–3.6855 in (93.631–93.639 mm)
4	3.6855–3.6858 in (93.639–93.646 mm)
5*	3.6858–3.6861 in (93.646–93.654 mm)
6*	3.6861–3.6864 in (93.654–93.662 mm)
(* Only grades 5 and 6 supplied in service)	
Oversize pistons available	0.0025 in (0.0635 mm), 0.015 in (0.381 mm), 0.030 in (0.762 mm). 0.045 in (1.14 mm), 0.060 in (1.52 mm)

Gudgeon pins

Type	Semi-floating, pressed into connecting rod
Material	Machined seamless steel tubing
Length	2.93–2.95 in (74.42–74.93 mm)
Outside diameter	0.9370–0.9373 in (23.793–23.806 mm)
Clearance in piston	0.0003–0.0005 in (0.0076–0.0127 mm) selective

Piston rings

Upper Compression Ring:	
Material	Cast iron and chrome plated
Type	Barrel face
Radial thickness	0.167–0.157 in (4.24–3.98 mm)
Width	0.077–0.078 in (1.956–1.981 mm)
Ring to groove clearance	0.002–0.004 in (0.0508–0.1016 mm)
Ring gap	0.010–0.020 in (0.254–0.508 mm)
Lower Compression Ring:	
Material	Cast iron, molybdenum coated
Type	Internally chamfered on the upper face
Radial thickness	0.163–0.184 in (4.14–4.67 mm)
Width	0.077–0.178 in (1.956–1.981 mm)
Ring to groove clearance	0.002–0.004 in (0.0508–0.1016 mm)
Ring gap	0.010–0.020 in (0.254–0.508 mm)
Oil Control Ring:	
Material	Cast iron
Type	'Micro-land' scraper with slotted channel
Radial thickness	0.150–0.160 in (3.81–4.06 mm)
Width	0.1855–0.1865 in (4.711–4.73 mm)
Ring to groove clearance	0.001–0.003 in (0.0254–0.0762 mm)
Ring gap	0.010–0.015 in (0.254–0.381 mm)
Oversize rings available	0.0025 in (0.0635 mm), 0.015 in (0.381 mm), 0.030 in (0.762 mm), 0.045in (1.14 mm), 0.060 in (1.52 mm)

Timing gears

Balance shaft gear fit	0–0.0016 in (0–0.046 mm)
Backlash - crankshaft to balance shaft gear	0.002–0.004 in (0.05–0.10 mm)
Camshaft gear fit	0–0.0013 in (0–0.033 mm)

Backlash:
  crankshaft to new camshaft gear .... 0.004–0.007 in (0.10–0.18 mm)
  crankshaft to used camshaft gear .... 0.002 in (0.05 mm) minimum
Crankshaft fit .... -0.0015–+0.0001 in (-0.038–+0.003 mm)
Backlash selective fit:

Colour Code	Crankshaft Gear Limit	Camshaft Gear Limit	Balance Shaft Gear Limit
Blue	Top	Bottom	Bottom
Yellow	Mean	Mean	Mean
Red	Bottom	Top	Top

Valves
Valve stem diameter:
  Inlet .... 0.3095–0.3105 in (7.861–7.887 mm)
  Exhaust .... 0.3086–0.3096 in (7.838–7.864 mm)
Valve stem to guide clearance:
  Inlet .... 0.0010–0.003 in (0.025–0.076 mm)
  Exhaust .... 0.0019–0.0039 in (0.048–0.099 mm)
Oversize stems available .... 0.003 in (0.076 mm), 0.015 in (0.38 mm), 0.030 in (0.76 mm)
Valve head diameter:
  Inlet .... 1.592–1.602 in (40.34–40.69 mm)
  Exhaust .... 1.428–1.438 in (36.27–36.52 mm)
Valve face angle .... 45°–45° 15'

Valve springs
Free length .... 2.028 in (51.51 mm)
Diameter .... 1.324–1.348 in (33.63–34.24 mm)
Total number of coils 6.75

Valve timing and clearances

	Inlet	Exhaust
Valve clearances (V4), hot	0.010 in (0.25 mm)	0.018 in (0.45 mm)
Valve clearances (V6), hot	0.013 in (0.33 mm)	0.020 in (0.50 mm)

Valve timing:

	V4	V6
Inlet opens	27° BTDC	29° BTDC
Inlet closes	65° ABDC	67° ABDC
Exhaust opens	69° BBDC	70° BBDC
Exhaust closes	23° ATDC	14° ATDC

Torque wrench settings

	lbf ft	kgf m
Main bearing cap bolts	55–60	7.6–8.3
Connecting rod bolts (V4)	25–30	3.5–4.1
Connecting rod bolts (V6)	38–43	5.3–6.0
Cylinder head bolts	65–70	9.0–9.7
Flywheel or drive plate to crankshaft bolts (V4)	45–50	6.2–6.9
Flywheel or intermediate plate (V6)	49–54	6.9–7.6
Sump	6–8	0.8–1.1
Rocker cover (re-torque after 2 mins to same torque)	2.5–3.5	0.3–0.4
Oil drain plug	20–25	2.8–3.5
Water jacket drain plug	18–21	2.1–2.9
Dry seal plugs:		
$\frac{1}{16}$ in pipe	3–4	0.4–0.5
$\frac{1}{8}$ in pipe	9–11	1.2–1.5
$\frac{1}{4}$ in pipe	18–22	2.1–3.0
$\frac{3}{4}$ in pipe	60–65	8.3–9.0
Servo connection	9–11	1.2–1.5
Heater connection	15–18	2.1–2.5
Oil pump to block	12–15	1.7–2.1
Carburettor attaching nuts	15–18	2.1–2.5
Intake manifold bolts	13–16	1.8–2.2
Oil filter mounting insert	20–30	2.8–4.1
Front cover bolts	11–13	1.5–1.8
Rear crankshaft oil seal retainer	11–13	1.5–1.8
Camshaft gear locking bolt	24–28	3.3–3.9
Balance shaft gear locking bolt	24–28	3.3–3.9
Crankshaft pulley nut	24–28	3.3–3.9

1 General description

The models covered by this manual may be fitted with a V6 engine having a capacity of 2500 or 3000cc or a V4 engine of 2000cc capacity. The original V4 engine was later discontinued and replaced by the 2000cc overhead camshaft ohc in-line engine as fitted to certain Cortina models.

The V6 and V4 engine overhaul procedures are given in Part A of this Chapter whilst the 2 litre ohc in-line engine overhaul procedures are described in Part B.

The large V6 engines are really six cylinder versions of the V4 engine but with the balance shaft deleted. The reason for this is that the primary reciprocation forces are automatically balanced out with a 6 cylinder V engine unlike the V4 engine which requires this additional shaft. Special balance weights are located in the front crankshaft

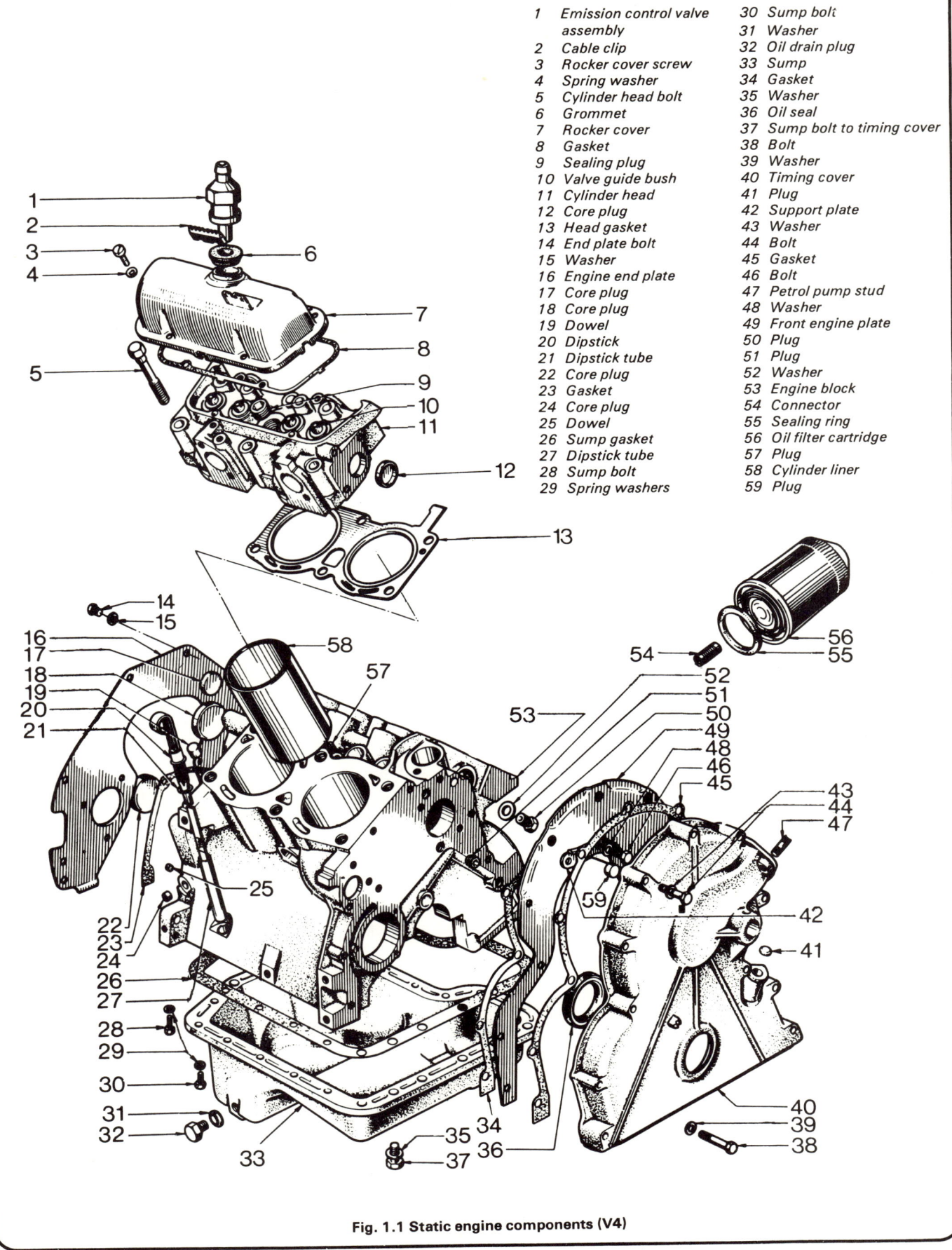

Fig. 1.1 Static engine components (V4)

pulley and flywheel and are heavier on the V6 than those incorporated in the V4 engine. It is therefore important that the crankshaft pulley and flywheel or drive plates are not interchanged between the V4 and V6 engines.

The engines have the cylinders arranged in a 60 degree formation and operate on the four stroke 'Otto' cycle.

The cylinder bores are machined directly into the cast iron cylinder block and have a common bore diameter, whilst the stroke for the 2 and 3 litre engines differs from that of the 2.5 litre engine.

The cylinder block is cast integral with the crankcase and incorporates full length water jackets for adequate cooling. On the V4 engine three main large diameter bearings are incorporated within the crankcase whilst on V6 engines there are four main large diameter bearings.

A cast iron crankshaft runs in the main bearings, which are fitted with detachable steel backed copper lead bearing shells. The endfloat of the crankshaft is controlled by thrust washers fitted at each side of the centre main bearing on the V4 engine and on the V6 engine they are located on either side of the front intermediate bearing.

Pressed in oil seals are incorporated in the front cover and rear oil seal carrier so as to prevent oil leaks from either the front or the rear of the crankshaft pulley hub. The rear oil seal in the carrier runs directly onto the crankshaft flange.

A fibre gear on the end of the camshaft is in direct mesh with a gear on the end of the crankshaft and is driven by the crankshaft at half engine speed. The camshaft runs in steel backed white metal bushes. Incorporated on the camshaft behind the front bearing journal is a skew gear and this drives the oil pump and distributor. Forward of the camshaft gear and retained by the fibre gear bolt is an eccentric which operates the mechanical lift fuel pump mounted onto the side of the front cover.

The valves are mounted overhead and are operated by a system of rockers, pushrods and tappets from the camshaft placed in the 'valley' between the two banks of cylinders. The inlet valves are of a larger diameter than those of the exhaust in order to improve engine breathing. The rocker arms are mounted individually on studs pressed into the cylinder heads and are retained in position by spherically faced fulcrum seats and self-locking nuts. The valve clearance is adjusted by the self locking nuts. The valve springs are of an unusual form with close coils at one end; these are fitted with the close coil adjacent to the cylinder head.

The connecting rods are H-section forgings and the big-ends are located by hollow dowels and secured with two bolts. Similar to the crankshaft main bearing, the big-end bearings are steel backed and copper lead lined.

The little-end, sometimes called the small-end, is not bearing lined but is shrunk onto the piston pin to secure the pin in position.

Mounted onto the rear end of the crankshaft is a cast iron flywheel and, for the V4 engine application, this is machined to accommodate an 8 inch diameter clutch, or for the V6 engine a 9 inch clutch, the larger diameter being necessary for the greater engine torque.

A steel starter ring gear is shrunk onto the outer periphery of the flywheel and engages with the starter motor drive during engine starting conditions. If an automatic transmission is fitted, the ring gear is shrunk onto an inertia ring which is attached to the torque converter. The torque converter is driven via a drive plate to the rear crankshaft flange instead of the normal flywheel.

Because the engines have 60° V formation the rotating and reciprocating masses do not entirely balance themselves out and there is an out of balance couple present which is more evident with V4 engines than V6 engines. This out of balance couple is controlled and balanced out by means of weights in the crankshaft pulley, crankshaft and the flywheel and, on the V4 engine, a balance shaft that revolves in the opposite direction to the crankshaft but at engine speed.

This balance shaft, which runs in steel backed white metal bearing bushes, is driven in constant mesh with the crankshaft gear. End thrust from the balance shaft is taken and controlled by a thrust plate located in between the balance shaft gear hub and the front bearing journal. It is bolted to the front face of the cylinder block and is made of sintered iron.

The engine oil sump is a steel pressing having a front well on the V6 engine application and a rear well on the V4 engine application. The drain plug is on the right-hand side of the pressing.

The hexagonal driveshaft from the distributor drives the oil pump which may be either of the sliding vane or eccentric bi-rotor design. Incorporated in the design of both pumps is an oil pressure relief valve. Oil under pressure is directed via a full flow oil filter to the tappets, main bearings, big-ends, camshaft and balance shaft (if fitted). As the tappets are hollow they control the amount of oil through the hollow pushrods to the rocker arms and valves.

On the V4 engine there is a drilling into the front journal of the balance shaft which passes oil onto the thrust plate and then into two jets that spray onto the timing gears. The V6 engine, not having the balance shaft, has a drilling into the cylinder block front face and this supplies lubrication to the timing gears.

The oil from the rocker arms drains from the cylinder head and into the tappet chamber so lubricating the cams and distributor drive gear as it returns to the oil sump at the base of the engine.

The cylinder bores are lubricated by one squirt of oil every crankshaft revolution emitting from a small drilling in each connecting rod web. The gudgeon pins are continuously lubricated by oil mist created by internal crankcase activity and on the downward stroke with oil scraped by the oil control rings from the cylinder bores.

Located on the left-hand rocker cover top is the oil filler cap and this incorporates a gauze filter for the positive crankcase ventilation system. Any crankcase fumes are discharged into the inlet manifold under the control of an emission valve located in the right-hand rocker cover.

2 Major operations with engine in place

The following major operations may be carried out without taking the engine from the car:
a) Removal and refitting of cylinder heads
b) Removal and refitting of sump (V4 only)
c) Removal and refitting of big-end bearings (V4 only)
c) Removal and refitting of pistons and connecting rods (V4 only)
e) Removal and refitting of timing gear
f) Removal and refitting of oil pump (V4 only)
g) Removal and refitting of front engine mountings
h) Removal and refitting of engine/gearbox rear mounting

3 Major operations with engine removed

Although it would be possible to carry out some of the following operations with the engine in the car, if the gearbox and clutch were removed, the author does not recommend it except as a last resort:
a) Removal and refitting of flywheel
b) Removal and refitting of rear main bearing oil seal
c) Removal and refitting of crankshaft and crankshaft bearings
d) Removal and refitting of camshaft and camshaft bearings
e) Removal and refitting of pistons and connecting rods
f) Removal and refitting of oil pump
g) Removal and refitting of sump
h) Removal and refitting of big-end bearings

4 Methods of engine removal

The engine may be lifted out together with the transmission or separated from the transmission and lifted out by itself. If the transmission is left attached the disadvantage is that the engine has to be tilted to a very steep angle to get it out. Unless both the engine and transmission are being repaired or overhauled together there is little reason for removing them as a unit.

5 Engine – removal without transmission

1 A do-it-yourself owner should be able to remove the engine from the car in about three hours. It is essential to have a good hoist. If an inspection pit is not available, two support stands (axle stands) will be required. In the later stages, when the engine is being separated from the transmission and lifted, the assistance of another person is most useful to help guide the engine and prevent it from swaying about and possibly causing damage.

2 Open the bonnet so as to expose the engine and ancillary components.

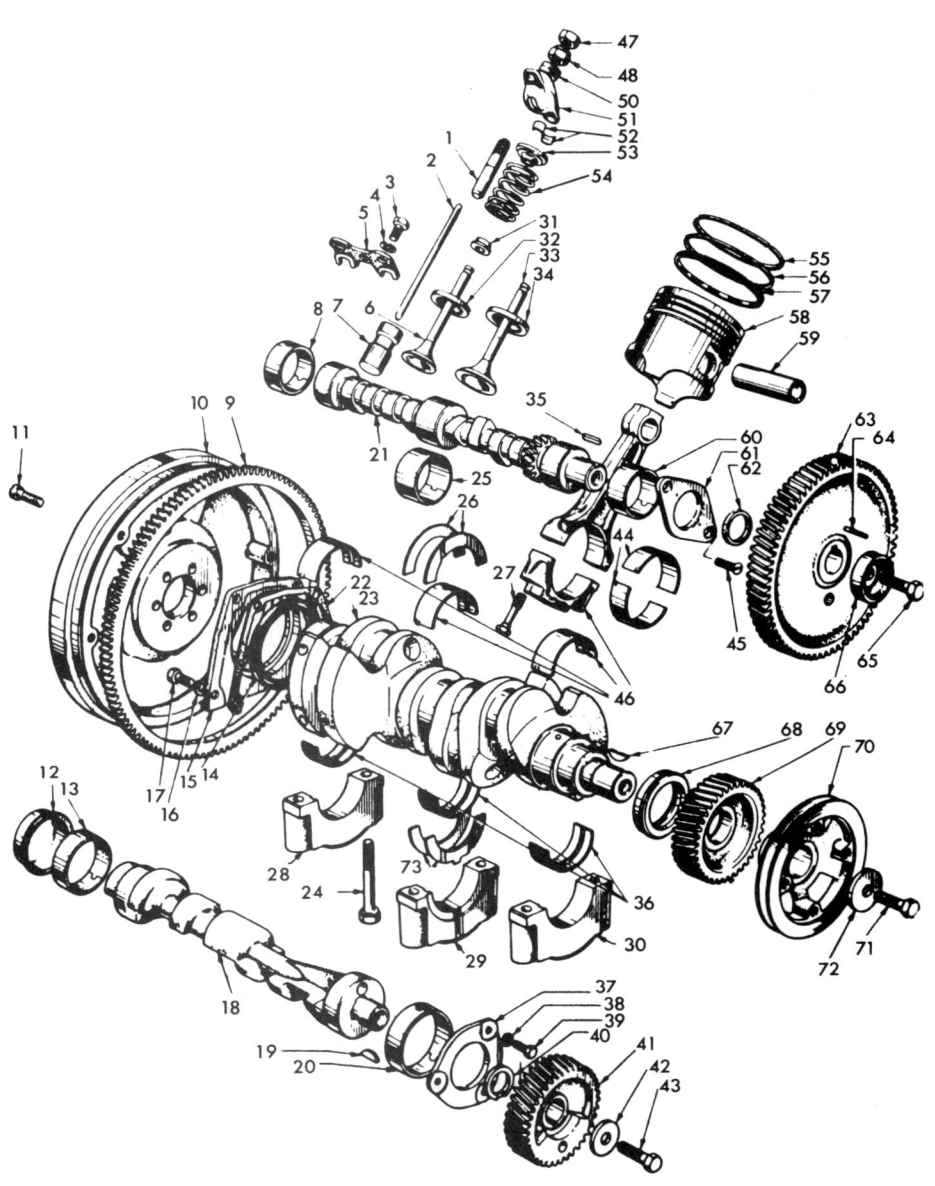

Fig. 1.2 Moving engine components (V4)

1 Rocker stud	20 Balance shaft bearing – front	lower
2 Pushrod	21 Camshaft	37 Balance shaft thrust plate
3 Bolt	22 Gasket	38 Stem washer
4 Washer	23 Crankshaft	39 Bolt
5 Pushrod guide	24 Bolt – main bearing	40 Spacer
6 Exhaust valve	25 Camshaft bearing – centre	41 Gear
7 Tappet	26 Crankshaft thrust washers	42 Washer
8 Camshaft bearing – rear	27 Bolt – big-end	43 Bolt
9 Starter ring	28 Main bearing cap – rear	44 Big-end bearing shells
10 Flywheel	29 Main bearing cap – centre	45 Camshaft thrust plate screw
11 Bolt	30 Main bearing cap – front	46 Main bearing shells – upper
12 Plug	31 Seal	47 Lock nut (if fitted)
13 Balance shaft bearing – rear	32 Valve seat insert – exhaust	48 Self-locking nut
14 Crankshaft oil seal	33 Valve – inlet	50 Pivot ball
15 Oil seal retainer	34 Valve seat insert – inlet	51 Rocker arm
16 Washer	35 Key	52 Collets
17 Bolt	36 Main bearing shells –	53 Valve collar
18 Balance shaft		54 Spring
19 Woodruff key		
		55 Upper compression ring
		56 Lower compression ring
		57 Oil control ring
		58 Piston
		59 Gudgeon pin
		60 Camshaft bearing – front
		61 Camshaft thrust plate
		62 Spacer
		63 Camshaft fibre gear
		64 Key
		65 Bolt
		66 Fuel pump drive cam
		67 Woodruff key
		68 Oil seal
		69 Crankshaft gear
		70 Pulley wheel
		71 Bolt
		72 Washer
		73 Crankshaft thrust washers

3 Place a container of suitable size under the radiator and another under the engine. Open the drain plug at the bottom of the radiator and the top of the cylinder block behind the oil filter.
4 Undo and remove the radiator filler cap. Do not drain the water in the garage or the place where the engine is to be removed if receptacles are not to hand to catch the water.
5 Place a container of at least 8 pints (4.55 litres) under the oil sump drain plug and remove the drain plug. Let the oil drain out for at least 10 minutes.
6 Place old blankets over the wings and across the cowl to prevent damage to the paintwork.
7 It is easier if two assistants are available so that the bonnet can be supported whilst the hinges are being released.
8 Using a pencil, mark the outline of the hinge bracket location on the underside of the bonnet to act as a datum for refitting.
9 Undo and remove the four bolts and washers securing the bonnet to the two hinges.
10 Carefully lift the bonnet up and over the front of the engine compartment, and place out of the way.
11 Disconnect the battery negative and positive terminals using an open-ended spanner. Note the second smaller terminal attached to the positive terminal post. Release the battery clamp and lift away the battery.
12 The air cleaner should next be removed. Undo and remove the top cover attachments and lift away the top cover. Recover the filter element.
13 Bend back the lock tabs, then undo and remove the four securing nuts and two tab washers. Also remove the two spacer tubes (photo).
14 The air cleaner body may now be lifted away.
15 Refer to Chapter 2, and remove the radiator and cowl assembly.
16 Slacken the hose clips and detach the hoses from the two-way union at the inlet manifold (photo).
17 Slacken the hose clip at the carburettor automatic choke union and detach the hose. This is the hose adjacent to the carburettor diaphragm body (photo).
18 Disconnect the engine hydraulic stabiliser and bracket from the rear of the engine and pivot it out of the way (photo).
19 Detach the throttle control cable socket from the relay shaft ball.
20 Disconnect the throttle relay shaft from the carburettor installation by releasing it from the spring clip.
21 Undo and remove the two bolts and spring washers securing the throttle relay shaft mounting bracket to the inlet manifold. Move the assembly to one side.
22 Detach the heater hose clip and hose from the rear of the water pump and position the hose out of the way.
23 Ease back the alternator terminal block retaining clip and detach the terminal block. Take care because this can be a little tight.
24 Undo and remove the four bolts and washers securing the fan to the front cover mounted hub. Lift away the fan assembly. 2.5 and 3.0 litre models fitted with automatic transmission have a viscous clutch located between the water pump pulley and the fan. To remove the fan complete with viscous clutch simply unscrew the central retaining bolt (photo).
25 **Power assisted steering (where fitted)**: Slacken off the power assisted steering pump mounting bolts and lift away the drivebelt (photo).
26 **Power assisted steering (where fitted)**: Remove the pump mounting bolts and pivot away from the engine (photo).
27 Undo and remove the earth strap to engine bolt and washer (photo).
28 Detach the high and low tension wire connections to the ignition coil.
29 Unscrew the oil pressure pipe union from the left-hand side of the engine directly beneath the thermostat housing. Tape the end of the pipe to stop the ingress of dirt (photo).
30 Undo and remove the two nuts and washers securing each exhaust downpipe to the exhaust manifold and separate the clamp halves (photo).
31 It will be necessary to remove the left-hand exhaust manifold. Undo and remove the securing bolts and lift away the manifold. Recover the small gaskets (photo). This is necessary to give better access to the starter motor.
32 Make a note of the electrical connections to the starter motor and then detach the cables from the rear of the starter motor.
33 Undo and remove the two bolts and washers securing the starter motor, carefully withdraw from the flywheel and lift away.
34 Disconnect the second heater hose from the engine and tuck back out of the way. On engines fitted with automatic choke carburettors the inlet hose connection to the water pump is blanked off and the hose from the thermostat housing is directed to the carburettor instead. This hose can be disconnected at this stage, as can the main fuel line from the fuel pump. Plug the end of the line to prevent further fuel leakage and the ingress of dirt.
35 Detach the electrical cable connection to the water temperature sender unit. Also detach the servo unit hose from the inlet manifold.
36 Place a jack under the transmission and support its weight.
37 Place a rope, or chains around the engine and support its weight using an overhead hoist or crane.
38 Undo and remove the nut securing the front engine mounting to the body mounted bracket on each side. It will probably be found that the retaining nut on the underside of the bracket will be easier to remove.
39 On automatic transmission models, disconnect the torque converter to engine intermediate plate retaining nuts/bolts. These are accessible through the starter motor housing aperture. Use a socket and extension (photo) and turn the crankshaft accordingly for each nut/bolt (4 off).
40 Undo and remove the bolts and spring washers securing the transmission bellhousing to the engine. For this a socket and universal joint will be of considerable assistance. During and after removal of the engine from the automatic transmission, it is essential that the torque converter is retained to the transmission. The converter should be retained by a means similar to that shown in the photo. We retained it with a block of wood and metal bar attached to the bellhousing. The transmission was supported by ropes attached to a bar positioned across the engine compartment on the inner wing panels.
41 The engine should now be ready for removal. Check that no hoses, cables or other items have been left connected and all is clear so that lifting out can begin.
42 Pull the unit forward and start to lift. Make sure that the transmission first motion shaft is clear of the clutch assembly.
43 Continue raising the engine through the engine compartment until it is free of the car (photo).
44 Move the car rearward or the engine forward until clear of the engine compartment and lower the engine to the floor. Suitably support so that it does not roll over.

6 Engine – removal with manual gearbox

1 Refer to Section 5 and follow the instructions given in paragraphs 1 to 16 inclusive.
2 Refer to Chapter 7. Remove the propeller shaft as directed, working from the underside of the car. This is particularly important where a split type propeller shaft is used.
3 Undo and remove the bolts securing the engine rear cover plate and bracket assembly to the clutch housing.
4 Detach the bracket assembly from the cylinder block and carefully swing it clear.
5 Undo and remove the nuts and bolts securing the exhaust downpipes to the front mounting brackets. Push the downpipes outward and tie out of the way of the gearbox.
6 If a centre console is fitted, this must be removed from inside the car. Directions will be found in Chapter 6.
7 Lift up the gear change lever gaiter and carefully remove the spring retainer.
8 Using a screwdriver prise open the locking tab and draw the gear change lever upward.
9 Refer to Chapter 5 and detach the clutch cable from the release arm.
10 Using a pair of circlip pliers or pointed pliers, compress the circlip retaining the speedometer cable to the side of the gearbox casing. Withdraw the speedometer cable assembly.
11 If a reversing light is fitted disconnect the lead from the gearbox mounted switch.
12 Disconnect the crossmember from the gearbox and then detach the crossmember from the underside of the body by undoing and removing the retaining bolts and washers.
13 The engine and gearbox assembly should now be ready for removal. Check that no hoses, cables or other items have been left connected and all is clear so that lifting out can begin.

5.13 The air cleaner body retaining nuts and spacer tubes

5.16 Disconnect the large and small hoses from the inlet manifold union

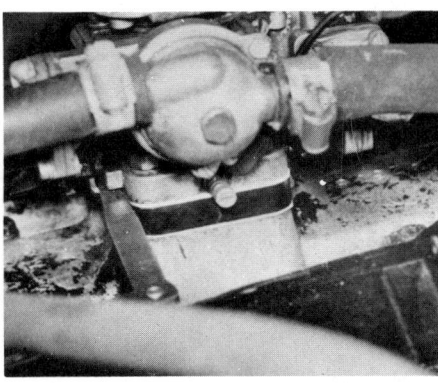
5.17 Detach the carburettor automatic choke hoses

5.18 Disconnect the engine stabilizer complete with clutch housing bracket

5.24 Remove the central bolt only on 2·5 and 3·0 litre models fitted with viscous clutch in fan unit

5.25 Lifting away the power assisted steering pump drivebelt

5.26 Remove pump mounting bolts

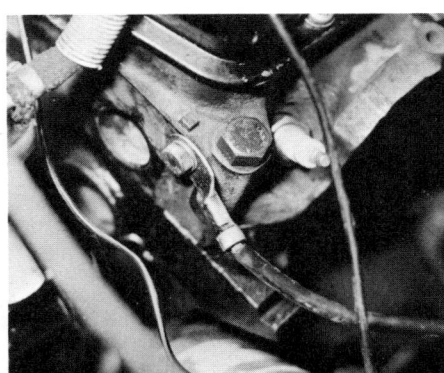
5.27 Remove the earth strap to engine (V6)

5.29 Remove the oil pressure pipe (V6)

5.30 Exhaust downpipe clamp

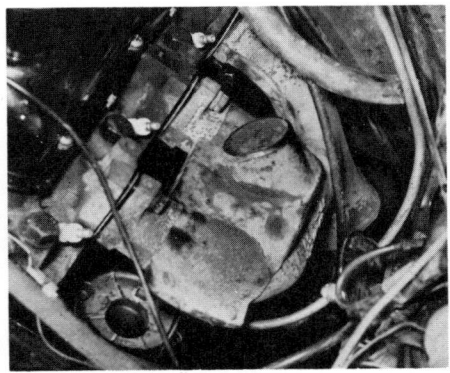
5.31 The left-hand exhaust manifold showing the heat duct to the air filter and, below, the starter motor

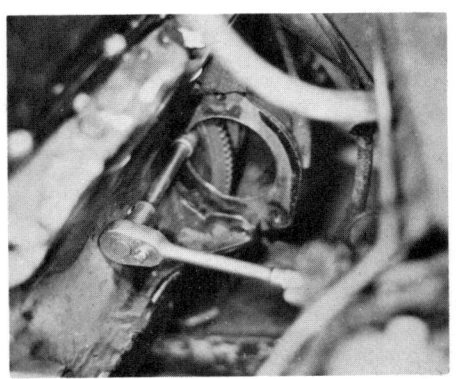
5.39 Unscrewing the engine intermediate plate to torque converter retaining nuts

5.40 Support the transmission and retain the torque converter (automatic transmission)

5.43 Raise the engine to clear the car

14 Lower the gearbox and raise the engine, drawing the unit forwards as much as possible.
15 It will now be necessary to tilt the unit at a steep angle and lift upward through the engine compartment. If there is not sufficient clearance it will be necessary to jack up the front of the car and support on stands.
16 Continue raising the unit until the gearbox can be lifted over the front body member.
17 Move the car rearward or the unit forward until clear of the engine compartment and lower the unit to the floor. Suitably support so that it does not roll over.

7 Engine removal – automatic transmission models

Due to weight considerations, if it is necessary to remove both the engine and the automatic transmission, it is advisable to remove each unit separately. Refer to Section 5 of this Chapter, and to Chapter 6.

8 Engine dismantling – general

1 Ideally, the engine is mounted on a proper stand for overhaul but it is anticipated that most owners will have a strong bench on which to place it. If a sufficiently large strong bench is not available then the work can be done at ground level. It is essential, however, that some form of substantial wooden surface is available. Timber should be at least $\frac{3}{4}$ inch thick, otherwise the weight of the engine will cause projections to punch holes straight through it.
2 It will save a great deal of time later if the engine is thoroughly cleaned down on the exterior before any dismantling begins. This can be done by using paraffin and a stiff brush or more easily, probably, by the use of a proprietary solvent such as Gunk which can be brushed on and then the dirt swilled off with a water jet. This will dispose of all the heavy grease and grit once and for all so that later cleaning of individual components will be a relatively clean process and the paraffin bath will not become contaminated with abrasive metal.
3 As the engine is stripped down, clean each part as it comes off. Try to avoid immersing parts with oilways in paraffin as pockets of liquid could remain and cause oil dilution in the critical first few revolutions after reassembly. Clean oilways with pipe cleaners, or preferably, an air jet.
4 Where possible, avoid damaging gaskets on removal, especially if new ones have not been obtained. They can be used as patterns if new ones have to be specially cut.
5 It is helpful to obtain a few blocks of wood to support the engine whilst it is in the process of dismantling. Start dismantling at the top of the engine and then turn the block over and deal with the sump and crankshaft etc, afterwards.

6 Nuts and bolts should be refitted in their locations where possible to avoid confusion later. As an alternative keep each group of nuts and bolts (all the timing gear cover bolts for example) together in a jar or tin. This is particularly important since the various components are retained and secured with a mixture of AF and metric nuts and bolts.
7 Many items dismantled must be refitted in the same position, if they are not being renewed. These include valves, rocker arms, tappets, pistons, pushrods, bearings and connecting rods. Some of these are marked on assembly to avoid any possibility of mixing them up during overhaul. Others are not, and it is a great help if adequate preparation is made in advance to classify these parts. Suitably labelled tins or jars and, for small items, egg trays, tobacco tins and so on, can be used. The time spent in this operation will be amply repaid later.
8 Before beginning a complete overhaul or if the engine is being exchanged for a works reconditioned unit the following items should be removed:

Fuel system components:
Carburettor
Inlet manifold
Exhaust manifolds
Fuel pump
Fuel lines
Ignition system components:
Spark plugs
Distributor
Electrical system components:
Generator or alternator and mounting brackets
Starter motor
Cooling system components:
Fan and hub
Water pump
Thermostat housing and thermostat
Water temperature sender unit
Engine:
Crankcase ventilation tube
Oil filter element
Oil pressure sender unit
Oil level dipstick
Oil filler cap
Engine mounting brackets
Oil pump
Clutch:
Clutch pressure plate assembly
Clutch friction plate assembly
All nuts and bolts associated with the foregoing.

Some of these items have to be removed for individual servicing or renewal periodically and details can be found under the appropriate Chapter.

9 Cylinder heads – removal with engine out of car

1 Remove the two valve rocker covers by undoing the four screws holding each one to its respective cylinder head. Disconnect the emission control valve pipe from the right-hand rocker cover.
2 Remove the distributor as detailed in Chapter 4.
3 Remove the carburettor as detailed in Chapter 3, and on automatic models detach the pipe from the thermostat housing.
4 *V4 engine:* Remove the inlet manifold by slackening the bolts, in the order shown in Fig.1.3 half a turn at a time until all bolts are free. The manifold casting may stick to the heads at the joint, in which case tap it on the ends in the centre with a soft faced hammer to release it.
5 *V6 engine:* Remove the inlet manifold by slackening the bolts, in the order shown in Fig.4 half a turn at a time until all bolts are free. The manifold casting may stick to the heads at the joint in which case tap it on the ends in the centre with a soft faced hammer to release it.
6 *V4 engine:* Taking each cylinder head in turn, remove the six holding-down bolts. The correct sequence is shown in Fig.1.5.
7 *V6 engine:* Taking each cylinder head in turn, remove the eight holding-down bolts. The correct sequence is shown in Fig.1.6.
8 When the head is sufficiently clear remove the four pushrods and note which valve they came from and which way up. Keep them in order and the right way up by pushing them through a piece of stiff paper or cardboard with the valve numbers marked and the top and bottom ends identified.
9 On occasions the heads stick to the block in which case they should be struck smartly using a block of wood and hammer or soft mallet in order to break the joint. However, the exhaust manifold should provide sufficient grip to provide the necessary lifting force required. Do not try and prise them off with a blade of any description or damage will be caused to the faces of the head or block or both. As a last resort in stubborn cases revolve the engine and the piston compression should lift the heads (make sure the sparking plugs are in place).
10 Lift the heads off carefully. Note which side each head comes from as they are identical and it is preferable to refit them on the same bank of cylinders. Place them where they cannot be damaged. Undo the bolts holding the exhaust manifold to each head.

10 Cylinder heads – removal with engine in car

1 The procedure described in Section 9 should be followed exactly but the following action must be completed first:

   a) *Disconnect the battery leads.*
   b) *Drain the cooling system as detailed in Chapter 2.*
   c) *Remove the top hose from the thermostat housing and the heater hose connection from the inlet manifold. Also remove the bypass hose connection at the thermostat. Full information will be found in Chapter 2.*
   d) *Remove the V-belt and the alternator as detailed in Chapter 10. The mounting brackets may also be removed but this is not essential.*
   e) *Disconnect the exhaust manifolds from the exhaust pipes by removing the two clamping rings.*
   f) *Disconnect the water temperature sender unit lead as detailed in Chapter 2.*
   g) *Remove the accelerator linkage cross-shaft.*

11 Cylinder heads – dismantling of rocker gear, valves and springs

1 With the cylinder head on the bench undo the nut from each rocker stud in the centre of the rocker arm. Lift out the hemispherical rocker pivot and then lift off the rocker arm.
2 Lay the cylinder head on its side and, using a proper valve spring compressor tool, place the 'U' shaped end over the valve collar (photo) and the screw on the valve head and compress the spring. Sometimes

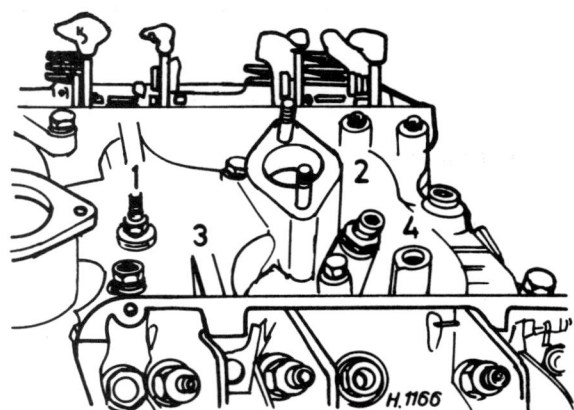

Fig. 1.3 Sequence for undoing or tightening V4 engine inlet manifold bolts (Secs. 9 and 48)

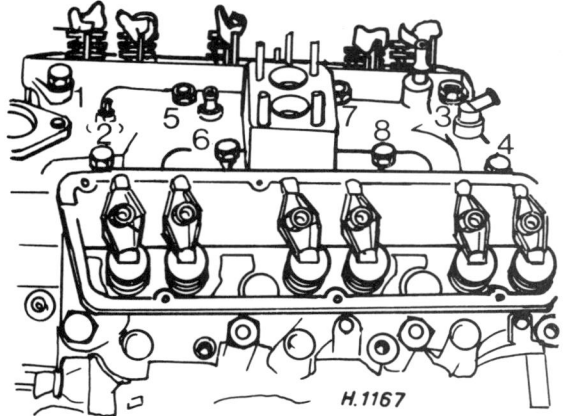

Fig. 1.4 Sequence for undoing or tightening V6 engine inlet manifold bolts (Secs. 9 and 53)

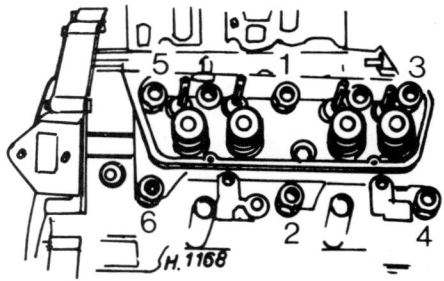

Fig. 1.5 Sequence for undoing or tightening V4 engine cylinder head bolts (Secs. 9 and 48)

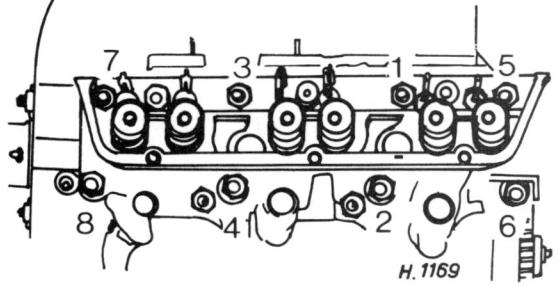

Fig. 1.6 Sequence for undoing or tightening V6 engine cylinder head bolts (Secs. 9 and 53)

the valve collar sticks, in which case, the end of the compressor over the spring should be tapped with a hammer to release the collar from the valve.

3 As the spring is pressed down the valve stem two tapered split collars (collets) will be revealed and these should be taken from the recess in the valve stem.

4 When the compressor is released the spring may be removed from the valve. Pull off the seal cap from the valve stem and then push the valve out of the head.

5 It is essential that the valves, springs, rocker arms and nuts are all kept in order so that they may be replaced in their original positions.

12 Tappets – removal

1 The tappets may now be removed from the cylinder block by pushing them up from the camshaft (which can be revolved if necessary to raise the tappets) and lifting them out. A piece of hooked wire inserted through the centre of the tappets will ease removal if they are sticky (photo).

2 If necessary, the pushrod bearing cups in each tappet can be taken out by first extracting the retaining circlip.

3 Make sure that all the tappets are kept in order so that they may be refitted in the location they came from.

13 Crankshaft pulley wheel – removal

1 Remove the bolt and washer locating the pulley to the front of the crankshaft. The pulley is keyed to the crankshaft and preferably must be drawn off with a proper sprocket puller. If a sprocket puller is not readily available, try lightly prising the pulley using suitable levers, but do not apply excessive pressure, or the timing cover, which is a light casting and comparatively fragile, may be damaged. Therefore unless the pulley is easily removed, a proper puller must be used.

2 The pulley may be removed with the engine in the car but it may be necessary to remove the radiator, depending on the type of pulley extractor used and the clearance it allows.

14 Flywheel or intermediate plate (automatic transmission) – removal

1 Remove the clutch assembly as described in Chapter 5.

2 The flywheel is retained to the crankshaft and flange by six bolts. One of these bolts is unevenly spaced so that the flywheel can only be located in one position.

3 Remove the six bolts, taking care to support the weight of the flywheel as they are loosened in case it slips off the flange.

4 Withdraw the flywheel, taking care not to damage the mating surfaces of the flywheel and crankshaft.

5 On automatic transmission models, unscrew the six bolts retaining the drive plate to the crankshaft flange, and lift it clear (photo).

15 Sump – removal

1 On V4 engines only, the sump may be removed with the engine in the car by undoing the bolts which hold it to the crankcase and timing cover at the front. With the engine out of the car, first invert the engine and then remove the bolts retaining the sump and the crankcase.

2 The sump may be stuck quite firmly to the engine if sealing compound has been used on the gasket. It is in order to lever it off in this case. The gasket should be removed anyway.

16 Timing gear and cover (V4) – removal

1 Invert the engine, remove the sump retaining bolts and lift off the sump. Remove the crankshaft pulley.

2 Take out the fixing bolts and lift off the cover.

3 The camshaft timing drive mechanism consists of a helical gear on the crankshaft and a large fibre gear on the camshaft. There is also another gear in mesh with the crankshaft gear which drives the balance shaft.

4 Remove the camshaft and balance shaft gears by removing the bolts and washers and drawing them off. They should not require the services of a puller to come off. Be careful with the large fibre gear as this can be damaged very easily if mishandled.

5 The crankshaft gear should be left in position as it is not normally detachable.

6 On the front of the fibre gear there is an eccentric boss held also by the locating bolt and this operates the fuel pump actuating lever.

17 Timing gear and cover (V6) – removal

1 Remove the crankshaft pulley wheel (see Section 13) and unscrew and remove the sump retaining bolts at the front (beneath the timing cover).

2 Take out the fixing bolts and lift off the front cover. If the engine is in the car the fuel pump and V-belt will first need removal.

3 The camshaft timing drive mechanism consists of a helical gear on the crankshaft and a large fibre gear on the camshaft.

4 Remove the camshaft gear by removing the centre bolt and drawing it off. It should not require a puller to release the gear. Be careful with the large fibre gear as this can be damaged very easily if mishandled.

5 The crankshaft gear should be left in position as normally it should not require removal.

6 On the front of the fibre gear is an eccentric boss held also by the locating bolt and this operates the fuel pump actuating lever.

18 Camshaft – removal

1 The camshaft cannot be conveniently removed with the engine in the car as the tappets will jam in position and therefore the valve rocker gear, pushrods and tappets all need to be removed in addition to the radiator, timing cover and gear. To remove sticky tappets, insert

11.2 Removing the valve collets by compressing the spring

12.1 Extract each tappet

14.5 The intermediate plate (automatic transmission)

a piece of hooked wire through them, extract them from their respective positions and keep them in order for correct refitting.
2   With the timing cover and gear removed, undo the bolts holding the front cover backplate. Note the pressure plate underneath the three bolts.
3   The camshaft thrust plate is held to the block by two countersunk cross-head screws and these will need removing with an impact screwdriver.
4   The camshaft may then be withdrawn. Take great care to avoid hitting the three bearing bushes with the cam lobes as this could damage them.

19 Oil pump – removal

1   Remove the sump.
2   Undo the two mounting bolts holding the pump to the crankcase and lift it out (photo). Note that the long hexagonal section driveshaft will come out with the pump. This is driven in turn from the distributor shaft.

20 Pistons, connecting rods and big-end bearings – removal

1   Pistons and connecting rods may be removed with the engine in the car on V4 engines only, provided the sump and cylinder heads are first removed. The bearing shells may be removed with the heads on.
2   Slacken the two bolts holding each bearing cap to the connecting rod. Use a good quality socket spanner for this work. A ring spanner may be used for removal only - not refitting, which calls for a special torque wrench. Having slackened the bolts two or three turns tap the bolt heads to dislodge the caps from the connecting rods. Hollow dowel pegs locate the caps in position. When the caps are free from the pegs they can be easily lifted off after the bolts are completely removed.
3   Each bearing cap normally has the cylinder number etched on one end as does the connecting rod. However, this must be verified and, if in doubt, the cap should be marked with a dab of paint, or punch mark, to ensure that its relationship with the connecting rod is not altered.
4   The piston and connecting rod may then be pushed out of the top of each cylinder.
5   The big-end bearing shells can be removed from the connecting rod and cap by sliding them round in the direction of the notch at the end of the shell and lifting them out. If they are not being renewed it is vital that they are not interchanged - either between pistons or between cap and connecting rod.

21 Piston rings – removal

1   Remove the pistons from the engine.
2   The rings come off over the top of the piston. Starting with the top one, lift one end of the ring out of the groove and gradually ease it out all the way round. With the second and third rings an old feeler blade is useful for sliding them over the other grooves. However, as rings are only normally removed if they are going to be renewed, it should not matter if breakages occur. If the original rings are to be refitted, keep them in their respective order to each piston.

22 Gudgeon pins – removal

1   The gudgeon pins will have to be removed if the pistons are to be separated from their respective connecting rods. This will, of course, be necessary when new pistons are being fitted.
2   New pistons are supplied with new pins for fitting to the existing connecting rods. The gudgeon pin is semi-floating - that is, it is a tight shrink fit with the connecting rod and a moving fit in the piston. To press it out requires considerable force and , under usual circumstances, a proper press and special tools are essential, otherwise piston damage will occur.
3   If damage to the pistons does not matter (ie they are being renewed anyway) then the pins may be pressed out using suitable diameter pieces of rod and tube between the jaws of a vice. However, this is not recommended as the connecting rod might be damaged also. It is recommended that gudgeon pins and pistons are removed

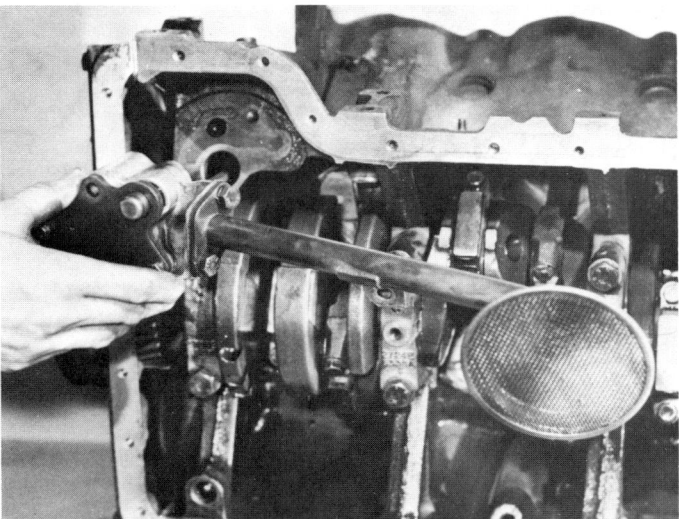

19.2 Remove the oil pump

from, and refitted to, connecting rods by Ford dealers with the necessary facilities.

23 Crankshaft rear oil seal – removal

1   The rear oil seal comprises a spring inset type flexible ring fitted in a separate carrier plate. This plate is bolted to the crankcase and the seal bears onto the crankshaft flange.
2   The engine rear plate may first be removed by undoing the bolts and lifting it away. Although this is not essential it is a simple operation and prevents the plate from becoming bent when the engine is being moved about.
3   Undo the four bolts holding the oil seal retainer plate to the engine and lift the plate away.

24 Main bearings and crankshaft (V4) – removal

1   The engine must be removed from the car, and the sump, cylinder heads, timing gears and pistons removed.
2   With a good quality socket spanner undo the six bolts holding the three main bearing caps in position.
3   When all bolts are removed lift out the caps. If they should be tight, tap the sides gently with a piece of wood or soft mallet to dislodge them. On removing each cap, check that its number is marked on it, and if not, punch or scribe its relative position for reassembly.
4   Lift out the crankshaft.
5   Slide out the bearing shells from the caps and also from the crankcase seats. Also take away the thrust washers on each side of the centre main bearing. The half which is on each side of the centre bearing cap is fitted with a tang to prevent rotation.

25 Main bearings and crankshaft (V6) – removal

1   The engine must be removed from the car and the sump cylinder heads, timing gears and pistons removed.
2   With a good quality socket spanner undo the eight bolts holding the four main bearing caps in position.
3   When all bolts are removed lift out the caps. If they are tight, tap the sides gently with a piece of wood or soft faced hammer to remove them. As each cap is removed, check that its number is marked on it, and if not, punch or scribe its position number on it.
4   Lift out the crankshaft.
5   Slide out the bearing shells from the caps and from the crankcase seats. Take away the thrust washers on each side of the centre main bearing. The half on each side of the centre bearing cap is fitted with a tang to prevent rotation.

26 Balance shaft (V4) – removal

1 If it is wished to remove the balance shaft, the engine need not be out of the car but the timing cover, radiator and grille should first be removed.
2 Remove the balance shaft gear retaining bolt and washer, then withdraw the gear. A puller will be required if levering from behind the gear does not release it. The key and spacer collar may be left in position on the shaft.
3 Undo the three bolts holding the thrust plate to the face of the block.
4 Withdraw the balance shaft carefully so as not to damage the bearing bushes in which it runs (photo).

27 Lubrication and crankcase ventilation system – description

1 A general description of the oil circulation system is given in Section 1 of this Chapter.
2 The oil pump may be of two types – the bi-rotor or sliding vane. Both types were fitted through the production of the V4 and V6 range and are interchangeable.
3 The oil is drawn through a gauze screen and tube which is below the oil level in the well of the sump. It is then pumped via the full-flow oil filter to the system of oil galleries in the block as previously described. The oil filter cartridge is mounted externally on the left-hand side of the block.
4 The crankcase is positively ventilated. Air enters through the oil filler cap in the left-hand rocker cover which is fitted with a washable gauze filter. Air enters directly under the rim of the cap or, as in the closed system, the cap is connected to the carburettor air filter by a pipe so that filtration of the air is done by the existing air filter.
5 Oil passes through the pushrod and drain channels in the tappet chamber and up the right-hand bank of the block to the right-hand rocker cover. The right-hand rocker cover is fitted with an outlet connected by a pipe to the engine intake manifold (V4 engines), and to the carburettor spacer (V6 engines). A tapered valve in the rocker cover outlet controls the outlet of fumes so that when manifold depression is high the valve closes partially, thus reducing the flow proportionally.

28 Crankcase ventilation system – routine maintenance

1 Every 6000 miles or when changing the oil, remove the oil filler cap (if fitted with gauze filter) and wash the whole unit thoroughly in petrol. Blow dry and apply a little clean engine oil to the gauze filter.
2 Clean the emission control valve. First remove the hose and then pull the valve out of the grommet in the right-hand rocker cover. Dismantle the valve by removing the circlip and taking out the valve seal, valve and spring, the components being shown in Fig. 1.7. Wash thoroughly in petrol, reassemble and refit.
3 Do not try and run the engine with any part of the emission valve or pipe disconnected as this will completely upset the fuel mixture due to the inlet manifold being opened to atmospheric pressure. It should be borne in mind that malfunctioning of the emission control valve may affect the fuel mixture to the engine.

29 Oil pump – overhaul

1 The oil pump maintains a pressure of about 50 lb/in² but any drop is not notified until it gets as low as 5 to 7 lb/in² when the warning light comes on. If an oil pressure gauge is fitted, earlier warning is given of falling oil pressure due to mechanical malfunction or failure.
2 At a major engine overhaul it is as well to check the pump and exchange it for a reconditioned unit if necessary. The efficient operation of the oil pump depends on the finely machined tolerances between the moving parts of the rotor (or vanes) and the body and reconditioning of these is generally not within the competence of the non-specialist owner.
3 To dismantle the pump first remove it from the engine as described in Section 19.
4 Remove the two bolts holding the end cover to the body and remove the cover and relief valve parts which will be released (except in early vane type pumps).

26.4 Withdraw the balance shaft (V4)

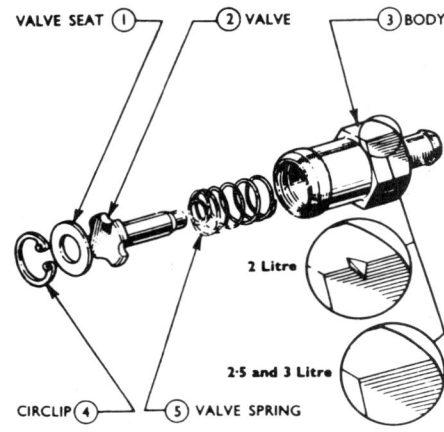

Fig. 1.7 Emission control valve components (Sec. 28)

5 The necessary clearances may now be checked using a machined straight edge (a good steel rule) and a feeler gauge.
6 On bi-rotor type pumps the critical clearances are between the lobes of the centre rotor and convex faces of the outer rotor, between the outer rotor and the pump body, and between both rotors and the end cover plate.
7 The rotor lobe clearances may be checked as shown (photo). The clearances should not exceed 0.006 inch (0.152 mm). The clearance between the outer rotor and pump body should not exceed 0.010 inch (0.254 mm) (photo).
8 The endfloat clearance can be measured by placing a steel straight edge across the end of the pump and measuring the gap between the rotors and the straight edge as shown (photo). The gap for either rotor should not exceed 0.005 inch (0.127 mm).
9 For vane type pumps check the end clearance of both the rotor and vanes as shown in Fig. 1.8 which should not exceed 0.005 inch (0.127 mm).
10 The clearances between vane and rotor, rotor and body, and vane and body must be checked with the rotor positioned as in Fig. 1.9. The gap between vane and rotor and rotor and body should not exceed 0.005 inch (0.127 mm). A maximum of 0.011 inch (0.279 mm) is permissible between the end of the vane and the pump body.
11 If the only excessive clearances are endfloat, it is possible to reduce them by removing the rotors and vanes from the pump body and lapping away the face of the body on a flat bed until the necessary clearances are obtained. It must be emphasised, however, that the faces of the body must remain perfectly flat and square to the axis of

Chapter 1 Part A V4 and V6 engines 31

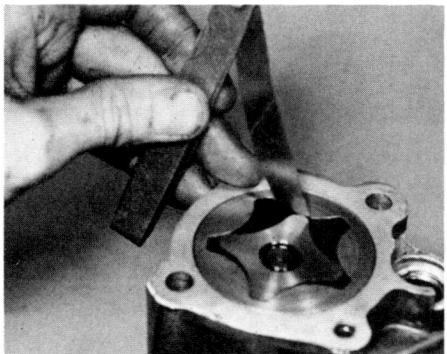

29.7a Checking the rotor to lobe clearance

29.7b Checking the body to outer rotor clearance

29.8 Checking the endfloat

the rotor spindle otherwise the clearances will not be equal and the end cover will not be a pressure tight fit to the body. It is worth trying, of course, if the pump is in need of renewal anyway, but unless done properly it could seriously jeopardise the rest of the overhaul. Any variations in the other clearances should be overcome with an exchange unit.

12 When reassembling the pump and refitting the end cover make sure that the interior is scrupulously clean and that the pressure relief valve parts are assembled in the correct positions as indicated in the illustrations.

30 Oil filter – removal and refitting

1 The oil filter element is of the disposable element type and is located on the left-hand side of the cylinder block.
2 To remove, simply unscrew the old unit, but be prepared for oil spillage and place a container or tray underneath when removing.
3 Wipe clean the mating surface at the cylinder block and the surrounding area. Before fitting the new element, smear the rubber O-ring on the new filter with a small amount of clean engine oil. Screw the new filter into position firmly by hand but do not overtighten. When the engine is restarted, check around the filter to ensure that it has sealed correctly.

31 Engine components – examination for wear

When the engine has been stripped down and all parts properly cleaned, decisions have to be made as to what needs renewal and the following sections tell the examiner what to look for. In any border line case it is always best to decide in favour of a new part. Even if a part may still be serviceable, its life will have been reduced by wear, and the degree of trouble needed to renew it in the future must be taken into consideration. However, these things are relative and it depends on whether a quick 'survival' job is being done or whether the car as a whole is being regarded as having many thousands of miles of useful and economical life remaining.

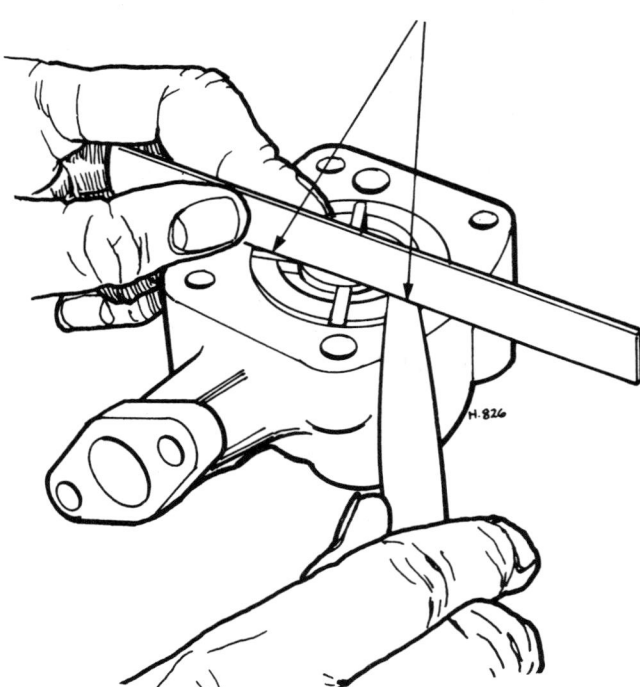

Fig. 1.8 Checking vane type oil pump endfloat clearances (Sec. 29)

32 Crankshaft – examination and renovation

1 Examine the main bearing journals and the crankpins, and if there are any scratches or score marks, the shaft will need regrinding. Such conditions will nearly always be accompanied by similar deterioration in the matching bearing shells.
2 Each bearing journal should also be round and can be checked with a micrometer or caliper gauge around the periphery at several points. If there is more than 0.001 inch of ovality, regrinding is necessary.
3 A main Ford agent or motoring engineering specialist will be able to decide to what extent regrinding is necessary and supply the special undersize shell bearings to match whatever may need grinding off.
4 Before taking the crankshaft for regrinding, check the cylinder bores and pistons as it may be advantageous to have all relevant components attended to at the same time.
5 The crankshaft oilways must be cleared. This can be done by

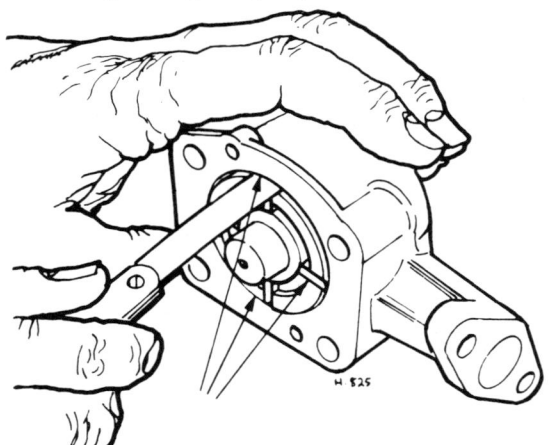

Fig. 1.9 Checking vane type oil pump rotor and vane clearance (Sec. 29)

33 Crankshaft (main) bearings and connecting rod (big-end) bearings – examination and renovation

1 With careful servicing and regular oil and filter changes bearings will last for a very long time, but they can still fail for unforeseen reasons. With big-end bearings the indication is a regular rhythmic loud knocking from the crankcase. The frequency depends on engine speed and is particularly noticeable when the engine is under load. This symptom is accompanied by a fall inoil pressure, although this is not normally noticeable unless an oil pressure gauge is fitted. Main bearing failure is usually indicated by serious vibration, particularly at higher engine revolutions, accompanied by a more significant drop in oil pressure and a 'rumbling' noise.

2 Bearing shells in good condition have bearing surfaces with a smooth, even matt silver/grey colour all over. Worn bearings will show patches of a different colour where the bearing metal has worn away and exposed the underlay. Damaged bearings will be pitted or scored. If the crankshaft is in good condition it is merely a question of obtaining another set of bearings the same size. A reground crankshaft will need new bearing shells as a matter of course.

3 The original bore in the cylinder block may have been standard or 0.015 inch (0.38 mm) oversize, in the latter instance this will be indicated by the bearing caps which will be marked with white paint.

4 The original size of the crankshaft main bearing journals may have been standard or 0.01 inch (0.25 mm) undersize. If the journals were undersize originally, this will be indicated by a green stripe on the first balance weight.

5 The original size of the big-end journal was either standard or 0.01 inch (0.25 mm) undersize. If undersize, the corresponding journal web will be marked with a green spot.

6 If the crankshaft is not being reground, but the bearings are to be renewed, take the old ones along to your supplier and this will act as a check that you are getting the correct size bearings. Undersize bearings are marked as such on the reverse face.

34 Cylinder bores – examination and renovation

1 A new cylinder is perfectly round and the walls parallel throughout its length. The action of the piston tends to wear the walls at right angles to the gudgeon pin due to side thrust. This wear takes place principally on that section of the cylinder swept by the piston rings.

2 It is possible to get an indication of bore wear by removing the cylinder heads with the engine still in the car. With the piston down in the bore first signs of wear can be seen and felt just below the top of the bore where the top piston ring reaches and there will be a noticeable lip (other than normal carbon build-up). If there is no lip it is fairly reasonable to expect that bore wear is not severe and any lack of compression or excessive oil consumption is due to worn or broken piston rings or pistons (See Section 35).

3 If it is possible to obtain a bore measuring micrometer, measure the bore in the thrust plane below the lip and again at the bottom of the cylinder in the same plane. If the difference is more than 0.003 inch (0.0762 mm) then a rebore is necessary. Similarly a difference of 0.003 inch (0.0762 mm) or more across the bore diameter is a sign of ovality calling for a rebore.

4 Any bore which is significantly scratched or scored will need reboring. This symptom usually indicates that the piston or rings are damaged. Even if only one cylinder is in need of reboring it will still be necessary for all four or six to be bored and fitted with new oversize pistons and rings. Your Ford agent or local motor engineering specialist will be able to rebore and obtain the necessary matched pistons. If the crankshaft is undergoing regrinding also, it is a good idea to let the same firm renovate and reassemble the crankshaft and pistons to the block. A reputable firm normally gives a guarantee for such work. In cases where engines have been rebored already to their maximum new cylinder liners are available which may be fitted. In such cases the same reboring processes have to be followed and the services of a specialist engineering firm are required.

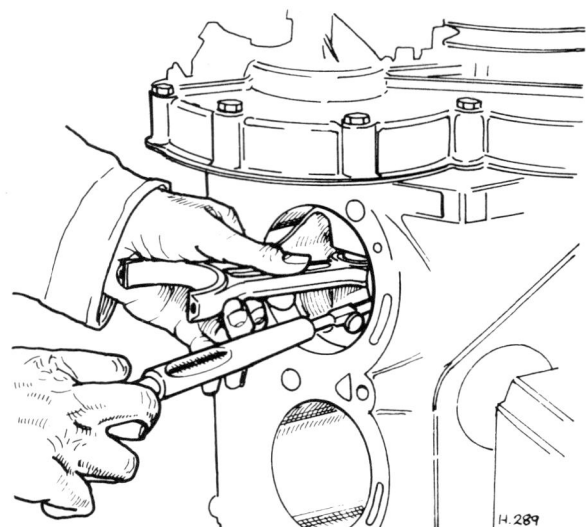

Fig. 1.10 Checking fit of piston in bore using a pull scale and feeler gauge

35 Pistons and pistons rings – examination and renovation

1 Worn pistons and rings can usually be diagnosed when the symptoms of excessive oil consumption and low compression occur and are sometimes, though not always, associated with worn cylinder bores. Compression testers that fit onto the spark plug holes are available and these can indicate where low compression is occurring. Wear usually accelerates the more it is left so when the symptoms occur early action can possibly save the expense of a rebore.

2 Another symptom of piston wear is piston slap - a knocking noise from the crankcase, not to be confused with big-end bearing failure. It can be heard clearly at low engine speed when there is no load (idling for example) and is much less audible when the engine speed increases. Piston wear usually occurs in the skirt or lower end of the piston and is indicated by vertical streaks in the worn area which is always on the thrust side. It can also be seen where the skirt thickness is different.

3 Piston ring wear can be checked by first removing the rings from the pistons as described in Section 21. Then place the rings in the cylinder bores from the top, pushing them down about 1½ inches with the head of a piston (from which the rings have been removed) so that they rest square in the cylinder. Then measure the gap at the ends of the ring with a feeler gauge. If it exceeds 0.020 inch (0.508 mm) for the two top compression rings, or 0.015 inch (0.381 mm) for the lower oil control ring then they need renewal.

4 The grooves in which the rings locate in the piston can also become enlarged in use. The clearance between ring and piston, in the groove, should not exceed 0.004 inch (0.102 mm) for the top two compression rings and 0.003 inch (0.0762 mm) for the lower oil control ring.

5 However, it is rare that a piston is only worn in the ring grooves and the need to renew them for this fault alone is hardly ever encountered. Wherever pistons are renewed the weight of the four piston/connecting rod assemblies should be kept within the limit variation of 8 gms. to maintain engine balance.

36 Connecting rods and gudgeon pins – examination and renovation

1 Gudgeon pins are a shrink fit into the connecting rods. Neither of these would normally need renewal unless the pistons were being changed, in which case the new pistons would automatically be supplied with new gudgeon pins.

2 Connecting rods are not subject to wear but in extreme circumstances such as engine seizure they could be distorted. Such conditions may be visually apparent but where doubt exists they should be checked for alignment and if necessary renewed or straightened. The bearing caps should also be examined for indications

Chapter 1 Part A V4 and V6 engines

of filing down which may have been attempted in the mistaken idea that bearing slackness could be remedied in this way. If there are such signs then the connecting rods should be renewed.

37 Camshaft and camshaft bearings – examination and renovation

1 The camshaft bearing bushes should be examined for signs of scoring and pitting. If they need renewal they will have to dealt with professionally, as, although it may be relatively easy to remove the old bushes, the correct fitting of new ones requires special tools. If they are not fitted evenly and square from the very start they can be distorted thus causing localised wear in a very short time. See your Ford dealer or local engineering specialist for this work.
2 The camshaft itself may show signs of wear on the bearing journals, cam lobes or the skew gear. The main decision to take is what degree of wear justifies renewal, which is costly. Any signs of scoring or damage to the bearing journals must be rectified, and, as undersize bearing bushes are not supplied, the journals cannot be reground. Renewal of the whole camshaft is the only solution. Similarly, excessive wear on the skew gear, which can be seen where the distributor driveshaft teeth mesh, will mean renewal of the whole camshaft.
3 The cam lobes themselves may show signs of ridging or pitting on the high points. If ridging is light then it may be possible to smooth it out with fine emery. The cam lobes, however, are surface hardened and once this is penetrated wear will be very rapid thereafter. The cams are offset and tapered to cause the tappets to rotate - thus ensuring that wear is even - do not mistake this condition for wear.

38 Tappets – examination and renovation

The faces of the tappets which bear on the camshaft should show no signs of pitting, scoring or other forms of wear. They should not be a loose fit in their housing. Wear is only normally encountered at very high mileages or in cases of neglected engine lubrication. Renew if necessary.

39 Valve and valve seats – examination and renovation

1 With the valves removed from the cylinder heads examine the heads for signs of cracking, burning away and pitting of the edge where it seats in the head. The seats of the valves in the cylinder head should also be examined for the same signs. Usually it is the valve that deteriorates first but if a bad valve is not rectified the seat will suffer and this is more difficult to repair.
2 Provided there are no obvious signs of serious pitting, the valve should be ground with its seat. This may be done by placing a smear of

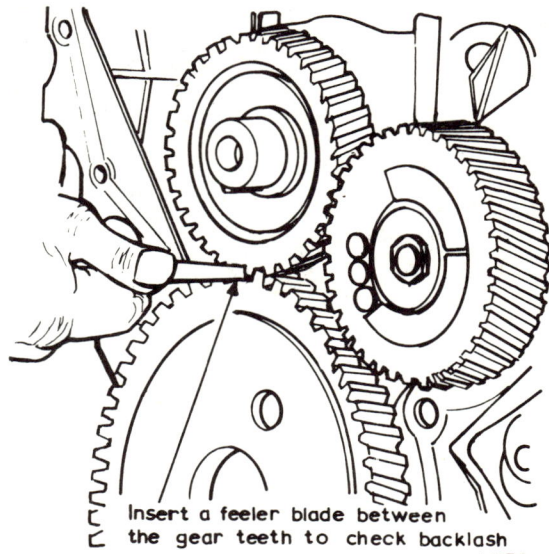

Fig. 1.11 Using feeler gauge to check camshaft gear backlash (V4 engines). The same principle is used for V6 engines

carborundum paste on the edge of the valve and, using a suction type valve holder, grinding the valve in situ. This is done with a semi-rotary action, rotating the handle of the valve holder between the hands and lifting it occasionally to redistribute the traces of paste. Use a coarse paste to start with graduating to a fine paste. As soon as a matt grey unbroken line appears on both the valve and seat the valve is 'ground in'. All traces of carbon should also be cleaned from the head and neck of the valve stem. A wire brush mounted in a power drill is a quick and effective way of doing this.
3 If the valve requires renewal it should be ground into the seat in the same way as an old valve.
4 Another form of valve wear can occur on the stem where it runs in the guide in the cylinder head. This can be detected by trying to rock the valve from side to side. If there is any movement at all it is an indication that the valve stem or guide is worn. Check the stem first with a micrometer at points along and around its length and if they are not within the specified size new valves will probably solve the problem. If the guides are worn, however, they will need reboring for oversize valves or for fitting guide inserts. The valve seats will need recutting to ensure they are concentric with the stems. This work should be given to your Ford dealer or local engineering works.
5 When valve seats are badly burnt or pitted, requiring renewal, inserts may be fitted - or renewed if already fitted once before - and

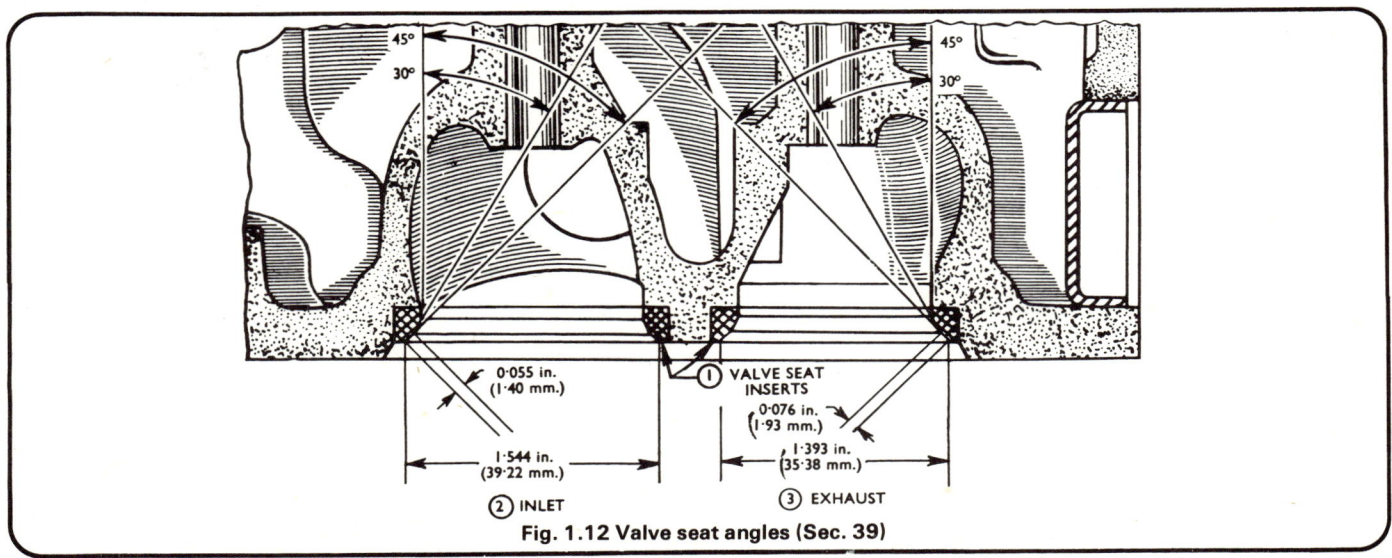

Fig. 1.12 Valve seat angles (Sec. 39)

once again this is a specialist task to be carried out by a suitable engineering firm.

6 When all valve grinding is completed it is essential that every trace of grinding paste is removed from the valves and ports in the cylinder head. This should be done by thorough washing in petrol or paraffin and blowing out with a jet of air. If particles of carborundum should work their way into the engine they would cause havoc with bearings or cylinder walls.

40 Timing gears – examination and renovation

Any wear which takes place in the timing mechanism will be on the teeth of the fibre gear which is driven from the crankshaft gear. The backlash, which can be measured with a feeler gauge between the gear teeth, should not exceed 0.004 inch (0.10 mm). The V4 balance shaft gear backlash should be the same but is not so critical. If the crankshaft gear to camshaft gear backlash is excessive the fibre gear wheel should be renewed.

41 Flywheel ring gear – examination and renovation

1 If the ring gear is badly worn or has missing teeth it should be renewed. The old ring can be removed from the flywheel by cutting a notch between two teeth with a hacksaw and then splitting it with a cold chisel.

2 To fit a new ring gear requires heating the ring to 400°F (204°C). This can be done by polishing four equally spaced sections of the gear, laying it on a suitable heat resistant surface (such as fire bricks) and heating it evenly with a blow lamp or torch until the polished areas turn a light yellow tint. Do not overheat or the hard wearing properties will be lost. The gear has a chamfered inner edge which should go against the shoulder when put on the flywheel. When hot enough place the gear in position quickly, tapping it home, if necessary, and let it cool naturally without quenching in any way.

42 Cylinder heads and piston crowns – examination and renovation

1 When cylinder heads are removed, either in the course of an overhaul or for inspection of bores or valve condition when the engine is in the car, it is normal to remove all carbon deposits from the piston crowns and heads.

2 This is best done with a cup shaped wire brush and an electric drill and is fairly straightforward when the engine is dismantled and the pistons removed. Sometimes hard spots of carbon are not easily removed except by a scraper. When cleaning the pistons with a scraper, take care not to damage the surface of the piston in any way.

3 When the engine is in the car certain precautions must be taken when decarbonising the piston crowns in order to prevent dislodged pieces of carbon falling into the interior of the engine which could cause damage to cylinder bores, pistons and rings - or if allowed into the water passage - damage to the water pump. Turn the engine so that the piston being worked on is at the top of its stroke and then mask off the adjacent cylinder bores and all surrounding water jacket orifices with paper and adhesive tape. Press grease into the gap all round the piston to keep carbon particles out and then scrape all carbon away by hand carefully. Do not use a power drill and wire brush when the engine is in the car as it will be virtually impossible to keep all the carbon dust clear of the engine. When completed carefully clear out the grease round the rim of the piston with a matchstick or something similar - bringing any carbon particles with it. Repeat the process on the other piston crown. It is not recommended that a ring of carbon is left round the edge of the piston on the theory that it will aid oil consumption. This was valid in the earlier days of long stroke low revving engines but modern engines, fuels and lubricants cause less carbon deposits anyway, and any left behind tends merely to cause hot spots.

43 Rocker gear – examination and renovation

1 The studs on which the rocker arms pivot are a press fit into the head and by placing a straight edge across the top of all four it can be seen if any have worked loose. If any have it will be necessary to have the hole bored out and an oversize stud fitted. This is a specialist task. The threads on the studs should be in good condition to ensure that the self-locking unit grips sufficiently tightly to prevent it working loose and altering the valve clearance.

2 If the torque required to turn any adjusting unit is less than 3 lbf ft (0.41 kgf m) on oiled threads the units should be renewed. If the torque is still inadequate it is possible to fit a second nut on the stud to lock the adjustment.

3 The rocker arms and fulcrum seats are matched and if either should show signs of ridging or pitting on the bearing surfaces both should be renewed.

44 Engine reassembly – general

All components of the engine must be cleaned of oil, sludge and old gaskets and the working area should also be cleared and clean. In addition to the normal range of good quality socket spanners and general tools which are essential the following must be available before reassembly begins:

Complete set of new gaskets
Supply of clean rags
Clean oil can full of clean engine oil
Torque wrench
All new spare parts as necessary

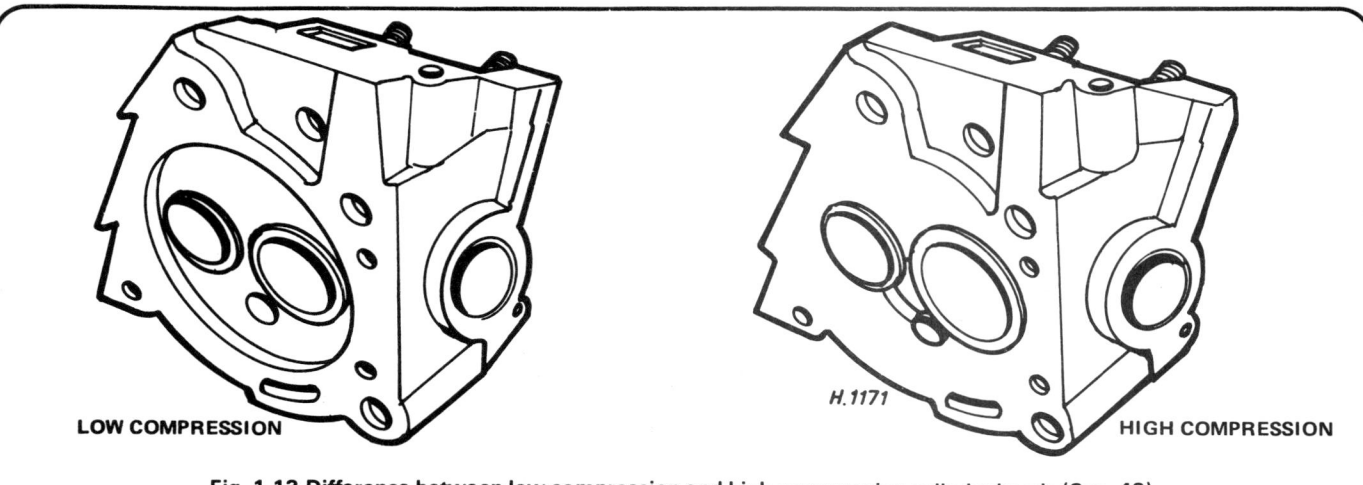

Fig. 1.13 Difference between low compression and high compression cylinder heads (Sec. 42)

45 Engine reassembly (V4) – balance shaft, camshaft, crankshaft and oil pump

1 Carefully refit the balance shaft into its bearing bushes and avoid hitting the bushes with any sharp edges (photo).
2 Refit the balance shaft thrust plate so that the oil hole in the block comes in the centre of the slot in the plate, both of which are arrowed (photo). Refit and tighten the bolts (photo).
3 Refit the camshaft carefully into the block, taking care not to let any of the cam lobes damage the bearing bushes (photo).
4 Refit the camshaft thrust plate and secure it with the two crosshead sunk screws (photo).
5 Refit the crankshaft bearing shells. The notches on the ends of the shells should locate in the cut-outs in the housing. It is essential that the two surfaces coming together are scrupulously clean (photo).
6 Lubricate the bearings generously with clean engine oil (photo).
7 Make sure that the crankshaft is scrupulously clean and lower it carefully into place on the bearing with the gearwheel towards the front of the engine (photo).
8 Take the two halves of the thrust washers which do not have tags on and very carefully slide them into position round the side of the centre main bearing. The grooves in the washers should face outward from the bearing (photo).
9 The end of the top half of the thrust washer can easily be pushed finally into position with a finger (photo).
10 Fit the plain halves of the main bearing shells into the caps (photo).
11 The centre bearing cap has machined recesses on each side to accept the lower halves of the thrust washers which have the tags on them to prevent rotation (photo).
12 Hold the thrust washers in place while fitting the centre bearing cap (photo) and check that the grooves on the washer are facing away from the cap.
13 When the crankshaft and centre bearing cap are in position the endfloat may be checked by pushing the crankshaft as far as it will go in either direction and checking the gap between the thrust washer and the crankshaft web with a feeler gauge (photo). The gap should be

45.1 Refitting the balance shaft

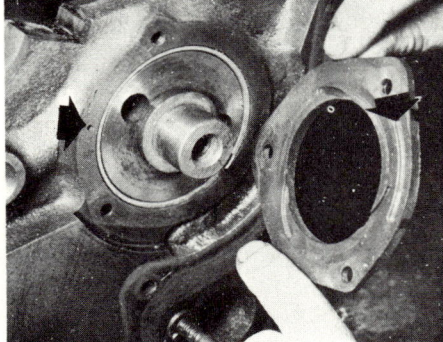
45.2a Balance shaft thrust plate

45.2b Tightening the thrust plate securing bolts

45.3 Inserting the camshaft into the cylinder block

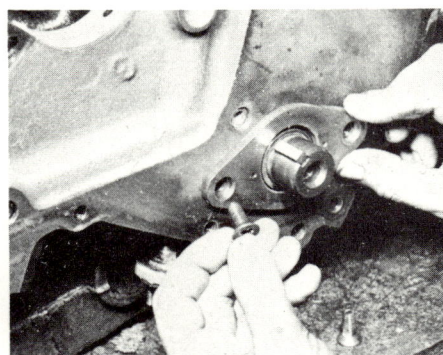
45.4 Refitting the camshaft thrust plate

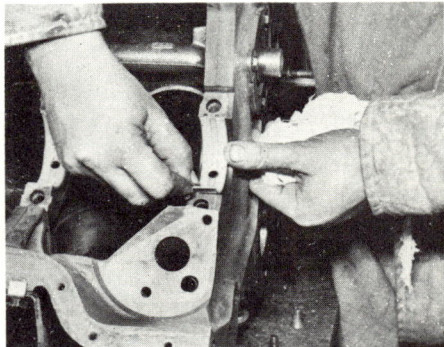
45.5 Refitting the crankshaft bearing shells

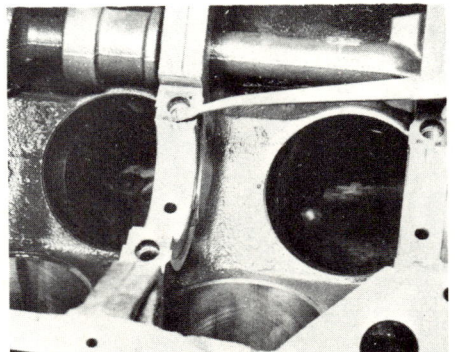
45.6 Lubricating the crankshaft bearing shells

45.7 Lowering the crankshaft into position

45.8 Refitting the crankshaft thrust washers

45.9 Correctly positioning the thrust washers

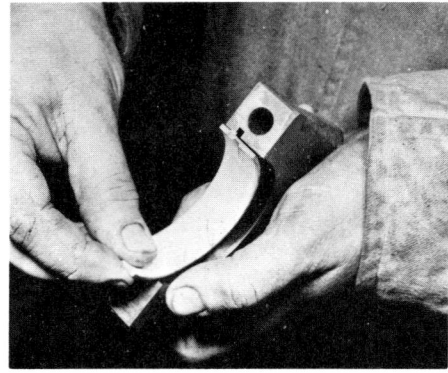
45.10 Fitting the shell bearing to the main bearing cap

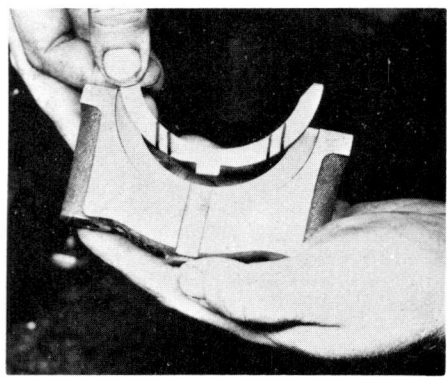
45.11 Fitting the thrust washer to the centre bearing cap

45.12 Fitting the centre bearing cap

45.13 Checking the crankshaft endfloat

45.14 Lining up the front main bearing cap

45.15 Tightening the main bearing cap bolts

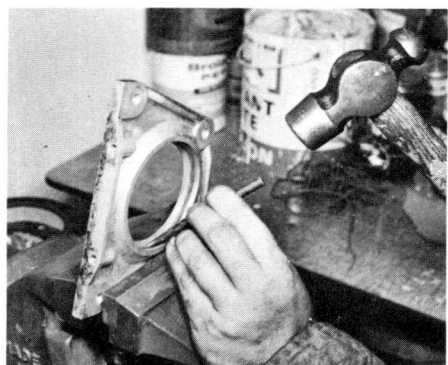
45.16 Removal of the oil seal from the rear seal carrier

45.17 Fitting the new seal to the carrier. The lip must face inwards

45.18 Tapping the seal into its final fitted position

45.19 Lubricating the crankshaft flange

45.20 The new carrier gasket fitted

between 0.003 inch and 0.011 inch (0.08 and 0.28 mm).
14 The front and rear main bearing caps do not automatically line up for bolting down and it may be necessary to tap them with a hammer handle or other soft weight to enable the bolts to pick up the threads (photo).
15 Make sure that the bolts are clean, and tighten them all down evenly to the specified torque (photo) with a torque wrench.
16 Although not absolutely necessary it is best to renew the rear crankshaft oil seal - it is provided in the gasket set anyhow. The old one can be removed from the seal carrier by carefully but firmly punching it out (photo).
17 Place the new seal squarely in position with the open lip facing away from the shoulder in the carrier bore (photo).
18 The seal can be tapped home squarely with a soft-headed mallet (photo). It is important to make sure that the seal is driven in squarely from the very start, otherwise it will buckle, so if one side tends to go in too far to start with pull it out and start afresh until it is squarely and firmly 'started' all round.
19 Lubricate the crankshaft flange well so that the seal will not run on a dry surface to start with and heat up (photo).
20 Fit the new carrier plate gasket (photo) and refit the plate.
21 Tighten the bolts to specified torque (photo).
22 Make sure the hexagonal driveshaft is located in the oil pump and refit the pump, tightening the two mounting bolts evenly to the specified torque (photo).

46 Engine reassembly (V4) – pistons, piston rings, connecting rods, big-end bearings, end plates, timing gear and front cover

1 The subsequent paragraphs on assembly assume that all the assemblies described in Section 45 have been carried out.
2 The assembly of new pistons to connecting rods should have been carried out by a Ford dealer as recommended in Section 22. The new pistons should be supplied with rings already fitted.
3 If new rings are being fitted to existing pistons the following procedure should be followed. Having removed the old rings make sure that each ring groove in the piston is completely free from carbon deposits. This is done most easily by breaking one of the old rings and using the sharp edge as a scraper. Be careful not to remove any metal from the groove. The new top ring should be stepped so as to clear the ridge in the cylinder bore left above the previous top ring. If a normal new ring is fitted, it will hit the ridge and break, because the new ring will not have worn in the same way as the old one, which will have worn in unison with the ridge.
4 The new piston rings - three for each piston - must first be checked in the cylinder bores as described in Section 35. It is assumed that the gap at the ends of the rings will not be too great. However, it is equally important that the gaps are not too small - otherwise the ends could meet when normal operating temperatures are reached and the ring would then break.
5 The minimum gap for all three rings is 0.010 inch (0.25 mm). If the gap is too small, one end of the ring must be filed to increase the gap. To do this the ring should be gripped carefully in a vice between thin pieces of soft metal in such a way that only the end to be filed is gripped and so that it only protrudes above the jaws of the vice a very small distance. This will eliminate the possibility of bending and breaking the ring while filing the end. Use a thin, fine file and proceed in easy stages - checking the gap by refitting the ring in the bore until the necessary minimum gap is obtained. This must be done with every ring - checking each one in the bore to which it will eventually be fitted. To avoid mistakes it is best to complete one set of rings at a time and refit the piston in the cylinder before proceeding to the next.
6 To fit the rings on to the piston calls for patience and care if breakages are to be avoided. The three rings for each piston must all be fitted over the crown so the first one to go on is the slotted oil control ring. Hold the ring over the top of the piston and spread the ends just enough to get it around the circumference. Then, with the fingers, ease it down, keeping it parallel to the ring grooves by 'walking' the ring ends alternately down the piston. Being wider than the compression rings no difficulty should be encountered in getting it over the first two grooves in the piston.
7 The lower compression ring, which goes on next. must be fitted one way up. It is marked 'TOP' to indicate its upper face (photo).
8 Start fitting this ring by spreading the ends to get it located over the top of the piston (photo).
9 The lower compression ring has to be guided over the top ring groove and this can be done by using a suitable cut piece of tin which can be placed so as to cover the top groove under the ends of the ring (photo).
10 Alternatively, a feeler blade may be slid around under the ring to guide it into its groove (photo).
11 The top ring may be fitted either way up as it is barrel faced.
12 When all the rings are in position on the piston rotate them fully in their respective grooves to ensure that they do not bind when compressed. Any tight spots are usually caused by carbon left on the ring band and this must therefore be cleaned off to enable the ring to expand and contract in its groove. Locate the piston ring gaps in the following manner:

Top: at 180° to bottom ring gap
Centre: at 90° to bottom ring gap
Bottom: in line with gudgeon pin

With the rings fitted, the piston/connecting rod assembly is ready for returning to the cylinder.
13 Each connecting rod and bearing cap should have been marked on removal (Section 20) but in any case the cylinder number is etched lightly on the end of the cap and connecting rod alongside. The piston and connecting rod are also marked to show which side faces the front of the engine (photo).
14 Start with No. 1 cylinder and remove the existing oil glaze from the bore by rubbing it down with very fine emery. This will break down the hardened skin and permit the new piston rings to bed down more quickly (photo). Wipe clean the cylinder bore after de-glazing.
15 Fit a new half shell bearing into the connecting rod of No. 1 piston so that the notch in the shell bearing locates in the connecting rod (photo). Lubricate with clean engine oil the piston/cylinder bore and big-end bearing.
16 Place the piston in the cylinder bore the correct way round until the oil control ring abuts the face of the block. Then, using a piston ring compressor or a large hose circlip as a compressor (photo), contract each ring in turn and tap the piston into the cylinder. Take great care to

45.21 Tightening the carrier securing bolts

45.22 Tightening the oil pump securing bolts

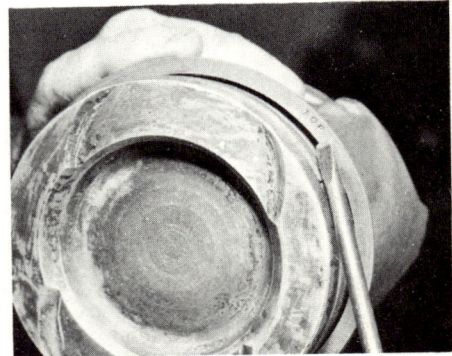
46.7 The new lower compression ring fitted correctly

46.8 Spreading the ring ends during fitment

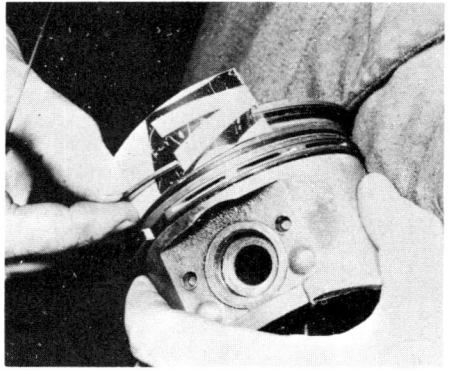
46.9 A piece of tin helps to slide the rings over the upper ring grooves

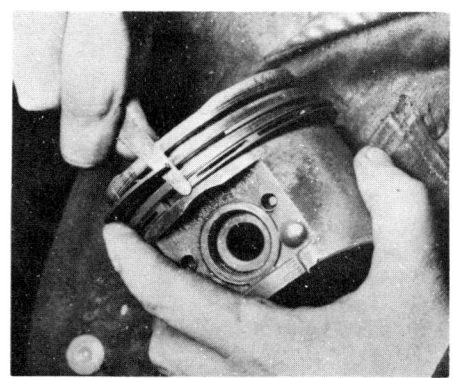
46.10 Using a feeler gauge to fit the rings

46.13 Connecting rod and piston identification

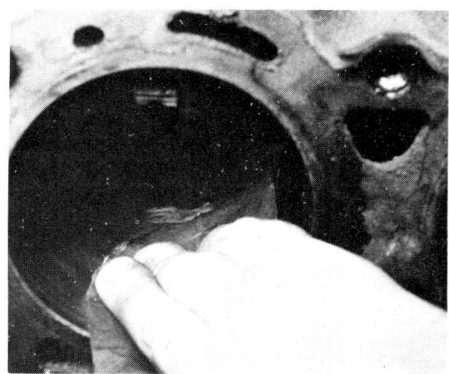
46.14 Cleaning off the oil glaze

46.15 Fitting the shell bearing half

46.16 Use of a jubilee clip to compress the piston rings

46.17 Lubricating the big-end journal

46.18 Refitting the connecting rod end cap

46.20 Tightening the end cap securing bolts

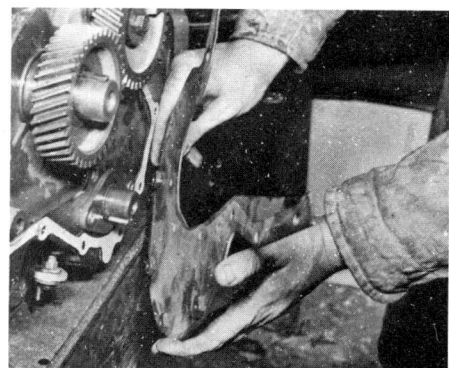
46.21 Fitting the front engine plate

46.22 Tightening the front engine plate securing bolts

Chapter 1 Part A V4 and V6 engines

be sure that the ring is not trapped on the top edge of the cylinder bore, and when tapping the piston in do not use any force as the rings could easily be broken.

17 When the piston has been fully located in the bore push it down so that the end of the connecting rod seats on the journal on the crankshaft. Make sure the journal is well lubricated with engine oil (photo).

18 Maintaining absolute cleanliness all the time, fit the other shell bearing half into the cap, once again with the notches in the bearing and cap lined up. Lubricate it with engine oil and fit it onto the connecting rod so that the hole in the cap fits in the dowels in the connecting rods (photo).

19 Refit all pistons and connecting rods in a similar manner and do not make any mistakes locating the correct No. 1 piston in the correct bore. Nos. 1 and 2 cylinders are front and rear respectively on the right-hand bank and Nos. 3 and 4 front and rear of the left-hand bank. However, due to the 'V' formation of the engine the big-end journals on the crankshaft starting at the front run 1, 3, 2, 4. This is different again from the firing order so make sure you have it all clear in your mind to start with.

20 When all caps are correctly fitted, tighten down the bolts to the specified torque wrench setting (photo).

21 Before refitting the camshaft timing gear the front engine plate must be fitted back. Select the new gasket and coat the clean face of the block with suitable gasket sealant; stick the gasket to it in position. Then offer up the engine plate (photo).

22 Bolt the cover plate up tight to the block, not forgetting to fit the support plate behind the three centre bolts (photo).

23 The timing gears are easily fitted but care must be taken to ensure that the marks line up properly. Both the balance shaft and camshaft gears are keyed on to their respective shafts. The crankshaft gear has two countersunk dimples machined in its periphery. Both these must match up simultaneously with the single dimple in each of the other two gears. The photograph shows how this should be. An arrow points to the crankshaft/camshaft marks and the finger to the crankshaft/balance shaft marks (photo).

24 Fit the camshaft gear and balance shaft gear so that the timing marks line up. Refit the camshaft gear locking bolt together with the eccentric boss that drives the fuel pump. Tighten the bolt to the specified torque. There is no special position for the boss, although it was marked by a pencil on the fibre gear in this photo before removal (photo).

25 Refit and tighten the bolt and washer (photo) holding the balance shaft gear to the specified torque.

26 If the crankshaft pulley wheel oil seal in the front cover is being renewed, care should be exercised when driving out the old seal as the cover is only a light alloy casting. As the old seal must be driven out from the front it is essential to find two pieces of wood thicker than the depth of the cover so that the immediate area near the seal ring may be supported (photo).

27 With the cover firmly supported inside, it can be laid on the bench and the old seal driven out with a punch (photo).

28 Turn the cover over and carefully tap in the new seal evenly with

46.23 Timing marks

46.24 Fitting the fuel pump eccentric

46.25 Refitting the balance shaft gear retaining bolt

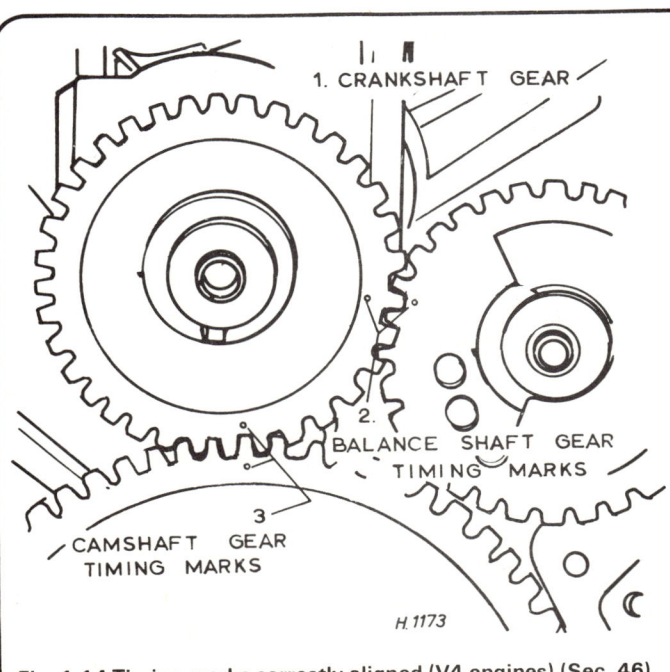
Fig. 1.14 Timing marks correctly aligned (V4 engines) (Sec. 46)

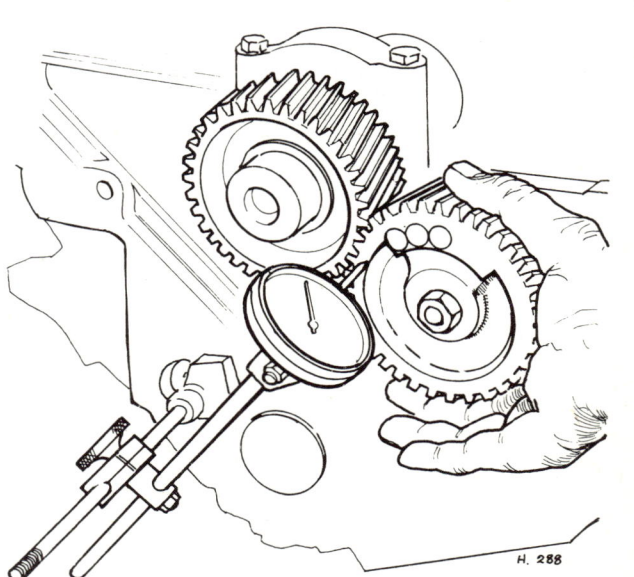
Fig. 1.15 Using dial indicator gauge to check endfloat of balance shaft and gear (V4 engines)

46.26 The correct method of supporting the rear of the cover

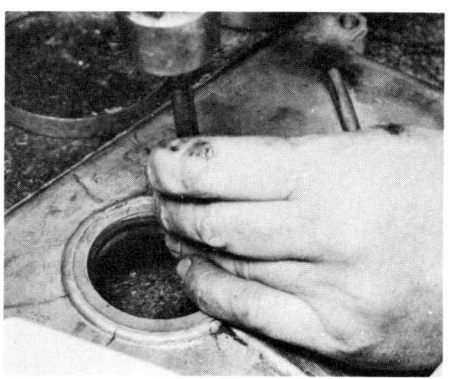
46.27 Driving out the old seal

46.28 The seal fitted the correct way round

46.29 Tapping the seal fully home

46.30 Fitting the front cover plate

46.31 Positioning the pulley onto the crankshaft

46.32 Tightening the front cover securing bolts

47.2 Tightening the crankshaft pulley securing bolt

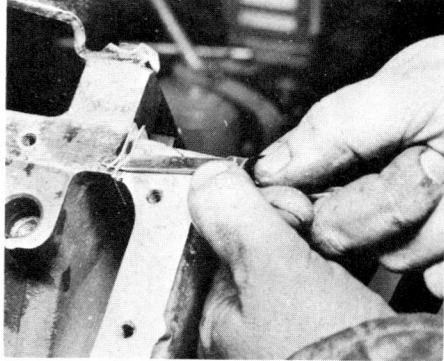
47.3 Trimming the front cover gasket ends

47.4 Trimming the rear oil seal carrier gasket

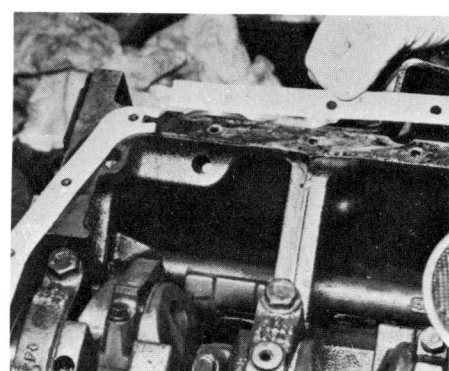
47.5 Fitting the new sump gasket

47.6 The new gasket correctly fitted

Chapter 1 Part A V4 and V6 engines

the inner lip facing away from the shoulder in the bore (photo).
29 Tap the seal home finally with a block of wood (photo).
30 Select the front cover gasket and, using a suitable gasket sealant, position it on the engine front plate and offer up the cover (photo).
31 Place the front cover bolts in position and screw them up loosely. Then fit the crankshaft pulley wheel onto the keyway of the crankshaft (photo). See that the boss of the pulley is lubricated where the oil seal runs.
32 The refitting of the crankshaft pulley, before tightening the cover bolts, centralises the seal to the pulley. The bolts holding the cover may then be tightened to the specified torque (photo).

47 Engine reassembly (V4) – rear plate, crankshaft pulley wheel, sump and flywheel

1 If the engine rear plate has been removed it should now be refitted. Make sure that both metal faces are quite clean before refitting. No gasket is used.
2 Refit the bolt and washer which locate the crankshaft pulley wheel, block the crankshaft with a piece of wood against the side of the crankcase and tighten the bolt to the specified torque (photo).
3 Trim the projecting pieces of the front cover and backplate gaskets at the sump face of the block and front cover (photo).
4 Trim the projecting edge of the rear oil seal carrier on the sump face at the rear of the crankcase (photo).
5 Clean all traces of old gasket which may remain from the sump joint faces and cover the faces of both the crankcase and sump with sealing compound. The sump gasket is in four sections which dovetail together and these should be carefully positioned and the joints interlocked (photo).
6 The engine is then ready for the sump to be refitted (photo).
7 Clean the interior of the sump thoroughly, apply sealer to the joint edge and place it in position (photo).
8 Refit all the sump bolts and tighten them evenly to the specified torque (photo).
9 The flywheel may now be refitted. Make sure that the mating flanges are clean and free from burrs and line up the bolt holes correctly. They are so positioned that they will only line up in one position. Do not hammer the flywheel into position if it should be difficult to get it fully onto the flange. Support it squarely and refit the bolts, tightening them evenly so as to draw the flywheel squarely onto its seat. There are no washers and the bolts should be tightened evenly and progressively to the specified torque (photo).

48 Engine reassembly (V4) – valve gear, cylinder heads and inlet manifold

1 When the cylinder heads have been decarbonised and the valves ground in, as described in Sections 39 and 42, the cylinder heads may be reassembled. If the valves have been removed as described in Section 11, there will be no confusion as to which valve belongs in which position.
2 Make sure all traces of carbon and grinding paste have been removed, lubricate the valve stem with engine oil and place it in the appropriate guide (photo).
3 It will then protrude through the top of the cylinder head (photo).
4 Fit a new seal cup over the valve stem (photo).
5 Place the valve spring over the valve stem with the close coils of the spring nearest the cylinder head (photo).
6 Fit the circular spring collar over the spring with the protruding centre boss of the collar downward (photo).
7 Using a proper valve spring compressor tool, compress the spring down the valve stem sufficiently far to enable the two halves of the split collar (collets) to be fitted into the groove in the valve stem (photo). If necessary the collets should be smeared with grease to keep them in position. The spring compressor may then be released. Watch to ensure that the collets stay together in position, as the spring collar comes past them. If the collar is a little off centre it may force one collet out of its groove in which case the spring must be re-compressed and the collet repositioned. When the compressor is finally released tap the head of the valve stem with a soft mallet to make sure the valve assembly is securely held in position.
8 Stand the engine the right way up on the bench and refit the tappets if they have been removed from the block. If these have been

47.7 Lowering the sump into position

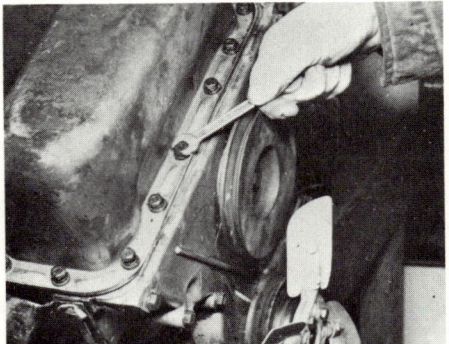
47.8 Refitting the sump bolts

47.9 Tightening the flywheel securing bolts

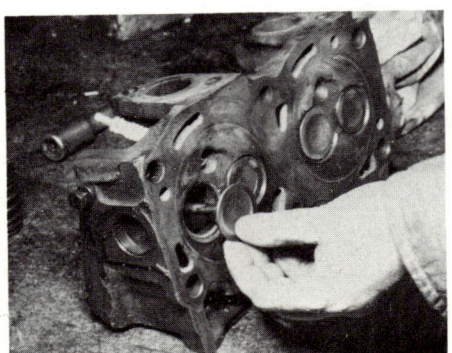
48.2 Inserting the valve into its guide

48.3 The valve stem projecting through the cylinder head

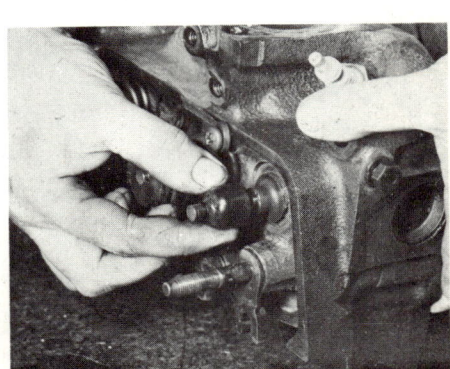
48.4 Fitting the valve oil seal

48.5 Fitting the valve spring

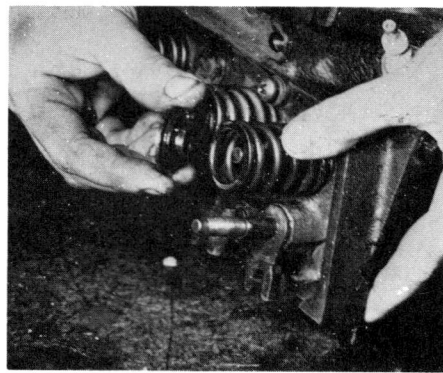
48.6 Refitting the circular collar

48.7 Refitting the collets with the spring compressed

48.10 Fitting a new cylinder head gasket

48.11 Lowering the cylinder head into position

48.12 Tightening the cylinder head bolts

48.13 Inserting the pushrods through the cylinder heads

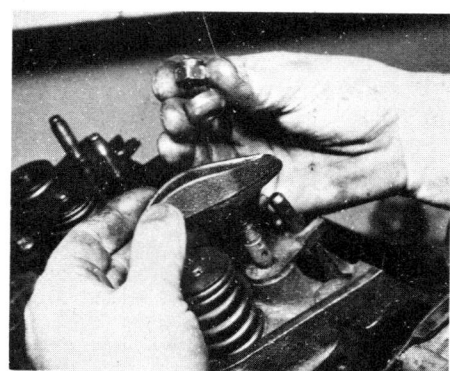
48.14 Refitting a rocker arm

48.15 Preparing the inlet manifold mating faces

48.16 Fitting the inlet manifold gasket

48.17 Location of the square port

48.18 Refitting the inlet manifold

kept in order on removal, as suggested, it will be a simple matter to refit them.

9 The two cylinder heads are identical so if they were marked left and right on removal they can be refitted on the same bank. If they have been muddled up no real harm will result but the pushrods will not be matched to their correct rocker arms. As these normally 'run in' together excessive wear could occur until such time as the two unfamiliar surfaces have bedded in.

10 Select a new cylinder head gasket and place it in position on the block on one bank. These gaskets are identical and can fit either bank but they can only go on one way - which is obvious from the way the bolt holes and cooling jacket holes line up (photo).

11 Locate the gasket over the protruding spigots in the block and then place the cylinder head in position (photo).

12 Make sure the cylinder head bolts are clean and lightly oiled and refit them. Nip them all down lightly and then tighten them in the sequence shown in Fig. 1.5. The bolts should be tightened down to progressive torque loadings, all to 50 lbf ft (6.9 kgf m) then all to 60 lbf ft (8.3 kgf m), and finally to the specified requirements of 65 - 70 lbf ft (9.0 - 9.7 kgf m) (photo).

13 Now fit the pushrods into position, making sure that they are refitted the same way as they came out and according to the original valve position. This will not be difficult if they have been kept in order as described in Sections 9 and 10. The pushrods are located at their upper ends in brackets bolted to the head (photo).

14 Locate the appropriate rocker arm over each stud so that the recessed end locates over the pushrod. Then place the fulcrum seat over the stud followed by the self-locking nut (photo).

15 When both heads are refitted and fully tightened down the inlet manifold may be fitted. In view of the large area to be sealed, it is a safety measure - if not essential - to use a jointing compound in addition to the gasket (photo) on the mating surfaces.

16 Place the inlet manifold gasket in position in the 'V' so that the single square hole (arrowed) is on the left-hand cylinder head (photo). The gasket is obviously incorrect if put on any other way, but this is a positive guide.

17 Apply jointing compound to the mating faces of the inlet manifold. Note the square port (arrowed) which matches the gasket hole and port in the left-hand cylinder head (photo).

18 Place the manifold in position with the thermostat housing to the front (photo).

19 Refit the six manifold securing bolts, ensuring that the gasket is lined up to permit them to pick up the threads in the cylinder heads, and screw them up lightly (photo).

20 With a torque wrench (photo) tighten the bolts down evenly in the sequence shown in Fig. 1.3 to the specified torque. This tightening should be done in stages - all being tightened to 5 lbf ft (0.7 kgf m), then to 10 lbf ft (1.4 kgf m), before finally reaching the specified figure. Any uneven or excessive tightening may crack the manifold casting so take care.

49 Valve rocker clearances (V4) – adjustment

1 The valve stem to rocker clearance, which is in effect the mechanical free play between the camshaft and the end of the valve stem, is important to the correct operation and performance of the engine. If the clearance is too great there is an increase in noise level and, since the opening is reduced, a consequent reduction in gas flow. If the clearance is too little the valve could open too much with the danger of it hitting the crown of the piston. The clearance is checked when the tappet is on the heel of the cam (opposite the highest point) and the valve therefore closed. This position coincides with certain other valves being fully open with their tappets on the highest point of the cam. This can be easily seen when the valve spring is fully compressed.

2 The table below shows the relationship between the fully open valves and the closed valves which are to be checked. The diagram shows the valve numbering - Nos. 1 - 4 front to rear on the right-hand bank and Nos. 5 - 8 front to rear on the left-hand bank.

Valves open (together)	Adjust
Nos. 1 and 4	Nos. 5 (inlet) and 8 (exhaust)
Nos. 2 and 6	Nos. 3 (exhaust) and 7 (inlet)
Nos. 5 and 8	Nos. 1 (exhaust) and 4 (inlet)
Nos. 3 and 7	Nos. 2 (inlet and 6 (exhaust)

Front of engine

LH Bank	RH Bank
5	1
6	2
7	3
8	4

The clearances after reassembly should be set at 0.012 inch (0.30 mm) for the inlet valves and 0.020 inch (0.51 mm) for exhaust valves for a cold engine. They should be checked later when the engine has reached normal running temperature, when they should be set at 0.010 inch (0.25 mm) for inlet valves and 0.018 inch (0.46 mm) for exhaust valves.

3 The actual adjustment procedure is straightforward. With the appropriate valve ready for checking place a feeler gauge of the required thickness (for exhaust or inlet valve) between the top of the valve stem and the rocker arm (photo). If it will not fit the clearance is too small so slacken off the self-locking nut on the stud until it will fit. If the clearance is too large the nut should be screwed down. The correct clearance is obtained when the feeler blade can be moved readily but a firm drag is felt.

4 It is a wise precaution to check each clearance measurement after the adjusting socket spanner has been removed from the nut. This is because the socket may possibly bind against the side of the rocker arm and tilt it, thus causing a false clearance measurement.

5 After the clearance adjustments are completed, refit the rocker covers, each fitted with a new gasket (photo).

6 Tighten down the screws firmly and evenly (photo).

Note: *The rocker cover with the oil filler cap goes on the left-hand bank. Rocker clearances should **NOT** be checked with a feeler gauge while the engine is running. In certain circumstances, the valve could be forced against the crown of the piston causing serious damage. If one rocker is noisy it is possible to identify which one by removing the rocker cover and pressing a finger on each rocker in turn. The noisy one will be quiet when pressed.*

48.19 Refitting the inlet manifold securing bolts

48.20 Tightening the inlet manifold securing bolts

49.3 Checking the valve rocker clearances

49.5 Refitting the rocker cover

49.6 Refitting the rocker cover securing bolts

50 Engine reassembly (V6) – crankshaft, pistons, piston rings, connecting rods and big-end bearings

Main bearings/crankshaft
1   Select the halves of the four main bearing shells which have the oil holes and grooves and place them in position in the crankcase (photo). The notches on the ends of the shells should locate in the cut-outs in the housing. It is essential that the two surfaces coming together are scrupulously clean.
2   Make sure that the oil holes in the bearings are in line with the drillings in the main bearing webs.
3   Lubricate the bearing generously with clean engine oil.
4   Make sure that the crankshaft is scrupulously clean and lower it carefully into place on the bearings with the gearwheel towards the front of the engine (photo).
5   Lubricate the crankshaft main bearing journals with clean engine oil.
6   Select the front main bearing half shell and, after checking that both mating surfaces are clean, fit the shell to the front main bearing cap with the notches in the shell corresponding with the groove in the cap.
7   It will be noted that on the end cap is a capital '**F**' and an arrow which indicates the correct way round that the end cap must be fitted (photo).
8   The intermediate front bearing cap has machined recesses on each side to accept the lower halves of the thrust washers which have tangs on them to prevent rotation. Apply a little grease on the thrust washer to bearing cap faces and place the thrust washers in position with the grooves on the washers facing away from the cap (photo).
9   Slide the two thrust washers without tags into position with the grooves on the washers facing toward the edge of the main bearing journal.
10   Holding the thrust washers in position fit the second or intermediate front main bearing to its location with the crankcase (photo).
11   Refit the two remaining bearing half shells into the main bearing caps and place in position in the crankcase.
12   The front intermediate and rear main bearing caps do not automatically line up for bolting down and it may be necessary to tap them with a hammer handle to enable the bolts to pick up the threads.
13   Make sure that all the bolts are clean, insert them in their respective caps and tighten them down evenly to the specified torque (photo).
14   The endfloat may now be checked by pushing the crankshaft as far as it will go in either direction and checking the gap between the thrust washer and the crankshaft with a feeler gauge. The gap should be between 0.003 and 0.011 inch (0.0762 and 0.2794 mm) (photo).

Pistons and connecting rods
15   The assembly of new pistons to connecting rods should have been carried out as recommended. The new pistons should be supplied with rings already fitted.
16   If new rings are being fitted to existing pistons, the following procedure should be followed. Having removed the old rings make sure that each ring groove in the piston is completely free from carbon deposits. This can be done most easily by breaking one of the old rings and using the sharp end as a scraper. Be careful not to remove any metal from the groove. The new top ring should be stepped so as to clear the ridge in the cylinder bore left above the previous top ring. If a normal new ring is fitted, it will hit the ridge and break, because the new ring will not have worn in the same way as the old one, which will have worn in unison with the ridge.
17   The new piston rings - three to each piston - must first be checked in the cylinder bores as described in Section 35. It is assumed that the gap at the ends of the rings will not be too great. However, it is equally important that the gaps are not too small - otherwise the ends could meet when normal operating temperatures are reached and the rings would then break.
18   The minimum gap for all three rings is 0.010 inch (0.25 mm). If the gap is too small, one end of the ring must be filed to increase the gap. To do this the ring should be gripped in a vice between two thin pieces of soft metal in such a way that only the end to be filed is gripped, and so that it only protrudes above the jaws of the vice a very small distance. This will eliminate the possibility of bending and breaking the ring while filing the end. Use a thin, fine file and proceed in easy stages checking the gap by refitting the ring in the bore until the necessary minimum gap is obtained. This must be done with every ring checking each one in the bore to which it will eventually be fitted. To avoid mistakes it is best to complete one set of rings at a time and refit the piston in the cylinder before proceeding to the next.
19   To refit the rings onto the pistons calls for patience and care if breakages are to be avoided. The three rings, for each piston, must all be fitted over the crown so obviously the first one to go on is the slotted oil control ring. Hold the ring over the top of the piston and spread the ends just enough to get it around the circumference. Then, with the fingers, ease it down, keeping it parallel to the ring grooves, by 'walking' the ring ends alternately down the piston. Being wider than the compression rings no difficulty should be encountered in getting it over the first two grooves in the piston.
20   The lower compression ring, which goes on next must only be fitted one way up. It is marked '**TOP**' to indicate its upper face (see photo).
21   Start fitting this ring by spreading the ends to get it located over the top of the piston (see photo 46.8)
22   The lower compression ring has to be guided over the top ring groove and this can be done by using a suitably cut piece of tin which can be placed so as to cover the top groove under the ends of the ring (see photo 46.9).
23   The top ring may be fitted either way up as it is barrel faced.
24   With the rings fitted the piston/connecting rod assembly is ready for refitting in the cylinder. However, first it will be necessary to locate the piston ring gaps in the following manner:

Top: at 180° to bottom ring gap
Centre: at 90° to bottom ring gap
Bottom: in line with gudgeon pin

25   Each connecting rod and bearing cap should have been marked on removal but, in any case, the cylinder number is etched lightly on the end of the cap and connecting rod. The piston and connecting rod are also marked to show which side faces the front of the engine.
26   Start with No.1 cylinder and remove the existing oil 'glaze' from the bore by rubbing it down with very fine emery. This will break down the hardened skin and permit the new piston rings to bed down more

Chapter 1 Part A V4 and V6 engines

50.1 Insert the main bearing shell and locate the upper half thrust washers with the oil grooves facing out

50.4 Lower the crankshaft carefully into position

50.7 Main bearing cap identification

50.8 Fit the thrust washer to the intermediate front bearing

50.10 Fit the intermediate front bearing

50.13 Tighten the end cap retaining bolts

50.14 Check the endfloat

50.20 Piston ring 'TOP' marking

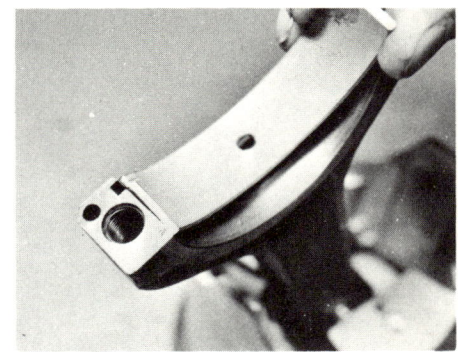

50.27 Fit the bearing shell

quickly (see photo 46.14).
27 Fit a new half shell bearing into the connecting rod of No. 1 piston so that the notch in the bearing shell locates in the groove in the connecting rod (photo).
28 Make sure that the hole in the half shell bearing aligns with the drilling in the connecting rod (photo).
29 Identify the connecting rod and piston front faces ('F' mark to front) and ensure that they are both on the same side (photos).
30 Place the piston in the cylinder bore the correct way round until the oil control ring abuts the face of the cylinder block (photo)
31 Whilst the connecting rod is being installed into the bore, line up the lower end with its respective crankshaft journal.
32 Using a large hose clip or piston ring compressor contract the piston rings and tap the piston into the cylinder. Take great care to be sure that the rings are not trapped on the top edge of the cylinder bore, and when tapping the piston in do not use any force. If this precaution is not taken the rings could easily be broken.
33 When the piston has been fully located in the bore push it down so that the end of the connecting rod seats on the journal on the crankshaft. Make sure that the journal is well lubricated with engine oil.
34 Maintaining absolute cleanliness all the time, fit the other half shell bearing into the cap, once again with the notches in the bearing and cap lined up. Lubricate it with engine oil and fit it onto the connecting rod so that the holes in the cap fit the dowels in the connecting rods (photo).
35 Refit all pistons and connecting rods in a similar manner. Do not make any mistake locating the correct number piston in the correct bore. No. 1, 2, and 3 cylinders are front to rear respectively on the right-hand bank and No. 4, 5, and 6 front to rear respectively on the left-hand bank.
36 When all the caps are correctly fitted tighten down the bolts to the specified torque (photo).

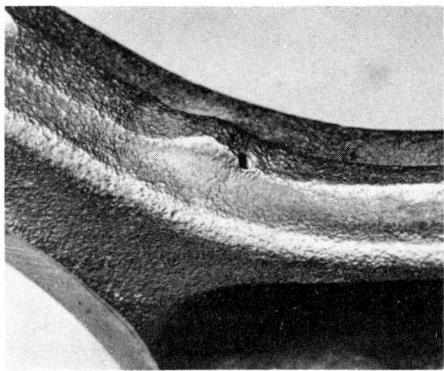
50.28 Connecting rod hole

50.29a Align 'F' mark on piston to ...

50.29b ... the 'FRONT' mark on connecting rod

50.30 Insert piston into bore – note ring compressor

50.34 Refit the end cap – note location dowel

50.36 Tighten the retaining bolts to the specified torque

51.1 Tap out the old seal

51.2 Correct oil seal position

51.5 Fit the retainer plate gasket

51.7 Centralise the seal housing

51.9 Insert the camshaft

51.10 Refit the camshaft thrust plate

Chapter 1 Part A V4 and V6 engines

51 Engine reassembly (V6) – crankshaft oil seals, oil pump, camshaft, timing gears, end plate, front and rear cover and crankshaft pulley

1 Although not absolutely necessary, it is best to renew the rear crankshaft oil seal. It is provided in the gasket set anyway. The old one can be removed from the seal carrier by using a screwdriver and carefully tapping it out (photo).
2 Tap the new seal squarely in position with the open lip facing away from the shoulder in the carrier bore (photo).
3 The seal can be tapped home using a hammer. It is important to make sure that the seal is driven in squarely from the very start, otherwise it will buckle. If one side tends to go in too far to start with, pull it out and start afresh until it is squarely and firmly 'started' all round.
4 Lubricate the crankshaft flange well so that the seal will not run on a dry surface to start with and heat up.
5 Fit the new retainer plate gasket, holding it in place with a little grease (photo).
6 Place the retainer plate in position on the engine.
7 Refit the four bolts with spring washers. Before tightening the bolts, centralise the seal housing using feeler gauges placed between the crankshaft flange and the location tabs of the housing (photo). Tighten to the specified torque wrench setting in a diagonal manner.
8 Ensure that the hexagonal driveshaft is located in the oil pump and refit the pump. Tighten the mounting bolts evenly to the specified torque.
9 Carefully insert the camshaft into the cylinder block making sure that the sharp lobes of the cams do not damage the bearing surfaces (photo).
10 Refit the camshaft thrust plate making sure that the countersunk securing screw holes face outwards (photo).
11 Refit the two camshaft thrust plate securing cross-head screws and tighten as tightly as possible, preferably using an impact screwdriver.
12 Fit a new front end plate gasket and retain in place with a little grease. Position the front end plate carefully so as not to dislodge the gasket.
13 Holding the front end plate in one hand refit the curved reinforcement plate and the three bolts with spring washers. Tighten these bolts securely (photo).
14 The timing gears are easily refitted providing that care is taken to ensure that all timing marks line up correctly. Both the crankshaft and camshaft gears are keyed on their respective shafts. First refit the crankshaft key and slide on the timing gear.
15 Screw the camshaft timing gear bolt into the end of the camshaft so that it may be rotated.
16 Rotate the crankshaft until the dot on the outer circumference of the gear opposite to the key is facing the camshaft.
17 Rotate the camshaft until the dot on the outer circumference of gear opposite to the key is facing the crankshaft and slide the gear onto the camshaft with the two dots exactly opposite each other (photo).
18 Remove the bolt from the end of the camshaft and fit the eccentric boss to the end of the camshaft. Secure in place with the bolt and tighten to the specified torque wrench setting. There is no special position for this boss although it was marked by a pencil on the fibre gear before removal. On some later models there is a location pin to the rear of the eccentric (photo).
19 If the crankshaft pulley wheel oil seal in the front cover is being renewed, care should be exercised when driving out the old seal as the cover is only a light alloy casting. As the old seal must be driven out from the front it is essential to find some piece of wood thicker than the depth of the cover so that the immediate area near the seal ring may be supported.
20 With the cover firmly supported inside, it can be laid on the bench and the old oil seal driven out with a chisel.
21 Turn the cover over and carefully tap in the new oil seal evenly with the inner lip facing away from the shoulder in the bore.
22 Lubricate the oil seal and position the front cover onto the new gasket fitted to the front of the engine. If necessary retain the gasket in place with a little grease. Screw the front cover retaining bolts with spring washers into their threaded holes but do not tighten yet.
23 Lubricate the front pulley with oil so that the oil seal will not be damaged upon initial starting of the engine.
24 Carefully insert the pulley so as to centralise the oil seal. If necessary tap the front cover with a soft-faced hammer (photo).
25 Refit the large plain washer and bolt that secures the pulley to the crankshaft (photo).
26 Tighten the bolt to the specified torque. If necessary lock the crankshaft with a piece of wood against the side of the crankcase.
27 Tighten the front cover retaining bolts to the specified torque wrench setting. The four short bolts are located at the top. Locate the crankshaft pulley and Woodruff key and secure with washer and bolt.
28 If the engine rear plate has been removed it should now be refitted. Make sure that both metal faces are quite clean before refitting. No gasket is used (photo).

52 Engine reassembly (V6) – sump and flywheel

1 Trim the projecting pieces of the front cover and backplate gaskets at the sump face of the block and front cover.
2 Trim the projecting edge of the rear oil seal carrier gasket on the sump face at the rear of the crankcase.
3 Clean all traces of old gasket which may remain from the sump joint faces and cover the faces of both the crankcase and sump with a gasket sealant. The sump gasket is in four sections which dovetail together and these should be carefully positioned and the joints interlocked (photo). The engine is now ready for the sump to be refitted.
4 Clean the interior of the sump thoroughly, apply sealer to the joint edge and place it in position (photo).
5 Refit all the sump bolts and tighten them evenly to the final torque wrench setting specified.
6 The flywheel or intermediate plate (automatic transmission models) may now be refitted. Make sure that the mating flanges are clean and free from burrs. Line up the bolt holes correctly; these are so designed as to line up in one position only. Do not hammer the flywheel or intermediate plate into position if it should be difficult to get it fully onto the flange. Support it squarely and refit the bolts,

51.13 Refit the curved plate and retaining bolts with spring washers

51.17 Align the gear marking dots

51.18 Relocate the eccentric lobe and retaining bolt. Note location dowel

51.24 Fit the crankshaft pulley

51.25 Refit the pulley retaining bolt and washer

51.29 Refit the rear plate

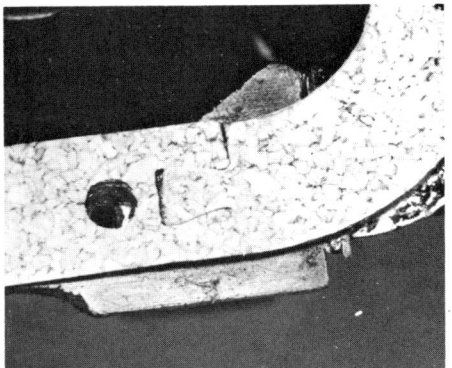
52.3 The sump gasket dovetail joint

52.4 Refit the sump

52.6 Tighten the flywheel or intermediate plate bolts to the specified torque

53.2 Insert each valve into its guide

53.4 Fit a new seal cup to each valve stem

53.5 Fit the valve spring

53.11 Locate the cylinder head gaskets over ...

53.12a ... the protruding spigots then ...

53.12b ... refit the cylinder head/s

tightening them evenly so as to draw the flywheel squarely onto its seat. There are no washers and the bolts should be tightened evenly and progressively to the final torque wrench setting specified (photo).

53 Engine reassembly (V6) – valve gear, cylinder heads and inlet manifold

1 When the cylinder heads have been decarbonised and the valves ground in as described in Sections 39 and 42, the cylinder heads may be reassembled. If the valves have been removed as described in Section 11 there will be no confusion as to which valve belongs in which position.
2 Make sure all traces of carbon and grinding paste have been removed, lubricate the valve stem with engine oil and place it in the appropriate guide (photo).
3 It will then protrude through the top of the cylinder head.
4 Fit a new seal cup over the valve stem (photo).
5 Place the valve spring over the valve stem with the close coils of the springs nearest the cylinder head (photo).
6 Fit the circular spring collar over the spring with the protruding centre boss of the collar downward.
7 Using a proper valve spring compressor tool, compress the spring down the valve stem sufficiently far to enable the two halves of the split collar (collets) to be fitted into the groove of the valve stem.
8 Insert the collets in the gap between the valve stem and circular spring collar. If necessary the collets should be smeared with grease to keep them in position. The spring compressor may then be released. Watch to ensure that the collets stay together in position as the spring collar comes past them. If the collar is a little off centre it may force one collet out of its groove in which case the spring must be re-compressed and the collet repositioned. When the compressor is finally released tap the head of the valve stem with a soft mallet to make sure the valve assembly is securely held in position.
9 Stand the engine the right way up on the bench and refit the tappets if they have been removed from the block. If they have been kept in order on removal as suggested it will be a simple matter to refit them.
10 The two cylinder heads are identical, so if they were marked left and right on removal they can be refitted on the same bank. If they have been mixed up no real harm will result but the pushrods will not be matched to their correct rocker arms. As these normally 'run in' together excessive wear could occur until such time as the two unfamiliar surfaces have bedded in.
11 Select a new cylinder head gasket and place it in position on the block on one bank. These gaskets are identical and can fit either bank but they can only go on the bank one way round, which is obvious from the way the bolt holes and cooling jacket holes line up (photo).
12 Locate the gasket over the protruding spigots in the block and then place the cylinder head in position (photos).
13 Make sure the cylinder head bolts are clean and lightly oiled and refit them. Nip them all down lightly and then tighten them in the sequence shown in Fig.1.6. The bolts should be tightened down to progressive torque settings - all to 50 lbf ft (6.9 kgf m) then all to 60 lbf ft (8.3 kgf m), and finally to the specified setting of between 65 to 70 lbf ft (9.0 - 9.7 kgf m) (photo).
14 Now fit the pushrods into position, making sure that they are refitted the same way up as they came out according to the original valve position. This will not be difficult if they have been kept in order as described in Sections 9 and 10. The pushrods are located at their upper ends in brackets bolted to the head (photo).
15 Locate the appropriate rocker arm over each stud so that the recessed end locates over the pushrod. Then place the fulcrum seat over the stud followed by the self-locking nut.
16 When both heads have been refitted and fully tightened down the inlet manifold may be refitted. In view of the large area to be sealed it is a safety measure, if not essential, to use a jointing compound in addition to the gasket on the mating surfaces.
17 Place the inlet manifold gasket in position in the 'V' so the single square hole (arrowed) is on the left-hand cylinder head (photo). The gasket is obviously incorrect if put on any other way but this is a positive guide.
18 Apply jointing compound to the mating faces of the inlet manifold. Note the square part which matches the gasket hole and port in the left-hand cylinder head.
19 Place the manifold in position with the thermostat housing to the front (photo).
20 Refit the manifold securing bolts (long bolts to inner position around manifold carburettor flange) ensuring that the gasket is lined up to permit them to pick up the threads in the cylinder heads, and screw them up lightly.
21 With a torque wrench tighten the bolts down evenly in the sequence shown in Fig. 1.4 to the specified torque. This tightening should be done in stages - all being tightened to 5 lbf ft (0.7 kgf m), then to 10 lbf ft (1.38 kgf m) before finally reaching the specified figure. Any uneven or excessive tightening may crack the manifold casting so take care.

54 Valve rocker clearances (V6) – adjustment

1 The valve stem to rocker clearance, which is in effect the mechanical free play between the camshaft and the end of the valve stem, is important to the correct operation and performance of the engine. If the clearance is too great there is an increase in noise level and, since the opening is reduced, a consequent reduction in gas flow. If the clearance is too little the valve would open too much with the danger of it hitting the crown of the piston. The clearance is checked when the tappet is on the heel of the cam (opposite the highest point) and the valve is therefore closed. This position coincides with certain other valves being fully open with their tappets on the highest point of the cam. This can be seen easily when the valve spring is fully compressed.
2 The table below shows the relationship between the fully open valves and the closed valves which are to be checked. The diagram shows the valve numbering No. 1 to 6 front to rear on the right-hand bank and Nos. 7 to 12 front to rear on the left-hand bank.

Valves open (together)	Adjust
Nos. 1 and 6	*Nos. 10 (exhaust) and 7 (inlet)*
Nos. 8 and 11	*Nos. 5 (exhaust) and 4 (inlet)*
Nos. 2 and 3	*Nos. 9 (inlet) and 12 (exhaust)*
Nos. 7 and 10	*Nos. 6 (inlet) and 1 (exhaust)*
Nos. 4 and 5	*Nos. 11 (inlet) and 8 (exhaust)*
Nos. 9 and 12	*Nos. 2 (inlet) and 3 (exhaust)*

53.13 Tighten the cylinder head bolts to the specified torque

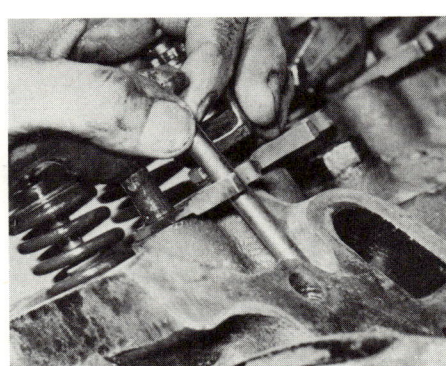

53.14 Refit the pushrods

53.17 Fit the new inlet manifold gasket – note square hole (arrowed)

53.19 Refit the inlet manifold

Front of engine

LH Bank	RH Bank
7	1
8	2
9	3
10	4
11	5
12	6

The clearance after reassembly should be set at 0.013 inch (0.33 mm) for the inlet valves and 0.020 inch (0.50 mm) for the exhaust valves. They should be checked later when the engine has reached normal running temperature when they should be reset again to the correct clearance.

3 The actual adjustment procedure is straightforward. With the appropriate valve ready for checking, place a feeler gauge of the required thickness (for exhaust or inlet valve) between the top of the valve stem and the rocker arm. If it will not fit the clearance is too small so slacken off the self-locking nut on the stud until it will fit. If the clearance is too large the nut should be screwed down. The correct clearance is obtained when the feeler blade can be moved readily but a firm drag is felt.

4 It is a wise precaution to check each clearance after the adjusting socket spanner has been removed from the nut. This is because the socket may possibly bind against the side of the rocker arm and tilt it, thus causing a false clearance to be recorded.

5 After the clearance adjustments are completed, refit the rocker covers, each fitted with a new gasket.

6 Tighten down the screw firmly and evenly.

Note: *The rocker cover with the oil filler cap goes on the left-hand bank. Rocker clearance should **NOT** be checked with a feeler gauge while the engine is running. In certain circumstances the valve could be forced against the crown of the piston causing serious damage. If one rocker is noisy it is possible to identify which one by removing the rocker cover and pressing a finger on each rocker in turn. The noisy one will be quiet when pressed.*

55 Engine reassembly – final ancillary components

1 To refit the distributor first turn the crankshaft until the correct timing mark on the timing cover is in line with the notch in the crankshaft pulley as No. 1 piston comes up on the compression stroke. The timing marks may be seen in Fig. 1.16. If there is doubt about the compression stroke place the thumb over the No. 1 spark plug hole and as the piston rises so pressure will be built up which can be felt.

2 Carefully line up the recessed end of the skew gear retaining pin with the groove on the lower part of the distributor body.

3 Position the distributor on the engine so that the vacuum unit faces forward (photo).

Fig. 1.16 Ignition timing marks (Sec. 55). For details of representation see Chapter 13

4 As the skew gears mesh the rotor arm will rotate until it points towards the No. 1 HT contact in the distributor cap. Check this by refitting the cap and noting the position of the rotor arm in relation to No. 1 HT segment (it will be seen that the correct segment in the cap is on the right-hand rear one when the distributor cap is fitted).

5 Refit the distributor pedestal securing bolt.

6 It will be necessary to accurately set the ignition timing. Full details of which are given in Chapter 4.

7 Fit a new oil filter canister to the engine and tighten firmly using the hands only (photo).

8 Fit a new fuel pump gasket cover over the two pump retaining studs and carefully ease the pump actuating arm over the top of the cam. Push the pump fully home and secure in position with two nuts and spring washers.

9 Fit a new water pump gasket and position with its three securing bolts and spring washers.

10 Refit the rubber hose connection to the insulator fitted between the carburettor and inlet manifold. Fit a new gasket and the top of the insulation (photo).

11 Refit the carburettor to the inlet manifold and secure in position with the nuts and spring washers.

12 Refit the left-hand exhaust manifold using new gaskets. Make sure that the gaskets are fitted the correct way round as they are not symmetrical (photos).

13 The various remaining ancillary equipment items (as listed in Section 8 of this Chapter) may now be refitted. Refer to the respective Chapter concerning the component to be refitted for further details. With the ancillary items reassembled, the engine is ready to be refitted into the car.

56 Engine – refitting without transmission

1 The engine must be positioned suitably so that the sling used to remove it can be easily refitted and the lifting tackle hooked on. Position the engine the right way round in front of the car and then raise it so that it may be brought into position over the car.

2 The transmission should be jacked up to its approximately normal position.

Manual gearbox

3 Lower the engine steadily into the engine compartment, keeping all ancillary wires, pipes and cables well clear of the sides. It is best to have a second person guiding the engine while it is being lowered, and to help align the engine with the gearbox.

4 The tricky part is finally mating the engine to the gearbox, which involves locating the gearbox input shaft into the clutch housing and flywheel. Provided that the clutch friction plate has been centred correctly as described in Chapter 5, there should be little difficulty. Grease the splines of the gearbox input shaft first. It may be necessary

Chapter 1 Part A V4 and V6 engines

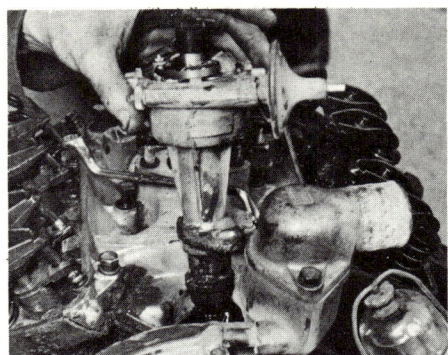
55.3 Refit the distributor

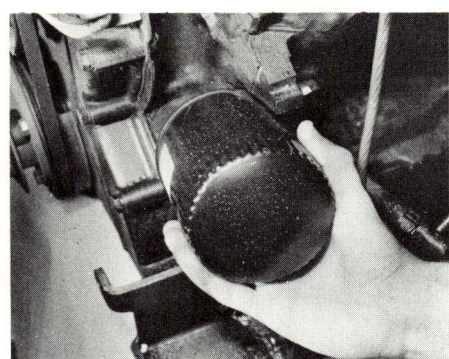
55.7 Replace the oil filter

55.10 Reconnect the rubber hose and use a new carburettor to manifold gasket

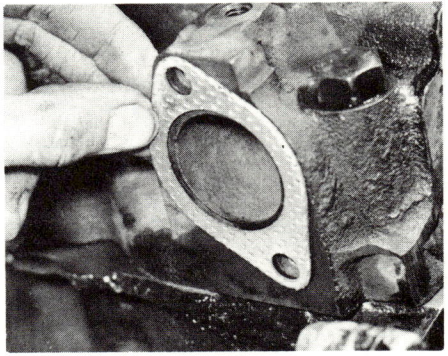
55.12a Locate the exhaust manifold gaskets and ..

55.12b ... manifold on the left bank

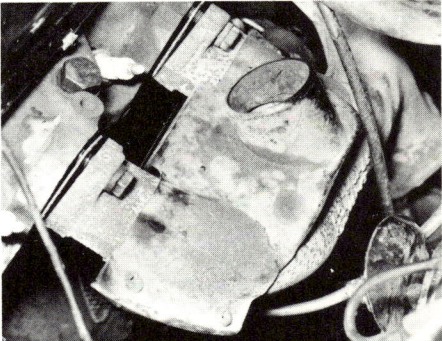
56.11 The exhaust manifold and air duct to the air filter

to rock the engine from side to side in order to get the engine fully home. Under no circumstances let any strain be imparted onto the gearbox input shaft. This could occur if the shaft was not fully located and the engine was raised or lowered more than the amount required for very slight adjustment of position.

5   As soon as the engine is fully up to the gearbox bellhousing refit the bolts holding the two together.

6   The final positioning of the engine brackets onto the mountings requires some attention because the positioning bolts on the mounting are angled inwards and therefore do not exactly line up with the holes in the brackets. However, they are flexibly mounted so, provided two people are doing the work, they may be levered into position whilst the engine is lowered.

Automatic transmission

7   Turn the torque converter in its housing so that the retaining studs are approximately aligned with the corresponding holes in the engine intermediate plate.

8   When the engine is lowered into position the converter can be further adjusted by turning the starter ring accordingly through the starter motor aperture. When the lower studs are aligned with the holes of the intermediate plate the engine can be pushed home to abut against the converter housing. The transmission may have to be raised or lowered further to enable the engine to mate with the transmission.

9   The four special self-locking nuts can now be fitted to secure the engine/transmission units. To gain access to each stud, turn the engine crankshaft pulley retaining nut in a clockwise direction (looking from front to rear) so that each stud in turn is accessible through the starter motor aperture and each nut can be fitted and fully tightened to secure.

All models

10 Insert and tighten the respective bellhousing/engine bolts.

11 Refit the starter motor generator, all electrical connections, the fuel lines and carburettor linkages, cooling system hoses and radiator in the reverse order as described in Section 5 and 6 (photo).

12 Reconnect the exhaust pipes to the manifolds and refit the plate covering the lower section of the bellhousing. Remove the supporting jack if this has not already been done.

13 Refill the engine with new oil and refill the cooling system. Check for signs of leaks.

57 Engine – refitting with transmission

1   The transmission should be refitted to the engine, taking the same precautions as regards the input shaft as mentioned in Section 56.

2   The general principles of lifting the engine/transmission assembly are the same as for the engine, but the transmission will tilt everything to a much steeper angle. Refitting will certainly require the assistance of a second person.'

3   Lift the transmission end of the unit into the engine compartment and then lower and guide the unit down. One of the first things to be done is to fit the propeller shaft into the transmission rear extension casing, so someone should be ready to lift and guide the propeller shaft into position as soon as the transmission is near enough. This cannot be done after the unit has been lowered past a certain position.

4   If a trolley jack is available this is the time to place it under the transmission so that, as the engine is lowered further, the rear end can be supported and raised as necessary - at the same time being able to roll back as required. Without such a jack, support the rear in such a way that it can slide if possible. In any case the transmission will have to be jacked and held up in position when the unit nears its final position.

5   Locate the front mounting brackets on the locating bolts as described in Section 56.

6   Refit the speedometer drive cable with the transmission drive socket and refit the clamping plate and bolt. This **MUST** be done before the gearbox supporting crossmember is refitted.

7   Fit the gearbox supporting crossmember to the transmission and secure it with the bolt which goes through the centre of the crossmember.

8   Using the jack, position the crossmember up to the body frame and refit and tighten the four securing bolts.

9   Refit the transmission remote control change lever and housing as described in Chapter 6.

10 *Manual gearbox models:* Reconnect the hydraulic pipe to the

clutch slave cylinder and bleeed the system as described in Chapter 5. The final connections should then be made to the engine as described in Section 56. In addition to the engine lubricant and coolant, the gearbox should be refilled with fresh oil.

11 *Automatic transmission models:* For refitting the automatic transmission and the engine as a unit, the instructions are similar to those for manual types, but when reconnecting the transmission unit, refer to Chapter 6, Section 8 and reverse the sequence of instructions. Reconnect the respective automatic transmission components and fittings as applicable.

58 Engine – initial start-up after overhaul or major repair

1 Make sure that the battery is fully charged and that all lubricants, coolants and fuel are replenished.

2 If the fuel system has been dismantled it will require several revolutions of the engine on the starter motor to get the petrol up to the carburettor. An initial 'prime' of about ⅓ of a cupful of petrol poured down the intake of the carburettor will help the engine to fire quickly, thus relieving the load on the battery. Do not overdo this, however, as flooding may result.

3 As soon as the engine fires and runs keep it going at a fast tickover only (no faster) and bring it up to normal working temperature.

4 As the engine warms up there will be odd smells and some smoke from parts getting hot and burning off oil deposits. The signs to look for are leaks of oil or water, which will be obvious if serious. Check also the clamp connections of the exhaust pipe to the manifolds as these do not always 'find' their exact gas tight position until the warmth and vibration have acted on them, and it is almost certain that they will need tightening further.

5 When running temperature has been reached adjust the idling speed as described in Chapter 3.

6 Stop the engine and wait a few minutes to see if any lubricants or coolant are dripping out when the engine is stationary.

7 Road test the car to check that the timing is correct and giving the necessary smoothness and power. Do not race the engine - if new bearings and/or pistons and rings have been fitted it should be treated as a new engine and run in at reduced revolutions for at least 500 miles (800 km).

59 Fault diagnosis – engine

Symptom	Reason/s	Remedy
Engine fails to turn over when starter operated		
No current at starter motor	Flat or defective battery	Charge or renew battery. Push-start car.
	Loose battery leads	Tighten both terminals and end of earth lead.
	Defective starter solenoid or switch or broken wiring	Run a wire direct from the battery to the starter motor or bypass the solenoid.
	Engine earth strap disconnected	Check and retighten strap.
Current at starter motor	Jammed starter motor drive pinion	Place care in gear and rock from side from side. Alternatively, free exposed square end of shaft with spanner.
	Defective starter motor	Remove and recondition.
Engine turns over but will not start		
No spark at spark plug	Ignition damp or wet	Wipe dry the distributor cap and ignition leads.
	Ignition leads to spark plugs loose	Check and tighten at both spark plug and distributor cap ends.
	Shorted or disconnected low tension leads	Check the wiring on the CB(-) and SW(+) terminals of the coil and to the distributor.
	Dirty, incorrectly set, or pitted contact breaker points	Clean, file smooth, and adjust.
	Faulty condenser	Check contact breaker points for arcing, remove and fit new.
	Defective ignition switch	Bypass switch with wire.
	Ignition leads connected wrong way round	Remove and refit leads to spark plugs in correct order.
	Faulty coil	Remove and fit new coil.
	Contact breaker point spring earthed or broken	Check spring is not touching metal part of distributor. Check insulator washers are correctly placed. Renew points if the spring is broken.
Excess of petrol in cylinder or carburettor flooding	Too much choke allowing too rich a mixture to wet plugs	Remove and dry spark plugs or with wide open throttle, push-start the car.
	Float damaged or leaking or needle not seating	Remove, examine, clean or renew float and and needle valve as necessary.
	Float lever incorrectly adjusted	Remove and adjust correctly.
Engine stalls and will not start		
No spark at spark plug	Ignition failure – sudden	Check over low and high tension circuits for breaks in wiring.
	Ignition failure – misfiring precludes total stoppage	Check contact breaker points, clean and adjust. Renew condenser if faulty.
	Ignition failure – in severe rain or after traversing water splash	Dry out ignition leads and distributor cap.

Chapter 1 Part A V4 and V6 engines

Symptom	Reason/s	Remedy
No fuel at jets	No petrol in petrol tank	Refill tank.
	Petrol tank breather choked	Remove petrol cap and clean out breather hole or pipe.
	Sudden obstruction in carburettor(s)	Check jets, filter, and needle valve in float chamber for blockage.
	Water in fuel system	Drain tank and blow out fuel lines.
Engine misfires or idles unevenly		
Intermittent spark at spark plugs	Ignition leads loose	Check and tighten as necessary at spark plug and distributor cap ends.
	Battery leads loose on terminals	Check and tighten terminal leads.
	Battery earth strap loose on body attachment point	Check and tighten earth lead to body attachment point.
	Engine earth lead loose	Tighten lead.
	Low tension leads to SW (+) and CB (-) terminals on coil loose	Check and tighen leads if found loose.
	Low tension lead from CB (-) terminal side to distributor loose	Check and tighten if found loose.
	Dirty, or incorrectly gapped plugs	Remove, clean and regap.
	Dirty, incorrectly set, or pitted contact breaker points	Clean, file smooth, and adjust.
	Tracking across inside of distributor cover	Remove and fit new cover.
	Ignition too retarded	Check and adjust ignition timing.
	Faulty coil	Remove and fit new coil.
No fuel at carburettor float chamber or at jets	No petrol in petrol tank	Refill tank!
	Vapour lock in fuel line (In hot conditions or at high altitude)	Blow into petrol tank, allow engine to cool or apply a cold wet rag to the fuel line.
	Blocked float chamber needle valve	Remove, clean and refit.
	Fuel pump filter blocked	Remove, clean and refit.
	Choked or blocked carburettor jets	Dismantle and clean.
	Faulty fuel pump	Remove, overhaul and refit.
Fuel shortage at engine	Mixture too weak	Check jets, float chamber needle valve, and filters for obstruction. Clean as necessary. Carburettor incorrectly adjusted.
	Air leak in carburettor	Remove and overhaul carburettor.
	Air leak at inlet manifold to cylinder head, or inlet manifold to carburettor	Test by pouring oil along joints. Bubbles indicate leak. Renew manifold gasket as appropriate.
Mechanical wear	Incorrect valve clearances	Adjust rocker arms to take up wear.
	Burnt out exhaust valves	Remove cylinder head and renew defective valves.
	Sticking or leaking valves	Remove cylinder head, clean, check and renew valves as necessary.
	Weak or broken valve springs	Check and renew as necessary.
	Worn valve guides or stems	Renew valve guides and valves.
	Worn pistons and piston rings	Dismantle engine, renew pistons and rings.
Lack of power and poor compression		
Fuel/air mixture leaking from cylinder	Burnt out exhaust valves	Remove cylinder head, renew defective valves.
	Sticking or leaking valves	Remove cylinder head, clean, check and renew valves as necessary.
	Worn valve guides and stems	Remove cylinder head and renew valves and valve guides.
	Weak or broken valve springs	Remove cylinder head, renew defective springs.
	Blown cylinder head gasket (accompanied by increase in noise)	Remove cylinder head and fit new gasket.
	Worn pistons and piston rings	Dismantle engine, renew pistons and rings.
	Worn or scored cylinder bores	Dismantle engine, rebore, renew pistons and rings.
Incorrect adjustments	Ignition timing wrongly set. Too advanced or retarded	Check and reset ignition timing.
	Contact breaker points incorrectly gapped	Check and reset contact breaker points.
	Incorrect valve clearances	Check and reset rocker arm to valve stem gap.
	Incorrectly set spark plugs	Remove, clean and regap.
	Carburation too rich or too weak	Tune carburettor for optimum performance.

Symptom	Reason/s	Remedy
Carburation and ignition faults	Dirty contact breaker points	Remove, clean and refit.
	Distributor automatic balance weights or vacuum advance and retard mechanisms not functioning correctly	Overhaul distributor.
	Faulty fuel pump giving top end fuel starvation	Remove, overhaul, or fit exchange reconditioned fuel pump.
Excessive oil consumption		
Oil being burnt by engine	Badly worn, perished or missing valve stem oil seals	Remove cylinder head, fit new oil seals to valve stems.
	Excessively worn valve stems and valve guides	Remove cylinder head and fit new valves and valve guides.
	Worn piston rings	Fit oil control rings to existing pistons or purchase new pistons.
	Worn pistons and cylinder bores	Fit new pistons and rings, rebore cylinders.
	Excessive piston ring gap allowing blow-by	Fit new piston rings and set gap correctly.
	Piston oil return holes choked	Decarbonise engine and pistons.
Oil being lost due to leaks	Leaking oil filter gasket	Inspect and fit new gasket as necessary.
	Leaking timing case gasket	Inspect and fit new gasket as necessary.
	Leaking sump gasket	Inspect and fit new gasket as necessary.
	Loose sump pump	Tighten, fit new gasket if necessary.
Unusual noises from engine		
Excessive clearances due to mechanical wear	Worn valve gear (noisy tapping from rocker box)	Inspect and renew rocker shaft, rocker arms, and ball pins as necessary.
	Worn big-end bearing (regular heavy knocking)	Drop sump, if bearings broken up clean out oil pump and oilways, fit new bearings. If bearings not broken but worn fit bearing shells
	Worn timing chain and gears (rattling from front of engine)	Remove timing cover, fit new timing wheels and timing chain.
	Worn main bearings (rumbling and vibration)	Drop sump, remove crankshaft; if bearings worn but not broken up, renew. If broken up strip oil pump and clean out oilways.
	Worn crankshaft (knocking rumbling and vibration)	Regrind crankshaft, fit new main and big-end bearings.

Chapter 1 Part B Four cylinder in-line engine

Contents

Auxiliary shaft and timing cover – refitting	46
Auxiliary shaft – removal	10
Cam followers – refitting	53
Camshaft, camshaft bearings and cam followers – examination and renovation	31
Camshaft drivebelt – refitting and timing	56
Camshaft drivebelt – removal (engine in car)	16
Camshaft drivebelt tensioner and thermostat housing – refitting	55
Camshaft – refitting	52
Camshaft – removal	18
Connecting rods and gudgeon pins – examination and renovation	30
Connecting rods to crankshaft – reassembly	43
Crankshaft and main bearings – removal	15
Crankshaft – examination and renovation	26
Crankshaft main and big-end bearings – examination and renovation	27
Crankshaft pulley, sprocket and timing cover – removal	13
Crankshaft rear oil seal – refitting	45
Crankshaft – refitting	39
Crankshaft sprocket and pulley, and auxiliary shaft sprocket – refitting	48
Cylinder bores – examination and renovation	28
Cylinder head and piston crowns – decarbonization	35
Cylinder head – refitting	54
Cylinder head – removal (engine in car)	8
Cylinder head – removal (engine on bench)	9
Engine components – examination for wear	25
Engine dismantling – general	7
Engine – initial start-up after major overhaul or repair	60
Engine reassembly – general	38
Engine – refitting with transmission	59
Engine – removal with transmission	6
Engine – removal without transmission	5
Engine – refitting without transmission	58
Fault diagnosis – engine	61
Flywheel and clutch – refitting	50
Flywheel and sump – removal	11
Flywheel ring gear – examination and renovation	34
General description	1
Gudgeon pin – removal	20
Lubrication and crankcase ventilation systems – description	22
Major operations possible with engine in place	2
Major operations requiring engine removal	3
Methods of engine removal	4
Oil filter – removal and refitting	24
Oil pump and strainer – removal	12
Oil pump – dismantling, inspection and reassembly	23
Oil pump – refitting	44
Piston rings – refitting	41
Piston rings – removal	21
Pistons and connecting rods – reassembly	40
Pistons and piston rings – examination and renovation	29
Pistons, connecting rods and big-end bearings – removal	14
Pistons – refitting	42
Sump – inspection	37
Sump – refitting	47
Thermostat housing and belt tensioner – removal	19
Timing gears and belt – examination and renovation	33
Valve clearances – checking and adjustment	57
Valve guides – inspection	36
Valves and valve seats – examination and renovation	32
Valves – refitting	51
Valves – removal	17
Water pump – refitting	49

Specifications

General

Engine type	Four cylinder in-line, single overhead camshaft
Firing order	1–3–4–2
Bore	3.575 in (90.8 mm)
Stroke	3.03 in (76.95 mm)
Cubic capacity	1993 cc (115.9 cu in)
Maximum continuous engine speed	5850
Engine bhp (DIN)	96 at 5200 rpm
Max torque (DIN)	111 lbf ft at 3500 rpm

Cylinder block

Cast identification marks	20
Number of main bearings	5
Cylinder bore dia. grades:	
Standard grade:	
1 in (mm)	3.5748–3.5752 (90.800–90.810)
2 in (mm)	3.5752–3.5756 (90.810–90.820)
3 in (mm)	3.5756–3.5760 (90.820–90.830)
4 in (mm)	3.5760–3.5764 (90.830–90.840)
Oversize A in (mm)	3.5949–3.5953 (91.310–91.320)
Oversize B in (mm)	3.5953–3.5957 (91.320–91.330)
Oversize C in (mm)	3.5957–3.5961 (91.330–91.340)
Standard supp. in service in (mm)	3.5760–3.5764 (90.830–90.840)
Oversize 0.5 in (mm)	3.5957–3.5961 (91.330–91.340)
Oversize 1.0 in (mm)	3.6154–3.6157 (91.830–91.840)
Centre main bearing width in (mm)	1.072–1.070 (27.22–27.17)
Main bearing liners fitted (inner diameter):	
Standard:	
Red in (mm)	2.2446–2.2456 (57.014–57.038)
Blue in (mm)	2.2442–2.2452 (57.004–57.028)
Crankshaft:	
Undersize:	
0.25 Red in (mm)	2.2348–2.2357 (56.764–56.788)
Blue in (mm)	2.2344–2.2354 (56.754–56.778)
0.50 in (mm)	2.2250–2.2263 (56.514–56.548)
0.75 in (mm)	2.2151–2.2164 (56.264–56.298)
1.00 in (mm)	2.2053–2.2066 (56.014–56.048)
Main bearing parent bore dia:	
Red in (mm)	2.3866–2.3870 (60.620–60.630)
Blue in (mm)	2.3870–2.3874 (60.630–60.640)

Crankshaft

Endfloat in (mm)	0.0032–0.0110 (0.08–0.28)
Main bearing journal diameters:	
Standard:	
Red in (mm)	2.2441–2.2437 (57.000–56.990)
Blue in (mm)	2.2437–2.2433 (56.990–56.980)
Undersize:	
0.25 in (mm)	2.2338–2.2335 (56.740–56.730)
0.50 in (mm)	2.2244–2.2240 (56.500–56.490)
0.75 in (mm)	2.2146–2.2142 (56.250–56.240)
1.00 in (mm)	2.2047–2.2043 (56.000–55.990)
Thrust washer thickness:	
Standard in (mm)	0.091–0.0925 (2.3–2.35)
Undersize in (mm)	0.098–0.100 (2.5–2.55)
Main bearing clearance in (mm)	0.0005–0.0019 (0.014–0.048)
Crankpin journal diameter:	
Standard:	
Red in (mm)	2.0472–2.0468 (52.000–51.990)
Blue in (mm)	2.0468–2.0465 (51.990–51.980)
Undersize:	
0.25 Red in (mm)	2.0374–2.0370 (51.750–51.740)
0.25 Blue in (mm)	2.0370–2.0366 (51.740–51.730)
0.50 in (mm)	2.0276–2.0272 (51.500–51.490)
0.75 in (mm)	2.0177–2.0173 (51.250–51.240)

Camshaft

Drive	Toothed belt
Thrust plate thickness:	
Type 1 in (mm)	0.158 (4.01)
Type 2 in (mm)	0.157 (3.98)
Width of camshaft groove in (mm)	$0.1600 {}^{+0.0028}_{-0.0000}$ $4.064 {}^{+0.070}_{-0.000}$
Cam lift in (mm)	0.2518 (6.397)
Cam heel to toe dimensions in (mm)	1.435–1.430 (36.46–36.32)
Journal diameter:	
Front in (mm)	1.6539–1.6531 (42.01–41.99)
Centre in (mm)	1.7606–1.7528 (44.72–44.52)
Rear in (mm)	1.7720–1.7713 (45.01–44.99)
Bearing – inside diameter:	
Front in (mm)	1.6557–1.6549 (42.055–42.035)
Centre in (mm)	1.7588–1.7580 (44.675–44.655)
Rear in (mm)	1.7381–1.7730 (45.055–45.035)
Camshaft endfloat in (mm)	0.002–0.0035 (0.05–0.09)
Identification colour	Yellow

Auxiliary shaft
Endfloat in (mm) 0.001–0.004 (0.04–0.12)

Pistons
Piston diameter:
  Standard grade:
    1 in (mm) 3.5730–3.5734 (90.755–90.765)
    2 in (mm) 3.5734–3.5738 (90.765–90.775)
    3 in (mm) 3.5738–3.5742 (90.775–90.785)
    4 in (mm) 3.5742–3.5746 (90.785–90.795)
  Standard supplied in service in (mm) 3.5740–3.5750 (90.780–90.805)
  Oversize supplied in service:
    0.5 in (mm) 3.5937–3.5947 (91.280–91.305)
    1.0 in (mm) 3.6134–3.6144 (91.780–91.805)
Piston clearance in cylinder bore in (mm) 0.001–0.0024 (0.025–0.060)
Ring gap (in situ):
  Top in (mm) 0.015–0.023 (0.38–0.58)
  Centre in (mm) 0.015–0.023 (0.38–0.58)
  Bottom in (mm) 0.0157–0.055 (0.4–1.4)

Gudgeon pins
Length in (mm) 2.83–2.87 (72.0–72.8)
Diameter:
  Red in (mm) 0.94465–0.94476 (23.994–23.997)
  Blue in (mm) 0.94476–0.94488 (23.997–24.000)
  Yellow in (mm) 0.94488–0.94500 (24.000–24.003)
Interference fit in piston in (mm) 0.0002–0.00043 (0.005–0.011)
Clearance in small end bush in (mm) 0.0007–0.00153 (0.018–0.039)

Connecting rods
Big-end bore:
  Red in (mm) 2.1653–2.1657 (55.00–55.01)
  Blue in (mm) 2.1657–2.1661 (55.01–55.02)
Small end bush diameter in (mm) 0.9434–0.9439 (23.964–23.976)
Inside diameter:
  Standard:
    Red in (mm) 2.0478–2.0487 (52.014–52.038)
    Blue in (mm) 2.0474–2.0483 (52.004–52.028)
  Undersize:
    0.25 Red in (mm) 2.0379–2.0388 (51.764–51.788)
    0.25 Blue in (mm) 2.0376–2.0385 (51.754–51.778)
    0.50 in (mm) 2.0281–2.0294 (51.514–51.548)
    0.75 in (mm) 2.0183–2.0196 (51.264–51.298)
    1.00 in (mm) 2.0084–2.0100 (51.014–51.048)
Crankpin to bearing liner clearance:
  Standard in (mm) 0.00055–0.0018 (0.014–0.048)
  Undersize in (mm) 0.00055–0.0023 (0.014–0.058)

Cylinder head
Cast identification number 0
Valve seat angle .... 44° 30'–45°
Valve guide inside diameter, inlet and exhaust:
  Standard in (mm) 0.3174–0.3184 (8.063–8.088)
  Oversize:
    0.2 in (mm) 0.3253–0.3263 (8.263–8.288)
    0.4 in (mm) 0.3332–0.3342 (8.463–8.488)
Parent bore for camshaft bearing liners:
  Front in (mm) 1.6557–1.6549 (42.055–42.035)
  Centre in (mm) 1.7589–1.7580 (44.675–44.655)
  Rear in (mm) 1.7738–1.7730 (45.055–45.035)

Valves
Valve clearances (cold):
  Inlet in (mm) 0.008 (0.20)
  Exhaust in (mm) 0.010 (0.25)

Inlet valve
Length in (mm) 4.3760 (111.15)
Valve head diameter in (mm) .... 1.654 ± 0.008 (42 ± 0.2)
Valve stem diameter:
  Standard in (mm) 0.3167–0.3159 (8.043–8.025)
  Oversize:
    0.2 in (mm) 0.3245–0.3238 (8.243–8.225)
    0.4 in (mm) 0.3324–0.3317 (8.443–8.425)
Valve stem to guide clearance in (mm) 0.0008–0.0025 (0.020–0.063)
Valve lift in (mm) 0.3993 (10.142)
Valve spring free length in (mm) 1.73 (44)

Exhaust valves

Length in (mm)	4.37 ± 0.19 (111 ± 0.5)
Valve head diameter in (mm)	1.42 ± 0.08 (36 ± 0.2)
Valve stem diameter:	
Standard in (mm)	0.3156–0.3149 (8.017–7.999)
Oversize:	
0.2 in (mm)	0.3235–0.3228 (8.217–8.199)
0.4 in (mm)	0.3314–0.3307 (8.417–8.399)
Valve stem to guide clearance in (mm)	0.0034–0.0035 (0.086–0.089)
Valve lift in (mm)	0.3992 (10.14)
Valve spring free length in (mm)	1.732 (44.0)

Engine lubrication and oil pump

Oil change without renewal of filter, Imp pints (litres)	5.3 (3.0)
Oil change with renewal of filter, Imp pints (litres)	6.6 (3.75)
Minimum oil pressure:	
At 700 rpm lbf in^2 (kp/cm^2)	16 (1.1)
At 1500 rpm lbf/in^2 (kp/cm^2)	36 (2.5)
Relief valve opens at lbf/in^2 (kp/cm^2)	57–67 (4.0–4.7)
Oil pump outer rotor and housing clearance in (mm)	0.006–0.012 (0.15–0.30)
Inner and outer rotor clearance in (mm)	0.002–0.008 (0.05–0.20)
Inner and outer rotor endfloat in (mm)	0.0012–0.004 (0.03–0.10)

Torque wrench settings

	lbf ft	kgf m
Main bearing caps	64.5–74.5	9.0–10.4
Flywheel	46.5–50.9	6.5–7.1
Oil pump	12–15	1.7–2.1
Oil pump cover	6.4–9.3	0.9–1.3
Oil sump:		
First stage	0.7–1.4	0.1–0.2
Second stage	4.3–5.7	0.6–0.8
Third stage	4.3–5.7	0.6–0.8
Oil drain plug	15–20	2.1–2.8
Cylinder head:		
First stage	30–40	4.1–5.6
Second stage	37–51	5.1–7.1
Third stage (after waiting 10 to 20 minutes)	63–69	8.7–9.7
Fourth stage (after engine has warmed up – 15 mins at 1000 rpm)	67–80	9.2–11.2
Rocker cover:		
1st to 6th bolt (Sequence 1)	3.6–5.0	0.5–0.7
7th and 8th bolt (Sequence 2)	1.4–1.8	0.2–0.25
9th and 10th bolt (Sequence 3)	3.6–5.0	0.5–0.7
7th and 8th bolt (Sequence 4)	3.6–5.0	0.5–0.7
Spark plugs	14.3–20	2.0–2.8
Big-end bearing cap	29–34	4.1–4.8
Crankshaft pulley	39–43	5.5–6.0
Camshaft/auxiliary shaft sprocket	32–36	4.5–5.0
Valve adjustment ball pin	32–36	4.5–5.0
Timing cover	10–12	1.3–1.7
Inlet manifold	12–15	1.7–2.1
Exhaust manifold	15–18	2.1–2.5
Clutch plate to flywheel	12–15	1.7–2.1
Thermostat housing	12–15	1.7–2.1

1 General description

In 1974 the 2.0 litre overhead camshaft (ohc) engine, as fitted to the Cortina range, became available in the Consul as an alternative to the V4 overhead valve (ohv) engine. Apart from a modified sump, the engine was the same as the Cortina power unit.

From April 1975 the ohc engine became available in the Granada range, replacing the 2.0 litre V4 ohv engine. The design layout of the 2.0 litre ohc engine is as follows.

The cylinder head is of the crossflow design with the inlet manifold one side and the exhaust manifold on the other. As flat top pistons are used the combustion chambers are contained in the cylinder head.

The combined crankcase and cylinder block is made of cast iron and houses the pistons and crankshaft. Attached to the underside of the crankcase is a pressed steel sump which acts as a reservoir for the engine oil. Full information on the lubricating system will be found in Section 22.

The cast iron cylinder head is mounted on top of the cylinder block and acts as a support for the overhead camshaft. The slightly angled valves operate directly in the cylinder head and are controlled by the camshaft via cam followers. The camshaft is operated by a toothed reinforced composite rubber belt from the crankshaft. To eliminate backlash and prevent slackness of the belt a spring loaded tensioner in the form of a jockey wheel is in contact with the back of the belt. It serves two further functions, to keep the belt away from the water pump and also to increase the contact area of the camshaft and crankshaft sprockets.

The drivebelt also drives the auxiliary shaft sprocket and it is from this shaft that the oil pump, distributor and fuel pump operate.

The inlet manifold is mounted on the left-hand side of the cylinder head and to this the carburettor is fitted. A water jacket is incorporated in the inlet manifold so that the petrol/air charge may be at the correct temperature before entering the combustion chambers.

The exhaust manifold is mounted on the right-hand side of the cylinder head and connects to a single downpipe and silencer system.

Aluminium alloy pistons are connected to the crankshaft by H-section forged steel connecting rods and gudgeon pins. The gudgeon pin is a press fit in the small end of the connecting rod but a floating fit in the piston boss. Two compression rings and one scraper ring, all located above the gudgeon pin, are fitted.

The forged crankshaft runs in five main bearings and endfloat is accommodated by fitting thrust washers either side of the centre main bearings.

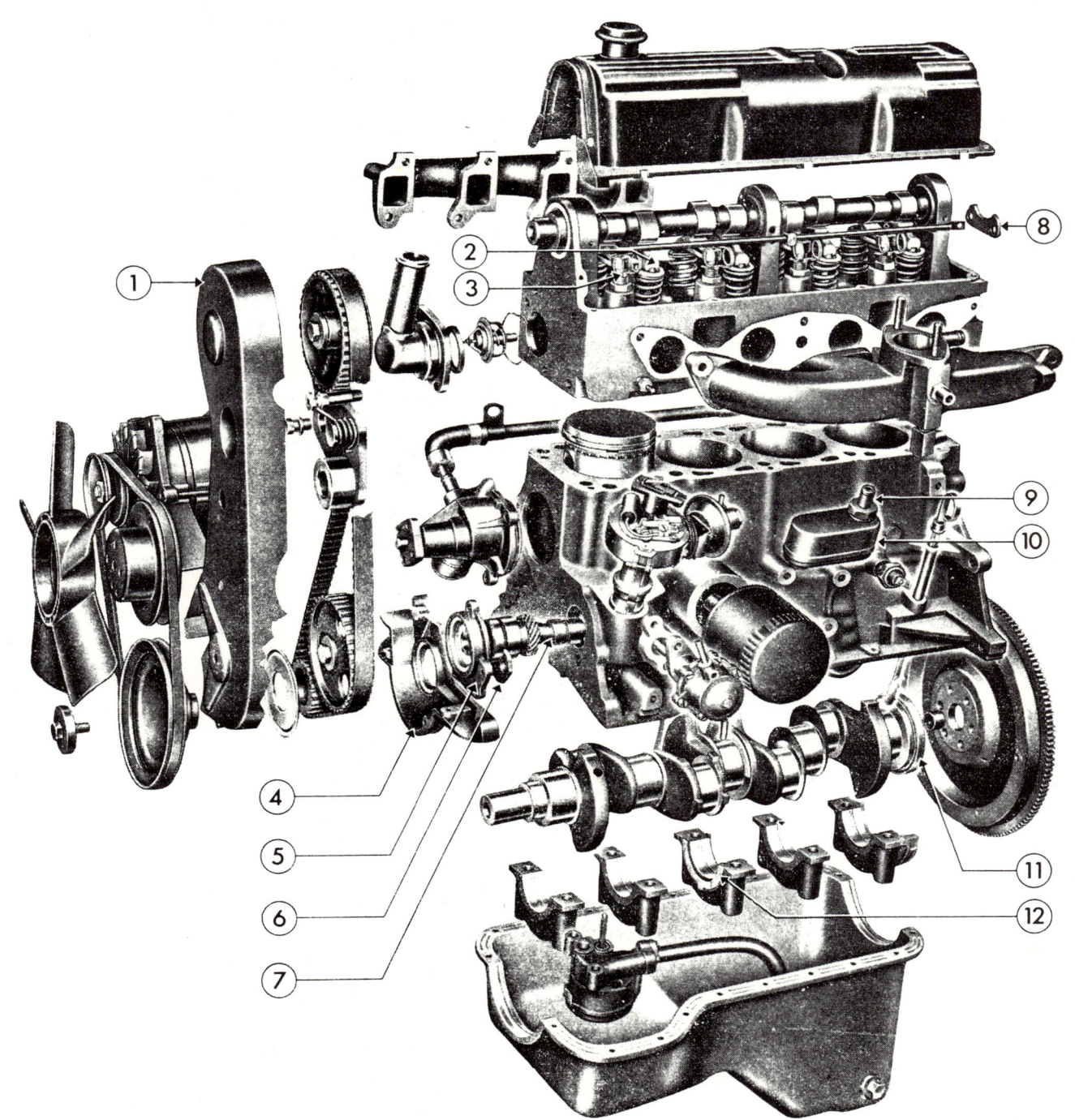

Fig. 1.1 Exploded view of the main engine components

1 Belt cover	5 Balance shaft timing cover	9 Ventilation valve
2 Cam follower	6 Balance shaft thrust plate	10 Oil separator
3 Cam follower spring	7 Balance shaft	11 Crankshaft oil seal
4 Crankshaft timing cover	8 Camshaft thrust plate	12 Lower crankshaft thrust washer

required to remove the cylinder head drive belt tensioner and oil pump.

2 Major operations possible with engine in place

The following major operations can be carried out to the engine with it in place:

   a) *Removal and refitting of camshaft.*
   b) *Removal and refitting of cylinder head.*
   c) *Removal and refitting of camshaft drivebelt*
   d) *Removal and refitting of oil pump*
   e) *Removal and refitting of engine front mountings*

3 Major operations requiring engine removal

The following major operations can be carried out with the engine out of the body frame on the bench or floor:

   a) *Removal and refitting of main bearings*
   b) *Removal and refitting of crankshaft*
   c) *Removal and refitting of flywheel*
   d) *Removal and refitting of crankshaft rear oil seal*
   e) *Removal and refitting of sump*
   f) *Removal and refitting of big-end bearings*
   g) *Removal and refitting of pistons and connecting rods*

4 Methods of engine removal

The engine may be lifted out either on its own or in unit with the transmission. On models fitted with automatic transmission it is recommended that the engine be lifted out on its own, unless a substantial crane or overhead hoist is available, because of the weight factor. If the engine and transmission are removed as a unit they have to be lifted out at a very steep angle, so make sure that there is sufficient lifting height available.

5 Engine - removal without transmission

1 The do-it-yourself owner should be able to remove the power unit fairly easily in about 4 hours. It is essential to have a good hoist and two axle stands if an inspection pit is not available.
2 The sequence of operations listed in this Section is not critical as the position of the person undertaking the work, or the tool in his hand, will determine to a certain extent the order in which the work is tackled. Obviously the power unit cannot be removed until everything is disconnected from it and the following sequence wil ensure that nothing is forgotten.
3 Open the bonnet and using a soft pencil mark the outline position of both the hinges at the bonnet to act as a datum for refitting.
4 With the help of a second person to take the weight of the bonnet undo and remove the hinge to bonnet securing bolts with plain and spring washers. There are two bolts to each hinge.
5 Lift away the bonnet and put it in a safe place where it will not be scratched. Remove the battery as described in Chapter 10.
6 Place a container having a capacity of at least 8 Imp. pints (4.55 litres) under the engine sump and remove the oil drain plug. Allow the oil to drain out and then refit the plug.
7 Refer to Chapter 3, and remove the air cleaner assembly from the top of the carburettor.
8 Mark the HT leads so that they may be refitted in their original positions and detach from the spark plugs.
9 Release the HT lead rubber moulding from the clip on the top of the distributor cover.
10 Spring back the clips securing the distributor cap to the distributor body. Lift off the distributor cap.
11 Detach the HT lead from the centre of the ignition coil. Remove the distributor cap from the engine compartment.
12 Refer to Chapter 2, and drain the cooling system.
13 Slacken the clips that secure the water hose to the thermostat from the radiator and detach the hose. Also disconnect the oil cooler pipes from the base of the radiator.
14 Slacken the clip that secures the heater hose to the heater unit. Pull off the hose.
15 Slacken the clip that secures the hoses to the automatic choke and pull off the two hoses.
16 Slacken the clip securing the water hose to the adaptor elbow on the side of the inlet manifold and pull off the hose.
17 Slacken the clip that secures the fuel feed pipe to the carburettor float chamber and pull off the hose. Plug the end to stop dirt ingress or fuel loss due to syphoning.
18 Detach the throttle control inner cable from the operating rod (photo) and place out of the way.
19 Unscrew the throttle control outer cable securing nut and detach the cable from the mounting bracket (photo).
20 Detach the vacuum pipe from the vacuum unit on the side of the distributor (photo). Remove the vacuum pipes from the manifold to brake servo unit and also the transmission vacuum hose (Auto transmission).
21 Undo and remove the four nuts and washers that secure the carburettor to the inlet manifold. Carefully lift the carburettor up and away from the studs on the manifold.
22 The combined insulation spacer and gasket may now be lifted from the studs. Note that it is marked 'TOP FRONT' and it must be refitted the correct way round.
23 Slacken the clip securing the hose to the manifold branch pipe adaptor and pull off the hose.
24 Slacken the clip securing the hose to the adaptor at the centre of the manifold and pull off the hose.
25 Undo and remove the self-lock nuts and bolts securing the inlet manifold to the side of the cylinder head.
26 Note that one of the manifold securing bolts also retains the air cleaner support bracket (photo).
27 Lift away the inlet manifold (photo) and gasket.
28 Undo and remove the two nuts securing the exhaust down pipe clamp plate to the manifold. Slide the clamp plate down the pipe.
29 Refer to Chapter 2 and remove the radiator.
30 Detach the temperature gauge cable from the sender unit in the inlet manifold side of the cylinder head.
31 Pull the crankcase ventilation valve and hose from the oil separator on the left-hand side of the cylinder block (photo).
32 Detach the oil pressure warning light cable from the switch located below the oil separator.
33 Disconnect the Lucar terminal connector from the starter motor solenoid (photo). Also detach the terminal connection from the rear of the alternator.
34 Take note of the electric cable connections to the starter motor solenoid and detach the cables (photos).
35 Undo and remove the distributor clamp bolt and clamp (photo) and lift the distributor clear.
36 Raise the car at the front and support with axle stands or blocks.
37 From underneath the car remove the starter motor.
38 Unscrew the clutch/converter housing lower bolts.
39 On automatic transmission models prise the rubber grommet from the cut away section of the starter motor aperture (certain models only) and then, using a suitable socket and extension, unscrew and remove the intermediate drive plate to torque converter retaining bolts (Fig. 1.2).
40 Place a jack or support under the transmission and remove the remaining clutch/converter housing to engine bolts.
41 Check that apart from the engine mountings, the respective components and fittings to the engine are disconnected and positioned out of the way.
42 Place the lifting sling in position round the engine and adjust the lifting tackle so that it is just supporting the weight of the engine.
43 Unscrew the engine mounting lower retaining nuts and remove with flat washers.
44 On removal of the engine from the automatic transmission, the torque converter should be retained by a means similar to that shown in photo 5.45 of Part A of this Chapter. We secured it with a piece of wood and metal bar which was attached to the bellhousing. The transmission was supported by ropes attached to a bar which was positioned across the engine compartment on the inner wing panels.
45 Carefully raise the engine from the car ensuring that it doesn't snag any of the surrounding components. When the sump is clear of the front grille panel the car can be wheeled out of the way, but remember that the transmission must be supported and provision must therefore be made for this.

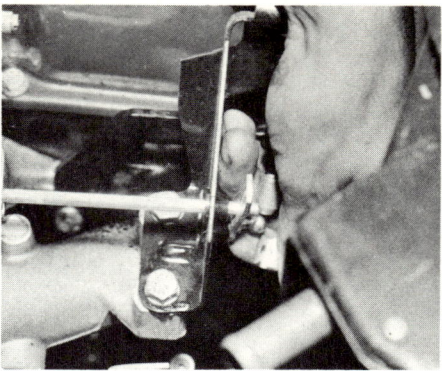
5.18 Detaching throttle cable from operating rod

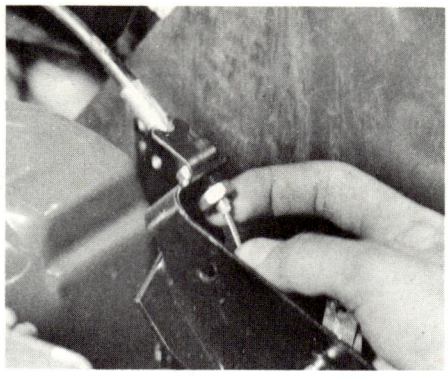
5.19 Detaching throttle cable assembly from mounting bracket

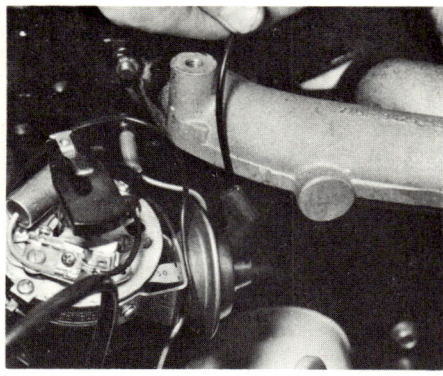
5.20 Detaching vacuum pipe from distributor

5.26 Air cleaner support bracket retained by one manifold bolt

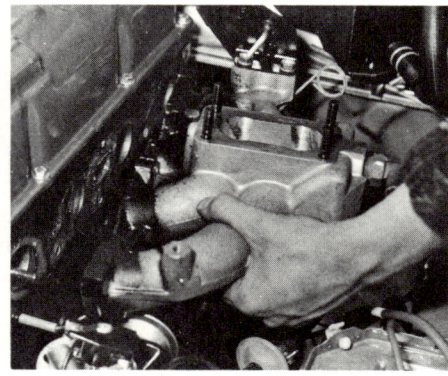
5.27 Lifting away inlet manifold

5.31 Crankcase ventilation valve

5.33 Removal of starter solenoid Lucar cable terminal

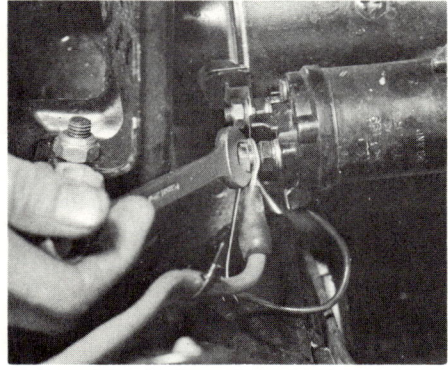
5.34a Detachment of cables at rear of solenoid

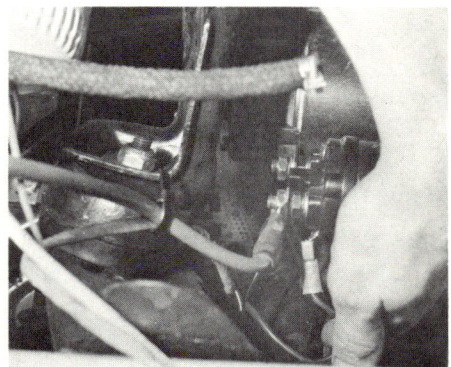
5.34b Detachment of third cable from rear of starter motor

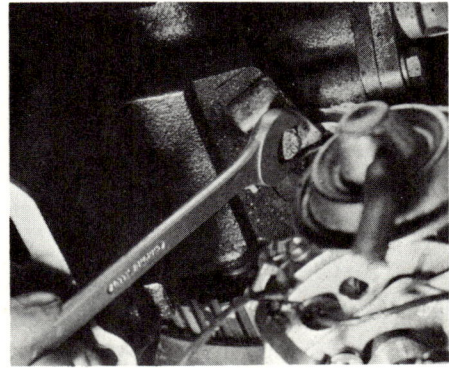
5.35 Removal of distributor clamp bolt

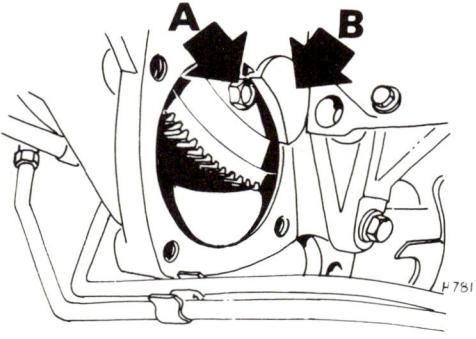
Fig. 1.2 With starter motor removed, prise out the seal grommet (B) (where fitted) and remove the intermediate drive plate to converter bolts (A) (Sec. 5)

6 Engine - removal with transmission

1 To remove the engine complete with manual transmission, first disconnect the engine attachments as described in the previous Section then refer to Part A of this Chapter, Section 6, paragraph 2 onwards.
2 Due to weight consideration, it is advisable to remove the automatic transmission and engine separately, as described in this Chapter and Chapter 6.

7 Engine dismantling - general

1 Refer to Part A of this Chapter, Section 8 for general information on dismantling the engine.
2 In addition it should also be noted that three special tools are required to complete the service operations of the cylinder head, the oil pump and the valves, (photo).

8 Cylinder head - removal (engine in car)

1 Although not absolutely necessary it is advisable to remove the bonnet as follows. Open the bonnet and, using a soft pencil, mark the outline of both the hinges at the bonnet to act as a datum for refitting.
2 With the help of a second person to take the weight of the bonnet undo and remove the hinge to bonnet securing bolts with plain and spring washers. There are two bolts to each hinge.
3 Lift away the bonnet and put in a safe place where it will not be scratched.
4 Disconnect the battery cables.
5 Place a container having a capacity of at least 8 Imp pints (4.55 litres) under the engine and sump and remove the oil drain plug. Allow the oil to drain out and then refit the plug.
6 Refer to Chapter 3 and remove the air cleaner assembly from the top of the carburettor.
7 Mark the HT leads so that they may be refitted in their original positions and detach from the spark plugs.
8 Release the HT lead rubber moulding from the clip on the top of the distributor cover.
9 Spring back the clips securing the distributor cap to the distributor body. Lift off the distributor cap.
10 Detach the HT lead from the centre of the ignition coil. Remove the distributor cap from the engine compartment.
11 Refer to Chapter 2, and drain the cooling system.
12 Refer to Chapter 3, and remove the carburettor.
13 The combined insulation spacer and gasket may now be lifted from the studs. Note that it is marked 'TOP FRONT' and it must be refitted the correct way round.
14 Slacken the clip securing the hose to the inlet manifold branch pipe adaptor and pull off the hose.
15 Slacken the clip securing the hose to the adaptor at the centre of the manifold and pull off the hose.
16 Undo and remove the self-lock nuts and bolts securing the inlet manifold to the side of the cylinder head. Note that one of the manifold securing bolts also retains the air cleaner support bracket.
17 Lift away the inlet manifold and recover the manifold gasket.
18 Undo and remove the two nuts that secure the exhaust downpipe and clamp plate to the exhaust manifold.
19 Slide the clamp plate down the exhaust pipe.
20 Detach the thermal transmitter electric cable from the inlet manifold side of the cylinder head (photo).
21 Slacken the radiator top hose clips and completely remove the hose (photo).
22 Undo and remove the bolts, spring and plain washers that secure the top cover to the cylinder head (photos).
23 Lift away the top cover (photo)
24 Undo and remove the two self-locking nuts that secure the heat deflector plate to the top of the exhaust manifold. Lift away the deflector plate (photo).
25 Undo and remove the bolts, spring and plain washers that secure the toothed drivebelt guard (photo).
26 Lift away the guard (photo).
27 Release the tension from the drivebelt by slackening the spring loaded roller mounting plate securing bolt (photo).
28 Lift the toothed drivebelt from the camshaft sprocket (photo)
29 Using the special tool (21-002) together with a socket wrench (photo), slacken the cylinder head securing bolts in a diagonal and progressive manner until all are free from tension. Remove in sequence (Fig. 1.3) the ten bolts, noting that because of the special shape of the bolt head, no washers are used. Unfortunately there is no other tool suitable to slot into the bolt head so do not attempt to improvise, which will only cause damage to the bolt.
30 The cylinder head may now be removed by lifting upwards (photo). If the head is stuck, try to rock it to break the seal. Under no circumstances try to prise it apart from the cylinder block with a screwdriver or cold chisel, as damage may be done to the faces of the cylinder head and block. If the head will not readily free, temporarily refit the battery and turn the engine over using the starter motor, as the compression in the cylinders will often break the cylinder head joint. If this fails to work, strike the head sharply with a plastic headed or wooden hammer, or with a metal hammer with an interposed piece of wood to cushion the blow. Under no circumstances hit the head directly with a metal hammer as this may cause the casting to fracture. Several sharp taps with the hammer, at the same time pulling upwards, should free the head. Lift the head off and place to one side (photo).

9 Cylinder head - removal (engine on bench)

The procedure for removing the cylinder head with the engine on the bench is similar to that for removal when the engine is in the car, with the exception of disconnecting the controls and services. Refer to Section 8 and follow the sequence given in paragraphs 22 to 30, inclusive.

10 Auxiliary shaft - removal

1 Using a metal bar lock the shaft sprocket, and with an open ended spanner undo and remove the bolt and washer that secures the sprocket to the shaft (photo).

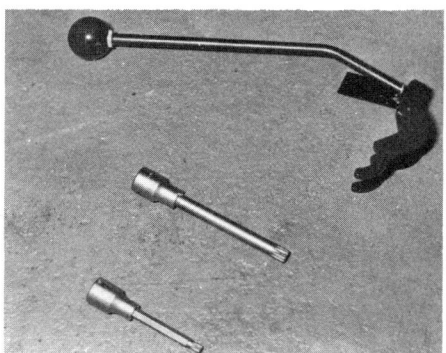

7.2 The three special tools necessary for dismantling

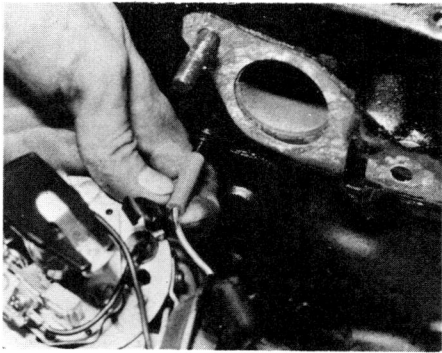

8.20 Thermal transmitter electric cable detachment

8.21 Slackening the radiator top hose clip

8.22a Removing top cover front securing bolts

8.22b Top cover flange securing bolts

8.23 Top cover removal

8.24 Removing heat deflector plate

8.25 Removing belt guard securing bolts

8.26 Belt guard removal

8.27 Retaining belt tensioner mounting plate securing bolt

8.28 Removing belt from camshaft sprocket

8.29 Slackening cylinder head securing bolts

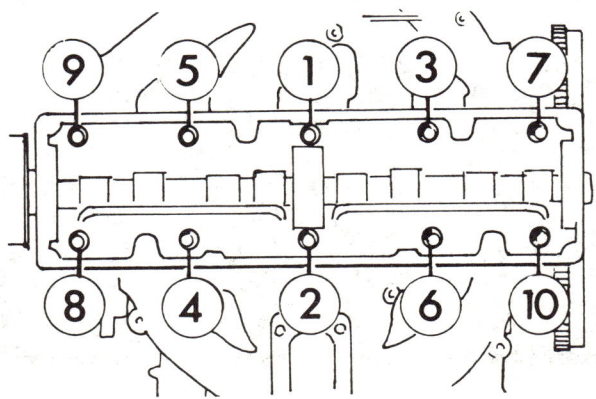
Fig. 1.3 Correct order for slackening or tightening cylinder head bolts (Sec. 8)

8.30a Cylinder head removal

8.30b Engine with cylinder head removed

10.1 Auxiliary shaft sprocket securing bolt removal

10.2 Removing auxiliary shaft timing cover securing bolts

10.3 Removing auxiliary shaft timing cover

10.4 Removing auxiliary shaft thrust plate securing screws

10.5 Lifting away thrust plate

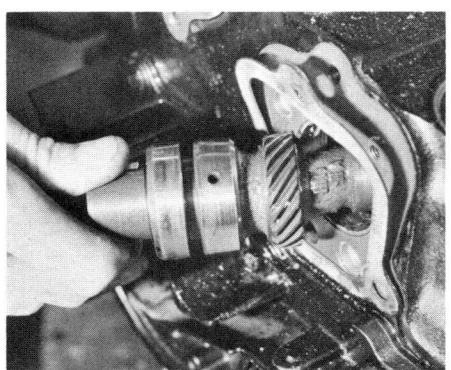
10.6 Withdrawal of auxiliary shaft

11.1 Removal of flywheel securing bolts

11.2 Lifting away flywheel

11.3 Backplate removal

11.4 Removal of sump securing bolts

11.5 Lifting away sump

Chapter 1 Part B Four cylinder in-line engine

2 Undo and remove the three bolts and spring washers that secure the shaft timing cover to the cylinder block (photo).
3 Lift away the timing cover (photo).
4 Undo and remove the two crosshead screws that secure the shaft thrust plate to the cylinder block (photo).
5 Lift away the thrust plate (photo).
6 The shaft may now be drawn forwards and then lifted away (photo).

11 Flywheel and sump - removal

1 With the clutch removed, as described in Chapter 5, lock the flywheel using a screwdriver in mesh with the starter ring gear and undo the six bolts that secure the flywheel to the crankshaft in a diagonal and progressive manner (photo). Lift away the bolts.
2 Mark the relative position of the flywheel and crankshaft and then lift away the flywheel (photo).
3 Undo the remaining engine backplate securing bolts and ease the backplate from the two dowels. Lift away the backplate (photo).
4 Undo and remove the bolts that secure the sump to the underside of the crankcase (photo).
5 Lift away the sump and its gasket (photo).

12 Oil pump and strainer - removal

1 Undo and remove the screw and spring washer that secures the oil pump pick-up pipe support bracket to the crankcase.
2 Using special tool (21-012) undo the two special bolts that secure the oil pump to the underside of the crankcase. Unfortunately there is no other tool suitable to slot into the screw head so do not attempt to improvise, which will only cause damage to the screw (photo).
3 Lift away the oil pump and strainer assembly (photo).
4 Carefully lift away the oil pump drive making a special note of which way round it is fitted (photo).

13 Crankshaft pulley, sprocket and timing cover - removal

1 Lock the crankshaft using a block of soft wood placed between a crankshaft web and the crankcase. Then, using a socket and suitable extension, undo the bolt that secures the crankshaft pulley. Recover the large diameter plain washer.
2 Using a large screwdriver ease the pulley from the crankshaft. Recover the large diameter thrust washer.
3 Again using the screwdriver ease the sprocket from the crankshaft (photo).
4 Undo and remove the bolts and spring washers that secure the timing cover to the front of the crankcase.
5 Lift away the timing cover and the gasket (photo).

14 Pistons, connecting rods and big-end bearings - removal

1 Note that the pistons have an arrow marked on the crown showing the forward facing side (photo). Inspect the big-end bearing caps and connecting rods to make sure identification marks are visible. This is to ensure that the correct end caps are fitted to the correct connecting rods and the connecting rods placed in their respective bores (Fig. 1.4)
2 Undo the big-end nuts and place to one side in the order in which they were removed.
3 Remove the big-end caps, taking care to keep them in the right order and the correct way round. Also ensure that the shell bearings are kept with their correct connecting rods unless the rods or shells are to be renewed (photo).
4 If the big-end caps are difficult to remove, they may be gently tapped with a soft hammer.
5 To remove the shell bearings, press the bearing opposite the groove in both the connecting rod and its cap, and the bearing will slide out easily.
6 Withdraw the pistons and connecting rods upwards and ensure they are kept in the correct order for refitting in the same bores as they were originally fitted.

12.2 Removal of oil pump securing bolts

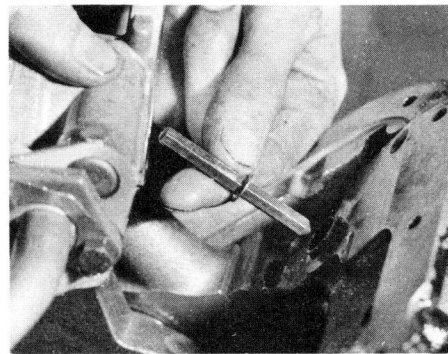
12.3 Lifting away oil pump and pick-up pipe

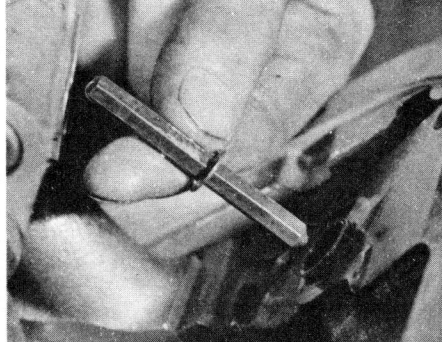
12.4 Oil pump driveshaft removal

13.3 Removal of sprocket from crankshaft

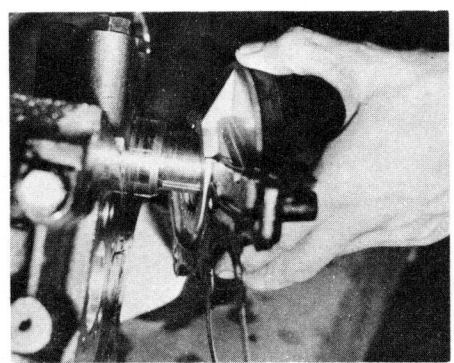
13.5 Removal of timing cover and gasket

14.1 Piston identification marks stamped on crown

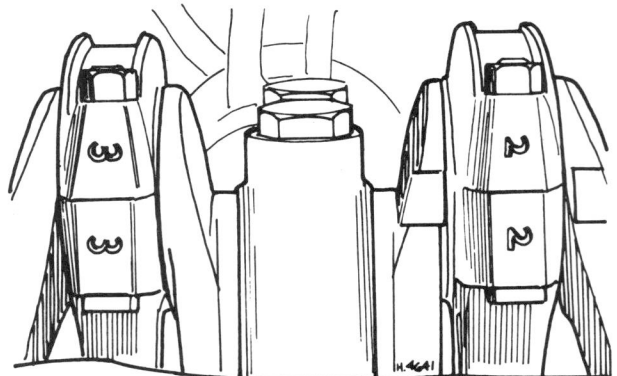

Fig. 1.4 Big-end bearing and connecting rod identification marks (Sec. 14)

15 Crankshaft and main bearings - removal

With the engine removed from the car and separated from the transmission, and the drivebelt, crankshaft pulley and sprocket, flywheel and backplate, oil pump, big-end bearings and pistons all dismantled, proceed to remove the crankshaft and main bearings.

1   Make sure that identification marks are visible on the main bearing end caps, so that they may be fitted in their original positions and also the correct way round (photo).
2   Undo by one turn at a time the bolts which hold the five bearing caps.
3   Lift away each main bearing cap and the bottom half of each bearing shell, taking care to keep the bearing shell in the right caps (photo).
4   When removing the rear main bearing end cap, note that this also retains the crankshaft rear oil seal (photo).
5   When removing the centre main bearing, note the bottom semi-circular halves of the thrust washers, one half lying on either side of

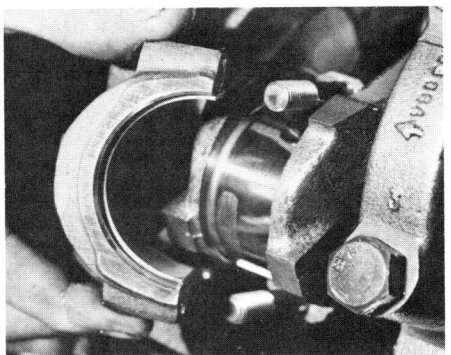

14.3 Lifting away big-end cap

15.1 Main bearing cap identification marks

15.3 Lifting away No. 2 main bearing cap

15.4 Rear main bearing cap removal

15.8 Lifting away crankshaft rear oil seal

15.9 Cylinder block and crankcase with crankshaft removed

16.6 Lifting away crankshaft pulley

16.8 Drivebelt removal

17.2 Cam follower spring removal

Chapter 1 Part B Four cylinder in-line engine

the main bearing. Lay them with the centre main bearing along the correct side.
6 As the centre and rear bearings end caps are accurately located by dowels it may be necessary to gently tap the end caps to release them.
7 Slightly rotate the crankshaft to free the upper halves of the bearing shells and thrust washers which can be extracted and placed carefully over the correct bearing cap.
8 Carefully lift away the crankshaft rear oil seal (photo).
9 Remove the crankshaft by lifting it away from the crankcase (photo).

16 Camshaft drivebelt - removal (engine in car)

It is possible to remove the camshaft drivebelt with the engine in-situ but experience is such that this type of belt is very reliable and unlikely to break or stretch considerably. However, during a major engine overhaul it is recommended that a new belt is fitted.
1 Refer to Chapter 2, and drain the cooling system. Slacken the top hose securing clips and remove the top hose.
2 Slacken the alternator mounting bolts and push the unit towards the engine. Lift away the fan belt.
3 Undo and remove the bolts that secure the drivebelt guard to the front of the engine. Lift away the guard.
4 Slacken the belt tensioner mounting plate securing bolt and release the tension on the belt.
5 Place the car in gear (manual gearbox only), and apply the brakes firmly. Undo and remove the bolt and plain washer that secure the crankshaft pulley to the nose of the crankshaft. On vehicles fitted with automatic transmission, the starter must be removed with the ring gear jammed to prevent the crankshaft rotating.
6 Using a screwdriver carefully ease off the pulley (photo).
7 Recover the plain large diameter thrust washer.
8 The drivebelt may now be lifted away (photo).

17 Valves - removal

1 To enable the valves to be removed a special valve spring compressor is required. This has a part number of 21 - 005. However it was found that it was just possible to use a universal valve spring compressor provided extreme caution was taken.
2 Make a special note of how the cam follower springs are fitted and, using a screwdriver, remove these from the cam followers (photo).
3 Back off fully the cam follower adjustment and remove the cam followers. Keep these in their respective order so that they can be refitted in their original positions.
4 Using the valve spring compressor, compress the valve springs and lift out the collets (photo).
5 Remove the spring cap and spring and, using a screwdriver, prise the oil retainer caps out of their seats. Remove each valve and keep in its respective order unless it is so badly worn that it is to be renewed. If valves are going to be used again, place them in a sheet of card having eight numbered holes corresponding with the relative positions of the valves when fitted. Also keep the valve springs, cups etc, in the correct order.

6 If necessary unscrew the ball head bolts.

18 Camshaft - removal

It is not necessary to remove the engine from the car in order to remove the camshaft. However, it will be necessary to remove the cylinder head first (Section 8) as the camshaft has to be withdrawn from the rear.
1 Undo and remove the bolts, and spring washers and bracket that secure the camshaft lubrication pipe. Lift away the pipe (photo).
2 Carefully inspect the fine oil drillings in the pipe to make sure that none are blocked (photo).
3 Using a metal bar, lock the camshaft drive sprocket then undo and remove the sprocket securing bolt and washer (photo).
4 Using a soft-faced hammer or screwdriver ease the sprocket from the camshaft (photo).
5 Undo and remove the two bolts and spring washers that secure the camshaft thrust plate to the rear bearing support (photo).
6 Lift away the thrust plate noting which way round it is fitted (photo).
7 Remove the cam follower springs and then the cam followers as detailed in Section 17 paragraphs 2 and 3.
8 The camshaft may now be removed by using a soft-faced hammer and tapping rearwards. Take care not to cut the fingers when the camshaft is being handled as the sides of the lobes can be sharp (photo).
9 Lift the camshaft carefully through the bearing inserts as the lobes can damage the soft metal bearing surfaces easily . (photo).
10 If the oil seal has hardened or become damaged, it may be removed by prising it out with a screwdriver (photo).

19 Thermostat housing and belt tensioner - removal

1 Removal of these parts will usually only be necessary if the cylinder head is to be completely dismantled.
2 Undo and remove the two bolts and spring washers that secure the thermostat housing to the front face of the cylinder head.
3 Lift away the thermostat housing and recover its gasket (photo).
4 Undo and remove the bolt and spring washer that secures the belt tensioner to the cylinder head. It will be necessary to override the tension using a screwdriver as a lever (photos).
5 Using tool number 21 - 012 (the tool for removal of the oil pump securing bolts) unscrew the tensioner mounting plate and spring shaped bolt and lift away the tensioner assembly (photo).

20 Gudgeon pin - removal

Interference fit type gudgeon pins are used and it is important that no damage is caused during removal and refitting. Because of this, should it be necessary to fit new pistons, take the parts along to the local Ford garage who will have the special equipment to do this job.

17.4 Compressing valve spring

18.1 Removing camshaft lubrication pipe (later models have a modified oil pipe)

18.2 Camshaft lubrication pipe oil holes (later models have a modified oil pipe)

18.3 Using a metal bar to lock camshaft sprocket

18.4 Removing camshaft sprocket

18.5 Removing camshaft thrust plate securing bolts

18.6 Camshaft thrust plate removal

18.8 Tapping camshaft through bearings

18.9 Camshaft removal

18.10 Camshaft oil seal removal

19.3 Thermostat housing removal

19.4a Removal of belt tensioner mounting plate securing bolt

19.4b Easing off the belt spring tension with a screwdriver

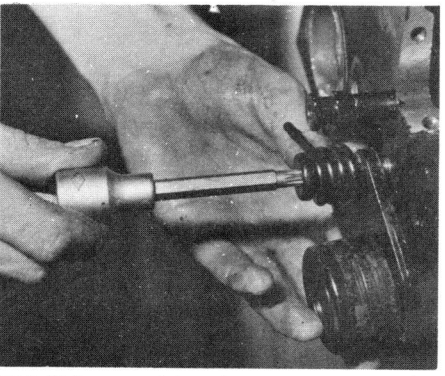
19.5 Using special tool to remove mounting plate and spring securing bolt from belt tensioner

Chapter 1 Part B Four cylinder in-line engine

21 Piston rings - removal

1 To remove the piston rings, slide them carefully over the top of the piston, taking care not to scratch the aluminium alloy; never slide them off the bottom of the piston skirt. It is very easy to break the cast iron piston rings if they are pulled off roughly, so this operation should be done with extreme care. It is helpful to make use of an old 0.020 inch (0.508 mm) feeler gauge.
2 Lift one end of the piston ring to be removed out of its groove and insert under it the end of the feeler gauge.
3 Turn the feeler gauge slowly round the piston and, as the ring comes out of its groove, apply slight upward pressure so that it rests on the land above. It can then be eased off the piston, with the feeler gauge stopping it from slipping into an empty groove if it is any but the top piston ring that is being removed.

22 Lubrication and crankcase ventilation systems - description

1 The pressed steel oil sump is attached to the underside of the crankcase and acts as a reservoir for the engine oil. The oil pump draws oil through a strainer located under the oil surface, passes it along a short passage and into the full flow oil filter. The freshly filtered oil flows from the centre of the filter element and enters the main gallery. Five small drillings connect the main gallery to the five main bearings. The big-end bearings are supplied with oil by the front and rear main bearings via skew oil bores. When the crankshaft is rotating, oil is thrown from the hole in each big-end bearing and splashes the thrust side of the piston and bore.
2 The auxiliary shaft is lubricated directly from the main oil gallery. The distributor shaft is supplied with oil passing along a drilling inside the auxiliary shaft.
3 A further three drillings connect the main oil gallery to the overhead camshaft. The centre camshaft bearing has a semi-circular groove from which oil is passed along a pipe running parallel with the camshaft. The pipe is drilled opposite to each cam and cam follower so providing the lubrication to the sump, via large drillings in the cylinder head and cylinder block.
4 A semi-enclosed engine ventilation system is used to control crankcase vapour. It is controlled by the amount of air drawn in by the engine when running and the throughput of the regulator valve (Fig. 1.7). The system is known as the PCV system (Positive Crankcase Ventilation) and the advantage of the system is that should the 'blow-by' exceed the capacity of the PCV valve, excess fumes are fed into the engine through the air cleaner. This is caused by the rise in crankcase pressure which creates a reverse flow in the air intake pipe.
5 Periodically, pull the valve and hose from the rubber grommet of the oil separator and inspect the valve for free movement. If it is sticky in action or is choked with sludge, dismantle it and clean the components.
6 Occasionally check the security and condition of the system connecting hoses.

23 Oil pump - dismantling, inspection and reassembly

1 If oil pump wear is suspected it is possible to obtain a repair kit. Check for wear as described later in this Section and, if confirmed, obtain an overhaul kit or a new pump. The two rotors are a matched pair and form a single replacement unit. Where the rotor assembly is to be re-used the outer rotor, prior to dismantling, must be marked on its front face in order to ensure correct reassembly.
2 Undo and remove the two bolts and spring washers that secure the intake cowl to the oil pump body. Lift away the cowl and its gasket (Fig. 1.8).
3 Note the relative position of the oil pump cover and body and then undo and remove the three bolts and spring washers. Lift away the cover.
4 Carefully remove the rotors from the housing.
5 Using a centre punch, tap a hole in the centre of the pressure relief valve sealing plug, and make a note to obtain a new one.
6 Screw in a self-tapping screw and, using an open-ended spanner, withdraw the sealing plug as shown in Fig. 1.9.

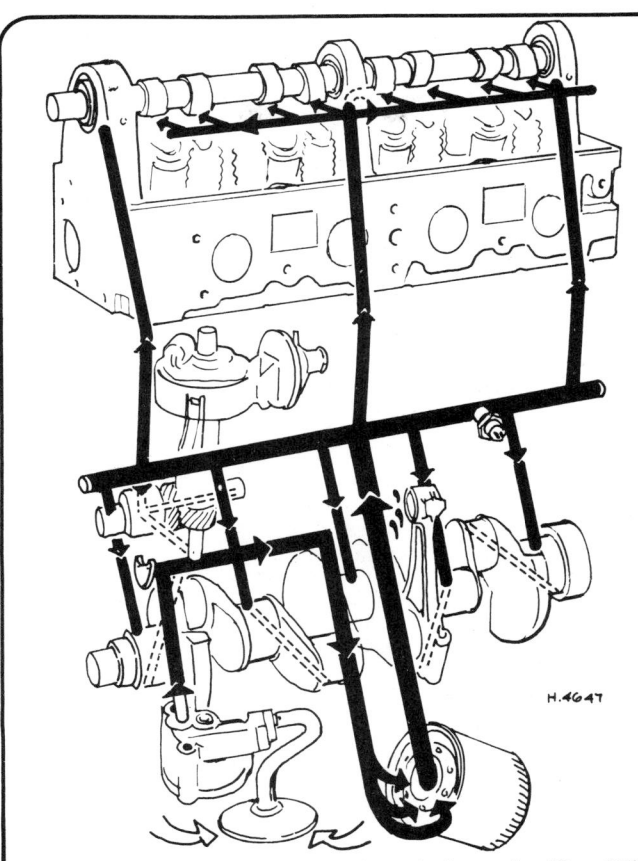

Fig. 1.5 Circulation of lubricant through the engine (Sec. 22)

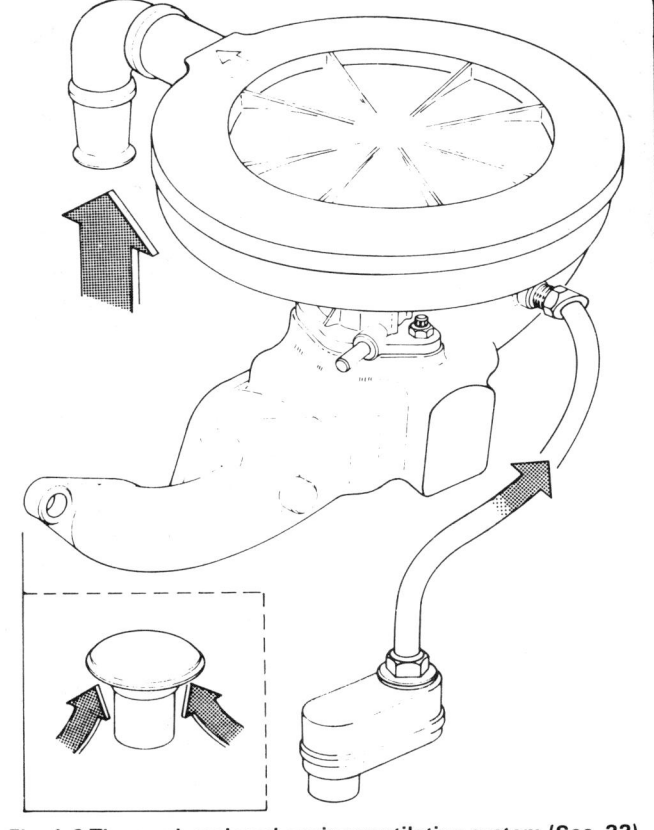

Fig. 1.6 The semi-enclosed engine ventilation system (Sec. 22)

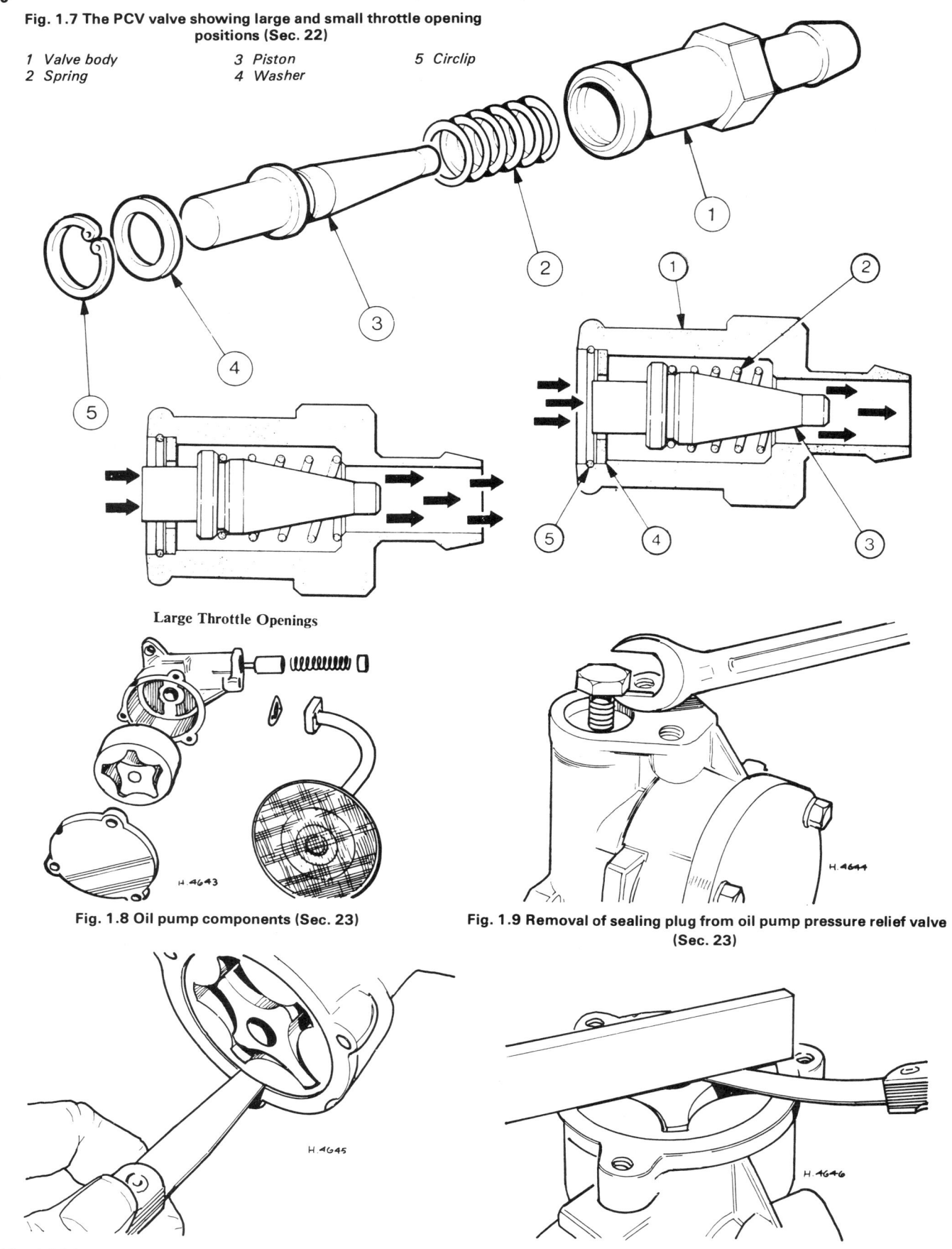

Fig. 1.7 The PCV valve showing large and small throttle opening positions (Sec. 22)

1 Valve body
2 Spring
3 Piston
4 Washer
5 Circlip

Large Throttle Openings

Fig. 1.8 Oil pump components (Sec. 23)

Fig. 1.9 Removal of sealing plug from oil pump pressure relief valve (Sec. 23)

Fig. 1.10 Checking oil pump outer rotor to body clearance (Sec. 23)

Fig. 1.11 Checking oil pump endfloat clearance (Sec. 23)

7 Thoroughly clean all parts in petrol or paraffin and wipe dry using a non-fluffy rag. The necessary clearances may now be checked using a machined straight-edge (a good steel rule) and a set of feeler gauges. The critical clearances are between the lobes of the centre rotor and convex faces of the outer rotor; between the outer rotor and the pump body; and between both rotors and the end cover plate.
8 The rotor lobe clearance may be checked using feeler gauges and should be within the limits specified.
9 The clearance between the outer rotor and pump body should be within the limits specified (Fig. 1.10).
10 The endfloat clearance may be measured by placing a steel straight edge across the end of the pump and measuring the gap between the rotors and the straight edge. The gap in either rotor should be within the limits specified as shown in Fig. 1.11.
11 If the only excessive clearances are endfloat it is possible to reduce them by removing the rotors lapping the face of the body on a flat bed until the necessary clearances are obtained. It must be emphasised, however, that the face of the body must remain perfectly flat and square to the axis of the rotor spindle otherwise the clearances will not be equal and the end cover will not be a pressure tight fit to the body. It is worth trying, of course, if the pump is in need of renewal anyway but unless done properly, it could seriously jeopardise the rest of the overhaul. Any variations in the other two clearances should be overcome with a new unit.
12 With all parts scrupulously clean, first refit the relief valve and spring and lightly lubricate with engine oil.
13 Using a suitable diameter drift, drive in a new sealing plug, flat side outwards until it is flush with the intake cowl bearing face.
14 Lubricate both rotors with engine oil and insert into the body. Fit the oil pump cover and secure with the three bolts in a diagonal and progressive manner to a final torque wrench setting as specified.
15 Fit the intermediate shaft into the rotor driveshaft and make sure that the rotor turns freely.
16 Fit the cowl to the pump body, using a new gasket and secure with two bolts.

24 Oil filter - removal and refitting

Refer to Part A, Section 30 of this Chapter.

25 Engine components - examination for wear

Refer to Part A, Section 31 of this Chapter.

26 Crankshaft - examination and renovation

Refer to Part A, Section 32 of this Chapter, but refer to Figs. 1.12 and 1.13 of this Part for the crankshaft and main bearing identification code information.

27 Crankshaft main and big-end bearings - examination and renovation

Refer to Part A Section 33, paragraphs 1 and 2 of this Chapter and refer to Fig. 1.13 of this Part for the big-end identification codes.

28 Cylinder bores - examination and renovation

Refer to Part A Section 34 of this Chapter.

29 Pistons and piston rings - examination and renovation

Refer to Part A Section 35 of this Chapter.

30 Connecting rods and gudgeon pins - examination and renovation

Refer to Part A Section 36 of this Chapter.

31 Camshaft, camshaft bearings and cam followers - examination and renovation

1 The camshaft bearing bushes should be examined for signs of scoring and pitting. If they need renewal they will have to be dealt with professionally as, although it may be relatively easy to remove the old bushes, the correct fitting of new ones requires special tools. If they are not fitted evenly and square from the very start they can be distorted thus causing localised wear in a very short time. See your Ford dealer or local engineering specialist for this work.
2 The camshaft itself may show signs of wear on the bearing journals, or cam lobes. The main decision to take is what degree of wear justifies renewal, which is costly. Any signs of scoring or damage to the bearing journals cannot be removed by regrinding. Renewal of the whole camshaft is the only solution. When overhauling the valve gear, check that oil is being ejected from the nozzzles onto the cam followers. Turn the engine on the starter to observe this.
3 The cam lobes themselves may show signs of ridging or pitting on the high points. If ridging is light then it may be possible to smooth it out with fine emery. The cam lobes however, are surface hardened and once this is penetrated wear will be very rapid thereafter.
4 The faces of the cam followers which bear on the camshaft should show no signs of pitting, scoring or other forms of wear. They should not be a loose sloppy fit on the ballheaded bolt. Inspect the face which bears onto the valve stem and if pitted the cam follower must be renewed.

32 Valves and valve seats - examination and renovation

Refer to Part A, Section 39 of this Chapter. Refer to Fig. 1.14 of this Part for the valve seat angles.

33 Timing gears and belt - examination and renovation

1 Any wear which takes place in the timing mechanism will be on the teeth of the drivebelt or due to stretch of the fabric. Whenever the engine is to be stripped for major overhaul a new belt should be fitted.
2 It is very unusual for the timing gears (sprockets) to wear at the teeth. If the securing bolts/nuts have been loose it is possible for the keyway or hub bore to wear. Check these two points and if damage or wear is evident a new gear must be obtained.

34 Flywheel ring gear - examination and renovation

Refer to Part A Section 41 of this Chapter.

35 Cylinder head and piston crowns - decarbonization

Refer to Part A Section 42 of this Chapter.

36 Valve guides - inspection

1 Examine each valve guide internal bore for signs of scoring and wear. Insert the respective valves and if they are a loose fit in the guides and/or they can be rocked laterally, either the valve stem or internal bore of the guide is badly worn.
2 Try a new valve in the guides and if it is still loose, then the guides must be reamed oversize and new valves fitted. This is a task that is best left to your Ford dealer.

37 Sump - inspection

Wash out the sump in petrol and wipe dry. Carefully inspect for signs of damage or distortion. Renew if required. Scrape away all of the old gasket and sealant solution from the cylinder block mating face.

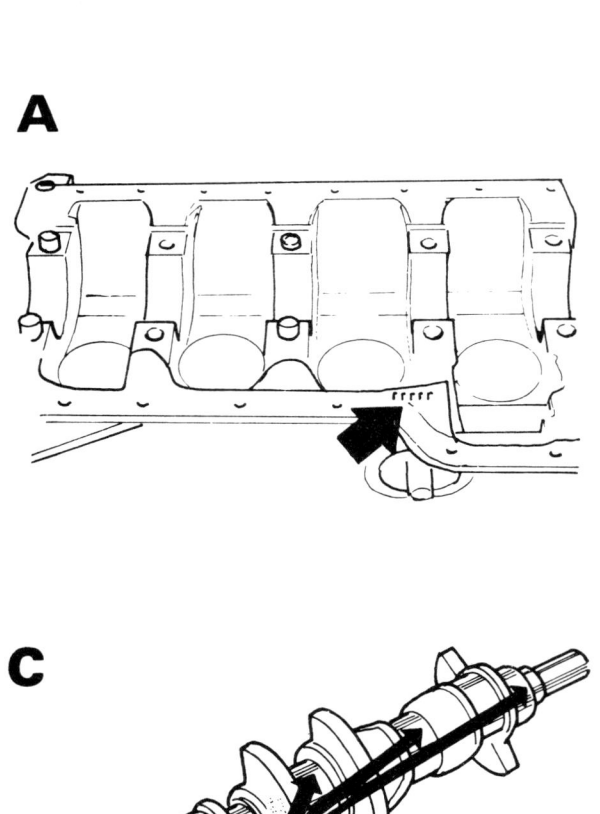
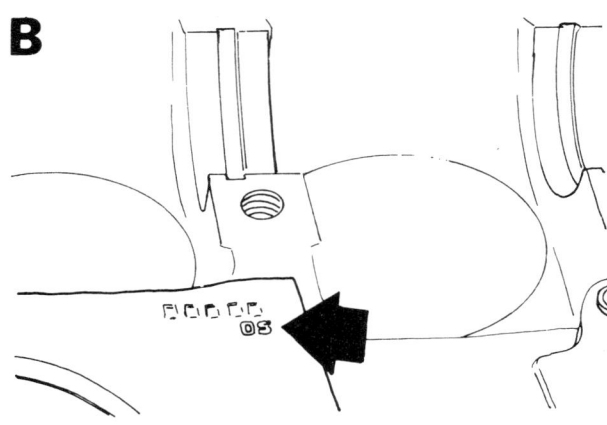
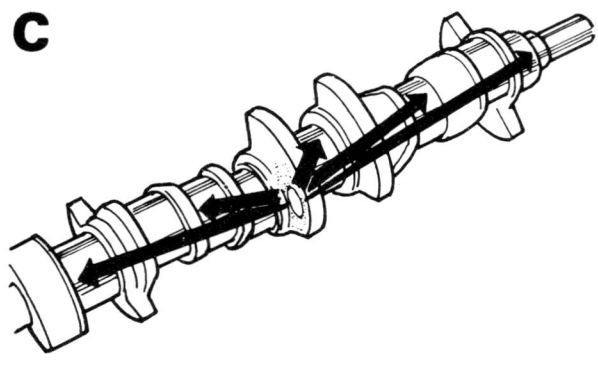
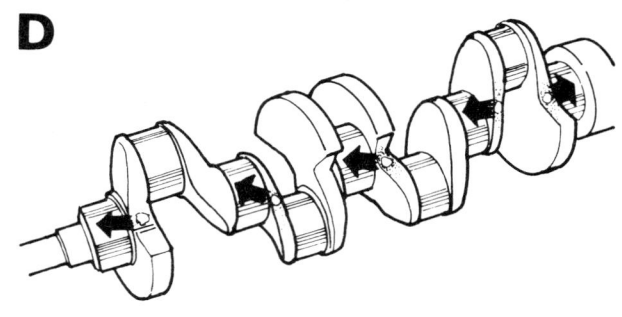
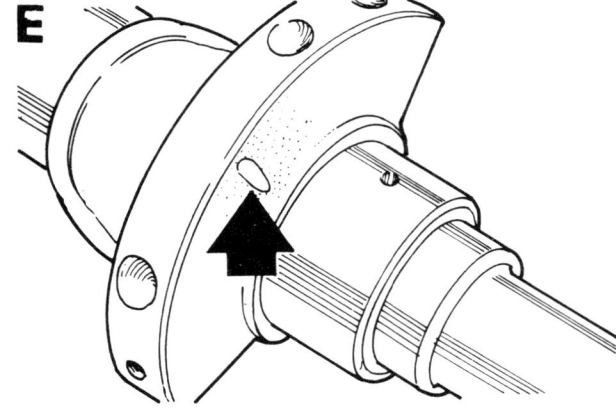

A   With either the crankshaft main or big-end bearings a bearing comprises the bore, crankshaft journal and two bearing liner halves. The main bearing bore and also the crankshaft journal are marked with blue colour if of minimum size within the tolerance grade, and with red colour if of maximum size within the tolerance grade. The parent bore in the cylinder block is marked with letters
r   red   b   blue

B   The parent bore identification letters are stamped on the oil sump side of the machined face of the cylinder block. Where the code letters are followed by the letters 'OS' the parent bores are of 0.4 mm oversize

C   If all main bearing journals are within the same tolerance grade, a red or blue colour mark is to be found on the crankshaft web behind the centre bearing

D   If the main bearing journals vary in tolerance the colour marks are to be found on the narrow side of the web behind the respective bearing, but for the rear bearing in front

E   If the main bearing journals have been ground to undersize a colour line is to be found on the front web

Fig. 1.12 Crankshaft, main bearings and big-end bearings identification codes (Part 1) (Sec. 26)

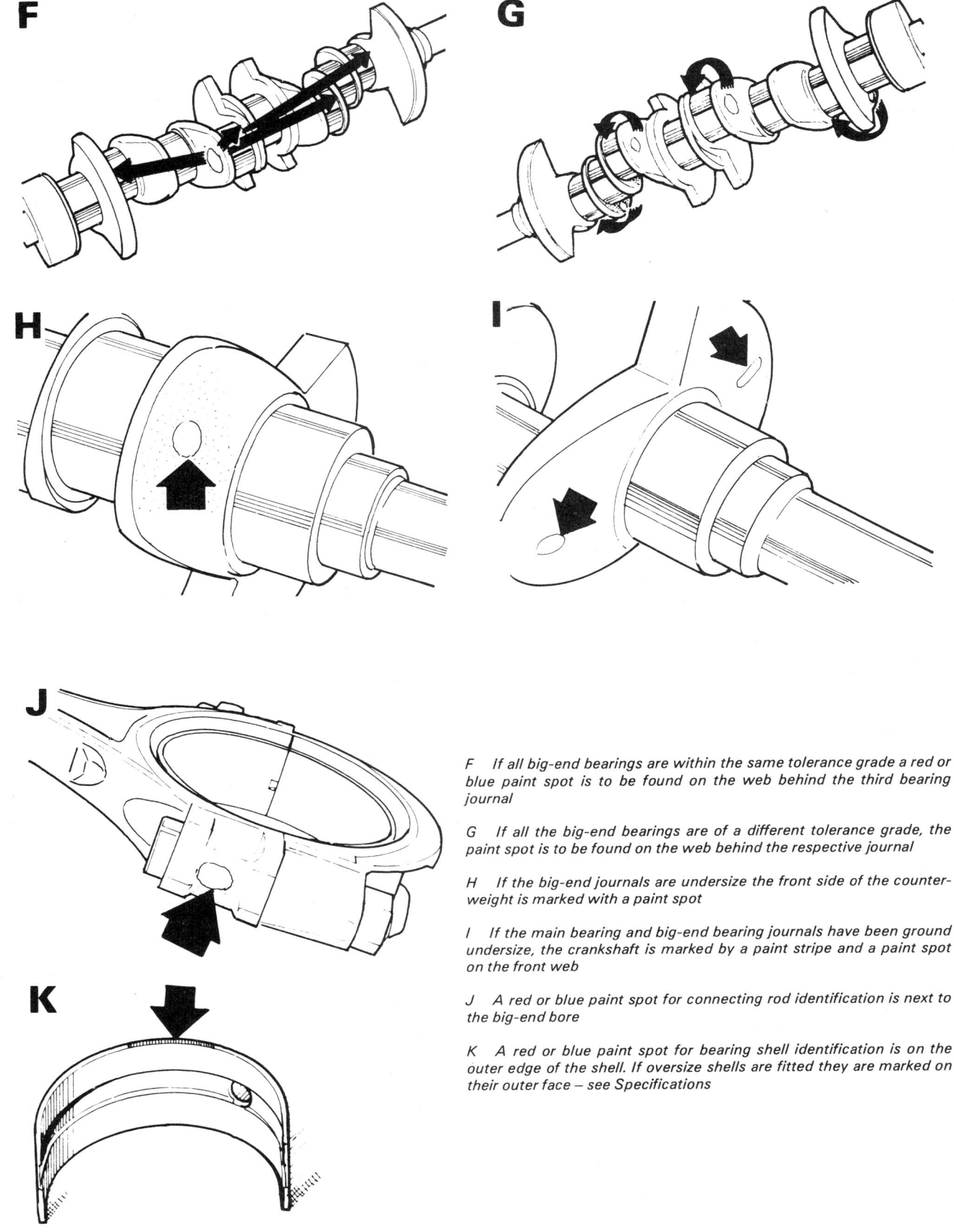

F If all big-end bearings are within the same tolerance grade a red or blue paint spot is to be found on the web behind the third bearing journal

G If all the big-end bearings are of a different tolerance grade, the paint spot is to be found on the web behind the respective journal

H If the big-end journals are undersize the front side of the counterweight is marked with a paint spot

I If the main bearing and big-end bearing journals have been ground undersize, the crankshaft is marked by a paint stripe and a paint spot on the front web

J A red or blue paint spot for connecting rod identification is next to the big-end bore

K A red or blue paint spot for bearing shell identification is on the outer edge of the shell. If oversize shells are fitted they are marked on their outer face — see Specifications

Fig. 1.13 Crankshaft, main bearings and big-end bearings identification codes (Part 2) (Sec. 26)

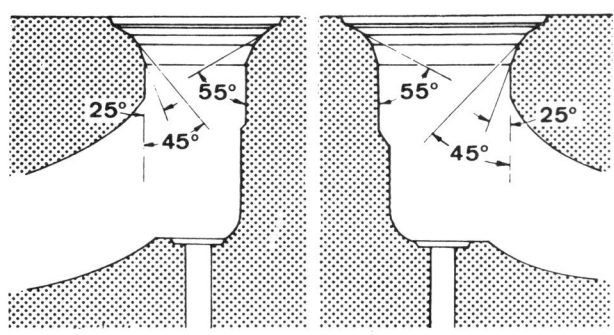

Fig. 1.14 Valve seat angles (Sec. 32)

38 Engine reassembly - general

1 All engine components must be cleaned of old oil, sludge and old gaskets. The work area should be cleaned also prior to reassembly. In addition to the normal range of essential tools the following must be available before reassembling the engine:

    a) Complete set of new gaskets (photo)
    b) Supply of clean rags
    c) Clean can full of engine oil of the correct grade
    d) Torque wrench
    e) All new spare parts as required
    f) A tube of gasket sealant solution

39 Crankshaft - refitting

Ensure that the crankcase is thoroughly clean and that all oilways

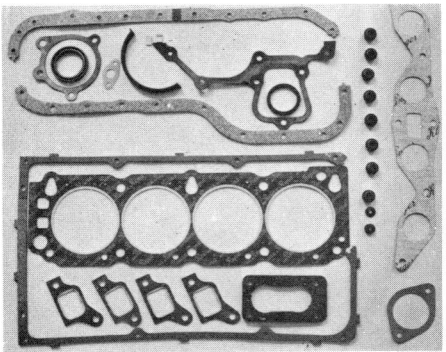

38.1 Items in gasket set

39.3 Inserting bearing shells into crankcase

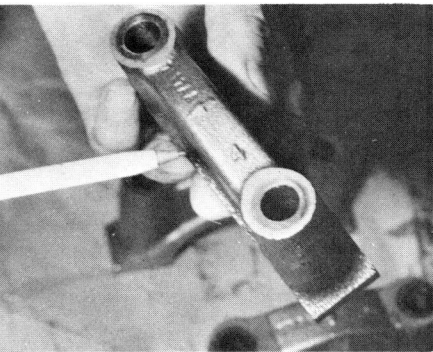

39.4 Main bearing cap identification marks

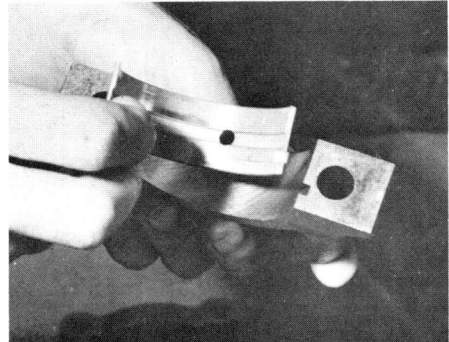

39.6 Fitting bearing shell to main bearing cap

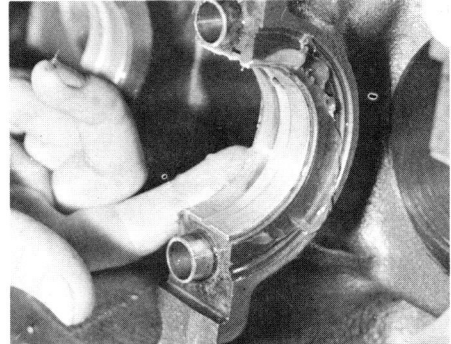

39.8 Applying grease to either side of centre main bearing

39.9 Fitting thrust washers to centre main bearing

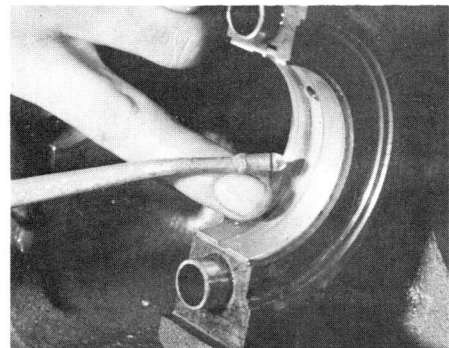

39.10 Lubricating bearing shells

39.11 Fitting crankshaft to crankcase

39.12 Refitting No. 1 main bearing cap. Note identification mark

Chapter 1 Part B Four cylinder in-line engine

are clear. A thin twist drill or a piece of wire is useful for cleaning them out. If possible blow them out with compressed air. Treat the crankshaft in the same fashion, and then inject engine oil into the crankshaft oilways. Commence work on rebuilding the engine by refitting the crankshaft and main bearings:

1 Wipe the bearing shell location in the crankcase with a soft, non-fluffy rag.
2 Wipe the crankshaft journals with a soft, non-fluffy rag.
3 If the old main bearing shells are to be renewed (not to do so is a false economy unless they are virtually new) fit the five upper halves of the main bearing shells to their location in the crankcase (photo).
4 Identify each main bearing cap and place in order. The number is cast onto the cap and with intermediate caps an arrow is also marked so that the cap is fitted the correct way round. (photo).
5 Wipe the end cap bearing shell location with a soft non-fluffy rag.
6 Fit the bearing half shell into each main bearing cap (photo).
7 Fit the bearing half shell into each location in the crankcase.
8 Apply a little grease to each side of the centre main bearing so as to retain the thrust washers (photo).
9 Fit the upper halves of the thrust washers into their grooves either side of the main bearing. The slots must face outwards (photo).
10 Lubricate the crankshaft journals and the upper and lower main bearing shells with engine oil (photo).
11 Carefully lower the crankshaft into the crankcase (photo).
12 Lubricate the crankshaft main bearing journals again and then fit No 1 bearing cap (photo). Fit the two securing bolts but do not tighten yet.
13 Apply a little gasket cement to the crankshaft rear main bearing end cap location (photo).
14 Next fit No 5 end cap (photo). Fit the two securing bolts but as before do not tighten yet.
15 Apply a little grease to either side of the centre main bearing end caps so as to retain the thrust washers. Fit the thrust washers with the tag located in the groove and the slots facing outwards (photo).
16 Fit the centre main bearing end cap and the two securing bolts. Then refit the intermediate main bearing end caps. Make sure that the arrows point towards the front of the engine (photo).
17 Lightly tighten all main cap securing bolts and then fully tighten in a progressive manner to a final torque wrench setting as specified (photo).
18 Using a screwdriver ease the crankshaft fully forwards and with feeler gauges check the clearance between the crankshaft journal side and the thrust washers. The clearance must not exceed that specified. Undersize thrust washers are available (photo).
19 Test the crankshaft for freedom of rotation. Should it be stiff to turn or possess high spots, a most careful inspection must be made with a micrometer, preferably by a qualified mechanic, to get to the root of the trouble. It is very seldom that any trouble of this nature will be experienced when fitting the crankshaft.

40 Pistons and connecting rods - reassembly

As a press type gudgeon pin is used (see Sections 20 and 30) this operation must be carried out by the local Ford garage.

41 Piston rings - refitting

1 Check that the piston ring grooves and oilways are thoroughly clean and unblocked. Piston rings must always be fitted over the head of the piston and never from the bottom.
2 The easiest method to use when fitting rings is to wrap a 0.020 in (0.5080 mm) feeler gauge round the top of the piston and place the rings one at a time, starting with the bottom oil control ring, over the feeler gauge.
3 The feeler gauge, complete with ring can then be slid down the piston over the other piston ring grooves until the correct groove is reached. The piston ring is then slid off the feeler gauge into the groove.
4 An alternative method is to fit the rings by holding them slightly open with the thumbs and both of the index fingers. This method requires a steady hand and great care as it is easy to open the ring too much and break it.

39.13 Applying gasket cement to rear main bearing cap location

39.14 Refitting rear main bearing cap

39.15 Fitting thrust washers to centre main bearing cap

39.16 All main bearing caps in position

39.17 Tightening main bearing cap securing bolts

39.18 Using feeler gauge to check endfloat

42 Pistons - refitting

The piston, complete with connecting rods, can be fitted to the cylinder bores in the following sequence:
1. With a wad of clean non-fluffy rag wipe the cylinder bores clean.
2. The pistons, complete with connecting rods, are fitted to their bores from the top of the block.
3. Locate the piston ring gaps in the following manner (photo):

Top: 150° to one side of the helical expander gap.
Centre: 150° to the opposite side of the helical expander gap.
Bottom: Helical expander: opposite the marked piston front side.
Intermediate rings: : 1 inch (25mm) each side of the helical expander gap.

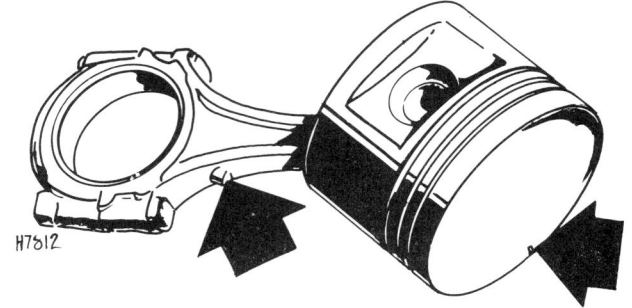

Fig. 1.15 Piston identification mark relative to piston lubrication jet hole (Sec. 42)

42.3 Positioning ring gaps

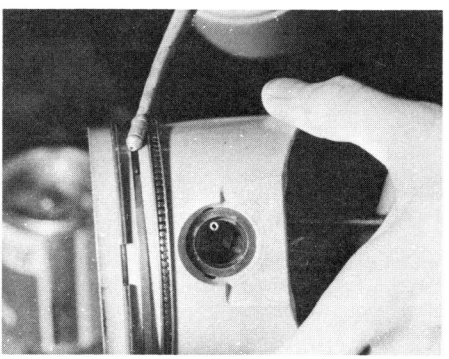

42.4 Lubricating pistons prior to refitting

42.5 Piston identification marks

42.6a Inserting connecting rod into cylinder bore

42.6b Piston ring compressor correctly positioned

42.7 Pushing piston down bore

43.6 Refitting big-end cap securing nuts

43.7 Tightening big-end cap securing nuts

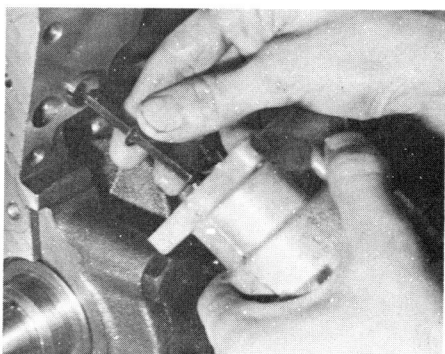

44.2 Inserting oil pump driveshaft

Chapter 1 Part B Four cylinder in-line engine

4 Lubricate the piston and rings with engine oil (photo).
5 Fit a universal piston ring compressor and prepare to insert the first piston into the bore. Make sure it is the correct piston connecting rod assembly for that particular bore, that the connecting rod is the correct way round and that the front of the piston is towards the front of the bore, ie towards the front of the engine (photo).
6 Again lubricate the piston skirt and insert into the bore up to the bottom of the piston ring compressor (photos).
7 Gently but firmly tap the piston through the piston ring compressor and into the cylinder bore with a wooden or plastic faced hammer (photo). Make certain that the rings do not jam against the block face and break.

43 Connecting rods to crankshaft - reassembly

1 Wipe clean the connecting rod half of the big-end bearing cap and the underside of the shell bearing and fit the shell bearing in position with its locating tongue engaged with the corresponding cut-out in the rod.
2 If the old bearings are nearly new and are being refitted then ensure they are refitted in their correct locations on the correct rods. Note that it is false economy not to fit new bearings unless the old ones are nearly new.
3 Generously lubricate the crankpin journals with engine oil and turn the crankshaft so that the crankpin is in the most advantageous position for the connecting rod to be drawn onto it.
4 Wipe clean the connecting rod bearing cap and back of the shell bearing, and fit the shell bearing in position ensuring that the locating tongue at the back of the bearing engages with the locating groove in the connecting rod cap.
5 Generously lubricate the shell bearing and offer up the connecting rod bearing cap to the connecting rod.
6 Refit the connecting rod nuts (photo).
7 Tighten the bolts with a torque wrench set to the specified torque (photo).
8 When all the connecting rods have been fitted, rotate the crankshaft to check that everything is free, and that there are no high spots causing binding.

44 Oil pump - refitting

1 Wipe the mating faces of the oil pump and underside of the cylinder block.
2 Insert the hexagonal driveshaft into the end of the oil pump (photo).
3 Offer up the oil pump and refit the two special bolts. Using the special tool (21-020) and a torque wrench tighten the two bolts to the specified torque (photo).
4 Refit the one bolt and spring washer that secures the oil pump pick-up pipe support bracket to the crankcase.

45 Crankshaft rear oil seal - refitting

1 Apply some gasket sealant to the slot on either side of the rear main bearing end cap and insert a rectangular shaped seal (photo).
2 Apply some gasket sealant to the slot in the rear main bearing end cap and carefully insert the shaped seal (photo).
3 Lightly smear some grease on the crankshaft rear oil seal and carefully ease it over the end of the crankshaft. The spring must be inwards (photo).
4 Using a soft metal drift carefully tap the seal into position (photo).

46 Auxiliary shaft and timing cover - refitting

1 Carefully insert the auxiliary shaft into the front face of the cylinder block (photo).
2 Position the thrust plate into its groove in the auxiliary shaft - countersunk faces of the holes facing outwards - and refit the two cross-head screws (photo).
3 Tighten the two cross-head screws using a cross-head screwdriver and an open-ended spanner (photo).
4 Smear some grease on to the cylinder block face of a new gasket

44.3 Tightening oil pump securing bolts

45.1 Refitting rectangular shaped seals to rear of crankshaft

45.2 Fitting seal into rear main bearing cap

45.3 Refitting crankshaft rear oil seal

45.4 Tapping crankshaft rear oil seal into position

46.1 Refitting auxiliary shaft

46.2 Locating auxiliary shaft thrust plate

46.3 Tightening auxiliary shaft thrust plate securing screws

46.4 Positioning new gasket on cylinder block front face

46.6a Refitting crankshaft timing cover

46.6b Tightening crankshaft timing cover securing bolts

46.8 Tightening auxiliary shaft timing cover securing bolts

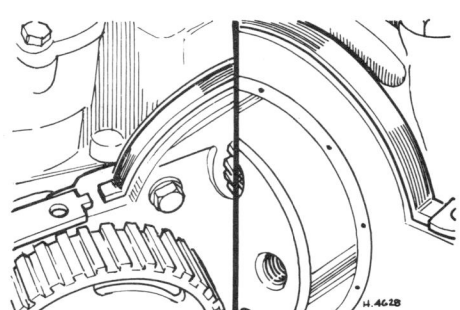
Fig. 1.16 Correct fitment of sump gasket at front and rear main bearing caps (Sec. 47)

47.4 New gaskets fitted to greased underside of crankcase ready for sump

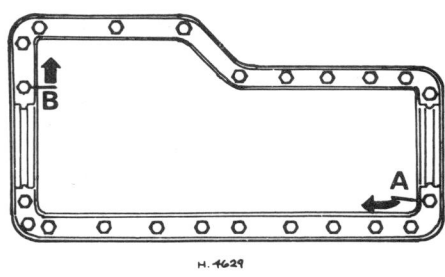
Fig. 1.17 Correct order for tightening sump bolts (Sec. 47)

48.1 Refitting Woodruff key to crankshaft

48.2 Sliding on crankshaft sprocket

48.3 Fitting drivebelt to crankshaft sprocket

and carefully fit into position (photo).
5 Apply some gasket sealant to the slot in the underside of the crankshaft timing cover. Insert the shaped seal.
6 Offer up the timing cover and secure with the bolts and spring washers (photos).
7 Smear some grease onto the seal located in the shaft timing cover and carefully ease the cover over the end of the auxiliary shaft.
8 Secure the auxiliary shaft timing cover with the four bolts and spring washers (photo).

47 Sump - refitting

1 Wipe the mating faces of the underside of the crankcase and the sump.
2 Smear some grease on the underside of the crankcase.
3 Fit the sump gasket making sure that the bolt holes line up (Fig. 1.16).
4 Offer the sump up to the gasket taking care not to dislodge the gasket and secure in position with the bolts (photo).
5 Tighten the sump bolts in a progressive manner to the torque wrench settings detailed in the Specifications (Fig. 1.17).

48 Crankshaft sprocket and pulley, and auxiliary shaft sprocket - refitting

1 Check that the keyways in the end of the crankshaft are clean and the keys are free from burrs. Fit the keys into the keyways (photo).
2 Slide the sprocket into position on the crankshaft. This sprocket is the small diameter one (photo).
3 Ease the drivebelt into mesh with the crankshaft sprocket (photo).
4 Slide the large diameter plain washer onto the crankshaft (photo).
5 Check that the keyway in the end of the auxiliary shaft is clean and the key is free of burrs. Fit the key to the keyway.
6 Slide the sprocket onto the end of the auxiliary shaft (photo).
7 Slide the pulley onto the end of the crankshaft (photo).
8 Refit the bolt and thick plain washer to the end of the crankshaft (photo).
9 Lock the crankshaft pulley with a metal bar and using a torque wrench fully tighten the bolt (photo).

49 Water pump - refitting

1 Make sure that all traces of the old gasket are removed and then smear some grease on the gasket face of the cylinder block.
2 Fit a new gasket to the cylinder block.
3 Offer up the water pump and secure in position with the four bolts and spring washers (photo).

50 Flywheel and clutch - refitting

1 Remove all traces of the shaped seal from the backplate and apply a little gasket sealant to the backplate. Fit a new seal to the backplate (photo).
2 Wipe the mating faces of the backplate and cylinder block and carefully fit the backplate to the two dowels (photo).
3 Wipe the mating faces of the flywheel and crankshaft and offer up the flywheel to the crankshaft, aligning the previously made marks unless new parts have been fitted.
4 Fit the six crankshaft securing bolts and lightly tighten.
5 Lock the flywheel using a screwdriver engaged in the starter ring gear and tighten the securing bolts in a diagonal and progressive manner to a final torque wrench setting as given in the Specifications (photo).
6 Refit the clutch disc and pressure plate assembly to the flywheel making sure the disc is the right way round (photo).
7 Secure the pressure plate assembly with the six retaining bolts and spring washers.
8 Centralise the clutch disc using an old input shaft or piece of wooden dowel and fully tighten the retaining bolts (photo).
9 On automatic transmission models, refit the intermediate drive plate and secure with the bolts.

48.4 Refitting large diameter plain washer

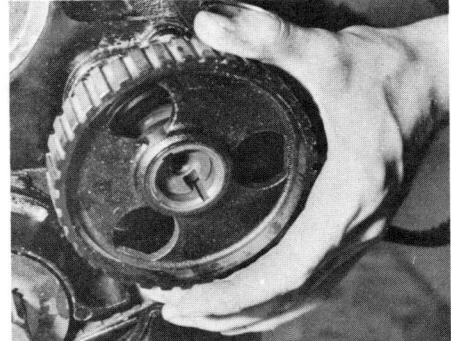
48.6 Fitting sprocket to auxiliary shaft

48.7 Refitting crankshaft pulley

48.8 Crankshaft pulley securing bolt and large washer

48.9 Tightening crankshaft pulley securing bolt

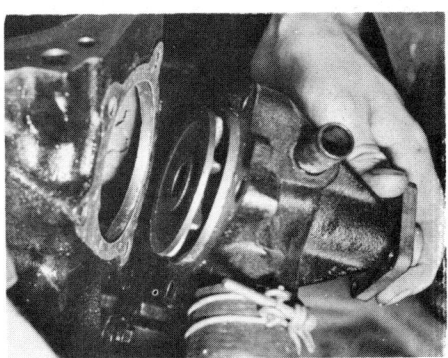
49.3 Water pump is offered up to mating fac fitted with new gasket

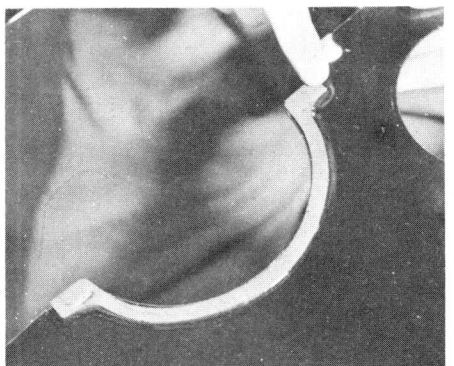
50.1 Fitting new gasket to backplate

50.2 Backplate located on dowels in rear of cylinder block

50.5 Fully tightening flywheel securing bolts

50.6 Refitting clutch

50.8 Fully tightening clutch securing bolts once disc has been centralised

51.1 Inserting valve into guide

51.2 Sliding seal down valve stem

51.3 Refitting valve spring cap

51.4 Refitting valve collets

52.1 Camshaft oil seal correctly fitted

52.3 Threading camshaft through bearings

52.4 Lubricating camshaft bearings

Chapter 1 Part B Four cylinder in-line engine

51 Valves - refitting

1 With the valves suitably ground in (See Section 32) and kept in their correct order, start with No. 1 cylinder and insert the valve into its guide (photo).
2 Lubricate the valve stem with engine oil and slide on a new oil seal. The spring must be uppermost as shown in the photo.
3 Fit the valve spring and cap (photo).
4 Using a universal valve spring compressor, compress the valve spring until the split collets can be slid into position (photo). Note these collets have serrations which engage in slots in the valve stems. Release the valve spring compressor.
5 Repeat this procedure until all eight valves and valve springs are fitted. Tap the head of each valve stem with a soft mallet to ensure correct seating.

52 Camshaft - refitting

1 If the oil seal was removed (Section 18) a new one should be fitted taking care that it is fitted the correct way round. Gently tap it into position so that it does not tilt (photo).
2 Apply some grease to the lip of the oil seal. Wipe the three bearing surfaces with a clean, non-fluffy rag.
3 Lift the camshaft through the bearings taking care not to damage the bearing surfaces with the sharp edges of the cam lobes. Also take care not to cut the fingers (photo).
4 When the journals are ready to be inserted into the bearings lubricate the bearings with engine oil (photo).
5 Push the camshaft through the bearings until the locating groove in the rear of the camshaft is just rearwards of the bearing carrier.
6 Slide the thrust plate into engagement with the camshaft taking care to fit it the correct way round as previously noted (photo).
7 Secure the thrust plate with the two bolts and spring washers (photo).
8 Check that the keyway in the end of the camshaft is clean and the key is free of burrs. Fit the key into the keyway (photo).
9 Locate the tag on the camshaft sprocket backplate and this must locate in the second groove in the camshaft sprocket (photo).
10 Fit the camshaft sprocket backplate, tag facing outwards (photo).
11 Fit the camshaft sprocket to the end of the camshaft and with a soft-faced hammer make sure it is fully home (photo).
12 Refit the sprocket securing bolt and thick plain washer (photo).

53 Cam followers - refitting

1 Undo the ball headed bolt locknut and screw down the bolt fully. This will facilitate refitting the cam followers (photo).
2 Rotate the camshaft until the cam lobe is away from the top of the cylinder head. Pass the cam follower under the back of the cam until the cup is over the ball headed bolt (photo).
3 Engage the cup with the ball headed bolt (photo).
4 Refit the cam follower spring by engaging the ends of the spring with the anchor on the ball headed bolt (photo).
5 Using the fingers pull the spring up and then over the top of the cam follower (photos).
6 Repeat the above sequence for the remaining seven cam followers.
7 Check that the jet holes in the camshaft lubrication pipe are free and offer up to the camshaft bearing pedestals (photo).
8 Refit the pipe securing bolts and spring washers.

54 Cylinder head - refitting

1 Wipe the mating faces of the cylinder head and cylinder block.
2 Carefully place a new gasket on the cylinder block and check to ensure that it is the correct way up, and the right way round (photo).
3 Gently lower the cylinder head being as accurate as possible first time, so that the gasket is not dislodged (photo).
4 Refit the cylinder head bolts taking care not to damage the gasket if it has moved (photo).
5 Using the special tool (21–002) lightly tighten all the bolts (photo).

52.6 Locating camshaft thrust plate

52.7 Tightening camshaft thrust plate retaining bolts

52.8 Fitting Woodruff key to camshaft

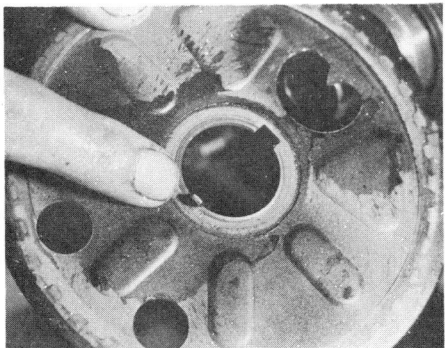
52.9 Camshaft sprocket backplate tag

52.10 Camshaft sprocket backplate refitted

52.11 Refitting camshaft sprocket

52.12 Camshaft sprocket securing bolt and washer

53.1 Slackening ball headed bolt locknut

53.2 Passing cam follower under camshaft

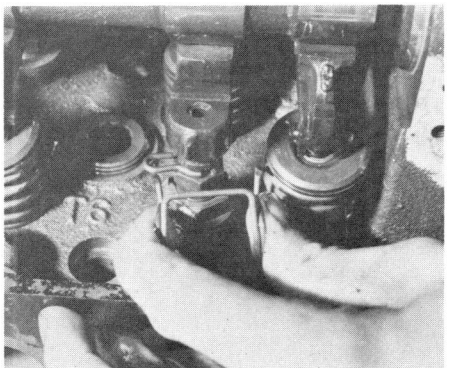
53.3 Cap located over ball headed bolt

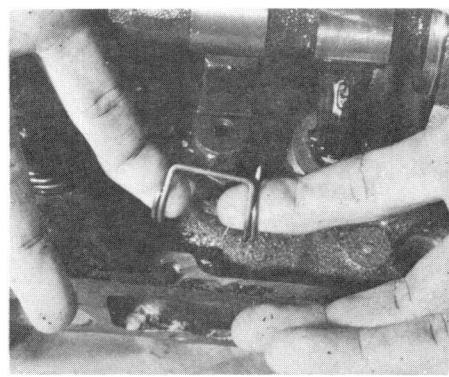
53.4 Cam follower spring engaged with the anchor

53.5a Cam follower spring being lifted over cam follower

53.5b Cam follower spring correctly fitted

53.7 Refitting lubrication pipe

54.2 Positioning cylinder head gasket in top of cylinder block

54.3 Lowering cylinder head onto gasket

54.4 Refitting cylinder head bolts

54.5 Special tool engaged in cylinder head bolt

Chapter 1 Part B Four cylinder in-line engine

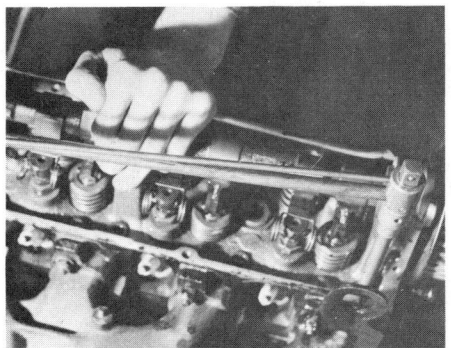

54.6 Tightening cylinder head bolts

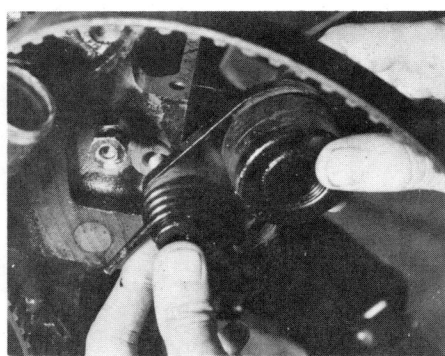

55.1 Refitting drivebelt tensioner

55.3 Using screwdriver to relieve tension of spring

6 Tighten the cylinder head bolts progressively to a final torque wrench setting as detailed in the Specifications (photo), in the order shown in Fig. 1.3.

55 Camshaft drivebelt tensioner and thermostat housing - refitting

1 Thread the shaped bolt through the spring and tensioner plate and screw the bolt into the cylinder head (photo).
2 Tighten the bolt securely using special tool 21-012.
3 Using a screwdriver to overcome the tension of the spring, position the plate so that its securing bolt can be screwed into the cylinder head (photo).
4 Clean the mating faces of the cylinder head and thermostat housing and fit a new gasket.
5 Offer up the thermostat housing and secure in position with the two bolts and spring washers.
6 Tighten the bolts to the specified torque.

56 Camshaft drivebelt - refitting and timing

1 Using a socket wrench on the crankshaft pulley bolt, turn the crankshaft until No 1 piston is at its TDC position. This is indicated by a mark on the crankshaft sprocket (see Fig. 1.18)
2 Rotate the camshaft until the pointer is in alignment with the dot mark on the front bearing pedestal (photo). To achieve this always rotate the camshaft in the direction shown in Fig. 1.18.
3 Engage the drivebelt with the crankshaft sprocket and auxiliary shaft sprocket. Pass the back of the belt over the tensioner jockey wheel and then slide it into mesh with the camshaft sprocket.
4 Slacken the tensioner plate securing bolt and allow the tensioner to settle by rotating the crankshaft twice. Retighten the tensioner plate securing bolt.
5 Line up the timing marks and check that these are correct indicating the belt has been correctly refitted (photo).
6 Refit the drivebelt guard, easing the guard into engagement with

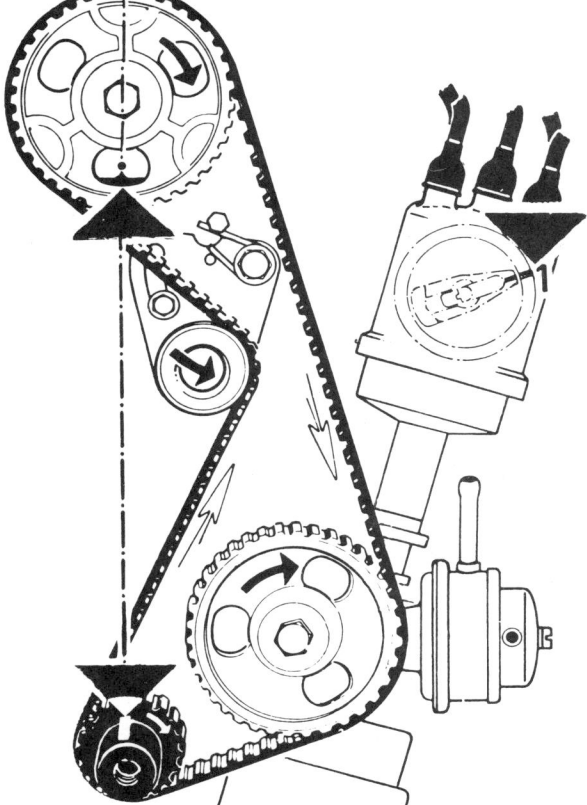

Fig. 1.18 Camshaft, ignition and crankshaft timing marks (Sec. 56)

56.2 Lining up camshaft timing marks

56.5 Drivebelt fitted

56.6a Refitting drivebelt guard

Chapter 1 Part B Four cylinder in-line engine

56.6b Locating guard between washer and pedestal

the bolt and large plain washer located under the water pump (photos).
7   Refit the guard securing bolts and tighten fully.

57 Valve clearances - checking and adjustment

1   With the engine top cover removed, turn the crankshaft until each cam in turn points vertically upwards. This will ensure that the cam follower will be at the back of the cam.
2   Using feeler gauges as shown in this photo check the clearance which should be as given in the Specifications.
3   If adjustment is necessary, using open ended spanners slacken the ball headed bolt securing locknut (photo).
4   Screw the ball headed bolt up or down as necessary until the required clearance is obtained (photo). Retighten the locknut.
5   An alternative method of adjustment is to work to the following table:

Valves open	Valves to adjust
1 ex and 4 in	6 in and 7 ex
6 in and 7 ex	1 ex and 4 in
2 in and 5 ex	3 ex and 8 in
3 ex and 8 in	2 in and 5 ex

57.2 Checking cam follower clearance

57.3 Slackening ball headed bolt locknut

57.4 Adjusting ball headed bolt

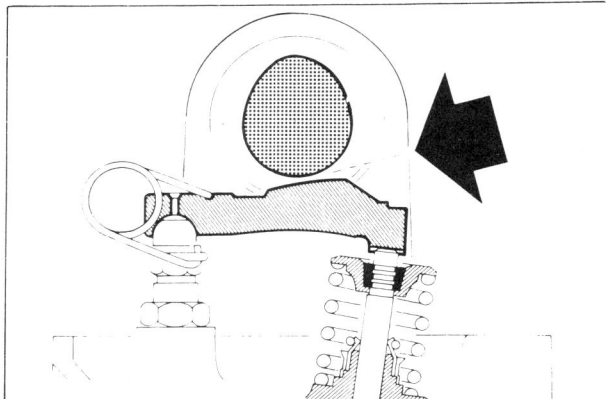

Fig. 1.19 Cam follower and camshaft clearance (Sec. 57)

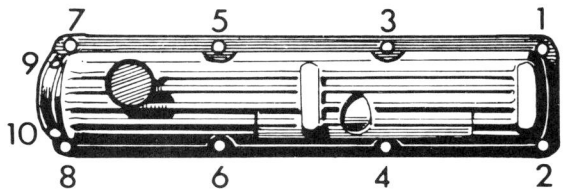

Fig. 1.20 Tightening order for engine top cover securing bolts (Sec. 57)

6   Refit the top cover and tighten the bolts in the order shown in Fig. 1.20 to the specified torque.

58 Engine - refitting without transmission

1   Commence refitting by referring to Section 56 in Part A of this Chapter and complete the operations in paragraphs 1 to 9 accordingly.
2   Complete the engine refitting by reversing the operations detailed in Section 5 of Part B of this Chapter, but note the following:
   a) *Ensure that all connections are made secure and tighten all fittings to the specified torque figures where given.*
   b) *Check that the respective electrical connections are clean, secure and that the cables and wires are retained away from the exhaust system and any moving parts against which they may chafe and short out at a later date.*
   c) *Do not overtighten fuel line connections but make sure that they are secure.*
   d) *Top up with oil and coolant of the correct grade and quantity and check for signs of leaks before starting up.*

59 Engine - refitting with transmission

Refer to Part A, Section 57 of this Chapter.

60 Engine - initial start-up after major overhaul or repair

1   Make sure that the battery is fully charged and that all lubricants,

Chapter 1 Part B Four cylinder in-line engine

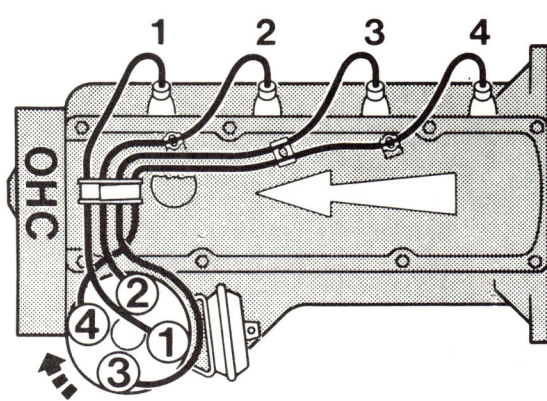

Fig. 1.21 Correct fitment of HT leads (Sec. 58)

coolant and fuel are replenished.
2   If the fuel system has been dismantled it will require several revolutions of the engine on the starter motor to pump the petrol up to the carburettor. An initial 'prime' of about $\frac{1}{3}$ of a cupful of petrol poured down the air intake of the carburettor will help the engine to fire quickly, thus relieving the load on the battery. Do not overdo this, however, as flooding may result.
3   As soon as the engine fires and runs, keep it going at a fast tickover only (no faster) and bring it up to normal working temperature.
4   As the engine warms up there will be odd smells and some smoke from parts getting hot and burning off oil deposits. The signs to look for are leaks of water or oil, which will be obvious if serious. Check also the exhaust pipe and manifold connections as these do not always find their exact gas tight position until the warmth and vibration have acted on them, and it is almost certain they they will need tightening further. This should be done, of course, with the engine stopped.
5   When normal running temperature has been reached, adjust the engine idle speed as described in Chapter 3.
6   Stop the engine and wait a few minutes to see if any lubricant or coolant is dripping out when the engine is stationary.
7   After the engine has run for 20 minutes remove the engine top cover and recheck the tightness of the cylinder head bolts. Also check the tightness of the sump bolts. In both cases use a torque wrench.
8   Road test the car to check that the timing is correct and that the engine is giving the necessary smoothness and power. Do not race the engine - if new bearings and/or pistons have been fitted it should be treated as a new engine and run in at a reduced speed for the first 1000 miles (1600 km).

61 Fault diagnosis - engine

See Section 59 of Part A of this Chapter.

Chapter 2 Cooling system

Contents

Antifreeze mixture ... 13	General description ... 1
Cooling system – draining ... 2	Radiator – removal, inspection, cleaning and refitting ... 5
Cooling system – filling ... 4	Temperature gauge and sender unit – removal and refitting ... 12
Cooling system – flushing ... 3	Temperature gauge – fault finding ... 11
Fan belt – removal, refitting and adjustment ... 10	Thermostat – removal, testing and refitting ... 6
Fan – removal, overhaul and refitting ... 9	Water pump – dismantling, overhaul and reassembly ... 8
Fault diagnosis – cooling system ... 14	Water pump – removal and refitting ... 7

Specifications

Type of system .... Pressurised, assisted by pump and fan

Thermostat
Type .... Wax capsule
Location .... Water outlet at front of inlet manifold
Opening temperature .... 85–89°C (185–192°F)
Fully open at .... 99–102°C (210–216°F)

Water pump
Type .... Centrifugal
Impeller to body clearance .... 0.020–0.040 in (0.508–1.016 mm)
Fit of pulley hub on shaft .... 0.0010–0.0025 in (0.025–0.0630 mm)*
Fit of impeller on shaft .... 0.0005–0.002 in (0.0127–0.058 mm)*

*Interference fit.

Fan belt
Free play .... 0.5 in (12.7 mm) movement midway between fan and alternator pulleys
Tension .... 40–50 lbf (18.4–22.18 kgf)

Radiator
Manual gearbox type .... Corrugated high efficiency fin
Automatic transmission type .... Corrugated high efficiency fin with integral oil cooler
Filler cap opening pressure .... 13 lbf/in^2 (0.91 kgf/cm^2)

Coolant capacity
2.0 litre V4 .... 14.0 Imp pints (7.95 litres)
2.0 litre ohc .... 12.5 Imp pints (7.1 litres)
2.5 and 3.0 litre V6 .... 20.0 Imp pints (11.36 litres)

Torque wrench settings

	lbf ft	kgf m
Fan blade (2.0 litre ohc)	5–7	0.69–0.97
Water pump bolts	5–7	0.69–0.97
Thermostat housing	12–15	1.66–2.07

1 General description

The engine cooling water is circulated by a thermo-syphon, water pump assisted system and the coolant is pressurised. This is both to prevent loss of water down the overflow pipe with the filler cap in position and to prevent premature boiling in adverse conditions.

The system comprises a radiator, a water pump, a fan mounted on the front cover, a thermostat, top and bottom hoses and heater hoses. There is one drain plug located at the side of the cylinder block and another at the bottom of the radiator (certain models only).

The system functions in the following manner: cool water in the bottom of the radiator circulates up the bottom hose to the water pump where it is directed round the various water passages in the cylinder block, which keep the cylinder bores and piston assemblies cool. On the 'V' series engines the water travelling from the water pump is directed into the right-hand tank of the cylinder block and then through to the left-hand tank.

The coolant then travels up to the cylinder head/s and is circulated around the combustion areas and valve seats. When the engine is operating at its correct operating temperature, the coolant is directed from the cylinder head through the thermostat and into the upper hose back into the radiator header tank.

Travelling down through the radiator, the coolant is rapidly cooled by the through-flow of cool air in the radiator core, which is created by the forward motion of the car and the cooling fan. The cycle of travel is then repeated through the engine, thus keeping the engine at its correct constant operating temperature.

To ensure a rapid engine warm-up period, the wax type thermostat and bypass system is in operation and the flow of water is confined to

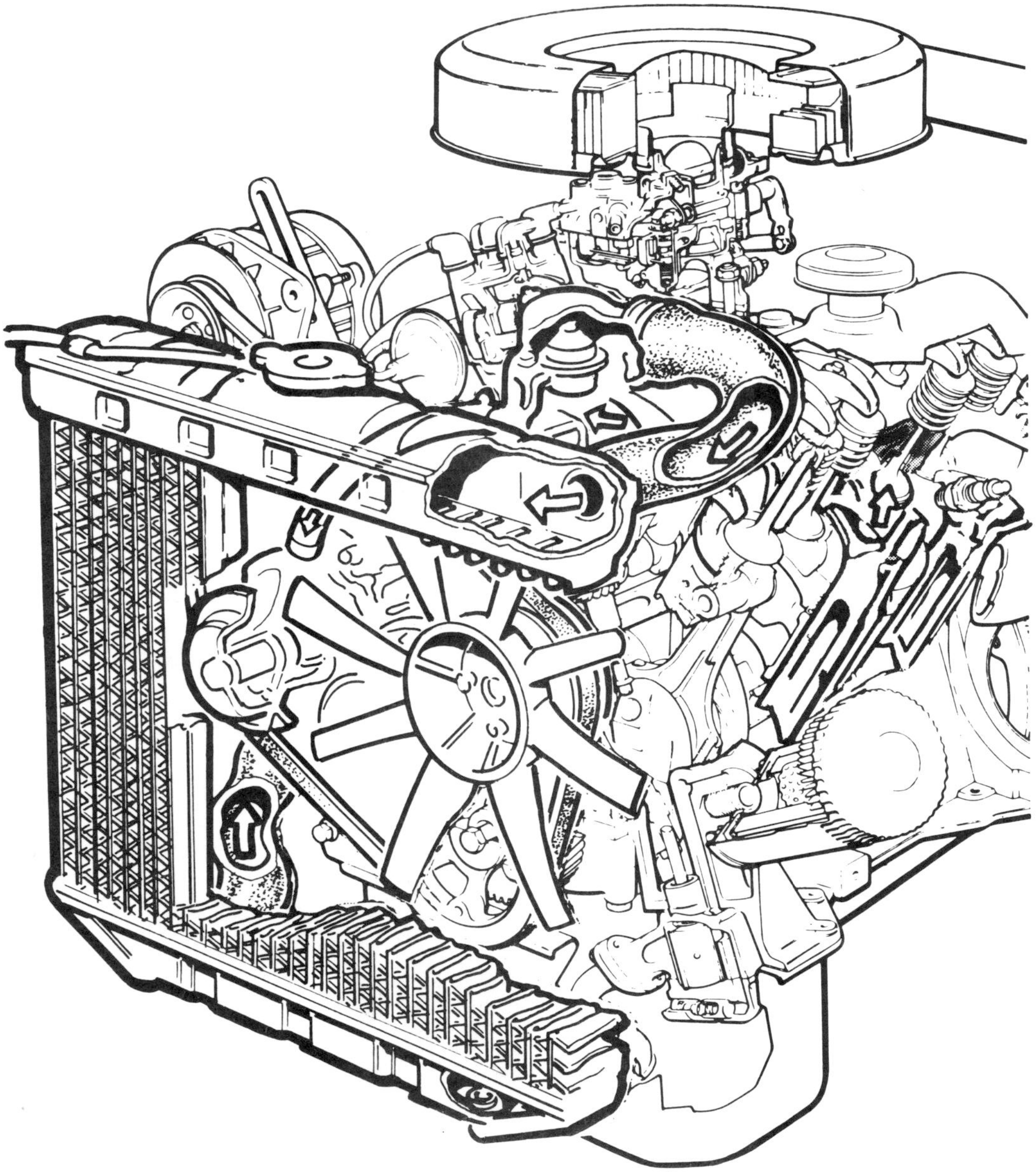

Fig. 2.1 The cooling system showing direction of flow on the 'V' series engines (Sec. 1)

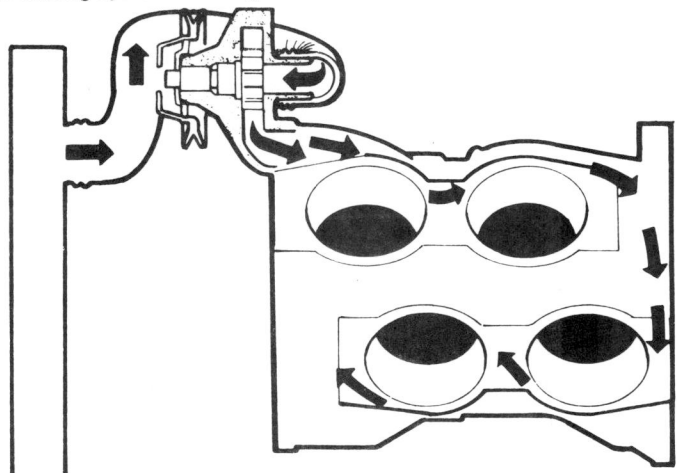

Fig. 2.2 The 'V' series engine cylinder block showing flow of coolant (Sec. 1)

the area around the engine, using the bypass hose to return the water to the inlet side of the pump via the automatic choke chamber of the carburettor installation. As the engine reaches normal operating temperature, the thermostat starts to open, so allowing water circulation around the complete cooling system. It should be appreciated that besides giving a rapid warm-up period the thermostat also controls the engine temperature.

The radiator cap is of the pressurised type which increases the coolant boiling point, thereby allowing the engine to operate at its most efficient operating temperature.

If the temperature of the water rises excessively, and the water boils, the pressure in the system forces the internal valve of the cap off its seat, thus exposing the overflow pipe down which the steam from the boiling water escapes, so relieving the pressure. The cap pressure rating is stamped into the top face (photo) and must be as specified.

Operation of the fan on models fitted with automatic transmission is slightly different from that fitted to manual models in that a viscous clutch is fitted between the water pump pulley and the fan. A drive disc, which is integral with the clutch body, is able to transmit torque through a silicone fluid to the clutch body. At higher engine speeds this fluid is able to permit the drive disc to turn relative to the clutch body and the overall effect is to limit the fan speed as the engine speed increases.

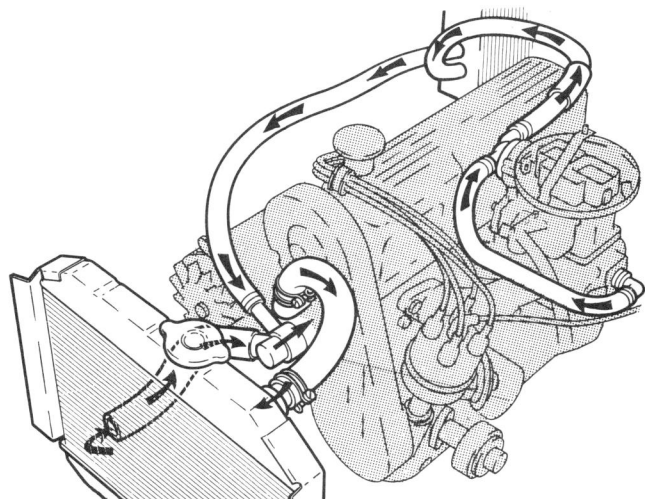

Fig. 2.3 The 2·0 litre ohc engine cooling system showing the coolant circulation (Sec. 1)

2 Cooling system – draining

With the car on level ground drain the system as follows:

1 If the engine is cold remove the radiator cap by turning it in an anti-clockwise direction. If the engine is hot, then turn the filler cap, suitably padded with a large amount of cloth over the top until the pressure in the system has had time to disperse. If with the engine very hot, the cap is released suddenly the drop in pressure can result in the water boiling. With the pressure released the cap can be removed.

2 If antifreeze is in the cooling system drain it into a clean container for re-use.

3 There are two drain points. On some models there is a tap located at the bottom of the radiator, whilst on others it is necessary to undo the bottom hose retaining clip and disconnect the hose from the radiator. The other drain point is in the cylinder block. On the 'V' series engines this will be found on the side of the crankcase to the rear of the oil filter. On the ohc engine it is located on the rear left-hand side of the cylinder block (photo).

4 When the coolant has finished running out, probe the drain point orifices with a short piece of wire to dislodge any particles of rust or sediment which may be blocking the holes so preventing any remaining coolant from running out.

1.1 The radiator cap pressure rating (arrowed)

3 Cooling system – flushing

1 With time the cooling system will gradually lose its efficiency as the radiator matrix becomes choked with rust, scale, deposits from the water and other sediment.

2 To clean the system out, first drain the coolant as described in the previous Section.

3 Insert a water hose into the filler cap neck and run water through the system for ten to fifteen minutes.

4 In very bad cases the radiator should be reverse flushed. This can be done in the car but it is better if the radiator can be removed as described in Section 5 of this Chapter.

5 Invert the radiator and place a hosepipe in the radiator lower tank connection, the gap between hose and connection suitably padded with cloth. Water under slight pressure is then forced through the radiator matrix in the reverse direction to normal flow so loosening any particles and passing them out through the radiator top tank hose connection.

6 The hose is then removed from the lower tank connection and with the radiator in its normal instead of inverted position fit the hose and padding to the top tank connection and flush in the normal water flow direction.

7 If the radiator still appears to be partially blocked a proprietory radiator cleaner may be used.

8 Once the radiator is clean it may be refitted as described in Section 6.

2.3 The cylinder block drain plug removal on the 2·0 litre ohc engine

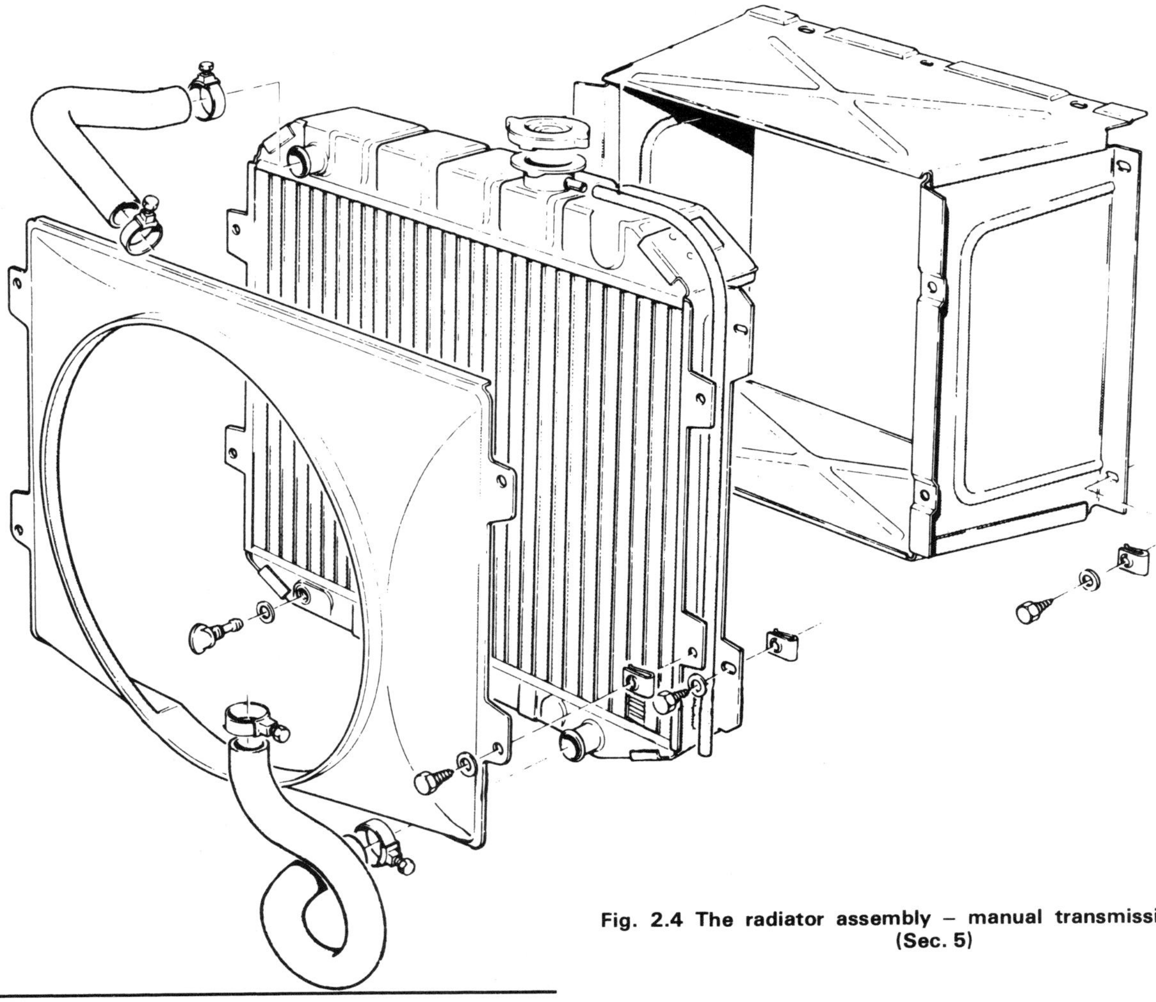

Chapter 2 Cooling system

Fig. 2.4 The radiator assembly – manual transmission models (Sec. 5)

4 Cooling system – filling

1   Refit the drain plug(s) and/or shut the tap or reconnect the bottom hose as applicable.
2   Move the temperature control of the heater and demister to the 'HOT' position.
3   Undo the clip and disconnect the bypass hose at its connection with the thermostat housing to ensure that there are no air locks.
4   Fill the cooling system slowly. The best type of water to use in the cooling system is rain water, so use this whenever possible if plain water is being used instead of antifreeze solution. Continue filling the system until the coolant begins to appear at both the disconnected bypass hose and thermostat housing. At this point reconnect the hose and tighten the clip.
5   Resume filling the cooling system until the level is 0·25 inch (6·35 mm) below the filler cap neck.
6   Refit the filler cap and turn it firmly in a clockwise direction to lock it in position.
7   Start the engine and allow to idle for two minutes. Carefully remove the radiator cap. Check the level and top up using warm water or antifreeze or alternatively allow to cool; if cold coolant is added to warm or hot water in the cooling system it can cause internal stress and damage in the water jacket surrounding metal due to sudden temperature changes.
8   Finally inspect for water leaks especially if any part of the cooling system has been disturbed for a new part fitment or overhaul.

5 Radiator – removal, inspection, cleaning and refitting

1   To remove the radiator first drain the cooling system as described in Section 2.

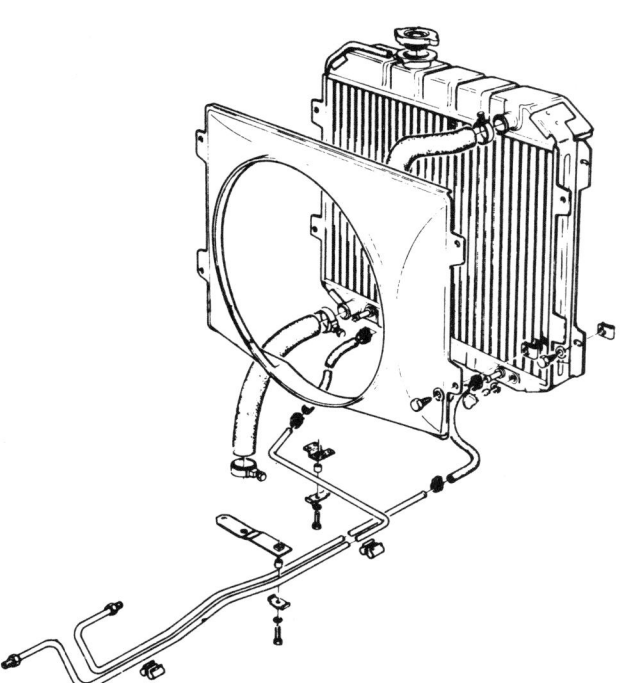

Fig. 2.5 The radiator assembly – automatic transmission models (Sec. 5)

2 Slacken the clip securing the hose to the top of the radiator. Detach the hose.
3 Slacken the clip securing the radiator bottom hose to the water pump and detach the hose.
4 *Automatic transmission only:* Wipe the oil cooler pipe unions at the base of the radiator and detach the two pipes. Plug the pipe ends to stop dirt ingress.
5 Undo and remove the bolts and washers securing the radiator to the front panel (photo).
6 The radiator may now be lifted up and away from the car, taking extreme car not to touch the matrix with the fan blades.
7 With the radiator away from the car any leaks can be soldered up or repaired with a proprietory repair substance. Clean out the inside of the radiator by flushing as described in Section 3.
8 Clean the exterior of the radiator by hosing down with a strong jet of water to clear away any road dirt, dead flies etc.
9 Inspect the radiator hoses for cracks, internal or external perishing, and damage caused by overtightening of the securing clips. Renew the hoses as necessary. Examine the radiator hose securing clips and renew them if they are rusted or distorted.
10 Refitting the radiator is the reverse sequence to removal.
11 Refill the cooling system as described in Section 4.

6 Thermostat – removal, testing and refitting

1 To remove the thermostat partially drain the cooling system (6 pints/3·4 litres is enough).
2 Slacken the hose clip securing the outlet hose to the water outlet on the top of the thermostat housing. Carefully ease off the hose.
3 Undo and remove the two bolts and spring washers securing the water outlet to the top of the thermostat housing.
4 The water outlet and its gasket may now be removed. Tap the side very gently if it has stuck to the thermostat housing gasket.
5 Carefully lift the thermostat from the housing (photo) easing it off its seating using a small screwdriver.
6 Test the thermostat for correct functioning by suspending it together with a thermometer in a container of cold water. Make sure they do not touch the sides of the container.
7 Heat the water and note when the thermostat begins to open, which should be within the limits quoted in the Specifications at the beginning of this Chapter.
8 Discard the thermostat if it opens too early. Allow the thermostat to cool down naturally and if it does not close fully, it should be discarded and a new one obtained.
9 If the thermostat is stuck open when cold this should have been apparent when initially removing it from the housing.
10 Refitting the thermostat is the reverse sequence to removal. It is recommended that a new paper gasket is fitted between the water outlet connection and the thermostat housing.
11 Clean the faces of the water outlet and the thermostat housing to ensure a water-tight joint. If the water outlet has corroded badly a new one should be fitted.
12 Refill the cooling system as described in Section 4, and finally check for water leaks.

7 Water pump – removal and refitting

1 Refer to Section 2 and drain the cooling system.
2 Slacken the respective alternator mounting bolts and hinge the alternator towards the engine, so that the fan belt can be removed from the water pump pulley.
3 On 2·0 litre ohc models, undo and remove the four bolts and washers securing the fan unit to the water pump spindle hub. Remove the fan and pulley, (Figs. 2.7, 2.8 and 2.9).
4 On 2·0 litre ohc engine models, remove the timing belt cover.
5 Detach the hoses at their connections to the pump.
6 Undo the bolts securing the pump to the cylinder block, and remove the pump (photo). Note the respective bolt positions for reassembly.
7 Refit in the reverse sequence to removal but note the following:

   a) *Ensure that the mating surfaces of the cylinder block and pump are clean and always use a new gasket.*
   b) *Tighten the pump securing bolts to the specified torque.*

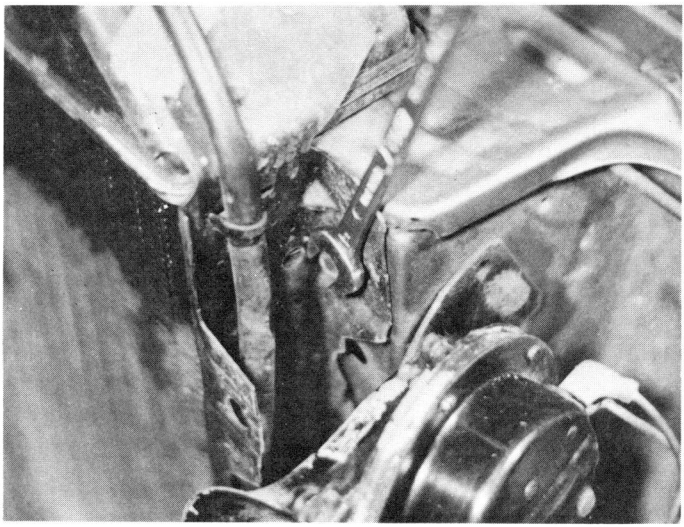
5.5 Remove the radiator retaining bolts

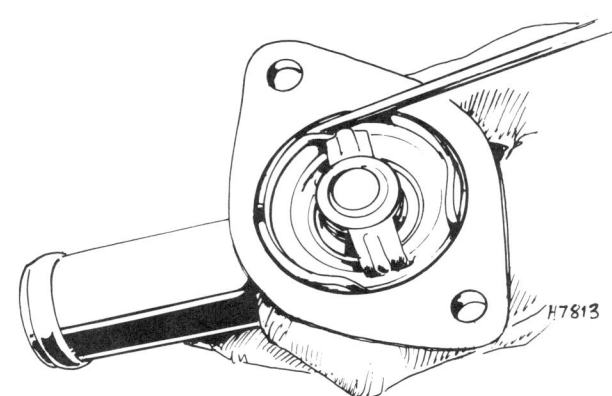
Fig. 2.6 Removal of thermostat retaining clip from housing (ohc engine) using a screwdriver as a lever (Sec. 6)

6.5 Removing the thermostat (V6 engine)

Chapter 2 Cooling system

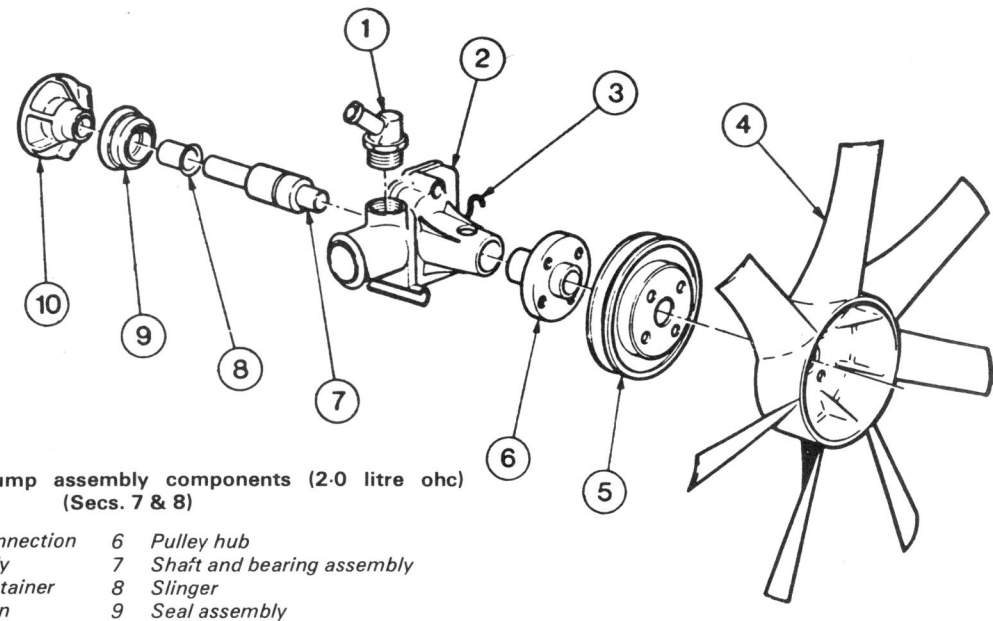

Fig. 2.7 Water pump assembly components (2·0 litre ohc) (Secs. 7 & 8)

1 Heater connection
2 Pump body
3 Bearing retainer
4 Cooling fan
5 Fan pulley
6 Pulley hub
7 Shaft and bearing assembly
8 Slinger
9 Seal assembly
10 Impeller

Fig. 2.8 Fan and pulley removal (2·0 litre ohc) (Sec. 7)

A Fan blades   B Pulley

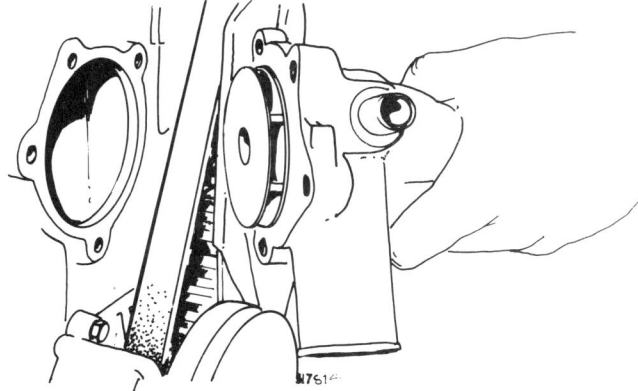

Fig. 2.9 Water pump removal (2·0 litre ohc) (Sec. 7)

c) On the 2.0 litre ohc models, tighten the fan and pulley retaining bolts to the specified torque.
d) Tension the fan belt as described in Section 10 of this Chapter. If the belt is too tight, undue strain will be imposed on the water pump and alternator bearings. If the belt is too loose it will slip causing premature wear to the belt, and the engine may overheat.

8 Water pump – dismantling, overhaul and reassembly

Prior to dismantling the water pump for overhaul, check that any parts necessary are readily available. It may well be quicker and more economical to renew the complete unit.

'V' Series engines

1 Refer to Section 7 and remove the water pump.
2 Undo and remove the four bolts that secure the rear cover to the pump housing and lift away the rear cover. Recover the gasket located between these two parts.
3 It should be appreciated that all the component parts are held together by a press fit. Obviously these fits are tight otherwise the pump would simply fly apart in use, so before proceeding any further it

7.6 Removing the water pump (V6 engine)

is essential that for pressing operations a wide opening vice and an assortment of drifts and hollow tubes for use as spacers are available. The use of hammers and blocks is possible but the force required is such that the likelihood of fracturing the pump is very high.

4 Draw off the fan belt pulley from the shaft with a hub puller.
5 Next press the shaft and bearing assembly, with impeller, seal and slinger, out of the housing. One way to do this is to support the housing with a piece of large diameter tube and then place the whole assembly in the vice jaws and press on the nose of the shaft. When the shaft is flush with the housing obtain a suitable piece of rod slightly smaller than the shaft diameter and use this to press it right through.
6 No further dismantling is necessary as all the components of the shaft and bearing come together as a repair kit.
7 Using a suitable length of tube press the slinger onto the longer end of the new shaft and bearing assembly in the vice so that the slinger flange abuts the bearing.
8 Next press the shaft and bearing into the housing, short end first, so that the bearing races comes flush with the end of the housing. A suitable sleeve will be needed to go over the pulley end of the shaft and up against the housing during the final pressing operation.
9 Press the pump seal into the housing with the carbon face away from the bearing.
10 With the flat face of the impeller supported by a piece of flat steel plate the shaft is now pressed into it. The correct distance is reached when the rear face of the housing has a 0 – 0·005 inch (0 – 0·13 mm) clearance from the plate supporting the impeller. Any over-pressing will dislodge the position of the bearing in the housing.
11 Refit the trapped bolt into its correct holes and refit the pulley to the shaft, recessed side over the housing. When pressing on the pulley care must be taken to ensure that support is such that the shaft is not dislodged in the housing. The pulley is in position when the centre line of the 'V' is 2·2 – 2·25 inch (56 – 57 mm) from the rear face of the housing.
12 Clean off the faces of the pump body and rear cover, fit a new gasket and refit the rear cover, tightening down the four bolts evenly but not too tightly, bearing in mind that the housing and cover are made from aluminium alloy.

2.0 litre ohc engine

13 Refer to Section 7 and remove the water pump.
14 Refer to Fig. 2.7 and using a universal three leg puller and suitable thrust block draw the hub from the shaft.
15 Carefully pull out the bearing retaining clip from the slot in the water pump housing. On some water pumps this clip is not fitted.
16 Using a soft-faced hammer drive the shaft and bearing assembly out towards the rear of the pump body.
17 The impeller vane is removed from the spindle by using a universal three leg puller and suitable thrust block.
18 Remove the seal and the slinger by splitting the latter with the aid of a sharp cold chisel.
19 Carefully inspect the condition of the shaft and bearing assembly and if it shows signs of wear or corrosion, new parts should be obtained. If it was found that coolant was leaking from the pump, a new seal should be obtained. If it was evident that the pulley hub or impeller were a loose fit they must be renewed. The repair kit available comprises a new shaft and bearing assembly, a slinger, seal, bush, clip and gasket.
20 To reassemble the water pump first fit the shaft and bearing assembly to the housing, larger end of the shaft to the front of the housing, and press the assembly into the housing until the front of the bearing is flush with the pump housing.
21 Refit the bearing locating wire.
22 Next press the pump pulley onto the front end of the shaft until the end of the shaft is flush with the end of the hub.
23 Press the new slinger (flanged end first) onto the shaft until the non-flanged end is approximately 0·5 in (13 mm) from the shaft end.

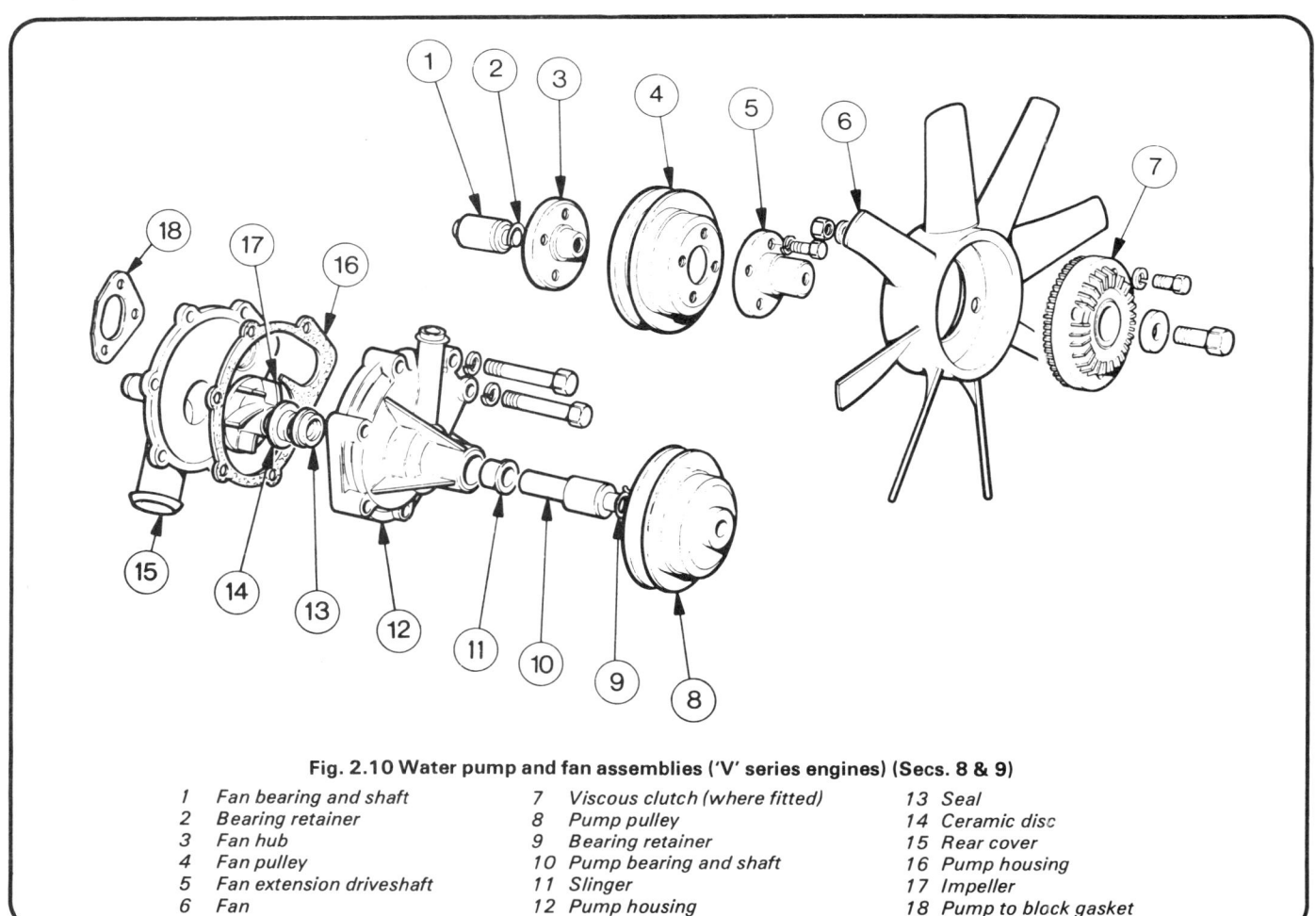

Fig. 2.10 Water pump and fan assemblies ('V' series engines) (Secs. 8 & 9)

1	Fan bearing and shaft	7	Viscous clutch (where fitted)
2	Bearing retainer	8	Pump pulley
3	Fan hub	9	Bearing retainer
4	Fan pulley	10	Pump bearing and shaft
5	Fan extension driveshaft	11	Slinger
6	Fan	12	Pump housing
13	Seal		
14	Ceramic disc		
15	Rear cover		
16	Pump housing		
17	Impeller		
18	Pump to block gasket		

Chapter 2 Cooling system

To act as a rough guide the flanged end on the slinger will be just in line with the impeller side of the window in the water pump body.
24 Place the new seal over the shaft and into the counterbore in the water pump housing and then the impeller into the shaft until a clearance of 0·03 inch (0·76 mm) is obtained between the impeller and the housing face (Fig. 2.11). Whilst this is being carried out the slinger will be pushed into its final position by the impeller.

9 Fan – removal, overhaul and refitting

For 2·0 litre ohc engines, details of fan removal and refitting will be found in Section 7, paragraph 3.
For 'V' series engines proceed as follows:

Manual transmission models
1 Refer to Section 10 and remove the fan belt.
2 Refer to Section 5 and remove the radiator.
3 Undo and remove the four bolts and washers securing the fan blade and pulley to the hub.
4 Refer to Chapter 1 and remove the engine front cover.
5 A circlip is located in a groove in the bearing and a corresponding groove in the housing. Remove this circlip using a pair of pointed nose pliers.
6 Press the shaft bearing and expansion plug together with the hub out of the front cover. The shaft can now be pressed out of the hub.
7 The new shaft and bearing assembly is first pressed into the housing so that the circlip grooves are in alignment.
8 Refit the circlip to lock the bearing.
9 The hub is next pressed on until the front face is 3.375 inch (85·8 mm) from the *rear* face of the front cover.
10 Fit a new expansion plug to the shaft bore in the rear face of the bearing housing.
11 Refit the front cover and refit the pulley and fan blades.
12 Refit the fan belt and adjust as described in Section 10.

Automatic transmission models
The procedure is basically identical to that for the manual transmission type except that the fan and viscous clutch unit is retained by a single centre bolt and flat washer/s. The extension shaft and pulley are secured to the pulley hub by four bolts and spring washers as shown in Fig. 2.10.

10 Fan belt – removal, refitting and adjustment

1 *Models fitted with power assisted steering:* Refer to Chapter 11 and remove the power assisted steering pump drivebelt.
2 Slacken the alternator mounting bolts and push in towards the engine. Lift the belt from the alternator pulley taking care not to damage the pulley. Lift away the belt from the crankshaft, fan and water pump pulleys.
3 To fit a new belt pass it over the pulleys, alternator last, and adjust the position of the alternator to give 0·5 inch (13 mm) total free movement of the fan belt on its longest span under normal finger pressure.
4 Tighten the alternator securing bolts.
5 *Power assisted steering:* Refit the steering pump drivebelt as described in Chapter 11.
6 The tension of the fan belt is of considerable importance because if it is too tight the water pump, alternator and fan bearings will be subjected to excessive strain – thus shortening their service life. If the fan belt is too slack it will slip and reduce the efficiency of the water pump and alternator output.

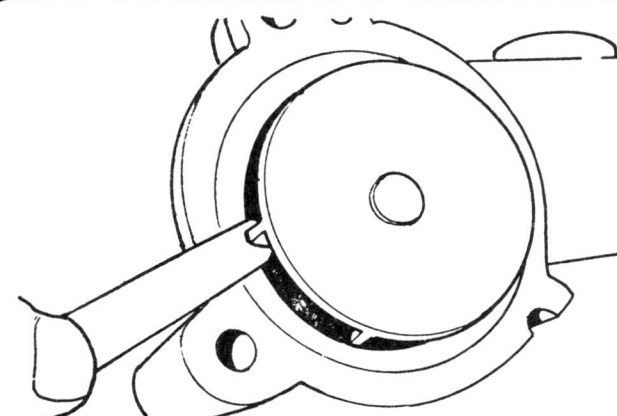

Fig. 2.11 Checking slinger clearance with feeler gauges (Sec. 8)

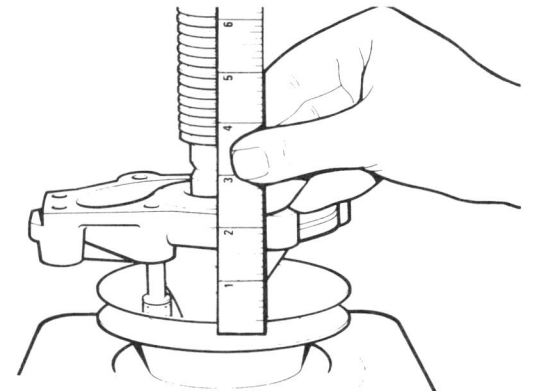

Fig. 2.12 Measurement of pulley relative to water pump body (Sec. 9)

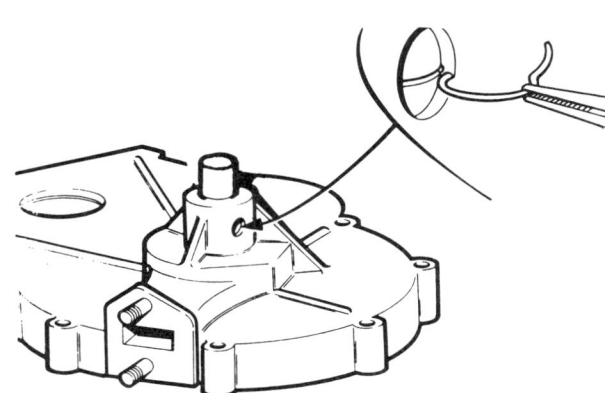

Fig. 2.13 Location of bearing retaining circlip (Sec. 9)

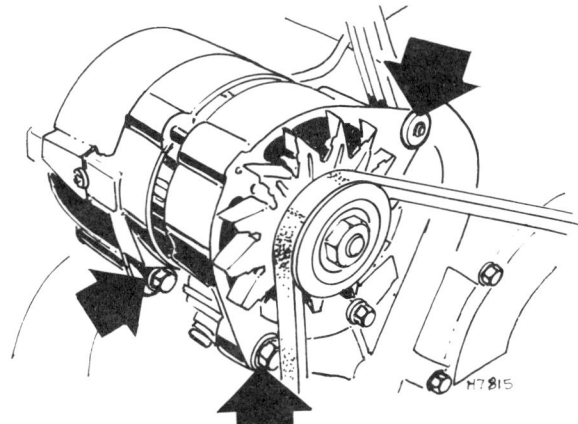

Fig. 2.14 The alternator attachment points (Sec. 10)

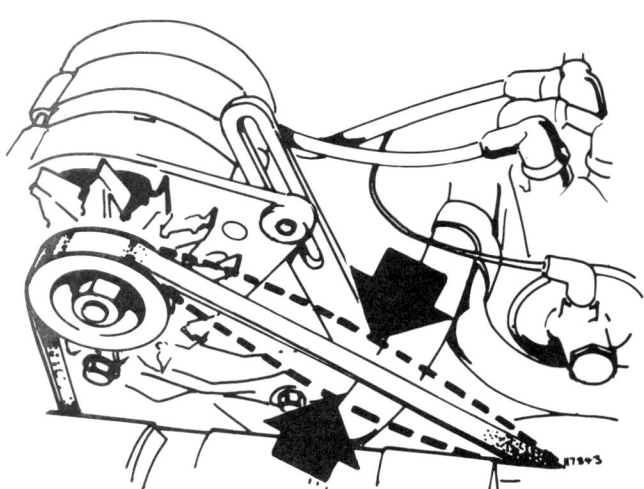

Fig. 2.15 The correct fan belt tension and check point (Sec. 10)

11 Temperature gauge – fault finding

1 If the temperature gauge fails to work, either the gauge, the sender unit, the wiring or the connections are at fault.
2 It is not possible to repair the gauge or sender unit and they must be renewed if at fault.
3 First check the wiring connections and if sound, check the wiring for breaks using an ohmmeter or test lamp.

12 Temperature gauge and sender unit – removal and refitting

1 For details of how to remove and refit the temperature gauge see Chapter 10.
2 To remove the sender unit, disconnect the wire leading into the unit at its connector and detach the sender unit from the inlet manifold.
3 Refitting is a reversal of the above procedure. It is recommended that a non-setting sealer is used on the threads.

13 Antifreeze mixture

1 In circumstances where it is likely that the temperature will drop to below freezing it is essential that some of the water is drained and an adequate amount of ethylene glycol antifreeze is added to the cooling system.
2 Never use an antifreeze with an alcohol base as evaporation is too high.
3 Any antifreeze can be left in the cooling system for up to two years, but after six months it is advisable to have the specific gravity of the coolant checked at your local garage, and thereafter once every three months.
4 Below are the amounts of antifreeze by percentage volume which should be added to ensure adequate protection down to the temperature given.

Amount of antifreeze	Protection to
50%	−37°C (−34°F)
40%	−25°C (−13°F)
30%	−16°C (+3°F)
25%	−13°C (+9°F)
20%	−9°C (+15°F)
15%	−7°C (+20°F)
10%	−4°C (+25°F)

Note: *Do not use antifreeze in the windscreen washer reservoir as it will cause damage to the paintwork when draining from the windscreen.*

14 Fault diagnosis – cooling system

Symptom	Cause	Remedy
Overheating	Insufficient water in cooling system	Top up radiator
	Fan belt slipping (accompanied by a shrieking noise on rapid engine acceleration)	Tighten fan belt to recommended tension or renew if worn.
	Radiator core blocked or radiator grille restricted	Reverse flush radiator, remove obstructions.
	Bottom water hose collapsed, impeding flow	Remove and fit new hose.
	Thermostat not opening properly	Remove and fit new thermostat.
	Ignition advance and retard incorrectly set (accompanied by loss of power, and perhaps misfiring)	Check and reset ignition timing.
	Carburettor incorrectly adjusted (mixture too weak)	Tune carburettor.
	Exhaust system partially blocked	Check exhaust pipe for constrictive dents and blockages.
	Oil level in sump too low	Top up sump to full mark on dipstick.
	Blown cylinder head gasket (water/steam being forced down the radiator overflow pipe under pressure)	Remove cylinder head, fit new gasket.
	Engine not yet run-in	Run-in slowly and carefully.
	Brakes binding	Check and adjust brakes if necessary.
Cool running	Thermostat jammed open	Remove and renew thermostat.
	Incorrect thermostat fitted allowing premature opening of valve	Remove and replace with new thermostat which opens at a higher temperature.
	Thermostat missing	Check and fit correct thermostat.
Loss of cooling water	Loose clips on water hose	Check and tighten clips if necessary.
	Top, bottom or bypass water hoses perished and leaking	Check and renew any faulty hoses.
	Radiator core leaking	Remove radiator and repair.
	Thermostat gasket leaking	Inspect and renew gasket.
	Radiator pressure cap spring worn or seal ineffective	Renew radiator pressure cap.
	Blown cylinder head gasket (pressure in system forcing water/steam down overflow pipe)	Remove cylinder head and fit new gasket.
	Cylinder wall or head cracked	Dismantle engine, despatch to engineering works for repair.

Chapter 3 Carburation, fuel and exhaust systems

Contents

Accelerator cable – removal and refitting	14	Exhaust system	29
Accelerator linkage – adjustment	15	Fault diagnosis – fuel system	30
Accelerator pedal and shaft – removal and refitting	13	Fuel gauge sender unit – removal and refitting	11
Air cleaner – removal, servicing and refitting	2	Fuel line filter – removal and refitting	12
Carburettor – accelerator pump adjustment (Ford)	22	Fuel pump – description	3
Carburettor – choke adjustment (Weber)	27	Fuel pump – dismantling, overhaul and reassembly (alternative type)	8
Carburettor – choke and fast idle adjustment (Ford)	21		
Carburettor – description	17	Fuel pump – dismantling, overhaul and reassembly (standard type)	7
Carburettor – dismantling and reassembly (Ford)	19		
Carburettor dismantling and reassembly – general	16	Fuel pump – removal and refitting	5
Carburettor – dismantling and reassembly (Weber)	25	Fuel pump – routine servicing	4
Carburettor float level height – adjustment (Ford)	23	Fuel pump – testing	6
Carburettor float level height – adjustment (Weber)	28	Fuel tank – cleaning	10
Carburettor – removal and refitting (Ford)	18	Fuel tank – removal and refitting	9
Carburettor – removal and refitting (Weber)	24	General description	1
Carburettor – slow running adjustment (Ford)	20		
Carburettor – slow running adjustment (Weber)	26		

Specifications

Fuel pump – 'V' series engines
Type .... Mechanical; driven from eccentric on front of camshaft
Delivery pressure .... 3.75 to 5.0 lbf/in² (0.26 to 0.35 kgf/cm²)
Inlet vacuum .... 8.5 in (21.60 cm) Hg

Fuel pump – 2.0 litre ohc engines
Type .... Mechanical; pushrod drive from auxiliary shaft
Delivery pressure .... 3.75 to 5.0 lbf/in² (0.26 – 0.35 kgf/m²)
Inlet vacuum .... 8.5 in (21.60 cm) Hg

Fuel Tank capacity
Saloon .... 14.3 galls (65 litres)
Estate .... 13.6 galls (62 litres)

Fuel octane rating 97

Air cleaner type .... Renewable paper element

Carburettor applications
a) 2.0 V4 and 2.0 ohc manual .... Ford 722F 9510 KAA
b) 2.0 V4 and 2.0 ohc automatic .... Ford 722F 9510 KBA
c) 2.5 V6 manual and automatic .... Weber 722F 9510 CA
d) 3.0 V6 manual with exhaust emission control .... Weber 722F 9510 AA
e) 3.0 V6 automatic with exhaust emission control .. Weber 722F 9510 BA
f) 3.0 V6 manual without exhaust emission control .. Weber 722F 9510 NA
g) 3.0 V6 automatic without exhaust emission control . Weber 722F 9510 RA
h) 2.0 ohc manual with exhaust emission control ... Weber 72HF 9510 AA
i) 2.0 ohc automatic with exhaust emission control .. Weber 72HF 9510 BA
j) 2.0 ohc manual with exhaust emission control ... Weber 76HF 9510 AB
k) 2.0 ohc automatic with exhaust emission control . Weber 76HF 9510 AA
l) 2.5 V6 manual and automatic with exhaust emission control .... Weber 742F 9510 AA
m) 3.0 V6 manual and automatic with exhaust emission control .... Weber 762F 9510 AA

Chapter 3 Carburation, fuel and exhaust systems

a) Ford 722F 9510 KAA
Throttle barrel diameter	1.42 in (36 mm)
Venturi diameter	1.11 in (28 mm)
Main jet	0.063 in (1.60 mm)
Idle speed (rpm)	700 to 740
Fast idle speed (rpm)	1700 to 1900
Float level	1.11 in (28.0 mm)
Float travel	0.276 in (7.0 mm)
Choke plate pull down	0.158 in ± 0.02 in (4.0 mm ± 0.5 mm)
De-choke	0.315 in (8.0 mm)
Accelerator pump stroke	0.145 in ± 0.005 in (3.68 mm ± 0.13 mm)
Vacuum piston link hole	Outer
Thermostatic spring slot	Centre

b) Ford 722F 9510 KBA
Throttle barrel diameter	1.42 in (36 mm)
Venturi diameter	1.11 in (28 mm)
Main jet	0.061 in (1.55 mm)
Idle speed (rpm)	700 to 740
Fast idle (rpm)	2100 to 2300
Float level	1.11 in (28.0 mm)
Float travel	0.276 in (7.0 mm)
Choke plate pull down	0.158 in ± 0.02 in (4.0 in ± 0.5 mm)
De-choke	0.315 in (8 mm)
Accelerator pump stroke	0.145 in ± 0.005 in (3.68 mm ± 0.13 mm)
Vacuum piston link hole	Outer
Thermostatic spring slot	Centre

c) Weber 722F 9510 CA
Venturi diameter:	
Primary	1.06 in (27 mm)
Secondary	1.06 in (27 mm)
Jet sizes:	
Main – Primary	0.057 in (1.45 mm)
Main – Secondary	0.057 in (1.45 mm)
Air correction – Primary	0.069 in (1.75 mm)
Air correction – Secondary	0.069 in (1.75 mm)
Idling – Primary	0.0197 in (0.5 mm)
Idling – Secondary	0.0197 in (0.5 mm)
Accelerator pump stroke	0.236 in (0.6 mm)
Emulsion tube type – Primary	F50
Emulsion tube type – Secondary	F50
Needle valve	0.10 in (2.50 mm)
Idle speed (rpm)	780 to 820
Fast idle speed (rpm)	3000
Float level – Upper	1.52 in (38.5 mm)
Float level – Lower	2.67 in (52.5 mm)
Choke plate pull down at extreme modulation	0.236 in (6.0 mm)

d) Weber 722F 9510 AA
Specifications same as carburettor c) but with the following exceptions:
Venturi diameter – Primary	1.02 in (26 mm)
Jet sizes:	
Main – Primary	0.055 in (1.4 mm)
Main – Secondary	0.053 in (1.35 mm)
Air correction – Primary	0.067 in (1.7 mm)
Air correction – Secondary	0.049 in (1.25 mm)
Idling – Primary	0.236 in (0.6 mm)
Accelerator pump stroke	0.0197 in (0.5 mm)
Needle valve	0.08 in (2.0 mm)
Idle speed (rpm)	680 to 720
Float level – Upper	1.86 in (47 mm)
Float level – Lower	1.97 in (50 mm)
Choke plate pull down at extreme modulation	0.256 in (6.5 mm)

e) Weber 722F 9510 BA
Specifications same as carburettor d) but with the following exceptions:
Jet size:	
Idling – Primary	0.0217 in (0.55 mm)
Float level – Upper	1.16 in (41 mm)

f) Weber 722F 9510 NA
Specifications same as carburettor c) but with following exceptions:
Jet sizes:	
Air correction – Primary	0.073 in (1.85 mm)
Air correction – Secondary	0.073 in (1.85 mm)

Idling – Primary	0.0177 in (0.45 mm)
Idling – Secondary	0.0177 in (0.45 mm)
Float level – Upper	1.57 in (40.0 mm)

g) Weber 722F 9510 RA
Specifications as per carburettor f)

h) Weber 72HF 9510 AA
Specifications as per carburettor d)

i) Weber 72HF 9510 BA
Specifications as per carburettor e)

j) Weber 76HF 9510 AB
Throttle barrel diameter:
    Primary .... 1.26 in (32 mm)
    Secondary .... 1.42 in (36 mm)
Venturi diameter:
    Primary .... 1.02 in (26 mm)
    Secondary .... 1.06 in (27 mm)
Main jet:
    Primary 137
    Secondary 127
Idle speed (rpm) .... 825 ± 25
CO percentage .... 1.5 ± 0.25
Fast idle (rpm) .... 2100 ± 100
Float level:
    Brass float .... 1.61 in ± 0.02 in (41.0 mm ± 0.5 mm)
    Plastic float .... 1.39 in ± 0.02 in (35.3 mm ± 0.5 mm)
Choke plate pull down .... 0.28 in ± 0.01 in (7.0 mm ± 0.25 mm)
Choke phasing .... 0.11 in ± 0.01 in (2.75 mm ± 0.25 mm)

k) Weber 76HF 9510 AA
Specifications as per carburettor j)

l) Weber 742F 9510 AA
Throttle barrel diameter:
    Primary and secondary .... 1.34 in (34 mm)
Venturi diameter:
    Primary and secondary .... 0.94 in (24 mm)
Main jet:
    Primary and secondary 122
Idle speed (rpm) .... 800 ± 25
CO percentage:
    Manual .... 2.0 ± 0.25
    Automatic .... 1.5 ± 0.25
Fast idle (rpm) .... 2100 ± 100
Float level:
    Brass float .... 1.57 in ± 0.02 in (40.0 mm ± 0.5 mm)
    Plastic float .... 1.39 in ± 0.02 in (35.3 mm ± 0.5 mm)
Choke plate pull down .... 0.20 in ± 0.01 in (5.0 mm ± 0.25 mm)
Choke phasing .... 0.09 in ± 0.01 in (2.3 mm ± 0.25 mm)

m) Weber 762F 9510 AA
Throttle barrel diameter:
    Primary and secondary .... 1.5 in (38 mm)
Venturi diameter:
    Primary and secondary .... 1.06 in (27 mm)
Main jet:
    Primary and secondary 142
Idle speed (rpm) .... 825 ± 25
CO percentage .... 1.75 ± 0.25
Fast idle (rpm) .... 2100 ± 100
Float level:
    Brass float .... 1.57 in ± 0.02 in (40.0 mm ± 0.5 mm)
    Plastic float .... 1.39 in ± 0.02 in (35.3 mm ± 0.5 mm)
Choke plate pull down .... 0.28 in ± 0.01 in (7.0 mm ± 0.25 mm)
Choke phasing .... 0.12 in ± 0.01 in (3.0 mm ± 0.25 mm)

Torque Wrench Settings

	lbf ft	kgf m
V4		
Air cleaner to carburettor	6 to 7	0.8 to 1.0
Air cleaner lid to body	5 to 7	0.7 to 1.0
Carburettor to inlet manifold	15 to 18	2.1 to 2.5
Fuel pump to engine	15 to 18	2.1 to 2.5

Chapter 3 Carburation, fuel and exhaust systems

V6

	lbf ft	kgf m
Air cleaner to carburettor	2 to 3	0.3 to 0.4
Air cleaner lid to body	5 to 7	0.7 to 1.0
Carburettor to inlet manifold	15 to 18	2.1 to 2.5
Fuel pump to engine	15 to 18	2.1 to 2.5

2.0 litre ohc

Air cleaner to carburettor	6 to 9	0.8 to 1.2
Air cleaner lid to body	2 to 3	0.3 to 0.4
Carburettor to inlet manifold	5 to 7	0.7 to 1.0
Fuel pump to engine	12 to 15	1.7 to 2.1
Manifold to cylinder head nuts	15 to 18	2.1 to 2.5
Exhaust front pipe to manifold nuts	14 to 19	2.0 to 2.7
Clamp nuts – front and rear	22 to 27	3.1 to 3.8

1 General description

The fuel system comprises a fuel tank, a mechanically operated fuel pump and a Ford or Weber carburettor.

The fuel tank is located beneath the luggage compartment at the rear, and is ventilated via the filler cap. The fuel outlet and gauge sender unit are situated in the front face of the tank.

The fuel pump is of the mechanical type, being operated by the eccentric on the front of the camshaft on the V6 and V4 models, whilst the 2·0 litre ohc engine fuel pump is driven via a pushrod from the auxiliary shaft.

Apart from the filter within the fuel pump, there is an additional filter provided in the fuel line between the pump and the carburettor and the fuel flow direction is indicated by an arrow on the housing.

The carburettor air cleaner fitted to all models, irrespective of carburettor type, is of the disposable paper element type. Some air filter inlets are provided with a summer/winter setting to increase or decrease the temperature of air flow into the carburettor accordingly, the respective positions being marked.

Exhaust emission control

Some later models have a thermostatically controlled air cleaner fitted. With this type of cleaner, the basic design remains the same but a heat sensor unit and a vacuum diaphragm unit are incorporated into the assembly, and these assist during the initial warming up from cold and reduce the exhaust emission levels. This type of cleaner unit is readily identified by the vacuum diaphragm unit which is located on the air intake spout.

Also on some later models the carburettors incorporate certain features which are designed to reduce the harmful exhaust emissions. The principle differences are as follows:

Motorcraft (Ford) carburettors

The bypass idle system differs in that, when idling, the majority of air flow and all of the fuel is supplied via the bypass system. Additional air flow is supplied via the Venturi butterfly. Refer to Fig. 3.2 for the principle features of this type of carburettor. This carburettor is readily identified by the number of screws securing the upper body – seven instead of the usual six previously employed.

Weber carburettor

A fuel return line has been added which enables any excess fuel being supplied to be returned to the fuel tank. A bypass idle system has been incorporated, and on automatic transmission models an anti-stall device is also fitted.

Although the adjustment and overhaul procedures are basically the same as for the standard type carburettors, the settings are more critical if the emission level at the exhaust is to be within the specified limits.

2 Air cleaner – removal, servicing and refitting

The renewable paper element type air cleaner is fitted onto the top of the carburettor installation and is retained by securing nuts on a flange at the top of the carburettor. To remove the air cleaner assembly proceed as follows:

1 Note the direction in which the air intake is pointing as on some models it is adjustable to a hot or cold weather position.
2 Undo and remove the nuts and spring washers or self-tapping

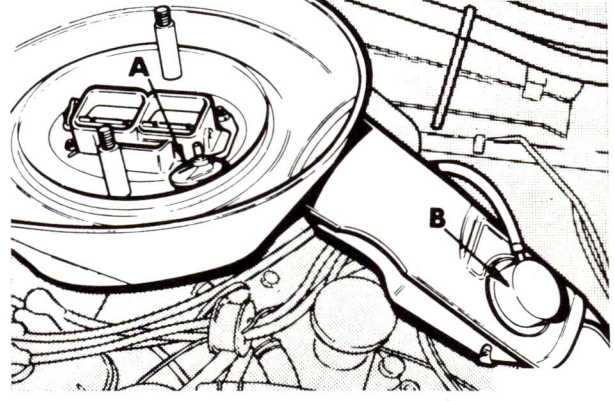

Fig. 3.1 The thermostatically controlled type air cleaner (Sec. 1)

A Heat sensor unit   B Vacuum diaphragm unit

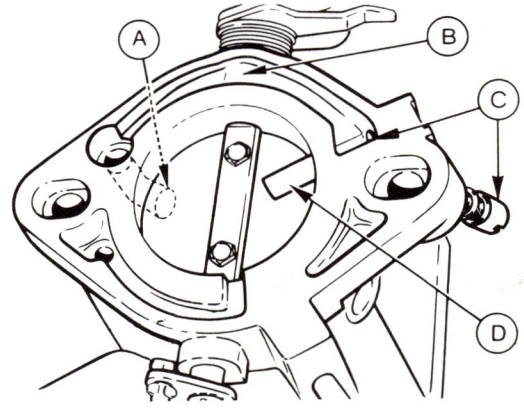

Fig. 3.2 The Motorcraft (Ford) bypass idle carburettor (Sec. 1)

A Air entry to bypass system   C Mixture screw
B Air distribution channel   D Sonic discharge tube

screws that secure the top cover to the main body. Lift away the top cover. Recover the two spacer tubes (photo).
3 The element may now be lifted out.
4 If it is necessary to remove the lower body, first bend back the lock tabs and then undo and remove the four securing nuts.
5 Lift away the two tab washers.
6 The lower body may now be lifted away from the top of the carburettor. Do not forget the paper gasket which should be renewed if damaged.
7 Refitting the air cleaner is the reverse sequence to removal. Make sure that the gasket and top cover sealing ring are located correctly.

2.2 Lift the top cover clear

2.10 The air cleaner Summer/Winter setting lever

To service the air cleaner, proceed as follows:
8 The element may be cleaned by using a compressed air jet in the reverse direction to air flow by holding the jet nozzle at least 5 inches (127 mm) away from the element at its centre and blowing outwards. Then hold the element in the vertical position and gently tap until all dirt and dust is removed.
9 Inspect the element for signs of splitting, cracking, pin holes or permanent distortion and, if evident, a new element should be fitted. A new element must be fitted after 15000 miles (25000 km) or earlier if the car is being operated in very dusty conditions.
10 On models having an adjustable air intake for summer or winter settings, a seasonal readjustment should be made accordingly at the appropriate time to increase or decrease the air temperature being drawn into the carburettor (photo).

3 Fuel pump – description

V4 and V6
The mechanical fuel pump is mounted on the right-hand side of the engine and operated through a spring-loaded rocker arm. One part of the arm bears against an eccentric in front of the camshaft gear and the other part operates a diaphragm pull rod.

As the engine camshaft rotates, the eccentric moves the pivoted rocker arms outward which, in turn, pulls the diaphragm pull rod and the diaphragm down against the pressure of the diaphragm spring. This creates sufficient vacuum in the pump chamber to draw in fuel from the tank through the fuel filter gauze and non-return valve.

The rocker arm is held in constant contact with the eccentric by an anti-rattle spring, and as the engine camshaft continues to rotate the eccentric allows the rocker arm to move inward. The diaphragm spring is thus free to push the diaphragm upward forcing the fuel in the pump chamber out to the carburettor through the non-return outlet valve.

When the float chamber in the carburettor is full the float chamber needle valve will close so preventing further flow from the fuel pump. The pressure in the delivery lines will hold the diaphragm downward against the pressure of the diaphragm spring, and it will remain in this position until the needle valve in the float chamber opens to admit more petrol.

Although one of two types of pump may be fitted the principle of operation is basically the same.

2·0 litre ohc
The mechanical fuel pump fitted to this engine is located on the left-hand side and is driven by an auxiliary shaft. It is not recommended that this type of pump be dismantled for repair other than cleaning the filter and sediment cap. One of two designs were fitted depending on availability at the time of production.

4 Fuel pump – routine servicing

1 At intervals of 3000 miles (5000 km) undo and pull the fuel pipe from the pump inlet tube. Although the sediment cap can be removed with the inlet tube in position, movement will be restricted.
2 Undo and remove the centre screw and O-ring and lift off the sediment cap, filter and seal (photo).
3 Thoroughly clean the sediment cap, filter and pumping chamber using a paintbrush and clean petrol to remove any sediment.
4 To reassemble is the reverse sequence to dismantling. Do not overtighten the centre screw as it could distort the sediment chamber cap.

Note: An alternative type of fuel pump may be fitted and is easily identifiable by the tall sediment and pumping chamber, this being retained by a clamp and knurled nut. Cleaning is accomplished by releasing the clamp and lifting away the sediment bowl. Recover the filter and seal. Cleaning is as described earlier in this Section and refitting is the reverse sequence to removal.

5 Fuel pump – removal and refitting

1 Remove the inlet and outlet pipes at the pump and plug the ends to stop petrol loss or dirt finding its way into the fuel system. (photo).

V4 and V6 engines
2 Undo and remove the two nuts and spring washers securing the fuel pump to the front cover.
3 Lift away the pump whilst at the same time lifting the rocker arm so as to clear both the eccentric at the front of the camshaft gear and the slotted hole in the front cover.
4 Lift away the gasket.
5 Before refitting the pump to the front cover first ensure that both mounting faces are clean and traces of old gasket or jointing compound have been removed.
6 Fit a new gasket onto the fuel pump mounting studs on the front cover.
7 Carefully insert the rocker arm through the slot in the front cover and position so that the rocker arm lies on the actuating eccentric on the front of the camshaft gear.
8 Refit the two nuts and spring washers and tighten to the specified torque.
9 Wipe the ends of the two fuel pipes, remove the plugs and connect the pipes to the pump.

2·0 litre ohc engine
10 Undo and remove the two bolts and spring washers securing the pump unit to the cylinder block.

Chapter 3 Carburation, fuel and exhaust systems

Fig. 3.3 Standard type fuel pump (Sec. 3)

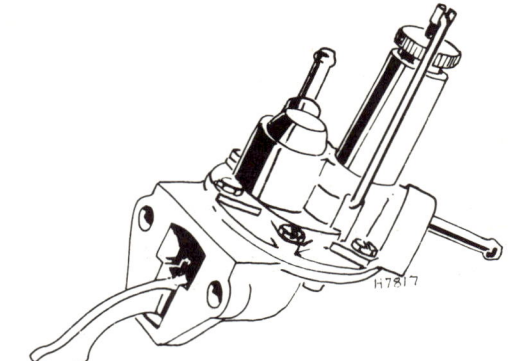

Fig. 3.4 Alternative type fuel pump (Sec. 3)

Fig. 3.5 Fuel filter removal (alternative type pump) (Sec. 4)

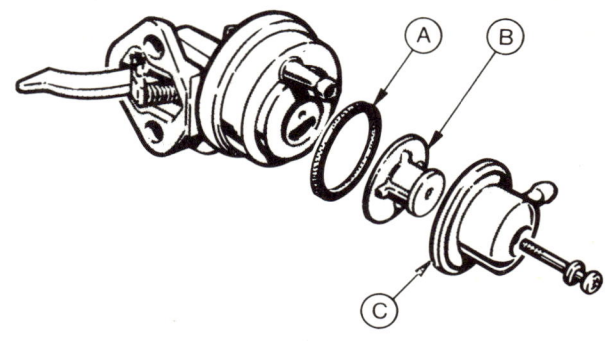

Fig. 3.6 Standard fuel pump components (Sec. 4)
A Seal   B Filter   C Cap

4.2 Remove the top cap to clean the filter

5.1 The fuel pump with inlet and outlet hoses detached

11 Carefully lift away the pump and gasket and recover the pushrod.
12 Refit the pump in the reverse order but note the following:

   a) Do not forget to refit the pushrod.
   b) Retighten the pump securing bolts to the specified torque.
   c) When reconnecting the fuel supply pipe from the tank, the end to be fitted to the pump must initially be lower than the tank so that fuel is allowed to flow through, then quickly connected to the pump inlet.
   d) Detach the fuel pipe from the carburettor and turn the engine over so that fuel is pumped through, and then reconnect the pipe to the carburettor union.

6 Fuel pump – testing

Assuming that the fuel lines and unions are in good condition and that there are no leaks anywhere, check the performance of the fuel pump in the following manner. Disconnect the fuel pipe at the carburettor inlet union, and the high tension lead to the coil and, with a suitable container or a large rag in position to catch the ejected fuel, turn the engine over on the starter. A good spurt of petrol should emerge from the end of the pipe every second revolution. Do not forget that the pump performance can be affected by a partially blocked fuel pipe or dirty in-line filter.

7 Fuel pump – dismantling, overhaul and reassembly (standard type)

If the performance of this pump is suspect, first clean the filter and sediment chamber as described in Section 4. Next test the pump performance as described in Section 6. Should the pump prove to be in need of attention it will have to be renewed as a complete unit as it is not possible to dismantle it or obtain spare parts.

8 Fuel pump – dismantling, overhaul and reassembly (alternative type)

1 With the pump removed from the engine and the exterior clean, first mark the upper and lower body halves to ensure correct alignment during assembly.
2 Undo and remove the six screws and spring washers securing the two halves of the body together.
3 Carefully separate the two halves of the body. It is possible for the diaphragm to stick to the mating flange faces so carefully release it with a knife or thin screwdriver.
4 Using a small sharp chisel remove the staking securing the rocker arm retaining pin.
5 The pin may now be tapped out with a suitable diameter parallel pin punch.
6 Detach the diaphragm pull rod from the rocker arm and carefully remove the diaphragm and lower oil seal. Note which way round the latter is fitted.
7 Release the clamp and lift away the sediment bowl from the top cover. Recover the filter and seal.
8 Thoroughly clean all parts and inspect the diaphragm for signs of perishing, hardening or other damage. Renew if necessary.
9 It is recommended that whenever the pump is overhauled a new oil seal is fitted.
10 If the valve assembly proves to be faulty, check that there is no dirt which could affect its operation. Unfortunately the valve assembly cannot be renewed so if this is the cause of any trouble a new pump will have to be obtained.
11 Reassembly of the pump is a direct reversal of the dismantling procedure. Before inserting the diaphragm pull rod into the oil seal, lubricate with a little engine oil.

9 Fuel tank – removal and refitting

1 The fuel tank is positioned at the rear of the car. If it is anticipated that the tank is to be removed allow the level to fall as low as possible.
2 Remove the filler cap and, using a length of rubber hose or plastic pipe approximately 0·25 inch (6·35 mm) bore, syphon as much petrol out as possible until the level is below the level of the sender unit.
3 Disconnect the battery earth terminal, release the fuel gauge sender unit wire and the fuel feed pipe from the sender unit. Slacken the filler pipe flexible hose clip.
4 Using two screwdrivers in the slots in the sender unit retaining ring turn the sender unit to detach it from the lugs on the tank. Lift away the sealing ring and the sender unit, noting that the float must hang downward.
5 Undo the tank strap retaining nuts and detach the strap hooks from the body. Lift away the tank protective tray and the tank.
6 Refitting is the reverse sequence to removal. Tighten the support strap securing nuts until 1·6 – 1·8 inch (40 – 45 mm) of thread is protruding through the nut.
7 Refill the fuel tank and reconnect the battery earth terminal. Test the operation of the fuel gauge sender unit by switching on the ignition. Wait 30 seconds and observe the gauge reading.

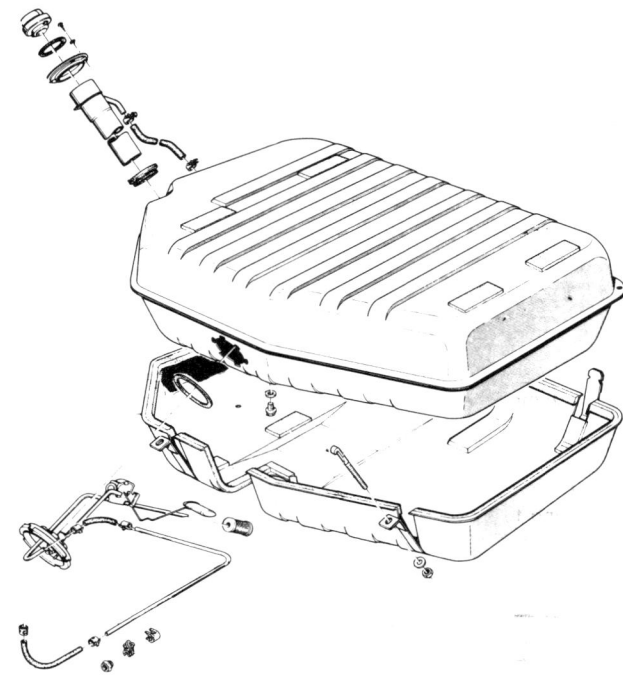

Fig. 3.7 The fuel tank and attachments (Sec. 9)

10 Fuel tank – cleaning

1 With time it is likely that sediment will collect in the bottom of the fuel tank. Condensation, resulting in rust and other impurities, will usually be found in the tank.
2 When the tank is removed it should be vigorously flushed out and turned upside down. If facilities are available at the local garage the tank may be steam cleaned and the exterior repainted with a lead based paint.
3 Never weld or bring a naked light close to an empty fuel tank unless it has been steam cleaned out for at least two hours or washed internally with boiling water and detergent and allowed to stand for at least three hours.
4 Any small holes may be repaired using a suitable repair kit, which gives satisfactory results provided that the instructions are rigidly adhered to.

11 Fuel gauge sender unit – removal and refitting

1 The fuel gauge sender unit can be removed with the fuel tank in position.
2 Disconnect the battery earth terminal.
3 Remove the filler cap and, using a length of rubber hose or plastic pipe approximately 0·25 in (6·35 mm) bore, syphon as much petrol out as possible until the level is below the level of the sender unit.
4 Release the fuel gauge sender unit wire and the fuel feed pipe from the sender unit.
5 Using two screwdrivers in the slots in the sender unit retaining ring turn the sender unit to detach it from the lugs on the tank. Lift away the sealing ring and the sender unit noting that the float will hang downward.
6 If the operation of the sender unit is suspect check that the rheostat is not damaged.
7 Refitting is a straightforward reversal of the removal sequence. Always fit a new seal to the recess in the tank to ensure that no leaks develop.
8 The float arm should hang downward. Test the operation of the fuel gauge sender unit by switching on the ignition. Wait 30 seconds and observe the gauge reading.

Chapter 3 Carburation, fuel and exhaust systems

12 Fuel line filter – removal and refitting

1   Slacken the two hose clips and ease off the inlet and outlet pipes. Plug the ends of the pipes to stop dirt ingress and loss of petrol. Lift away the filter.
2   The filter should be renewed at intervals of 18000 miles (30000 km) or when fuel starvation symptoms are experienced.
3   Refitting the fuel line filter is the reverse sequence to removal. There is an arrow on the filter body which indicates the direction of fuel flow and the correct way of fitting.

13 Accelerator pedal and shaft – removal and refitting

1   Release the accelerator cable retaining clip from the top of the accelerator pedal lever assembly.
2   Detach the cable socket from the lever balljoint.
3   Withdraw the shaft retaining spring clip and slide out the shaft. Recover the two shaft bushes.
4   Inspect the pedal shaft bushes and if worn they should be renewed.
5   Refitting the pedal is the reverse sequence to removal. It will be necessary to check the adjustment as described in Section 15.

14 Accelerator cable – removal and refitting

1   Working under the bonnet slide the clip from the inner cable socket and the throttle shaft ball so as to disconnect the inner cable.
2   Slacken the adjustment nut and slide the outer cable from the support bracket.
3   Withdraw the clip and disconnect the inner cable socket from the balljoint on the top of the accelerator pedal lever.
4   The cable may now be drawn through the aperture in the bulkhead.
5   Refitting and reconnecting the accelerator cable is the reverse sequence to removal.
6   It will now be necessary to adjust the linkage as described in Section 15.

15 Accelerator linkage – adjustment

1   Working under the bonnet first remove the air cleaner top cover so that the throttle disc can be seen.
2   An assistant should now depress the accelerator pedal and hold it in the fully open position.
3   The throttle disc should now be fully open. If necessary turn the outer cable adjustment nut in the required direction until the required setting is obtained.
4   Release the accelerator pedal and refit the air cleaner top cover.

16 Carburettor – dismantling and reassembly – general

1   With time the component parts of the carburettor will wear and petrol consumption will increase. The diameter of the drillings and jets may alter due to erosion. Air and fuel leaks may develop around the spindle and other moving parts. Because of the high degree of precision, it is best to purchase an exchange rebuilt carburettor. This is one of the few instances where it is better to take this course rather than rebuild the component itself.
2   It may be necessary to partially dismantle the carburettor to clear a blocked jet or renew a gasket. Provided care is taken there is no reason why the carburettor may not be completely reconditioned at home, but ensure a full repair kit can be obtained before you strip the carburettor down. NEVER poke out jets with wire. To clean them out blow them out with compressed air or with air from a car tyre pump. Always use the right tool for the job when overhauling the carburettor and never overtighten the retaining screws, nuts or fittings.

Fig. 3.8 The fuel line filter (fuel flows in direction of arrow) (Sec. 12)

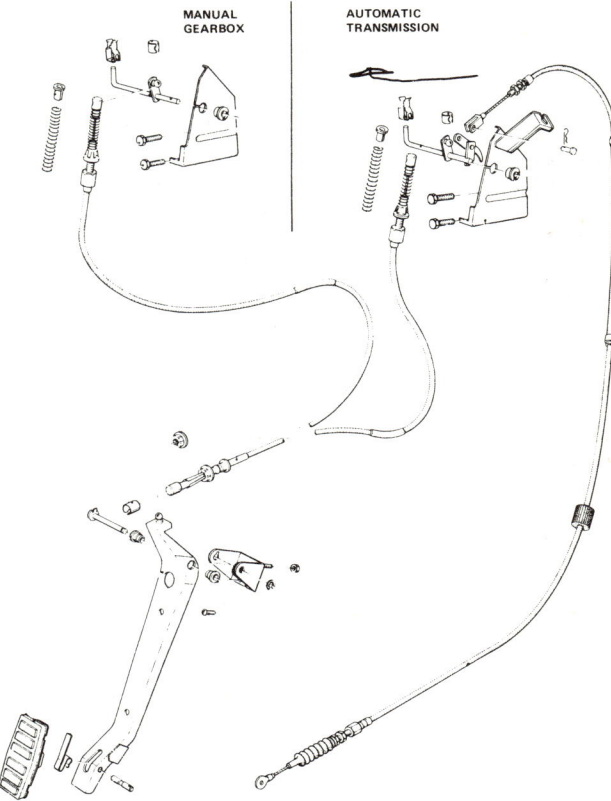

Fig. 3.9 The accelerator pedal and cable assemblies (Sec. 13)

17 Carburettor – description

One of two basic types of carburettor are used on models covered by this manual, the application depending on the specification.

Ford

The component parts of this carburettor are shown in Fig. 3.10 and it will be seen that it is of the single venturi down-draught design incorporating an accelerator pump and power valve as well as the usual engine idle and main systems. A fully automatic strangler type choke system is fitted to ensure easy starting whilst the engine is cold.

The carburettor body comprises two parts, the upper and lower bodies with a two piece cast housing for the automatic choke system.

The upper body incorporates the float chamber cover, float pivot brackets, fuel inlet connection tube, spring-loaded needle, needle valve, air intake, choke plate, the main and power valve system with the discharge beak, engine idle jet, fast idle air bleed, ventilator tube connection and accelerator pump discharge nozzle.

The fully automatic choke system comprises an inner and outer housing which is attached to the carburettor upper body. Inside the housing is a bi-metal (thermostatic) spring which is mounted on a hub in the housing. Engine cooling water from the bypass tube is allowed

Chapter 3 Carburation, fuel and exhaust systems

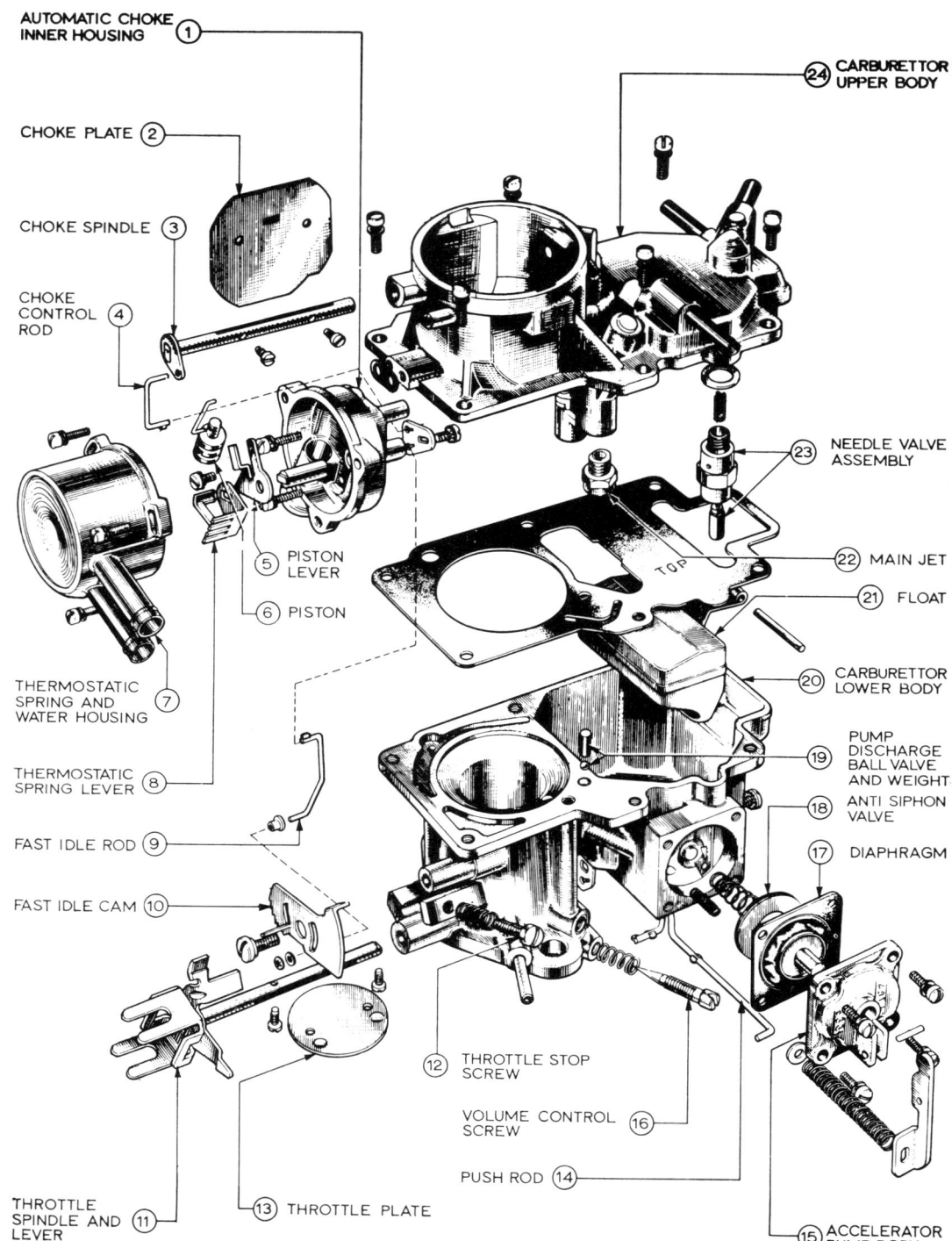

Fig. 3.10 The Ford carburettor components (Sec. 17)

to pass through the housing.

Located in the inner housing is a lever and shaft assembly which is able to transmit the thermostatic spring movement to the choke plate. Also incorporated in the housing is a vacuum pull down piston and lever.

The lower body incorporates the throttle barrel with integral choke tube, throttle and lever, idling discharge orifice and progression slot, float chamber, adjustment screws, accelerator pump and anti-syphon valve, distributor automatic advance vacuum connection and the choke linkage fast idle cam.

Weber

The Weber carburettor is of the dual barrel, vertical down-draught type incorporating a fully automatic strangler type choke to ensure easy starting whilst the engine is cold.

The component parts of this carburettor are shown in Fig. 3.11 and upon inspection it will be seen that the main and idling systems are duplicated and each barrel has separate systems, each being supplied from a single float chamber.

A single accelerator pump of the diaphragm type supplies both barrels so that smooth acceleration is obtained from engine idle speed

Chapter 3 Carburation, fuel and exhaust systems 105

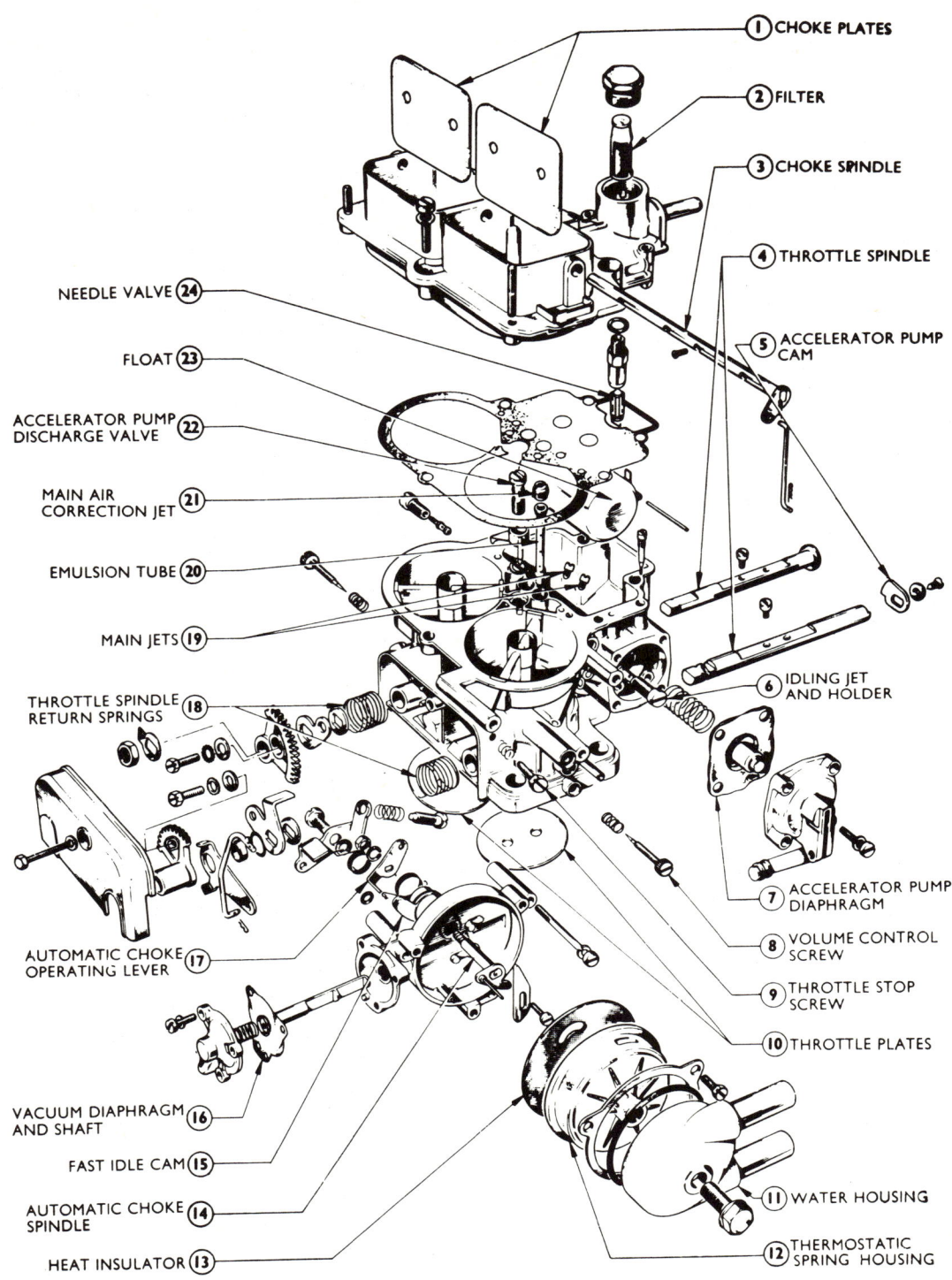

Fig. 3.11 The Weber carburettor components (Sec. 17)

until the main system is in full operation.

There is a vacuum pipe connection for the distributor automatic advance system, and also a metered return pipe to the fuel tank and a gauze filter fitted onto the fuel inlet to the float chamber. Internal ventilation of the float chamber is incorporated in this type of carburettor.

The main body of the carburettor, comprising the float chamber, throttle barrels, main venturis and the accelerator pump body, is cast as one piece and accommodates the main air correction jets, emulsion tubes, idling air correction jets and the accelerator pump discharge valve, and its double jet, all being positioned on the top face of the body.

The main jets are positioned in the bottom of the emulsion tube wells inside the float chamber. The engine idle jets and their holders and the volume control screws are located on each side of the casting.

Located in the top of each barrel and above the main venturis are the small auxiliary venturis which incorporate the main system beaks.

There are two throttle spindles which are interconnected by gear sectors and these open and close the throttle plates simultaneously as each barrel feeds one of the two banks of cylinders through the ducts

17.10a The Weber carburettor showing A) vacuum diaphragm unit, B) automatic choke thermostat housing, C) accelerator pump unit

17.10b The Weber carburettor showing A) volume control screws, B) sectors (note alignment marks), C) throttle stop screw

18.11a Fit new gaskets to each face of the intermediate flange

cast in the dual inlet manifold. There is an idle stop screw which operates on the right-hand spindle. This spindle has a cam attached to it and operates the accelerator pump through a roller and lever system.

Incorporated in the float chamber cover is the fuel feed inlet connection and the fuel return pipe connection to return fuel back to the fuel tank. The float assembly pivots on brackets and controls the needle valve which ensures a constant level of fuel in the float chamber. Also in the cover are the twin air intakes to the two barrels and the mounting studs for the air cleaner.

The fully automatic choke system is located on the right-hand side of the carburettor body and comprises a bi-metal (thermostatic) spring which is attached by its inner end to a housing connected in series with the engine cooling system bypass tube, therefore being heated by the engine coolant. A shaft passing through the housing incorporates a crankpin, which locates in the free end of the spring, and transmits spring movement by a lever and connecting linkage to the two offset choke plates mounted on a spindle which passes through the carburettor air intakes (photos).

An engine fast idle cam, which pivots on a bush positioned around the automatic choke shaft, is connected to the operating lever by a spring. A lever, which has an adjustment screw, bears against this fast idle cam and is mounted onto the automatic choke housing below the shaft. It is connected to a lever pivoting about the right-hand throttle spindle and has lugs which loosely embrace the gear sector so that, after opening the throttle for the first time with a cold engine, a fast idle setting is obtained. The fast idle interconnecting linkage has an overriding system for the choke when the throttle is opened. There is a vacuum diaphragm, connected by internal drillings to the throttle barrel below the butterfly, to automatically open the choke plates by a pre-determined amount when the engine is first started.

18 Carburettor – removal and refitting (Ford)

1 Open the bonnet and remove the air cleaner assembly as detailed in Section 2 of this Chapter.
2 Before disconnecting the automatic choke coolant hoses, the cooling system must be de-pressurised by removing the radiator cap. When any pressure in the system is fully released, refit the cap into position. This normally only applies if the engine has been run recently, in which case extra care must be taken when removing the cap, as described in Chapter 2, Section 2.
3 Slacken the clips securing the hoses to the automatic choke housing and carefully detach them from the housing. To prevent coolant loss each hose must be positioned facing upwards on removal, or alternatively plugged or clamped.
4 Disconnect the throttle linkage from the carburettor installation.
5 Release the distributor automatic advance pipe from the side of the carburettor.
6 Slacken the fuel pipe retaining clip at the float chamber and detach the flexible hose. Crimped type hose clips must be cut free and renewed on reassembly (preferably with a screw type clip).
7 Disconnect the engine ventilation tube.
8 Detach the ventilation tube from the top of the float chamber.
9 Undo the nuts securing the carburettor flange and remove the nuts and spring washers.
10 Carefully lift away the carburettor and its gasket.
11 Refitting is a straightforward reversal of the removal sequence but note the following additional points:

   a) *Remove all traces of the old carburettor gasket clean the mating flanges and fit a new gasket in place (photo).*
   b) *Top up the cooling system, and after the engine has been restarted and run for a couple of minutes, recheck the coolant level in the radiator and top up further if necessary.*
   c) *If a spacer is fitted, refit it with the chamfer upward and facing the front of the engine. Tighten the nuts to the specified torque.*
   d) *Check for petrol and coolant leaks on restarting the engine, and readjust the carburettor as necessary.*

19 Carburettor – dismantling and reassembly (Ford)

1 Before dismantling wash the exterior of the carburettor and wipe dry using a non-fluffy rag. Select a clean area of the work-bench and lay several layers of newspaper on the top. Obtain several small containers for putting in some of the small parts that could easily be lost. Whenever a part is to be removed look at it first so that it may be refitted in its original position. As each part is removed place it in order along one edge of the newspaper so that by using this method reassembly is made easier.
2 All parts of the carburettor are shown in Fig. 3.10.
3 Undo and remove the shoulder screw that secures the fast idle cam and assembly to the lower body.
4 Undo and remove the six screws that hold the upper body to the lower carburettor body and separate the two parts. As the two halves are being separated check that the gasket is released from the lower carburettor body and is lifted away with the upper body.
5 Using the fingers, withdraw the float arm pivot pin. Lift away the float from the upper body.
6 Lift away the needle valve from the needle valve housing.
7 Lift away the gasket from the upper body.
8 Invert the lower body and remove the accelerator pump discharge ball valve weight and ball.
9 Using a box spanner undo and remove the needle valve housing filter and washer.
10 With an open-ended spanner undo and remove the main jet from the upper body.
11 Undo and remove the three screws and spring washers securing the thermostatic spring and water housing to the choke inner housing. Lift away the housing.
12 Undo and remove the two screws and spring washers that secure the choke inner housing to the carburettor body and lift away the inner housing and its gasket from the carburettor body.
13 Undo and remove the screw securing the thermostatic spring lever. Lift out the thermostatic spring lever, choke piston lever, choke piston link and piston from the choke inner housing.
14 Remove the choke control lever and shaft assembly and the choke

Chapter 3 Carburation, fuel and exhaust systems

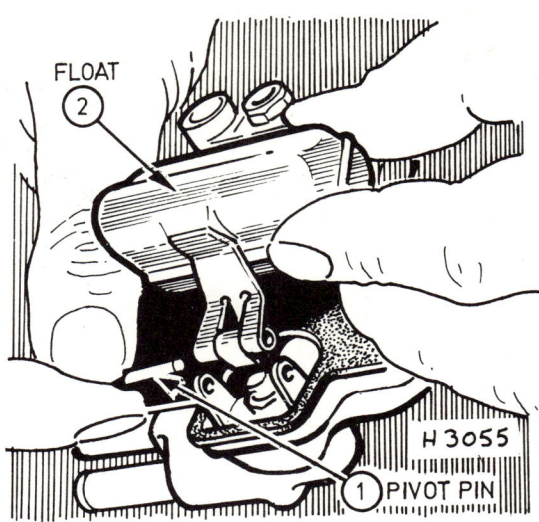

Fig. 3.12 Float pin removal (Ford) (Sec. 19)

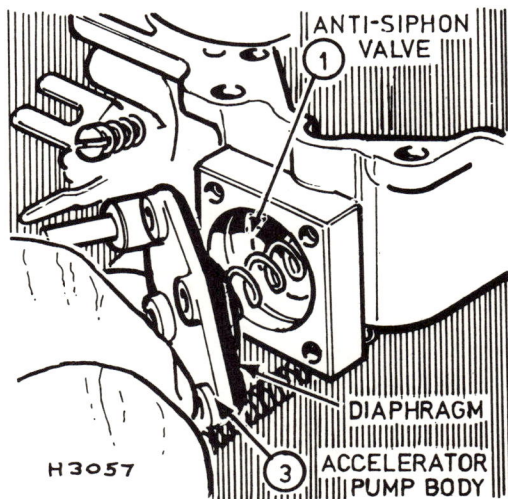

Fig. 3.13 Accelerator pump removal (Ford) (Sec. 19)

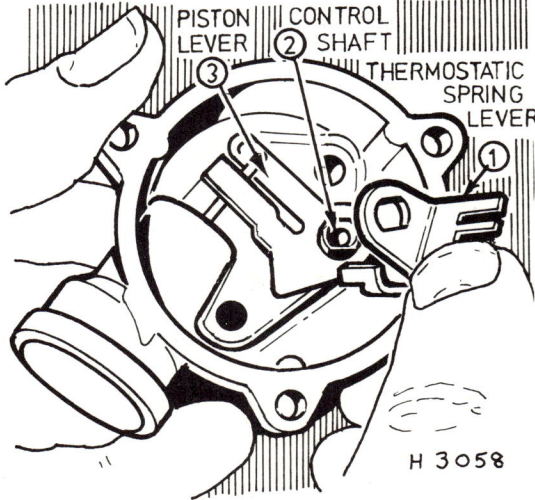

Fig. 3.14 Refitting the thermostat spring lever (Ford) (Sec. 19)

control rod from the inner housing. Locate the 'Teflon' bushing and carefully remove this.

15 Should it be necessary to remove the choke plate and its shaft first remove the two air cleaner retainer pins using sharp side cutters and lift away the air cleaner retainer.

16 Next undo and remove the two screws that secure the choke plate to the shaft. Lift away the choke plate and withdraw the choke spindle and lever assembly.

17 Undo and remove the four screws securing the accelerator pump in position and lift away the accelerator pump body, operating arm, diaphragm, return spring, anti-syphon valve and spring.

18 Carefully disconnect the accelerator pump pushrod and spring assembly from the pump operating lever and the arm on the throttle spindle.

19 Separate the accelerator pump pushrod arm from the throttle spindle.

20 Undo and remove the two screws securing the throttle plate to the spindle and lift away the plate.

21 Withdraw the throttle spindle from the carburettor lower body.

22 Unscrew the volume control needle screw and spring.

23 Finally remove the throttle stop screw and spring.

24 Dismantling is now complete and all parts should be thoroughly washed and cleaned in petrol. Remove any sediment in the float chamber and drillings but take care not to scratch the fine drillings whilst doing so. Remove all traces of old gaskets using a sharp knife.

25 The main components to check are the float, which should be inspected for signs of leakage, the pump diaphragm for splits or damage of any description and the mixture screw, throttle spindle and needle valve, which may show signs of wear. Renew any components where necessary, and commence reassembly as follows:

26 Insert the throttle spindle into the carburettor lower body. Slide the throttle plate into the spindle with the two indentations in the throttle plate face in the same way as the screw head recesses in the throttle shaft. Rotate the spindle several times to centralise the plate and secure the plate with the two screws. Peen over the ends of the screws so that they cannot work loose.

27 Fit the spring onto the volume control screw and refit the volume control screw. Tighten, without any force, so that it is just seated and then turn the screw back one complete turn to give an approximate setting.

28 Fit the spring onto the throttle stop screw and refit the screw.

29 Refit the accelerator pump pushrod arm onto the throttle spindle.

30 Reconnect the accelerator pump rod and spring assembly to the arm and to the accelerator pump operating lever. The spring tapers outwards.

31 Carefully fit the diaphragm and plunger into the accelerator pump cover and position the anti-syphon valve return spring in the bore. Refit the valve and diaphragm return spring making sure that its smaller diameter is fitted into the recess within the pump housing.

32 Refit the cover and retain it in position with the four screws and spring washers.

33 Refit the accelerator pump discharge ball bearing and weight to the lower body.

34 Fit the choke shaft and lever assembly into the carburettor upper body and slide the choke plate into the slot in the shaft with the indentation on the plate facing the same way as the recesses in the shaft.

35 Rotate the shaft several times to centralise the choke plate and secure the plate with the two screws. Peen over the ends of the screws so that they cannot work loose, or apply locking compound to the threads before fitting.

36 Refit the air cleaner and secure the two pins or rivets squeezed into the holes. As an alternative small nuts and bolts can be used.

37 Fit the choke control lever and shaft assembly to the inner choke housing whilst at the same time refitting the 'Teflon' bush.

38 Refit the piston, piston lever and link, which should be assembled to the outer position of the lever, into the inner housing. Place the piston lever onto the shaft and attach the thermostatic spring lever and screw to the control lever shaft.

39 Fit the inner housing, with the choke control and fast idle rods positioned in the choke control lever. Fit the vacuum housing gasket and secure the housing in place with the two screws.

40 Refit the thermostatic spring and water housing assembly and engage the thermostatic spring with the central slot in the lever.

41 Carefully align the mark with the central mark on the inner housing and secure the housing with the three screws. The screw holes in the

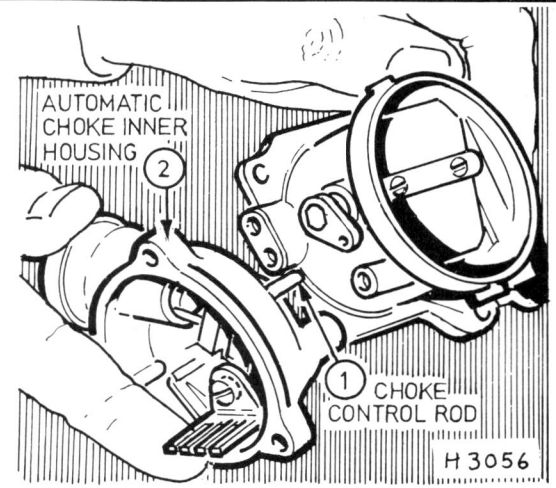
Fig. 3.15 Refitting the automatic choke inner housing (Ford) (Sec. 19)

Fig. 3.18 Removing the automatic choke outer housing (Ford) (Sec. 21)

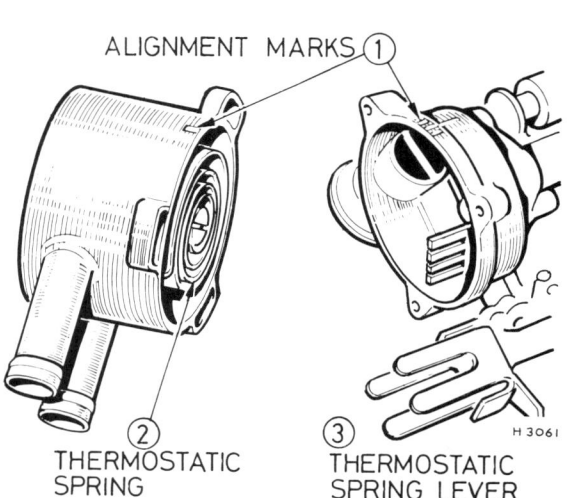
Fig. 3.16 Thermostatic spring housing alignment marks (Ford) (Sec. 19)

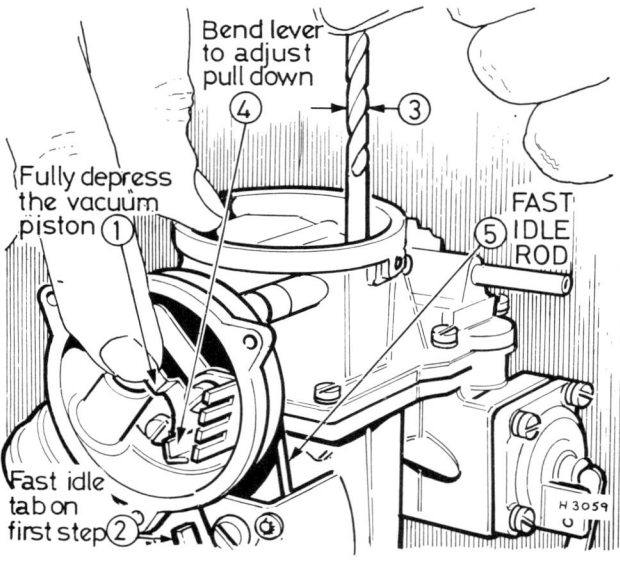
Fig. 3.19 Choke plate pull down adjustment (Ford) (Sec. 21)

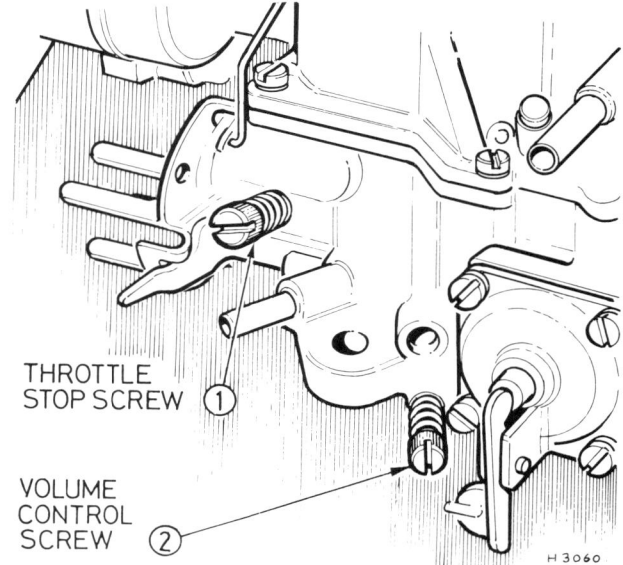
Fig. 3.17 Slow running adjustment screws (Ford) (Sec. 20)

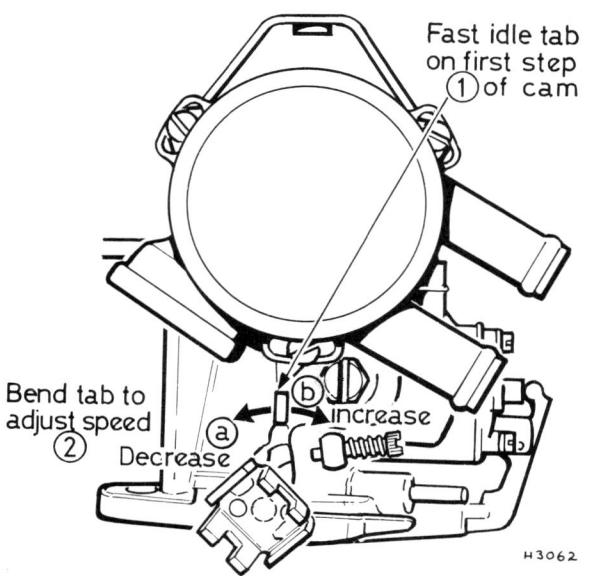
Fig. 3.20 Fast idle adjustment position (Ford) (Sec. 21)

Chapter 3 Carburation, fuel and exhaust systems

housing are slotted to allow for accurate alignment.
42 Using an open-ended spanner refit the main jet to the upper housing.
43 Refit the fuel filter gauze screen into the needle valve housing and refit the needle valve housing.
44 Carefully insert the needle valve into the housing with the needle end upward.
45 Fit a new gasket to the upper body of the carburettor.
46 Refit the float and retain in position using the float arm pivot pin. Check the float setting as detailed in Section 23.
47 Refit the carburettor upper body to the lower body and secure with the six screws and spring washers.
48 Refit the fast idle cam and secure it in position with the screw.

20 Carburettor – slow running adjustment (Ford)

1 If available the idling adjustment is best made with the aid of a vacuum gauge. This connection can be made by disconnecting the blanking plug on the inlet manifold and connecting a suitable adaptor and vacuum gauge.
2 Ensure the engine is at its normal operating temperature and then turn the throttle stop screw to obtain a fast idle.
3 Turn the volume control screws in either direction until a maximum reading is obtained on the vacuum gauge.
4 Readjust the idling speed as required and continue the adjustments until the maximum reading is obtained with the engine running smoothly. See Specifications for recommended speed.
5 To adjust the slow running without a vacuum gauge turn the throttle stop screw clockwise so that the engine is running at a fast idle, then turn the volume control screw in either direction until the engine just runs evenly. Continue the adjustments until the engine will run as slowly as possible, but smoothly, with regular firing and no hint of stalling.
6 On some later models fitted with emission control equipment, the mixture screw is fitted with a sealing plug, the initial correct adjustment position being set up at the factory. If the cap is removed (by prising it out) a new one must be pressed into position over the mixture screw after the adjustment has been made. In countries having strict emission control regulations, the adjustments of the carburettor must be made using a CO meter (exhaust gas analyser) to ensure that the carbon monoxide given off by the exhaust does not exceed the specified reading.

21 Carburettor – choke and fast idle adjustment (Ford)

1 To check the choke control first take off the air cleaner described in Section 2 of this Chapter.
2 It is important that the automatic choke is correctly adjusted so that its operation is reliable at all times. There are four individual adjustments to the system which may be made as follows:
3 **Bi-metal (thermostatic) spring tension.** The position of the housing governs the operating temperature range, although it is pre-set during manufacture and marks are incorporated on the housing to assist with correct reassembly. It should not be necessary to alter the correct setting as indicated by the alignment of the marks, but under certain circumstances it may be adjusted by not more than $\frac{1}{8}$ inch (3·175 mm) in either direction. The bi-metal spring should not, under normal circumstances, need re-positioning from the original location in the spring lever positioned in the centre slot.
4 **Choke plate pull down.**

  a) Remove the air cleaner as detailed in Section 2.
  b) Remove the thermostatic spring and water housing and check that the piston link is fitted to the outer hole in the lever.
  c) With the throttle sufficiently opened so that the fast idle lever tab clears the cam, hold the piston down in its fully depressed position and manually close the choke plate until its movement is stopped by the linkage.
  d) Check the clearance between the lower edge of the choke plate and the inside of the carburettor air intake. This should be between 0.27 and 0.29 inch (6.858 and 7.366 mm) for models fitted with manual transmission and between 0.24 and 0.26 inch (6.096 and 6.604 mm) for models with automatic transmission. A twist drill of suitable size is ideal for this check.
  e) Should this clearance require adjustment, carefully bend the extension of the choke thermostatic spring lever at the part which rests against the choke piston lever until the correct adjustment is obtained.
  f) Check that when the throttle is closed in the pull down position the throttle lever fast idle tab is in the first or high speed stop of the fast idle cam. The position of the stop relative to the tab may be adjusted by bending the fast idle rod at its existing bend.
  g) Carefully align the marks with the centre mark on the inner housing before tightening the screws.

5 **Fast idle.** The fast idle must only be checked with the engine at normal operating temperature and once the choke plate pull down has been tested and set as necessary.
It is recommended that an electric tachometer be obtained and connected into the ignition system. Test and reset the engine idle speed as necessary referring to Section 20.
The throttle lever fast idle tab should next be positioned on the first step of the cam and the tachometer should give the speeds as given in the Specifications. If the readings indicate adjustment is necessary, bend the little tab that contacts the fast idle cam to a new position.
6 **De-choke.** This may only be checked with the choke system fully assembled. Open the throttle fully and hold it against its stop where it should be seen that the choke plate should open from the closed position to give a clearance of 0·315 inch (8·0 mm) between the lower edge of the choke plate and the inside of the carburettor air intake on all models. Use a suitable twist drill as shown in Fig. 3.21 to check this dimension.
Should adjustment be necessary the clearance can be altered by bending the projection on the fast idle cam which is operated by the throttle lever arm.

22 Carburettor – accelerator pump adjustment (Ford)

1 It should not be necessary to adjust the accelerator pump as it is set during manufacture to give the best engine performance at normal ambient temperatures. The stroke of pump can be adjusted as follows:

  a) Screw out the throttle stop screw until the throttle plate is fully closed and depress the diaphragm plunger.
  b) Check the accelerator pump stroke and compare the reading obtained with the figures given in the Specifications at the beginning of this Chapter.
  c) If adjustment is necessary close the gooseneck to lengthen the stroke or expand it to shorten the stroke.

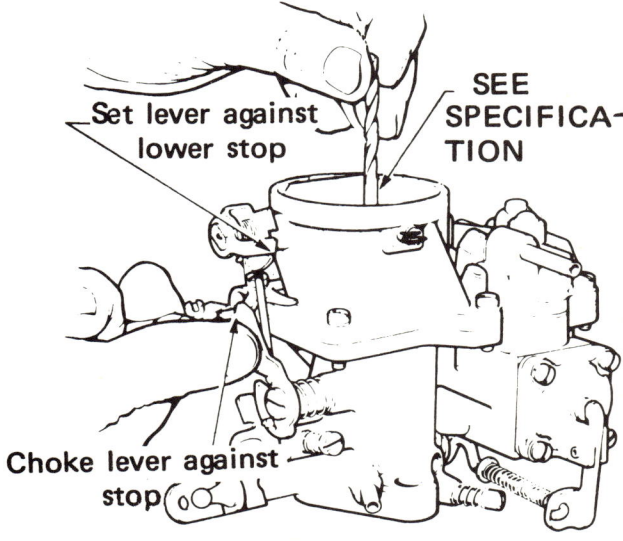

Fig. 3.21 Choke plate de-choke setting (Ford) (Sec. 21)

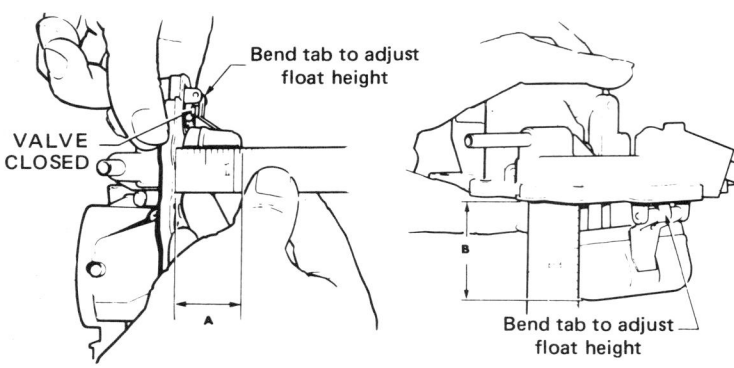

Fig. 3.22 Float and fuel level settings (Ford). Dimensions A and B are given in the Specifications (Sec. 23)

23 Carburettor float level height – adjustment (Ford)

1 Since the height of the float is important to the maintenance of a correct flow of fuel, the correct height is obtained by measurement and adjustment.
2 First remove the air cleaner as detailed in Section 2.
3 Undo and remove the six screws and spring washers that secure the upper body to the lower body of the carburettor.
4 Carefully lift up the upper body and at the same time disconnect the choke link and also ensure that the gasket is not sticking to the lower body.
5 It is important to observe that the accelerator pump discharge valve is exposed in its bore now that the upper body has been removed. Take care that when the throttle is being operated the valve and weight are not ejected and go down the venturi into the engine, necessitating the cylinder heads being removed for recovery!
6 Carefully examine the float for signs of puncture which may be checked by inserting in warm water and watching for air bubbles. Inspect the float arm for signs of fracture, damage or bending and, if satisfactory, the setting should be checked. The correct level and travel dimensions are given in the Specifications at the beginning of this Chapter.
7 If necessary the position of the float may be adjusted by bending the tab that rests on the fuel inlet needle valve and also by bending the tab that rests on the needle valve housing (Fig. 3.22).

24 Carburettor – removal and refitting (Weber)

1 Open the bonnet and remove the air cleaner assembly as detailed in Section 2 of this Chapter.
2 Remove the radiator drain plug and partially drain the cooling system into a container of suitable size.
3 Slacken the clips securing the hoses to the automatic choke housing and carefully separate the hoses from the housing.
4 Disconnect the throttle linkage from the carburettor installation.
5 Release the distributor automatic advance pipe from the side of the carburettor.
6 Slacken the fuel pipe retaining clip at the float chamber and detach the flexible hose.
7 Detach the ventilation tube from the top of the float chamber.
8 Undo the four nuts securing the carburettor flange and remove the nuts and spring washers.
9 Carefully lift away the carburettor and its gasket.
10 Refitting is a straightforward reversal of the removal sequence but note the following additional points:

   a) *Remove all traces of the old carburettor gasket, clean the mating flanges and fit a new gasket in place.*
   b) *Refill the cooling system as detailed in Chapter 2.*
   c) *Check the fuel line and coolant hoses (to automatic choke) for signs of leakage when the engine is running.*

25 Carburettor – dismantling and reassembly (Weber)

1 Before dismantling wash the exterior of the carburettor and wipe dry using a non-fluffy rag. Select a clean area of the workbench and lay several layers of newspaper on the top. Obtain several small containers for putting in some of the small parts that could easily be lost. Whenever a part is to be removed look carefully at it first so that it may be refitted in its original position. As each part is removed place it in order along one edge of the newspaper so that by using this method reassembly is made easier.
2 All parts of the carburettor are shown in Fig. 3.11.
3 Extract the spring clip securing the choke plate connecting rod at its lower end and disconnect the rod at this point.
4 Undo and remove the screws with spring washers securing the float chamber cover to the main body and carefully lift away the cover and its gasket.
5 Carefully extract the float pivot pin and lift out the float assembly followed by the needle valve.
6 Using a box spanner unscrew the needle valve carrier.
7 Undo and remove the three screws from the thermostatic spring and coolant housing retaining ring and lift away the ring, housing and insulating spacer.
8 Disconnect the fast idle connecting rod from the lever on the end of the throttle spindle.
9 Undo and remove the three screws that secure the automatic choke to the carburettor body and lift away the automatic choke.
10 If trouble has been experienced with the automatic choke it may be dismantled. First undo and remove the three screws and spring washers securing the diaphragm cover. Lift away the cover, diaphragm and spring. The stop must be released before the diaphragm rod can be withdrawn. Undo and remove the single screw to remove the fast idle adjustment lever and washer. Next release the return spring and then undo the nut and remove the choke plate operating lever and return spring. Finally remove the washer and withdraw the spindle. Note: *As the cam and stop plate are retained by a brass bush, which is pressed into the housing, it should not be removed.*
11 Obtain a selection of screwdrivers with the ends in good condition and square so that the jets may be removed without damage.
12 Remove the following jets: idling (2), main jet (2), main air correction jet (2), emulsion tube (2), accelerator pump jet (1) (Fig. 3.23).
13 Remove the secondary venturis and the discharge beaks.
14 Undo and remove the single screw and lift away the cover from the end of the throttle spindles. Carefully bend back the locking tab and unscrew the nut on the left-hand spindle.
15 Unscrew the adjusting screw and lift away the gear quadrant. Next remove the lever, return spring and spacer. Then unscrew the two screws securing the throttle plate to the spindle and lift away the throttle plate. Finally the first spindle may be withdrawn.
16 Bend back the second locking tab and unscrew the nut on the right-hand spindle. Lift away the operating lever.
17 Unscrew the adjusting screw and lift away the second gear quadrant, wave washer, choke link and bush. Also remove the stop lever return spring and spacer.
18 Undo the two screws securing the throttle plate to the spindle and lift away the throttle plate. Withdraw the second spindle.
19 Undo the screw at the end of the accelerator pump cam and lift away the screw, retainer and cam.
20 Disconnect the connecting rod at the end of the choke spindle lever. Undo the two screws securing the choke plate to the spindle and lift away the choke plate. Repeat this operation for the second choke plate and withdraw the choke spindle.
21 Undo the fuel filter retainer and lift away the retainer washer and filter from the top cover.

Chapter 3 Carburation, fuel and exhaust systems

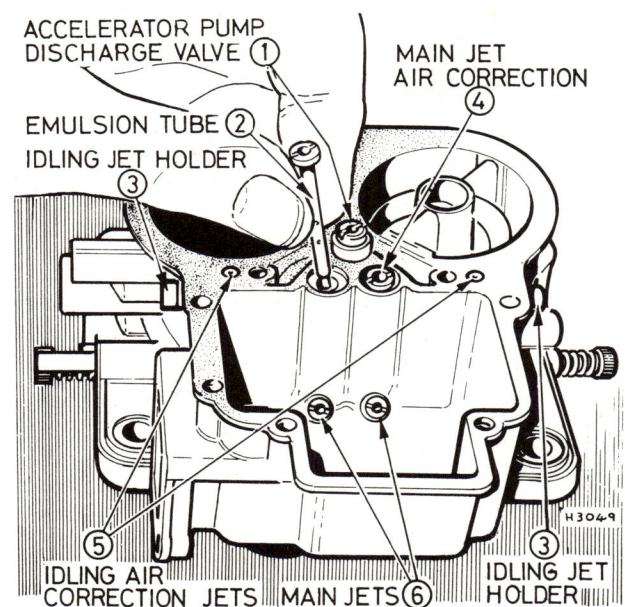

Fig. 3.23 The jet positions (Weber) (Sec. 25)

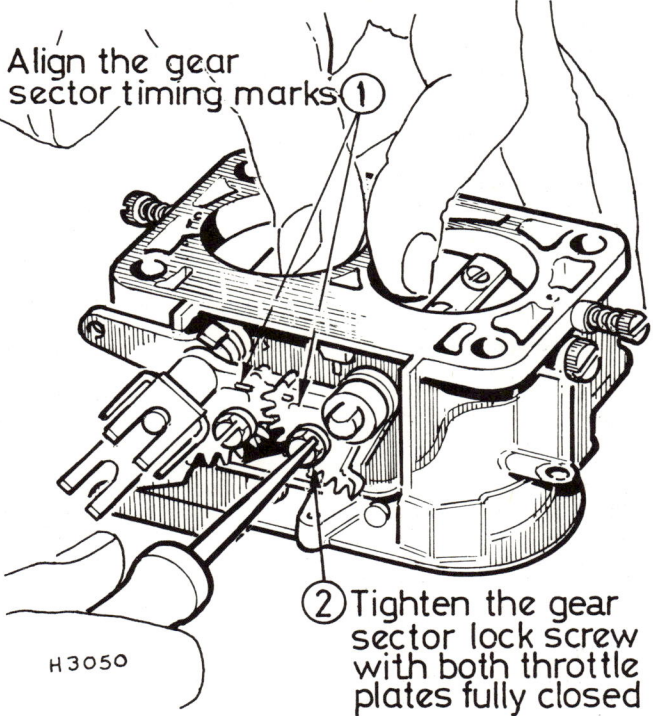

Fig. 3.24 Synchronise the throttle plates (Weber) (Sec. 25)

22 Dismantling is now complete and all parts should be thoroughly washed and cleaned in petrol. Remove any sediment in the float chamber and drillings but take care not to scratch the fine drillings whilst doing so. Remove all traces of old gaskets using a sharp knife. When all parts are clean reassembly can begin.
23 Fit a new gauze filter into the filter housing in the top cover and secure with the filter housing plug and a new washer.
24 Insert the choke spindle into the bores in the body through the air intakes from the right-hand side.
25 Insert one choke plate into its slot in the spindle with the offset portion to the rear. Rotate the spindle several times to centralise the plate and secure the plate with the two screws. Peen over the ends of the screws or apply a locking compound to the threads so that they cannot work loose.
26 Repeat the previous operation for the second choke plate refitment.
27 Insert the right-hand throttle spindle into the bore in the throttle barrel from the float chamber side. This spindle, is the one with the accelerator pump cam attached to one end. The spindle should be positioned so that the countersunk holes are away from the choke tube and the pump cam will then be inclined away from the accelerator pump.
28 Select the right-hand coiled return spring and locate it on the cast spindle boss with the straight tab anchored under the cast lug in the base of the throttle spindle gear sector housing.
29 Fit the thrust washer and stop lever pointing upward onto the spindle and hook the return spring to the lever. Fit the bush and wave washer onto the end of the spindle and then place the fast idle lever onto the bush with the lugs facing away from the carburettor body and the lever to the right-hand side.
30 Fit the gear sector with the extended boss to the right-hand spindle so that it lies within the housing. Next fit the star and plain washers to the lockscrew and centralise it in the slotted hole in the gear sector. Screw the lockscrew into the stop lever.
31 Refit the throttle control lever and secure with a lockplate and nut. Bend the lockplate tab across one of the flats on the nut.
32 Slide one of the throttle plates into the slot in the spindle the correct way round so that the chamfered edge of the plate will completely close the throttle barrel when the idling stop screw is backed off. For information, the angle of the chamfer is 78°, and this is stamped in the face of the plates and should be on the underside of the plate when fitted and facing toward the adjacent throttle barrel.
33 Back off the idling stop screw and rotate the throttle spindle several times so as to centralise the plate in the barrel and on the spindle. Secure the plate with the two screws applying a locking compound to the threads or peening over the ends to stop them working loose.
34 Insert the left-hand throttle spindle into the spindle bore in the throttle barrel with the countersunk holes away from the choke tube.
35 Select the left-hand coiled return spring and locate it on the cast spindle boss with the straight tab anchored under the cast lug in the base of the throttle spindle gear sector housing.
36 Fit the thrust washer and adjustment arm in the manner as detailed in paragraph 29.
37 Fit the gear sector on the spindle and mesh the two sectors so that the two marks are in alignment (Fig. 3.24).
38 Refit the lockplate and nut on the spindle but do not at this stage tighten fully. Refit the star and plain washers to the lockscrew and fit the lockscrew into the slotted hole in the sector. Screw it into the arm on the stop lever but do not tighten fully yet.
39 Fit the throttle plate to the spindle as detailed in paragraphs 32 and 33.
40 Close both throttle plates fully. Tighten the lockscrews and retaining nuts and bend the lockplate tab across one of the flats on the nut.
41 Refit the sector cover and secure with the one countersunk screw.
42 To fit the secondary venturis and discharge beaks into place, locate the arms in the slots in the carburettor barrel and gently press into place. Check that the mixture channels correctly align with the corresponding channels in the carburettor body.
43 Refit the jets.
44 Position the idling jets in their jet holders and fit one to each side of the float chamber. Screw the main jets into position in the float chamber. Insert the emulsion tubes into the emulsion tube well and retain in position with the air correction jets. Finally position the accelerator pump jets, not forgetting to fit a new gasket beneath the assembly, and retain in position with the discharge valve.
45 If the automatic choke assembly was dismantled it should be reassembled next. Slide the automatic choke spindle into the housing. Locate the preload spring on the bush and hook one end onto the fast idle cam. Position the operating lever on the spindle with the lug facing toward the crankpin and adjacent to the tab of the fast idle cam, at the same time engaging the lug with the preload spring hook. Secure with a nut and spring washer.
46 Fit the fast idle relay lever return spring on the cast boss below the fast idle cam locating the spring tab behind the fast idle cam lug. Next fit the washer and relay lever with the lug toward the housing and below the tab of the fast idle cam and secure with the pivot screw.
47 Slide the diaphragm shaft into the housing, locating the diaphragm on the vacuum tube, and fit the cover, retaining it with

three screws and spring washers. Position the adjusting plate in the position from which it was removed and lock with the one securing screw.
48 Refit the automatic choke housing to the carburettor body and secure in position with the three screws and spring washers.
49 Reconnect the fast idle link.
50 Position the heat insulator over the crankpin and onto its dowel. Engage the thermostatic spring with the crankpin and fit the thermostatic spring and water housing in place carefully aligning the mixture setting marks.
51 Refit the locking ring and secure with the three bolts and spring washers.
52 Refit the needle valve housing in the float chamber cover, insert the needle valve and refit the float assembly, securing with the pivot pin to the pivot bracket. Refer to Section 28 and check the float level setting.
53 Refit the float chamber cover to the carburettor body and secure with the five screws and spring washers.
54 Reconnect the choke link and lock with the spring clip.
55 The carburettor is now ready for refitting.

26 Carburettor – slow running adjustment (Weber)

1 If available the idling adjustment is best made with the aid of a vacuum gauge. This connection can be made by disconnecting the blanking plug on the inlet manifold and connecting a suitable adaptor and the carburettor body.
4 To adjust this setting remove the water housing and gently depress the vacuum shaft inward to its maximum travel whilst holding the choke plate towards the closed position using light finger pressure. Move the adjusting plate in either direction as necessary so as to alter the travel of the shaft.

28 Carburettor float level height – adjustment (Weber)

1 Since the height of the float is important in the maintenance of a correct flow of fuel, the correct height is obtained by measurement and adjustment.
2 First remove the float chamber cover retaining screws and lift away from the carburettor body. Carefully examine the float for signs of puncture which may be tested by inserting in warm water and watching for air bubbles.
3 Inspect the float arm for signs of fracture, damage, or bending and, if satisfactory, using a ruler or test gauge with the cover held vertically, check the distance between the float and cover with gasket in place (Fig. 3.28 - left-hand side).
4 If any adjustment is necessary bend the arm between the pivot and the float at the float end to obtain this measurement. Once this setting has been obtained check the float travel (Fig. 3.28 - right-hand side). If necessary the position of the tab that abuts the needle valve housing should be adjusted accordingly.

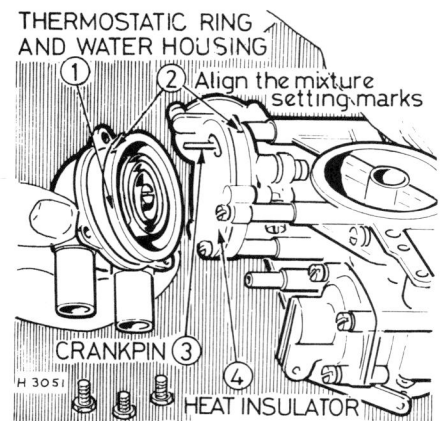

Fig. 3.25 Checking the thermostatic spring and water housing (Weber) (Sec. 25)

Fig. 3.26 Slow running adjustment screws (Weber) (Sec. 26)

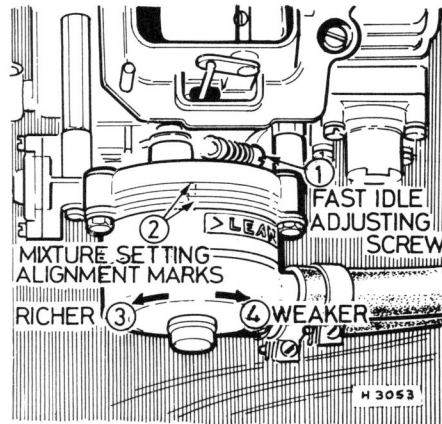

Fig. 3.27 The fast idle and automatic choke adjustment positions (Weber) (Sec. 27)

and vacuum gauge.
2 Ensure the engine is at its normal operating temperature and then turn the throttle stop screw (Fig. 3.26) to obtain a fast idle.
3 Turn the two volume control screws, in either direction until a maximum reading is obtained on the vacuum gauge.
4 Readjust the idling speed as required and continue these adjustments until the maximum vacuum reading is obtained with the engine running smoothly at about 600 rpm.
5 To adjust the slow running without a vacuum gauge turn the throttle stop screw clockwise so that the engine is running at a fast idle, then turn the two volume control screws in either direction until the engine just runs evenly. Continue the adjustments until the engine will run as slowly as possible, but smoothly, with regular firing and no hint of stalling.

27 Carburettor – choke adjustment (Weber)

1 To check the choke control first take off the air cleaner as described in Section 2 of this Chapter.
2 The throttle plate should be open 0·031 to 0·035 in (0·8 to 0·9 mm) when in the fast idle starting position. The measurement of this distance should be between the edge of the throttle plates and the carburettor body whilst the fast idle adjusting screw is on the top stop of the fast idle cam.
3 The choke plate vacuum opening should be set at 0·12 in (3 mm) and this is the distance between the lower edge of the choke plates

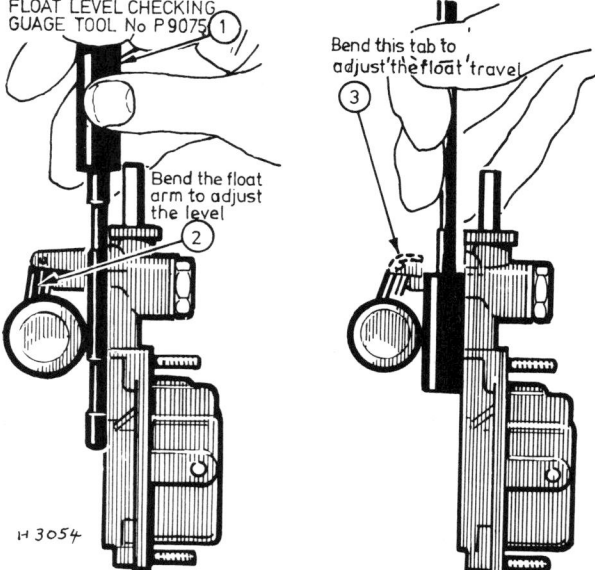

Fig. 3.28 The float level check position (Weber) (Sec. 28)

Chapter 3 Carburation, fuel and exhaust systems

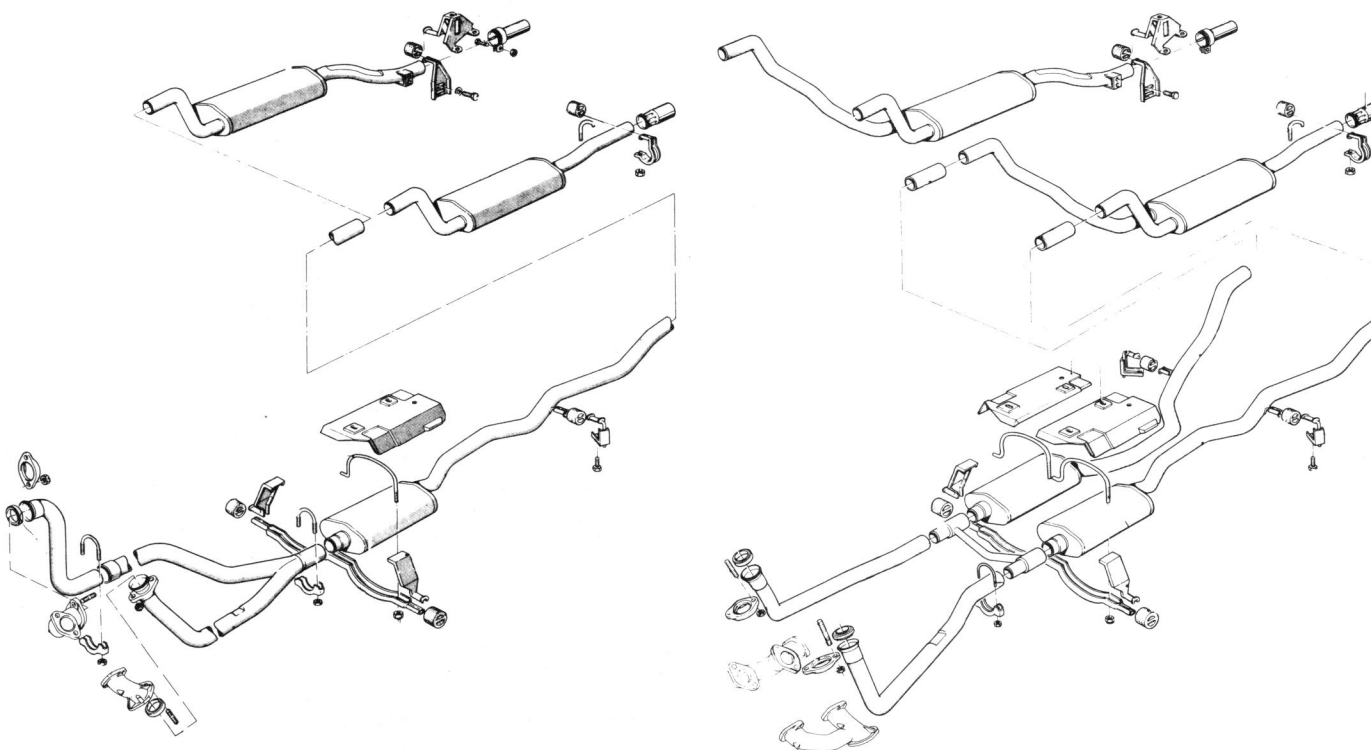

Fig. 3.29 The single pipe exhaust system (Sec. 29)

Fig. 3.30 The twin pipe exhaust system (Sec. 29)

29 Exhaust system

1 The exhaust system layout differs according to model and year, and therefore when the time comes for the renewal of part of the system, it is advisable to remove the offending section and take it along to your Ford agents or local exhaust specialist for renewal. In this manner you will be certain of obtaining the correct part.

2 However, before detaching any part of the exhaust system for repair or renewal, take a closer look at the rest of the system. It's a good bet that if part of the system has rusted through or badly deteriorated then the rest will not be too far behind. In this case consideration should be given to renewing the complete system.

3 Exhaust specialists are to be found in most areas now, and since they usually offer a free fitting service it's not really worth getting your hands soiled.

4 If you wish to do the job yourself or just want to renew part of the system, first obtain the part.

5 If a pit or ramps are not available jack up the car and firmly support with axle stands or blocks before attempting to work underneath the car.

6 Old sections of pipe are usually best cut free with a hacksaw. Apply plenty of penetrating oil to rusted bolts/nuts and joints to assist in freeing them.

7 When installing the new parts, apply some exhaust sealer solution to the joints and always use new pipe clamps.

8 Ensure that the pipes are secure and do not rub against the bodywork and fittings. On restarting the engine, check for leaks around the respective joints.

See overleaf for 'Fault diagnosis – fuel system'.

30 Fault diagnosis – fuel system

Symptom	Reason/s	Remedy
Fuel consumption excessive	Air cleaner choked and dirty giving rich mixture	Remove, clean or renew air cleaner.
	Fuel leaking from carburettor, fuel pump or fuel lines	Check for and eliminate all fuel leaks. Tighten fuel line union nuts.
	Float chamber flooding	Check and adjust float level.
	Generally worn carburettor	Remove, overhaul or renew
	Distributor condenser faulty	Remove and fit new unit.
	Balance weights or vacuum advance mechanism in distributor faulty	Remove and overhaul distributor.
	Carburettor incorrectly adjusted mixture too rich	Tune and adjust carburettor.
	Idling speed too high	Adjust idling speed.
	Contact breaker gap incorrect	Check and reset gap.
	Valve clearances incorrect	Check valve clearances and adjust as necessary.
	Incorrectly set spark plugs	Remove, clean and re-gap.
	Tyres under-inflated	Check tyre pressures and inflate if necessary.
	Wrong spark plugs fitted	Remove and renew with correct units.
	Brakes dragging	Check and adjust brakes.
Insufficient fuel delivery or weak mixture due to air leaks	Petrol tank air vent restricted	Remove petrol cap and clean out air vent.
	Partially clogged filters in pump and carburettor	Remove and clean filters. Remove and clean out float chamber and needle valve assembly.
	Incorrectly seating valves in fuel pump	Remove, overhaul or renew fuel pump.
	Fuel pump diaphragm leaking or damaged	Remove, overhaul or renew fuel pump.
	Gasket in fuel pump damaged	Remove, overhaul or renew fuel pump.
	Fuel pump valves sticking due to petrol gumming	Remove and thoroughly clean fuel pump.
	Too little fuel in fuel tank (prevalent when climbing steep hills)	Refill fuel tank.
	Union joints of pipe connection loose	Tighten joints and check for air leaks.
	Split in fuel pipe on suction side of fuel pump	Examine, locate and repair.
	Inlet manifold to block or inlet manifold to carburettor gasket leaking	Test by pouring oil along joints – bubbles indicate leak. Renew gasket as appropriate.

Chapter 4 Ignition system

Contents

Condenser – removal and refitting	4
Contact breaker points – adjustment	2
Contact breaker points – removal and refitting	3
Distributor (Bosch) – dismantling	8
Distributor (Bosch) – reassembly	11
Distributor (Ford) – dismantling	7
Distributor (Ford) – reassembly	10
Distributor – inspection and repair	9
Distributor – lubrication	5
Distributor – removal and refitting	6
Fault diagnosis – engine fails to start	16
Fault diagnosis – engine misfires	17
General description	1
Ignition system – fault finding	14
Ignition system – fault symptoms	15
Ignition timing	13
Spark plugs and leads	12

Specifications

Spark plugs
Type:
- V4 and V6 .... Motorcraft AGR 22 DB–14 mm
- 2.0 litre ohc .... Motorcraft BF32–18 mm taper seat

Gap:
- V4 and V6 .... 0.025 in (0.64 mm)
- 2.0 litre ohc .... 0.025 in (0.64 mm)

Ignition coil
Type .... Low voltage used in conjunction with 1.5 ohm ballast resistor

Resistance at 20°C (68°F):
- Primary .... 0.95 to 1.6 ohms
- Secondary .... 5000–9300 ohms

Distributor (V4 and V6)
Type .... Motorcraft or Bosch
Automatic advance .... Mechanical and vacuum
Rotation .... Clockwise when viewed from top
Shaft endfloat .... 0.0005–0.00075 in (0.013–0.019 mm)

Colour code:
- 2.0 litre V4 .... Red
- 2.5 litre V6 .... Green
- 3.0 litre V6 .... Red

Initial advance .... Up to 1975, 10° BTDC (all models); 1975 on, 14° BTDC (V6 models only)

Condenser capacity .... 0.21–0.25 mfd

Contact breaker points gap:
- Motorcraft .... 0.025 in (0.64 mm)
- Bosch (V6) .... 0.012–0.016 in (0.3–0.4 mm)

Dwell angle:
- V4 .... 48°–52°
- V6 .... 36°–40°

Distributor (2.0 litre ohc)
Type .... Bosch
Automatic advance .... Mechanical and vacuum
Rotation .... Clockwise when viewed from top
Shaft endfloat .... 0.021–0.052 in (0.55–1.31 mm)
Colour code .... Blue

Initial advance:
- Consul .... 4° BTDC
- Granada from 1975 .... 8° BTDC

Condenser capacity .... 0.18–0.26 mfd
Contact breaker points gap .... 0.016–0.020 in (0.4–0.5 mm)
Dwell angle .... 50° ± 2°

Firing order
- V4 and 2.0 litre ohc 1–3–4–2
- V6 1–4–2–5–3–6

Chapter 4 Ignition system

1 General description

In order that a petrol engine can run correctly, it is necessary for an electrical spark to ignite the fuel/air mixture in the combustion chamber at exactly the right moment in relation to engine speed and load. The ignition system is based on feeding low tension voltage from the battery to the coil where it is converted into high tension voltage. The high tension voltage is powerful enough to jump the spark plug gap in the cylinders many times a second under high compression pressures.

The ignition system is divided into two circuits. The low tension (LT) circuit and the high tension (HT) circuit. These are shown in Fig. 4.1.

The low tension circuit (sometimes known as the primary circuit) consists of the battery, ignition switch, ignition coil low tension windings, contact breaker points and condenser in the distributor.

The high tension circuit consists of the high tension windings in the ignition coil, the rotor arm, spark plugs and associated HT cables.

The system fuctions in the following manner: Low tension voltage is changed in the coil into high tension voltage by the opening and closing of the contact breaker points in the low tension circuit. High tension voltage is then fed via the carbon brush in the centre of the distributor cap to the rotor arm in the distributor cap, and each time it comes into line with one of the metal segments in the cap, which are connected to the spark plug leads, the opening and closing of the contact breaker points causes the high tension voltage to build up, jump the gap from the rotor arm to the appropriate segment and so to the spark plug, where it finally jumps the spark plug gap before going to earth.

The ignition is advanced and retarded automatically, to ensure that the spark occurs at just the right instant for the particular load at the prevailing engine speed.

The ignition advance is controlled both mechanically and by a vacuum operated system. The mechanical governor mechanism comprises two weights, which move out from the distributor shaft as the engine speed rises due to centrifugal force. As they move outwards they rotate the cam relative to the distributor shaft and so advance the spark. The weights are held in position by two light springs and it is the tension of the springs which is largely responsible for correct spark advancement.

The vacuum control consists of a diaphragm, one side of which is connected via a small bore tube to the carburettor, and the other side to the contact breaker plate. Depression in the inlet manifold and carburettor, which varies with engine speed and throttle opening, causes the diaphragm to move, so moving the contact breaker plate, and advancing or retarding the spark. A fine degree of control is achieved by a spring in the vacuum assembly.

To facilitate cold engine starting a high output ignition coil, incorporating a series resistance wire is fitted. When the starter motor is operated the series resistor is disconnected and full battery is fed to the ignition coil. When the starter motor stops the resistor automatically operates to reduce the current to the coil.

2 Contact breaker points – adjustment

1 To adjust the contact breaker points to the correct gap, first release the two spring clips securing the distributor cap to the distributor body, and lift away the cap. Clean the cap inside and out with a dry cloth. It is unlikely that the four segments will be badly burned or scored, but if they are the cap will have to be renewed. Light carbon deposits can be cleaned from the segments by scraping with a penknife.
2 Inspect the carbon brush contact located in the top of the cap see that it is unbroken and stands proud of the plastic surface.
3 Check the contact spring on the top of the rotor arm. It must be clean and have adequate tension to ensure good contact.
4 Gently prise the contact breaker points open to examine the condition of their faces. If they are rough, pitted, or dirty, it will be necessary to remove them for re-surfacing, or for new points to be fitted.
5 Assuming that the points are satisfactory, or that they have been cleaned and renewed, measure th gap between the points by turning the engine over until the heel of the breaker arm is on the highest point of the cam (photo).
6 A feeler gauge of the specified thickness should now just fit between the points.
7 If the gap varies from this amount slacken the contact plate securing screws.
8 Adjust the contact gap by inserting a screwdriver in the shaped hole in the breaker plate. Turn clockwise to increase and anti-clockwise to decrease the gap. When the gap is correct tighten the securing screws and check the gap again (photo).
9 Making sure the rotor is fully in position refit the distributor cap and clip the spring blade retainers into position.

3 Contact breaker points – removal and refitting

1 If the contact breaker points are burned, pitted or badly worn, they must be removed and either renewed or their faces must be filed smooth. The contact breaker points fitted are mounted on the breaker plate and the assembly must be renewed as a complete unit.
2 Lift off the rotor arm by pulling it straight up from the top end of

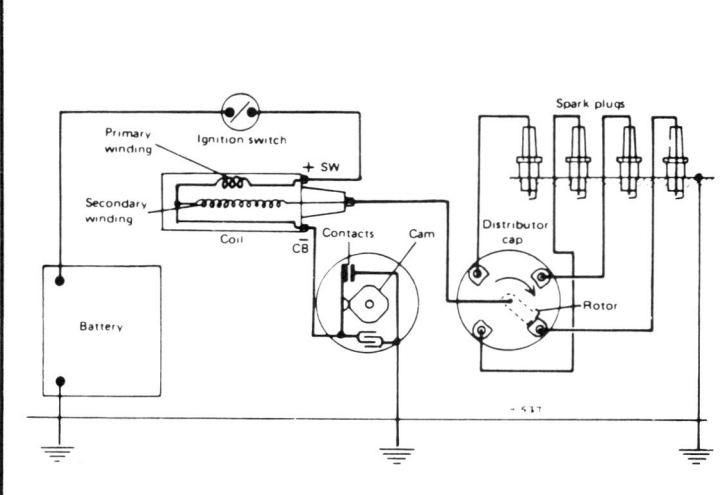
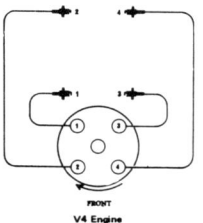
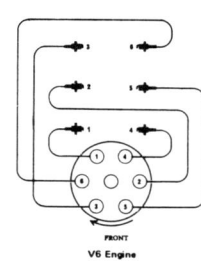

Fig. 4.1 Ignition system theoretical wiring diagram. The in-line ohc engine arrangement is shown, but theory is the same for V4 and V6 engines. HT lead arrangements for 'V' series engines shown inset (Sec. 1)

Chapter 4 Ignition system

2.5 Checking the contact breaker points gap

2.8 Resetting the points gap

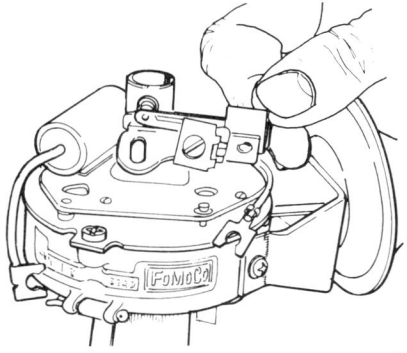

Fig. 4.2 Removing the contact breaker points assembly (Ford distributor) (Sec. 3)

the cam spindle.
3 Slacken the self-tapping screw securing the condenser and low tension lead to the contact breaker point assembly. Slide out the forked ends of the lead terminals.
4 Undo and remove the two screws which secure the contact breaker points baseplate to the distributor baseplate. Lift away the points assembly.
5 To refit the points is the reverse sequence to removal. Smear a trace of grease onto the cam to lubricate the moving point heel, and then reset the gap as described in Section 2.
6 Should the contact breaker points be badly worn, a new set must be fitted. As an emergency measure clean the faces with fine emery paper folded over a thin steel rule. When the surfaces are flat a feeler gauge can be used to reset the gap.
7 Finally refit the rotor arm and distributor cap. Retain in position with the two clips.

4 Condenser – removal and refitting

1 The purpose of the condenser (sometimes known as a capacitor) is to ensure that when the contact breaker points open there is no sparking across them which would waste voltage and cause rapid wear.
2 The condenser is fitted in parallel with the contact breaker points. If it develops a short circuit, it will cause ignition failure as the contact breaker points will be prevented from correctly interrupting the low tension circuit.
3 If the engine becomes very difficult to start or begins to miss after several miles of running and the breaker points show signs of excessive burning then the condition of the condenser must be suspect. One further test can be made by separating the points by hand with the ignition switched on. If this is accompanied by a bright flash, it is indicative that the condenser has failed.
4 Without special test equipment the only safe way to diagnose condenser trouble is to replace a suspected unit with a new one and note if there is any improvement.
5 To remove the condenser from the distributor take off the distributor cap and rotor arm.
6 Slacken the self-tapping screw holding the condenser lead and low tension lead to the contact breaker points. Slide out the forked terminal on the end of the condenser low tension lead. Undo and remove the condenser retaining screw and remove the condenser from the breaker plate.
7 To refit the condenser, simply reverse the order of removal.

5 Distributor – lubrication

1 It is important that the distributor cam is lubricated sparingly with petroleum jelly or grease at 3000 miles (5000 km) or 3 monthly intervals. Also the automatic timing control weights and cam spindle are lubricated with engine oil.
2 Great care should be taken not to use too much lubricant as any excess that finds its way onto the contact breaker points could cause burning and misfiring.
3 To gain access to the cam spindle, lift away the distributor cap and rotor arm. Apply no more than two drops of engine oil onto the felt pad. This will run down the spindle when the engine is hot and lubricate the bearings.
4 To lubricate the automatic timing control allow a few drops of oil to pass through the holes in the contact breaker baseplate through which the four-sided cam emerges. Apply not more than one drop of oil to the pivot post of the moving contact breaker point. Wipe away excess oil and refit the rotor arm and distributor cap.

6 Distributor – removal and refitting

1 To remove the distributor from the engine, first mark the spark plug leads for correct identification for refitting, and pull off the terminals from the spark plugs. Release the Lucar connector which connects the low tension lead to the lead emerging from the side of the distributor body. Also disconnect the high tension lead from the centre of the coil.
2 Disconnect the vacuum line from the vacuum unit on the side of the distributor.
3 Rotate the engine until the appropriate timing marks on the crankshaft pulley and timing cover line up as No. 1 piston is coming up on the compression stroke. Check that the right stroke is obtained by removing the spark plug, and with the thumb over the spark plug hole the compression pressure should be felt (Figs. 4.3a and 4.3b).
4 Mark the position of the rotor in relation to the distributor body to facilitate refitting of the distributor, assuming of course that the crankshaft will not be turned over to alter the position whilst the distributor is removed.
5 Undo the bolt that secures the shaped clamp to the distributor body pedestal. Lift away the bolt, spring washer and the shaped clamp. The distributor may now be lifted away from the engine.
6 To refit the distributor check the engine timing marks are in alignment as detailed in paragraph 3 of this Section.
7 Line up the recessed end of the skew gear retaining pin with the groove on the lower part of the distributor body.
8 Place the distributor in position on the engine so that the vacuum advance unit faces forward. As the two skew gears mesh the rotor arm should rotate until it points towards the No. 1 HT segment in the distributor cap. This may be checked by refitting the cap and noting the position of the rotor arm relative to No. 1 HT lead. Take care, however, to remember that No. 1 HT segment is the right-hand rear one when the distributor is correctly fitted.
9 Refit the shaped clamp on top of the wire clip fitted to the distributor body pedestal and secure the clamp in place with the bolt and spring washer.
10 Refit the distributor cap and reconnect the high tension cables to the spark plugs in their correct order as previously identified. Reconnect the vacuum pipe to the vacuum unit on the side of the distributor.
11 Refer to Section 13 and accurately set the ignition timing.

7 Distributor (Ford) – dismantling

1 With the distributor on the bench pull off the two spring clips retaining the cover and lift the cover off. (See Fig. 4.4 for the position of the relative parts).
2 Pull the rotor arm off the distributor cam spindle.

Chapter 4 Ignition system

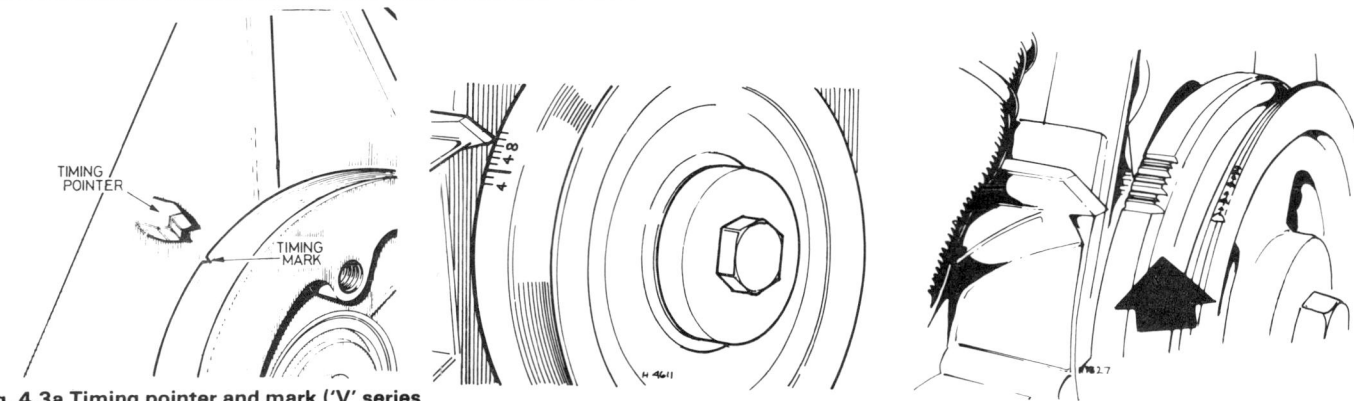

Fig. 4.3a Timing pointer and mark ('V' series engines) (Sec. 6). For details of representation see Chapter 13

Fig. 4.3b Timing marks (2·0 litre ohc engine) – alternative types shown (Sec. 6)

3 Remove the points from the breaker plates as detailed in Section 3.
4 Undo the condenser retaining screw and take off the condenser (photo).
5 Next prise off the small circlip from the vacuum unit pivot post.
6 Take out the two screws holding the breaker plate to the distributor body and lift away.
7 Take off the circlip, flat washer and wave washer from the pivot post. Separate the two plates by bringing the holding-down screw through the keyhole slot in the lower plate. Be careful not to lose the spring now left on the pivot post.
8 Pull the low tension wire and grommet from the lower plate.
9 Undo the two screws holding the vacuum unit to the body. Take off the unit (photo).
10 To dismantle the vacuum unit unscrew the bolt on the end of the unit and withdraw the vacuum spring, stop and shims.
11 The mechanical advance is next removed, but first make a careful note of the assembly, particularly which spring fits which post and the position of the advance springs. Then remove the advance springs.
12 Prise off the circlips from the governor weight pivot pins and take out the weights.
13 Dismantle the shaft by taking out the felt pad in the top of the spindle. Expand the exposed circlip and take it out (photo).
14 Now mark which slot in the mechanical advance plate is occupied by the advance stop which stands up from the action plate, and lift off the cam spindle (photo).
15 It is necessary to remove the lower shaft and action plate only if it is excessively worn. If this is the case, with a small punch drive out the gear retaining pin and remove the gear with the two washers located above it.
16 Withdraw the shaft from the distributor body and take off the two washers from below the action plate. The distributor is now completely dismantled.

7.4 The V6 distributor with cap and rotor removed

A – Contact breaker points retaining screws
B – Condenser retaining screw
C – Pivot post, C-clip and washer

8 Distributor (Bosch) – dismantling

1 With the distributor removed to the workbench, release the two spring clips retaining the cap and lift the cap clear.
2 Withdraw the rotor arm from the distributor cam spindle.
3 Refer to Section 3 and remove the contact breaker points.
4 Unscrew and remove the condenser retaining screw and detach the condenser with connector.
5 Carefully remove the 'U' shaped clip from the vacuum unit pull rod.
6 The vacuum unit is now removed from the distributor body by

7.9 Vacuum unit retaining screws (A) and advance springs (B)

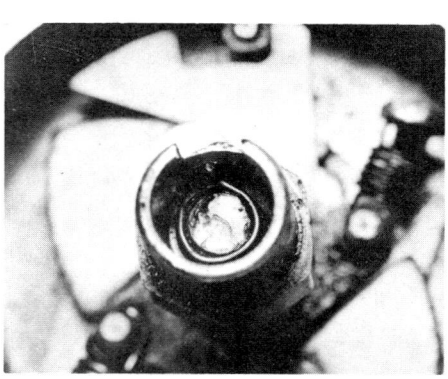

7.13 Extracting the spindle retaining clip

7.14 Removing the cam spindle

Chapter 4 Ignition system

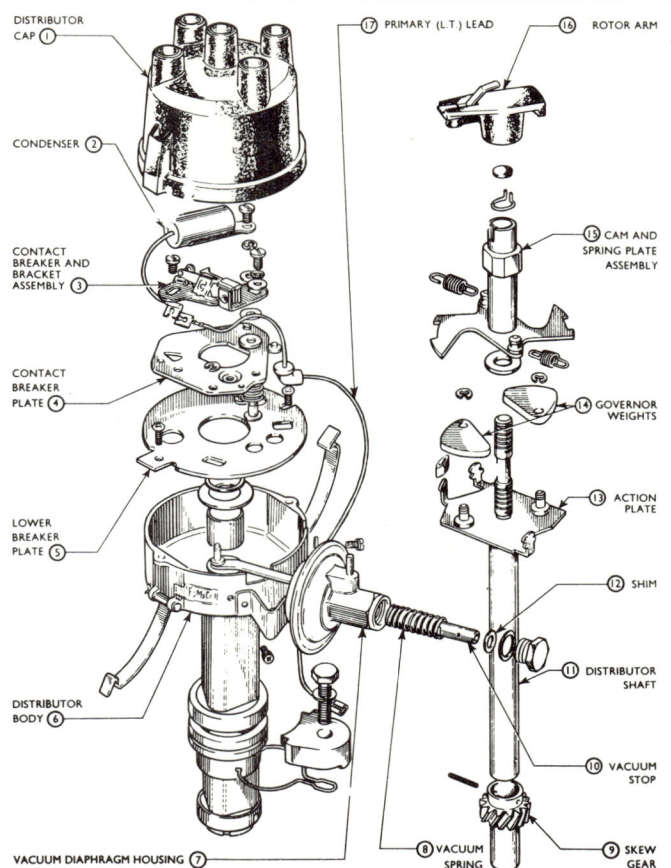

Fig. 4.4 The Motorcraft (Ford) distributor component parts. The distributor shown is for V4 engine – that for V6 is similar except for cam and cap (Sec. 7)

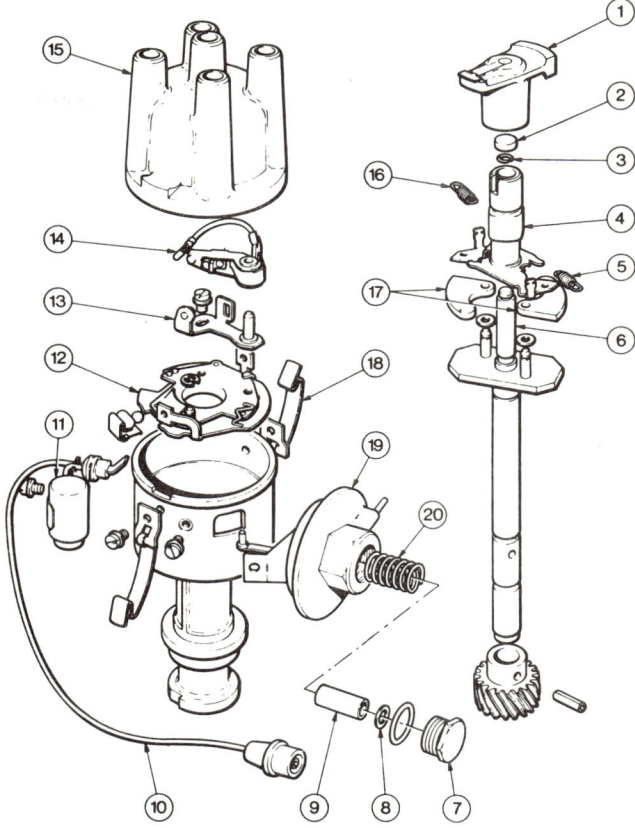

Fig. 4.5 Component part of Bosch distributor*

1	Rotor	11	Condenser
2	Felt	12	Base plate
3	Circlip	13	Points assembly
4	Cam	14	Points assembly
5	Advance spring	15	Cap
6	Shaft	16	Spring
7	Plug	17	Advance weights
8	Plate	18	Clip
9	Spacer	19	Vacuum unit
10	LT lead	20	Spring

* Distributors may differ slightly in detail.

undoing the two retaining screws and lifting the unit clear.
7 To release the breaker plate assembly, undo and remove the distributor cap spring clip retaining screws and lift clear.
8 From inside the distributor body lift clear the breaker plate assembly.
9 Remove the spring clip securing the lower and upper plates together.
10 Before removing the primary and secondary springs of the automatic advance system, they must be marked so that on reassembly they are correctly repositioned. Mark the springs and weights in their respective relation to the upper plate.
11 Referring to Fig. 4.6, unhook the springs from the posts on the centrifugal weights.

12 Release the cam from the spindle using a suitable screwdriver as a lever as shown in Fig. 4.7. Recover the felt pad, lock-ring and thrust

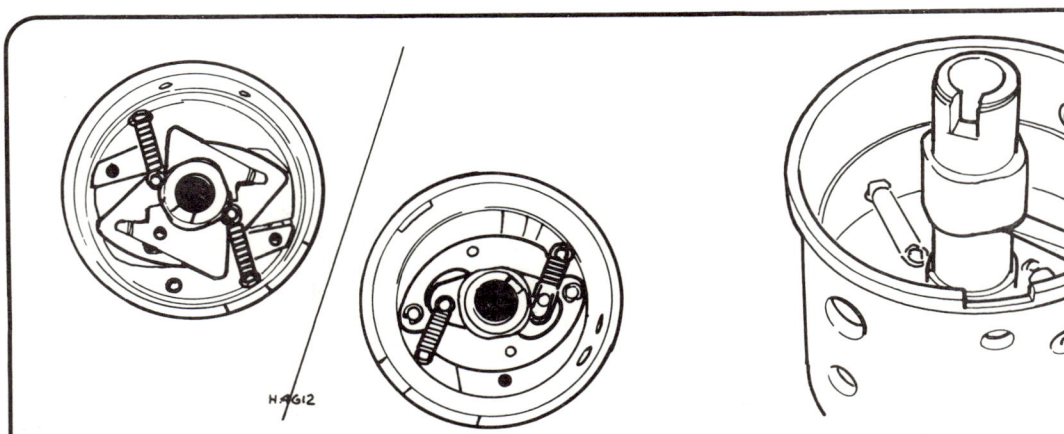

Fig. 4.6 The correct spring location (Bosch distributor) (Sec. 8)

Left – early type   *Right – later type*

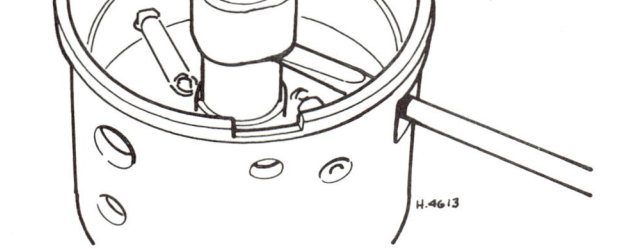

Fig. 4.7 Removal of cam from cam spindle (Bosch) (Sec. 8)

washers. Unhook the two springs from the cam plate and withdraw the centrifugal weights and washers.

13 If removing the drive gear, use a suitable diameter parallel pin punch and drive out the gear lock pin, taking care not to damage the teeth of the gear. Support the gear and shaft during removal.

14 To withdraw the gear from the shaft, having removed the pin, use a universal puller as shown in Fig. 4.8.

15 Finally remove the shaft from the distributor body.

9 Distributor – inspection and repair

1 Check the points as described in Section 2. Check the distributor cap for signs of tracking, indicated by a thin black line between the segments. Renew the cap if any signs of tracking are found.

2 If the metal portion of the rotor arm is badly burned or loose, renew the arm. If only slightly burned, clean the end with a fine file. Check that the contact spring has adequate pressure and the bearing surface is clean and in good condition.

3 Check that the carbon brush in the distributor cap is unbroken and stands proud of its holder.

4 Examine the weights and pivots for wear and the advance springs for slackness. They can best be checked by comparing with new parts. If they are slack they must be renewed.

5 Check the points assembly for fit on the breaker plate and the cam follower for wear.

6 Examine the fit of the lower shaft in the distributor body. If this is excessively worn it will be necessary to fit a new assembly.

10 Distributor (Ford) – reassembly

1 Reassembly is a straightforward reversal of the dismantling process, but there are several points which must be noted.

2 Lubricate with engine oil the weights and other parts of the mechanical advance mechanism, the distributor shaft, and the portion of the shaft on which the cam bears, during assembly. Do not oil excessively, but ensure these parts are adequately lubricated.

3 When fitting the lower shaft, first refit the thrust washers below the action plate before inserting into the distributor body. Next fit the wave washer and thrust washer at the lower end and refit the drive gear. Secure it with a new pin.

4 Assemble the upper and lower shaft with the advance stop in the correct slot (the one which was marked) in the mechanical advance plate.

5 After assembling the advance weights and springs, check that they move freely without binding.

6 Before assembling the breaker plates make sure that the three nylon bearing studs are properly located in their holes in the upper breaker points, and that the small earth spring is fitted on the pivot post.

7 As you refit the upper breaker plate pass the holding-down spindle through the keyhole slot in the lower plate (photo).

8 Hold the upper plate in position by refitting the spring clip (photos).

9 When all is assembled, remember to set the contact breaker gap to that specified as described in Section 2.

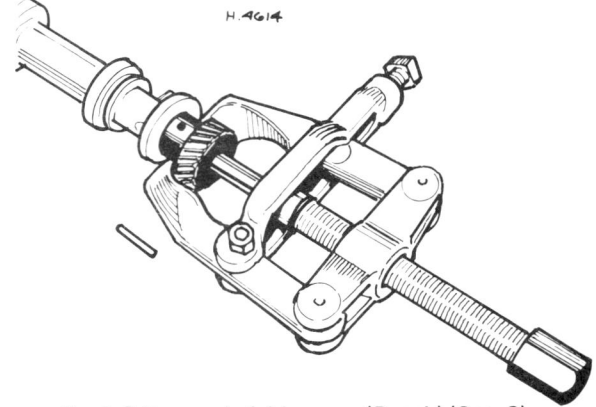

Fig. 4.8 Removal of drive gear (Bosch) (Sec. 8)

10 If a new gear and/or shaft are to be fitted, a new pin hole will have to be drilled. If fitting a new gear to a used shaft, ensure that the shaft is not badly worn or buckled. If the shaft is worn or distorted in any way fit a new one, as the new gear will otherwise suffer from premature wear and possible tooth breakage. To fit a new gear and/or shaft proceed as follows:

11 Make a 0.004 inch (0.10 mm) forked shim to slide over the driveshaft.

12 Assemble the shaft, wave washer, thrust washer, shim and gear wheel in position in the distributor body.

13 Hold the assembly in a large clamp such as a vice or carpenter's clamp using only sufficient pressure to take up all end play.

14 There is a pilot hole in a new gear wheel for drilling the new hole. Set this pilot at 90° to the existing hole if the old shaft is being reused. Drill $\frac{1}{8}$ inch (3.18 mm) hole through both gear and shaft.

15 Fit a new pin in the hole. Release the clamp and remove the shim. The shaft will now have the correct amount of clearance.

16 When fitting an existing gear wheel still in good condition to a new shaft drill a new pin hole through the gear wheel at 90° to the existing hole. Secure with a new pin.

11 Distributor (Bosch) – reassembly

1 To reassemble first refit the two centrifugal weight washers onto the cam spindle. Smear a little grease onto the centrifugal weight contact faces and pivots and refit the weights in their original positions.

2 Lubricate the upper end of the spindle with engine oil and slide on the cam. Hold the two springs onto the weight retainers so that they are refitted in their original positions.

3 Position the thrust washer and lock-ring in the cam. Carefully manipulate the lock-ring into position using a thin electrician's screwdriver.

4 Refit the felt pad and thoroughly soak with engine oil.

5 Lubricate the distributor spindle with engine oil and insert it into the housing. The gear may now be tapped into position taking care to

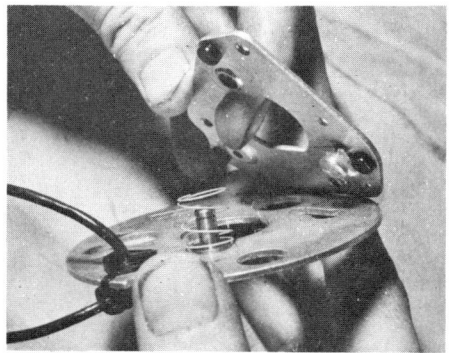

10.7 Reassembling the breaker plate

10.8a Refitting the spring clip to the breaker plate post

10.8b The breaker plate correctly assembled

Measuring plug gap. A feeler gauge of the correct size (see ignition system specifications) should have a slight 'drag' when slid between the electrodes. Adjust gap if necessary

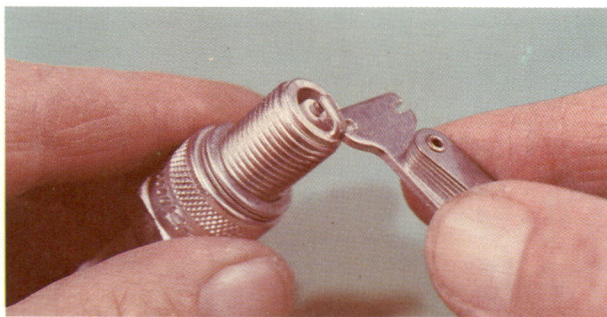

Adjusting plug gap. The plug gap is adjusted by bending the earth electrode inwards, or outwards, as necessary until the correct clearance is obtained. Note the use of the correct tool

Normal. Grey-brown deposits lightly coated core nose. Gap increasing by around 0.001 in (0.025 mm) per 1000 miles (1600 km). Plugs ideally suited to engine and engine in good condition

Carbon fouling. Dry, black, sooty deposits. Will cause weak spark and eventually misfire. Fault: over-rich fuel mixture. Check: carburettor mixture settings, float level and jet sizes; choke operation and cleanliness of air filter. Plugs can be re-used after cleaning

Oil fouling. Wet, oily deposits. Will cause weak spark and eventually misfire. Fault: worn bores/piston rings or valve guides; sometimes occurs (temporarily) during running-in period. Plugs can be re-used after thorough cleaning

Overheating. Electrodes have glazed appearance, core nose very white - few deposits. Fault: plug overheating. Check: plug value, ignition timing, fuel octane rating (too low) and fuel mixture (too weak). Discard plugs and cure fault immediately

Electrode damage. Electrodes burned away; core nose has burned, glazed appearance. Fault: initial pre-ignition. Check: as for 'Overheating' but may be more severe. Discard plugs and remedy fault before piston or valve damage occurs

Split core nose (may appear initially as a crack). Damage is self-evident, but cracks will only show after cleaning. Fault: pre-ignition or wrong gap-setting technique. Check: ignition timing, cooling system, fuel octane rating (too low) and fuel mixture (too weak). Discard plugs, rectify fault immediately

line up the lock pin holes in the gear and spindle. Support the spindle whilst performing this operation.

6 Fit a new lock pin to the gear and spindle and make sure that it is symmetrically positioned.

7 Locate the lower breaker plate in the distributor body. Fit the distributor cap retaining spring clip and retainers on the outside of the distributor body and secure the retainers and lower breaker plate with the two screws.

8 Position the contact breaker point assembly in the breaker plate in such a manner that the entire lower surface of the assembly contacts the plate. Refit the contact breaker point assembly securing screw but do not fully tighten yet.

9 Hook the diaphragm assembly pull rod into contact with the pivot pin.

10 Secure the diaphragm to the distributor body with the two screws. Also refit the condenser to the terminal side of the diaphragm bracket securing screw. The condenser must firmly contact its lower stop on the housing.

11 Apply a little grease or petroleum jelly to the cam and also to the heel of the breaker lever.

12 Reset the contact breaker points, as described in Section 2, and then refit the rotor arm and distributor cap.

12 Spark plugs and leads

1 The correct functioning of the spark plugs is vital for the correct running and efficiency of the engine.

2 At intervals of 6000 miles (10000 km) the plugs should be removed, examined, cleaned, and if worn excessively, renewed. The condition of the spark plugs will also tell much about the overall condition of the engine (refer to illustrations on page 121).

3 If the insulator nose of the spark plug is clean and white, with no deposits, this is indicative of a weak mixture, or too hot a plug.

4 If the tip and insulator nose is covered with hard black-looking deposits, then this is indicative that the mixture is too rich. Should the plug be black and oily, then it is likely that the engine is fairly worn, as well as the mixture being too rich.

5 If the insulator nose is covered with light tan to greyish brown deposits, then the mixture is correct and it is likely that the engine is in good condition.

6 If there are any traces of long brown tapering stains on the outside of the white portion of the plug, then the plug will have to be renewed, as this shows that there is a faulty joint between the plug body and the insulator, and compression is being allowed to leak away.

7 Plugs should be cleaned by a sand blasting machine, which will free them from carbon deposits more thoroughly than cleaning by hand. The machine will also test the condition of the plugs under compression. Any plug that fails to spark at the recommended pressure should be renewed.

8 The spark plug gap is of considerable importance, as if it is too large or too small, the size of the spark and its efficiency will be seriously impaired. The spark plug gap should be set to the figure given in the Specifications at the beginning of this Chapter.

9 To set it, measure the gap with a feeler gauge, and then bend open, or close, the outer plug electrode until the correct gap is achieved. The centre electrode should never be bent as this may crack the insulation and cause plug failure if nothing worse.

10 When refitting the plugs, remember to refit the leads from the distributor in the correct firing order as given in the Specifications.

11 The plug leads require no routine attention other than being wiped over regularly and kept clean. At intervals of 6000 miles (10000 km), however, pull the leads off the plugs and distributor one at a time and make sure no water has found its way onto the connections. Remove any corrosion from the brass ends, wipe the collars on top of the distributor, and refit the leads.

13 Ignition timing

1 When a new distributor gear has been fitted or the engine has been rotated, or if a new distributor assembly is being fitted it will be necessary to re-time the ignition. Carry it out this way:

2 Look up the initial advance for the particular model in the Specifications at the beginning of the Chapter.

3 Turn the engine until No. 1 piston is coming up to TDC on the compression stroke. This can be checked by removing No. 1 spark plug and feeling the pressure being developed in the cylinder. The engine can be turned by engaging top gear and edging the car along (manual gearbox only), or rotating the crankshaft pulley retaining bolt.

4 Continue turning the engine until the appropriate timing marks on the timing cover and crankshaft pulley line up. This setting must be correct for the initial advance for the engine, as given in the Specifications.

5 Place the distributor in position on the engine so that the vacuum advance unit faces forward. As the two skew gears mesh the rotor arm should rotate until it points toward the No. 1 HT segment in the distributor cap. This may be checked by refitting the cap and noting the position of the rotor arm relative to No. 1 HT lead. Take care to remember that No. 1 HT segment is the right-hand rear one when the distributor is correctly fitted.

6 Fit the clamp plate retaining bolt and spring washer and lightly tighten it.

7 Gently turn the distributor body until the contact breaker points are just opening when the rotor is pointing at the contact in the distributor cap which is connected to No. 1 spark plug. A convenient way is to put a mark on the outside of the distributor body in line with the terminal on the cap, so that it shows when the cap is removed.

8 If this position cannot easily be reached check that the drive gear has meshed on the correct tooth by lifting out the distributor once more. If necessary, rotate the driveshaft one tooth and try again.

9 Tighten the distributor clamp plate retaining bolt fully.

10 Set in this way the timing should be correct, but small adjustments may be made by slackening the distributor clamp bolt once more and rotating the distributor body clockwise to advance and anti-clockwise to retard.

11 The setting of a distributor, including the amount of vacuum and mechanical advance, can be accurately carried out only on an electronic tester. Alterations to the vacuum advance shims or tension on the mechanical advance unit springs will change the characteristics of the unit.

12 Since the ignition timing setting enables the firing point to be correctly related to the grade of fuel used, the fullest advantage of a change of grade from that recommended for the engine will only be achieved by readjustment of the ignition setting.

14 Ignition system – fault finding

By far the majority of breakdowns and running troubles are caused by faults in the ignition system, either in the low tension or high tension circuits.

15 Ignition system – fault symptoms

There are two main symptoms indicating ignition faults. Either the engine will not start and fire, or the engine is difficult to start and misfires. If it is a regular misfire, ie the engine is running on only two or three cylinders, the fault is almost sure to be in the secondary, or high tension circuit. If the misfiring is intermittent, the fault could be either the high or low tension circuits. If the car stops suddenly, or will not start at all, it is likely that the fault is in the low tension circuit. Loss of power and overheating, apart from faulty carburation settings, are normally due to faults in the distributor or incorrect ignition timing.

16 Fault diagnosis – engine fails to start

1 If the engine fails to start and the car was running normally when it was last used, first check there is fuel in the petrol tank. If the engine turns over normally on the starter motor and the battery is evidently well charged, then the fault may be in either the high or low tension circuits. First check the HT circuit. **Note:** *If the battery is known to be fully charged, the ignition light comes on, and the starter motor fails to turn the engine, check the tightness of the leads on the battery terminals and also the secureness of the earth lead to its connection to the body. It is quite common for the leads to have worked loose, even if they look and feel secure. If one of the battery terminal posts gets very hot when trying to work the starter motor this is a sure indication of a faulty connection to that terminal.*

2 One of the commonest reasons for bad starting is wet or damp

Chapter 4 Ignition system

spark plug leads and distributor. Remove the distributor cap. If condensation is visible internally dry the cap with a rag and also wipe over the leads. Refit the cap.

3 If the engine still fails to start, check that current is reaching the plugs, by disconnecting each plug lead in turn at the spark plug end, and holding the end of the cable about $\frac{1}{4}$ in (6 mm) away from the cylinder block. Spin the engine on the starter motor.

4 Sparking between the end of the cable and the block should be fairly strong with a regular blue spark. (Hold the lead with rubber to avoid electric shocks). If current is reaching the plugs, then remove them, clean and regap them. The engine should now start.

5 If there is no spark at the plug leads take off the HT lead from the centre of the distributor cap and hold it to the block as before. Spin the engine on the starter once more. A rapid succession of the blue sparks between the end of the lead and the block indicate that the coil is in order and that the distributor cap is cracked, the rotor arm faulty, or the carbon brush in the top of the distributor cap is not making good contact with the spring on the rotor arm. Possibly, the points are in bad condition. Clean and reset them as described in this Chapter, Sections 2 and 3.

6 If there are no sparks from the end of the lead from the coil check the connections at the coil end of the lead. If it is in order start checking the low tension circuit.

7 Use a 12v voltmeter on a 12v bulb and two lengths of wire. With the ignition switched on and the points open, test between the low tension wire to the coil (it is marked SW or +) and earth. No reading indicates a break in the supply from the ignition switch. Check the connections at the switch to see if any are loose. Refit them and the engine should run. A reading shows a faulty coil or condenser, or broken lead between the coil and the distributor.

8 Take the condenser wire off the points assembly and with the points open test between the moving point and earth. If there now is a reading then the fault is in the condenser. Fit a new one and the fault is cleared.

9 With no reading from the moving point to earth, take a reading between earth and the CB or - terminal of the coil. A reading here shows a broken wire which will need to be renewed between the coil and distributor. No reading confirms that the coil has failed and must be renewed, after which the engine will run once more. Remember to refit the condenser wire to the points assembly. For these tests it is sufficient to separate the points with a piece of dry paper while testing with the points open.

17 Fault diagnosis – engine misfires

1 If the engine misfires regularly, run it at a fast idling speed. Pull off each of the plug caps in turn and listen to the note of the engine. Hold the plug cap in a dry cloth or with a rubber glove as additional protection against a shock from the HT supply.

2 No difference in engine running will be noticed when the lead from the defective circuit is removed. Removing the lead from one of the good cylinders will accentuate the misfire.

3 Remove the plug lead from the end of the defective plug and hold it about $\frac{1}{4}$ inch (6 mm) away from the block. Re-start the engine. If the sparking is fairly strong and regular the fault must lie in the spark plug.

4 The plug may be loose, the insulation may be cracked, or the electrodes may have burnt away giving too wide a gap for the spark to jump. Worse still, one of the electrodes may have broken off. Either renew the plug, or clean it, reset the gap, and then test it.

5 If there is no spark at the end of the plug lead, or if it is weak and intermittent, check the ignition lead from the distributor to the plug. If the insulation is cracked or perished, renew the lead. Check the connections at the distributor cap.

6 If there is still no spark, examine the distributor cap carefully for tracking. This can be recognised by a very thin black line running between two or more electrodes, or between an electrode and some other part of the distributor. These lines are paths which now conduct electricity across the cap thus letting it run to earth. The only answer is a new distributor cap.

7 Apart from the ignition timing being incorrect, other causes of misfiring have already been dealt with under the section dealing with the failure of the engine to start. To recap, these are that:

   a) *the coil may be faulty giving an intermittent misfire*
   b) *there may be a damaged wire or loose connection in the low tension circuit*
   c) *the condenser may be short circuiting*
   d) *there may be a mechanical fault in the distributor (broken driving spindle or contact breaker spring).*

8 If the ignition timing is too far retarded, it should be noted that the engine will tend to overheat, and there will be a quite noticeable drop in power. If the engine is overheating and the power is down, and the ignition timing is correct, then the carburettor should be checked, as it is likely that this is where the fault lies.

Chapter 5 Clutch

Contents

Clutch – adjustment	2
Clutch cable – removal and refitting	6
Clutch – dismantling and inspection	4
Clutch faults	9
Clutch pedal – removal and refitting	8
Clutch – refitting	5
Clutch release bearing – removal and refitting	7
Clutch – removal	3
General description	1

Specifications

Type .... Single dry plate, diaphragm spring, cable operated

V4 and 2.0 litre ohc models
Make .... Laycock
Disc diameter .... 8.5 in (216 mm)
Vibration damper torsion springs 6
Diaphragm spring force .... 990 lbf (450 kgf)

V6 models
Make .... Borg and Beck
Disc diameter .... 9.5 in (242 mm)
Vibration diameter torsion springs 6
Diaphragm spring face .... 1262 lbf (574 kgf)

Total pedal stroke .... 6.7 in (170 mm)

Clearance (nut and cable bush collar) ..... 0.12–0.14 in (3.05–3.56 mm)

Torque wrench settings
	lbf ft	kgf m
Clutch to flywheel bolts	12–17	1.6–2.1
Bellhousing to gearbox	40–45	5.5–6.2

1 General description

All manual gearbox versions are fitted with a single dry plate, diaphragm spring clutch. The unit comprises a steel cover which is dowelled and bolted to the rear face of the flywheel and contains the pressure plate and diaphragm spring.

The clutch disc is free to slide along the spindled first motion shaft (gearbox input shaft) and is held in position between the flywheel and the pressure plate by the pressure of the pressure plate spring. Friction lining material is riveted to the clutch disc and it has a spring cushioned hub to absorb transmission shocks and to help ensure a smooth take off.

The clutch is actuated by a cable controlled by the clutch pedal. The clutch release mechanism consists of a release fork and bearings which are able to contact the release fingers on the pressure plate assembly. There should therefore never be any free play at the release fork. Wear of the friction material in the clutch is adjusted out by means of a cable adjuster at the lower end of the cable where it passes through the bellhousing.

Depressing the clutch pedal actuates the clutch release arm by means of the cable. The release arm pushes the release bearing forward to bear against the release fingers so moving the centre of the diaphragm spring inwards. As the centre of the spring is pushed in, the outside of the spring is pushed out, so moving the pressure plate backward and disengaging the pressure plate from the clutch disc.

When the clutch pedal is released the diaphragm spring forces the pressure plate into contact with the high friction linings on the clutch disc and at the same time pushes the clutch disc a fraction of an inch forward on its splines so engaging the clutch disc with the flywheel. The clutch disc is now firmly in contact with and between the pressure plate and the flywheel so the drive is taken up.

2 Clutch – adjustment

1 Every 6000 miles (10 000 km) it will probably be necessary to adjust the clutch cable to compensate for wear in the linings.
2 The clutch is adjusted until the clearance between the nut and cable bush collar is as specified.
3 This adjustment is obtained by pulling the clutch pedal hard against the back stop and retaining in position with a suitable block of wood, or if an assistant is on hand, get him/her to hold the pedal back.
4 Working under the car take up any slack in the system by pulling the adjuster end of the outer cable forward.
5 Turn the adjuster nut as necessary until the specified clearance is obtained. Slide the adjustment nut into the bush, remove the wood block and operate the pedal several times. Check the clearance again.
6 When a new clutch friction plate (disc) has been fitted it will be found that the cable will require fairly extensive adjustment particularly if the old friction plate was well worn before renewal.

3 Clutch – removal

This job may be carried out with the engine either in or out of the car. The gearbox must be detached from the rear of engine as described in Chapter 6. Then proceed as follows:

Chapter 5 Clutch 125

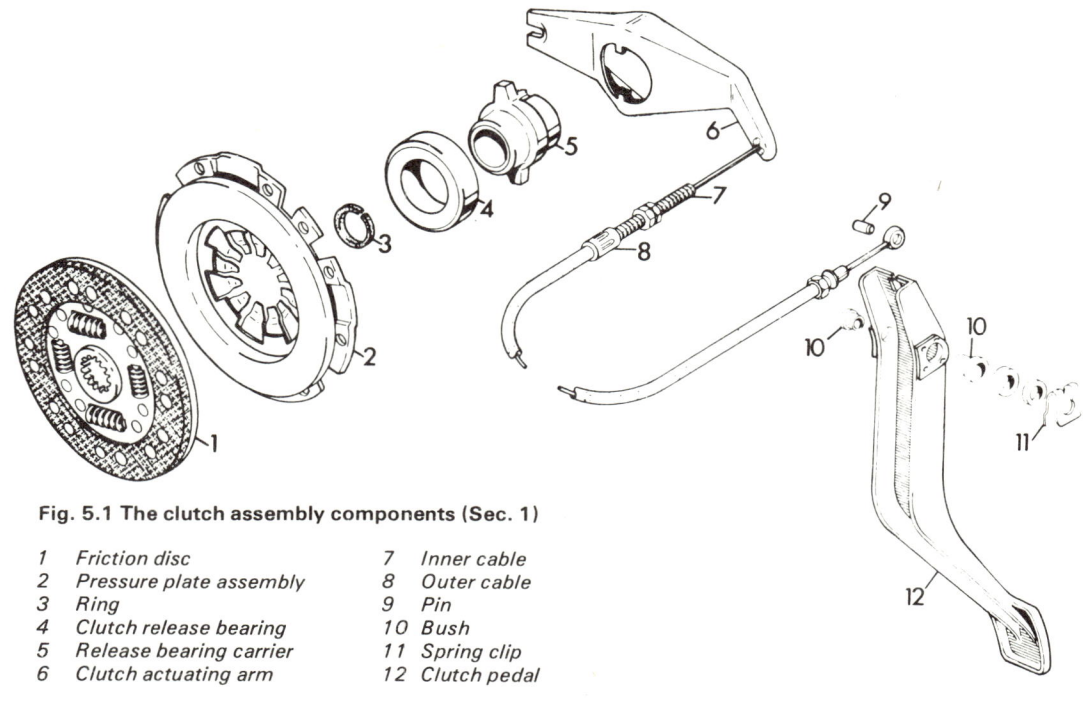

Fig. 5.1 The clutch assembly components (Sec. 1)

1 Friction disc
2 Pressure plate assembly
3 Ring
4 Clutch release bearing
5 Release bearing carrier
6 Clutch actuating arm
7 Inner cable
8 Outer cable
9 Pin
10 Bush
11 Spring clip
12 Clutch pedal

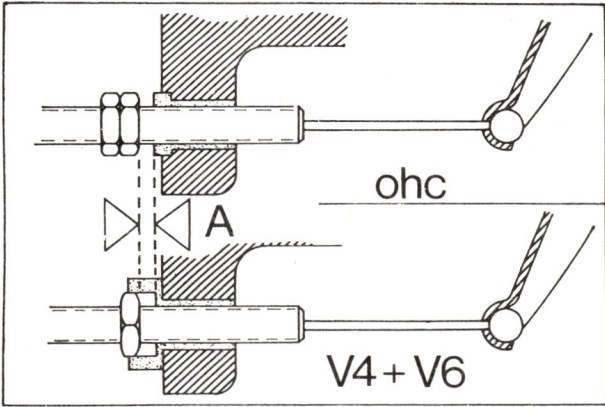

Fig. 5.2 The clutch clearance (A) (Sec. 2)

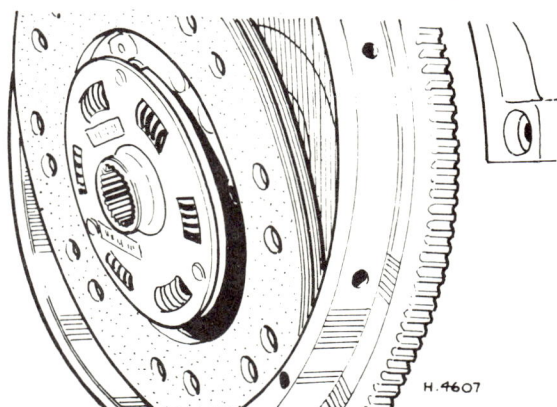

Fig. 5.3 Withdraw the clutch friction disc (Sec. 3)

1 With a file or scriber mark the relative position of the clutch cover and flywheel which will ensure identical positioning on refitting. This is not necessary if a new clutch is to be fitted.
2 Undo and remove, in a diagonal and progressive manner, the six bolts and spring washers which secure the clutch cover to the flywheel. This will prevent distortion of the cover and the cover suddenly flying off.
3 With all the bolts removed lift the clutch assembly from the locating dowels. Note which way round the friction disc is fitted and lift away from the cover.

4 Clutch – dismantling and inspection

1 It is not practicable to dismantle the Borg and Beck pressure plate assembly although it is possible to dismantle the Laycock type provided that individual parts are available. Further information will be found later in this Section. Normally the term dismantling is used for simply fitting a new clutch friction plate and cover assembly.
2 Thoroughly clean all parts by wiping with a rag to remove any dust. Do not inhale the dust as it is harmful to the lungs!
3 Examine the clutch disc friction lining for wear, loose or broken springs and rivets. The linings must be proud of the rivets and light in appearance, with the material structure visible. If it is dark in appearance, further investigation is necessary as it is a sign of oil contamination caused by oil leaking past the crankshaft rear seal.
4 Check the machined faces of the flywheel and pressure plate for signs of grooving. If evident new parts should be fitted. Inspect the pressure plate for signs of hair line cracks usually caused by overheating, and if evident a new unit must be fitted.
5 Fit the disc to the gearbox input shaft, and check that it is free to slide up and down the splines without signs of binding.
6 Check the release bearing for smoothness of operation. There should be no harshness or slackness in it. It should spin reasonably freely bearing in mind it has been pre-packed with grease.
7 To dismantle the Laycock cover and driving plate assembly first locate the rivets on the cover and drill these out. It will not be necessary to renew the rivets during reassembly as they are used to keep the parts together during bulk manufacture.
8 To separate the pressure plate from the driving plate remove the diaphragm spring retaining ring using a screwdriver.
9 Lift away the four anti-rattle springs.
10 Using a scriber or file, mark the driving plate, pressure plate and diaphragm spring and then separate the parts.
11 Upon reassembly apply a little molybdenum disulphide grease sparingly to the sides of the pressure plate lugs, fulcrum points for the

Chapter 5 Clutch

diaphragm spring on the pressure plate, driving plate and cover.
12 Line up the previously made marks making sure the depressions in the cover and driving plate coincide as one of them is offset.
13 Make sure the retaining ring is refitted with the flat sections under the pressure plate lugs and the curved sections against the edge of the diaphragm spring.

5 Clutch – refitting

1 It is important that no oil or grease gets on the clutch plate friction linings or on the pressure plate and flywheel faces. It is advisable to refit the clutch with clean hands and to wipe down the pressure plate and flywheel faces with a clean rag before assembly begins.
2 Place the clutch friction disc against the flywheel, ensuring that it is the correct way round. The flywheel side of the clutch disc is clearly marked near the centre. If the disc is fitted the wrong way round it will be quite impossible to operate the clutch (photo).
3 Refit the clutch cover assembly loosely on the dowels. Refit the six bolts and spring washers and tighten them finger tight so that the clutch plate is gripped but can still be moved.
4 The clutch disc must now be centralised so that when the engine and gearbox are mated the gearbox first motion shaft splines will pass through the splines in the centre of the driven plate.
5 Centralisation can be carried out quite easily by inserting a round bar or long screwdriver through the hole in the centre of the clutch, so that the end of the bar rests in the small hole in the end of the crankshaft containing the spigot bush. Ideally an old Ford first motion shaft should be used.
6 Using the first motion shaft spigot bush as a fulcrum, moving the bar sideways or up and down will move the clutch disc in whichever direction is necessary to achieve centralisation.
7 Centralisation is easily judged by removing the bar and viewing the driven plate hub in relation to the hole in the centre of the clutch cover plate diaphragm spring. When the hub appears exactly in the centre of the hole, all is correct. Alternatively the old first motion shaft will fit the bush and centre of the clutch hub exactly obviating the need for visual alignment.
8 Tighten the clutch cover securing bolts firmly in a diagonal sequence to ensure that the cover plate is pulled down evenly and without distortion of the flange. Finally tighten the bolts down to the specified torque.

5.2 The friction disc directional marking

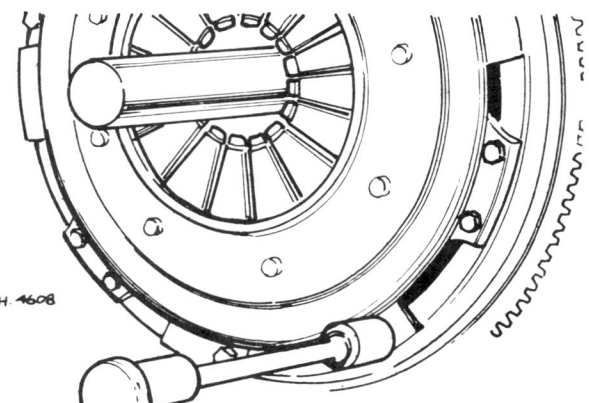

Fig. 5.4 Tighten the clutch securing bolts, then remove the centralisation bar (Sec. 5)

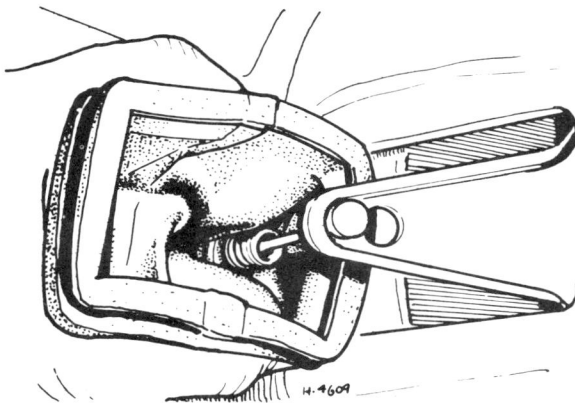

Fig. 5.5 Remove the rubber grommet from the clutch bellhousing (sec. 6)

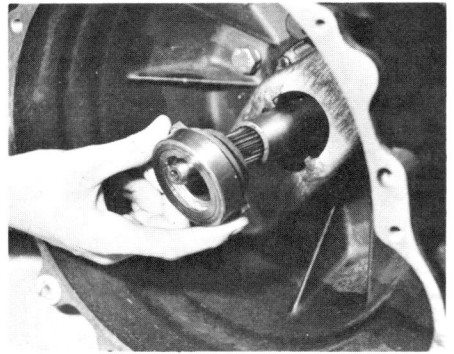

7.4a Release bearing removal

7.4b Release arm removal

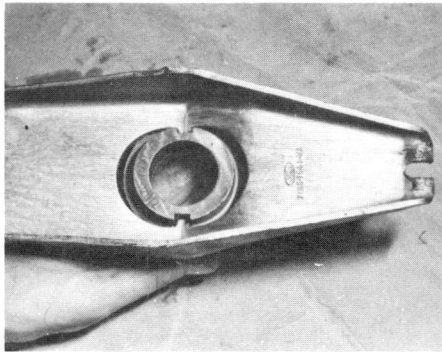

7.5 Removal of clutch release bearing by rotating through 90°

6 Clutch cable – removal and refitting

1 Open the bonnet and for safety reasons disconnect the battery.
2 Carefully prise out the rubber bung from the upper bulkhead over the pedal assembly.
3 Chock the rear wheels, jack up the front of the car and support on firmly based stands. Ease off the rubber grommet from the side of the clutch housing located as shown in Fig. 5.5.
4 Push the clutch pedal hard against the stop, and with an open-ended spanner back off the cable adjustment nut. This is located on the clutch bellhousing.
5 It will now be possible to lift the cable ball end from the slotted end of the release lever. Whilst this is being done take great care not to accidentally disengage the release lever from the bearing hub.
6 Lever the cable eye end and pin from the cable retention bush in the pedal with a small screwdriver.
7 Withdraw the pin from the eye and withdraw the cable assembly from the abutment tube in the dash panel.
8 Refitting of the cable is a straightforward reversal of the removal sequence. Lubricate the pivot pin. Refer to Section 2 and adjust the cable.

7 Clutch release bearing – removal and refitting

1 With the gearbox and engine separated to provide access to the clutch, attention can be given to the release bearing located in the bellhousing, over the input shaft.
2 The release bearing is a relatively inexpensive but important component and unless it is nearly new it is false economy not to renew it during overhaul of the clutch.
3 To remove the release bearing, first pull off the release arm rubber gaiter.
4 The release bearing and arm can be separately withdrawn from the clutch housing. Alternatively they may be renewed as an assembly (photos).
5 To free the bearing from the release arm simply unhook it and then, with the aid of two wood blocks and a vice press off the release bearing from its hub. Note which way round the bearing is fitted (photo).
6 Refitting is a straightforward reversal of removal.

8 Clutch pedal – removal and refitting

1 The clutch pedal is removed and refitted in the same manner as the brake pedal, once the cable has been released from the pedal.
2 A full description of how to remove and refit the brake pedal can be found in Chapter 9.

9 Clutch faults

There are four main faults to which the clutch and release mechanism are prone. They may occur by themselves or in conjunction with other faults. They are clutch squeal, slip, spin and judder.

Clutch squeal
1 If, on taking up the drive or when changing gear, the clutch squeals this is a sure indication of a badly worn clutch release bearing.
2 As well as regular wear due to normal use, wear of the clutch release bearing is much accentuated if the clutch is ridden, or held down for long periods in gear, with the engine running. To minimise wear of this component the car should always be taken out of gear at traffic lights and for similar hold-ups.

Clutch slip
3 Clutch slip is a self-evident condition which occurs when the clutch friction plate is badly worn, when oil or grease have got onto the flywheel or pressure plate faces, or when the pressure plate itself is faulty.
4 The reason for clutch slip is that, due to one of the faults listed above, there is either insufficient pressure from the pressure plate, or insufficient friction from the friction plate to ensure solid drive.
5 If oil gets onto the clutch in small amounts, it will be burnt off under the heat of clutch engagement, and in the process, gradually darken the linings. Excessive oil on the clutch will burn off leaving a carbon deposit which can cause quite bad slip, fierceness, spin or judder.
6 If clutch slip is suspected, and confirmation of this condition is required, there are several tests which can be made.
7 With the engine in second or third gear and pulling lightly up a moderate incline sudden depression of the accelerator pedal may cause the engine to increase its speed without any increase in road speed. Easing off on the accelerator will then give a definite drop in engine speed without the car slowing.
8 In extreme cases of clutch slip the engine will race under normal acceleration conditions.
9 If slip is due to oil or grease on the linings a temporary cure can sometimes be effected by squirting carbon tetrachloride through the release arm aperture into the clutch assembly. The permanent cure is, of course, to renew the clutch driven plate and trace and rectify the oil leak.

Clutch spin
10 Clutch spin is a condition which occurs when the release arm travel is excessive, there is an obstruction in the clutch either on the primary gear splines or the release lever itself, or the oil may have partially burnt off the clutch linings and have left a resinous deposit which is causing the clutch disc to stick to the pressure plate or flywheel.
11 The reason for clutch spin is that, due to any or a combination of, the faults just listed, the clutch pressure plate is not completely freeing from the centre plate even with the clutch pedal fully depressed.
12 If clutch spin is suspected, the condition can be confirmed by extreme difficulty in engaging first gear from rest, difficulty in changing gear, and very sudden take up of the clutch drive at the fully depressed end of the clutch pedal travel as the clutch is released.
13 Check that the clutch cable is correctly adjusted and, if in order, the fault lies internally in the clutch. It will then be necessary to remove the clutch for examination, and to check the gearbox input shaft for distortion.

Clutch judder
14 Clutch judder is a self-evident condition which occurs when the gearbox or engine mountings are loose or too flexible, when there is oil on the face of the clutch friction plate, or when the clutch pressure plate has been incorrectly adjusted during assembly.
15 The reason for clutch judder is, due to one of the faults just listed, the clutch pressure plate is not freeing smoothly from the friction disc, and is snatching.
16 Clutch judder normally occurs when the clutch pedal is released in first or reverse gears, and the whole car shudders as it moves backward or forward.

Chapter 6 Manual gearbox and automatic transmission

Contents

Automatic transmission – fluid level and maintenance	7
Automatic transmission – general description	6
Automatic transmission – removal and refitting	8
Downshift cable – removal, refitting and adjustment	13
Fault finding – automatic transmission	17
Fault finding – manual gearbox	18
Intermediate band – adjustment	15
Low and reverse band – adjustment (C4 transmission only)	16
Manual gearbox – dismantling	3
Manual gearbox – general description	1
Manual gearbox – inspection	4
Manual gearbox – reassembly	5
Manual gearbox – removal and refitting	2
Selector cable – removal and refitting	11
Selector lever assembly – overhaul	10
Selector lever assembly – removal and refitting	9
Selector rod – removal and refitting	12
Starter inhibitor switch – removal, refitting and adjustment	14

Specifications

Manual gearbox

Number of gears	4 forward, 1 reverse
Type of gears	Helical, constant mesh
Synchromesh	All forward gears
Layshaft gear train endfloat	0.006–0.018 in (0.15–0.45 mm)
Thrust washer thickness	0.061–0.062 in (1.55–1.60 mm)
Layshaft diameter	0.6818–0.6823 (17.317–17.329 mm)
Oil capacity:	
2.0 litre	2.91 pints (1.66 litres)
2.5 and 3.0 litre	3.48 pints (1.98 litres)

Gear ratios:

	2.5 litre (saloon only) and 2.0 litre	2.5 litre (estate only) and 3.0 litre
First	3.651 : 1	3.163 : 1
Second	1.968 : 1	1.950 : 1
Third	1.368 : 1	1.401 : 1
Top	1.000 : 1	1.000 : 1
Reverse	3.660 : 1	3.346 : 1

Automatic transmission

Types:	
Early models	Ford C4
Later models	Ford C3 (Bordeaux)
Oil capacity (including oil cooler and torque converter):	
C4:	
9.5 in (24 cm) converter	10.7 pints (6.1 litres)
10.25 in (26 cm) converter	12.3 pints (7.0 litres)
C3 (except 3.0 litre models)	11.4 pints (6.5 litres)
C3 (3.0 litre models)	13.2 pints (7.5 litres)
Selector positions	P R N D 2 1
Torque converter type	Trilock (hydraulic)
Torque converter ratio range	Infinitely variable between 1 : 1 and 2 : 1 operating in all gears
Oil cooler type	Twin tube

Gear ratios:

	C4	C3
First	2.46 : 1	2.47 : 1
Second	1.46 : 1	1.47 : 1
Third	1.00 : 1	1.1 : 1
Reverse	2.20 : 1	2.11 : 1

Torque wrench settings

	lbf ft	kgf m
Manual gearbox		
Gearbox top cover	8–9	1.1–1.3
Gearbox spigot bearing	8–9	1.1–1.3
Extension housing to gearbox	33–36	4.6–5.0

Chapter 6 Manual gearbox and automatic transmission

Automatic transmission – C4

	lbf ft	kgf m
Torque converter to drive plate bolts	20–29	2.8–4.0
Starter inhibitor switch locknut	5–6	0.64–0.86
Oil pan to transmission housing bolts	12–16	1.6–2.2
Drain plug	9–12	1.3–1.6

Automatic transmission – C3 (Bordeaux)

Converter to drive plate bolts	26–30	3.6–4.1
Oil pan to transmission housing	12–17	1.6–2.4
Downshift cable bracket	12–17	1.6–2.4
Outer downshift lever nut	7–11	1.0–1.5
Inner downshift lever nut	30–39	4.1–5.4
Starter inhibitor switch	12–14	1.6–2.0
Oil cooler line to connector	12–14	1.6–2.0
Converter housing to engine	22–27	3.0–3.7
Drain plug	20–29	2.8–4.0

1 Manual gearbox – general description

The manual gearbox fitted to the Consul and Granada models throughout the production period has remained basically the same, although two types of selector mechanism have been used according to the model. The selector mechanism is either a single rail type as fitted to the 2·0 litre V4 and ohc engine models and the 2·5 litre V6 saloon, or a three rail type as fitted to the 2·5 litre V6 estate models and the 3·0 litre versions.

The manual gearbox contains four constant mesh, helically cut, forward gears and one spur cut reverse gear. Synchromesh is fitted on all forward gears. The separate bellhousing and main gearbox casing are of cast iron whereas the extension housing is of cast aluminium and incorporates the remote control gear change system.

The gearbox is of a simple design using a minimum number of components. Where close tolerances and limits are required, manufacturing tolerances are compensated for and excessive endfloat or backlash is eliminated by the fitting of selective circlips, located as shown in Fig. 6.1. When overhauling the gearbox always use new circlips, never refit ones that have already been used.

2 Manual gearbox – removal and refitting

1 The gearbox can be removed in unit with the engine through the engine compartment as described in Chapter 1. Alternatively the gearbox can be separated from the rear of the engine at the bellhousing and the gearbox lowered from under the car. The latter method is easier and quicker than the former.
2 If a hoist or an inspection pit are not available then run the back of the car up a pair of ramps or jack it up and support on firmly based axle stands.
3 For safety reasons disconnect the battery earth terminal.
4 Working inside the car push the front seats rearward as far as possible.
5 Remove the spring retainer from the top of the gear change lever rubber gaiter.
6 Carefully ease the gaiter from the body panel and slide it up the gear lever (photo).
7 Using a screwdriver bend back the locking tabs on the lock-ring and very carefully unscrew the lock-ring and gear lever retainer (photo).

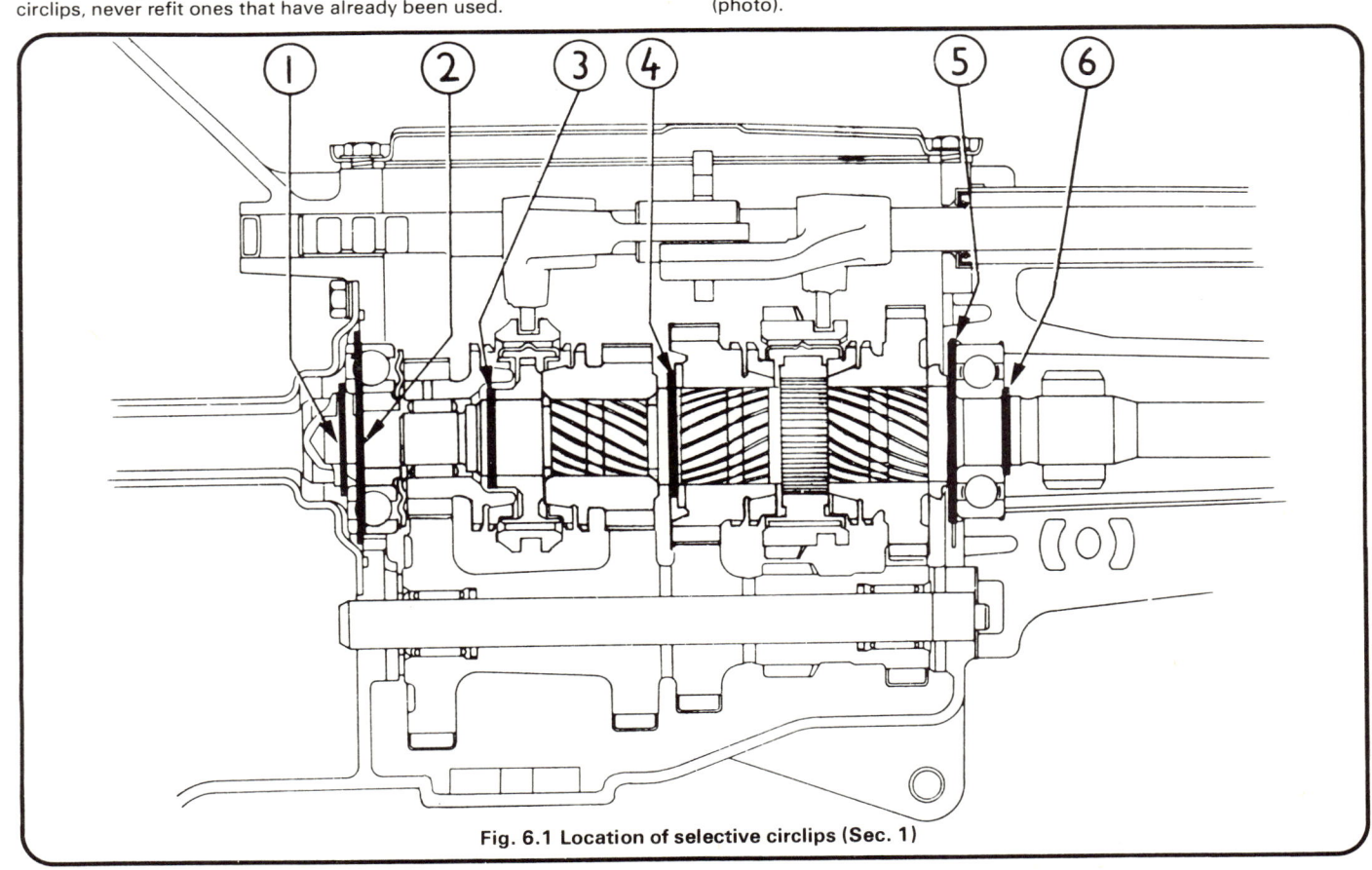

Fig. 6.1 Location of selective circlips (Sec. 1)

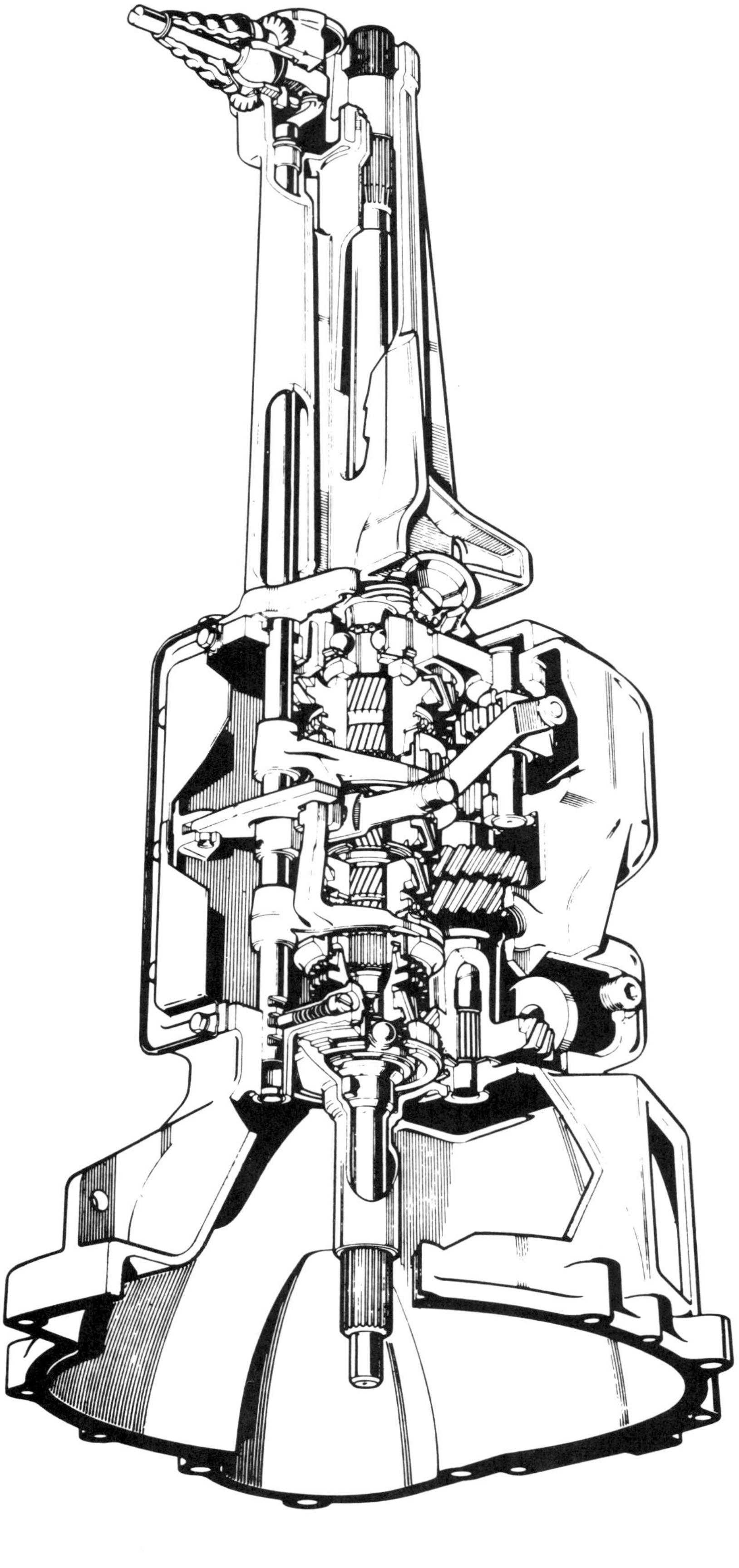

Fig. 6.2 Cutaway view of manual gearbox with single rail selector (Sec. 1)

Chapter 6 Manual gearbox and automatic transmission

2.6 Slide gaiter up gear lever

2.7 Bending back lock-ring tabs with screwdriver

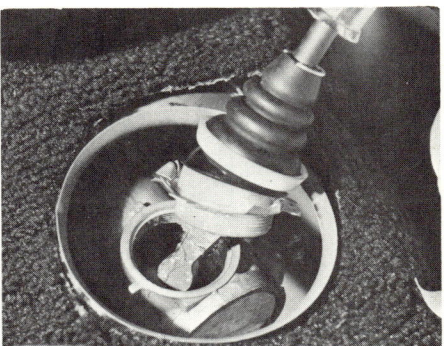
2.8 Lifting away gear change lever

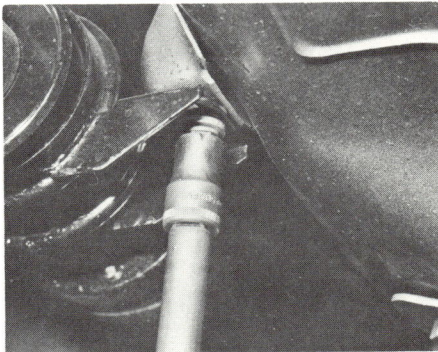
2.10 Centre bearing retainer securing bolt removal

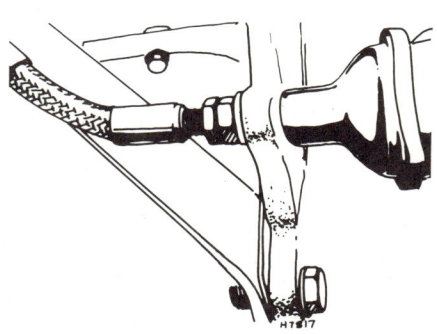
Fig. 6.3 Location of bracket between engine and clutch housing (Sec. 2)

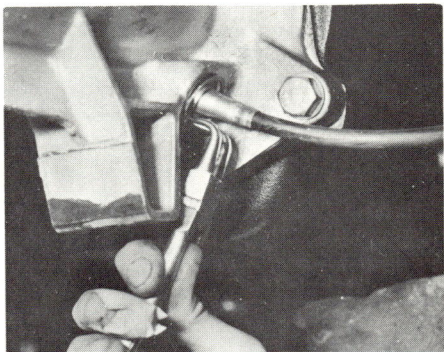
2.17 Speedometer cable retaining circlip removal

8 The gear change lever can now be lifted upward and away from the gearbox (photo).
9 Mark the mating flanges of the propeller shaft and final drive so that they may be reconnected in their original positions and undo and remove the four securing bolts.
10 Where a split type propeller shaft is fitted, undo and remove the centre bearing retainer securing bolts, spring and plain washers (photo).
11 Draw the propeller shaft rearward so detaching the front end from the rear of the gearbox and lift away from under the car.
12 Wrap some polythene around the end of the gearbox and secure with string or wire to stop any oil running out.
13 Make a note of the cable connections to the starter motor and detach the cables.
14 Undo and remove the two bolts that secure the starter motor to the gearbox flange. Lift away the starter motor. It will be easier to remove the starter motor if the exhaust downpipe unit is removed first.
15 Remove the rear engine cover plate and bracket assembly from the clutch housing. Detach the bracket assembly from the cylinder block and swing it back out of the way. This bracket is shown in Fig. 6.3.
16 Pull off the plug attached to the reverse light switch located on the side of the remote control housing.
17 Using a pair of circlip pliers remove the circlip retaining the speedometer drive cable end to the gearbox extension housing (photo).
18 Pull the speedometer drive cable away from the side of the extension housing.
19 Pull back the clutch cable and release arm rubber gaiter from the clutch bellhousing and, using a pair of pliers, detach the clutch operating cable from the release arm which protrudes from the side of the clutch housing (photo).
20 Pull the clutch cable assembly through the locating hole in the flange on the clutch housing.
21 Suitably support the weight of the gearbox by either using a jack or an axle stand. Insert a wooden chock between the sump and engine support, so that the engine does not drop when the gearbox is removed.

22 Undo and remove the remaining bolts securing the clutch bellhousing to the rear of the engine.
23 Undo and remove the exhaust pipe securing nuts at the exhaust manifolds and the exhaust mounting brackets. Push the assemblies away from the gearbox and tie back with string.
24 Undo and remove the one bolt which secures the rubber mounting to the gearbox extension housing.
25 Undo and remove the four bolts, spring and plain washers securing the gearbox support crossmember to the body (photo).
26 Lift away the crossmember (photo).
27 The assistance of a second person is now required who should be ready to help in taking the weight of the gearbox.
28 Do NOT allow the weight of the gearbox to hang on the input shaft (first motion shaft) as it is easily bent. Carefully separate the gearbox from the engine by sliding it rearwards. It will be necessary to lower the jack or stand to give clearance of the gearbox from the underside of the body.
29 If major work is to be undertaken on the gearbox it is recommended that the exterior be washed with paraffin or a proprietary grease solvent and dried with a non-fluffy rag.
30 Refitting the gearbox is the reverse sequence to removal but the following additional points should be noted:
   a) *Make sure that the engine cover plate gasket is correctly positioned (if fitted).*
   b) *Adjust the clutch control cable in such a manner that after two or more pedal applications, the specified clearance exists between the adjuster nut and its abutment.*
   c) *Before refitting the gear change lever, lubricate the fork ends with grease.*
   d) *Refill the gearbox with the recommended amount of lubricant.*

3 Manual gearbox – dismantling

1 Place the complete unit on a firm bench or table and ensure that you have the following available, in addition to the normal range of spanners, etc.

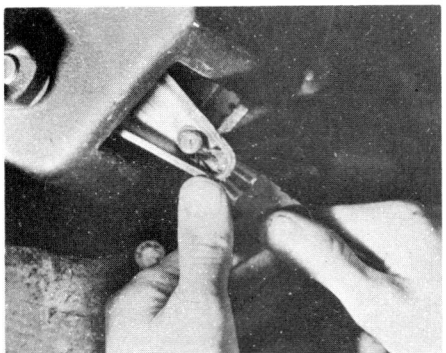
2.19 Detaching clutch inner cable from actuating arm

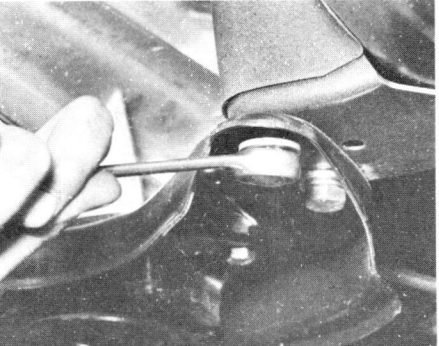
2.25 Gearbox support crossmember to body securing bolt removal

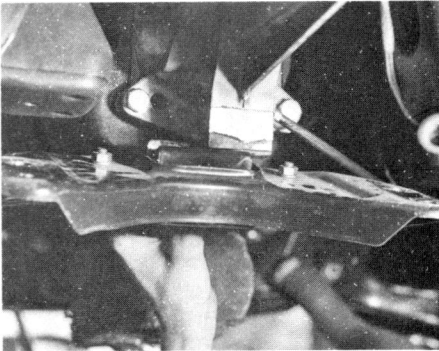
2.26 Crossmember removal

a) Good quality circlip pliers, 2 pairs – 1 expanding and 1 contracting.
b) Copper-headed mallet, at least 2 lb (0.14 kg).
c) Drifts, steel and brass, 0.375 inch (4.525 mm) diameter.
d) Small containers for needle rollers.
e) Engineer's vice mounted on firm bench.
f) Selection of metal tubing.

Any attempt to dismantle the gearbox without the foregoing is not impossible, but will certainly be very difficult and inconvenient.

2 Read the whole of this Section before starting work.
3 The internal parts of the gearbox are shown in Fig. 6.4.
4 Detach the clutch release bearing from the release lever by turning the carrier through 90° and pulling forward (photo).
5 This photo shows the cut-outs in the release bearing carrier which have to be lined up with the two protrusions on the release lever to enable removal of the bearing carrier.
6 Undo and remove the four bolts and spring washers that secure the clutch housing to the gearbox main case (photo).
7 Draw the clutch housing forward away from the main case.

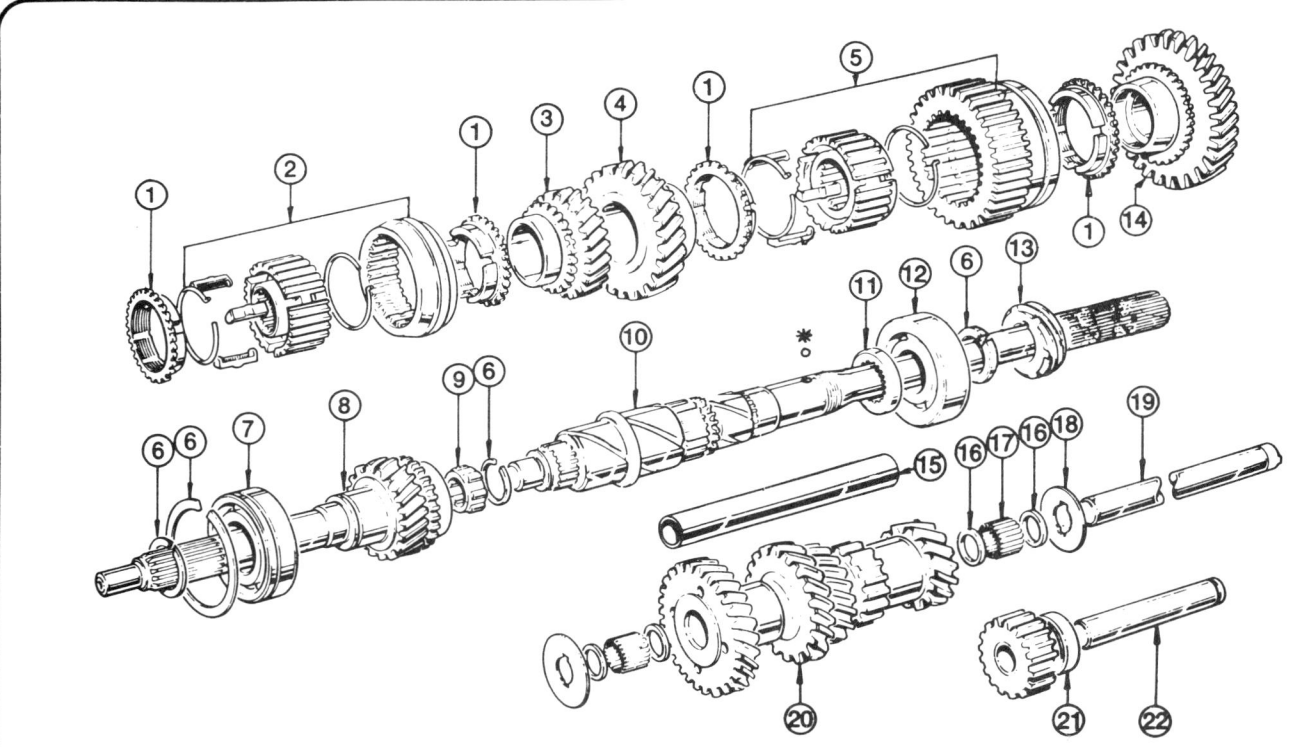

Fig. 6.4 Gearbox internal components (Sec. 3)

1 Synchroniser sleeve
2 Synchroniser hub (3rd/top gear)
3 3rd gear
4 2nd gear
5 Synchroniser hub (1st/2nd gear)
6 Circlip
7 Input shaft bearing
8 Input shaft
9 Needle roller bearing
10 Mainshaft
11 Oil scoop ring
12 Mainshaft bearing
13 Speedometer worm
14 1st gear
15 Spacer sleeve (single rail gearbox only)
16 Spacer shim
17 Needle roller (19 off)
18 Thrust washer
19 Layshaft
20 Layshaft gear train
21 Reverse idler gear
22 Idler shaft

* Speedometer worm locating ball fitted to the 3 rail gearbox

Chapter 6 Manual gearbox and automatic transmission

3.4 Release bearing removal

3.5 Release bearing located in release lever

3.6 Clutch housing to gearbox securing bolts removal

Selector unit dismantling – single rail selector gearbox

8 Undo and remove the bolts and shakeproof washers that secure the top cover to the main casing.
9 Lift away the top cover and its gasket (photo).
10 Using a suitable size Allen key unscrew the side plug that retains the selector rail blocker bar (photo).
11 Withdraw the spring and blocker bar (photo).
12 Using a suitable diameter parellel pin punch, tap out the spring pin securing the reverse selector boss to the selector rail (photo). Allow to drop into the bottom of the gearbox main case.
13 Again using a parallel pin punch and working through the gear change lever aperture, tap out the extension housing rear cover

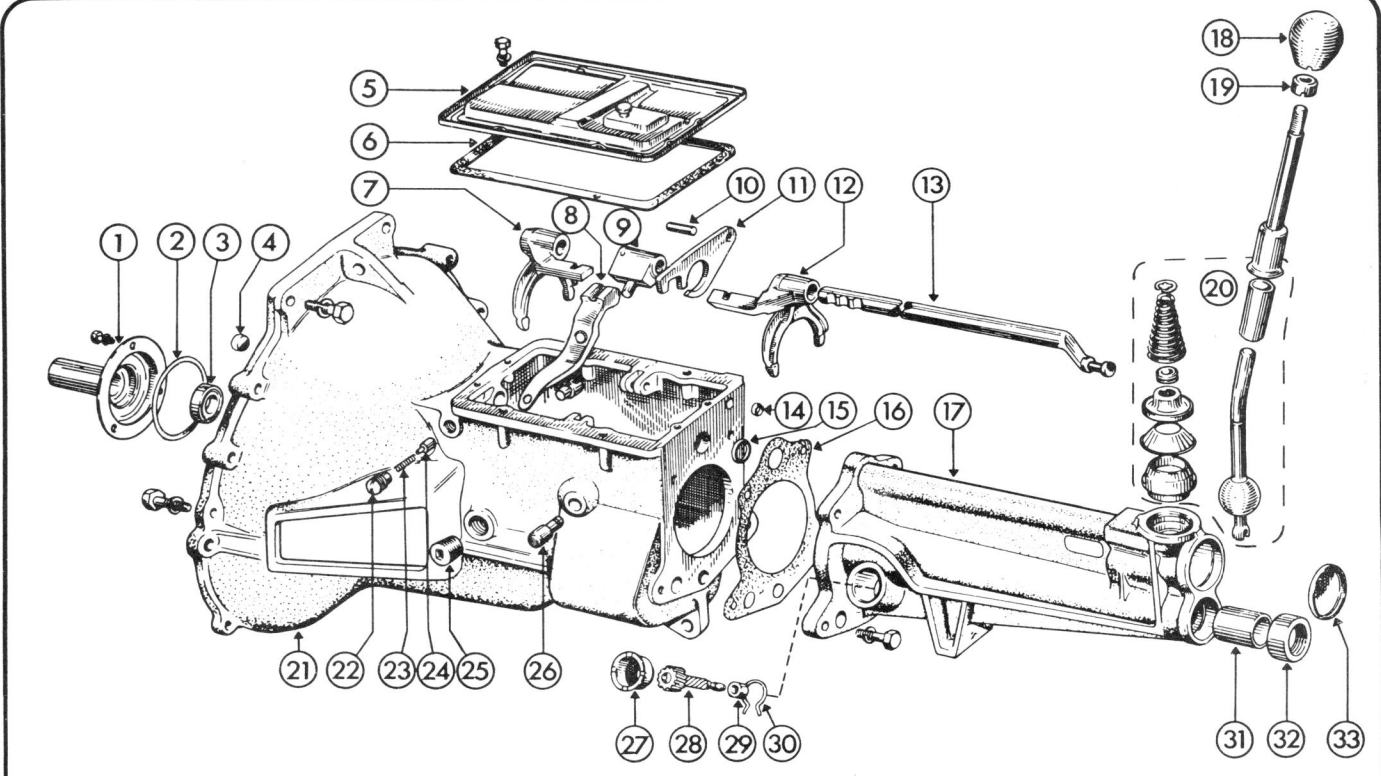

Fig. 6.5 The single rail selector mechanism components (Sec. 3)

1 Spigot bearing retainer
2 O-ring
3 Oil seal
4 Blanking plug
5 Cover – transmission housing
6 Gasket
7 Selector fork 3–4 gear
8 Selector fork reverse gear
9 Selector finger
10 Swivel pin
11 Selector lockplate
12 Selector fork 1–2 gear
13 Gear shift lever shaft
14 Blanking plug
15 Sealing ring
16 Gasket
17 Extension housing
18 Gear knob
19 Locking nut
20 Gear lever assembly
21 Transmission casing
22 Locking bolt
23 Spring
24 Selector shaft locking pin
25 Oil filler plug
26 Pin (gearbox reverse relay lever)
27 Speedometer drive cover
28 Speedometer driven gear
29 Sealing ring
30 Circlip
31 Bushing
32 Sealing ring
33 Gearbox extension housing plug

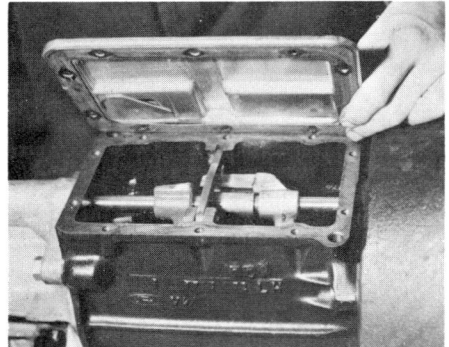
3.9 Gearbox top cover removal

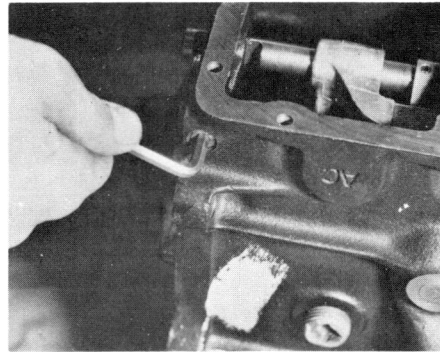
3.10 Selector rail blocker bar plug removal

3.11 Blocker bar and spring removal

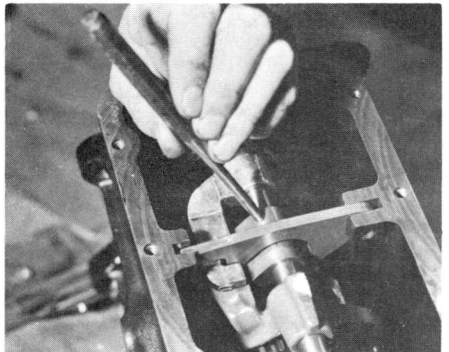
3.12 Reverse selector boss spring pin removal

3.13 Extension housing rear cover removal

3.15 Selector rail removal

3.16 Selector forks correctly located in main casing

3.17 Selector fork removal

3.18 Detaching selector forks from lockplate

3.19 Lockplate spring pin removal

(photo).
14 Undo and remove the four bolts and spring washers that secure the extension housing to the main casing.
15 Carefully pull the selector rail through the extension housing. It will be found necessary to ease each selector fork boss from the selector rail as it is withdrawn (photo).
16 This photo shows the selector forks in position but with the selector rail removed.
17 Lift the selector forks up which will at the same time pivot the lockplate up (photo).
18 Detach the selector forks from the lockplate (photo).
19 Using a suitable diameter rod, tap out the spring pin on which the lockplate pivots (photo).

Selector unit dismantling – three rail selector gearbox
20 Remove the four bolts and washers retaining the top cover in position on the main casing.
21 Carefully remove the top cover and gasket.

Chapter 6 Manual gearbox and automatic transmission

22 Unscrew the four bolts and remove the extension housing top cover.
23 Using a suitable bar magnet or bar smeared with grease, extract the selector detent balls and springs from the top front gearbox face.
24 Unscrew and remove the selector fork retaining bolt and slide the fork free of the shaft.
25 Unscrew and remove the two shift rod bridge support retaining bolts through the extension housing aperture.
26 Unscrew the three bolts and remove the gear lever and housing from the extension. The selector shaft can now be extracted.
27 With a suitable pin punch, drive out the reverse gear relay lever roll pin from its location in the side of the extension housing.
28 The respective selector forks are located on the rails with roll pins. Tap the pins out using a suitable pin punch and withdraw the selector rails to the rear through the extension housing. Note that 3rd/4th gear selector rod also has a circlip fitted and this must be removed before the rail can be withdrawn. Remove the plunger and interlock pins from each rail during removal. As each rail is removed, extract the respective selector forks and relocate on their rails for inspection and/or refitting.
29 Remove the following from the extension housing:

a) Use a pair of screwdrivers and prise the speedometer pinion from its housing
b) Unscrew the plug on the side housing and extract the plunger
c) Bend over the reverse gear interlock tab washer and unscrew and remove the interlock assembly comprising of bolt, spring, ball and plunger
d) Unscrew the reverse light switch and remove.

30 Unscrew the four bolts and detach the extension housing from the gearbox.
31 The extension housing oil seal can be removed by prising or drifting it out of its aperture.

Gearcase dismantling – all models

32 Undo and remove the bolts and spring washers securing the spigot bearing retainer to the front face of the main case.
33 Lift away the spigot bearing retainer from over the input shaft. Recover the O-ring (photo).
34 Working in the small space between the mainshaft constant mesh gear teeth and the main case, compress the circlip using a pair of

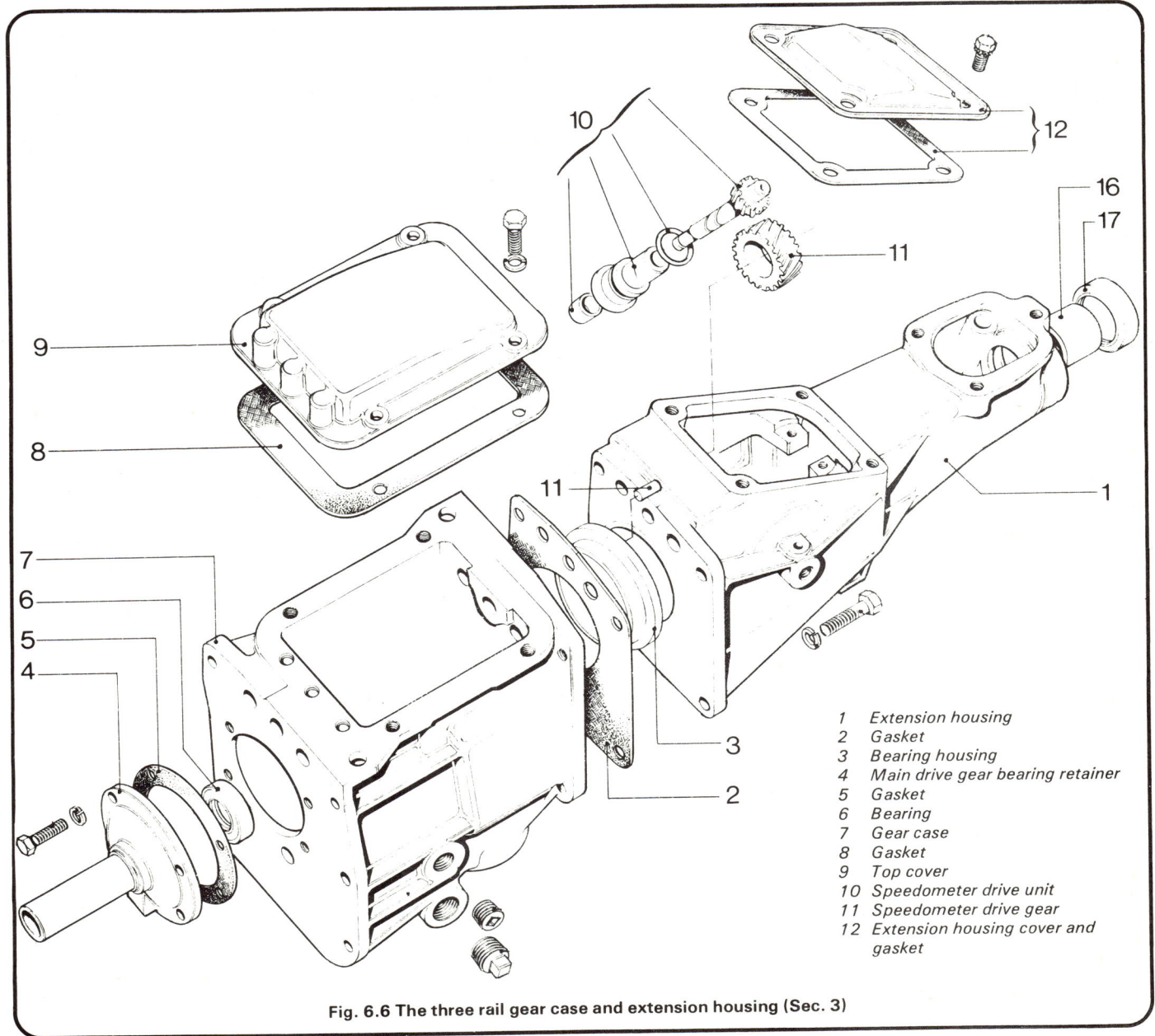

1 Extension housing
2 Gasket
3 Bearing housing
4 Main drive gear bearing retainer
5 Gasket
6 Bearing
7 Gear case
8 Gasket
9 Top cover
10 Speedometer drive unit
11 Speedometer drive gear
12 Extension housing cover and gasket

Fig. 6.6 The three rail gear case and extension housing (Sec. 3)

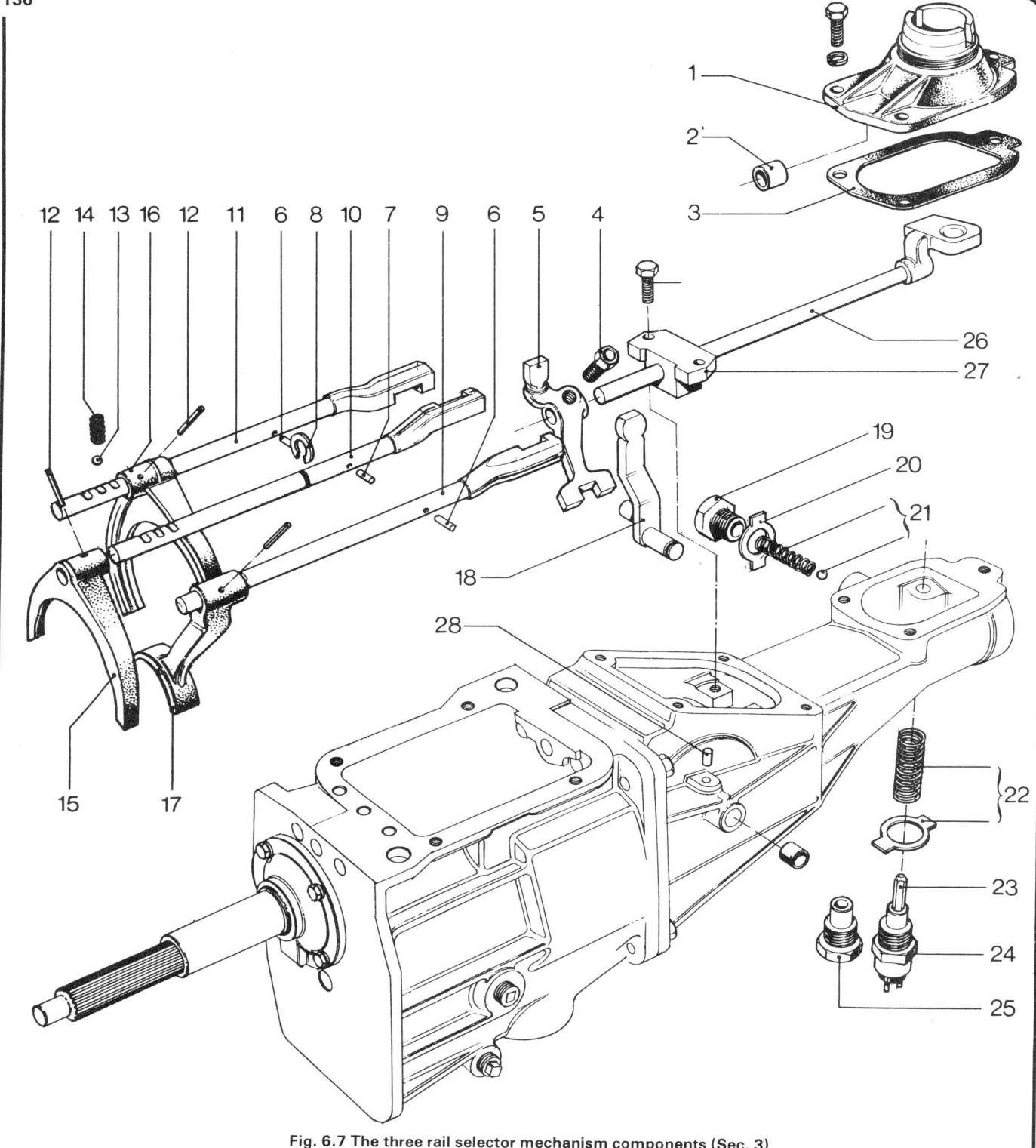

Fig. 6.7 The three rail selector mechanism components (Sec. 3)

1. Gear shift housing
2. Bush
3. Gasket
4. Selector fork adjustment screw
5. Selector fork
6. Plunger
7. Shift shaft interlock pin
8. Circlip
9. Reverse gear shift rail
10. 3rd/4th gear shift rail
11. 1st/2nd gear shift rail
12. Roll pin
13. Ball
14. Spring
15. 3rd/4th speed selector fork
16. 1st/2nd speed selector fork
17. Reverse selector fork
18. Reverse gear relay lever
19. Banjo bolt
20. Locking washer
21. Spring and ball
22. Gear selection plunger spring and locking washer
23. Selector lock plunger
24. Reverse light switch
25. Plug
26. Gear change shaft
27. Bridge support
28. Reverse relay arm roll pin

Chapter 6 Manual gearbox and automatic transmission

pointed pliers and release it from its location groove in the main case (photo).
35 On single rail selector gearboxes, rotate the extension housing until the cut-away is in such a position that the layshaft can be drawn from the main casing. This position is shown in photo 3.37.
36 Using a suitable diameter soft metal drift, tap the layshaft rearwards until it is possible to pull it from the rear face of the main case (photo) but before removing note its horizontal position in the rear face of the housing.
37 Remove the layshaft from the main case (photo).
38 Allow the layshaft gear train to drop to the bottom of the main case.
39 Using a parallel pin punch or a tapered soft metal drift, tap the outer track of the input shaft bearing forward until there is a gap between the circlip located in the outer circumference of the outer track (photo).
40 Using a screwdriver with the blade between the circlip and main case gently prise the bearing from the face of the main case (photo).

41 Lift the caged bearing from the spigot end of the mainshaft (photo).
42 Lift the synchroniser sleeve from the 3rd and top synchroniser hub (photo).
43 The extension housing and mainshaft assembly may now be drawn rearward from the main case (photo).
44 Lift the layshaft gear train from inside the main case. Note which way round it is fitted (photo). Recover the two layshaft gear train thrust washers, then remove the needle roller bearings. On single rail selector gearboxes remove the spacer sleeve.
45 Using a suitable diameter drift, carefully tap the idler shaft rearwards (photo).
46 Note which way round the idler shaft and reverse idler gear are fitted and lift away the shaft, gear and spacer sleeve.
47 To separate the mainshaft from the extension housing, use a pair of pointed pliers to compress the circlip located in the space between the 1st gear and the extension housing face. Carefully disengage it from its groove (photo).

3.33 Spigot bearing and O-ring removal

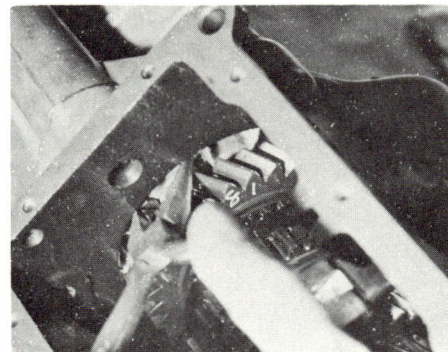
3.34 Rear bearing retaining circlip removal

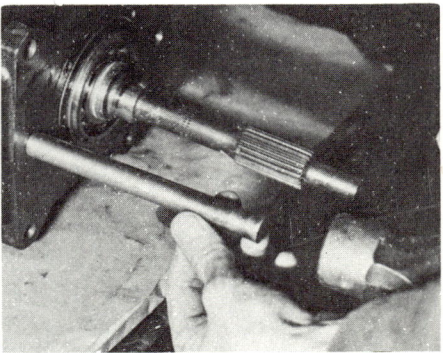
3.36 Layshaft removal using a drift

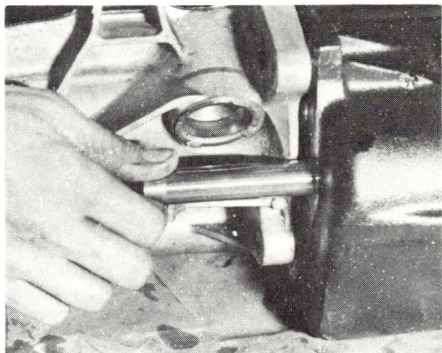
3.37 Lifting away layshaft

3.39 Using pin punch to move input shaft bearing outer track

3.40 Prising bearing outer track from main casing with screwdriver

3.41 Mainshaft caged bearing removal

3.42 Synchroniser sleeve removal

3.43 Removal of extension housing and mainshaft assembly

3.44 Layshaft gear train removal

3.45 Idler shaft removal

3.47 Clip being released from extension housing

3.48 Mainshaft being tapped through extension housing

3.49 Lifting away mainshaft

3.52 Circlip removal from end of mainshaft

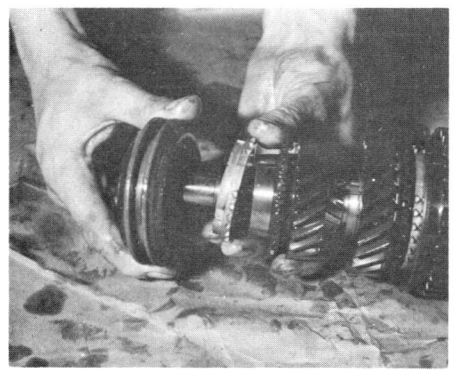
3.53 Removing 3rd and top synchromesh sleeve and hub assembly

3.55 2nd speed gear and thrust washer retaining circlip removal

3.56 Lifting away circlip and thrust washer

3.57 2nd speed gear and synchroniser sleeve removal

3.58 Mainshaft rear bearing retaining circlip removal

3.62 Lifting away speedometer drive gear, small circlip, bearing, oil scoop ring, large circlip, 1st gear and synchroniser sleeve

Chapter 6 Manual gearbox and automatic transmission

48 Using a soft-faced hammer, tap the end of the mainshaft so releasing the mainshaft bearing outer track from its bore in the extension housing (photo).
49 Lift the mainshaft forward and away from the extension housing (photo).
50 The gearbox is now completely stripped out from the main casing and extension housing.
51 Clean out the interior thoroughly and check for dropped needle rollers and spring pins.
52 With the mainshaft on the bench, using a pair of circlip pliers expand the circlip retaining the 3rd and top synchromesh hub on the mainshaft. Lift away the circlip (photo).
53 Lift the 3rd and top synchromesh sleeve and hub assembly from the end of the mainshaft. Note which way round it is fitted. Lift away the synchromesh sleeve from the coned face of the 3rd gear (photo). Keep these parts together and if possible do not separate the synchromesh sleeve from the hub.
54 Slide the 3rd speed gear from the mainshaft.
55 Using a pair of circlip pliers expand the circlip retaining the 2nd speed gear and thrust washer on the mainshaft (photo).
56 Slide the circlip and the thrust washer from the mainshaft (photo).
57 The 2nd speed gear and synchronizer sleeve may next be lifted away from the mainshaft (photo).
58 Using a pair of circlip pliers, expand the circlip located at the rear of the mainshaft bearing, lift it from its groove and slide it down the mainshaft toward the speedometer drive gear (photo).
59 Place the mainshaft between soft faces placed on the jaws of a bench vice so that the rear end is uppermost and the face of the 1st gear is on the drive. Note the exact location of the speedometer drive gear.
60 Using a soft-faced hammer drive the mainshaft through the gear and bearing assembly. It may be found that the speedometer drive gear is tight and in extreme cases it may be necessary to gently heat it with a blow torch. On three rail selector gearboxes the drive gear is located with a detent ball.
61 It should be noted that the 1st and 2nd gear synchroniser hub is an integral part of the mainshaft and no attempt should be made to remove it (see photo 3.64).
62 Lift away the speedometer drive gear, small circlip, bearing, oil scoop ring, large circlip, 1st gear and synchroniser sleeve (photo).
63 This photo shows the order of the parts as they are removed from the mainshaft.
64 The mainshaft is now dismantled with the exception of the synchroniser hub which stays on (photo). Mark the synchromesh sleeve, hub and blocker bars for each synchromesh unit so that they may be refitted in their original positions.
65 Slide the synchromesh sleeve from the hub and lift away the blocker bars and springs.
66 The input shaft assembly may be dismantled by first removing the circlip using a pair of circlip pliers (photo).
67 Place the drive gear on the top of the vice with the outer track of the race resting on soft faces.
68 Using a soft-faced hammer drive the input shaft through the race inner track. The strain placed on the bearing does not matter, as the bearing would not be removed unless it was being renewed. Alternatively use a three legged puller.
69 Lift away the race from the input shaft noting that the circlip groove on the outer track is offset towards the front.

4 Manual gearbox – inspection

1 It is assumed that the gearbox has been dismantled for reasons of excessive noise, lack of synchromesh on certain gears, or for failure to stay in gear. If anything more drastic than this exists (eg total failure, seizure or gear case cracked) it would be better to leave well alone and look for a replacement, either a second hand or exchange unit.
2 Examine all gears for excessively worn, chipped, pitted or damaged teeth. Any such gears should be renewed. It will usually be found that if a tooth is damaged in the layshaft gear train the mating gear teeth on the mainshaft will also be damaged.
3 Check all synchroniser sleeves for wear on the bearing surface which normally have clearly defined oil reservoir grooves in them. If these are smooth or obviously uneven, renewal is essential. When fitted to their mating cones – as they would be in operation – there should be no rock. This would signify ovality, or lack of concentricity. One of the most satisfactory ways of checking is by comparing the fit of a new sleeve on the hub with the old one. If the grooves of the sleeve are obviously worn or damaged (causing engagement difficulties) the sleeve should be renewed.
4 All ball bearings should be checked for clatter. It is advisable to renew these anyway, even though they may not appear to be too badly worn.
5 Circlips, which in this particular gearbox, are all important in locating bearings, gears and hubs, should also be checked to ensure that they are not distorted or damaged. In any case a selection of new circlips of varying thickness should be obtained to compensate for variations in new components fitted, or wear in old ones.
6 The thrust washers at the ends of the layshaft gear train should also be renewed as they will almost certainly have worn if the gearbox is of any age.
7 The caged bearing between the input shaft and the mainshaft will usually be found in good order, but if in any doubt renew the needles as necessary.
8 The sliding hubs themselves are also subject to wear and where the fault has been failure of any gear to remain engaged, or actual difficulty in engagement, then the hub is one of the likely suspects.
9 The ends of the splines are machined in such a way as to form a 'Keystone' effect on engagement with the corresponding mainshaft gear. Do not confuse this with wear. Check that the blocker bars (sliding keys) are not sloppy and move freely. If there is any rock or backlash between the inner and outer sections of the hub, the whole assembly must be renewed, particularly if there has been a complaint of jumping out of gear.

5 Manual gearbox – reassembly

1 To reassemble the input shaft, place the race against soft metal (eg. an old shell bearing suitably straightened) on the top of the jaws of the vice and, using a drift located in the mainshaft spigot bearing hole in the rear of the input shaft, drive the shaft into the bearing. Make

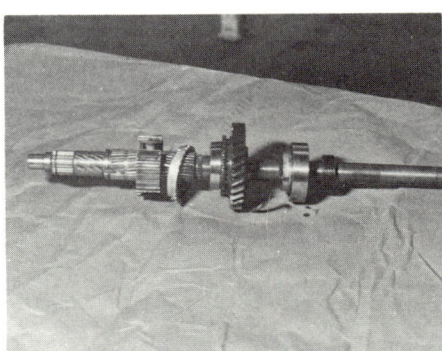

3.63 Mainshaft with components of photo 3.62 in correct order

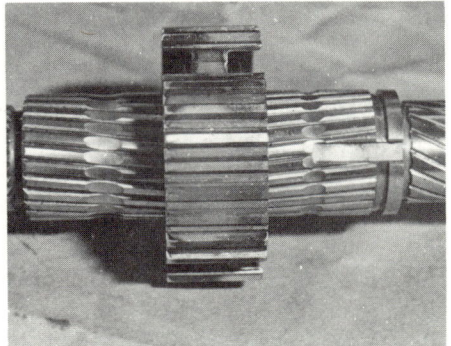

3.64 Synchroniser hub which cannot be removed from mainshaft

3.66 Input shaft bearing circlip removal

sure the bearing is the correct way round. Alternatively use a piece of long tube of suitable diameter (photo).
2 Refit the circlip that secures the bearing and also the one located in the bearing outer track.
3 To reassemble the mainshaft fit the two springs into the synchromesh hub which is part of the mainshaft (photo).
4 Fit the blocker bars into the grooves in the hub and grasp using the thumb and index finger (photo).
5 Carefully slide the sleeve onto the hub so retaining the blocker bars. The grooved end should be toward the front of the mainshaft (photo).
6 Fit the synchroniser sleeve and 1st gear to the mainshaft (photo).
7 Slide the oil scoop ring, larger diameter to the rear of the mainshaft, and bearing onto the mainshaft (photo).
8 Using a piece of suitable diameter tube drift the bearing into position on the mainshaft (photo).
9 Slide the 2nd gear synchroniser sleeve and 2nd gear onto the mainshaft (photo).
10 Fit a new circlip into the groove on the mainshaft so retaining the 2nd gear.
11 Fit a new circlip into the groove on the mainshaft at the rear of the bearing (photo).
12 Using a suitable diameter tube locate the speedometer drive gear into position on the mainshaft as noted during removal (photo). Ensure that the detent ball is correctly located where fitted.
13 Slide the 3rd gear, synchroniser sleeve and hub assembly onto the front of the mainshaft (photo).
14 Retain the assembly with a new circlip. Make sure that it is correctly seated in its groove (photo).
15 Using a screwdriver ease a new large diameter circlip over the mainshaft bearing and into the gap between 1st gear and the bearing (photo).
16 Now that the mainshaft assembly is complete, in the single rail selector type gearbox it can be refitted to the extension housing (paragraph 17 on). The three rail selector type gearbox mainshaft unit should be put to one side and will be inserted direct into the gearbox after the layshaft has been 'semi located' in the gear case (proceed from paragraph 23).
17 Lay the extension housing on its side and carefully insert the mainshaft (photo).
18 Place the extension housing on the edge of the bench so that the mainshaft end can protrude when fully home. Using a soft-faced hammer drive the mainshaft bearing into the extension housing bore (photo).
19 Using a pair of pointed pliers and small screwdriver refit the bearing retaining circlip. This is a fiddle and can take time (photo).
20 Apply grease to the mating face of the extension housing and fit a new gasket (photo).
21 Check to see that the reverse relay arm is free yet without signs of wear, otherwise it should be renewed (photo).
22 Place the reverse idler gear into its location in the main casing and engage it with the reverse relay arm. Slide in the idler shaft, plain end first, and push fully home (photo).
23 The layshaft gear train needle roller bearings are now reassembled (photo).
24 Slide the spacer tube into the layshaft gear train bore (single rail selector gearbox only).
25 Smear some general purpose grease in either end of the bore.
26 Insert one of the spacer shims (photo).
27 Refer to photo 5.23 and it will be seen that the longer needle rollers are fitted to the smaller diameter end of the layshaft gear train bore.
28 Fit the smaller needle rollers into the forward end of the bore. Do not handle the needle rollers more than absolutely necessary as they will warm up and therefore not adhere to the grease (photo).
29 With the first set of needle rollers in position carefully fit the second spacer shim (photo).
30 Obtain a piece of bar or tube having approximately the same diameter as the layshaft and the same length as the layshaft gear train. Slide this halfway into the bore of the layshaft gear train so acting as a retainer for the needle rollers.
31 Insert a spacer shim into the rear end of the layshaft gear train bore and fit the second set of needle rollers in the same manner as for the first set (photo).

5.1 Input shaft bearing refitting

5.3 Fitting springs into synchromesh hub

5.4 Fitting blocker bars to synchromesh hub

5.5 Synchromesh sleeve being slid onto hub

5.6 Fitting synchroniser sleeve and 1st gear onto mainshaft

5.7 Fitting oil scoop ring and bearing onto mainshaft

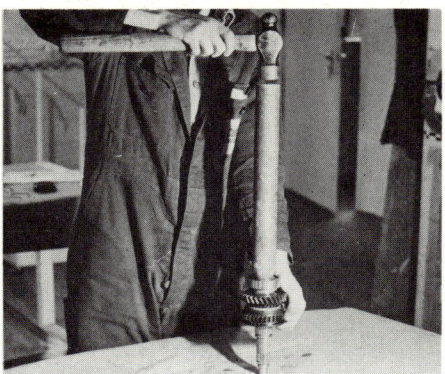

5.8 Drifting bearing onto mainshaft

5.9 2nd gear synchroniser sleeve and 2nd gear being fitted to mainshaft

5.11 Rear bearing retaining circlip refitting

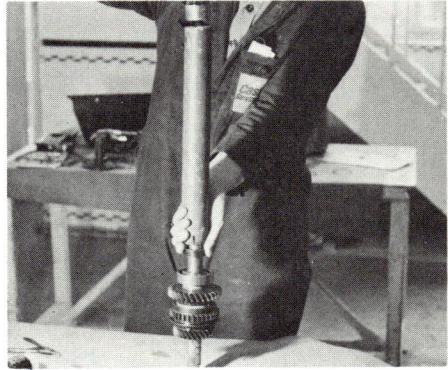

5.12 Drifting speedometer drive gear onto mainshaft

5.13 3rd gear, synchroniser sleeve and hub assembly

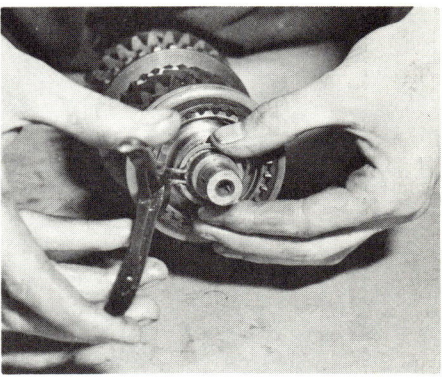

5.14 Fitting circlip to mainshaft to retain 3rd gear assembly

5.15 Easing circlip over mainshaft bearing and into position between 1st gear and bearing

5.17 Fitting mainshaft into extension housing – Stage 1

5.18 Drifting mainshaft bearing into extension housing – Stage 2

5.19 Fitting bearing retaining circlip

5.20 Fitting new gasket to greased face of extension housing

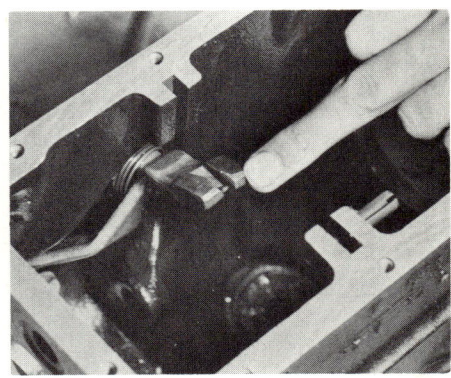

5.21 Reverse relay arm

5.22 Fitting reverse idler gear and shaft into main casing

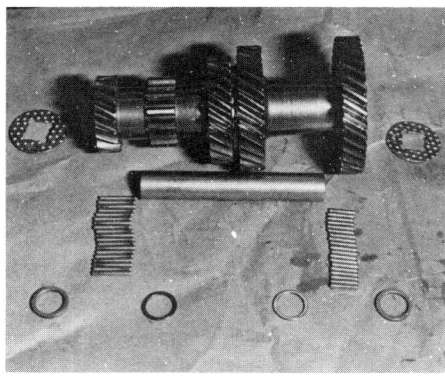

5.23 Component parts of layshaft

5.26 Inserting spacer shim into layshaft bore

5.28 Fitting needle rollers into layshaft bore

5.29 Inserting second spacer shim into layshaft bore

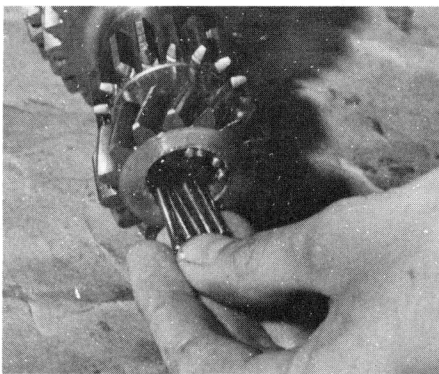

5.31 Fitting second set of needle rollers into layshaft bore

5.34a Fitting thrust washers to greased face of layshaft gear train

5.34b Fitting layshaft gear train into main casing

5.35 Inserting mainshaft into main casing

5.36 Fitting caged bearing into input shaft

5.38 Drifting input shaft into its final fitted position

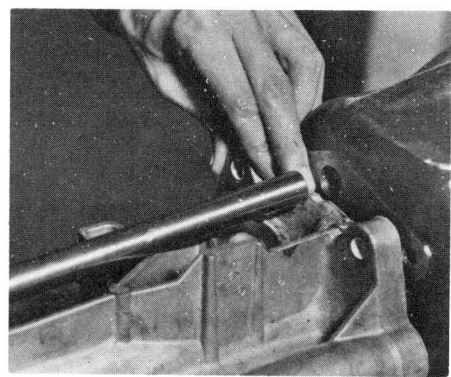

5.40 Inserting layshaft into main casing

Chapter 6 Manual gearbox and automatic transmission

32 Fit the last spacer shim and push the previously obtained bar or tube through the second set of needle roller bearings.
33 Smear general purpose grease on each thrust washer face of the layshaft gear train.
34 Fit the thrust washers to the layshaft gear train, (photo), then carefully lower the layshaft gear train into the main casing making sure that the thrust washers are not dislodged (photo).
35 Support the main casing on the bench so that it is upright and then insert the mainshaft through the rear face of the main casing (photo).
36 Apply some general purpose grease to the caged bearing that fits into the bore in the rear of the input shaft. Fit the bearing into the bore (photo).
37 Fit the synchroniser sleeve to the taper on the rear of the input shaft and insert the input shaft into the front face of the main case. Manipulate the mainshaft spigot so that it enters the caged bearing in the rear of the input shaft.
38 Using a soft-faced hammer on the spigot at the front of the input shaft, tap the shaft until the bearing outer track circlip is fully home in its recess in the main casing (photo).
39 On the single rail selector gearbox, it will be necessary to invert the gearbox and turn the extension housing, so that its away section is positioned to allow the layshaft to be inserted through the rear face of the gear case.
40 Turn the input shaft and mainshaft so that the layshaft gear train can drop into engagement. Visually line up the layshaft bore hole in the main case with the centre of the layshaft gear train and slide the layshaft into position. The milled end of the layshaft is toward the rear of the main case (photo).
41 Turn the layshaft until it is positioned as shown in the photo. Tap in until the main part of the shaft is flush with the rear face (photo).
42 Check that the idler shaft and layshaft protrusions will line up with the slots in the extension housing.
43 On the single rail type gearbox push the extension housing up to the rear face of the main casing.
44 On the three rail type gearbox, the extension housing is now fitted over the protruding mainshaft and bolted into position against the main casing. Position a new gasket between the gear case and extension mating faces and ensure that the speedometer driven gear bearing and O-ring are in position in the extension before refitting the extension housing.
45 Secure the extension housing with the bolts and spring washers.
46 Smear some general purpose grease on the groove in the front face of the main casing and fit a new O-ring seal (photo).
47 Slide the spigot bearing over the input shaft. Make sure that the slight internal recess is toward the bottom, or line up the marks made during dismantling (photo).
48 Secure the spigot bearing with the four bolts and spring washers (photo). Tighten in a diagonal manner to ensure that the O-ring seals correctly.

Single rail selector mechanism – reassembly

49 Slide the selector rail through the extension housing until the end protrudes into the main casing (photo).
50 The selector forks may next be fitted into the main casing as shown in this photo. Check to ensure that the fork ends engage into the sleeve grooves.
51 Slide the reverse selector boss into the lockplate (photo).
52 The selector rail can now be passed through the selector fork bosses until the cut-away is just at the rear of the front face (photo).
53 Line up the hole in the reverse selector boss and selector rail and insert the spring pin to lock the two parts together (photo).
54 Fit the spring pin to the lockplate mounting and tap fully home (photo).
55 Refit the blanking plug to the main case rear face (photo).
56 Insert the selector rail blocker bar and spring into the drilling in the front left-hand side of the main case (photos 3.10 and 3.11).
57 Screw in the side plug and tighten with an Allen key.
58 Fit the extension housing rear cover, smearing some sealing compound on the outer circumference. Do not tap it down the bore more than necessary otherwise it could cause problems in selecting gears.
59 Smear some grease on the top face of the main case, fit the new gasket and then refit the top cover (photo).
60 Secure the top cover with the ten bolts and shakeproof washers.

5.41 Correct positioning of layshaft cutaway

5.46 Fitting new O-ring to front face of main casing

5.47 Sliding spigot bearing over input shaft

5.48 Securing spigot bearing to main casing

5.49 Fitting selector rail into extension housing

5.50 Fitting selector forks to main casing

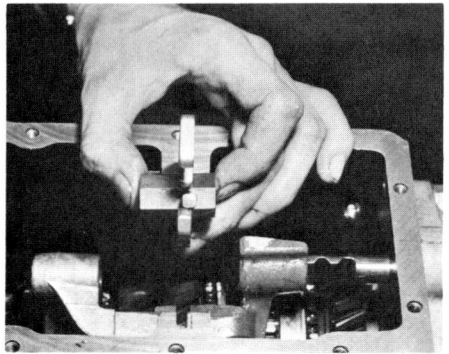
5.51 Sliding reverse selector boss into the lock plate

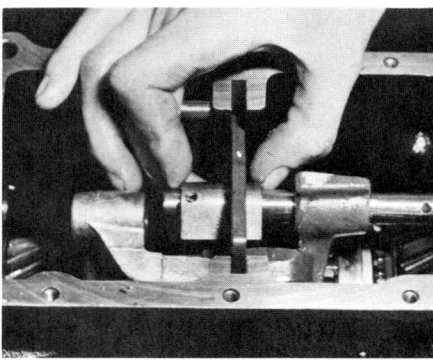
5.52 Sliding selector rail through selector forks

5.53 Fitting spring pin to reverse selector boss and rail

5.54 Fitting lockplate mounting spring pin

5.55 Fitting blanking plug to main case rear face

5.59 Fitting new gasket and top cover

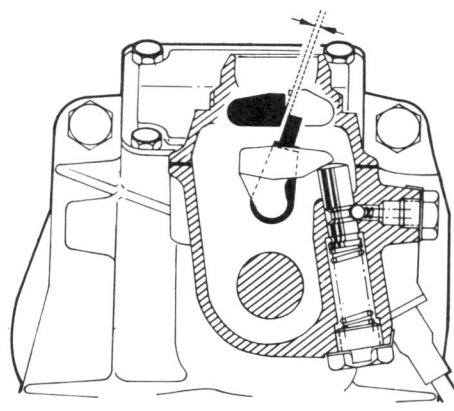
Fig. 6.8 Check the selector fork finger to 3rd/4th gear selector rail clearance, at point indicated (Sec. 5)

5.73 Securing clutch housing with bolts and spring washers

Three rail selector mechanism – reassembly

61 Reassemble the speedometer drive pinion, the reverse gear interlock assembly and new oil seal into the extension housing. Be sure to fit a new O-ring seal to the speedometer drive, use a new tab washer and bend it over the bolt head to secure the interlock assembly. If fitting a new oil seal, lubricate it to ease assembly and drift it into position carefully and evenly so that it is not distorted.

62 Place the respective selector forks into position. Now carefully slide the 1st/2nd selector rail into its bore (right-hand side) in the rear of the case and pass it through to locate in the selector fork. Align the holes in fork and rail and insert the roll pin to secure. Insert the interlock plunger.

63 Repeat the above procedure with the 3rd/4th selector and rail, inserting through the central bore in the case, and with the pin fitted, insert the circlip and roll pin to secure, (use a new circlip).

64 The reverse selector rail can be refitted and located with its fork in the same manner. Apply some sealant to a new pin plug and drive into position.

65 Relocate the reverse gear relay lever and retain with a new roll pin.
66 Slide the selector shaft into its housing and refit the cover with a new gasket, but do not fully tighten the bolts at this stage.
67 Relocate the selector shaft bracket and retaining bolts.
68 Refit the selector fork onto the shaft and secure with stud bolt.
69 Insert the respective detent bolts and springs (lubricate with a medium grease) into their respective locating bores in the front face of the gearbox. Fit a new gasket smeared with sealant solution to the gearbox cover, and position the cover onto the top of the gearbox, retaining with the bolts.
70 Before refitting the extension housing cover, check the clearance between the selector fork finger and third and top gear selector rail. To do this, position the selector shaft at the reverse gear stop, then, using a suitable lever, move the 3rd/4th gear selector rail to the rear and check the clearance between the selector fork finger and the selector (Fig. 6.8) using a feeler gauge. The clearance should be 0·035 in (0·9 mm). Any adjustment to this clearance is made by fitting an alternative reverse gear interlock plunger, which are available with varying

Chapter 6 Manual gearbox and automatic transmission

tolerances to suit.
71 Use a new gasket and smear with sealant when refitting the extension housing cover.

Final assembly

72 Wipe the mating faces of the clutch housing and main casing and offer up the clutch housing.
73 Secure the clutch housing with the four bolts and spring washers (photo).
74 Fit the clutch release arm to the clutch housing and then the release bearing to the release arm. Turn through 90° to lock.
75 The gearbox is now ready for refitting. Do not forget to refill the gearbox with the correct amount and grade of oil upon refitting.

6 Automatic transmission – general description

An automatic transmission unit may be fitted as a factory option. It takes the place of the clutch and manual gearbox, which are, of course, mounted behind the engine.
The system comprises two main components:

a) *A three element hydrokinetic torque converter coupling, capable of torque multiplication at an infinitely variable ratio between 2:1 and 1:1.*
b) *A torque/speed responsive and hydraulic epicyclic gearbox comprising a planetary gearset providing three forward ratios and one reverse ratio.*

Due to the complexity of the automatic transmission unit, if performance is not up to standard, or overhaul is necessary, it is imperative that this be left to the local Ford main agents who will have the special equipment and knowledge for fault diagnosis and rectification.

7 Automatic transmission – fluid level and maintenance

1 It is important that transmission fluid manufactured only to the correct specification is used. The capacity of the complete unit is given in the Specifications. Drain and refill capacity will be less as the torque converter cannot be completely drained, but this operation should not be necessary except for repairs.
2 Every 6000 miles (10 000 km) or more frequently, check the automatic transmission fluid level. The car must be standing on level ground and with the engine at its normal operating temperature. Move the selector lever through all positions at least three times. Select the 'P' position and wait for at least 1 minute. With the engine idling withdraw the dipstick, wipe it clean and refit it. Quickly withdraw it again and note the level. If necessary top-up with the specified automatic transmission fluid. The difference between the LOW and FULL marks on the dipstick is 1 pint (0·57 litres). If required, top up the fluid level through the dipstick tube.
3 If the unit has been drained, it is recommended that only new fluid is used. Fill up to the correct FULL level by gradually refilling the unit. The exact amount will depend on how much was left in the converter after draining.
IMPORTANT: Do NOT under any circumstances run the engine when there is no hydraulic fluid in the transmission.
4 Ensure that the exterior of the converter housing and gearbox is always kept free from dust or mud, otherwise over-heating will occur.

8 Automatic transmission – removal and refitting

Any suspected faults must be referred to the main agent before unit removal, as with this type of transmission the fault must be confirmed, using specialist equipment, before it has been removed from the car.
1 For safety reasons disconnect the battery earth terminal.
2 Jack up the car and support on firmly based axle stands if a lift or pit are not available.
3 Mark the mating flanges of the propeller shaft and final drive so that they may be reconnected in their original positions and undo and remove the four securing bolts.
4 If a split type propeller shaft is fitted, undo and remove the centre bearing retainer securing bolts, spring and plain washers.

5 Draw the propeller shaft rearward so detaching the front end from the rear of the transmission unit and lift away from under the car.
6 Wrap some polythene around the end of the transmission and secure with string or wire to stop any fluid running out.
7 Undo and remove the nuts securing the exhaust downpipes to the exhaust manifolds. Detach the exhaust pipes from their mounting brackets and tie back away from the transmission unit.
8 Make a note of the cable connections to the starter motor and detach the cables.
9 Undo and remove the two bolts securing the starter motor to the transmission flange. Lift away the starter motor (and heat shield if fitted).
10 On early models, release the spring clip and withdraw the clevis pin securing the selector cable to the selector lever. Detach the selector cable mounting from the transmission. On later models, detach the two clips retaining the selector rod and withdraw the rod.
11 Detach the downshift cable from the accelerator linkage and then from the transmission housing (Fig. 6.8a).
12 Detach the vacuum pipes from the vacuum diaphragm.
13 Make a note of the electrical cable connections to the starter inhibitor switch. Detach the leads from the switch.
14 Wipe the area around the oil cooler pipes at the transmission unit and then detach the pipes. To prevent dirt ingress plug the ends of the pipes and unions.
15 Disconnect the speedometer cable from the side of the transmission unit.
16 Detach the engine damper/s from the engine and body mountings and lift away the damper/s.
17 Disconnect the filler pipe securing bracket from the torque converter housing and withdraw the pipe from the transmission casing.
18 It should be noted that on FOB (Ford of Britain) models the filler tube will have to be disconnected from the oil sump.
19 Plug the opening to stop loss of hydraulic fluid or place a container under the unit to catch the fluid. Then plug the end to stop any fluid draining out when the unit is being removed.
20 Undo and remove the four bolts and spring washers securing the converter housing bottom plate. Lift away the bottom plate.
21 Working through the starter motor aperture undo and remove the four bolts securing the torque converter to the drive plate (photo). On some models, remove the rubber bung from the aperture cut-out to align the socket with the bolt/nut head (Fig. 6.11). For this to be accomplished it will be necessary to turn the crankshaft. Remove the bolts in a progressive manner, one turn at a time.
22 Place a piece of soft wood on the saddle of a jack and support the weight of the transmission unit.
23 Place two wooden blocks between the engine and crossmember so that when the transmission is being removed the engine does not drop too far.
24 Undo and remove the two bolts and spring washers that secure the transmission to the crossmember. Also remove the four bolts and washers securing the crossmember to the floor panel. Lift away the crossmember (Fig. 6.12).
25 Slowly lever the jacks until there is sufficient clearance between the top of the converter housing and the underside of the floor for the transmission to be satisfactorily withdrawn.

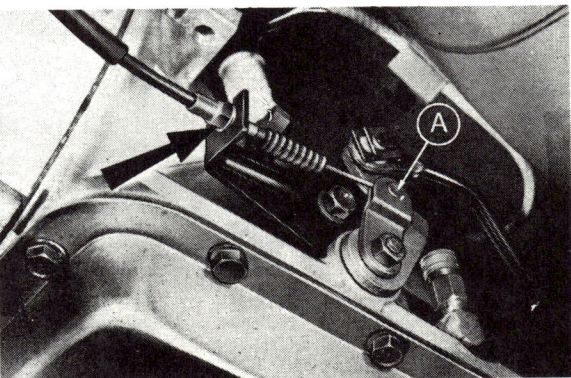

Fig. 6.9 Downshift cable attachment (arrowed) and downshift lever (A) (Sec. 8)

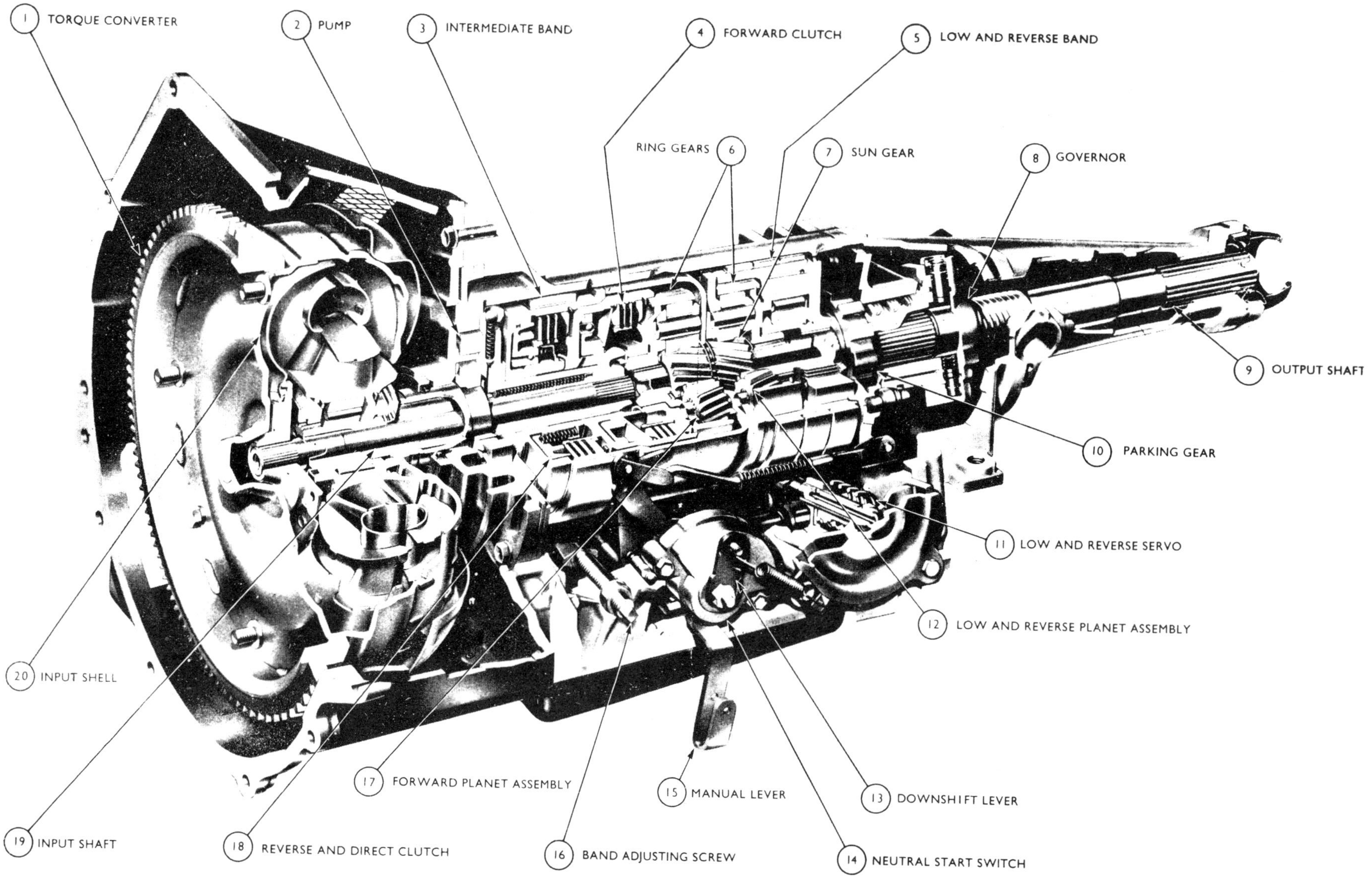

Fig. 6.10 Cross sectional view of C4 automatic transmission

Chapter 6 Manual gearbox and automatic transmission

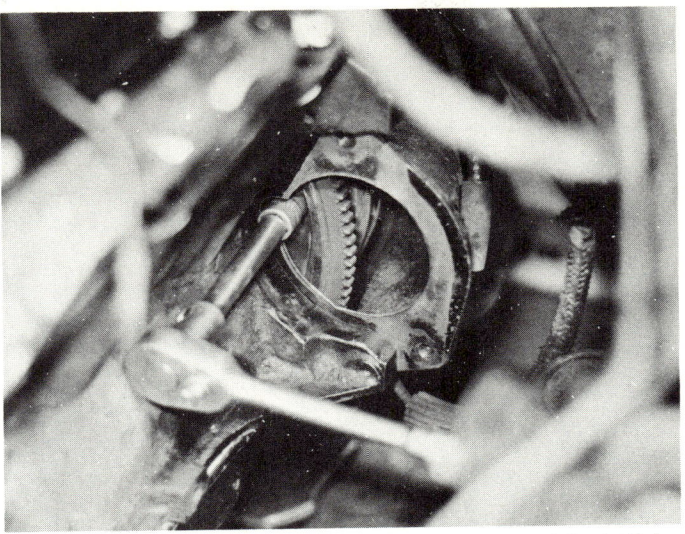

8.21 Removing the torque converter to drive plate retaining bolts/nuts

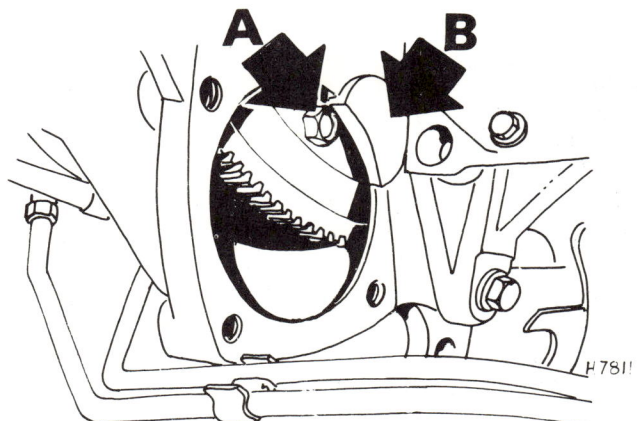

Fig. 6.11 Remove the rubber grommet (B) for access to the drive plate bolts (A) (Sec. 8)

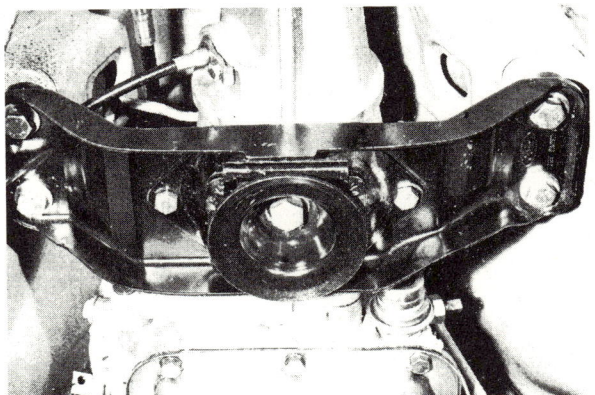

Fig. 6.12 Transmission crossmember (Sec. 8)

26 Undo and remove the bolts and spring washers securing the converter housing to the rear of the engine.
27 The assistance of at least one other person is now required because of the weight of the complete unit. Carefully pull the unit rearward and hold the converter in place in the housing, as it will still be full of hydraulic fluid.
28 Finally withdraw the unit from under the car and place on wooden blocks so that the selector lever is not damaged or bent.

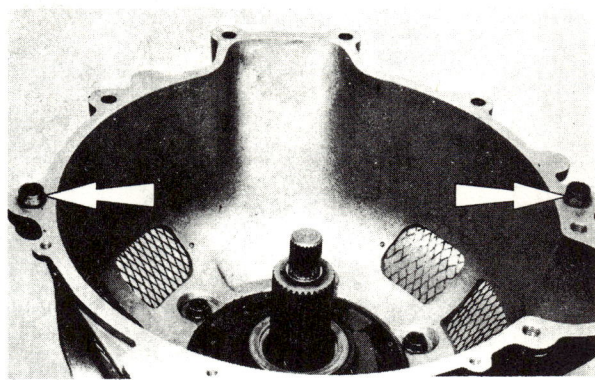

Fig. 6.13 Location of alignment dowels (Sec. 8)

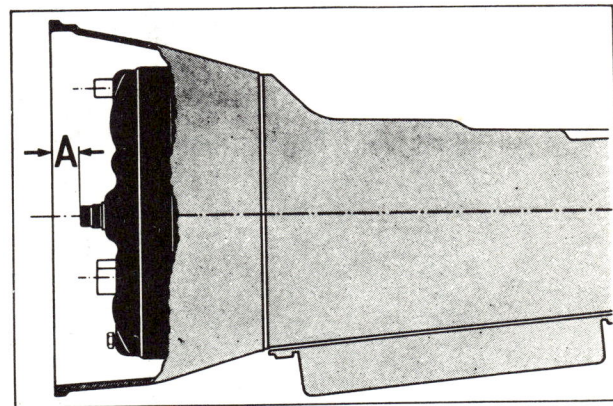

Fig. 6.14 Converter face flange to central stub face clearance (A) (Sec. 8)

29 To separate the converter housing from the transmission case first lift off the converter from the transmission unit, taking suitable precautions to catch the fluid upon separation.
30 Undo and remove the six bolts and spring washers which secure the converter housing to the transmission case. Lift away the converter housing.
31 Refitting the automatic transmission unit is the reverse sequence to removal, but there are several additional points which will assist.

   a) It is recommended that the front band adjustment is checked before the unit is refitted.
   b) If the torque converter has been removed, before refitting it will be necessary to align the front pump drive tangs with the slots in the inner gear and then carefully refit the torque converter. Take care not to damage the oil seal.
   c) Before mounting the transmission on the engine remove the two dowel pins from the converter housing flange and push them in the engine block. (Fig. 6.3).
   d) The oil drain plug must align with the drive plate opening.
   e) When the torque converter hub is fully engaged in the pump gear, the distance between the converter facing flange and the central stub face must be at least 0.4 in (10 mm) as shown in Fig. 6.14.
   f) Adjust the manual selector linkage, the throttle downshift cable and the inhibitor switch. Full details of these adjustments will be found in subsequent Sections.
   g) Refer to Section 7 and check the fluid level, and top up if required. Check for signs of leaks particularly in the oil cooler pipes and connections.

9 Selector lever assembly – removal and refitting

1 Carefully lift the quadrant cover from its mounting bracket.
2 *Granada models:* The centre console must be removed. Further

information will be found in Chapter 12.

3   The gear shift gate may next be removed followed by the dial light assembly from the holder on the selector lever assembly.

4   Chock the front wheels, jack up the rear of the car and support on firmly based stands.

5   Working under the car withdraw the spring pin retaining the clevis pin to the bottom of the selector arm. Withdraw the clevis pin and detach the selector cable. On later models a rod is fitted instead of the cable and this is removed by unclipping the retaining clip from the lever.

6   Undo and remove the four nuts and spring washers securing the selector lever casing and lift away the complete assembly.

7   Refitting the selector lever assembly is the reverse sequence to removal. The following additional points should be noted:

   a) Lubricate all moving parts with engine oil.
   b) Adjust the selector cable rod as described in Section 11.

10 Selector lever assembly – overhaul

1   Refer to Section 9 and remove the lever assembly.

2   Carefully remove the rubber plugs on the selector lever casing.

3   Undo and remove the nuts and carefully tap the lever arm from the casing. Recover the bushes.

4   Undo and remove the operating cable lower nuts and then remove the locking bush and springs from the selector lever.

5   Using an Allen key remove the grub screw from the top of the selector lever handle. Remove the handle.

6   The release button may now be withdrawn from the handle.

7   Using a suitable diameter parallel pin punch remove the roll pin from the release unit and remove the release unit complete with the operating cable from the lever arm.

8   Reassembly of the selector lever is the reverse sequence to removal. It will, however, be necessary to adjust the operating cable.

9   Move the selector lever to the 'D' position and, using feeler gauges set to 0·005 – 0·010 inch (0.13 – 0.25 mm) between the locking pins and stop in the casing, adjust the operating cable to obtain the required clearance.

11 Selector cable – removal and refitting

1   Release the spring clip and withdraw the clevis pin attaching the cable to the lever arm on the side of the transmission unit. Now remove the cable locknut.

2   Slacken the cable retaining locknut and disconnect the cable from the manual selector lever. To do this withdraw the spring pin and the clevis pin.

3   Slacken the nut on the cable on the upper holder. The cable may now be removed from the car.

4   To refit the cable move the manual selector lever to the 'P' position. Position the cable on the car and secure it to the upper holder and the manual selector lever.

5   Secure the cable holder to the bracket and position the cable in the lower bracket. Adjust the cable in the lower bracket until the bolts can be inserted into the lever arm of the transmission without any difficulty.

6   Now mount the cable on the transmission lever arm. Move the manual selector lever, and check to ensure that all gear positions can be obtained and also that the lever is retained in each position. Tighten all attachments.

12 Selector rod – removal and refitting

1   Unclip each of the retaining clips from the shift rod and remove the rod.

2   The rod guide bushes must be renewed in the transmission and selection lever if badly worn.

3   To refit, the shift lever must be in the 'D' position (see Fig. 6.6) which is two notches back from the front stop position.

4   Relocate the rod to the lever arm and secure with the clip.

5   The rod is now adjusted to length so that it can be fitted without undue strain. Tighten the locknut.

6   Check that the gear shift rod adjustable end is in the vertical position and reconnect the shift rod to the selector arm, and retain with the clip.

7   Operate the manual shift lever and ensure that it can engage each of the shift positions. Readjust the shift rod if necessary.

13 Downshift cable – removal, refitting and adjustment

1   Working under the car detach the cable from the downshift lever on the side of the transmission unit. Detach the outer cable from the support bracket.

2   The return spring on the reverse lever should be allowed to hang down.

3   Now working under the bonnet detach the cable from the carburettor operating shaft and the outer cable from the bracket.

4   Detach and remove the return spring.

5   To refit the downshift cable, working under the car connect the outer cable to the bracket and the inner cable to the downshift lever on the side of the transmission unit. Tighten the two nuts in the centre of the thread length.

6   Reconnect the inner cable to the operating shaft of the carburettor and the outer cable to the bracket. Screw back the inner locknut completely.

7   Turn the operating shaft into the completely open throttle position and put the downshift lever of the transmission into the kickdown position.

Adjustment – early models

8   Adjust the setting nut until the downshift cable is under moderate tension. Now tighten the locknut.

9   Using 0·004 – 0·01 inch (0.1 – 0.25 mm) feeler gauges measure the play between the full throttle stop and the throttle stop lever of the carburettor. If necessary re-set the adjustment nut.

10 Refit the return spring and then check that the throttle valve opens fully so that the kickdown position can be obtained.

Adjustment – later models

11 Check that the throttle plate/s can be fully opened by depressing the accelerator pedal, then holding the plate/s open to make the adjustment.

12 Using a screwdriver, press the downshift cable connection lever from the operating shaft lever.

13 Refer to Fig. 6.17 and check the clearance between the two levers, which should be 0·02 to 0·05 in (0.5 to 1.3 mm). Adjustment is made by the nut arrowed in the illustration. Loosen the locknut and turn the adjustment nut as required, then retighten the locknut. Reconnect the return springs and check that the throttle valve fully opens during kickdown.

14 Starter inhibitor switch – removal, refitting and adjustment

Early models

1   Working under the car detach and allow the selector cable return spring to hang down and then detach the downshift cable from the lever on the side of the transmission unit.

2   Unscrew the downshift lever from the transmission unit.

3   Unscrew and remove the inhibitor switch securing bolts and withdraw the switch.

4   Make a note of the cable connections to the switch and detach the cables.

5   To refit the inhibitor switch first reconnect the cables and slide the switch onto the selector shaft making a note of the guide slots.

6   Refit the two switch securing bolts together with the downshift cable bracket and tighten hand-tight.

7   Refit the lever and selector cable return spring.

8   Move the selector lever to the 'D' position and now carefully line up the switch in such a manner that a 0·086 inch (2.2 mm) diameter drill shank can be inserted into the switch locking hole without signs of binding. (Fig. 6.18). Tighten the two securing bolts.

9   Reconnect the downshift cable to the lever on the side of the transmission and check the adjustment as described in Section 13.

10 Check that the engine can only be started in the 'P' and 'N' selector lever positions and that the reverse light only operates in the 'R' position.

Chapter 6 Manual gearbox and automatic transmission

149

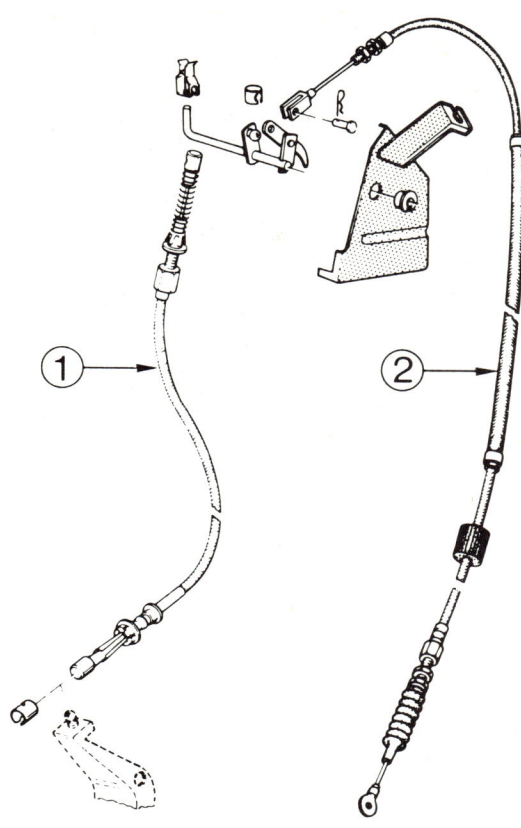

Fig. 6.15 Downshift cable assembly (Sec. 11)

1 Operating cable from accelerator pedal to carburettor
2 Downshift cable

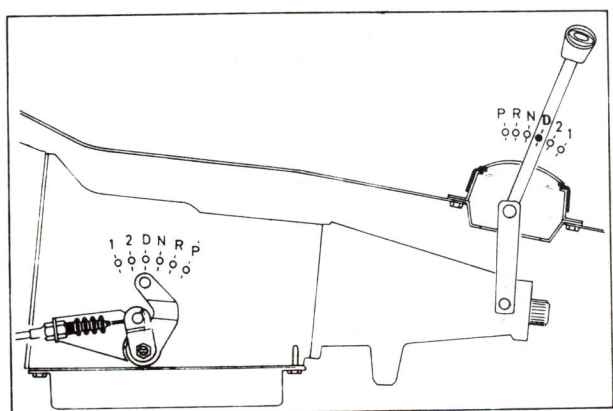

Fig. 6.16 The transmission and manual selector levers in the 'D' position (Sec. 12)

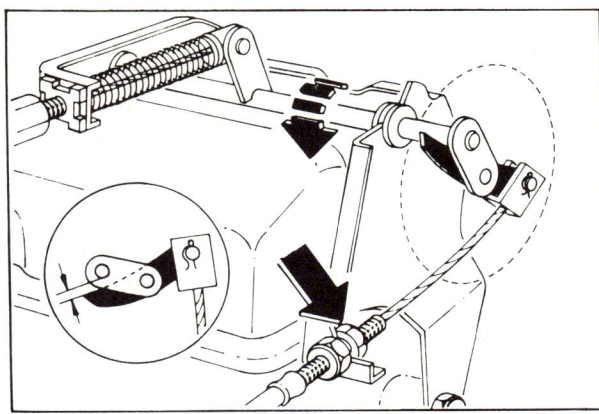

Fig. 6.17 Downshift cable adjustment (Sec. 13)

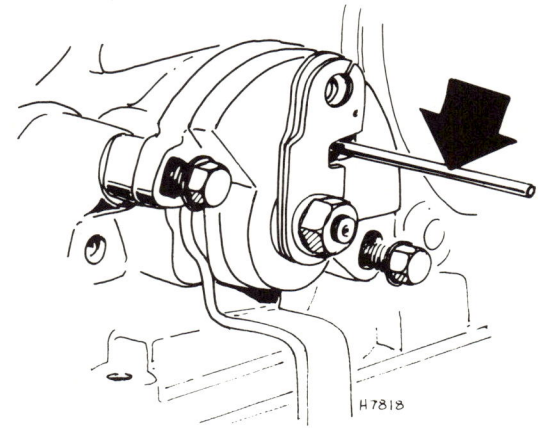

Fig. 6.18 The starter inhibitor switch setting (arrow indicates drill inserted) – early models (Sec. 14)

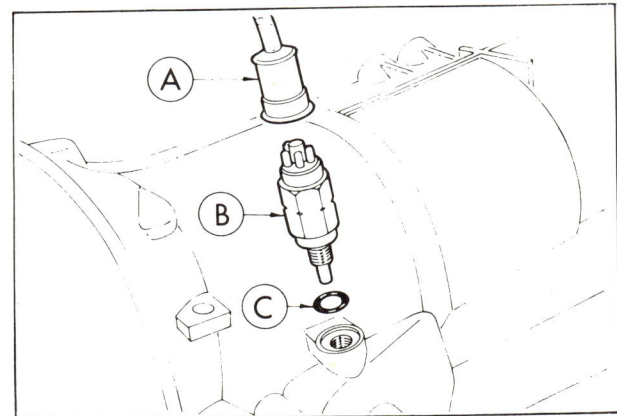

Fig. 6.19 The starter inhibitor switch – later models (Sec. 14)

A Connector   B Inhibitor switch
C O-ring

Later models

11 Referring to Fig. 6.19, disconnect the cable plug from the switch which is located in the transmission housing.
12 The starter inhibitor switch is now removed by unscrewing from the housing. Remove the O-ring seal and discard.
13 Using a new O-ring seal, screw the replacement switch into position and tighten to the specified torque.
14 Reconnect the cable plug to the switch and check that the starter only operates when the selector is in the 'N' or 'P' position. Also check that the reversing light operates only when 'R' is selected.

15 Intermediate band – adjustment

1 The intermediate or front band is used to hold the sun gear stationary so as to give the second gear ratio. If it is not correctly adjusted there will be noticeable slip during first to second gear change or from third to second gear change. The first symptoms of these conditions will be a very sluggish gear change instead of the usual crisp action.
2 To adjust the intermediate band, undo and remove the adjustment

screw locknut located on the left-hand side of the transmission case. Tighten the adjusting screw using a torque wrench set to 10 lbf ft (1·4 kgf m) and then slacken off the adjustment screw 1¾ turns for the C4 type transmission, or 1½ turns for the later C3 type transmission. A new locknut should be fitted and tightened to a torque wrench setting of 35 – 45 lbf ft (4·8 – 6·22 kgf m) (photo).

16 Low and reverse band – adjustment (C4 transmission only)

1   The low and reverse band or rear band is in action when 'L' or 'R' position of the selector lever is obtained to hold the low and reverse pinion carrier stationary. If it is not correctly adjusted, there will be a noticeable malfunction of the automatic transmission unit, whereby there will be no drive with the selector lever in the 'R' position, also associated with no engine braking on first gear when the selector lever is in the 'L' position.
2   To adjust the rear band undo and remove the adjusting screw locknut located on the right-hand side of the transmission case. Tighten the adjusting screw using a torque wrench set to 10 lbf ft (1·4 kgf m) and then slacken off the adjustment screw exactly 3 turns. A new locknut should be fitted and tightened to a torque wrench setting of 35 – 45 lbf ft (4·8 – 6·22 kgf m).

17 Fault finding – automatic transmission

As has been mentioned elsewhere in this Chapter, no service repair should be considered by anyone without the specialist knowledge and equipment required to undertake such work. This is

15.2 The intermediate (front) band adjustment screw and locknut

also relevant to fault diagnosis. If a fault is evident carry out the various adjustments previously described and if the fault still exists consult the local main dealer.

18 Fault finding – manual gearbox

Symptom	Reason/s	Remedy
Weak or ineffective synchromesh	Synchronising cones worn, split or damaged	Dismantle and overhaul gearbox. Fit new gear wheels and synchronising cones.
	Baulk ring synchromesh dogs worn, or damaged	Dismantle and overhaul gearbox. Fit new baulk ring synchromesh.
Jumps out of gear	Broken gear change fork rod spring	Dismantle and renew spring.
	Gearbox coupling dogs badly worn	Dismantle gearbox. Fit new coupling dogs.
	Selector fork rod groove badly worn	Fit new selector fork rod.
	Selector fork rod securing screw and locknut loose	Remove side cover, tighten securing screw and locknut.
Excessive noise	Incorrect grade of oil in gearbox or oil level too low	Drain, refill or top up gearbox with correct grade of oil.
	Bush or needle roller bearings worn or damaged	Dismantle and overhaul gearbox. Renew bearings.
	Gear teeth excessively worn or damaged	Dismantle, overhaul gearbox. Renew gear wheels.
	Laygear thrust washers worn allowing excessive end play	Dismantle and overhaul gearbox. Renew thrust washers.
Excessive difficulty in engaging gear	Clutch pedal adjustment incorrect	Adjust clutch pedal correctly.

Chapter 7 Propeller shaft

Contents

Fault diagnosis- propeller shaft 6
General description 1
Hardy flexible disc – removal and refitting 4
Propeller shaft centre bearing – removal and refitting 3
Propeller shaft – removal and refitting 2
Universal joints – test for wear 5

Specifications

Type .... Single or two piece according to model

Universal joint type .... Needle bearing or flexible coupling according to model

Torque wrench settings
	lbf ft	kgf m
Propeller shaft to drive pinion flange	41–49	5.8–6.8
Centre bearing support bolts	13–17	1.8–2.3
Flexible disc securing bolts	34	4.7

1 General description

Drive is transmitted from the gearbox to the rear axle by a finely balanced tubular propeller shaft. This may be of the single piece or split type depending on the vehicle specification.

Where the split type is fitted an intermediate bearing is used, this is secured to the underside of the floor panels.

Fitted at each end of the shaft is a universal joint which allows for vertical movement of the rear axle, each universal joint comprises a four legged centre spider, four needle roller bearing sets and two yokes. On some models a Hardy flexible coupling replaces the front universal joint.

Fore and aft movement of the rear axle is absorbed by a sliding spline in the front of the propeller shaft which slides over a mating spline on the rear of the gearbox mainshaft.

All models are fitted with the sealed type of universal joint which requires no maintenance.

The propeller shaft assembly is a relatively simple component and therefore reliable in service. Unfortunately it is not possible to obtain spare parts for the conventional universal joints, therefore when these are worn a new assembly must be fitted.

2 Propeller shaft – removal and refitting

Single piece propeller shaft
1 Jack up the rear of the car, or position the rear of the car over a pit or on a ramp.
2 If the rear of the car is jacked up, supplement the jack with support

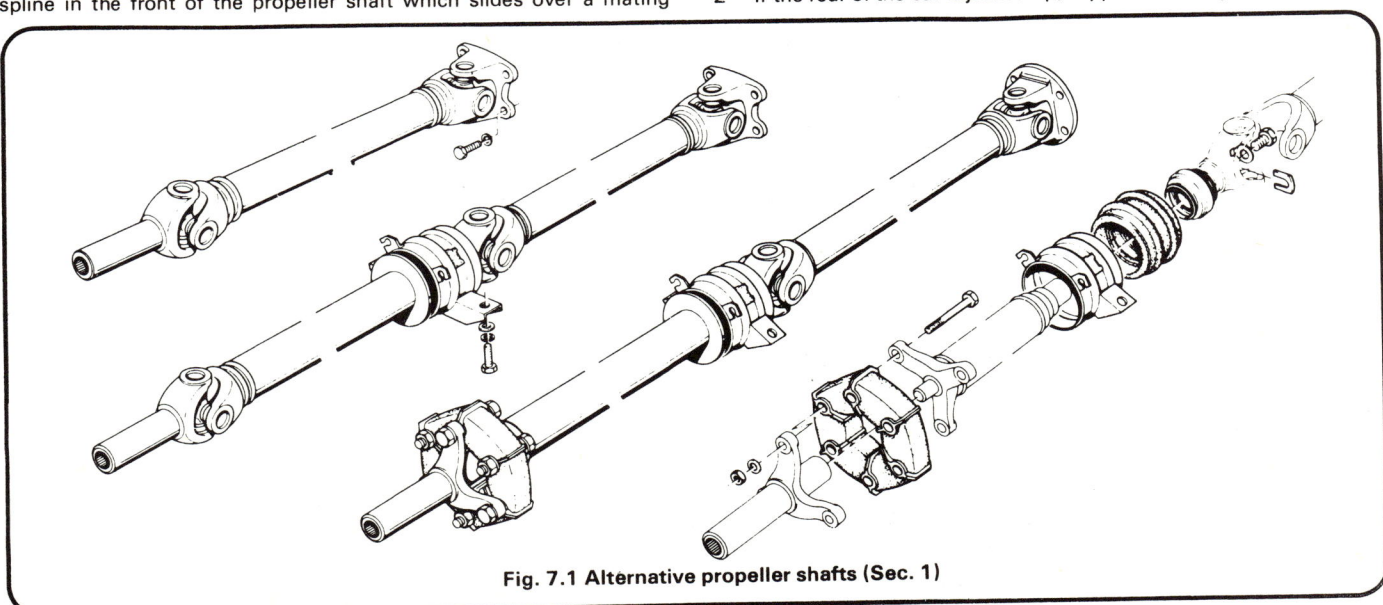

Fig. 7.1 Alternative propeller shafts (Sec. 1)

blocks so that danger is minimised should the jack collapse.
3 If the rear wheels are off the ground place the car in gear (automatic transmission P) and apply the handbrake to ensure that the propeller shaft does not turn when an attempt is made to loosen the four bolts securing the propeller shaft to the rear axle.
4 The propeller shaft is balanced to fine limits and it is important that it is refitted in exactly the same position it was in prior to removal. Scratch marks on the propeller shaft and rear axle flange to ensure accurate mating when the time comes for reassembly (photo).
5 Unscrew and remove the four bolts and spring washers which hold the flange on the propeller shaft to the flange on the rear axle.
6 Slightly push the shaft forward to separate the two flanges, and then lower the end of the shaft and pull it rearwards to disengage the gearbox mainshaft splines.
7 Place a large can or a tray under the rear of the gearbox extension to catch any oil which is likely to leak past the oil seal when the propeller shaft is removed.
8 Refitting the propeller shaft is a reversal of the above procedure. Ensure that the mating marks scratched on the propeller shaft and rear axle flanges line up and always use new spring washers. Check the oil level in the gearbox and top up if necessary.

Split type propeller shaft

9 The removal sequence is basically identical to that for the single piece propeller shaft with the exception that the cable bearing support must be detached from the underside of the body. This should be done before the rear flange securing bolts and spring washers are removed. Support the centre of the propeller shaft during removal.
10 To detach the centre bearing support, undo and remove the two bolts, spring and plain washers securing it to the underside of the body. Retain and refit any shims which are found between the bearing support and the floor as these control the driveline angles.
11 Refitting is the reverse sequence to removal.

3 Propeller shaft centre bearing – removal and refitting

1 Refer to Section 2 and remove the complete propeller shaft assembly.
2 Using a blunt chisel carefully prise open the centre bearing support retaining bolt locking tab.
3 Slacken the bolt in the end of the yoke and with a screwdriver ease out the 'U' shaped retainer through the side of the yoke. These parts are shown in Fig. 7.2, 7.3 and 7.6.
4 Mark the propeller shaft and yoke for correct refitting. Disconnect the propeller shaft from the yoke and lift off the insulator rubber together with collar from the ball race.
5 Part the insulator rubber from the collar.
6 Refer to Fig. 7.4 and using a universal two leg puller draw the bearing together with cup from the end of the propeller shaft.
7 To fit a new bearing and cup onto the end of the propeller shaft use a piece of suitable diameter tube and drive into position.
8 With a pair of pliers bend the six metal tongues of the collar slightly outward and carefully insert the insulator rubber. It is important that the flange of the insulator rubber, when fitted into the support, is uppermost. See Fig. 7.5.
9 Using a pair of 'parrot jaw' pliers or a chisel bend the metal

2.4 Clean the mating flanges and look for an alignment mark. Scribe a mark if necessary (A)

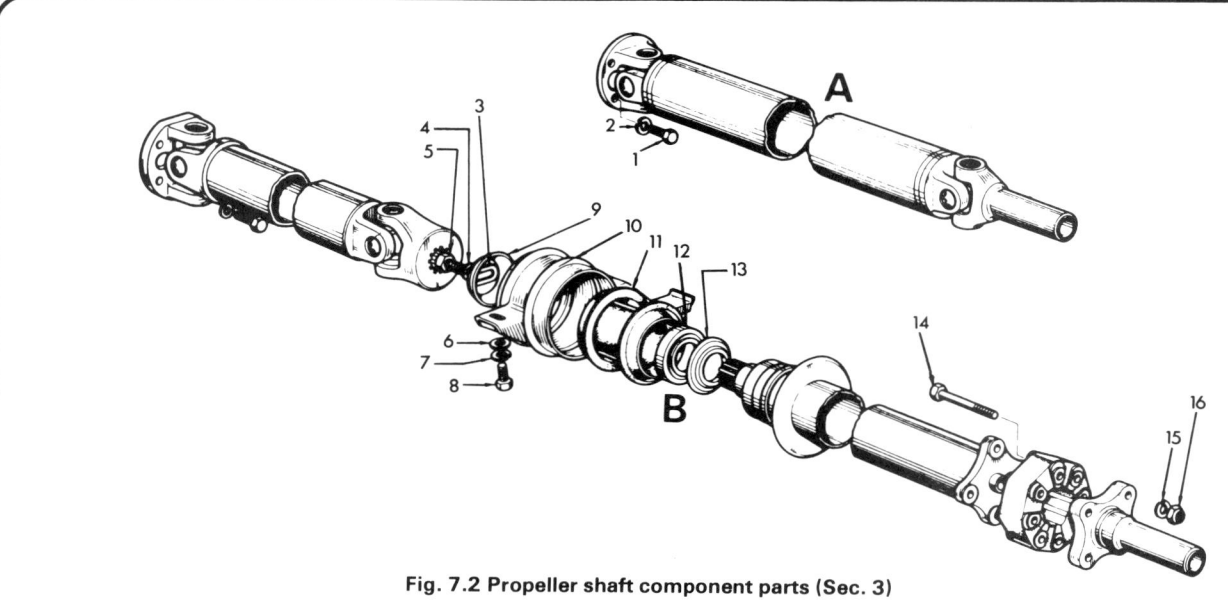

Fig. 7.2 Propeller shaft component parts (Sec. 3)

A	Single piece propeller shaft	4	Bolt	9	Dust cover	13	Dust cover
B	Two piece propeller shaft	5	Nut	10	Bearing housing and retainer	14	Bolt
1	Bolt	6	Plain washer			15	Nut
2	Spring washer	7	Spring washer	11	Rubber bush	16	Spring washer
3	'U' shaped retainer	8	Bolt	12	Bearing		

Chapter 7 Propeller shaft

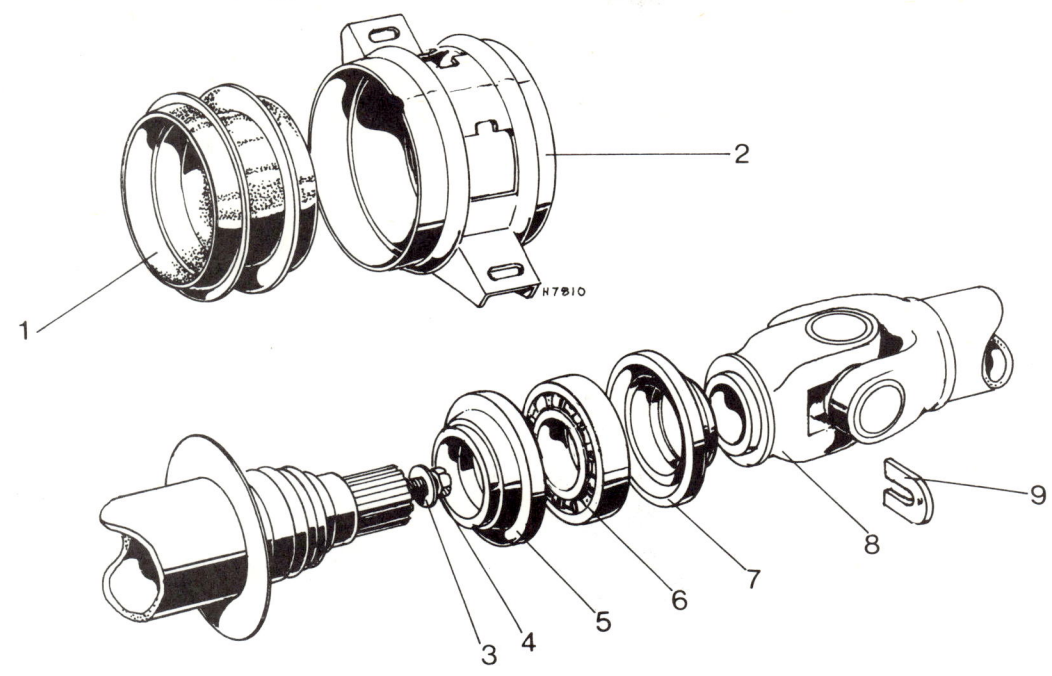

Fig. 7.3 Centre bearing components (Sec. 3)

1 Rubber bush
2 Bearing housing and retainer
3 Washer
4 Bolt
5 Dust cover
6 Ball race
7 Dust cover
8 Yoke
9 'U' shaped retainer

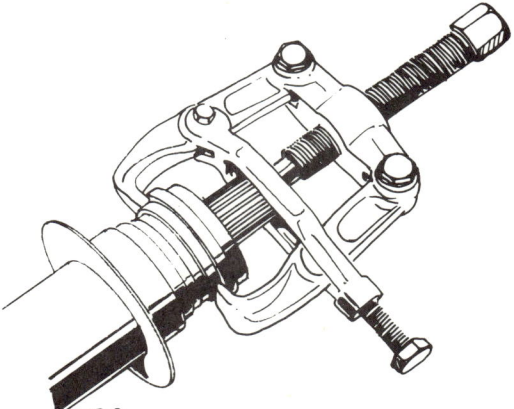

Fig. 7.4 Using universal puller to withdraw centre bearing (Sec. 3)

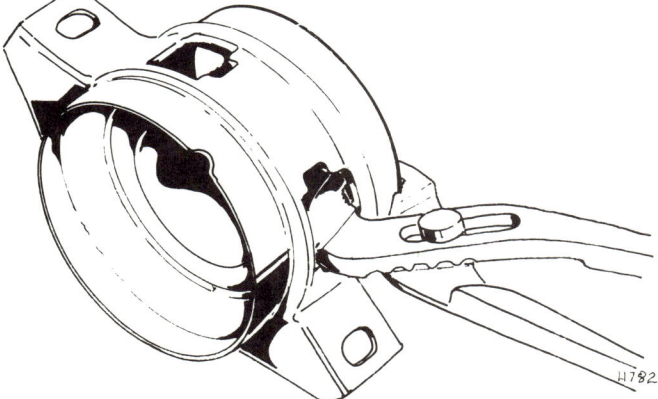

Fig. 7.5 Using parrot jaw pliers to bend over rubber bush locking tabs in housing (Sec. 3)

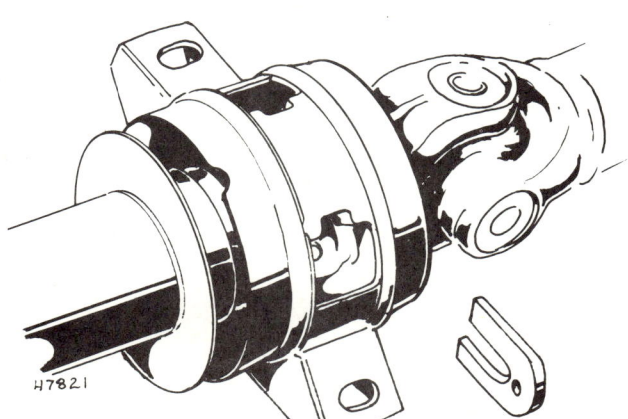

Fig. 7.6 The centre bearing and 'U' shaped retainer (Sec. 3)

tongues rearward over the rubber lip as shown in Fig. 7.5.
10 Next slide the support with the insulator rubber over the ball race. The semi circular recess in the support periphery must be positioned toward the front end of the car when fitted. (Fig. 7.6).
11 Screw in the bolt together with locking tab into the propeller shaft forward end bearing leaving just sufficient space for the 'U' shaped retainer to be inserted.
12 Assemble the two propeller shaft halves in their original positions as denoted by the two previously made marks or by the double tooth (Fig. 7.2).
13 Refit the 'U' shaped retainer with the tagged end towards the splines (Fig. 7.6).
14 Finally tighten the retainer securing bolt and bend over the lockwasher (Fig. 7.7).

4 Hardy flexible disc – removal and refitting

1 Refer to Section 2 and remove the propeller shaft.
2 It will be very much easier to remove and refit the flexible disc

Chapter 7 Propeller shaft

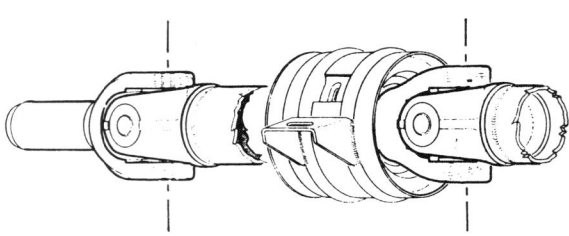

Fig. 7.7 The correct relative positions of the propeller shaft forward and centre yokes. Note semi-circular recess on the periphery of the support (Sec. 3)

which is fitted under compression if a compressor is available. However, if this is not available, jubilee clips joined end to end will serve the purpose equally well. **Note**: *new discs are usually supplied in a compressed state. If this is the case leave the compressing band in position until the disc has been fitted.*

3   Fit the compressor around the circumferences of the disc and tighten it until it just begins to compress the disc.
4   Make a note of the relative positions of the flanges and then progressively slacken and remove the six nuts, spring washers and bolts. Note which way round each bolt is fitted.
5   The disc can now be removed. If the disc is to be refitted leave the compressor in position.
6   To refit the disc is the reverse sequence to removal. The following additional points should however be noted:

a) *Always connect the flanges in their same relative positions as noted during disconnection.*
b) *Always fit the nuts and bolts the same way round as noted during disconnection.*
c) *Tighten the disc securing bolts to the torque wrench setting given in the Specifications.*
d) *Do not forget to remove the compressor otherwise the disc will not last long.*

5   Universal joints – tests for wear

1   Wear in the needle roller bearings is characterised by vibration in the transmission, 'clonks' on taking up the drive, and, in extreme cases of lack of lubrication, metallic squeaking and ultimately grating and shrieking sounds as the bearings break up.
2   It is easy to check if the needle roller bearings are worn with the propeller shaft in position, by trying to turn the shaft with one hand, the other hand holding the rear axle flange when the rear universal joint is being checked, and the front half coupling when the front universal joint is being checked. Any movement between the propeller shaft and the front and the rear half coupling is indicative of considerable wear. If worn, a new assembly will have to be obtained. Check by trying to lift the shaft and noticing any movement of the joints.
3   The centre bearing is a little more difficult to test for wear when mounted on the car. Undo and remove the two support securing bolts, spring and plain washers and allow the propeller shaft centre to hang down. Test the centre bearing for wear by gripping the support and rocking it. If movement is evident the bearing is probably worn and should be renewed as described in Section 3.
4   When a Hardy flexible disc is fitted to the front of the propeller shaft carefully inspect for signs of oil contamination or the rubber breaking up. If this condition is evident the disc must be renewed as described in Section 4.

6   Fault diagnosis – Propeller shaft

Symptom	Reason/s
Vibration	Wear in sliding sleeve splines
	Worn universal joint bearings
	Propeller shaft out of balance
	Distorted propeller shaft
Knock or 'clunk' when taking up drive	Worn universal joint bearings
	Worn rear axle drive pinion splines
	Loose rear drive flange bolts
	Excessive backlash in rear axle gears

Chapter 8 Rear axle

Contents

Fault diagnosis – rear axle 4
Final drive assembly – dismantling, overhaul
and reassembly 3
Final drive – removal and refitting 2
General description 1

Specifications

Final drive ratio:
2.0 ohc Saloon/Estate
    Manual transmission .... 4.11 : 1
    Automatic transmission .... 4.44 : 1
V4 2000 cc .... 3.89 : 1 (optional 4.11 : 1)
V6 2500 cc .... 3.64 : 1
V6 3000 cc .... 3.45 : 1

Oil capacity
3.4 pints (1.95 litres)

Lubricant
EP SAE 90

Drive pinion bearing pre-load
12–15 lbf ft (8.40 kgf m)

Crownwheel tooth backlash
0.004–0.008 in (0.12–0.22 mm)

Torque wrench settings

	lbf ft	kgf m
Drive pinion nut (maximum)	361	50
Crownwheel to differential carrier bolts	93–101	13–14
Bearing cap to differential housing bolts	72–86	10–12
Cover plate to differential housing bolts	32–37	4.5–5
Driveshaft to extension shaft flange bolts	41–49	5.8–6.8

1 General description

The rear axle and suspension assembly is of independent rear suspension design and the contents of this Chapter are confined to the overhaul and repair of the final drive unit whilst details of the suspension and driveshaft are given in Chapter 11. The complete layout is shown in Fig. 8.1 and it will be seen that the final drive unit is mounted on the rear suspension crossmember at the front and a large rubber mounting at the rear.

The differential unit is of the two pinion design and is driven by a hypoid crownwheel and pinion.

Engine torque is transmitted from the propeller shaft to the drive pinion via an extension shaft which is supported by a conventional ball race. A splined coupling connects the extension shaft to the drive pinion. This has two roller bearings which are pre-loaded with a collapsible spacer. The correct drive pinion/crownwheel mesh is adjusted using a selective shim between the drive pinion and rear taper roller bearing.

The crownwheel is bolted to the differential carrier and the whole assembly is fitted with taper roller bearings which are pre-loaded with selective shims between the bearings and differential housing. Engine torque is transmitted from the differential assembly through two pinion gears to the side gears. These side gears are secured with circlips as well as being splined to the side drive shafts.

2 Final drive – removal and refitting

1 Because of the design of the rear suspension system and engine exhaust system it is easier to remove the final drive assembly together with the rear suspension rather than to try to remove it on its own. Although it may appear to be involved and complicated upon first inspection, it is not as bad as it looks.
2 Chock the front wheels, jack up the rear of the car and support on firmly based axle stand. Remove the road wheels.
3 Mark the relative positions of the propeller shaft and extension shaft flanges with a scriber or file (if not already marked), and then undo and remove the four securing bolts. Separate the two parts and tie the propeller shaft back out of the way (Fig. 8.2).
4 Mark the relative positions of the half shaft and stub axle coupling flanges and then undo and remove the securing bolts.
5 Undo and remove the speed nuts retaining the brake drums to the hub. Release the handbrake and remove the brake drums. If tight tap outwards on the outer circumference (Fig 8.3).
6 Refer to Chapter 9 and detach the handbrake cables from the brake shoes and control arms.
7 Again referring to Chapter 9, disconnect the brake line at the rear junction and plug the ends to stop dirt ingress (Fig. 8.4).
8 Undo the nut and bolt and second nut retaining each exhaust pipe support to the rear suspension crossmember (Fig. 8.5).

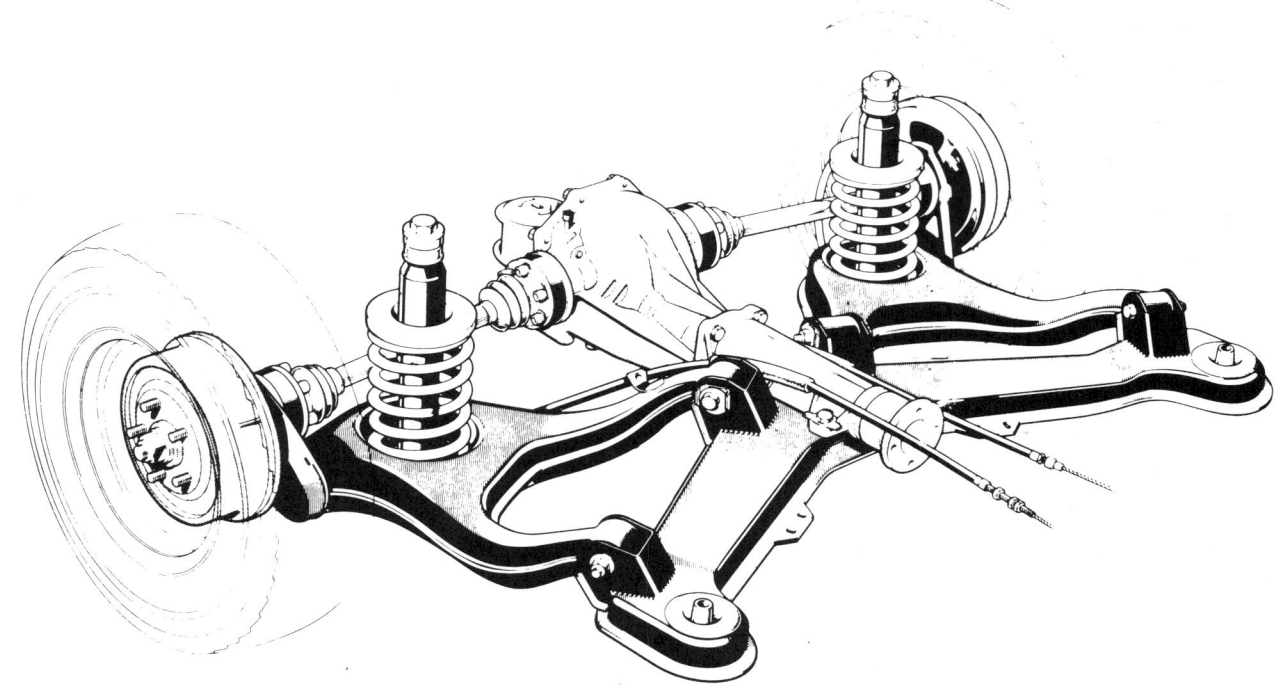

Fig. 8.1 Final drive unit mounted on rear suspension crossmember (Sec. 1)

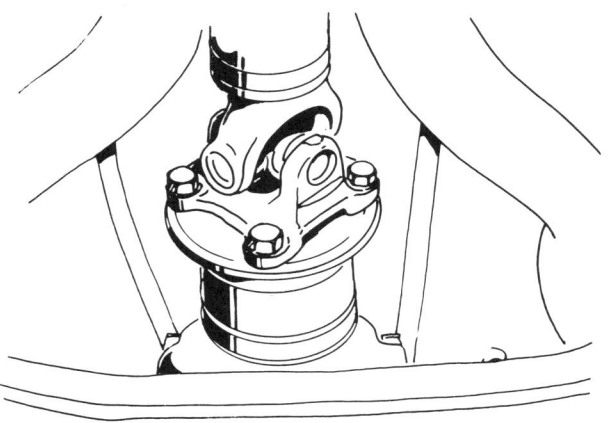

Fig. 8.2 Propeller shaft attached to extension shaft (Sec. 2)

Fig. 8.3 Removal of brake drum (Sec. 2)

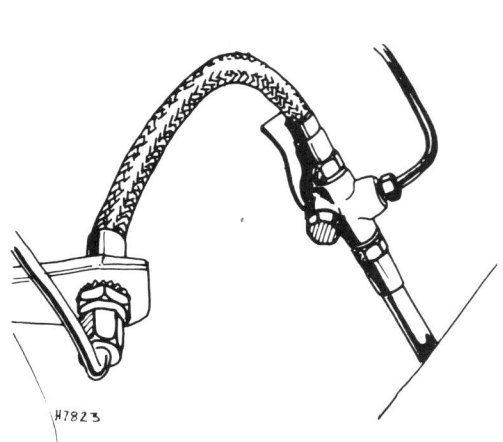

Fig. 8.4 Location of brake line rear junction (Sec. 2)

Fig. 8.5 Exhaust pipe support attached to rear suspension (Sec. 2)

Chapter 8 Rear axle

9 Refer to Chapter 11 and detach the rear shock absorbers from the body and rear suspension. Lift away the shock absorbers and suitably mark so that they may be refitted in their original positions.
10 With the suspension arms lowered lift away the coil springs and rubber seats. Mark these in the same way as the shock absorbers.
11 Position a jack at the centre of the final drive housing.
12 Carefully bend back the locking tab and then unscrew the centre bolt nut. It may be necessary to hold the centre bolt, access to which may be made from the boot/luggage compartment. Lift away the nut and withdraw the bolt.
13 Undo and remove the hanger bracket retaining bolts and lift away the hanger bracket.
14 Carefully bend back the locking tabs of both crossmember retainer brackets and remove the retaining bolts, centre bolt and bracket from the floor assembly.
15 Carefully lower the complete rear suspension assembly and withdraw rearward from under the car.
16 Undo and remove the four nuts, bolts and plain washers securing the final drive assembly to the rear suspension crossmember.
17 Refitting the final drive assembly is the reverse sequence to removal. Do not forget to refill with 3.4 pints (1.95 litres) of the specified type of oil. Whenever possible always use new lockwashers. Top up the fluid level in the brake master cylinder and bleed the brakes as described in Chapter 9.

3 Final drive assembly – dismantling, overhaul and reassembly

Most garages will prefer to fit a complete set of gears, bearings, spacers and thrust washers rather than renew parts which may have worn. To do the job properly requires the use of special and expensive tools which the majority of garages do not have.

The primary object of these special tools is to enable the mesh of the crownwheel to the pinion to be set very accurately and thus ensure that noise is kept to a minimum. If any increase in noise cannot be tolerated (provided that the final drive is not already noisy due to a defective part) then it is best to allow a Ford garage to carry out the repairs.

Final drive units have been rebuilt without the use of special tools so if the possibility of a slight increase in noise can be tolerated then it is quite possible for any do-it-yourself mechanic to successfully recondition this final drive unit without special tools.

The final drive unit must first be removed from the car as described in Section 2 and and then proceed as follows:
1 Wash down the final drive housing area to remove all traces of dirt and oil. Wipe dry with a non-fluffy rag.
2 Undo and remove the ten bolts and spring washers that secure the differential housing cover plate to the main housing. Lift away the cover and gasket and be prepared to catch the oil once the cover is removed.
3 Using a pair of angle end circlip pliers remove the extension shaft retaining circlip. This is located behind the flange.
4 Use a slide hammer if available and drive off the flange and extension shaft. If a slide hammer is not available use a soft faced hammer and tap it off.
5 Undo and remove the four bolts and spring washers that secure the extension housing to the differential housing. Lift away the extension housing.
6 Using a universal two leg puller and thrust block carefully draw the splined coupling from the drive pinion.
7 If the bearing is to be renewed, using a pair of circlip pliers, remove the circlip from the end of the extension shaft and with the bearing held in a vice drift the extension shaft through the bearing inner track. Take care not to damage the splined end (Fig 8.12).
8 Using a pair of angled circlip pliers remove the circlip from the inner end of each side drive shaft (Fig.8.14). Withdraw the drive shafts and note which way round they are fitted. Normally they have a letter L or R stamped on the flange fitted to the side as seen in the direction of car travel.
9 Mark the differential bearing caps and then undo and remove the

Fig. 8.6 Rear suspension coil spring and rubber seal (Sec. 2)

Fig. 8.7 Final drive rear mounting (Sec. 2)

Fig. 8.8 Rear suspension crossmember retainer bracket (Sec. 2)

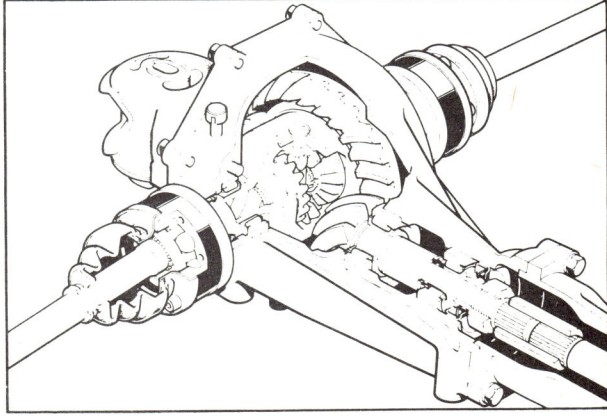

Fig. 8.9 Sectional view of final drive (Sec. 3)

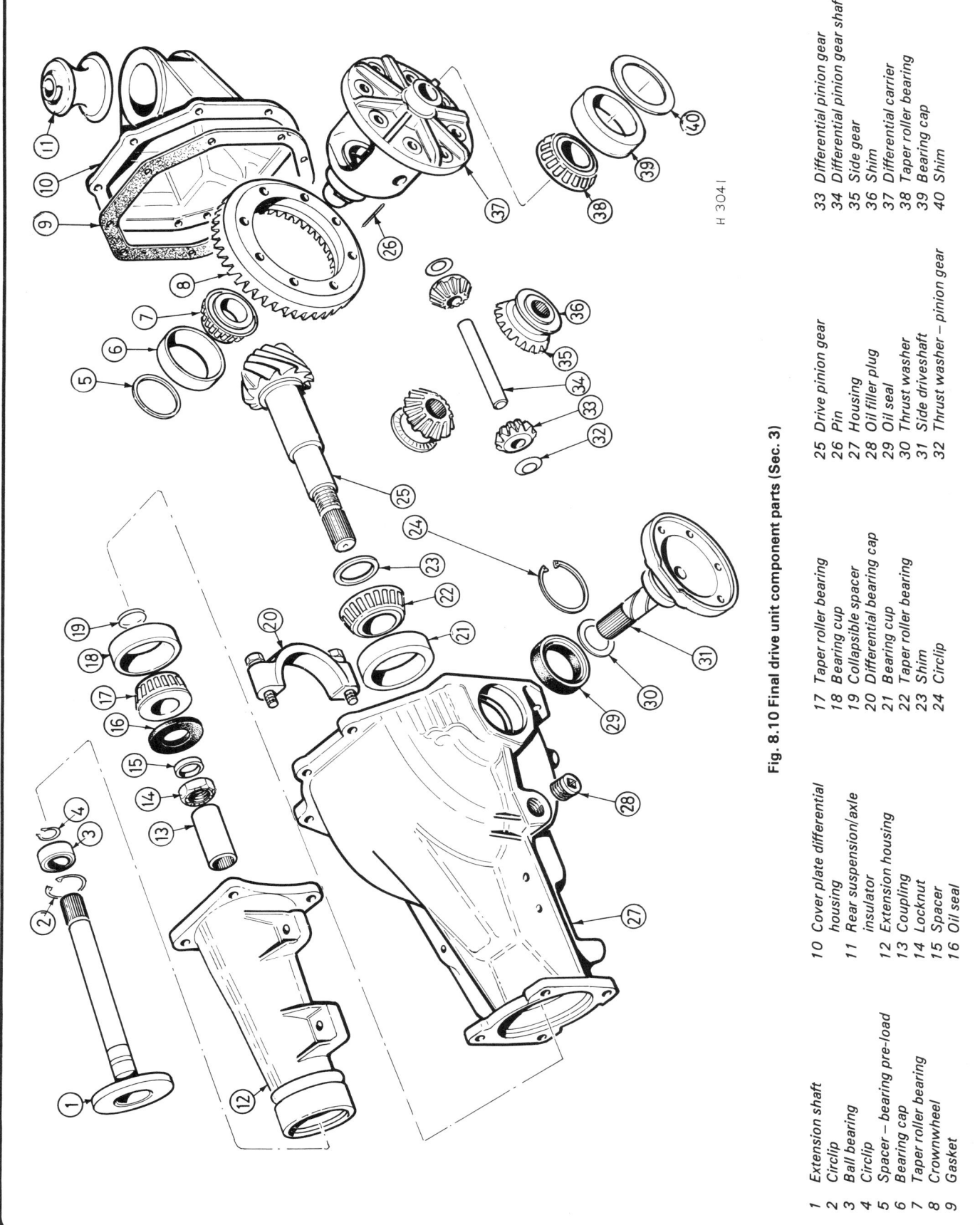

Fig. 8.10 Final drive unit component parts (Sec. 3)

1 Extension shaft
2 Circlip
3 Ball bearing
4 Circlip
5 Spacer – bearing pre-load
6 Bearing cap
7 Taper roller bearing
8 Crownwheel
9 Gasket
10 Cover plate differential housing
11 Rear suspension/axle insulator
12 Extension housing
13 Coupling
14 Locknut
15 Spacer
16 Oil seal
17 Taper roller bearing
18 Bearing cup
19 Collapsible spacer
20 Differential bearing cap
21 Bearing cup
22 Taper roller bearing
23 Shim
24 Circlip
25 Drive pinion gear
26 Pin
27 Housing
28 Oil filler plug
29 Oil seal
30 Thrust washer
31 Side driveshaft
32 Thrust washer – pinion gear
33 Differential pinion gear
34 Differential pinion gear shaft
35 Side gear
36 Shim
37 Differential carrier
38 Taper roller bearing
39 Bearing cap
40 Shim

Chapter 8 Rear axle

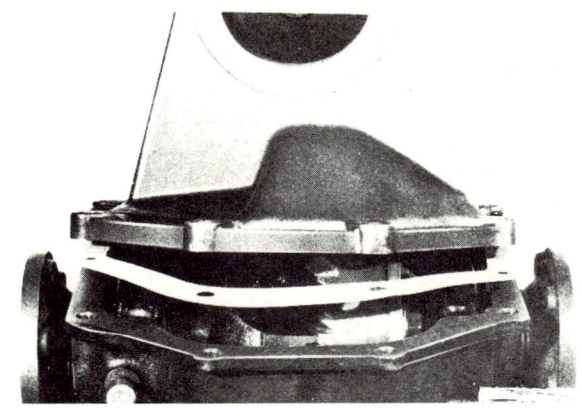

Fig. 8.11 Lifting away differential housing cover plate (Sec. 3)

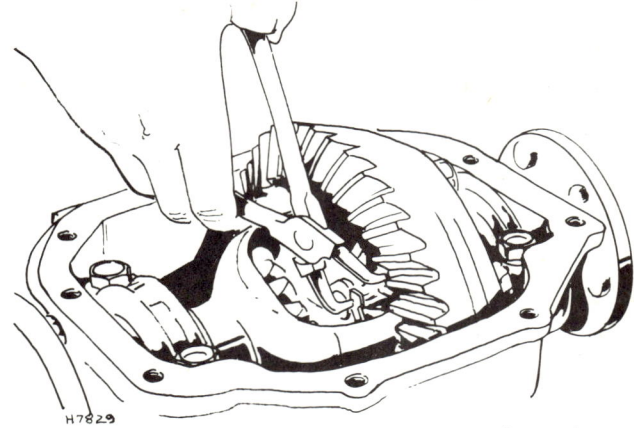

Fig. 8.14 Removal of driveshaft retaining clip (Sec. 3)

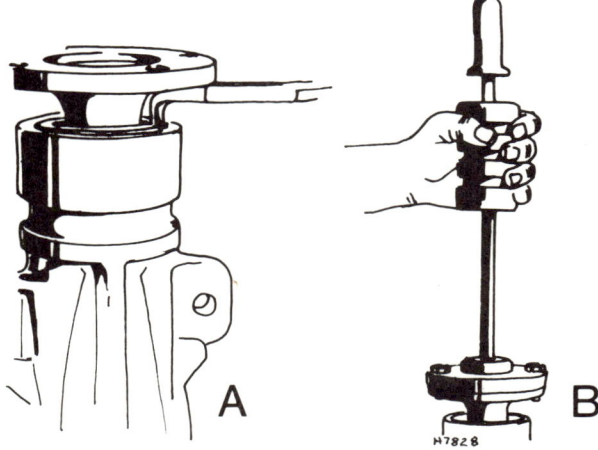

Fig. 8.12 Removal of extension shaft circlip (A) and withdrawing extension shaft (B) (Sec. 3)

Fig. 8.15 Differential bearing cap identification (Sec. 3)

Fig. 8.13 Removal of extension housing securing bolts (Sec. 3)

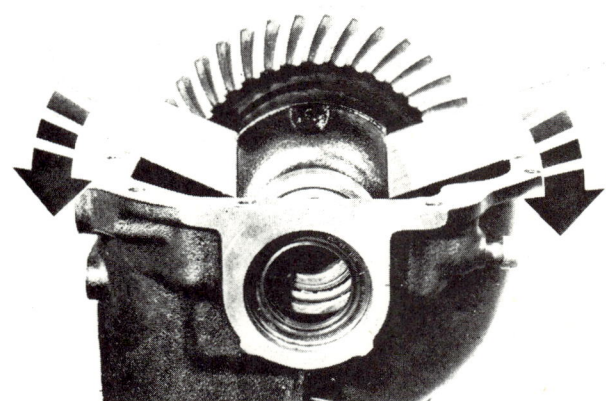

Fig. 8.16 Removal of differential assembly (Sec. 3)

four securing bolts. Lift away the bearing caps (Fig. 8.15).
10 Obtain two pieces of tapered wood and carefully ease out the differential carrier from the main housing. Recover any shims used between the bearing outer track side and the main housing.
11 Using a suitable tapered drift tap out the oil seals noting which way round they are fitted. Once removed, discard them and fit new ones on reassembly.
12 It is now necessary to remove the pinion locknut. For this a special tool is required to hold the pinion but it is possible to lock the pinion teeth to the main housing using a piece of hard wood with a strong nail to engage between two teeth.
13 The pinion may now be tapped into the main housing and lifted away.

14 If the large taper roller bearing is to be renewed it will have to be either pressed out or 'dismantled' with a large sharp chisel. Do not damage the shim behind the pinion head.
15 To remove the smaller taper roller bearing and oil seal use a suitable metal drift and tap outward. The seal will, of course have to be renewed on reassembly.
16 When new roller bearings are to be fitted the old cups (outer tracks) must be removed using a tapered drift and driven outward from the main housing.
17 Turning to the differential assembly, use a suitable two leg universal puller and draw each taper roller bearing from the differential case.
18 Mark the relative position of the crownwheel and differential case

unless a new crownwheel is to be fitted and then undo and remove the eight bolts. Carefully tap off the crownwheel.

19 Using feeler gauges measure the side gear to differential housing clearance. If the play exceeds 0.006 inch (0.15 mm) new shims will be required on reassembly (Fig. 8.17).

20 Using a suitable diameter parallel pin punch carefully tap out the differential shaft roll pin (Fig. 8.18).

21 Remove the differential shaft using a suitable diameter drift and lift away the pinion gear shaft and gears and side gears noting their locations. Keep any thrust washers used matched with their respective gears (Fig. 8.19).

22 The final drive assembly is now dismantled and should be washed and dried with a clean non-fluffy rag ready for inspection.

23 Carefully inspect all the gear teeth for signs of pitting or wear and, if evident, new parts must be obtained. The crownwheel and pinion are a matched pair so if one of the two requires renewal a new matched pair must be obtained. If wear is evident on one or two of the differential pinion gears or side gears it is far better to obtain all four gears rather than just renew the worn ones.

24 Inspect the thrust washers for signs of score marks or wear and, if evident, obtain new ones. Before the bearings were removed they should have been inspected for wear and usually if one bearing is worn it is far better to fit a complete new set.

25 With new parts obtained as required, reassembly can begin. First fit the thrust washers to the side gears and place them in position in the differential housing.

26 Place the thrust washers behind the differential pinion gears and mesh these two gears with the side gears through the two apertures in the differential housing. Make sure that they are diametrically opposite to each other. Rotate the differential pinion gears through 90° so bringing them into line with the pinion gear shaft bore in the housing.

27 Insert the pinion gear shaft with the locking pin hole in line with the pin hole in the housing. Tap the shaft into position with a soft metal drift.

28 Using feeler gauges measure the side gear to differential housing clearance. This should not exceed the upper limit of 0.006 inch (0.15 mm). If necessary adjust the clearance using different thickness shims.

29 Lock the pinion gear shaft using the pin which should be tapped fully home using a suitable diameter parallel pin punch.

30 The crownwheel may next be refitted. Wipe the mating faces of the crownwheel and differential housing and if original parts are being used, place the crownwheel into position with the previously made marks aligned. Refit the bolts that secure the crownwheel and tighten these in a progressive and diagonal manner to the torque wrench setting given in the Specifications.

31 Using a piece of suitable diameter tube, very carefully fit the differential housing bearings with the smaller diameter of the taper outward. The bearing cage must not be damaged in any way.

32 Place the shim behind the head of the pinion gear and using a suitable diameter tube, very carefully fit the larger taper roller bearing onto the pinion shaft. The larger diameter of the bearing must be next to the pinion head.

33 Using suitable diameter tubes fit the two taper roller bearing cones into the final drive housing, making sure that they are fitted the correct way round.

34 Fit the smaller taper roller bearing into the differential housing. Apply a little grease between the two lips of a new oil seal and a little jointing compound to the outer circumference. Using a suitable diameter tube fit the oil seal.

35 Slide a new collapsible spacer onto the pinion and insert the pinion shaft into the main housing.

36 Refit the oil seal sleeve and a new locknut. Hold the pinion and tighten the locknut. If should be possible to pre-load the pinion to a torque wrench setting of 1.7 lbf ft (0.23 kgf m). This is the measured torque required to turn the pinion and NOT the final tightening torque of the locknut. If the figure is exceeded a new collapsible spacer will be required.

37 Fit the bearing cones to the differential housing bearings and carefully ease the housing into the main housing.

38 Insert the shims previously removed from between the differential housing bearings and the main housing (Fig. 8.21).

39 Refit the bearing caps in their original positions. Smear a little jointing compound on the threads of each cap securing bolt and fit into position. When all four bolts have been refitted tighten these up in a diagonal and progressive manner to the final torque wrench setting given in the Specifications.

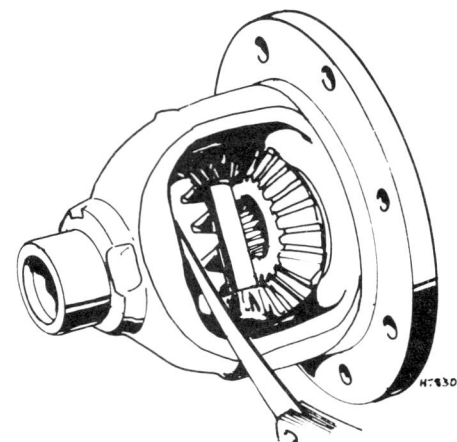

Fig. 8.17 Measurement of side gear clearance (Sec. 3)

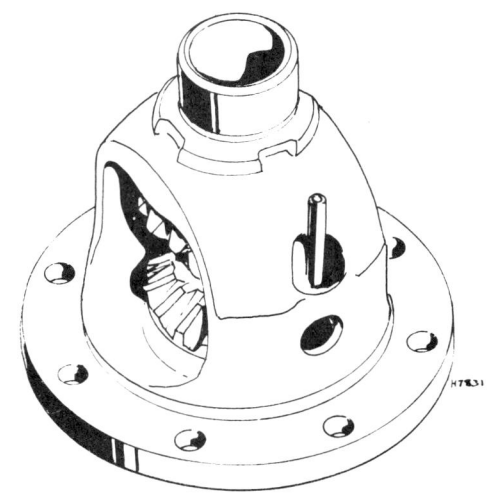

Fig. 8.18 Differential shaft roll pin partially removed (Sec. 3)

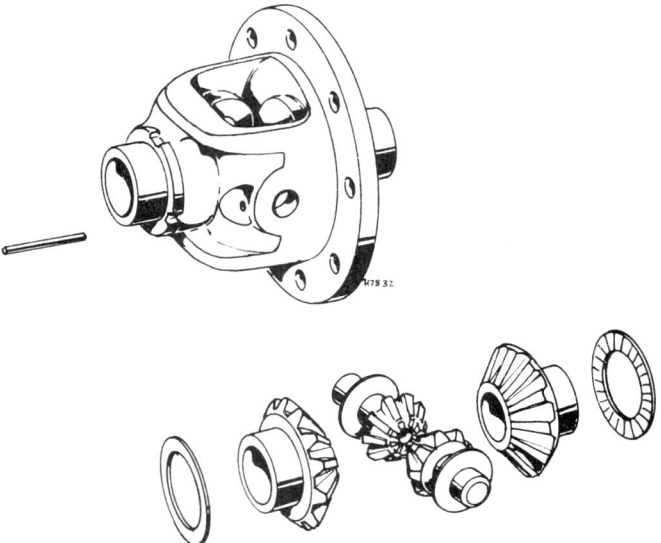

Fig. 8.19 Components of differential housing (Sec. 3)

Chapter 8 Rear axle

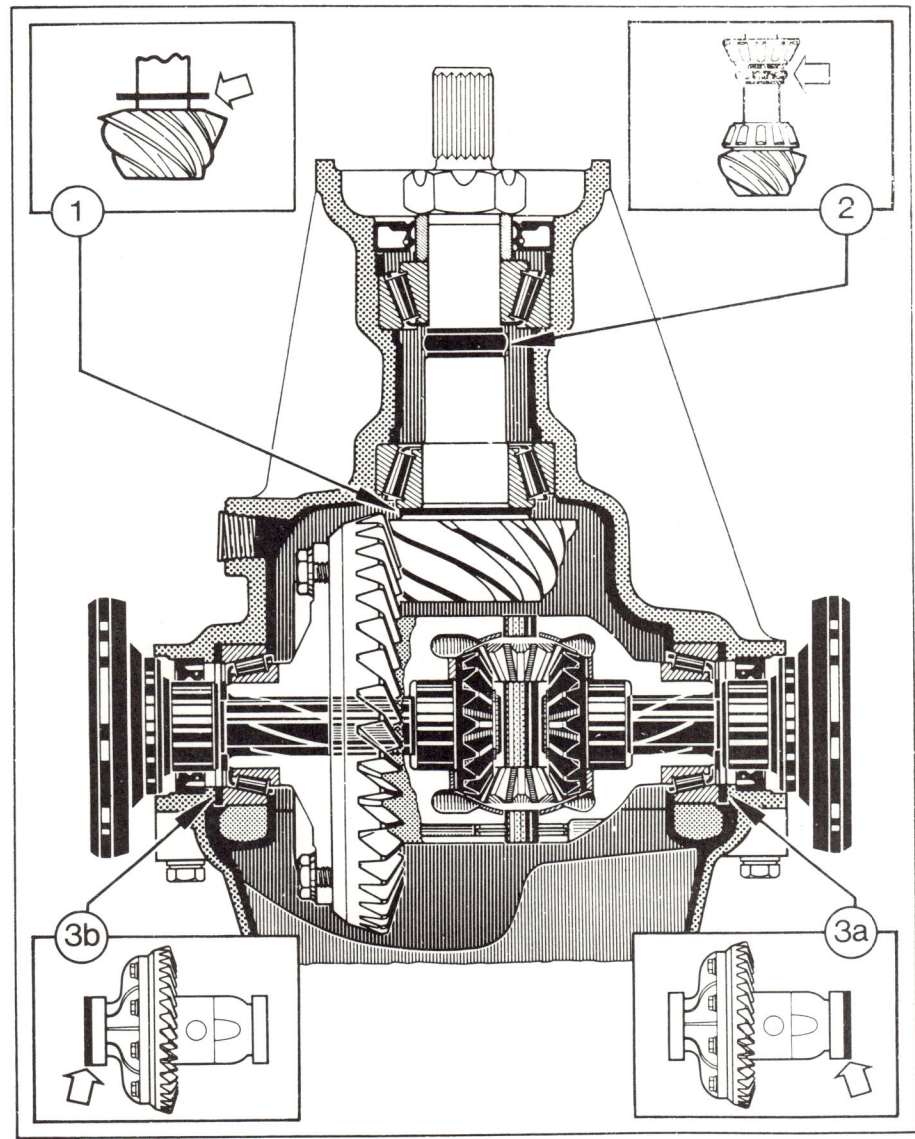

Fig. 8.20 Location of adjustment shims (Sec. 3)

1 Determine the required drive pinion shim thickness
2 Install the drive pinion (determine the pinion bearing pre-load)
3 Determine the shims required for both ends of the differential unit as shown: (a) Crownwheel side (b) Side at the rear of the crownwheel

40 If possible mount a dial indicator gauge so that the probe is resting on one of the teeth of the crownwheel and pinion. The backlash may be varied by decreasing the thickness of the shims behind one differential housing bearing and increasing the thickness of shims behind the other, thus moving the crownwheel into or out of mesh as required. The total thickness of the shims must not be changed.
41 The best check the do-it-yourself enthusiast can make to ascertain the correct meshing of the crownwheel and pinion is to smear a little engineer's blue onto the crownwheel and then rotate the pinion. The contact mark should appear right in the middle of the crownwheel teeth. Refer to Fig. 8.22 where the correct tooth pattern is shown. Also given are incorrect tooth patterns and the method of obtaining the correct pattern. Obviously this will take time and further dismantling, but will be worth it.
42 Lightly grease the side drive shaft oil seals between the two lips and refit the oil seals using a suitable diameter tube.
43 The two side drive shafts are not interchangeable and care must be taken not to interchange them. They are marked 'L' and 'R' respectively and must be installed together with a spacer.
44 Secure the side drive shafts with their circlips. If possible select a circlip such that the axial play does not exceed 0.118 inch (0.30 mm).

Fig. 8.21 Inserting differential housing bearing shims (Sec. 3)

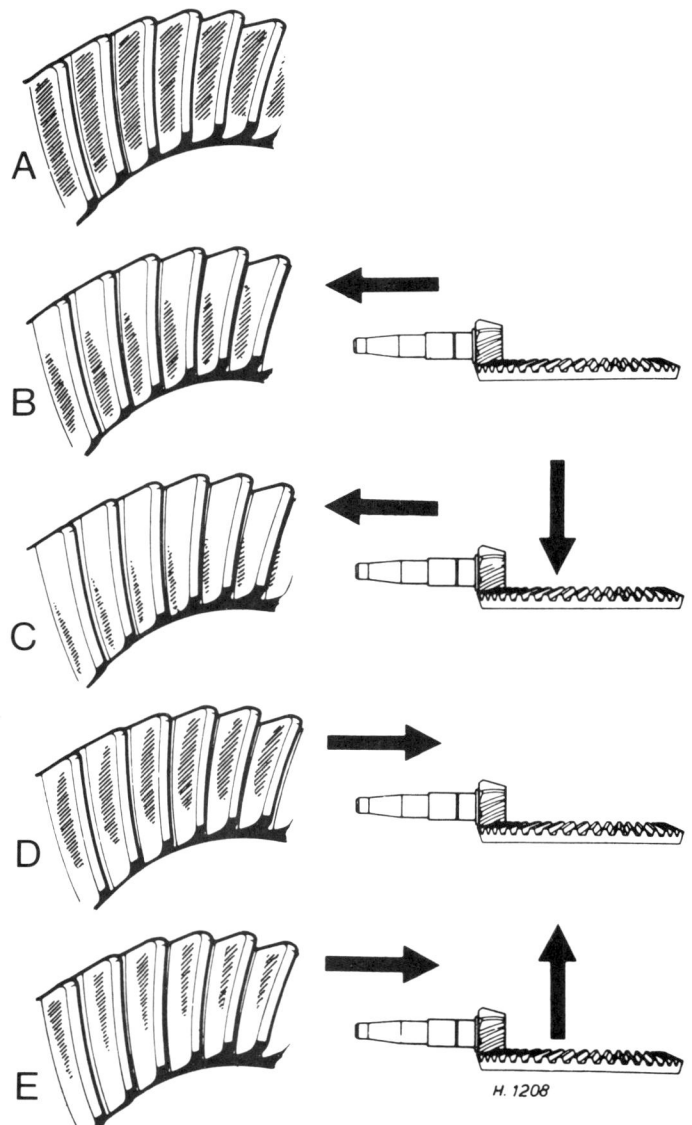

Fig. 8.22 Correct meshing of crownwheel and pinion and repositioning guide for incorrect tooth meshing (Sec. 3)

- A Correct tooth contact
- B Heavy contact at tooth toe, towards the centre. Move pinion away from crownwheel
- C Heavy contact with toe, at tooth flank bottom. Move pinion away from crownwheel and crownwheel from pinion
- D Heavy contact at tooth heel and towards the centre. Move pinion towards crownwheel
- E Heavy contact on heel, at tooth face. Move pinion towards crownwheel and crownwheel towards pinion

45 Before refitting the rear cover make sure that the mating faces are free from traces of the old gasket or joining compound.
46 Fit a new gasket and then the rear cover and secure with the ten bolts and spring washers.
47 Tighten the cover securing bolts to the torque wrench setting given in the Specifications.
48 Fit the bearing onto the extension shaft using a bench vice, soft faces and a soft faced hammer and then insert the shaft into the housing.
49 Fit the retaining circlip and slide the splined coupling onto the extension shaft.
50 Wipe the mating faces of the main housing and the extension housing, fit a new gasket and position the extension housing on the gasket. Secure with four bolts and spring washers and tighten to a torque setting of 50 – 57 lbf ft (7.0 – 8.0 kgf m).
51 The final drive assembly is now ready for refitting. Do not forget to refill with the specified amount and type of oil, and check for leaks after initial mileage.

4 Fault diagnosis – rear axle

Symptom	Reason/s	Remedy
Oil leakage	Faulty pinion oil seal	Renew
	Faulty axle-shaft oil seals	Renew
	Defective cover gasket	Renew
Noise	Lack of oil	Top-up
	Worn bearings	Renew
	General wear	Have assembly reconditioned or purchase new unit
'Clonk' on taking up drive and excessive backlash	Incorrectly tightened pinion nut	Check (see Section 3)
	Worn components	Renew or recondition unit
	Worn axle-shaft splines	Renew unit
	Elongated roadwheel bolt holes	Renew wheels

Chapter 9 Braking system

Contents

Bleeding the hydraulic system	2
Brake master cylinder – dismantling, examination and reassembly	14
Brake master cylinder – removal and refitting	13
Brake pedal – removal and refitting	15
Differential valve assembly – dismantling and reassembly	22
Differential valve assembly – removal and refitting	21
Drum brake back plate – removal and refitting	10
Drum brake shoes – removal, inspection and refitting	8
Drum brake wheel cylinder – removal, inspection and overhaul	9
Fault diagnosis – braking system	23
Flexible hoses – inspection, removal and refitting	3
Front brake caliper – dismantling and reassembly	6
Front brake caliper – removal and refitting	5
Front brake disc and hub – removal and refitting	7
Front brake pads – inspection, removal and refitting	4
General description	1
Handbrake – adjustment	11
Handbrake cable – removal and refitting	12
Handbrake lever – removal and refitting	16
Hydraulic pipes and hoses	20
Vacuum servo unit – description	17
Vacuum servo unit – dismantling, inspection and reassembly	19
Vacuum servo unit – removal and refitting	18

Specifications

Brake system type .... Hydraulic, servo assisted on all four wheels
Front .... Dual line disc. Self adjusting
Rear .... Dual line drum. Self adjusting
Handbrake .... Mechanical, on rear wheels only

Front
Disc diameter .... 10.3 in (262 mm)
Max disc runout .... 0.002 in (0.05 mm)
Cylinder diameter .... 2.13 in (54.0 mm)
Pad swept area .... 212.0 in² (13632.0 cm²)
Minimum pad thickness .... 0.059–0.118 in (1.5–3.0 mm)

Rear
Drum diameter:
  Saloon .... 9.0 in (228.6 mm)
  Estate .... 10.0 in (254.0 mm)
Shoe swept area:
  Saloon – 2000 cc .... 94.67 in² (61080.0 mm²)
  2500, 3000 cc .... 122.8 in² (79241.0 mm²)
  Estate .... 138.6 in² (89479.0 mm²)
Wheel cylinder diameter:
  Saloon – 2000 cc .... 0.812 in (20.64 mm)
  2500, 3000 cc .... 0.70 in (17.78 mm)
  Estate – 2000 cc .... 0.749 in (19.05 mm)
  3000 cc .... 0.70 in (17.78 mm)
Minimum lining thickness .... 0.06 in (1.52 mm)

Vacuum servo unit
Type .... Mechanical
Boost ratio:
  Saloon and estate (except 2000 cc saloon) .... 4.5 : 1
  2000 cc saloon .... 3.02 : 1

Torque wrench settings

	lbf ft	kgf m
Brake caliper to front suspension	45–50	6.2–6.9
Brake disc to hub	40–50	5.5–6.9
Rear brake backplate to axle housing	30–36	4.1–5.1
Hydraulic unions	8–10	1.1–1.4
Bleed valves	8–10	1.1–1.4
Master cylinder to servo	17	2.3
Wheel cylinder to backplate	4–5	0.55–0.69
Splash shield to front spindle	15–18	2.0–2.5
Rear hub centre nut	180–200	24.9–27.6
Tipping valve securing nut	27–35	4.8–6.22

1 General description

Disc brakes are fitted to the front wheels and drum brakes to the rear. All are operated under servo assistance from the brake pedal, this being connected to the master cylinder and servo assembly mounted on the bulkhead.

The hydraulic system is of the dual line principle whereby the front disc brake calipers have a separate hydraulic system from that of the rear drum brake wheel cylinders so that if failure of the hydraulic pipes to the front or rear brakes occurs half the braking system still operates. Servo assistance in this condition is still available.

The front brake disc is secured to the hub flange and the caliper mounted on the steering knuckle and wheel stub, so that the disc is able to rotate in between the two halves of the calipers. Inside each half of the caliper is a hydraulic cylinder interconnected by a drilling which allows hydraulic fluid pressure to be transmitted to both halves. A piston operates in each cylinder, and is in contact with the outer face of the brake pad. By depressing the brake pedal, hydraulic fluid pressure is increased by the servo unit and transmitted to the caliper by a system of metal and flexible hoses; the pistons are moved outward so pushing the pads onto the face of the disc and thus slowing down the rotational speed of the disc.

The rear drum brakes have one cylinder operating two shoes. When the brake pedal is depressed hydraulic fluid pressure, increased by the servo unit, is transmitted to the rear brake wheel cylinders by a system of metal and flexible pipes. The pressure moves the pistons outward so pushing the shoe linings into contact with the inside circumference of the brake drum and slowing down the rotational speed of the drum.

The handbrake provides an independent means of rear brake application.

Also, attached to each of the brake units is an automatic adjuster which operates in conjunction with the handbrake mechanism.

Whenever it is necessary to obtain spare parts for the braking system great care must be taken to ensure that the correct parts are obtained because of the varying types of braking systems fitted to the Consul/Granada range of cars.

2 Bleeding the hydraulic system

1 Removal of all the air from the hydraulic system is essential to the correct working of the braking system, and before undertaking this, examine the fluid reservoir cap to ensure that the vent hole is clear. Check the level of fluid in the reservoir and top up if required.
2 Check all brake line unions and connections for possible seepage, and at the same time check the condition of any rubber hoses.
3 If the condition of the caliper or wheel cylinders is in doubt, check for possible signs of fluid leakage.
4 If there is any possibility that incorrect fluid has been used in the system, drain all the fluid out and flush through with methylated spirits. Renew all piston seals and cups since they will be affected and could possibly fail under pressure.
5 Gather together a clean glass jar, a 12 inch (300 mm) length of tubing which fits tightly over the bleed screws and a tin of the correct brake fluid.
6 To bleed the system, clean the area around the bleed valves and start on the front right-hand bleed screw by first removing the rubber cup over the end of the screw.
7 Place the end of the tube in the clean jar which should contain sufficient fluid to keep the end of the tube below the surface during the operating.
8 Open the bleed screw $\frac{1}{4}$ turn with a spanner and depress the brake pedal. After slowly releasing the pedal, pause for a moment to allow the fluid to recoup in the master cylinder and then depress it again. This will force air from the system. Continue until no more air bubbles can be seen coming from the tube. At intervals make certain that the reservoir is kept topped up, otherwise air will enter at the point again (photo).
9 Finally press the pedal down fully and hold it there whilst the bleed screw is tightened. To ensure correct seating it should be tightened to the torque wrench setting given in the Specifications.
10 Repeat this operation on the second front brake, and then the rear brakes, starting with the right-hand brake unit.
11 When completed check the level of the fluid in the reservoir and then check the feel of the brake pedal, which should be firm and free from any 'spongy' action, which is normally associated with air in the system.
12 It will be noticed that during the bleeding operation the effort required to depress the pedal the full stroke will increase because of the loss of vacuum assistance as it is destroyed by repeated operation of the servo unit. Although the servo unit will be inoperative as far as assistance is concerned it does not affect the brake bleed operation.
13 If difficulty is experienced in bleeding the system refer to Section 21, paragraph 6.

3 Flexible hose – inspection, removal and refitting

1 Inspect the condition of the flexible hydraulic hoses leading to each of the front disc brake calipers and the one at the front of the rear axle. If they are swollen, damaged or chafed, they must be renewed (photo).
2 Wipe the top of the brake master cylinder reservoir and unscrew the cap. Place a piece of polythene sheet over the top of the reservoir and refit the cap. This is to stop hydraulic fluid syphoning out during subsequent operations.
3 To remove a front flexible hose, wipe the union and brackets free from dust and undo the union nuts from the metal pipe ends.
4 Undo and remove the locknuts and plain washers securing each flexible hose end to the bracket and lift away the hose.
5 To remove the rear flexible hose follow the instructions for the front hose.
6 Refitting in both cases is the reverse sequence to removal. It will be necessary to bleed the brake hydraulic system as described in Section 2. If one hose has been removed it is only necessary to bleed either the front or rear brake hydraulic system.
7 If new hoses are fitted they must be located so that they do not chafe or rub against any parts of the body/suspension or steering, and an allowance must be made for the movement of these parts when the car is in motion.

4 Front brake pads – inspection, removal and refitting

1 Jack up the front of the car and place on firmly based axle stands. Remove the front wheel.
2 Inspect the amount of friction material left on the pads. The pads must be renewed when the thickness has been reduced to the minimum given in the Specifications.
3 If the fluid level in the master cylinder reservoir is high, when the pistons are moved into their respective bores to accommodate new pads, the level could rise sufficiently for the fluid to overflow. Place absorbant cloth around the reservoir or syphon a little fluid out so preventing paintwork damage caused by being in contact with the hydraulic fluid.
4 Using a pair of long nosed pliers extract the two small spring clips that hold the main retaining pins in place.
5 Remove the main retaining pins which run through the caliper and the metal backing of the pads and the shims.
6 Lift away the anti-rattle clips. It may be found that the wire clips will fly off the retaining pins so take care.
7 On some models the main retaining pins do not use small spring clips but are drifted into the main body. In this case drift out the pins using a suitable diameter parallel pin punch and lift away the cruciform anti-rattle clip (photo).
8 The friction pads can now be removed from the caliper. If they prove difficult to remove by hand a pair of long nosed pliers can be used. Lift away the shims (photo).
9 Carefully clean the recesses in the caliper in which the friction pads and shims lie, and the exposed faces of each piston from all traces of dirt or rust.
10 Using a piece of wood carefully retract the pistons.
11 Fit new friction pads and shims, and refit the clips.
12 When fitting the shims the directional arrow must point upwards (photo).
13 Insert the main pad retaining pins and where applicable, secure with spring clips (photo).
14 Refit the road wheel and lower the car. Tighten the wheel nuts securely and refit the wheel trim.
15 To correctly seat the pistons, pump the brake pedal several times

Chapter 9 Braking system

2.8 Opening bleed screw

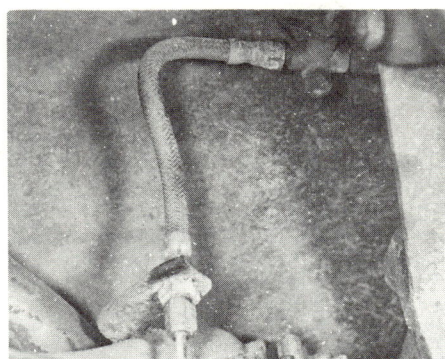

3.1 Clean and inspect the flexible hydraulic hoses and connections

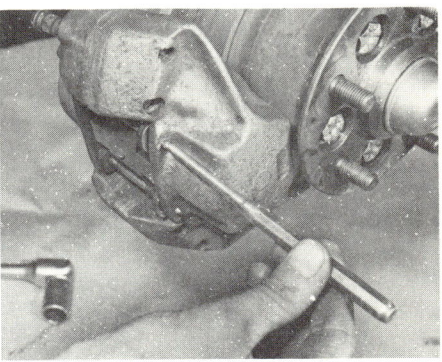

4.7 Drifting out pad retaining pins

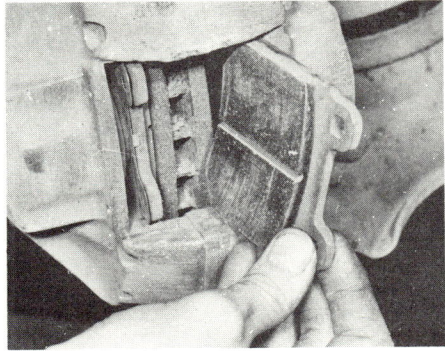

4.8 Remove the friction pads

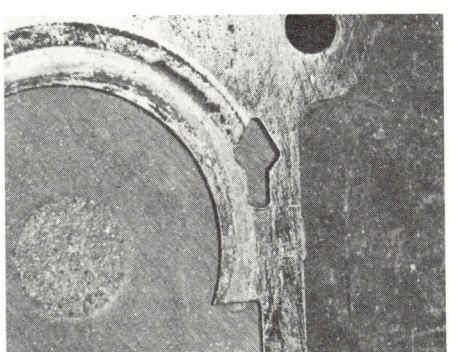

4.12 The directional arrow on the shim

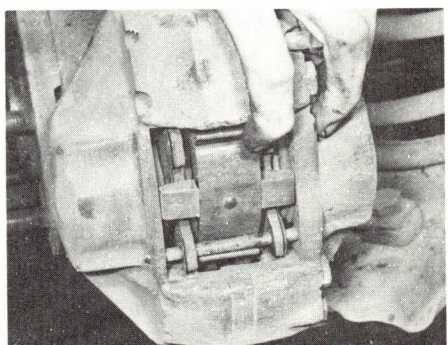

4.13 Refit the retaining pins

and finally top up the hydraulic fluid level in the master cylinder reservoir as necessary.

5 Front brake caliper – removal and refitting

1 Jack up the front of the car and place on firmly based axle-stands. Remove the front wheel.
2 Wipe the top of the brake master cylinder reservoir and unscrew the cap. Place a piece of polythene sheet over the top of the reservoir and refit the cap. This is to stop hydraulic fluid syphoning out during subsequent operations.
3 Remove the friction pads as described in Section 4.
4 If it is intended to fit new caliper pistons and/or seals, depress the brake pedal to bring the pistons into contact with the disc and so assist subsequent removal of the pistons.
5 Wipe the area clean around the flexible hose bracket and detach the pipe as described in Section 3. Tape up the end of the pipe to stop the possibility of dirt ingress.
6 Using a screwdriver or chisel bend back the tabs on the locking plate and undo the two caliper body mounting bolts. Lift away the caliper from its mounting flange on the steering knuckle and wheel stub.
7 To refit the caliper, position it over the disc and move it until the mounting bolt holes are in line with the two front holes in the steering knuckle and wheel stub mounting flange.
8 Fit the caliper retaining bolts through the two holes in a new locking plate and insert the bolts through the caliper body. Tighten the bolts to the torque wrench setting given in the Specifications.
9 Using a screwdriver, pliers or chisel, bend up the locking plate tabs so as to lock the bolts.
10 Remove the tabs from the end of the flexible hydraulic pipe and reconnect it to the union on the hose bracket. Be careful not to cross thread the union nut during the initial turns. The nut should be tightened securely, if possible using a torque wrench and special slotted end ring spanner attachment set to the setting given in the Specifications.
11 Push the pistons into their respective bores so as to accommodate the pads. Watch the level of hydraulic fluid in the master cylinder reservoir as it can overflow if too high whilst the pistons are being retracted. Place absorbant cloth around the reservoir or syphon a little fluid out so preventing paintwork damage caused by being in contact with the hydraulic fluid.
12 Fit the pads into their respective original positions, if being refitted. If new pads are being used it does not matter which side they are fitted. Refit the shims and clips.
13 Insert the two pad and shim retaining pins and secure in position with the spring clips, (if fitted).
14 Bleed the hydraulic system as described in Section 2. Refit the road wheel and lower the car.

6 Front brake caliper – dismantling and reassembly

1 The pistons should be removed first. (See Fig. 9.1 for the location of the various parts). To do this, half withdraw one piston from its bore in the caliper body.
2 Carefully remove the securing circlip and extract the sealing bellows from its location in the lower part of the piston skirt. Completely remove the piston.
3 If difficulty is experienced in withdrawing the pistons use a jet of compressed air or a foot pump to move it out of its bore.
4 Remove the sealing bellows from its location in the annular ring machined in the cylinder bore.
5 Remove the piston sealing ring from the cylinder bore using a small screwdriver but do take care not to scratch the fine finish of the bore.
6 To remove the second piston repeat paragraphs 1 – 5 inclusive.
7 It is important that the two halves of the caliper are not separated under any circumstances. If hydraulic fluid leaks are evident from the joint, the caliper must be renewed.
8 Thoroughly wash all parts in methylated spirits or correct hydraulic fluid. During reassembly new rubber seals must be fitted and these should be well lubricated with clean hydraulic fluid.
9 Inspect the pistons and bores for signs of wear, score marks or damage, and if evident, new parts, or a new caliper, should be

Chapter 9 Braking system

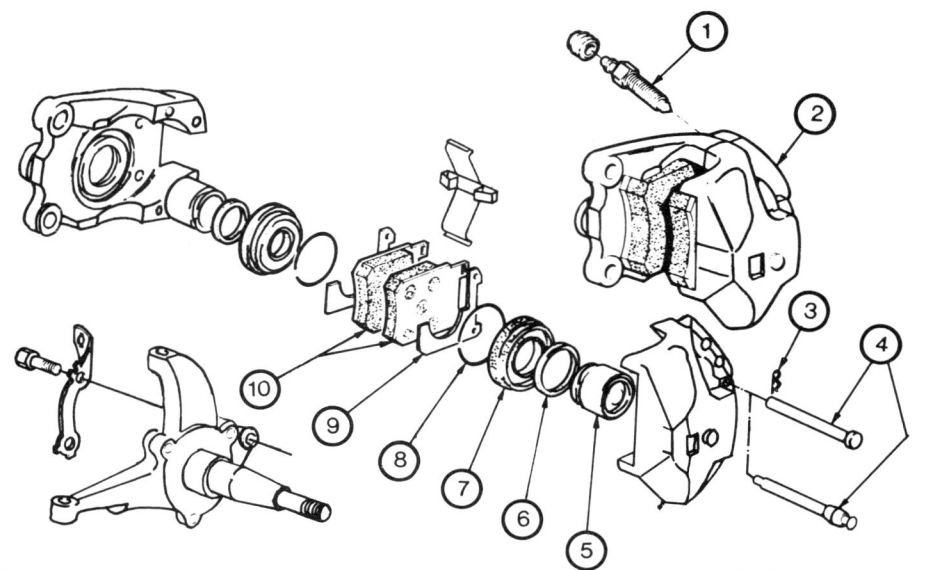

Fig. 9.1 Front disc caliper components

1 Bleed nipple
2 Caliper body
3 Pad retainer clip
4 Pad retainer pins (Top pin with clip is for M16 caliper. Bottom pin for S54/S54J caliper)
5 Piston
6 Piston seal
7 Piston bellows
8 Piston bellows retainer
9 Pad shim
10 Brake pad

obtained ready for fitting.
10 To reassemble, fit one of the piston seals into the annular groove in the cylinder bore.
11 Fit the rubber bellows to the cylinder bore groove so that the lip is turned outwards.
12 Lubricate the seal and rubber bellows with correct hydraulic fluid. Push the piston, crown first, through the rubber sealing bellows and then into the cylinder bore. Take care as it is easy for the piston to damage the rubber bellows.
13 With the piston half inserted into the cylinder bore fit the inner edge of the bellows into the annular groove in the piston skirt.
14 Push the piston down the bore as far as it will go. Secure the rubber bellows to the caliper with the circlip.
15 Repeat paragraphs 10 to 14 inclusive for the second piston.
16 The caliper is now ready for refitting. It is recommended that the hydraulic pipe end is temporarily plugged to stop any dirt ingress whilst being refitted, before the pipe connection is made.

7 Front brake disc and hub – removal and refitting

1 After jacking up the car and removing the front wheel, remove the caliper as described in Section 5.
2 By judicious tapping and levering, remove the dust cap from the centre of the hub.
3 Remove the split pin from the nut retainer and lift away the adjusting nut retainer.
4 Unscrew the adjusting nut and lift away the thrust washer and outer tapered bearing.
5 Pull off the complete hub and disc assembly from the stub axle.

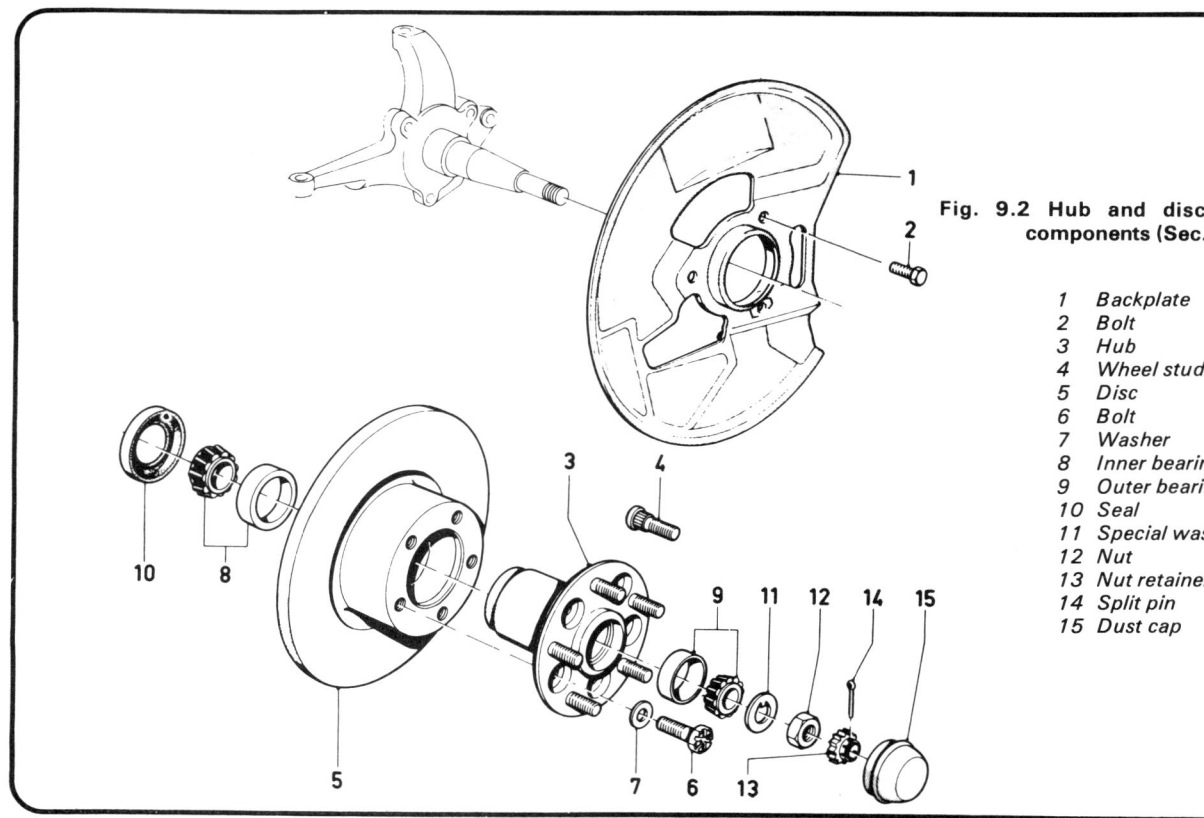

Fig. 9.2 Hub and disc assembly components (Sec. 7)

1 Backplate
2 Bolt
3 Hub
4 Wheel stud
5 Disc
6 Bolt
7 Washer
8 Inner bearing
9 Outer bearing
10 Seal
11 Special washer
12 Nut
13 Nut retainer
14 Split pin
15 Dust cap

Chapter 9 Braking system

6 From the back of the hub assembly carefully prise out the grease seal and lift away the inner tapered bearing.
7 Carefully clean out the hub and wash the bearings with petrol making sure that no grease or oil is allowed to get onto the brake disc.
8 Should it be necessary to separate the disc from the hub for renewal or regrinding, first bend back the locking tabs and undo the four securing bolts. With a scriber mark the relative positions of the hub and disc to ensure refitting in their original positions and separate the disc from the hub.
9 Thoroughly clean the disc and inspect for signs of deep scoring or excessive corrosion. If these are evident, the disc may be reground but no more than a maximum total of 0.060 inch (1.524 mm) may be removed. It is, however, desirable to fit a new disc.
10 To reassemble make quite sure that the mating faces of the disc and hub are very clean and place the disc on the hub, lining up any previously made marks.
11 Fit the four securing bolts and two new tab washers and tighten the bolts in a progressive and diagonal manner to the final torque wrench setting given in the Specifications. Bend up the locking tabs.
12 Work some grease well into the bearing, fully pack the bearing cages and rollers. **Note:** *leave the hub and grease seal empty to allow for subsequent expansion of the grease.*
13 To reassemble the hub, first fit the inner bearing and then gently tap the grease seal back into the hub. A new seal must always be fitted as during removal it was probably damaged. The lip must face inward to the hub.
14 Replace the hub and disc assembly on the stub axle and slide on the outer bearing and thrust washer.
15 Refit the adjusting nut and tighten it to a torque wrench setting of 27 lbf ft (3.7 kgf m) whilst rotating the hub and disc to ensure free movement and centralisation of the bearings. Slacken the nut back by 90° which will give the required endfloat of 0.001 – 0.005 inch (0.03 – 0.13 mm). Fit the nut retainer and a new split pin but at this stage do not lock the split pin.
16 If a dial indicator gauge is available, it is advisable to check the disc for run out. The measurements should be taken as near to the edge of the worn yet smooth part of the disc as possible, and must not exceed 0.002 inch (0.05 mm). If the figure obtained is found to be excessive, check the mating surfaces of the disc and hub for dirt or damage and also check the bearings and cups for excessive wear or damage.
17 If a dial indicator gauge is not available the runout can be checked by means of a feeler gauge placed between the casting of the caliper and the disc. (Fig. 9.3) Establish a reasonably tight fit with the feeler gauge between the top of the casting and the disc and rotate the disc and hub. Any high or low spot will immediately become obvious by extra tightness or looseness of the fit of the feeler gauge. The amount of runout can be checked by adding or subtracting feeler gauges as necessary. It is only fair to point out that this method is not as accurate as when using a dial indicator gauge owing to the rough nature of the caliper casting.
18 Once the disc runout has been checked and found to be correct bend the ends of the split pin back and refit the dust cap.
19 Reconnect the brake hydraulic pipe and bleed the brakes as described in Section 2 of this Chapter.

8 Drum brake shoes – removal, inspection and refitting

After high mileages, it will be necessary to fit new shoes with new linings. Refitting new brake linings to shoes is not considered economic, or possible, without the use of special equipment. However, if the services of a local garage or workshop having brake re-lining equipment are available then there is no reason why the original should not be successfully relined. Ensure that the correct specification linings are fitted to the shoes.
1 Chock the front wheels, jack up the rear of the car and place on firmly based axle stands. Remove the road wheel.
2 Release the handbrake and then unscrew the speed nut from the wheel stud.
3 Release the handbrake, remove the brake drum retaining screw.
4 Using a soft faced hammer on the outer circumference of the brake drum, remove the brake drum (photo).
5 Should the situation exist whereby the shoes foul the drum making removal impossible, the shoes must be collapsed by detaching the handbrake cable from the body mounted brackets and then the plunger assembly removed from the backplate (photo). Whenever the

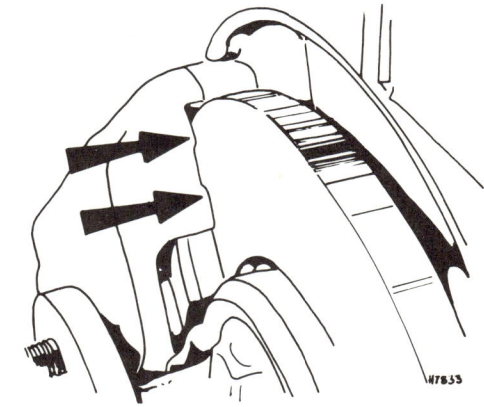

Fig. 9.3 Disc run-out check points using feeler gauges (Sec. 7)

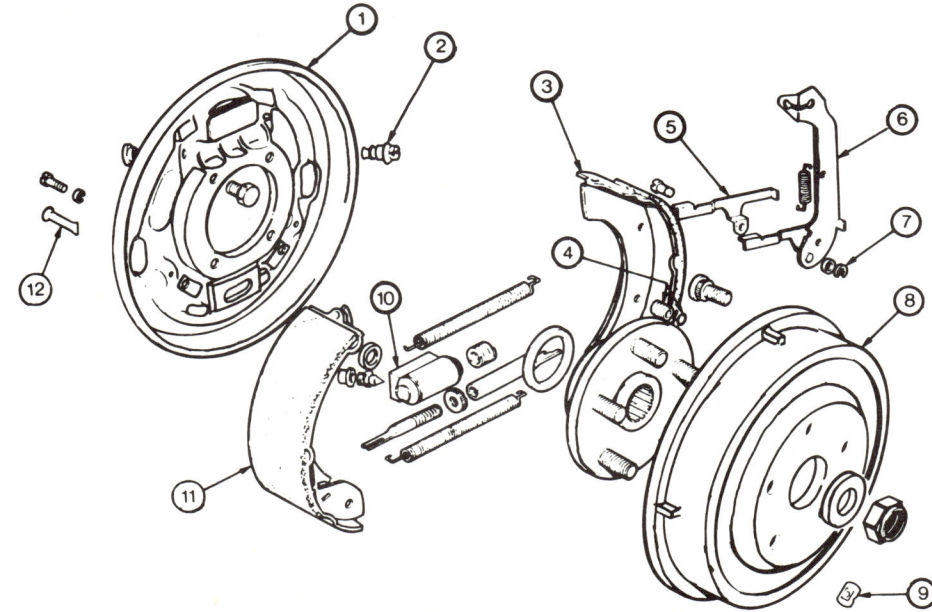

Fig. 9.4 Rear brake drum components (Sec. 8)

1 Backplate
2 Handbrake adjustment plunger
3 Trailing shoe
4 Hold down spring and washer
5 Self-adjusting lever
6 Handbrake relay lever
7 'U' clip
8 Drum
9 Drum retainer clip
10 Wheel cylinder
11 Leading shoe
12 Shoe hold down pin

8.4 Remove the drum for brake inspection

8.5 Removing handbrake cable

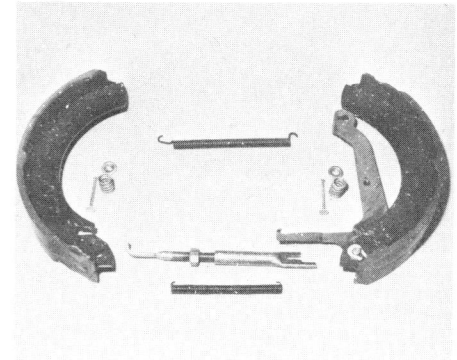
8.15 Rear brake components removed for cleaning

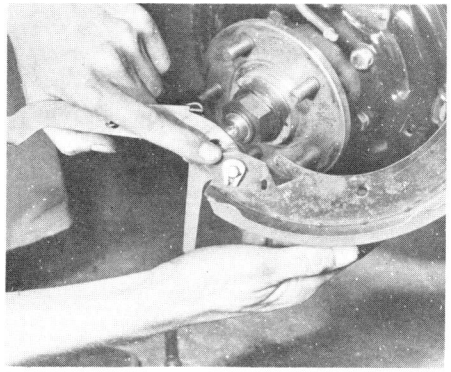
8.18a 'U' clip securing relay lever to shoe web

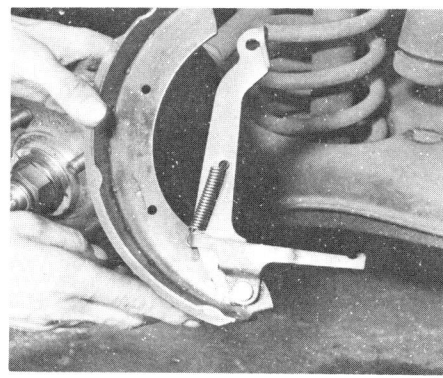
8.18b Relay lever correctly assembled to shoe web

8.19a Fitting lower retracting spring to shoe

8.19b Fitting lower retracting spring to second shoe

8.19c Fitting upper retracting spring

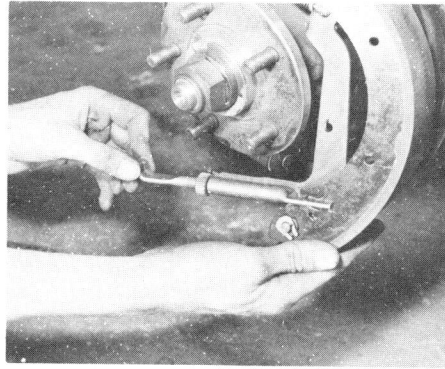
8.19d Refitting the adjuster pushrod

8.19e Fitting adjuster pushrod to second shoe

8.20a Fitting rear shoe to backplate

8.20b Place shoes in position ready to hook onto abutment

Chapter 9 Braking system

plunger is removed it must be discarded and a new one obtained.
6   The brake linings should be renewed if they are so worn that the rivet heads are flush with the surface of the lining. If bonded linings are fitted, they must be renewed when the lining material has worn down to 0.6 inch (1.52 mm) at its thinnest part.
7   Depress each shoe holding down spring and rotate the spring retaining washer through 90° to disengage it from the pin secured to the backplate. Lift away the washer and spring.
8   Ease each shoe from its location slot in the fixed pivot and then detach the other end of each shoe from the wheel cylinder.
9   Note which way round and into which holes in the shoes the two retracting springs fit and detach them.
10 Lift away the front shoe followed by the self adjusting pushrod and ratchet assembly.
11 Completely remove the handbrake cable from the body mounted brackets and disconnect the cable from the relay lever.
12 Lift away the rear shoe together with the self adjusting mechanism.
13 If the shoes are to left off for a while, place a warning on the steering wheel as accidental depression of the brake pedal will eject the pistons from the wheel cylinder.
14 To remove the relay lever assembly, using a screwdriver prise open the U clip on the rear brake shoe and lift away the assembly. The U-clip must be discarded and a new one obtained ready for reassembly.
15 Thoroughly clean all traces of dust from the shoes, backplates and brake drums using a stiff brush (photo). Brake dust can cause judder or squeal and it is therefore important to remove all traces. It is recommended that compressed air is **NOT** used for this operation as this increases the possibility of the dust being inhaled.
16 Check that the pistons are free in the cylinder, that the rubber dust covers are undamaged and in position, and that there are no hydraulic fluid leaks.
17 Prior to reassembly smear a trace of Castrol PH Brake Grease on the shoe support pads, brake shoe pivots and on the ratchet wheel face and threads.
18 To reassemble first it the relay lever assembly to the rear brake shoe and retain in position using a new U-clip. A pair of pliers close to the end of the clips will assist this action (see photos).
19 Fit the retracting springs to the shoe webs in the same position as was noted during removal (photos). Refit the adjusting pushrod (photos).
20 Position the rear brake shoe on the fixed pivot and wheel cylinder piston extension and using a screwdriver ease the front shoe into position on the brake backplate and wheel cylinder piston extension (photos).
21 Reconnect the handbrake cable to the relay lever taking care to ensure that it does not foul the adjustment plunger (photo).
22 Refit the handbrake cable to the body mounted brackets.
23 Place each shoe holding down clip on its pin followed by the washer, dished face inwards. Depress and turn the washer through 90° to lock position. Make sure that each shoe is firmly seated on the backplate (photo).
24 Rotate each adjusting pushrod ratchet until all slack in the pushrod is removed. Check that the adjusting arm positively locates in the ratchet wheel serrations.
25 Refit the brake drum and push it onto the studs as far as it will go.
26 The shoes must next be centralised by the brake pedal being depressed firmly several times.
27 Operate the handbrake lever several times until it is no longer possible to hear the clicking noise of the ratchet being turned by the adjusting arm.
28 Refit the road wheel and lower the car. Road test to ensure correct operation of the rear brakes.

9   Drum brake wheel cylinder – removal, inspection and overhaul

If hydraulic fluid is leaking from the brake wheel cylinder, it will be necessary to dismantle and renew the seals. Should brake fluid be found running down the side of the wheel, or if it is noticed that a pool of liquid forms alongside one wheel or the level in the master cylinder drops it is also indicative of failed seals.
1   Refer to Section 8 and remove the brake drum and shoes. Clean down the rear of the backplate using a stiff brush. Place a quantity of rag under the backplate to catch any hydraulic fluid which may issue

8.20c Lever shoe into abutment

8.20d The shoes reassembled

8.21 Connect the handbrake cable to relay lever

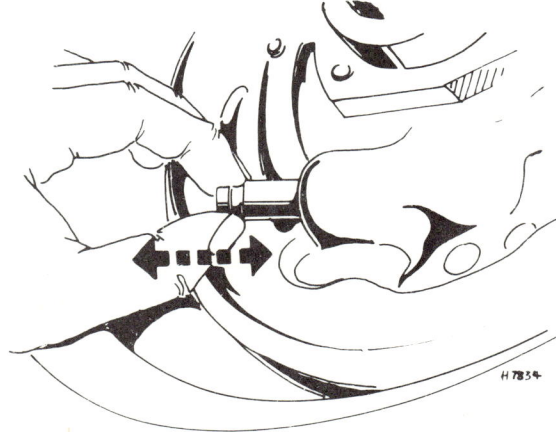
Fig. 9.5 Check movement of adjustment plungers (Sec. 8)

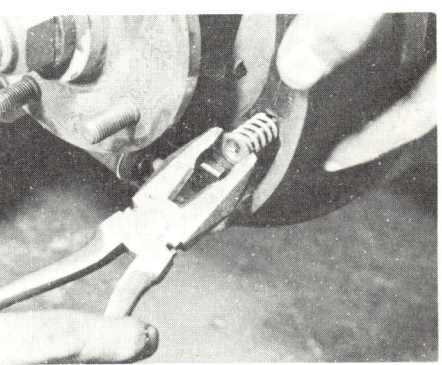
8.23 Refit the spring and washer

from the open pipe or wheel cylinder.
2   Wipe the top of the brake master cylinder reservoir and unscrew the cap. Place a piece of polythene sheet over the top of the reservoir and refit the cap. This is to stop hydraulic fluid syphoning out.
3   Using an open ended spanner, carefully unscrew the hydraulic pipe union/s to the rear of the wheel cylinder. To prevent dirt ingress tape over the pipe end.
4   Undo and remove the two bolts and washers that secure the wheel cylinder to the brake backplate.
5   Withdraw the wheel cylinder from the front of the brake backplate.
6   To dismantle the wheel cylinder first ease off each rubber dust cover retaining ring and lift away each dust cover.
7   Carefully lift out each piston together with seal from the wheel cylinder bore. Recover the return spring.
8   Using the fingers only, remove the piston seal from each piston, noting which way round it is fitted (Fig. 9.6). Do not use a metal screwdriver as this could scratch the piston.
9   Inspect the inside of the cylinder for score marks caused by impurities in the hydraulic fluid. If any are found, the cylinder and pistons will require renewal. **Note**: *if the wheel cylinder requires renewal always ensure that the replacement is exactly the same as the one removed.*
10   If the cylinder is sound, thoroughly clean it out with fresh hydraulic fluid.
11   The old rubber seals will probably be swollen and visibly worn. Smear the new rubber seals with hydraulic fluid and refit to the pistons making sure they are the correct way round with the flap face of the seal adjacent to the piston rear shoulder.
12   Wet the cylinder bore and insert the return spring. Carefully insert the piston seal end first into the cylinder, making sure that the seals do not roll over as they are initially fitted into the bore.
13   Position the rubber boots on each end of the wheel cylinder and secure in position with the retaining rings.
14   Fit a new ring seal onto the rear of the wheel cylinder and position this in its slot in the backplate. Secure in position with the two bolts and washers.
15   Reconnect the brake/pipe(s) to the rear of the wheel cylinder, taking care not to cross thread the union nuts. On the left-hand wheel cylinder make sure the pipes are connected the correct way round as noted during removal.
16   Refit the brake shoes and drum as described in Section 8.
17   Refer to Section 2 and bleed the brake hydraulic system.

10 Drum brake backplate – removal and refitting

1   To remove the backplate refer to Chapter 11 and remove the halfshaft and drive shaft flange.
2   Detach the handbrake cable from the handbrake relay lever.
3   Wipe the top of the brake master cylinder reservoir and unscrew the cap. Place a piece of polythene sheet over the top of the reservoir and refit the cap. This is to stop hydraulic fluid syphoning out.
4   Using an open ended spanner, carefully unscrew the hydraulic pipe union to the rear of the wheel cylinder. To prevent dirt ingress tape over the pipe end.
5   The brake backplate may now be lifted away once the four securing bolts have been removed.
6   Refitting is the reverse sequence to removal. It will be necessary to bleed the brake hydraulic system as described in Section 2.

11 Handbrake – adjustment

1   It is important to check that lack of adjustment is not caused by the cable becoming detached from the body mounted clips, that equaliser bracket and pivot points are adequately lubricated and that the rear shoe linings have not worn excessively.
2   Chock the front wheels. Jack up the rear of the car and support on firmly based axle-stands located under the rear axle. Release the handbrake.
3   Check the adjustment of the handbrake by measuring the amount of movement of the adjustment plungers located in the brake backplate. This should be 0.020 – 0.039 in (0.5 – 1.0 mm). If the results obtained differ from one another the difference may be equalised by gripping the handbrake cable at the equaliser bracket and adjusting the position of the cable.

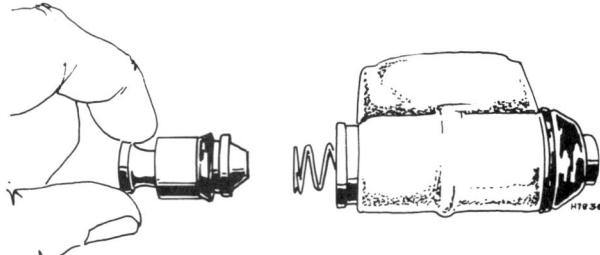

Fig. 9.6 Dismantling wheel cylinder (note which way round seal is fitted) (Sec. 9)

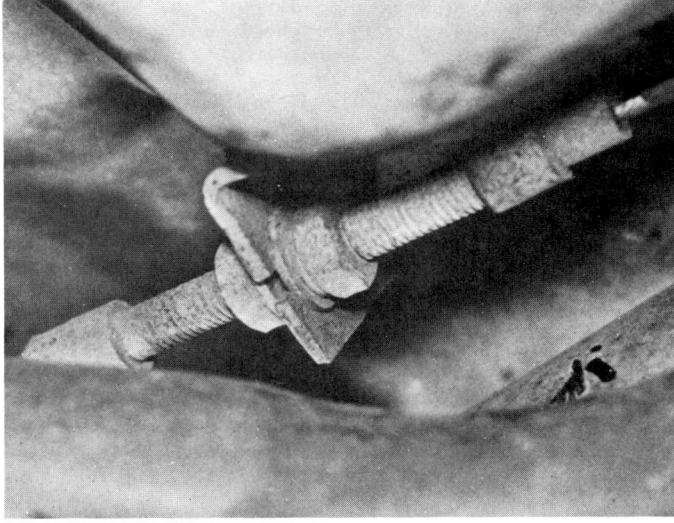

11.7 Handbrake cable adjustment location on body mounted bracket

4   If the movement of the adjustment plungers is correct operate the handbrake lever several times until it is no longer possible to hear the clicking noise of the ratchet being turned by the adjusting arm.
5   If the movement of the adjustment plungers is incorrect the cable may then be adjusted as described in the following paragraphs.
6   Make sure that the handbrake is in the full off position.
7   Remove all free movement of the adjustment plungers by slackening off the cable as necessary at the right-hand cables to body abutment bracket. (photo). The relay levers in the rear brake units will automatically return to the fully 'off' position.
8   Now adjust the cable at the right-hand cable to body abutment bracket so as to give a plunger free movement of 0.020 – 0.039 inch (0.5 – 1.0 mm) on each brake backplate.
9   Equalise the movement of the plungers by gripping the handbrake cable at the equaliser bracket and adjusting the position of the cable.
10   Should adjustment of the cable not alter the plunger free movement, it is an indication that the cable is binding or the automatic brake adjuster is not operating correctly – usually due to seizure of the moving parts within the brake unit. It could also be that the adjustment plungers have seized in their locations in the backplate. Further investigation will therefore be necessary.
11   When adjustment is correct tighten the adjuster locknuts.
12   Operate the handbrake lever several times until it is no longer possible to hear the clicking noise of the ratchet being turned by the adjuster arm.
13   Remove the axle stands and lower the car to the ground.
14   Handbrake operation can be regarded as satisfactory if the lever travel does not exceed 10 notches of the ratchet.

12 Handbrake cable – removal and refitting

1   Chock the front wheels, jack up the rear of the car and support on firmly based axle-stands located under the rear axle. Release the handbrake. Remove the two rear wheels.
2   Using a pair of pliers, remove the spring clip and withdraw the clevis pin and wave washer securing the handbrake cable to the handbrake lever. Detach the cable from the lever.

Chapter 9 Braking system

3   Undo the cable adjuster nuts and then detach the cable from the clips located under the body and suspension arm.
4   Remove the brake drums. If they are tight they may be removed using a soft faced hammer on the outer drum circumference and tapping outward.
5   Detach the brake cable from each brake unit relay lever and pull the cable rearward through the backplate.
6   To refit the cable first feed the cable ends through the rear of the backplate and reconnect to the relay levers. Refit the brake drums.
7   Attach the cable to the underbody brackets and clips on the radius arms. Take care to make sure that the adjuster is correctly located in its bracket. A white paint mark is provided on each cable to identify the clip location on the suspension arm.
8   Position the handbrake cable onto the handbrake lever and retain with the clevis pin, wave washer and spring clips.
9   Refit the rear wheels and referring to Section 11 adjust the handbrake cable.
10   Remove the axle-stands and lower the car to the ground.

13 Brake master cylinder – removal and refitting

1   Apply the handbrake and chock the front wheels. Drain the fluid from the master cylinder reservoir and master cylinder by attaching a plastic bleed tube to one of the brake bleed screws. Undo the screw one turn and then pump the fluid out into a clean glass container by means of the brake pedal. Hold the brake pedal against the floor at the end of the each stroke and tighten the bleed screw. When the pedal has returned to its normal position loosen the bleed screw and repeat the process until the reservoir is empty.
2   Wipe the area around the two union nuts on the side of the master cylinder body and using an open ended spanner undo the two union nuts. Tape over the ends of the pipes to stop dirt ingress (Fig. 9.7).
3   Undo and remove the two nuts and spring washers that secure the master cylinder to the rear of the servo unit. Lift away the master cylinder taking care that no hydraulic fluid is allowed to drip onto the paintwork.
4   Refitting is the reverse sequence to removal. Always start with the union nuts before finally tightening the master cylinder nuts. It will be necessary to bleed the hydraulic system: Full details will be found in Section 2.

14 Brake master cylinder – dismantling, examination and reassembly

If a new master cylinder is to be fitted, it will be necessary to lubricate the seals before fitting to the car as they have a protective coating when originally assembled. Remove the blanking plugs from the hydraulic pipe union seatings. Inject clean hydraulic fluid into the master cylinder and operate the primary piston several times so that the fluid spreads over all the internal working surfaces.

If the master cylinder is to be dismantled after removal proceed as follows.
1   Undo and remove the two screws and spring washers holding the reservoir to the master cylinder body. Lift away the reservoir. Using a suitable sized Allen key, or wrench, unscrew the tipping valve nut and lift away the seal. Using a suitable diameter rod, push the primary plunger down the bore, this operation enabling the tipping valve to be withdrawn.

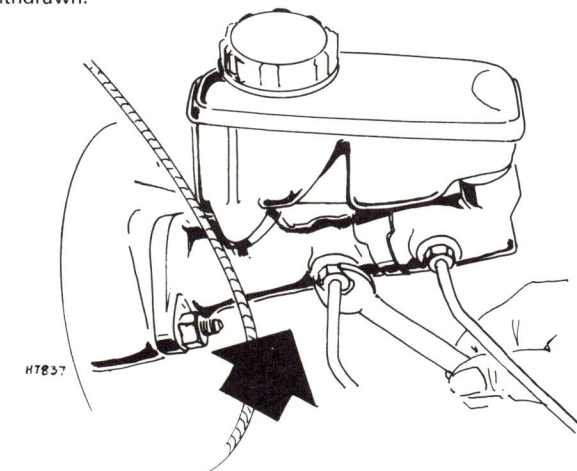

Fig. 9.7 Release brake pipe unions from master cylinder (Sec. 13)

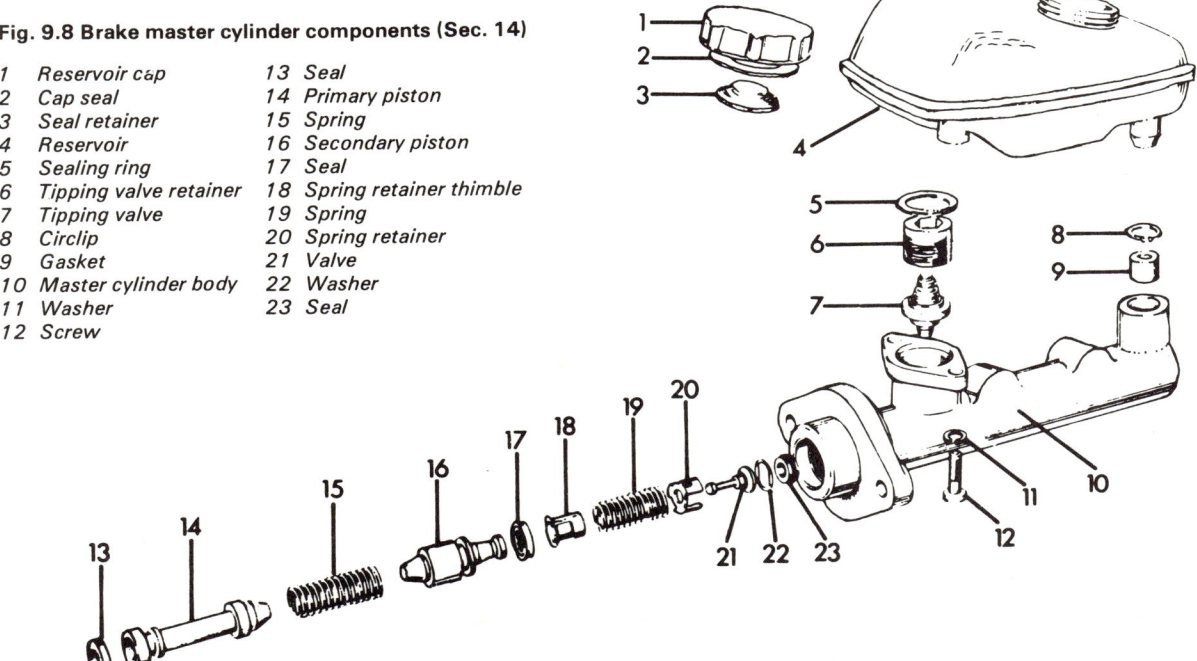

Fig. 9.8 Brake master cylinder components (Sec. 14)

  1 Reservoir cap
  2 Cap seal
  3 Seal retainer
  4 Reservoir
  5 Sealing ring
  6 Tipping valve retainer
  7 Tipping valve
  8 Circlip
  9 Gasket
 10 Master cylinder body
 11 Washer
 12 Screw
 13 Seal
 14 Primary piston
 15 Spring
 16 Secondary piston
 17 Seal
 18 Spring retainer thimble
 19 Spring
 20 Spring retainer
 21 Valve
 22 Washer
 23 Seal

2 Using a compressed air jet, very carefully applied to the rear outlet connection, blow out all the master cylinder internal components. Alternatively, shake out the parts. Take care that adequate precautions are taken to ensure all parts are caught as they emerge.
3 Separate the primary and secondary plungers from the intermediate spring. Use the fingers to remove the gland seal from the primary plunger.
4 The secondary plunger assembly should be separated by lifting the thimble leaf over the shouldered end of the plunger. Using the fingers, remove the seal from the secondary plunger.
5 Depress the secondary spring, allowing the valve stem to slide through the keyhole in the thimble, thus releasing the tension on the spring.
6 Detach the valve spacer, taking care of the spring washer which will be found located under the valve head.
7 Examine the bore of the cylinder carefully for any signs of scores or ridges. If this is found to be smooth all over new seals can be fitted. If however, there is any doubt of the condition of the bore, then a new cylinder must be fitted.
8 If examination of the seals shows them to be apparently oversize, or swollen, or very loose on the plungers, suspect oil contamination in the system. Oil will swell these rubber seals, and if one is found to be swollen, it is reasonable to assume that all seals in the braking system will need attention.
9 Thoroughly clean all parts in clean hydraulic fluid or methylated spirits. Ensure that the by pass ports are clear.
10 All components should be assembled wet by dipping in clean brake fluid. Using fingers only, fit new seals to the primary and secondary plunger ensuring that they are the correct way round. Place the dished washer with the dome against the underside of the valve seat. Hold it in position with the valve spacer ensuring that the legs face towards the valve seal.
11 Refit the plunger return spring centrally on the spacer. Insert the thimble into the spring, and depress until the valve stem engages in the keyhole of the thimble.
12 Insert the reduced end of the plunger into the thimble, until the thimble engages under the shoulder of the plunger, and press home the thimble leaf. Refit the intermediate spring between the primary and secondary plungers.
13 Check that the master cylinder bore is clean and smear with clean brake fluid. With the complete assembly suitably wetted with brake fluid, carefully insert it into the bore. Ease the lips of the piston seals into the bore taking care that they do not roll over. Push the assembly fully home.
14 Refit the tipping valve assembly, and seal, to the cylinder bore and tighten the securing nut to the torque wrench setting given in the Specifications.
15 Using a clean screwdriver push the primary piston in and out checking that the recuperating valve opens when the screwdriver is withdrawn and closes again when it is pushed in.
16 Check the condition of the front and rear reservoir gaskets and if there is any doubt as to their condition they must be renewed.
17 Refit the hydraulic fluid reservoir and tighten the two retaining screws.
18 The master cylinder is now ready for refitting to the servo unit. Bleed the complete hydraulic system and road test the car.

15 Brake pedal – removal and refitting

1 For safety reasons disconnect the battery.
2 Refer to Chapter 12 and remove the crash pad lower insulation.
3 Withdraw the spring clip from the brake servo pushrod to brake pedal clevis pin. Remove the clevis pin and the two bushes.
4 Detach the brake pedal return spring from the brake pedal and bracket.
5 Remove the spring clip and D-washer from the shaft. Push the shaft through the pedal and bracket until the pedal can be removed.
6 Remove the bushes from the pedal. Renew the bushes if there is any evidence of wear.
7 Refitting the brake pedal is the reverse sequence to removal. Lubricate all moving parts with engine oil.

16 Handbrake lever – removal and refitting

1 If a handbrake warning light is fitted, disconnect the battery for safety reasons.
2 Undo and remove the six screws securing the handbrake lever gaiter to the floor.
3 Remove the spring clip, clevis pin and wave washer that secure the primary cable to the lower end of the handbrake lever. Access to this is gained by working under the car. Note that the wave washer locates inside the clevis pin yoke.
4 If a handbrake warning light is fitted, pull the connectors from the switch.
5 Undo and remove the two bolts that secure the handbrake lever to the floor and lift away.
6 Refitting is the reverse sequence to removal. Smear the clevis pin with a little high melting point grease.

17 Vacuum servo unit – description

1 A vacuum servo unit is fitted in to the brake hydraulic circuit in series with the master cylinder, to provide assistance to the driver when the brake pedal is depressed. This reduces the effort required by the driver to operate the brakes under all braking conditions.

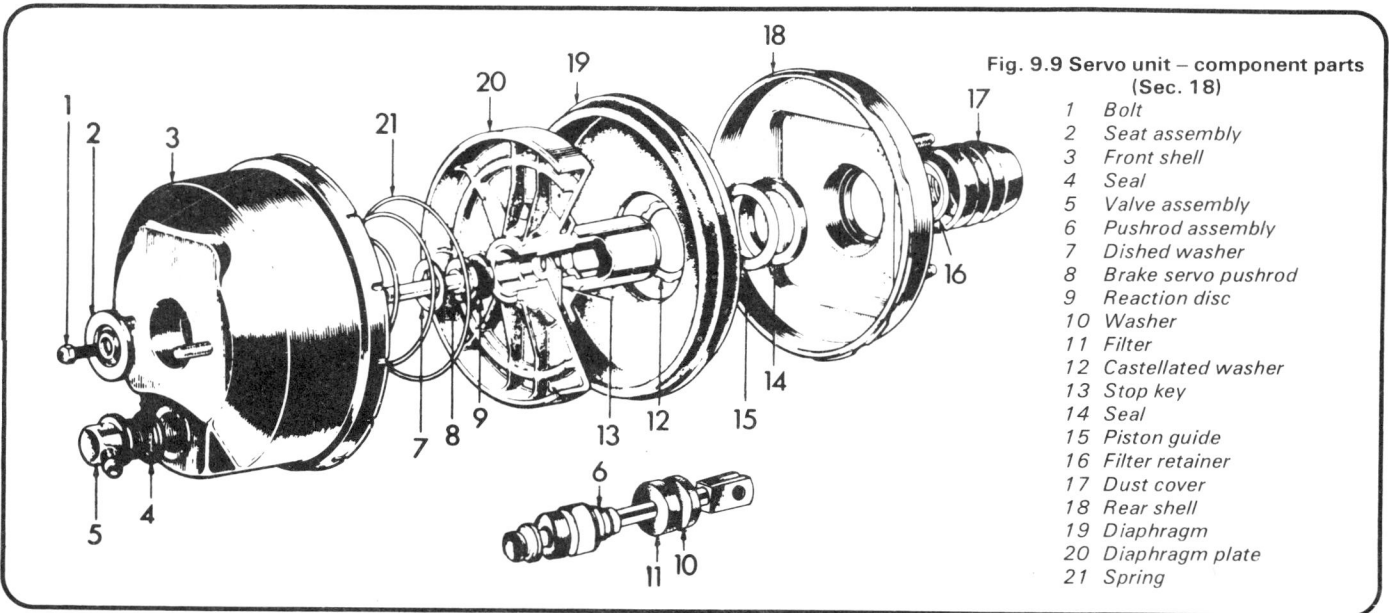

Fig. 9.9 Servo unit – component parts (Sec. 18)

1 Bolt
2 Seat assembly
3 Front shell
4 Seal
5 Valve assembly
6 Pushrod assembly
7 Dished washer
8 Brake servo pushrod
9 Reaction disc
10 Washer
11 Filter
12 Castellated washer
13 Stop key
14 Seal
15 Piston guide
16 Filter retainer
17 Dust cover
18 Rear shell
19 Diaphragm
20 Diaphragm plate
21 Spring

Chapter 9 Braking system

2 The unit operates by vacuum obtained from the induction manifold and comprises basically a booster diaghragm and check valve. The servo unit and hydraulic master cylinder are connected together so that the servo unit piston rod acts as the master cylinder pushrod. The driver's braking effort is transmitted through another pushrod to the servo unit piston and its built in control system. The servo unit piston does not fit tightly into the cylinder, but has a strong diaphragm to keep its edges in constant contact with the cylinder wall, so ensuring an air tight seal between the two parts. The forward chamber is held under vacuum conditions created in the inlet manifold of the engine and, during periods when the brake pedal is not in use, the controls open a passage to the rear chamber so placing it under vacuum conditions as well. When the brake pedal is depressed, the vacuum passage to the rear chamber is cut off and the chamber opened to atmospheric pressure. The consequent rush of air pushes the servo piston forward in the vacuum chamber and operates the main pushrod to the master cylinder.

3 The controls are designed so that assistance is given under all conditions and, when the brakes are not required, vacuum in the rear chamber is established when the brake pedal is released. All air from the atmosphere entering the rear chamber is passed through a small air filter.

4 Under normal operating conditions the vacuum servo unit is very reliable and does not require overhaul except at very high mileages. In this case it is far better to obtain a service exchange unit, rather than repair the original unit.

18 Vacuum servo unit – removal and refitting

1 Slacken the clip securing the vacuum hose to the servo unit and carefully draw the hose from its union.
2 Refer to Section 13 and remove the master cylinder.
3 Refer to Chapter 12 and remove the crash pad lower insulation.
4 Pull out the spring clip and withdraw the clevis pin together with the two half bushes.
5 Disconnect the push rod from the brake pedal.
6 Working in the engine compartment, undo and remove the two nuts securing the servo bracket to the bulkhead (Fig. 9.10).
7 Working in the passenger compartment undo and remove the two nuts securing the servo unit to the bulkhead. Lift away the bracket and servo unit.
8 Undo and remove the four retaining nuts and washers and remove the bracket from the servo unit.
9 Inspect the condition of the bracket to bulkhead panel seal and renew if necessary.
10 Refitting the servo unit is the reverse sequence to removal. The following additional points should be noted:

(a) Use an impact adhesive to secure the gasket to the servo bracket.
(b) Apply a sealer to the bracket to bulkhead mating faces.
(c) Bleed the brake hydraulic system as described in Section 2.

19 Vacuum servo unit – dismantling, inspection and reassembly

Thoroughly clean the outside of the unit using a stiff brush and wipe with a non-fluffy rag. It cannot be too strongly emphasised that cleanliness is important when working on the servo. Before any attempt is made to dismantle, refer to Fig. 9.11 where it will be seen that two items of equipment are required. Firstly, a base plate must be made to enable the unit to be safely held in a vice. Secondly, a lever must be made similar to the form shown. Without these items it is impossible to dismantle satisfactorily. In addition to these items, special lubricants number 64949008 EM – IC – 14/and 15 will be required for use during the overhaul procedures.

To dismantle the unit proceed as follows:
1 Refer to Fig. 9.11 and, using a file or scriber, make a line across the two halves of the unit to act as a datum for alignment.
2 Fit the previously made base plate into a firm vice and attach the unit to the plate using the master cylinder studs.
3 Fit the lever to the four studs on the rear shell as shown in Fig. 9.11.
4 Use a piece of long rubber hose and connect one end to the

Fig. 9.10 Removal of servo unit upper mounting nuts (Sec. 18)

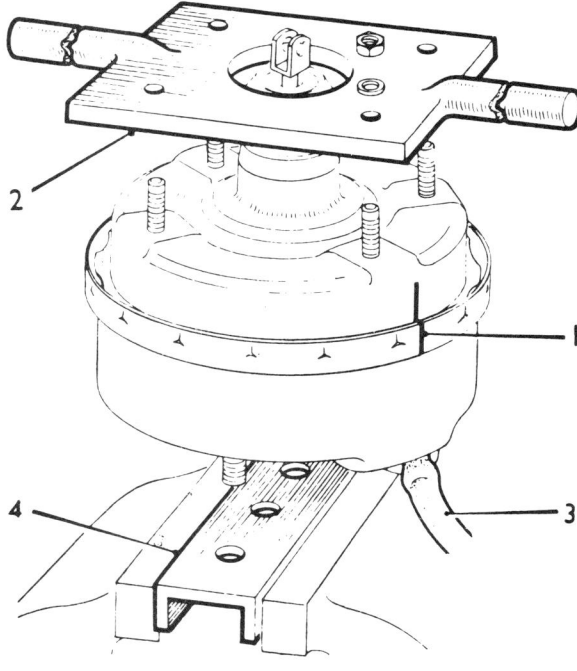

Fig. 9.11 Special tools required to dismantle servo unit (Sec. 19)

1 Scribe line   3 Vacuum applied
2 Lever   4 Base plate

adaptor on the engine inlet manifold and the other end to the non-return valve. Start the engine and this will create a vacuum in the unit so drawing the two halves together.
5 Rotate the lever in an anticlockwise direction until the front shell indentations are in line with the recesses in the rim of the rear shell. Then press the lever assembly down firmly whilst an assistant stops the engine and quickly removes the vacuum pipe from the inlet manifold connector. Depress the operation rod so as to release the vacuum, whereupon the front and rear halves should part. If necessary, use a soft faced hammer and lightly tap the front half to break the bond.
6 Lift away the rear shell followed by the diaphragm return spring, the dust cap, end cap and filter. Also withdraw the diaphragm. Press down the valve rod and shake out the valve retaining plate. Then separate the valve rod assembly from the diaphragm plate.
7 Gently ease the spring washer from the diaphragm plate and withdraw the push rod and reaction disc.
8 The seal and plate assembly in the end of the front shell are a press fit. It is recommended that, unless the seal is to be renewed, they

be left in situ.
9   Thoroughly clean all parts. Inspect all parts for signs of damage, stripped threads etc., and obtain new parts as necessary. All seals should be renewed and for this a 'Major Repair Kit' should be purchased. This kit will also contain two separate greases which must be used as directed and not interchanged.
10 To reassemble first smear the seal and bearing with grease numbered 64949008 EM – IC – 14 and refit the rear shell positioning it such that the flat face of the seal is towards the bearing. Press into position and refit the retainer.
11 Lightly smear the disc and hydraulic pushrod with the same grease. Refit the reaction disc and pushrod to the diaphragm plate and press in the large spring washer. The small spring washer supplied in the 'Major Repair Kit' is not required. It is important that the length of the pushrod is not altered in any way and any attempt to move the adjustment bolt will strip the threads. If a new hydraulic pushrod has been required, the length will have to be reset. Details of this operation are given at the end of this Section.
12 Lightly smear the outer diameter of the diaphragm plate neck and the bearing surfaces of the valve plunger again using the same grease. Carefully fit the valve rod assembly into the neck of the diaphragm and fix with the retaining plate.
13 Fit the diaphragm into position and also the non-return valve to the front shell. Next smear the seal and plate assembly with grease numbered 64949008 EM – IC – 15 and press into the front shell with the plate facing inward.
14 Fit the front shell to the base plate and the lever to the rear shell. Reconnect the vacuum hose to the non-return valve and the adaptor on the engine inlet manifold. Position the diaphragm return spring in the front shell. Lightly smear the outlet head of the diaphragm with grease numbered 64949008 EM – IC – 14 and locate the diaphragm assembly in the rear shell. Position the rear shell assembly on the return spring and line up the previously made scribe marks.
15 The assistant should start the engine. Watching one's fingers very carefully press the two halves of the unit together and, using the lever tool, turn clockwise to lock the two halves together. Stop the engine and disconnect the hose.
16 Press a new filter into the neck of the diaphragm plate, refit the end cap and position the dust cover onto the special lugs of the rear shell.
17 Hydraulic pushrod adjustment only applies if a new pushrod has been fitted. It will be seen from Fig. 9.12 that there is a bolt screwed into the end of the pushrod. The amount of protrusion has to be adjusted in the following manner: Remove the bolt and coat the threaded portion with Loctite Grade B. Reconnect the vacuum hose to the adaptor on the inlet valve and non-return valve. Start the engine and screw the prepared bolt into the end of the pushrod. Adjust the position of the bolt head so that it is 0.011 to 0.016 inch (0.28 – 0.40 mm) below the face of the front shell as shown by dimension 'A' in Fig. 9.12. Leave the unit for a minimum of 24 hours to allow the Loctite to set hard.
18 Refit the servo unit to the car as described in the previous Section. To test the servo unit for correct operation after overhaul, first start the engine and run for a minimum period of two minutes and then switch off. Wait for ten minutes and apply the footbrake very carefully, listening to hear the rush of air into the servo unit. This will indicate that vacuum was retained and, therefore, operating correctly.

20 Hydraulic pipes and hoses

1   Periodically all brake pipes, pipe connections and unions should be carefully examined (Figs.9.13 and 9.14).
2   First examine for signs of leakage where the pipe unions occur. Then examine the flexible hoses for signs of chafing and fraying and, of course, leakage. This is only a preliminary part of the flexible hose inspection, as exterior condition does not necessarily indicate the interior condition, which will be considered later.
3   The steel pipes must be examined carefully and methodically. They must be cleaned off and examined for any signs of dents, or other damage and rust and corrosion. Rust and corrosion should be scraped off and, if the depth of pitting in the pipes is appreciable, they will need renewing. This is particularly likely in those areas underneath the car body and along the rear axle where the pipes are exposed to full force of road and weather conditions.
4   If any section of pipe is to be taken off, first wipe and then remove

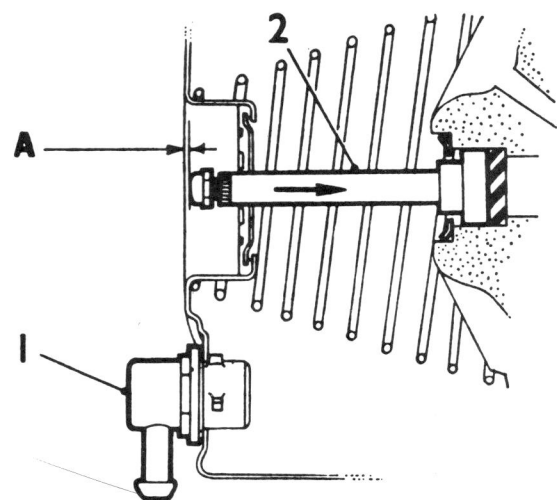

Fig. 9.12 The correct pushrod setting (Sec. 19)

A Pushrod setting to 0.011 – 0.016 in (0.28 – 0.40 mm)
1 Vacuum applied
2 Pushrod against reaction disc

the fluid reservoir cap and place a piece of polythene over the reservoir. Refit the cap. This will stop syphoning during subsequent operations.
5   Rigid pipe removal is usually quite straightforward. The unions at each end are undone, the pipe and union pulled out, and the centre sections of the pipe removed from the body clips. The joints may sometimes be very tight. As one can only use an open ended spanner and the unions are not large, burring of the flats is not uncommon when attempting to undo them. For this reason a self-locking grip wrench (mole) is often the only way to remove a stubborn union.
6   Removal of flexible hoses is described in Section 3.
7   With the flexible hose removed, examine the internal bore. If it is blown through first, it should be possible to see through it. Any specks of rubber which come out, or signs of restriction in the bore, means that the rubber lining is breaking up and the pipe must be renewed.
8   Rigid pipes which need renewal can usually be purchased at any garage where they have the pipe, unions and special tools to make them up. All they need to know is the total length of the pipe, the type of flare used at each end with the union, and the length and thread of the union.
9   Fitting the pipes is a straightforward reversal of the removal procedure. If the rigid pipes have been made up it is best to get all the sets (bends) in them before trying to install them. Also if there are any acute bends, ask your supplier to put these in for you on a special tube bender. Otherwise you may kink the pipe and thereby decrease the bore area and fluid flow.
10 With the pipes refitted remove the polythene from the reservoir cap and bleed the system as described in Section 2.

21 Differential valve assembly – removal and refitting

1   Place some absorbent cloth under the valve to stop brake hydraulic fluid touching the paintwork.
2   Wipe the area around the valve assembly and then undo the four pipe unions from the valve. Tape the ends of the pipes to prevent dirt ingress or loss of hydraulic fluid.
3   Unscrew and remove the self tapping screw holding the valve assembly to the body.
4   Disconnect the cable connection to the valve warning light switch. Lift the valve assembly from the car.
5   Refitting the differential valve assembly is the reverse sequence to removal. It will be necessary to bleed the brake hydraulic system as described in Section 2.
6   Should difficulty be experienced in bleeding the brakes it could be that the valve pistons are stuck and not in the central position.

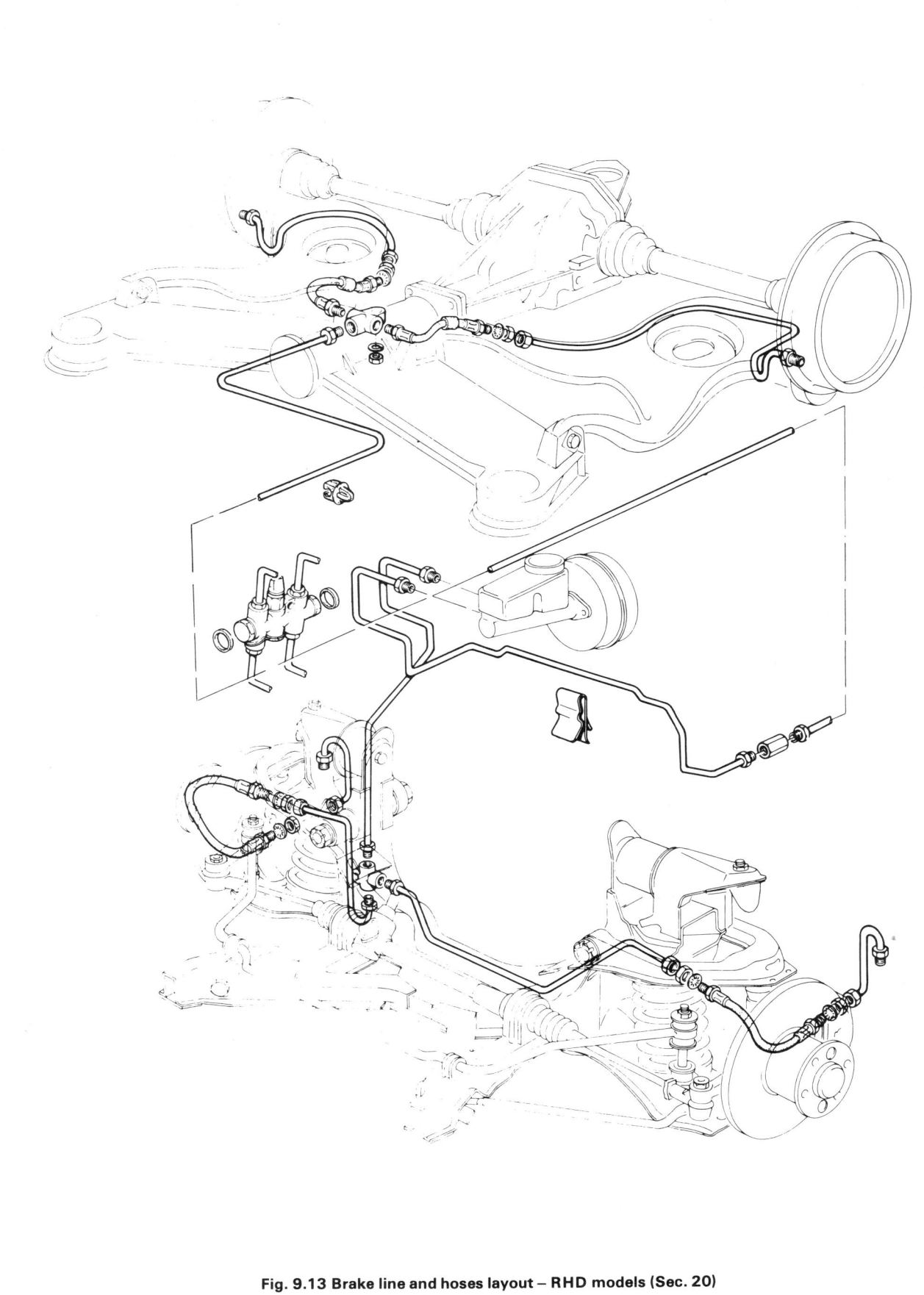

Fig. 9.13 Brake line and hoses layout – RHD models (Sec. 20)

176 Chapter 9 Braking system

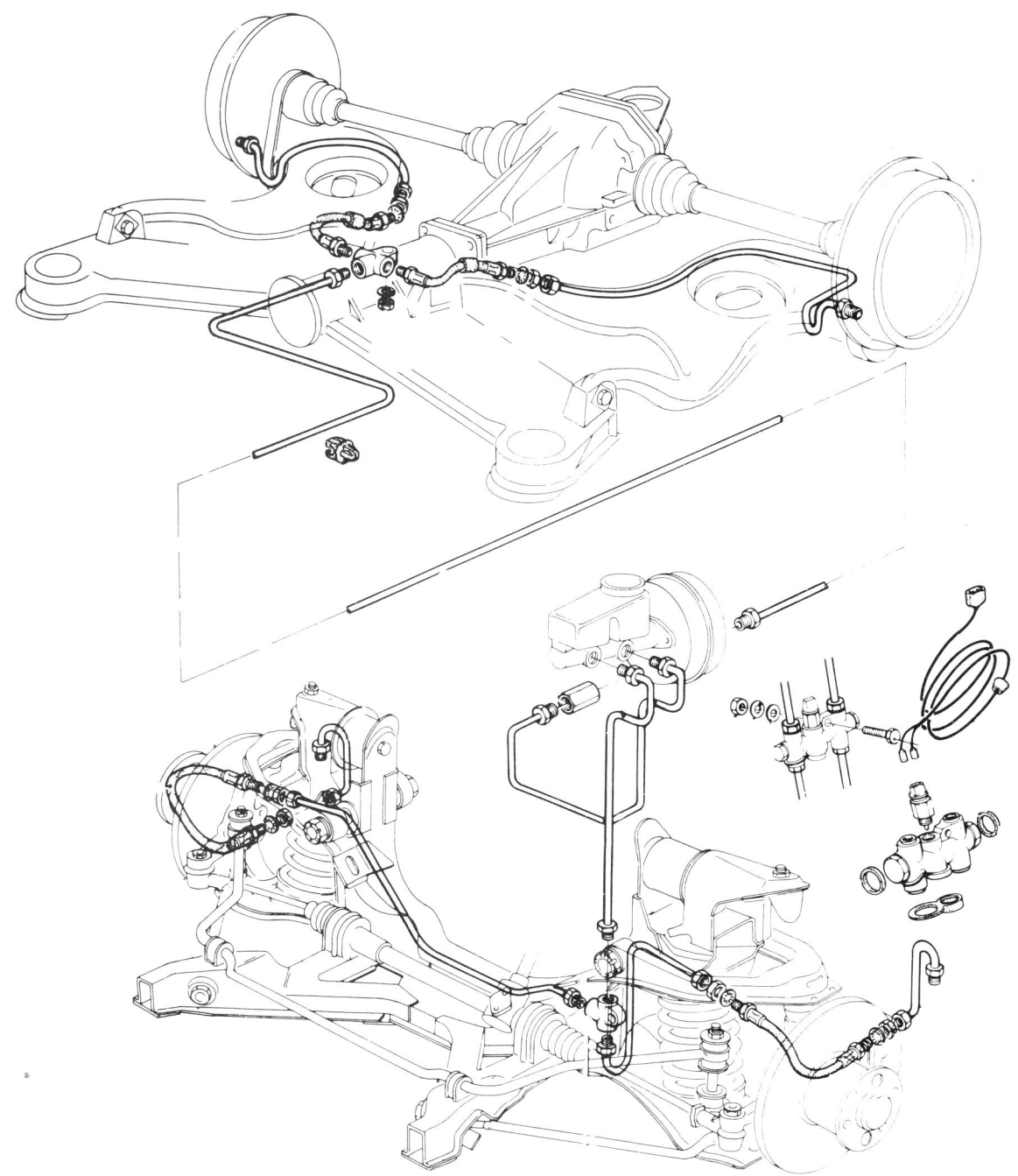

Fig. 9.14 Brake line and hoses layout – LHD models (Sec. 20)

22 Differential valve assembly – dismantling and reassembly

1 Refer to Section 21 and remove the differential valve assembly.
2 Before commencing dismantling obtain an overhaul kit.
3 Unscrew the two end plugs and discard the copper washers. These must not be refitted.
4 Unscrew the plastic switch assembly.
5 The pistons may now be pushed out of the bore. Take great care not to damage the bore surface finish.
6 Using the fingers remove the seals from the pistons and discard.
7 Pull off the rubber dust cover and discard.
8 Thoroughly wash all parts in methylated spirits or clean hydraulic fluid and inspect the surfaces of the pistons and bores for signs of scoring or damage. If wear is evident a new assembly should be obtained.
9 To reassemble, wet the seals in clean hydraulic fluid and fit to pistons. The larger diameter of each seal must be adjacent to the slotted end of the respective pistons.
10 Wet the pistons and insert the longer piston into the bore, the slotted end must be outermost, until the groove in the piston is opposite the switch aperture.
11 Refit the switch assembly.
12 Insert the second piston onto the bore with the slotted end outermost.
13 Fit new copper washers to the end plugs and screw them into their respective ends. Note the thread sizes are different.
14 Fit a new dust cover. The unit is now ready for refitting to the car.

Chapter 9 Braking system

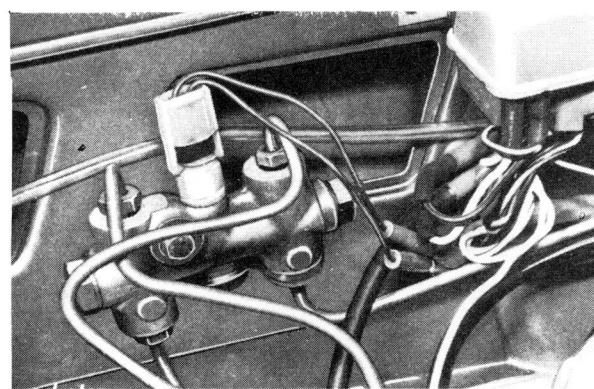

Fig. 9.15 Pressure differential valve assembly (Sec. 22)

23 Fault diagnosis – braking system

Symptom	Reason/s	Remedy
Pedal travels almost to floorboards before brakes operate	Brake fluid level too low	Top up master cylinder reservoir. Check for leaks
	Caliper leaking	Dismantle caliper, clean, fit new rubbers and bleed brakes
	Master cylinder leaking (bubbles in master cylinder fluid)	Dismantle master cylinder, clean and fit new rubbers. Bleed brakes
	Brake flexible hose leaking	Examine and fit new hose if old hose leaking. Bleed brakes
	Brake line fractured	Replace with new brake pipe. Bleed brakes
	Brake system unions loose	Check all unions in brake system and tighten as necessary. Bleed brakes
	Pad or shoe linings over 75° worn	Fit new pads or shoes
	Brakes badly out of adjustment	Jack up car and adjust brakes
Brake pedal feels springy	New linings not yet bedded-in	Use brakes gently until springy pedal feeling leaves
	Brake discs or drums badly worn or cracked	Fit new brake discs or drums
	Master cylinder securing nuts loose	Tighten master cylinder securing nuts. Ensure spring washers are fitted
Brake pedal feels spongy and soggy	Caliper or wheel cylinder leaking	Dismantle caliper or wheel cylinder, clean, fit new rubbers and bleed brakes
	Master cylinder leaking (bubbles in master cylinder reservoir)	Dismantle master cylinder, clean and fit new rubbers and bleed brakes. Replace cylinder if internal walls scored
	Brake pipe line or flexible hose leaking	Fit new pipeline or hose
	Unions in brake system loose	Examine for leaks, tighten as necessary
Excessive effort required to brake car	Pad or shoe linings badly worn	Fit replacement brake shoes and linings
	New pads or shoes recently fitted – not yet bedded-in	Use brakes gently until braking effort normal
	Harder linings fitted than standard causing increase in pedal pressure	Remove pads or shoes and fit standard units
	Linings and brake drums contaminated with oil, grease or hydraulic fluid	Rectify source of leak, clean brake drums, fit new linings
Brakes uneven and pulling to one side	Linings and discs or drums contaminated with oil, grease or hydraulic fluid	Ascertain and rectify source of leak, clean discs or drums, fit new pads or shoes
	Tyre pressures unequal	Check and inflate as necessary
	Radial ply tyres fitted at one end of the car only	Fit radial ply tyres of the same make to all four wheels
	Brake caliper loose	Tighten backplate securing nuts and bolts
	Brake pads or shoes fitted incorrectly	Remove and fit correct way round
	Different type of linings fitted at each wheel	Fit the pads or shoes specified by the manufacturer all round
	Anchorage for front suspension or rear suspension loose	Tighten front and rear suspension pick-up points including spring anchorage
	Brake discs or drums badly worn, cracked or distorted	Fit new brake discs or drums
Brakes tend to bind, drag or lock-on	Brake pads or shoes adjusted too tightly	Slacken off brake shoe adjusters. Check if caliper piston seized.

Chapter 10 Electrical system

Contents

Alternator brushes – removal, inspection and refitting (Bosch)	12
Alternator brushes – removal, inspection and refitting (Lucas)	11
Alternator – fault finding and repair	10
Alternator – general description	6
Alternator – removal and refitting	9
Alternator – routine maintenance	7
Alternator – special procedures	8
Auxiliary lamp assembly – removal and refitting	43
Auxiliary light beam adjustment	45
Auxiliary light bulb – removal and refitting	44
Battery charging	5
Battery electrolyte replenishment	4
Battery maintenance and inspection	3
Battery – removal and refitting	2
Cigarette lighter assembly – removal and refitting (Type A)	62
Cigarette lighter assembly – removal and refitting (Type B)	74
Direction indicator switch – removal and refitting	65
Electric clock – removal and refitting	61
Fault diagnosis – electrical system	76
Flasher circuit – fault tracing and rectification	20
Fog lamp assembly – removal and refitting	40
Fog light beam alignment	42
Fog light bulb – removal and refitting	41
Front direction indicator bulb assembly – removal and refitting	38
Front direction indicator light bulb – removal and refitting	39
Front side light bulb – removal and refitting	37
Fuel gauge – removal and refitting (Type A)	59
Fuel gauge – removal and refitting (Type B)	72
Fuses – general (all models)	75
General description	1
Headlamp alignment	36
Headlamp bulb – removal and refitting	35
Headlamp lens and reflector assembly – removal and refitting	34
Horn-fault tracing and rectification	32
Horn slip ring contact finger – removal and refitting	33
Ignition switch – removal and refitting	63
Instrument cluster bezel – removal, dismantling and refitting	67
Instrument cluster bulb – removal and refitting	56
Instrument cluster glass – removal and refitting (Type A)	54
Instrument cluster glass – removal and refitting (Type B)	70
Instrument cluster printed circuit – removal and refitting (Type A)	53
Instrument cluster printed circuit – removal and refitting (Type B)	69
Instrument cluster – removal and refitting (Type A)	52
Instrument cluster – removal and refitting (Type B)	68
Instruments – general	50
Instrument voltage regulator – removal and refitting	55
Interior bulbs – removal and refitting	51
Light switch – removal and refitting (Type A)	64
Light switch – removal and refitting (Type B)	73
Oil pressure gauge – removal and refitting (Type A)	60
Rear lamp assembly bulb – removal and refitting	48
Rear lamp assembly (estate) – removal and refitting	47
Rear lamp assembly (saloon) – removal and refiting	46
Rear number plate lamp bulb – removal and refitting	49
Rear windscreen washer pump – removal and refitting	31
Rear windscreen wiper motor – removal and refitting	30
Speedometer head – removal and refitting (Type A)	57
Speedometer head – removal and refitting (Type B)	71
Speedometer inner and outer cable – removal and refitting	58
Starter motor – general description	13
Starter motor (M35J) – dismantling and reassembly	16
Starter motor (M35J) – removal and refitting	15
Starter motor (M35J) – testing on engine	14
Starter motor (2M100) – dismantling and reassembly	19
Starter motor (2M100) – removal and refitting	18
Starter motor (2M100) – testing on engine	17
Switches (general) – removal and refitting	66
Windscreen washer jets – removal and refitting	29
Windscreen washer pump – removal and refitting	28
Windscreen wiper arms – removal and refitting	23
Windscreen wiper blades – removal and refitting	22
Windscreen wiper linkage – removal and refitting	27
Windscreen wiper mechanism – fault diagnosis and rectification	24
Windscreen wiper mechanism – maintenance	21
Windscreen wiper motor – brush renewal	26
Windscreen wiper motor – removal and refitting	25

Specifications

Battery
Type	Lead acid 12 volt, negative (-) earth
Rate	44 or 55 amp hr according to model
Specific gravity charged	1.270–1.290 at temperature of 25°C (77°F)

Starter motor
V4 and V6
Make .... Lucas

Chapter 10 Electrical system

Type	M35J	2M 100
Number of brushes	4	4
Minimum brush length	0.4 in (10 mm)	0.4 in (10 mm)
Brush spring pressure	1.8 lb (0.8 kg)	2.2 lb (1.0 kg)
Armature end play	0.01 in (0.25 mm)	0.01 in (0.25 mm)
Drive pinion engagement	Inertia	Solenoid
Maximum current draw	380 amps	440 amps

2.0 ohc

Make	Lucas	
Type	M35 G	M 100 and M 35J
Number of brushes	4	4
Min brush length	0.35 in (9.0 mm)	0.38 in (9.5 mm)
Brushes spring pressure	14.9 oz (420 gm)	17 oz (480 gm)
Commutator min. diameter	1.338 in (34 mm)	–
Armature endfloat	0.005–0.015 in (0.1–0.3 mm)	0.005–0.015 in (0.1–0.3 mm)
Type of drive	Solenoid	Solenoid
Maximum output	620 watts	750 watts (M 100); 700w (M 35 J)

Alternator

Type .... Lucas 15ACR or 17ACR
Bosch 35 K1 or 28 G1

Application:
    2.0 V4 standard .... Lucas 15ACR
            optional .... Lucas 17ACR
    2.0 ohc standard .... Bosch 28 G1
            optional .... Bosch 35 K1
    2.5 V6 standard .... Lucas 15ACR
            optional .... Lucas 17ACR
    3.0 V6 standard .... Lucas 17ACR or Bosch 35 K1
Output – Lucas 15ACR .... 28 amps
         Lucas 17ACR .... 35 amps
         Bosch 35 K1 .... 35 amps
         Bosch 28 G1 .... 28 amps

Windscreen wipers
Two speed electric

Fuses
See Section 75

Bulb application:

Bulb	Quantity	Fitting	Rating (watts)
Headlamps	2	Spring clip	45/40
Side lamps	2	Bayonet	4
Front direction indicators	2	Bayonet	21
Rear direction indicators	2	Bayonet	21
Rear stop/tail lamps	2	Bayonet	21/5
Rear number plate	2	Bayonet	4
Interior lamp	1+ 2++	Festoon	10
Instrument panel warning light	5* 4**	Wedge base	3
Instrument panel illumination	3* 8**	Bayonet	3
Automatic gear change illumination	1	Bayonet	2.2
Fog lamp	2	Spring clip	55
Driving lamp	2	Spring clip	55

+ Saloon
++ Estate
* Consul
** Granada

Torque wrench settings

	lbf ft	kgf m
Front indicator lamp to body aperture nuts	26–43 lbf in	0.3–0.5 gmf cm
Fog lamp body securing screws	18–26 lbf in	0.21–0.30 gmf cm
Fog lamp body securing bolt	6–7	0.8–1.0
Auxiliary lamp retaining bolt	30–33	4.0–4.5
Fog lamp shroud retaining screws	13–17	0.15–0.2
Wiper linkage to motor shaft locknut	5–6 lbf in	0.7–0.8 gmf cm
Wiper motor to bracket bolts	3–4	0.4–0.5
Wiper arm spindle securing nut	7–8	1.0–1.1
Washer jet securing screws	3–4	0.4–0.5
Horn to horn bracket bolts	15–18	2.0–2.5
Headlamp securing screw	13–23 lbf in	0.15–0.25 gmf cm
Starter motor retaining bolts	20–25	2.76–3.46
Alternator fan pulley nut	25–29	3.5–4.0
Alternator mounting bolts	15–18	2.07–2.49
Alternator mounting brackets	20–25	2.76–3.46

Chapter 10 Electrical system

1 General description

The electrical system is of the 12 volt negative earth type and the major components comprise a 12 volt battery of which the negative terminal is earthed, an alternator which is driven from the crankshaft pulley, a starter motor, a coil, distributor and spark plugs.

The battery supplies a steady amount of current for the ignition, lighting and other electrical circuits and provides a reserve of electricity when the current consumed by the electrical equipment exceeds that being produced by the alternator.

The alternator has its own integral regulator which ensures a high output if the battery is in a low state of charge or the demand from the electrical equipment is high, and a low output if the battery is fully charged and there is little demand for the electrical equipment.

When fitting electrical accessories to cars with a negative earth system it is important, if they contain silicone diodes or transistors, that they are connected correctly, otherwise serious damage may result to the components concerned. Items such as radios, tape recorders, electronic ignition systems, electronic tachometer, automatic dipping etc, should all be checked for correct polarity.

It is important that the battery negative lead is always disconnected if the battery is to be boost charged, also if body repairs are to be carried out using electric arc welding equipment — the alternator must be disconnected otherwise serious damage can be caused. Whenever the battery has to be disconnected it must always be reconnected with the negative terminal earthed.

2 Battery – removal and refitting

1 The battery is secured on a carrier fitted to the left-hand wing inner panel of the engine compartment. It should be removed once every three months for cleaning and testing. Disconnect the negative and then the positive leads from the battery terminals by undoing and removing the plated nuts and bolts. Note that two cables are attached to the positive terminal.

2 Unscrew and remove the bolt and plain washer that secure the battery clamp plate to the carrier. Lift away the clamp plate. Carefully lift the battery from its carrier holding it upright to ensure that none of the electrolyte is spilled.

3 Refitting is a direct reversal of this procedure. **Note:** *Refit the positive lead before the negative lead and smear the terminals with vaseline to prevent corrosion.* **Never** *use an ordinary grease.*

3 Battery – maintenance and inspection

1 Normal weekly battery maintenance consists of checking the electrolyte level of each cell to ensure that the separators are covered by $\frac{1}{4}$ inch (6 mm) of electrolyte. If the level has fallen, top up the battery using distilled water only. Do not overfill. If a battery is overfilled or any electrolyte spilled, immediately wipe away the excess using an alkaline solution (see para. 4) as electrolyte attacks and corrodes any metal it comes into contact with very rapidly.

2 If the battery has the Auto-fil device as fitted on original production of the car, a special topping up sequence is required. The white balls in the Auto-fil battery are part of the automatic topping up device which ensures correct electrolyte level. The vent chamber should remain in position at all times except when topping up or taking specific gravity readings. If the electrolyte level in any of the cells is below the bottom of the filling tube top up as follows:

(a) *Lift off the vent chamber cover (photo).*
(b) *With the battery level, pour distilled water into the trough until all the filling tubes and troughs are full.*
(c) *Immediately refit the cover to allow the water in the trough and tubes to flow into the cells. Each cell will automatically receive the correct amount of water.*

3 As well as keeping the terminals clean and covered with petroleum jelly, the top of the battery, and especially the top of the cells, should be kept clean and dry. This helps prevent corrosion and ensures that the battery does not become partially discharged by leakage through dampness and dirt.

4 Once every three months remove the battery and inspect the

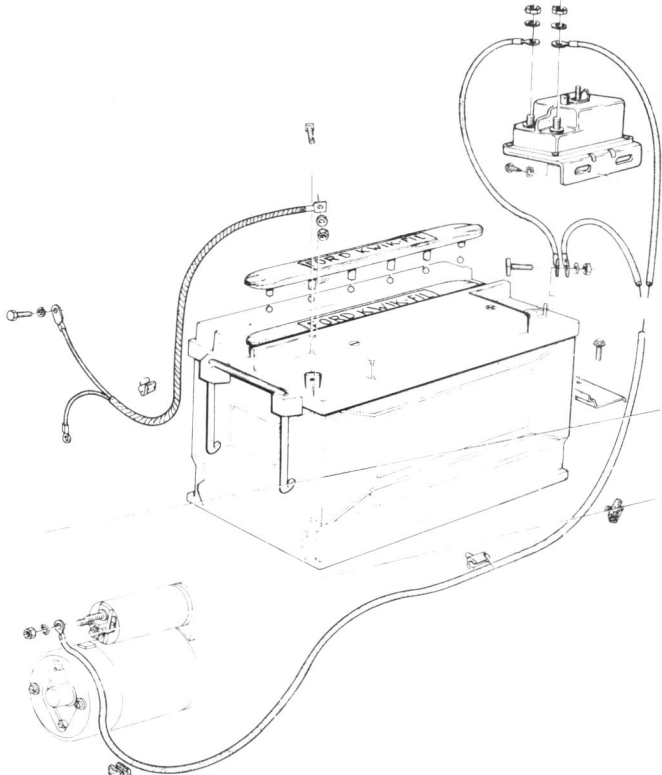

Fig. 10.1 Battery and heavy duty cable attachments

3.2a The battery with vent chamber cover removed for checking

battery securing bolts, the battery clamp plate, tray and battery leads for corrosion (white fluffy deposits on the metal which are brittle to touch). If any corrosion is found clean off the deposit with ammonia and paint over the clean metal with an anti-rust anti-acid paint.

5 At the same time inspect the battery case for cracks. If a crack is found, clean and plug it with one of the proprietary compounds marketed by such firms as Holts for this purpose. If leakage through the crack has been excessive then it will be necessary to refill the appropriate cell with fresh electrolyte as detailed later. Cracks are frequently caused to the top of the battery case by pouring in distilled water in the middle of winter *after* instead of *before* a run. This gives the water no chance to mix with the electrolyte and so the former freezes and splits the battery case.

6 If topping up the battery becomes excessive and the case has

been inspected for cracks that could cause leakage, but none are found, the battery is being overcharged and the voltage regulator will have to be checked and reset.

7 With the battery on the bench at the three monthly interval check, measure the specific gravity with a hydrometer to determine the state of charge and condition of the electrolyte. There should be very little variation between the different cells and, if a variation in excess of 0·025 is present it will be due to either:

(a) *Loss of electrolyte from the battery at some time caused by spillage or a leak, resulting in a drop in the specific gravity of the electrolyte when the deficiency was replaced with distilled water instead of fresh electrolyte.*
(b) *An internal short circuit caused by buckling of the plates or similar malady pointing to the likelihood of total battery failure in the near future.*

8 The specific gravity of the electrolyte for fully charged conditions at the electrolyte temperature indicated, is listed in Table A. The specific gravity of a fully discharged battery, at different temperatures of the electrolyte is given in Table B.

TABLE A
Specific gravity – battery fully charged
1·268 at 100°F or 38°C electrolyte temperature
1·272 at 90°F or 32°C electrolyte temperature
1·276 at 80°F or 27°C electrolyte temperature
1·280 at 70°F or 21°C electrolyte temperature
1·284 at 60°F or 16°C electrolyte temperature
1·288 at 50°F or 10°C electrolyte temperature
1·292 at 40°F or 4°C electrolyte temperature
1·296 at 30°F or –1·5°C electrolyte temperature

TABLE B
Specific gravity – battery fully discharged
1·098 at 100°F or 38°C electrolyte temperature
1·102 at 90°F or 32°C electrolyte temperature
1·106 at 80°F or 27°C electrolyte temperature
1·110 at 70°F or 21°C electrolyte temperature
1·114 at 60°F or 16°C electrolyte temperature
1·118 at 50°F or 10°C electrolyte temperature
1·122 at 40°F or 4°C electrolyte temperature
1·126 at 30°F or –1·5°C electrolyte temperature

4 Battery – electrolyte replenishment

1 If the battery is in a fully charged state and one of the cells maintains a specific gravity reading which is 0·025 or more lower than the others, and a check of each cell has been made with a voltmeter (a four to seven second test should give a steady reading of between 1·2 to 1·8 volts), then it is likely that electrolyte has been lost from the cell with the low reading at sometime.

2 Top up the cell with a solution of 1 part sulphuric acid to 2·5 parts of water. If the cell is already fully topped up draw some electrolyte out of it with a pipette. The total capacity of each cell is ¾ pint.

3 When mixing the sulphuric acid and water **never add water to sulphuric acid** – always pour the acid slowly into the water in a glass container. **If water is added to sulphuric acid it will explode.**

4 Top up the cell with the freshly made electrolyte, which should have been allowed to cool since heat is generated during the mixing process, and then recharge the battery and check the hydrometer readings.

5 Battery charging

1 In winter time when heavy demand is placed upon the battery, eg starting from cold, and much electrical equipment is continually in use, it is a good idea to occasionally have the battery fully charged from an external source at the rate of 3·5 to 4 amps.

2 Continue to charge the battery at this rate until no further rise in specific gravity is noted over a four hour period.

3 Alternatively, a trickle charge charging at the rate of 1·5 amps can be safely used overnight.

4 Specially rapid 'boost' charges which are claimed to restore the power of the battery in 1 to 2 hours are most dangerous as they can cause serious damage to the battery plates through over-heating.

5 While charging the battery note that the temperature of the electrolyte should never exceed 100°F.

6 Alternator – general description

The main advantage of the alternator lies in its ability to provide a high charge at low revolutions. Driving slowly in heavy traffic with a dynamo invariably means no charge is reaching the battery. In similar conditions even with the wiper, heater, lights and perhaps radio switched on the alternator will ensure a charge reaches the battery.

An important feature of the alternator is a built in output control regulator, based on 'thick film' hybrid integrated micro-circuit technique which results in the alternator being a self contained generating and control unit.

The system provides for direct connection of a charge indicator light, and eliminates the need for a field switching relay or warning light control unit, necessary with former systems.

The alternator is of rotating field, ventilated design. Its two main components are a laminated stator on which is wound a star connected three phase output winding and a twelve pole rotor carrying the field windings. Each end of the rotor shaft runs in a ball race bearing which is lubricated for life. The unit is completed by natural finish die cast aluminium end brackets which carry the mounting lugs, a rectifier pack which converts the AC output into DC for battery charging, and an output control regulator.

The rotor is belt driven from the engine through a pulley keyed to the rotor shaft. A pressed steel fan adjacent to the pulley draws cooling air through the machine. This fan forms an integral part of the alternator specification. It has been designed to provide adequate air flow with minimum noise, and to withstand the high stresses associated with the maximum speed. Rotation is clockwise viewed on the drive end. Maximum continuous rotor speed is 12500 rpm.

Rectification of the alternator output is achieved by six silicone diodes housed in a rectifier pack and connected as a 3-phase full wave bridge. The rectifier pack is attached to the outer face of the slip ring end bracket and contains also three 'field' diodes; at normal operating speeds, rectified current from the stator output windings flows through these diodes to provide the self excitation of the rotor field, via brushes bearing on face type slip rings.

The slip rings are carried on a small diameter moulded drum attached to the rotor shaft outboard of the slip ring end bearing. The inner ring is centred on the rotor shaft axle, while the outer ring has a mean diameter of approximately ¾ inch. By keeping the mean diameter of the slip rings to a minimum, relative speeds between brushes and rings, and hence wear, are also minimal. The slip rings are connected to the rotor field windings by wires carried in grooves in the rotor shaft.

The brush gear is housed in a moulding screwed to the outside of the slip ring end bracket. This moulding thus encloses the slip ring and brush gear assembly, and together with the shielded bearing, protects the assembly against the entry of dust and moisture.

The regulator is set during manufacture and requires no further attention. Briefly, the 'thick film' regulator comprises resistors and conductors screen printed onto a 1 inch square alumina substrate. Mounted on the substrate are Lucas semi-conductor dice consisting of three transistors, a voltage reference diode and a field recirculation diode, and two capacitors. The internal connections between these components and the substrate are made by special Lucas patented connectors. The whole assembly is 0·0625 inch (1·588 mm) thick, and is housed in a recess in an aluminium heat sink, which is attached to the slip ring end bracket. Complete hermetic sealing is achieved by a silicone rubber encapsulant to provide environmental protection.

Electrical connections to external circuits are brought out to Lucar connector blades, these are grouped to accept a moulded connector socket which ensures correct connection.

The Bosch alternator operates on the same principles as the Lucas alternator and only differs in design as may be seen when Fig. 10.2 and Fig. 10.3 are compared.

7 Alternator – routine maintenance

1 The equipment has been designed for minimum maintenance in

Chapter 10 Electrical system

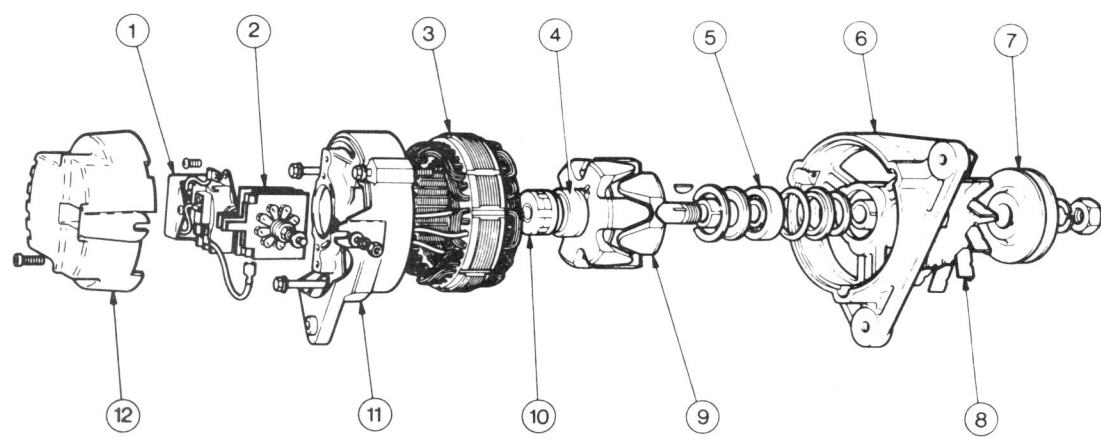

Fig. 10.2 Lucas alternator components (Sec. 6)

1 Brushgear and regulator assembly
2 Rectifier pack
3 Stator
4 Ball race bearing
5 Ball race bearing
6 Drive end bracket
7 Pulley
8 Fan
9 12 pole rotor
10 Slip ring
11 Slip ring end bracket
12 Cover

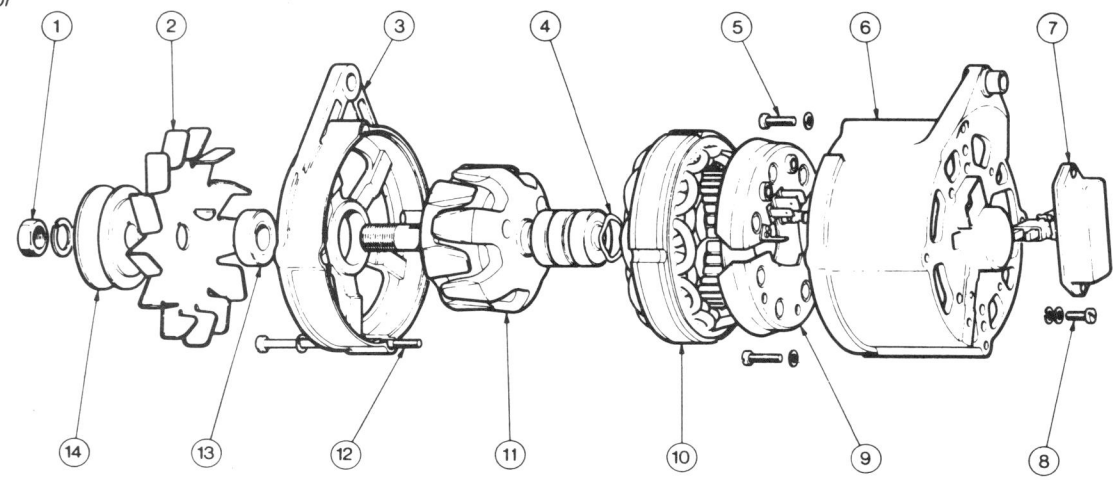

Fig. 10.3 Bosch alternator components (Sec. 6)

1 Nut
2 Fan
3 Drive end bracket
4 Washer
5 Retaining screw
6 Brush end housing
7 Brush box
8 Brush box retaining screw
9 Diode support
10 Stator
11 Rotor
12 Through-bolt
13 Bearing
14 Pulley

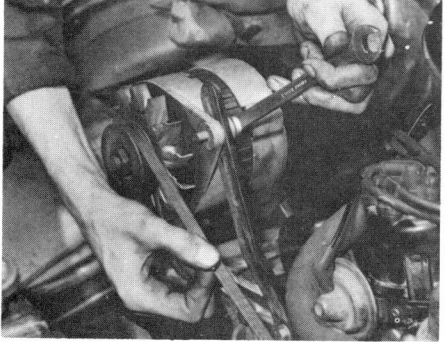

7.3 Check the fan belt adjustment

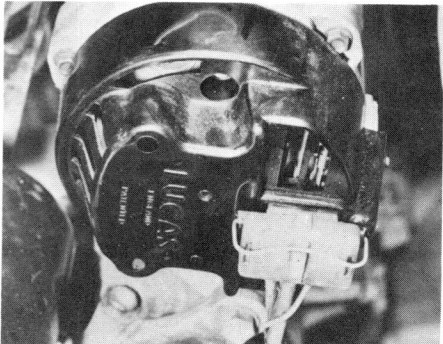

9.2 Disconnect the alternator multi pin plug

9.3 The alternator showing the mounting bracket and adjustment arm

service, the only items subject to wear being the brushes and bearings.
2 Brushes should be examined after about 75,000 miles (120,000 km) and renewed if necessary. The bearings are pre-packed with grease for life, and should not require further attention.

3 Check the fan belt every 3,000 miles (5,000 km) for correct adjustment which should be 0·5 inch (13 mm) total movement at the centre of the run between the alternator and water pump pulleys (photo).

Chapter 10 Electrical system

8 Alternator – special procedures

Whenever the electrical system of the car is being attended to, or external means of starting the engine are used, certain precautions must be taken otherwise serious and expensive damage can result.
1   Always make sure that the negative terminal of the battery is earthed. If the terminal connections are accidentally reversed or if the battery has been reverse charged the alternator diodes will burn out.
2   The output terminal on the alternator marked 'BAT' must never be earthed but should always be connected directly to the positive terminal of the battery.
3   Whenever the alternator is to be removed or when disconnecting the terminals of the alternator circuit, always disconnect the battery earth terminal first.
4   The alternator must never be operated without the battery to alternator cable connected.
5   If the battery is to be charged by external means always disconnect both battery cables before the external charger is connected.
6   Should it be necessary to use a booster charger or booster battery to start the engine always double check that the negative cables are connected to negative terminals and positive cables to positive terminals.
7   If electric arc welding equipment is to be used to repair any part of the car, disconnect the connector from the alternator and detach the battery terminal connectors.

9 Alternator – removal and refitting

1   Disconnect the battery leads.
2   Note the terminal connections at the rear of the alternator and disconnect the plug or multi pin connector (photo).
3   Undo and remove the alternator adjustment arm bolt, slacken the alternator mounting bolts and push the alternator inward towards the engine. Lift away the fan belt from the pulley (photo).
4   Remove the remaining two mounting bolts and carefully lift the alternator away from the car.
5   Take care not to knock or drop the alternator otherwise this can cause irreparable damage.
6   Refitting the alternator is the reverse sequence to removal. Adjust the fan belt so that it has 0·5 inch (13 mm) total movement at the centre of the run between the alternator and water pump pulleys.

10 Alternator – fault finding and repair

Due to the specialist knowledge and equipment required to test or service an alternator it is recommended that if the performance is suspect, the car be taken to an automobile electrician who will have the facilities for such work. Because of this recommendation, information is limited to the inspection and renewal of the brushes. Should the alternator not charge or the system be suspect the following points may be checked before seeking further assistance:
1   Check the fan belt tension as described in Section 7.
2   Check the battery as described in Section 3.
3   Check all electrical cable connections for cleanliness and security.

11 Alternator brushes – removal, inspection and refitting (Lucas)

1   Refer to Fig. 10.2, undo and remove the two screws that hold on the end cover. Lift away the end cover.
2   To inspect the brushes correctly the brush holder moulding should be removed by undoing the two securing bolts and disconnecting the 'Lucar' connector to the diode plates.
3   With the brush holder moulding removed and the brush assemblies still in position check that they protrude from the face of the moulding by at least 0·2 inch (5 mm). Also check that when depressed, the spring pressure is 7 – 10 oz (198 – 283 gms) when the end of the brush is flush with the face of the brush moulding. To be done with any accuracy this requires a push type spring scale.
4   Should either of the foregoing requirements not be fulfilled the spring assemblies must be renewed. This can be done by simply removing the holding screws of each assembly, discarding the old ones, and fitting the new assemblies.
5   With the brush holder moulding removed the slip rings on the face end of the rotor are exposed. These can be cleaned with a petrol soaked cloth and any signs of burring may be removed very carefully with fine glass paper. On no account should any other abrasive be used or any attempt at machining be made.
6   Reassembly is the reverse order of dismantling. Make sure that leads which may have been connected to any of the screws are reconnected correctly.

12 Alternator brushes – inspection, removal and refitting (Bosch)

1   Undo and remove the two screws, spring and plain washers that secure the brush box to the rear of the brush end housing. Lift away the brush box.
2   Check that the carbon brushes are able to slide smoothly in their guides without binding.
3   Measure the length of the brushes and if they have worn down to 0·35 inch (9 mm) or less, they must be renewed.
4   Hold the brush wire with a pair of engineer's pliers and unsolder it from the brush box. Lift away the two brushes.
5   Insert the new brushes and check to make sure that they are free to move in their new guides. If they bind lightly polish with a very fine file.
6   Solder new brush wire ends to the brush box taking care that solder is allowed to pass to the stranded wire.
7   Whenever new brushes are fitted new springs should be fitted.
8   Refitting the brush box is the reverse sequence to removal.

13 Starter motor – general description

1   The starter motor fitted to engines on models covered by this manual is one of two types, these being either inertia or pre-engaged. Both types are of Lucas manufacture (photo).
2   With the inertia type starter motor, when the ignition is switched 'on', current flows from the battery to the starter motor solenoid switch which becomes energised. The internal plunger is pulled inward by the field and closes the switch, so allowing full starting current to flow from the battery to the starter motor. This causes a powerful magnetic field to be induced into the field coils which causes the armature to rotate.
3   Mounted on helical splines is the drive pinion which, because of the sudden rotation of the armature, is thrown forward along the armature shaft and so into engagement with the flywheel ring gear. The engine crankshaft will then be rotated until the engine starts to operate on its own and, at this point, the drive pinion is thrown out of mesh with the flywheel ring gear.
4   The pre-engaged starter motor operates by a slightly different method using end face commutator brushes instead of brushes

13.1 The starter motor in position (V6 engine)

Chapter 10 Electrical system

located on the side of the commutator.

5 The method of engagement on the pre-engaged starter motor differs considerably in that the drive pinion is brought into mesh with the starter ring gear before the main starter current is applied.

6 With the ignition switched on, current flows from the solenoid which is mounted on the top of the starter motor body. The plunger in the solenoid moves inward so causing a centrally pivoted engagement lever to move in such a manner that the forked end pushes the drive

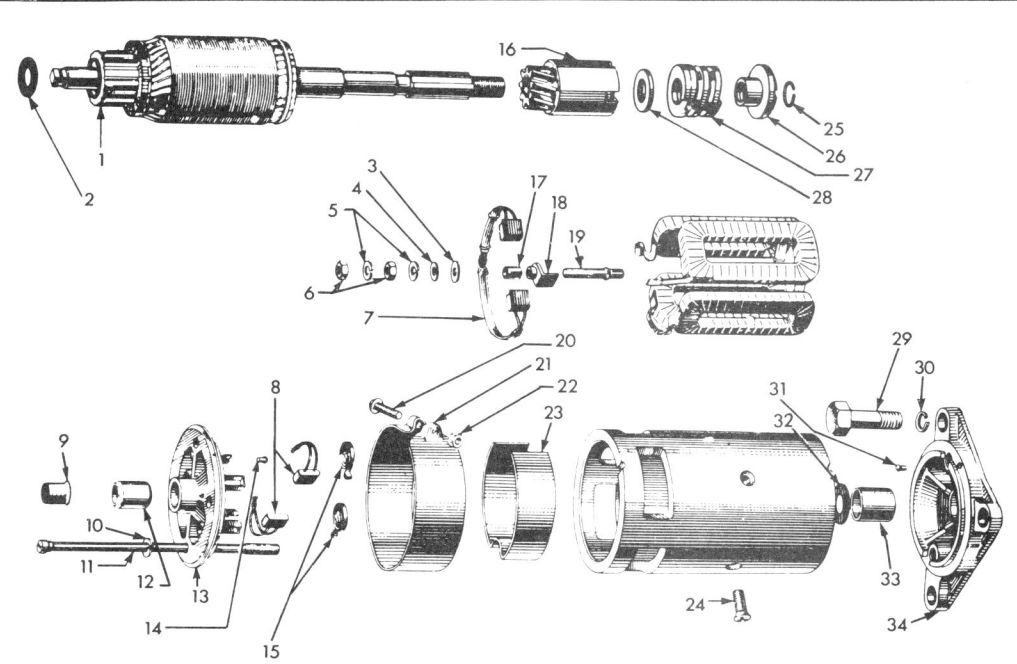

Fig. 10.4 Inertia type starter motor components (Sec. 13)

1	Armature	10	Lockwasher	18	Terminal insulator	27	Spring
2	Washer	11	Starter motor through-bolt	19	Terminal	28	Washer
3	Washer	12	Bush	20	Screw	29	Starter motor – bell-housing bolt
4	Washer	13	End plate	21	Starter motor band		
5	Lockwashers	14	Rivet	22	Nut	30	Lockwasher
6	Nuts	15	Brush retaining springs	23	Field coil insulator	31	Rivet
7	Brush assembly	16	Pinion	24	Field coil retaining screw	32	Washer
8	Brush assembly	17	Spacer	25	Circlip	33	Bush
9	Cap			26	Spring retaining cup	34	End plate

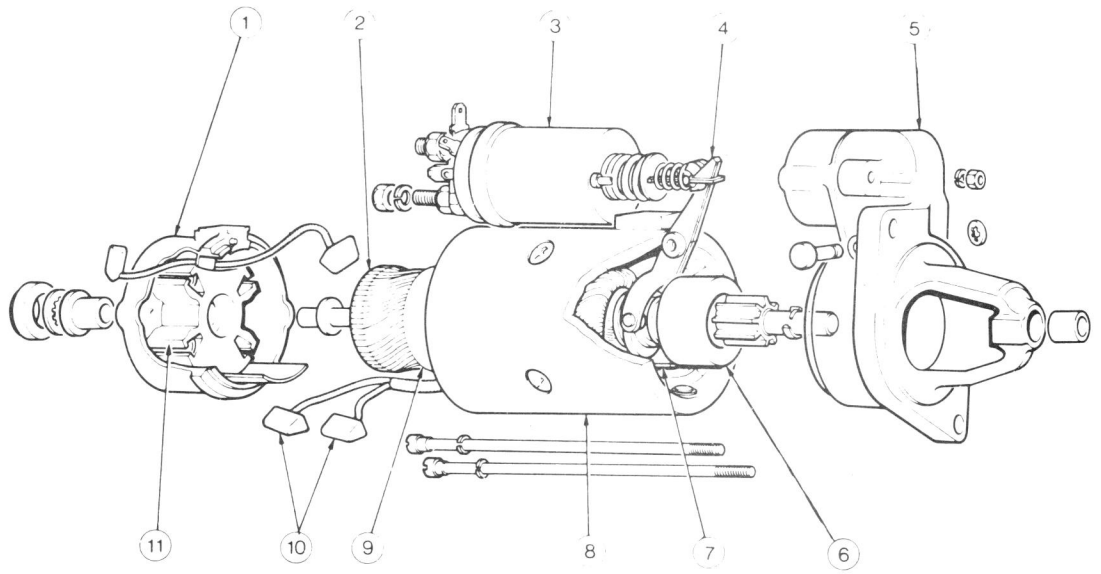

Fig. 10.5 Pre-engaged type starter motor components (Sec. 13)

1	Commutator end bracket	4	Engagement lever	7	Pole shoe	10	Brush
2	Commutator	5	Drive end bracket	8	Yoke	11	Brush box moulding
3	Solenoid	6	Drive assembly	9	Armature		

Chapter 10 Electrical system

pinion into mesh with the starter ring gear. When the solenoid plunger reaches the end of its travel, it closes an internal contact and full starting current flows to the starter field coils. The armature is then able to rotate the crankshaft so starting the engine.

7 A special one way clutch is fitted to the starter drive pinion so that when the engine fires and starts to operate on its own, it does not drive the starter motor.

14 Starter motor (M35J) – testing on engine

1 If the starter motor fails to operate, then check the condition of the battery by turning on the headlamps. If they glow brightly for several seconds and then gradually dim, the battery is in a discharged condition.

2 If the headlamps glow brightly and it is obvious that the battery is in good condition then check the tightness of the battery wiring connections (and in particular the earth lead from the battery terminal to its connection on the bodyframe). Check the tightness of the connections at the relay switch and at the starter motor. Check the wiring with a voltmeter for breaks or shorts.

3 If the wiring is in order then check that the starter motor switch is operating. To do this press the rubber covered button in the centre of the relay switch under the bonnet (manual transmission only). If it is working, the starter motor will be heard to 'click' as it tries to rotate. Alternatively check it with a voltmeter.

4 If the battery is fully charged, the wiring in order and the switch working, but the starter still fails to operate then it will have to be removed from the car for examination.

Before this is done, however, ensure that the starter pinion has not jammed in mesh with the flywheel. Check by turning the square end of the armature shaft with a spanner. This will free the pinion if it is stuck in engagement with the flywheel teeth.

15 Starter motor (M35J) – removal and refitting

1 Disconnect the positive and then the negative terminals from the battery. Also disconnect the starter motor cable from the terminal on the end cover.

2 Undo and remove the two bolts which secure the starter motor to the engine backplate. Lift it away by manipulating the drive gear from the ring gear area and then from the engine compartment.

3 Refitting is the reverse procedure to removal. Make sure that the starter motor cable, when secured in position by its terminal, does not touch any part of the body or engine which could damage the insulation.

16 Starter motor (M35J) – dismantling and reassembly

1 With the starter motor on the bench, first mark the relative positions of the starter motor body to the two end brackets.

2 Undo and remove the two screws and spring washers securing the drive end bracket to the body. The drive end bracket, complete with armature and drive, may now be drawn forward from the starter motor body.

3 Lift away the thrust washer from the commutator end of the armature shaft.

4 Undo and remove the two screws securing the commutator end bracket to the starter motor body. The commutator end bracket may now be drawn back about an inch allowing sufficient access to disengage the field bushes from the bracket. Once these are free, the end bracket may be completely removed.

5 With the starter motor stripped, the brushes and brush gear may be inspected. To check the brush spring tension, fit a new brush into each holder in turn and, using an accurate spring balance, push the brush on the balance tray until the brush protrudes approximately $\frac{1}{16}$ inch (1·587 mm) from the holder. Make a note of the reading which should be approximately 28 ounces. If the spring pressures vary considerably the commutator end bracket must be renewed as a complete assembly.

6 Inspect the brushes for wear and fit new brushes if the existing ones are nearing the minimum length of $\frac{3}{8}$ inch (9·525 mm). To renew the end bracket bushes, cut the brush cables from the terminal posts, and with a small file or hacksaw, slot the head of the terminal posts to a sufficient depth to accommodate the new heads. Solder the new brush head to the post.

7 To renew field winding brush, cut the brush head approximately $\frac{1}{4}$ inch (6·35 mm) from the field winding junction and carefully solder the new brush head to the remaining stump, making sure that the insulation sleeve provides adequate cover.

8 If the commutator surface is dirty or blackened, clean it with a petrol dampened rag. Carefully examine the commutator for signs of excessive wear, burning or pitting. If evident it may be reconditioned by having it skimmed at the local engineering works or Ford garage which possesses a centre lathe. The thickness of the commutator must not be less than 0·08 inch (2·032 mm). For minor reconditioning, the commutator may be polished with glass paper, this should be done whilst rotating the commutator otherwise flats may occur. **Do not undercut the mica insulators between the commutator segments.**

9 With the starter motor dismantled, test the field coils for open circuit. Connect a 12 volt battery with a 12 volt bulb in one of the leads between each of the field brushes and a clean part of the body. The lamp will light if continuity is satisfactory between the brushes, windings and body connections.

10 Renewal of the field coils calls for the use of a wheel operated screwdriver, a soldering iron, caulking and riveting operations and is beyond the scope of the majority of owners. The starter motor body should be taken to an automobile electrical engineering works for new field coils to be fitted. Alternatively, purchase an exchange Lucas starter motor.

11 Check the condition of the bushes and they should be renewed when they are sufficiently worn to allow visible side movement of the armature shaft.

12 To renew the commutator end bracket bush, drill out the rivets securing the brush box moulding and remove the moulding, bearing seal retaining plate and felt washer seal.

13 Screw in a $\frac{1}{2}$ inch tap and withdraw the bush with the tap.

14 As the bush is phosphor bronze it is essential that the new bush is allowed to stand in engine oil for at least 24 hours before fitment. Alternatively soak in oil at 100°C for 2 hours.

15 Using a suitable diameter drift, drive the new bush into position. Do not ream the bush as its self lubricating properties will be impaired.

16 To remove the drive end bracket bush it will be necessary to remove the drive gear as described in paragraphs 18 and 19.

17 Using a suitable diameter drift remove the old bush and fit a new one as described in paragraphs 14 and 15.

18 To dismantle the starter motor drive, first use a press to push the retainer clear of the circlip which can then be removed. Lift away the retainer and main spring.

19 Slide off the remaining parts with a rotary action of the armature shaft.

20 It is most important that the drive gear is completely free from oil, grease, and dirt. With the drive gear removed, clean all parts thoroughly in paraffin. **Under no circumstances oil the drive components.** Lubrication of the drive components could easily cause the pinion to stick.

21 Reassembly of the starter motor drive is the reverse sequence to dismantling. Use a press to compress the spring and retainer sufficiently to allow a new circlip to be fitted to its groove in the shaft. Remove the drive from the press.

22 Reassembly of the starter motor is the reverse sequence to removal.

17 Starter motor (2M100) – testing on engine

The testing procedure is similar to the inertia engagement type as described in Section 14. However, note the following instructions before finally deciding to remove the starter motor.

Ensure that the pinion gear has not jammed in mesh with the flywheel due either to a broken solenoid spring or dirty pinion gear splines. To release the pinion, engage a low gear (manual gearbox only) and, with the ignition switched off, rock the car backward and forward which should release the pinion from mesh with the ring gear. If the pinion still remains jammed the starter motor must be removed for further examination.

18 Starter motor (2M100) – removal and refitting

1 Disconnect the negative and then the positive terminals from the battery.
2 Make a note of the electrical connections at the rear of the solenoid and disconnect the top heavy duty cable. Also release the Lucar terminals from the rear of the solenoid. There is no need to undo the lower heavy duty cable at the rear of the solenoid.
3 Undo and remove the securing bolts and spring washers which hold the starter motor in place and lift away. If difficulty is experienced in removing the top bolt it will be found advantageous to remove the left-hand exhaust manifold.
4 Refitting is a straightforward reversal of the removal sequence. Ensure that the electrical cable connections are clean and firmly attached to their respective terminals.

19 Starter motor (2M100) – dismantling and reassembly

1 Undo and remove the nut and spring washer securing the connecting link between the solenoid and starter motor at the solenoid 'STA' terminal. Carefully ease the connecting link out of engagement of the terminal post on the solenoid.
2 Undo and remove the two nuts and spring washers that secure the solenoid to the drive end bracket.
3 Carefully ease the solenoid back from the drive end bracket, lift the solenoid plunger and return spring from the engagement lever, and completely remove the solenoid.
4 Recover the shaped rubber block between the solenoid and starter motor body.
5 Carefully remove the end cap seal from the commutator end cover.
6 Ease the armature shaft retaining ring (spire nut) from the armature shaft. **Note**: *The retaining ring must not be reused, but a new one obtained ready for fitting.*
7 Undo and remove the two long through bolts and spring washers.
8 Detach the commutator end cover from the yoke, at the same time disengaging the field brushes from the brush box moulding.
9 Lift away the thrust washer from the armature shaft.
10 The starter motor body may now be lifted from the armature and drive end assembly.
11 Ease the retaining ring (spire nut) from the engagement lever pivot pin. **Note**: *The retaining ring must not be reused, but a new one obtained ready for fitting.*
12 Using a parallel pin punch of suitable size, remove the pivot pin from the engagement lever and drive end bracket.
13 Carefully move the thrust collar clear of the jump ring, and slide the jump ring from the armature shaft.
14 Slide off the thrust collar, and finally remove the roller clutch drive and engagement lever assembly from the armature shaft.
15 For inspection and servicing information of the brush gear, commutator and armature, refer to Section 16 paragraphs 5 to 8 inclusive.
16 To test the field coils refer to Section 16 paragraphs 9 and 10.
17 Check the condition of the brushes and if they show signs of wear remove the old ones and fit new as described in Section 16, paragraphs 11 to 17. Disregard the reference in paragraph 16 to the removal of the drive gear as this will have already been done.
18 Whilst the motor is apart, check the operation of the drive clutch. It must provide instantaneous take up of the drive in one direction and rotate easily and smoothly in the opposite direction.
19 Make sure that the drive moves smoothly on the armature shaft splines without binding or sticking.
20 Reassembling the starter motor is the reverse sequence to dismantling. The following additional points should be noted.
21 When assembling the drive end bracket always use a new retaining ring (spire nut) to secure the engagement lever pivot pin.
22 Make sure that the internal thrust washer is fitted to the commutator end of the armature shaft before the armature end cover is fitted.
23 Always use a new retaining ring (spire nut) onto the armature shaft to a maximum clearance of 0·010 inch (0·254 mm) between the retaining ring and the bearing bush shoulder. This will be the armature endfloat.
24 Tighten the through bolts to a torque wrench setting of 8 lbf ft (1·11 kgf m) and the nuts securing the solenoid to the drive bracket to 4·5 lbf ft (0·61 kgf m).

20 Flasher circuit – fault tracing and rectification

1 The flasher unit consists of a small alloy container positioned on the pedal bracket.
2 If the flasher unit works twice as fast as usual when indicating either right or left turns, this is an indication that there is a broken filament in the front or rear indicator bulb on the side operating too quickly.
3 If the external flashers are working but the internal flasher warning light has ceased to function, check the filament of the warning bulb and renew as necessary.
4 With the aid of the wiring diagram check all the flasher circuit connections if a flasher bulb is sound but does not work.
5 Connect a voltmeter between the positive terminal of the flasher unit and earth. Switch 'on' the ignition; the voltmeter should indicate 12 volts. If this condition obtains then switch 'off' the ignition, disconnect the voltmeter. Connect the two flasher unit terminals together, switch on the ignition and operate the direction indicator switch. Should one of the flasher warning lights indicate then the flasher unit is faulty and must be changed.

21 Windscreen wiper mechanism – maintenance

1 Renew the windscreen wiper blades at intervals of 12,000 miles (20,000 km) or 12 months, or more frequently if found necessary.
2 The washer round the wheelbox spindle can be lubricated with several drops of glycerine every 6,000 miles (10,000 km). The windscreen wiper linkage may be lubricated with a little engine oil (photo).

22 Windscreen wiper blades – removal and refitting

1 Lift the wiper arm away from the windscreen and remove the old blade by turning it in towards the arm and then disengage the arm from the slot in the blade.
2 To fit a new blade, slide the end of the wiper arm into the slotted spring fasten ring in the centre of the blade. Push the blade firmly onto the arm until the raised portion of the arm is fully home in the hole in the blade.

23 Windscreen wiper arms – removal and refitting

1 Before removing a wiper arm, turn the windscreen wiper switch on and off to ensure the arms are in their normal parked position parallel with the bottom of the windscreen.
2 To remove the arm, use an open ended spanner undo and remove the retaining bolt and pull the arm from the spindle (photo).
3 When replacing an arm, position it so that it is in the correct parked position and then press the head onto the spindle until it is fully home (see Fig. 10.7).
4 Refit the retaining bolt and tighten fully.

24 Windscreen wiper mechanism – fault diagnosis and rectification

1 Should the windscreen wipers fail, or work very slowly, then check the terminals on the motor for loose connections and make sure the insulation of all wiring has not been damaged thus causing a short circuit. If this is in order then check the current the motor is taking by connecting an ammeter in series in the circuit and turning on the wiper switch. Consumption should be between 2·3 and 3·1 amps.
2 If no current is passing through the motor, check that the switch is operating correctly.
3 If the wiper motor takes a very high current check the wiper blades for freedom of movement. If this is satisfactory check the gearbox cover and gear assembly for damage.
4 If the motor takes a very low current ensure that the battery is fully charged. Check the brush gear and ensure the brushes are bearing on the commutator. If not, check the brushes for freedom of movement and, if necessary, renew the tension springs. If the brushes are very worn they should be replaced with new ones. Check the armature by

Chapter 10 Electrical system

21.2 The windscreen wiper and linkage

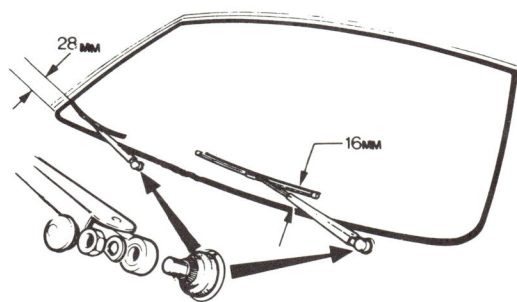

Fig. 10.7a Correct setting of windscreen wiper blades (RHD) (Sec. 23)

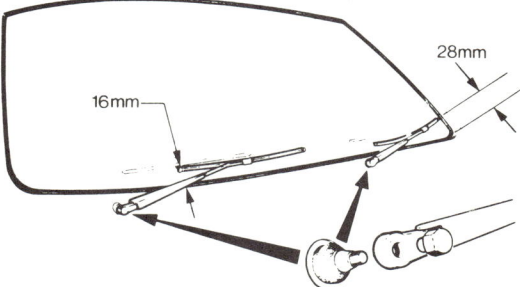

Fig. 10.7b Correct setting of windscreen wiper blades (LHD) (Sec. 23)

substitution if this part is suspect.

25 Windscreen wiper motor – removal and refitting

1 For safety reasons disconnect the battery.
2 Undo and remove the nut securing the linkage to the wiper motor drive shaft.
3 Carefully lever off the linkage and place to one side.
4 Undo and remove the three bolts and washers that secure the wiper motor to the support bracket. Note that one of the bolts also retains the earth lead.
5 Move the wiper motor away from the support bracket and detach the wiring loom multi pin connector. Lift away the wiper motor.
6 Refitting the wiper motor is the reverse sequence to removal. Make sure that the tang on the linkage engages with the keyway on the wiper motor drive shaft.

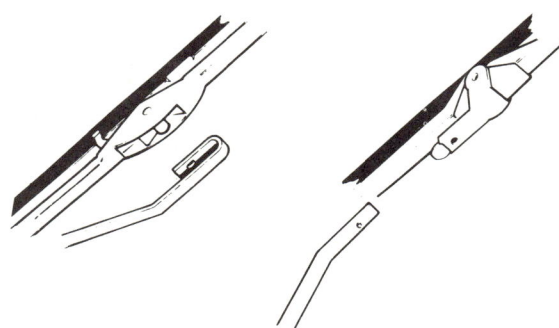

Fig. 10.6 Windscreen wiper blade attachments (Sec. 22)

LH alternative   RH standard

26 Windscreen wiper motor – brush renewal

1 Refer to Section 25 and remove the windscreen wiper motor.
2 Undo and remove the two screws securing the armature outer casing and then withdraw the casing (Fig. 10.8).
3 Undo and remove the five screws retaining the gear cover. Lift away the gear cover and gasket.
4 Now push out the driven gear.
5 Slacken the screws that secure the armature to the housing and carefully slide back the locking plate.
6 Push the brushes against their springs so as to clear the bearing and slide the cam out of the housing.
7 Carefully remove the three rubber pegs and remove the brush assembly.
8 Using a small soldering iron unsweat the brush wires and detach the brushes.
9 To fit new brushes resolder the new brushes in position on the plate.
10 Refit the brushes to the assembly and secure the assembly to the housing by pulling home the rubber securing pegs.
11 Refit the armature to the housing and lock in position. Tighten the securing screws.
12 Refit the brush springs and bend back the ends of the brush holding boxes.

23.2 Remove the retaining bolt from the windscreen wiper arm/spindle

Chapter 10 Electrical system

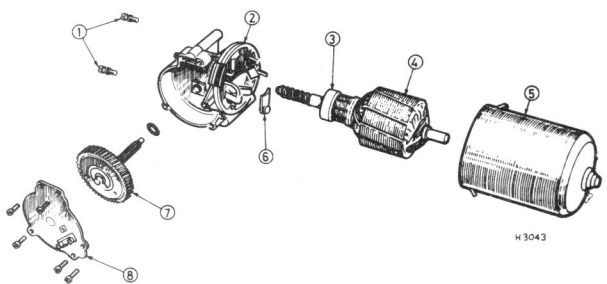

Fig. 10.8 Windscreen wiper motor components (Sec. 26)

1 Armature casing securing screws
2 Brush housing
3 Bearing
4 Armature
5 Armature casing
6 Armature locking plate
7 Driven gear
8 Gear cover

27 Windscreen wiper linkage – removal and refitting

1 Refer to Section 23 and remove the windscreen wiper arms and blades.
2 Remove the rubber sleeves from each spindle.
3 Undo and remove the nut that secures the linkage to the windscreen wiper motor drive shaft. Carefully lever the linkage from the drive shaft.
4 Undo and remove the nut, washer and seal assembly holding each spindle to the cowl panel.
5 The linkage may now be lifted away from the car.
6 Refitting the windscreen wiper linkage is the reverse sequence to removal. Make sure that the tang on the linkage engages with the keyway on the wiper motor drive shaft.

13 Slide the driven gear back into position.
14 Apply a little grease to the gear and refit the gasket and gear cover plate.
15 Secure the gear cover plate with the five retaining screws.
16 Refit the outer casing and secure with the two screws.

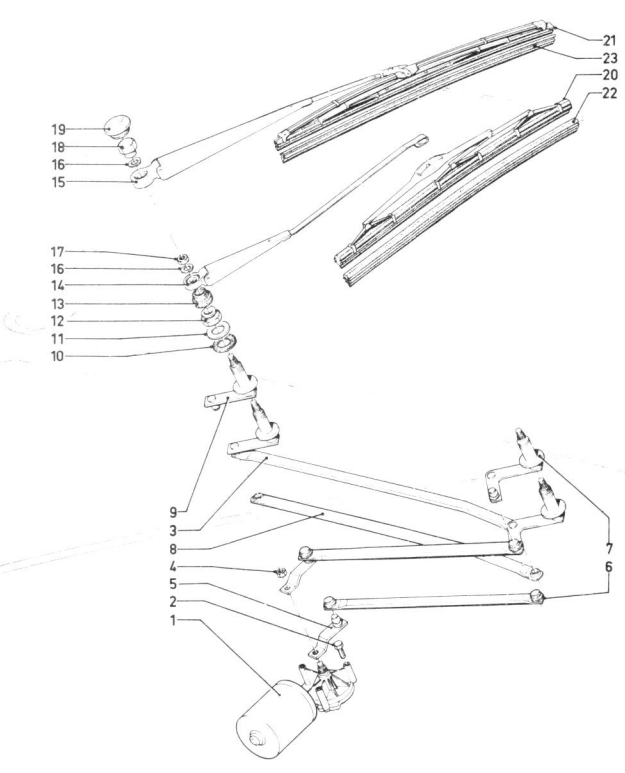

Fig. 10.9 Windscreen wiper linkage components (Sec. 27)

1 Motor and drive assembly
2 Bolt
3 Linkage assembly
4 Nut
5 Arm assembly
6 Link assembly
7 Arm and pivot assembly
8 Link assembly
9 Arm and pivot assembly
10 Gasket
11 Washer
12 Nut
13 Seal
14 Arm assembly
15 Arm assembly
16 Spring washer
17 Nut
18 Bolt
19 Plug
20 Blade assembly
21 Blade assembly
22 Blade insert
23 Blade insert

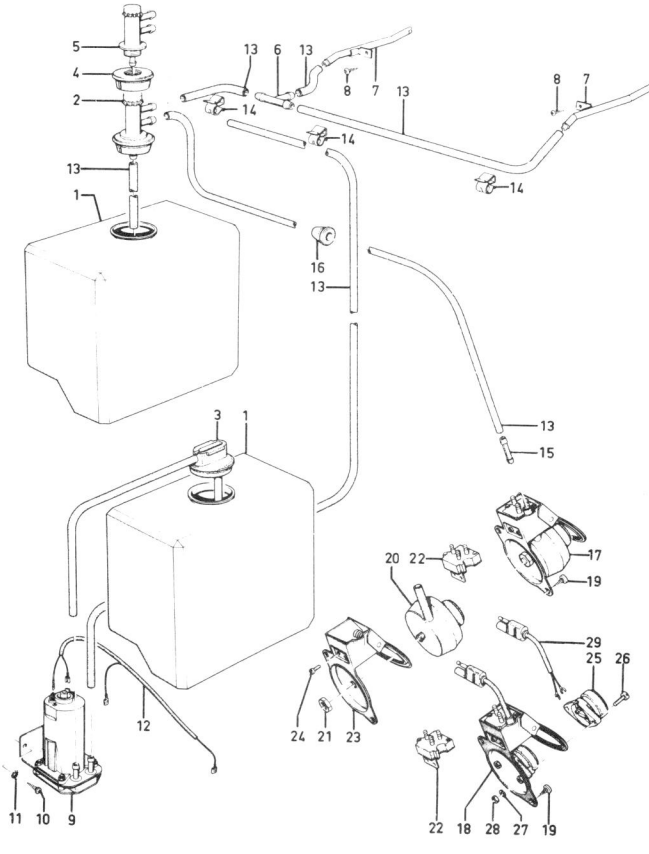

Fig. 10.10 Windscreen washer assembly (Sec. 28)

1 Reservoir
2 Cover and valve
3 Cover and hose
4 Cover
5 Valve
6 'T' connector
7 Jet
8 Screw
9 Motor and pump
10 Screw
11 Lockwasher
12 Wiring
13 Hose
14 Clip
15 Connection
16 Grommet
17 Pump and switch
18 Switch
19 Screw
20 Pump (foot operated)
21 Nut
22 Switch
23 Plate
24 Screw
25 Switch
26 Screw
27 Lockwasher
28 Nut
29 Wiring

28 Windscreen washer pump – removal and refitting

Foot operated type:
1 Disconnect the plastic hose from the pump inlet and outlet connections.
2 Undo and remove the two crosshead screws securing the pump to the floor mounted bracket. Lift away the pump (photo).
3 Refitting the foot operated pump is the reverse sequence to removal.

Electrically operated type:
4 Undo and remove the two crosshead screws and shakeproof washers securing the motor and pump assembly to the front fender apron.
5 Disconnect the multi pin connector and hoses from the motor and pump assembly. Make a note of the location of the hoses and multi pin connector.
6 Refitting the electrically operated windscreen washer motor and pump is the reverse sequence to removal.

29 Windscreen washer jets – removal and refitting

1 Working under the bonnet undo and remove the self tapping screw and washer securing each jet to the top cowl.
2 Pull off the water hose and lift away the jet.
3 Refitting the jet is the reverse sequence to removal. Adjust the position of the jet before finally tightening the retaining screw.

30 Rear windscreen wiper motor – removal and refitting

1 Disconnect the battery terminals.

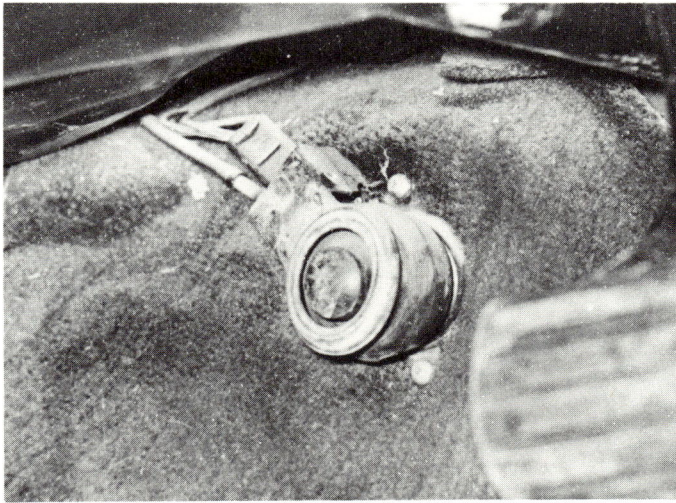

28.2 The foot operated windscreen washer pump

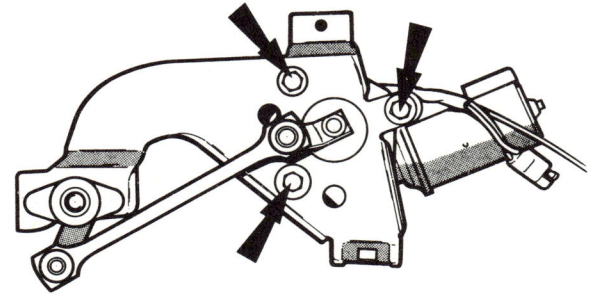

Fig. 10.11 Rear screen wiper motor and bracket – arrows indicate motor securing bolts (Sec. 30)

2 Detach the wiper arm and blade from the tailgate in similar fashion to that described in Section 23.
3 Open and remove the trim panel from the tailgate.
4 Note the wiring connections to the wiper motor and disconnect them.
5 Unscrew and remove the wiper spindle securing nut, and then the three screws retaining the motor bracket in position.
6 Extract the motor unit complete with linkage from the tailgate.
7 To separate the motor from the bracket, unscrew and remove the three securing bolts. Unclip the circlip from the wiper spindle and detach the linkage.
8 Refitting is a direct reversal of removal but to ensure that the motor is correctly positioned the bracket is adjustable as shown in Fig. 10.12.
9 Check the motor operation before refitting the trim panel to the tailgate.

31 Rear windscreen washer pump – removal and refitting

1 Disconnect the battery terminals
2 Open the tailgate and then remove the spare wheel cover to expose the pump unit.
3 Unscrew the pump unit bracket retaining screws and detach the wire connections and hoses.
4 Carefully remove the pump and bracket, disengaging the retaining rubbers in the process.
5 Refitting is the reversal of removal but ensure that the pump operates correctly before fitting the spare wheel cover.

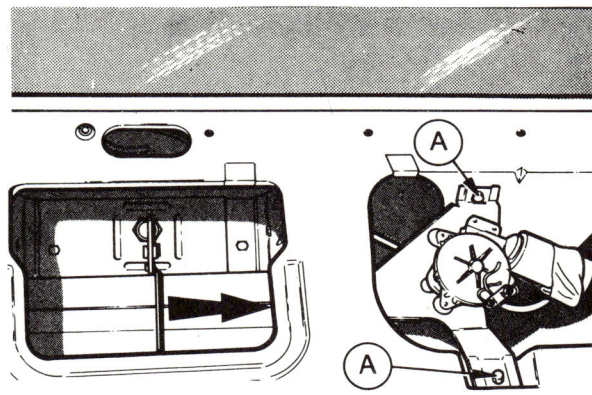

Fig. 10.12 Rear screen wiper motor in position in tailgate. The securing bolts are marked 'A' (Sec. 30)

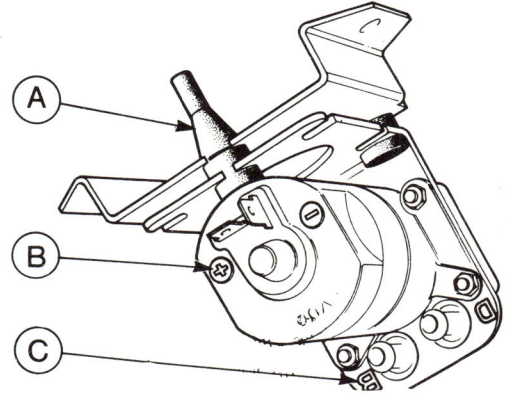

Fig. 10.13 Rear windscreen washer pump (Sec. 31)

A Rubber mounting   C Inlet and outlet tubes
B Multi-plug location

32 Horn – fault tracing and rectification

1 If the horn works badly or fails completely, first check the wiring leading to the horn for short circuits and loose connections. Also check that the horn is firmly secured and that there is nothing lying on the horn body.
2 Using a test lamp check the wiring to the number 5 fuse on the fuse box. Check that the fuse has not blown.
3 If the fault is an internal one it will be necessary to obtain a new horn.
4 To remove the horn undo and remove the three crosshead screws securing the radiator grille. Lift away the radiator grille.
5 Disconnect the wiring loom connections to the horn (photo).
6 Undo and remove the one bolt and lock washer securing the horn to the bracket. Lift away the horn.
7 Refitting the horn is the reverse sequence to removal.

33 Horn slip ring contact finger – removal and refitting

1 With time the contact finger will wear and a new one will be required. The usual indication of wear is intermittent operation at different steering wheel positions.
2 Undo and remove the four screws that secure the steering column shroud. Lift away the shroud and ignition switch surround.
3 Disconnect the lead from the contact finger and remove the finger by pushing in towards the steering wheel. Rotate through 90° and draw out away from the back of the steering wheel.
4 Refitting the horn slip ring contact finger is the reverse sequence to removal.

34 Headlamp lens and reflector assembly – removal and refitting

1 Undo and remove the six screws securing the headlamp bezel and lift away the bezel (Fig. 10.16).
2 Undo and remove the screw that secures the lamp assembly to the body and draw the whole assembly forward by a sufficient amount to gain access to the rear.
3 Detach the side light bulb and headlamp multi pin plug from the assembly and lift away the complete unit.
4 Remove the rubber grommet surrounding the rear of the bulb.
5 Release the spring clips and detach the bulb retaining ring and bulb.
6 Release the adjustment screw retaining clips from their locations on the assembly and unscrew the adjustment screws from the headlamp body.
7 To reassemble first screw the adjustment screws into their locations by a sufficient amount for the light clips to engage their locations on the lamp body.
8 Refit the headlamp bulb and secure with the retaining ring and spring clip.
9 Refit the headlight bulb grommet and reconnect the multi pin plug. Refit the side light bulb socket to the headlamp body.
10 Check that the seals are securely fitted to prevent water ingress.
11 Offer up the assembly to the body engaging the lower retaining clips on the aperture and secure the assembly with the retaining screw.
12 Refit the headlamp bezel and secure with the six screws.
13 It will now be necessary to reset the headlight beam alignment. Further information will be found in Section 36.

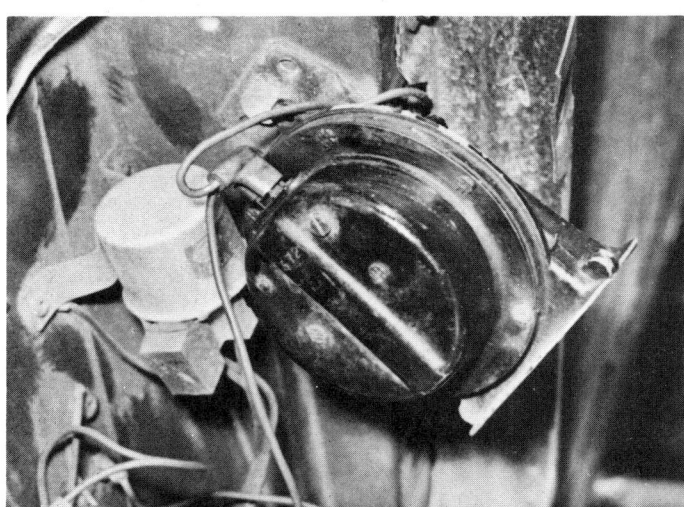

32.5 The horn showing wiring connections

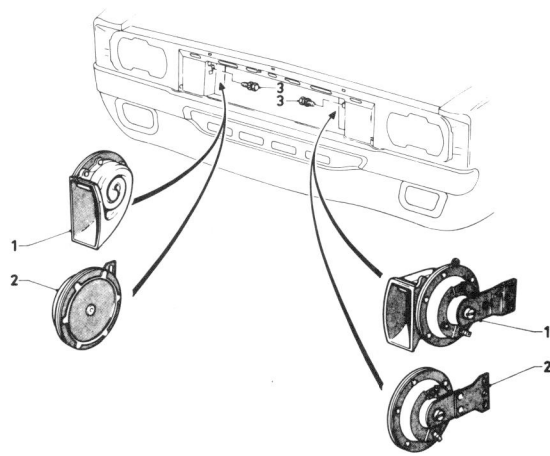

Fig. 10.14 Horns and mountings (Sec. 32)

1 Standard   2 Alternative   3 Securing bolts

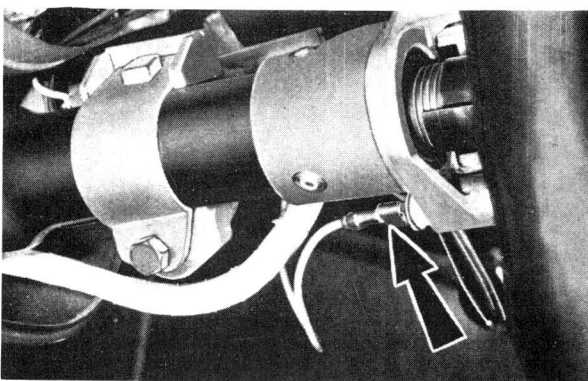

Fig. 10.15 Horn slip ring contact finger (arrowed) (Sec. 33)

Fig. 10.16 Headlamp unit bezel attachments (Sec. 34)

Chapter 10 Electrical system

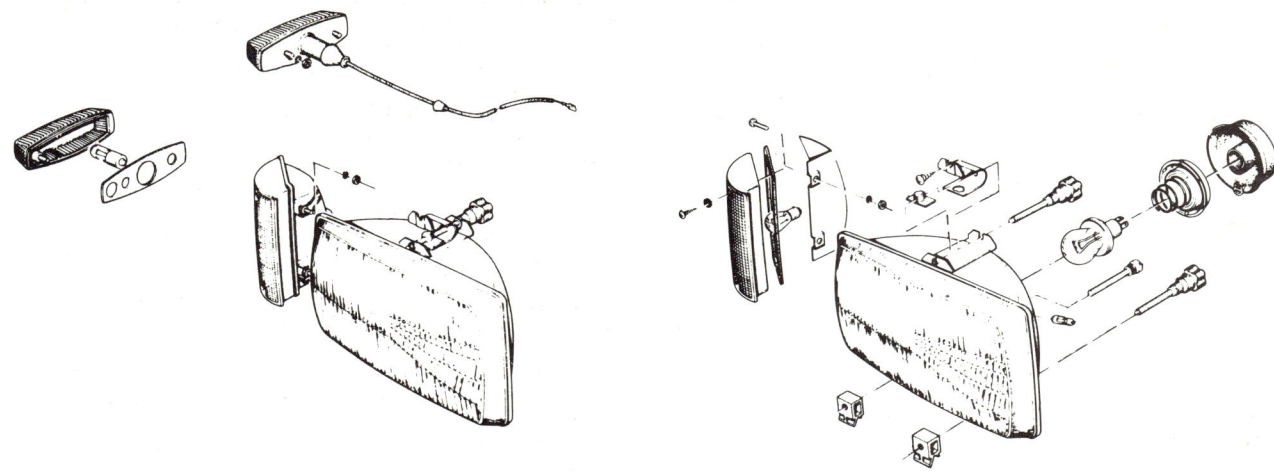

Fig. 10.17 Headlamp, sidelight and flasher light assemblies (Sec. 35)

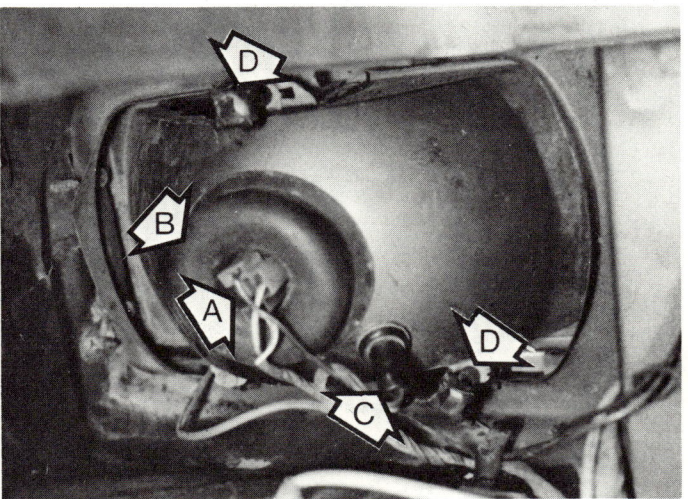

35.2 The rear side of the headlight showing:
  A) Multi pin connector
  B) Rubber grommet
  C) Side light bulb holder
  D) The light adjuster knobs for beam alignment

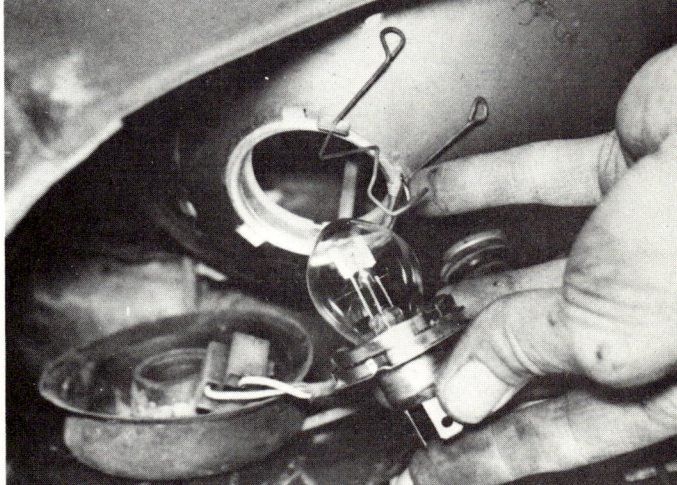

35.3 The headlamp bulb removed

36 Headlight alignment

1 It is always advisable to have the headlights aligned using special optical beam setting equipment but if this is not available the following procedure may be used.
2 Place the car on level ground and locate a white board marked up as shown in Fig. 10.18, 10 ft (3 m) in front of the car.
3 Check the tyre pressures and adjust as necessary.
4 Remove any luggage in the boot/luggage compartment and then bounce the front of the car to ensure correct settlement of the suspension and measure the height 'H' from the ground to the centre of the headlights.
5 Mark the centre of the front and rear windscreens with a wax crayon and position the aiming board so that the vertical centre line and the marks on the glass are exactly in line when viewed through the rear glass. The horizontal line must be set at a height 'H–X' from the ground. (See caption to Fig. 10.18)
6 Adjust each headlight by means of the vertical and horizontal adjustment screws as described in the following paragraphs.
7 Cover over one headlight to prevent glare when adjusting the second headlight beam.
8 Adjust the horizontal position of the headlight until the point 'C' is in the same vertical plane as the cross on the aiming board.
9 Adjust the vertical position of the headlight so that the light/dark boundary of the beam pattern just touches the dotted line shown on the aiming board.
10 Repeat the operations described in paragraphs 7 to 9 inclusive for the second headlight.

35 Headlamp bulb – removal and refitting

1 Working inside the wheel arch remove the dust and road dirt from the area around the rear of the headlamp unit.
2 Disconnect the multi pin connector and then remove the rubber grommet (photo).
3 Disengage and remove the bulb retaining spring clips and detach the bulb retaining ring and bulb. **Note:** *If halogen bulbs are fitted the glass must not be touched with the fingers. If it is touched, the bulbs should be washed in methylated spirits and dried with a clean soft cloth* (photo).
4 To refit the bulb first locate it in the reflector making sure that the dimple on the bulb flange engages with the cut out on the reflector body.
5 Locate and re-engage the retaining spring clips and bulb retaining ring on the reflector body cut-outs.
6 Make sure that the rubber grommet is clean and not damaged and refit over the bulb. Always renew this grommet if damaged otherwise a complete new unit will be necessary later if damaged by water ingress.
7 Refit the multi pin connector and recheck that the rubber grommet is correctly seating.

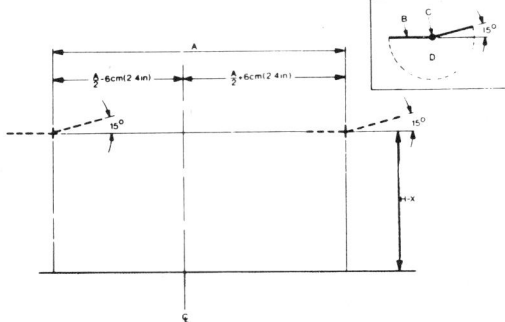

Fig. 10.18 Headlight aiming board markings (Sec. 36)
NOTE: Chart for LHD cars shown
For RHD cars distances A/2 − 6 cm and A/2 + 6 cm should be reversed and the 15° beam inclination line should be transposed from right to left

A = Distance between headlamps centres
B = Light/dark boundary
C = Beam centre (dipped)
D = Dipped beam pattern
H = Height from ground to centre of headlamps
X = 5.5 cm (2.2 in) for saloon – 4.5 cm (1.75 in) for estate car

37.2 The sidelight bulb removed

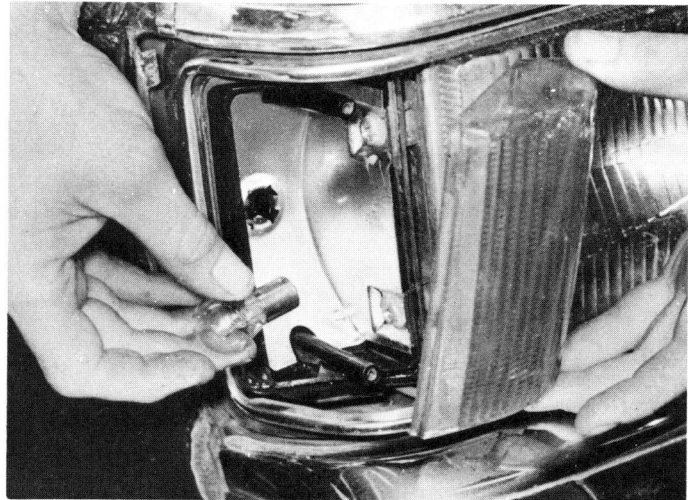

39.2 The front indicator bulb replacement

37 Front side light bulb – removal and refitting

1 Working inside the wheel arch remove the dust and road dirt from the area around the rear of the headlamp unit.
2 Pull the side light bulb assembly from its location in the headlamp body (photo).
3 Remove the bulb by depressing, twisting and withdrawing from the holder.
4 Refitting the side light bulb and holder is the reverse sequence to removal. Make sure that the rubber boot fits tightly against the reflector. If it has perished always fit a new one otherwise a complete new unit will be necessary later if damaged by water ingress.

38 Front direction indicator lamp assembly – removal and refitting

1 Refer to Section 34 and remove the headlamp lens and reflector assembly.
2 Undo and remove the two nuts and washers securing the indicator light assembly to the body and pull the assembly away from the aperture.
3 Disconnect the lead and remove the assembly.
4 Refitting the front direction indicator lamp assembly is the reverse sequence to removal.

39 Front direction indicator light bulb – removal and refitting

1 Undo and remove the crosshead screws securing the lens to the lamp assembly. Lift away the lens.
2 Remove the bulb by depressing, twisting and withdrawing from the holder (photo).
3 Refitting the bulb and lens is the reverse sequence to removal. Make sure that the lens gasket is correctly seated to prevent dirt or water ingress.

40 Fog lamp assembly – removal and refitting

1 For safety reasons disconnect the battery.
2 Working under the wheel arch remove the dust and road dirt from the area around the rear of the fog lamp assembly.
3 Undo and remove the one self tapping screw and disconnect the earth cable from the radiator panel.
4 Disconnect the wiring loom connections from inside the engine compartment.
5 Carefully push the lamp cables and grommet through the aperture in the fender apron.
6 Working from the front of the assembly, undo and remove the two screws that secure the shroud. Lift away the shroud.
7 Undo and remove the two crosshead screws and one bolt that

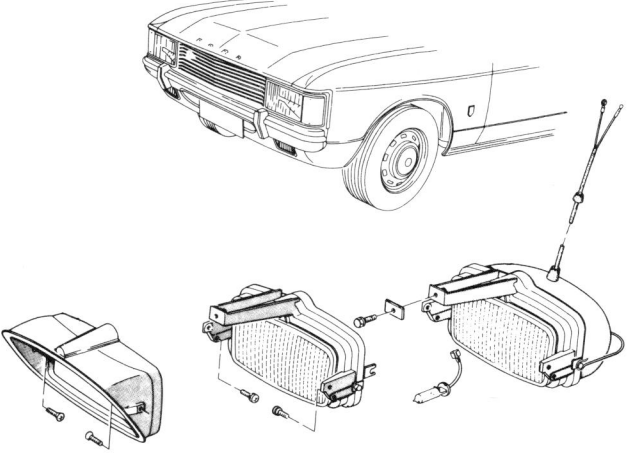

Fig. 10.19 Fog lamp assembly (Sec. 40)

Chapter 10 Electrical system

secures the assembly to the body. Lift away the assembly and gasket.
8 Refitting the assembly is the reverse sequence to removal but the following additional points should be noted:

   (a) Remove all traces of old sealing compound from the shroud and aperture.
   (b) Apply a little Bostik Sealer to both sides of the gasket before refitting.
   (c) Apply a little Bostik Sealer to the rear face of the shroud.
   (d) Refer to Section 42 and reset the fog light beam.

41 Fog light bulb – removal and refitting

1 Working under the wheelarch remove the dust and road dirt from the area around the rear of the fog lamp assembly.
2 Pull down the spring retainer and detach the rear of the body (photo).
3 Detach the spring clip that retains the bulb in the lens. Lift away the bulb.
4 Refitting the fog light bulb is the reverse sequence to removal. Make sure that the gasket is clean and correctly seated to prevent dirt or water ingress.

42 Fog light beam alignment

1 It is always advisable to have the fog lights aligned using special optical beam setting equipment but if this is not available the following procedure may be used.
2 Place the car on level ground and locate a white board marked up as shown in Fig. 10.20, 16·5 ft (5 m) from the centre point of one fog light at 90° to the car axis.
3 The centre point 'A' must be exactly in line with the centre of the fog light assembly.
4 Check the tyre pressures and adjust as necessary.
5 Remove any luggage in the boot/luggage compartment and then bounce the front of the car to ensure correct settlement of the suspension.
6 Cover the headlights and second fog light to prevent glare whilst carrying out the adjustment.
7 Adjust the beam so that the centre point is 'A' and cut off line of beam touches the line 'B' of the aiming board.
8 Adjust the second fog light beam in a similar manner as for the first one.

43 Auxiliary lamp assembly – removal and refitting

1 Open the bonnet and disconnect the battery for safety reasons.
2 Undo and remove the bolt that secures the assembly bracket to the radiator mounting panel.
3 Lift away the assembly and recover the washers, reinforcement plate and bracket.
4 Detach the cable from the wiring loom and completely remove the lamp assembly.
5 Refitting the assembly is the reverse sequence to removal. Reset the auxiliary light beam as described in Section 45.

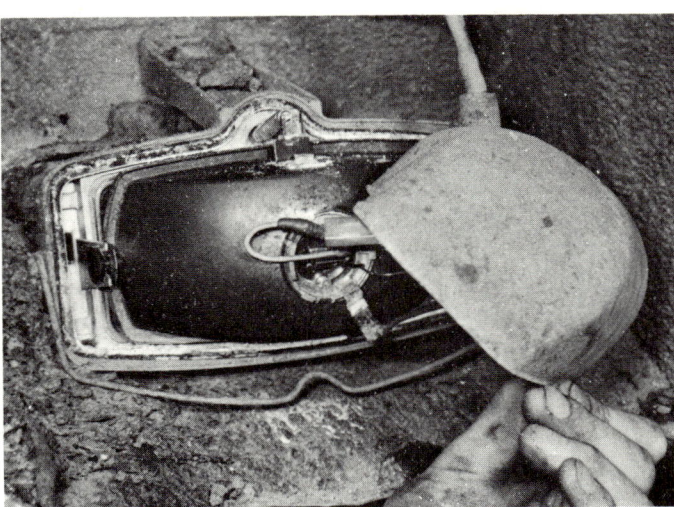

41.2 Remove the cover

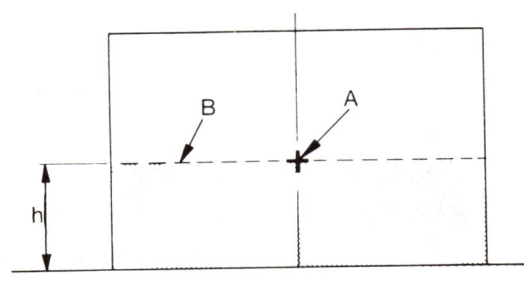

Fig. 10.20 Fog light beam alignment (Sec. 42)

A = Centre point of fog light beam
B = Beam cut off line
h = Saloon 6 in (150 mm)
   = Estate 8 in (200 mm)

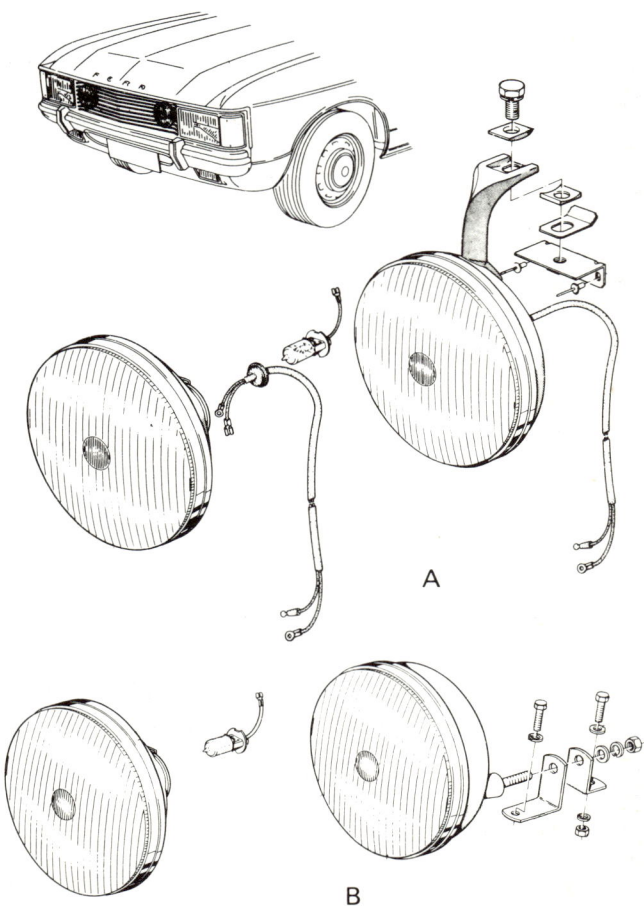

Fig. 10.21 Auxiliary lamps (Sec. 43)

A Standard   B Alternative

44 Auxiliary light bulb – removal and refitting

1 Undo and remove the crosshead screw on the lens rim and draw the lens assembly forward from the lamp body.
2 Disconnect the cable connection at the terminal inside the assembly.
3 Release the spring clip and lift away the bulb.
4 Refitting the bulb and lens is the reverse sequence to removal.

45 Auxiliary light beam alignment

1 It is always advisable to have the auxiliary lights aligned using special optical beam setting equipment but if this is not available the following procedure may be used.
2 Place the car on level ground and locate a white board marked up as shown in Fig. 10.22, 33 ft (10 m) from the centre point of one auxiliary light at 90° to the car axis.
3 The centre point 'A' must be exactly in line with the centre of the auxiliary light assembly.
4 Check the tyre pressures and adjust as necessary.
5 Remove any luggage in the boot/luggage compartment and then bounce the front of the car to ensure correct settlement of the suspension.
6 Cover the headlights and second auxiliary light to prevent glare whilst carrying out the adjustment.
7 Adjust the beam so that the centre of the pencil of light coincides with the point 'A' on the aiming board.
8 Adjust the second auxiliary light beam in a similar manner as for the first one.

46 Rear lamp assembly (saloon) – removal and refitting

1 Working inside the boot compartment undo and remove the two nuts and washers that secure the lamp assembly.
2 Make a note of the cable terminal connections and disconnect.
3 The assembly may now be lifted away from the car.
4 Refitting the assembly is the reverse sequence to removal. The correct cable connections are as follows:

Bulb	Left	Right
Rear lamp	Grey/black	Grey/red
Stop lamp	Black/red (2)	Black/red
Direction indicator	Black/white	Black/green
Reverse lamp	Black (2)	Black (2)

47 Rear lamp assembly (estate) – removal and refitting

1 Open the tailgate and remove the load spare side trim panel.
2 Undo and remove the screws that secure the lens to the lamp body. Lift away the lens.
3 Remove all three bulbs noting their locations.
4 Working inside the luggage compartment undo and remove the two nuts and washers that secure the assembly body to the rear panel.
5 Draw the lamp body from the rear panel and make a note of the cable terminal connections. Disconnect these cables.
6 The body may now be lifted away.
7 Refitting the assembly is the reverse sequence to removal. The following additional points should be noted.

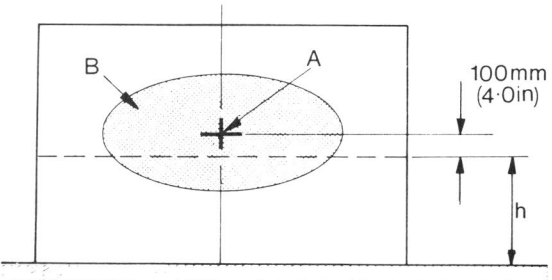

Fig. 10.22 Auxiliary light beam alignment (Sec. 45)
A = Centre point of beam
B = Beam pattern
h = 6.75 in (170 mm)

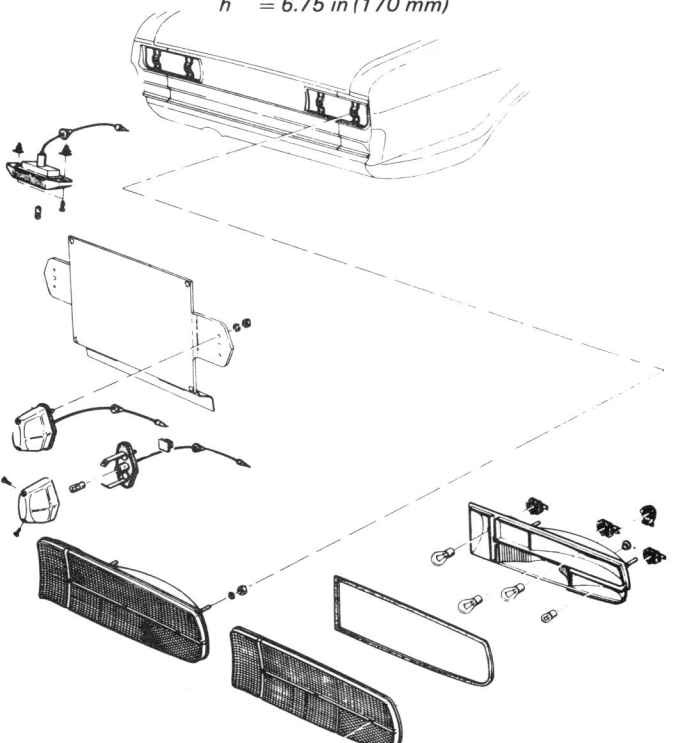

Fig. 10.23 Rear lamp assembly (saloon) (Sec. 46)

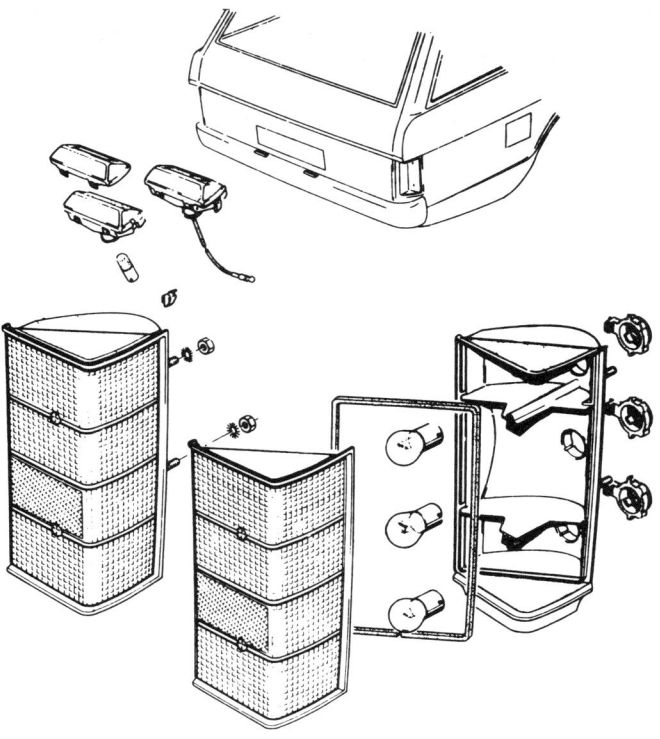

Fig. 10.24 Rear lamp assembly (estate) (Sec. 47)

Chapter 10 Electrical system

(a) Apply some caulking tape (Bostik) around the periphery of the body. Make the joint at the lower edge.
(b) The correct cable connections are as follows:

Bulb	Left	Right
Rear light	Multi pin plug	Multi pin plug
Stop light		
Direction indicator	Black/white	Black/green
Reverse	Black (2)	Black

48 Rear lamp assembly bulb – removal and refitting

1 The rear lamp assembly incorporates the following bulbs: a) rear, stop, b) direction indicator and c) reverse.
2 Undo and remove the crosshead screws securing the lens to the rear lamp assembly body.
3 Lift away the lens. The relevant bulb is removed by depressing, turning anti-clockwise and withdrawing from the holder (photo).
4 Refitting a bulb and lens is the reverse sequence to removal.

48.3 Remove the lens to replace the rear light cluster bulbs (Saloon)

49 Rear number plate lamp bulb – removal and refitting

1 Undo and remove the two crosshead screws that secure the assembly to the rear bumper.
2 Lift away the lens and then remove the bulb.
3 Refitting the bulb and lens is the reverse sequence to removal.

50 Instruments – general

The instruments fitted to the basic Consul model comprise a combined temperature and fuel gauge, a speedometer and warning lights for the direction indicators, oil pressure, alternator/ignition, main beam and handbrake. In the following Sections any specific service instructions are designated **Type B**.
The instruments fitted to the Consul GT and Granada models have a tachometer in place of the combined temperature and fuel gauge. Four additional instruments, an ammeter, oil pressure gauge, temperature gauge and fuel gauge are mounted in pairs on either side of the speedometer. All Granada models incorporate an odometer and trip meter within the speedometer head.
The panel was modified slightly for the 1976 range in that the instrument cluster layout was revised, although the removal instructions remain the same. In the following Sections any specific service instructions are designated **Type A**.
Note: *Where specific instructions for Type B do not appear refer to Type A.*

51 Interior bulbs – removal and refitting

Interior light bulb
1 Carefully prise the lamp assembly from its location in the roof panel. It is best to use a screwdriver in the cut-out on the sides.
2 Make a note of the electrical cable connections and detach.
3 Release the bulb from its clip.
4 Refitting the bulb and assembly is the reverse sequence to removal.

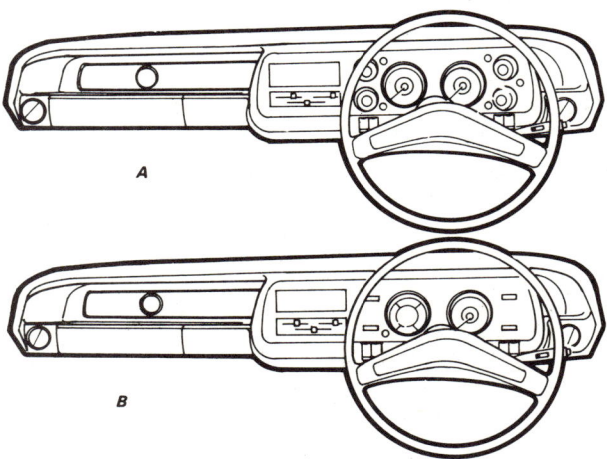

Fig. 10.25 Instrument panel layout and identification (Sec. 50)

Top   Type A   Consul GT and Granada
Bottom   Type B   Consul

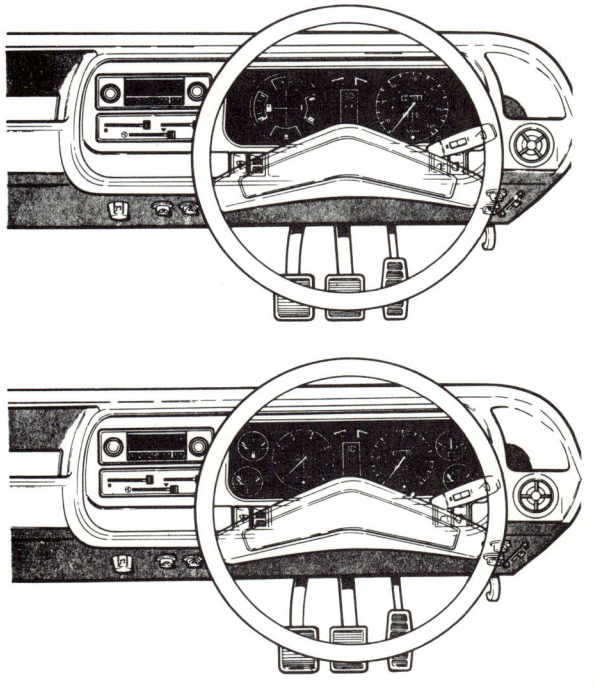

Fig. 10.26 Instrument panel layout and identification for the 1976 models

Glove compartment light bulb

5 Carefully pull the lens assembly from its location at the rear of the glove compartment.
6 Disconnect the leads and then detach the bulb and holder. Remove the bulb.
7 Refitting is the reverse sequence to removal. Push the assembly into the aperture aligning the lugs with the cut-outs in the aperture.

Heater control illumination bulb

8 Refer to Section 52 and remove the instrument cluster.
9 Reach through the instrument cluster aperture and remove the bulb from the holder located behind the heater control panel.
10 Refitting is the reverse sequence to removal.

Quadrant light bulb (automatic transmission)

11 Carefully ease the quadrant up and away from the floor.
12 Pull the bulb holder off the locating tang.
13 Part the two halves of the holder and lift away the bulb.
14 Refitting the bulb and quadrant is the reverse sequence to removal.

Heated rear window warning light bulb

15 Remove the instrument cluster bezel by carefully easing away from the facia.
16 Pull the switch assembly from its location, then disconnect the multi pin plug and finally remove the bulb.
17 Refitting the bulb and switch is the reverse sequence to removal.

52 Instrument cluster – removal and refitting (Type A)

1 For safety reasons disconnect the battery.
2 Ease off the radio control knobs.
3 Remove the instrument cluster bezel by carefully easing away from the facia.
4 Undo and remove the four screws that secure the instrument cluster assembly to the facia panel and draw the assembly away from the facia as far as possible.
5 Disconnect the oil pressure pipe union, speedometer cable and multi pin connector from the rear of the cluster. Lift away the cluster assembly.
6 Refitting the instrument cluster is the reverse sequence to removal.

53 Instrument cluster printed circuit – removal and refitting (Type A)

1 Refer to Section 52 and remove the instrument cluster.
2 Remove the instrument cluster illumination bulbs from the rear by simply pulling out.
3 Undo and remove the screw that secures the voltage regulator to the rear of the cluster and detach the regulator and radio suppressor filter.
4 Undo and remove the small nuts that secure the printed circuit to the rear of the instrument cluster.
5 Undo and remove the rheostat switch assembly screws and washers and lift away the switch.
6 The printed circuit may now be lifted away from the rear of the instrument cluster.
7 Refitting the instrument cluster is the reverse sequence to removal.

54 Instrument cluster glass – removal and refitting (Type A)

1 Remove the instrument cluster bezel by carefully easing away from the facia.
2 Undo and remove the self tapping screws securing the glass to the cluster. It will be noted that there are five for the main instruments and two for the auxiliary instruments. Two main instrument lower screws hold the cluster to the facia.
3 Refitting the instrument cluster glass is the reverse sequence to removal. Do not forget to remove all traces of dust before refitting.

55 Instrument voltage regulator – removal and refitting

1 Refer to Section 52 and remove the instrument cluster.
2 Undo and remove the screw that secures the voltage regulator to the rear of the cluster and detach the regulator and radio suppressor filter.
3 Refitting the unit is the reverse sequence to removal.

56 Instrument cluster bulb – removal and refitting

1 Refer to Section 52 paragraphs 1 to 4 inclusive.
2 Carefully pull the relevant bulb holder from its location at the rear of the instrument cluster and remove the bulb.
3 Refitting the bulb and instrument cluster is the reverse sequence to removal.

57 Speedometer head – removal and refitting (Type A)

1 Refer to Section 52 and remove the instrument cluster.
2 Undo and remove the six self tapping screws that secure the two halves of the cluster body together.
3 Separate the two halves of the instrument cluster.
4 Undo and remove the two screws securing the speedometer head to the cluster. Lift away the speedometer head.
5 Refitting the speedometer head and instrument cluster is the reverse sequence to removal. When fitting the two halves of the cluster together, place the front half on a flat surface making sure that the metal trim plates are correct. Place the rear half of the cluster on the front half making sure that the locating tags, odometer and rheostat switch shafts are correctly located. Secure the two halves with the six self tapping screws.

58 Speedometer inner and outer cable – removal and refitting (Type A)

1 Refer to Section 52 and remove the instrument cluster.
2 Chock the front wheels, jack up the rear of the car and support on firmly based stands.
3 Undo and remove the two nuts and washers holding the washer and clip OR remove the cable retainer circlip using a pair or circlip pliers depending on the type of transmission fitted.
4 Detach the speedometer cable assembly from its securing clips and carefully pull through the bulkhead.
5 Refitting the speedometer cable assembly is the reverse sequence to removal but the following additional points should be noted: On RHD models the cable should be routed from the instrument cluster and secured by one clip on the apron panel and two clips on the side member. The colour bands on the cable must register with the rubber dash panel grommets and frontmost sidemember clip. Position the cable to the underside of the floor panel with the body mounted clip.

59 Fuel gauge – removal and refitting (Type A)

1 Refer to Section 52 and remove the instrument cluster.
2 Undo and remove the six self tapping screws that secure both halves of the instrument cluster together. Separate the two halves.
3 Undo and remove the two nuts and washers that secure the fuel gauge to the cluster body. Lift away the fuel gauge.
4 Refitting the fuel gauge and instrument cluster is the reverse sequence to removal. Refer to Section 57, second half of paragraph 5 for information on assembling the two halves of the instrument cluster.

60 Oil pressure gauge – removal and refitting (Type A)

1 Refer to Section 52 and remove the instrument cluster.
2 Undo and remove the six self tapping screws that secure both halves of the instrument cluster together. Separate the two halves.
3 Carefully pull the two bulb holders located immediately above the oil pressure gauge away from the rear of the cluster.
4 Gently ease the printed circuit from its location so as to expose the

Chapter 10 Electrical system

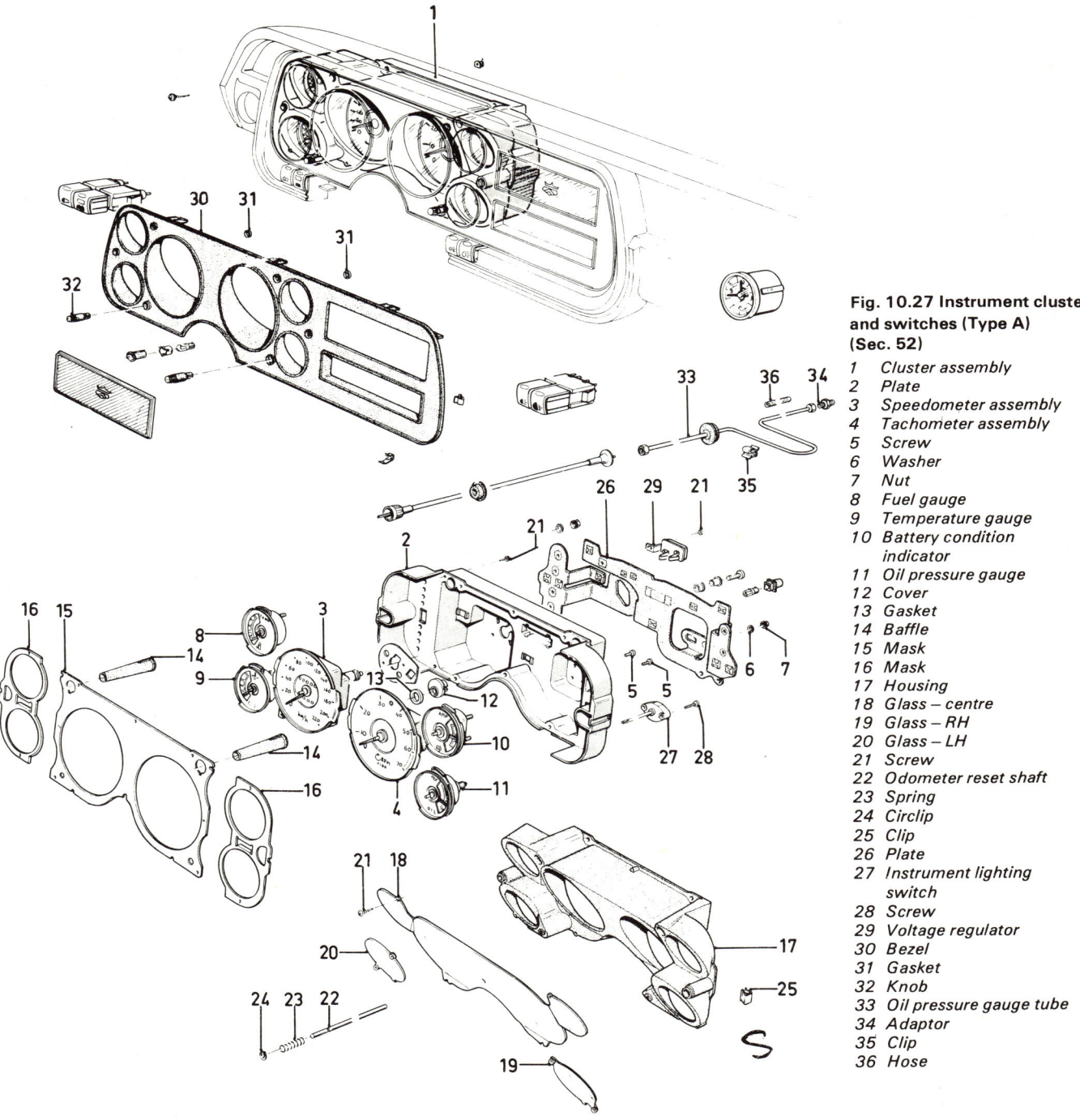

Fig. 10.27 Instrument cluster and switches (Type A) (Sec. 52)

1 Cluster assembly
2 Plate
3 Speedometer assembly
4 Tachometer assembly
5 Screw
6 Washer
7 Nut
8 Fuel gauge
9 Temperature gauge
10 Battery condition indicator
11 Oil pressure gauge
12 Cover
13 Gasket
14 Baffle
15 Mask
16 Mask
17 Housing
18 Glass – centre
19 Glass – RH
20 Glass – LH
21 Screw
22 Odometer reset shaft
23 Spring
24 Circlip
25 Clip
26 Plate
27 Instrument lighting switch
28 Screw
29 Voltage regulator
30 Bezel
31 Gasket
32 Knob
33 Oil pressure gauge tube
34 Adaptor
35 Clip
36 Hose

upper gauge securing screw.
5 Undo and remove the exposed screw and the lower retaining screw. Lift away the oil pressure gauge.
6 Refitting the oil pressure gauge and instrument cluster is the reverse sequence to removal. Refer to Section 57, second half of paragraph 5 for information on assembling the two halves of the instrument cluster.

61 Electric clock – removal and refitting

1 Refer to Chapter 12 and remove the lower crash pad insulation.
2 For safety reasons disconnect the battery.
3 Working from the rear of the crash pad carefully push the clock out of its location. To prevent the clock bezel being displaced hold it in position whilst the clock is being removed.
4 Pull out the bulb holder, make a note of the cable connector positions and detach from the rear of the clock. Lift away the clock.
5 Refitting the clock is the reverse sequence to removal.

62 Cigarette lighter assembly – removal and refitting (Type A)

1 For safety reasons disconnect the battery.
2 Pull the centre console cover plates away from the console so as to disengage the locating pegs.
3 Undo and remove the two screws that secure the ashtray mounting panel and pull the panel forward.

4 Remove the lighter from its socket and then undo and remove the locknut and washer securing the socket retainer to the tray panel.
5 Make a note of the electrical connections at the rear of the socket and detach.
6 Depress the sides of the bulb holder and detach from the socket. Lift away the socket.
7 Refitting the cigarette lighter is the reverse sequence to removal.

63 Ignition switch – removal and refitting

1 For safety reasons disconnect the battery.
2 Undo and remove the four screws that secure the steering column shroud. Part and remove the two halves of the shroud.
3 Using a suitable diameter drill, carefully drill out the shear bolt that secures the two halves of the lock to the column.
4 Lift away the two lock halves from the column.
5 Undo and remove the two screws that secure the wiring loom connection to the switch and completely lift away the switch.
6 To refit the ignition switch first line up the loom connection to the base of the switch and secure with the two screws.
7 Check that the pawl of the switch is projecting and then engage the pawl with the cut-out in the column.
8 Place the switch halves around the column and fit a new shear bolt. Tighten the shear bolt until the head parts from the shank.
9 Refit the steering column shroud and secure with the four screws.
10 Reconnect the battery.

64 Light switch – removal and refitting (Type A)

1 Refer to Section 52 and remove the instrument cluster.
2 Working from the rear of the crash pad carefully push the switch and wiring loom assembly from its housing in the facia. It will be found easier if one works through the cluster aperture.
3 Disconnect the light switch multi pin plug and lift away the switch.
4 Refitting the light switch is the reverse sequence to removal.

65 Direction indicator switch – removal and refitting

1 Refer to Section 52 and remove the instrument cluster.
2 Undo and remove the four screws securing the steering column shroud. Part and remove the two halves of the shroud.
3 Locate and then disconnect the three wiring loom multi-pin plugs for the switch.
4 Undo and remove the two screws that secure the switch to the steering column. Lift away the switch.
6 Refitting the direction indicator switch is the reverse sequence to removal.

66 Switches – general – removal and refitting

Instrument cluster light
1 Refer to Section 52 and remove the instrument cluster.
2 Working at the rear of the instrument cluster, remove the two self tapping screws that secure the rheostat to the cluster.
3 The rheostat and shaft may now be lifted from the cluster.
4 Refitting the instrument cluster is the reverse sequence to removal.

Courtesy light
5 Ease the switch from the door pillar and detach it from the holder.
6 Refitting the switch is the reverse sequence to removal.

Handbrake warning light
7 Undo and remove the six screws that secure the handbrake control rubber gaiter. Remove the gaiter.
8 Apply the handbrake and disconnect the cable terminal connector from the switch.
9 Undo and remove the two screws that secure the switch to the handbrake. Lift away the switch.
10 Refitting the handbrake warning light switch is the reverse sequence to removal.

Stop light
11 Disconnect the battery for safety reasons.
12 Working inside the car remove the lower trim panel insulation from the driver's side.
13 Disconnect the two terminal connectors from the switch and then undo and remove the front locknut securing the switch to the mounting bracket. Lift away the switch.
14 Refitting the switch is the reverse sequence to removal. It will be necessary to adjust its position to give correct operation.

Brake warning light
15 Clean the area around the brake differential valve body.
16 Carefully prise open the clips and disconnect the leads from the switch.
17 Wipe the top of the brake master cylinder reservoir, unscrew the cap and place a piece of polythene over the top of the reservoir neck. Refit the cap. This is to prevent loss of hydraulic fluid during subsequent operations.
18 Unscrew the switch assembly from the differential valve body.
19 Refitting the brake warning light switch is the reverse sequence to removal. It will be necessary to bleed the brake hydraulic system as described in Chapter 9.

Emergency flasher lights
20 Carefully ease the switch and lamp assembly from its location in the instrument panel.
21 Disconnect the multi pin connector from the rear of the switch and light assembly.
22 Refitting the emergency flasher light is the reverse sequence to removal.

67 Instrument cluster bezel – removal, dismantling and refitting

1 For safety reasons disconnect the battery.
2 Remove the instrument cluster bezel by carefully pulling forward from the facia panel.
3 Disconnect the instrument panel light switch and warning light leads. Lift away the instrument cluster bezel.
4 Undo and remove the self tapping screw from each warning light housing. Detach the housings from the bezel.
5 Carefully press out the radio aperture cover.
6 Undo and remove the two self tapping screws securing the light switch assembly and detach it from the bezel.
7 Remove the six spring clips from the mounting lugs on the rear of the bezel.
8 Reassembling and refitting the instrument cluster bezel is the reverse sequence to removal and dismantling.

68 Instrument cluster – removal and refitting (Type B)

1 For safety reasons disconnect the battery.
2 Remove the instrument cluster bezel by carefully pulling forwards from the facia panel.
3 Disconnect the instrument panel light switch and warning light leads. Lift away the instrument cluster bezel.
4 Undo and remove the four self tapping screws that secure the instrument cluster to the facia.
5 Disconnect the multi pin plug connector and also the speedometer from the rear of the instrument cluster. Lift away the instrument cluster.
6 Refitting the instrument cluster is the reverse sequence to removal.

69 Instrument cluster printed circuit – removal and refitting

1 Refer to Section 68 and remove the instrument cluster.
2 Remove the instrument cluster illumination bulbs from the rear by simply pulling out.
3 Undo and remove the screw that secures the voltage regulator to the rear of the cluster and detach it from the cluster.
4 Undo and remove the four nuts and washers securing the printed

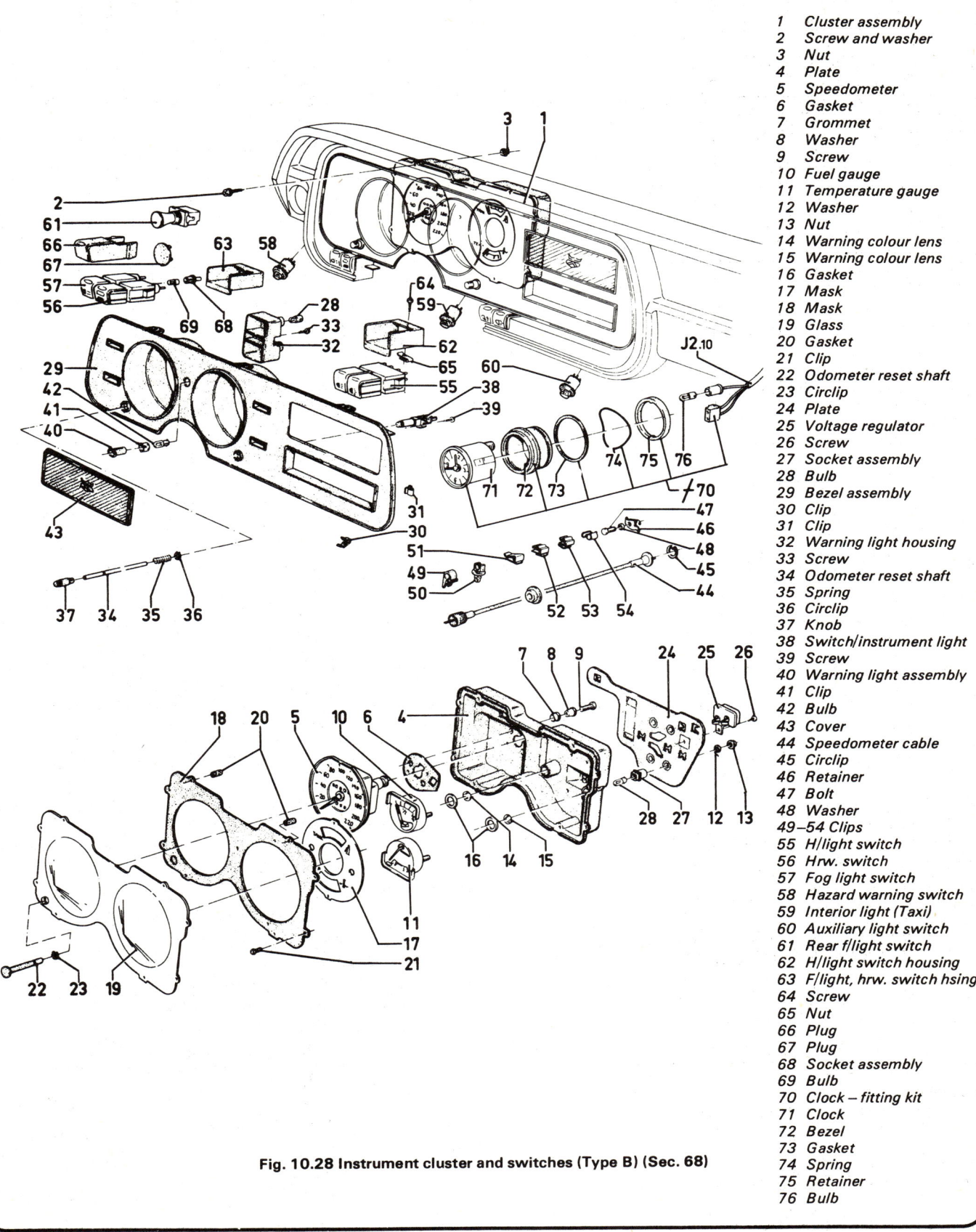

Fig. 10.28 Instrument cluster and switches (Type B) (Sec. 68)

1 Cluster assembly
2 Screw and washer
3 Nut
4 Plate
5 Speedometer
6 Gasket
7 Grommet
8 Washer
9 Screw
10 Fuel gauge
11 Temperature gauge
12 Washer
13 Nut
14 Warning colour lens
15 Warning colour lens
16 Gasket
17 Mask
18 Mask
19 Glass
20 Gasket
21 Clip
22 Odometer reset shaft
23 Circlip
24 Plate
25 Voltage regulator
26 Screw
27 Socket assembly
28 Bulb
29 Bezel assembly
30 Clip
31 Clip
32 Warning light housing
33 Screw
34 Odometer reset shaft
35 Spring
36 Circlip
37 Knob
38 Switch/instrument light
39 Screw
40 Warning light assembly
41 Clip
42 Bulb
43 Cover
44 Speedometer cable
45 Circlip
46 Retainer
47 Bolt
48 Washer
49–54 Clips
55 H/light switch
56 Hrw. switch
57 Fog light switch
58 Hazard warning switch
59 Interior light (Taxi)
60 Auxiliary light switch
61 Rear f/light switch
62 H/light switch housing
63 F/light, hrw. switch hsing
64 Screw
65 Nut
66 Plug
67 Plug
68 Socket assembly
69 Bulb
70 Clock – fitting kit
71 Clock
72 Bezel
73 Gasket
74 Spring
75 Retainer
76 Bulb

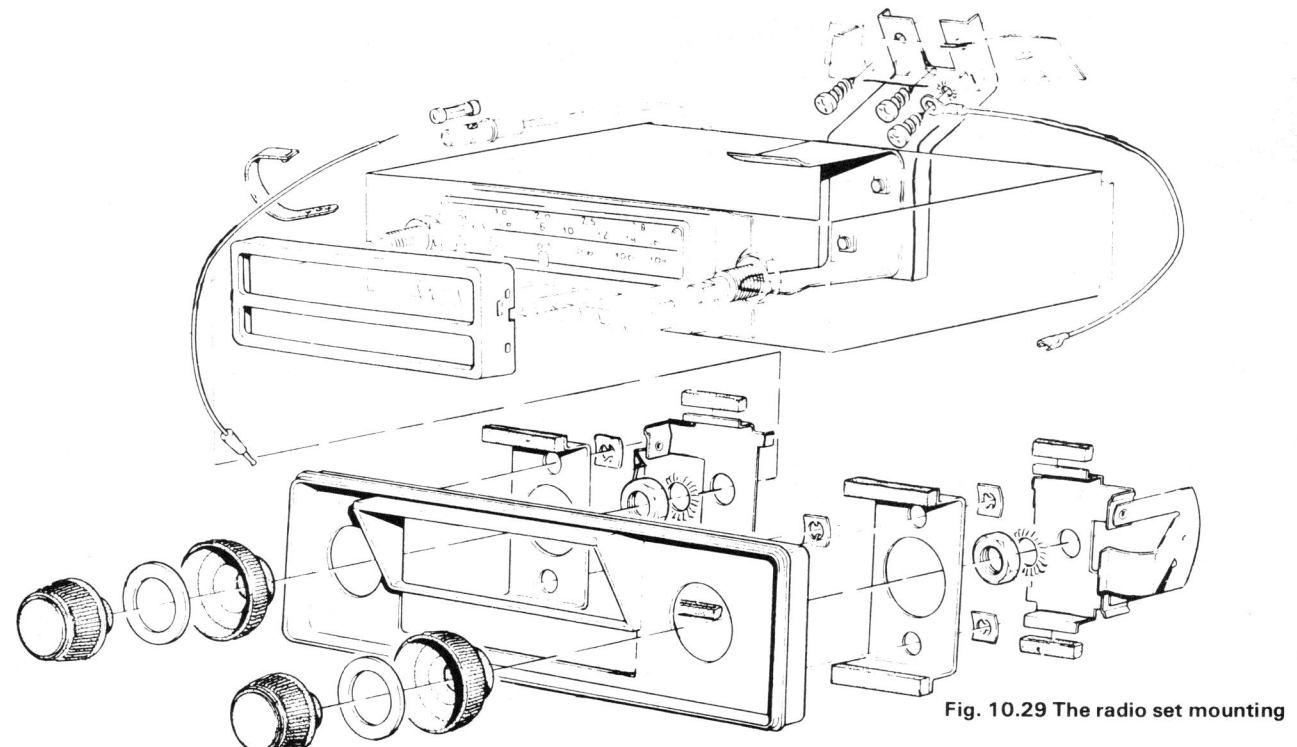

Fig. 10.29 The radio set mounting

circuit to the rear of the instrument cluster.
5   Carefully lift off the printed circuit.
6   Refitting the printed circuit and instrument cluster is the reverse sequence to removal.

70 Instrument cluster glass – removal and refitting (Type B)

1   Refer to Section 68 and remove the instrument cluster.
2   Carefully remove the five plastic pegs retaining the glass to the cluster by applying pressure to the rear of the pegs.
3   Lift off the glass.
4   Refitting the instrument cluster glass is the reverse sequence to removal. Do not forget to remove all traces of dust before refitting.

71 Speedometer head – removal and refitting

1   Refer to Section 70 and remove the instrument cluster glass.
2   Remove the instrument face plate.
3   Working at the rear of the instrument cluster undo and remove the two screws that secure the speedometer head to the cluster body. Lift away the speedometer head.
4   Refitting the speedometer head and instrument cluster is the reverse sequence to removal.

72 Fuel gauge – removal and refitting

1   Refer to Section 70 and remove the instrument cluster glass.
2   Carefully lift the two rubber distance pieces from the instrument face plate retaining pins and remove the face plate.
3   Working at the rear of the instrument cluster undo and remove the two nuts and washers securing the fuel gauge to the instrument cluster bezel. Lift away the fuel gauge.
4   Refitting the fuel gauge and instrument cluster is the reverse sequence to removal.

73 Light switch – removal and refitting (Type B)

1   Refer to Section 67 and remove the instrument cluster bezel.

2   Working from the rear of the crash pad carefully push the switch and wiring loom assembly from its housing in the facia. It will be found easier if one works through the instrument cluster aperture.
3   Disconnect the light switch multi pin plug and lift away the switch.
4   Refitting the light switch is the reverse sequence to removal.

74 Cigarette lighter assembly – removal and refitting (Type B)

1   Disconnect the battery for safety reasons.
2   Undo and remove the screws that secure the parcel tray to the tunnel.
3   Remove the gear lever knob and gaiter.
4   Disconnect the cigarette lighter leads and remove the parcel tray.
5   Undo and remove the locknut and washer securing the socket retainer to the tray.
6   Remove the socket from the tray by unscrewing the illumination ring on the opposite side of the tray.
7   Remove the bulb housing by depressing the sides and removing the bulb.
8   Refitting the cigarette lighter assembly is the reverse sequence to removal.

75 Fuses – general (all models)

The fuses are mounted in a block in the engine compartment.
There are seven fuses and the circuits protected are indicated on the plastic cover (photos).

Rating	Circuit
1 16 amp	Cigar lighter, clock, interior lights, glove box light, hazard light system.
2 8 amp	Number plate light, instrument illumination. Automatic change quadrant illumination (where fitted).
3 8 amp	Tail light/side light – RHS
4 8 amp	Tail light/side light – LHS

Chapter 10 Electrical system

75 a Remove the black fuse cover and then ...

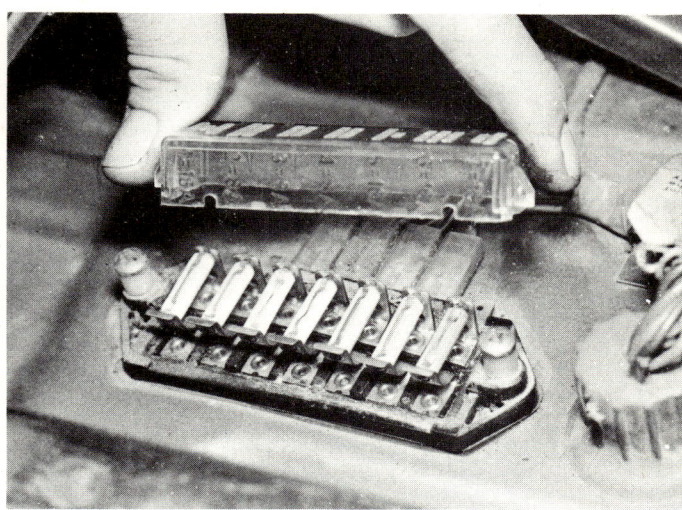

75 b ... the clear plastic cover to replace a fuse. Note the fuse values marked on the side of the cover

75 c To check the headlight fuses, remove the screws ...

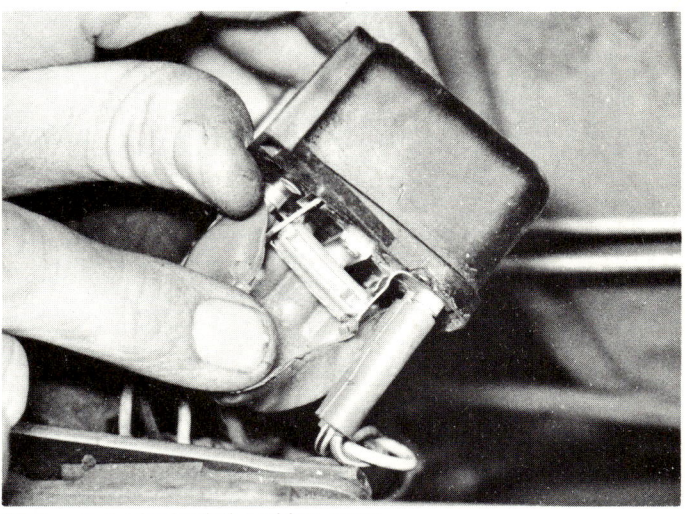

75 d ... and prise back the rubber cover

Rating		Circuit
5	16 amp	Horn, heater fan motor, primary circuit. Heated rear window.
6	16 amp	Wiper motor. Reverse lights. Instrument cluster.
7	16 amp	Direction indicators. Stop lights.

There are also three unused connections on the fuse block which correspond to fuses 1, 2 and 7 and these may be used to supply additional accessories. Fuses 1 and 2 are alive all the time whilst fuse 7 is connected via the ignition switch and only alive when the ignition is switched on.

The headlight fuses are located at the headlight relay positioned on the right-hand inner wing (photos).

Rating		Circuit
8	16 amp	Headlight, dipped beam, LHS.
9	16 amp	Headlight, dipped beam, RHS.
10	16 amp	Headlight, main beam RHS. Consul GT: left-hand spot light.
11	16 amp	Headlight, main beam LHS. Consul GT: right-hand spot light.

Before any fuse that has blown is renewed, it is important to find the cause of the trouble and for it to be rectified, as a fuse acts as a safety device and protects the electrical equipment against expensive damage should a fault occur.

See overleaf for 'Fault diagnosis – electrical system'

Chapter 10 Electrical system

76 Fault diagnosis – electrical system

Symptom	Reason/s	Remedy
Horn emits intermittent or unsatisfactory noise	Cable connections loose	Check and tighten all connections
Lights do not come on	If engine not running, battery discharged	Push/start car (not automatics) charge battery
	Light bulb filament burnt out or bulbs broken	Test bulbs in live bulb holder
	Wire connections loose, disconnected or broken	Check all connections for tightness and wire cable for breaks
	Light switch shorting or otherwise faulty	By-pass light switch to ascertain if fault is in switch and fit new switch as appropriate
Lights come on but fade out	If engine not running battery discharged	Push/start car and charge battery (not automatics)
Lights give very poor illumination	Lamp glasses dirty	Clean glasses
	Reflector tarnished or dirty	Fit new reflectors
	Lamps badly out of adjustment	Adjust lamps correctly
	Incorrect bulb with too low wattage fitted	Remove bulb and replace with correct grade
	Existing bulbs old and badly discoloured	Renew bulb unit
	Electrical wiring too thin not allowing full current to pass	Re-wire lighting system
Lights work erratically – flashing on and off, especially over bumps	Battery terminals or earth connections loose	Tighten battery terminals and earth connection
	Lights not earthing properly	Examine and rectify
	Contacts in light switch faulty	By-pass light switch to ascertain if fault is in switch and fit new switch as appropriate
Wiper motor fails to work	Blown fuse	Check and renew fuse if necessary
	Wire connections loose, disconnected or broken	Check wiper wiring. Tighten loose connections
	Brushes badly worn	Remove and fit new brushes
	Armature worn or faulty	If electricity at wiper motor, remove and overhaul and fit new armature
	Field coils faulty	Purchase reconditioned wiper motor
Wiper motor works very slowly and takes excessive current	Commutator dirty, greasy or burnt	Clean commutator thoroughly
	Drive to wheelboxes too bent or unlubricated	Examine drive and straighten out severe curvature. Lubricate
	Wheelbox spindle binding or damaged	Remove, overhaul or fit new spindle
	Armature bearings dry or unaligned	Replace with new bearings correctly aligned
	Armature badly worn or faulty	Remove, overhaul, or fit new armature
Wiper motor works slowly and takes little current	Brushes badly worn	Remove and fit new brushes
	Commutator dirty, greasy or burnt	Clean commutator thoroughly
	Armature badly worn or faulty	Remove and overhaul or fit new armature
Wiper motor works but wiper blades remain static	Driving cable rack disengaged or faulty	Examine and if faulty, renew
	Wheelbox gear and spindle damaged or worn	Examine and if faulty, renew
	Wiper motor gearbox parts badly worn	Overhaul or fit new gearbox
Starter motor fails to turn engine	Battery discharged	Charge battery
	Battery defective internally	Fit new battery
	Battery terminal leads loose or earth lead not securely attached to body	Check and tighten leads
	Loose or broken connections in starter motor circuit	Check all connections and tighten any that are loose
	Starter motor switch or solenoid faulty	Test and replace faulty components with new
	Starter motor pinion jammed in mesh with flywheel gear ring	Disengage pinion by turning squared end of armature shaft
	Starter brushes badly worn, sticking, or brush wires loose	Examine brushes, renew as necessary, tighten down brush wires
	Commutator dirty, worn or burnt	Clean commutator, recut if badly burnt
	Starter motor armature faulty	Overhaul starter motor, fit new armature
	Field coils earthed	Overhaul starter motor
Starter motor turns engine very slowly	Battery in discharged condition	Charge battery
	Starter brushes badly worn, sticking, or brush wires loose	Examine brushes, replace as necessary, tighten down brush wires
	Loose wires in starter motor circuit	Check wiring and tighten as necessary

Chapter 10 Electrical system

Symptom	Reason/s	Remedy
Starter motor operates without turning engine	Starter motor pinion sticking on the screwed sleeve	Remove starter motor, clean starter motor drive
	Pinion or flywheel gear teeth broken or worn	Fit new gear to flywheel, and new pinion to starter motor drive
Starter motor noisy or excessively rough engagement	Pinion or flywheel gear teeth broken or worn	Fit new gear teeth to flywheel, or new pinion to starter motor drive
	Starter drive main spring broken	Dismantle and fit new main spring
	Starter motor retaining bolts loose	Tighten starter motor securing bolts. Fit new spring washer if necessary
Battery will not hold charge for more than a few days	Battery defective internally	Removal and fit new battery
	Electrolyte level too low or electrolyte too weak due to leakage	Top up electrolyte level to just above plates Repair leak
	Plate separators no longer fully effective	Remove and fit new battery
	Battery plates severely sulphated	Remove and fit new battery
	Fan/alternator belt slipping	Check belt for wear, renew if necessary, and tighten
	Battery terminal connections loose or corroded	Check terminals for tightness, and remove all corrosion
	Alternator not charging properly	Take car to specialist
	Short in lighting circuit causing continual battery drain	Trace and rectify
	Regulator unit not working correctly	Take car to specialist
Ignition light fails to go out, battery runs flat in a few days	Fan belt loose and slipping or broken	Check, renew and tighten as necessary
	Alternator faulty	Take car to specialist

Failure of individual electrical equipment to function correctly is dealt with alphabetically, item by item, under the headings listed below

Symptom	Reason/s	Remedy
Fuel gauge gives no reading	Fuel tank empty!	Fill fuel tank
	Electric cable between tank sender unit and gauge earthed or loose	Check cable for earthing and joints for tightness
	Fuel gauge case not earthed	Ensure case is well earthed
	Fuel gauge supply cable interrupted	Check and renew cable if necessary
	Fuel gauge unit broken	Renew fuel gauge
Fuel gauge registers full all the time	Electric cable between tank unit and gauge broken or disconnected	Check over cable and repair as necessary
Horn operates all the time	Horn push either earthed or stuck down	Disconnect battery earth. Check and rectify source of trouble
	Horn cable to horn push earthed	Disconnect battery earth. Check and rectify source of trouble
Horn fails to operate	Blown fuse	Check and renew if broken. Ascertain cause
	Cable or cable connection loose, broken or disconnected	Check all connections for tightness and cables for breaks
	Horn has an internal fault	Remove and overhaul horn

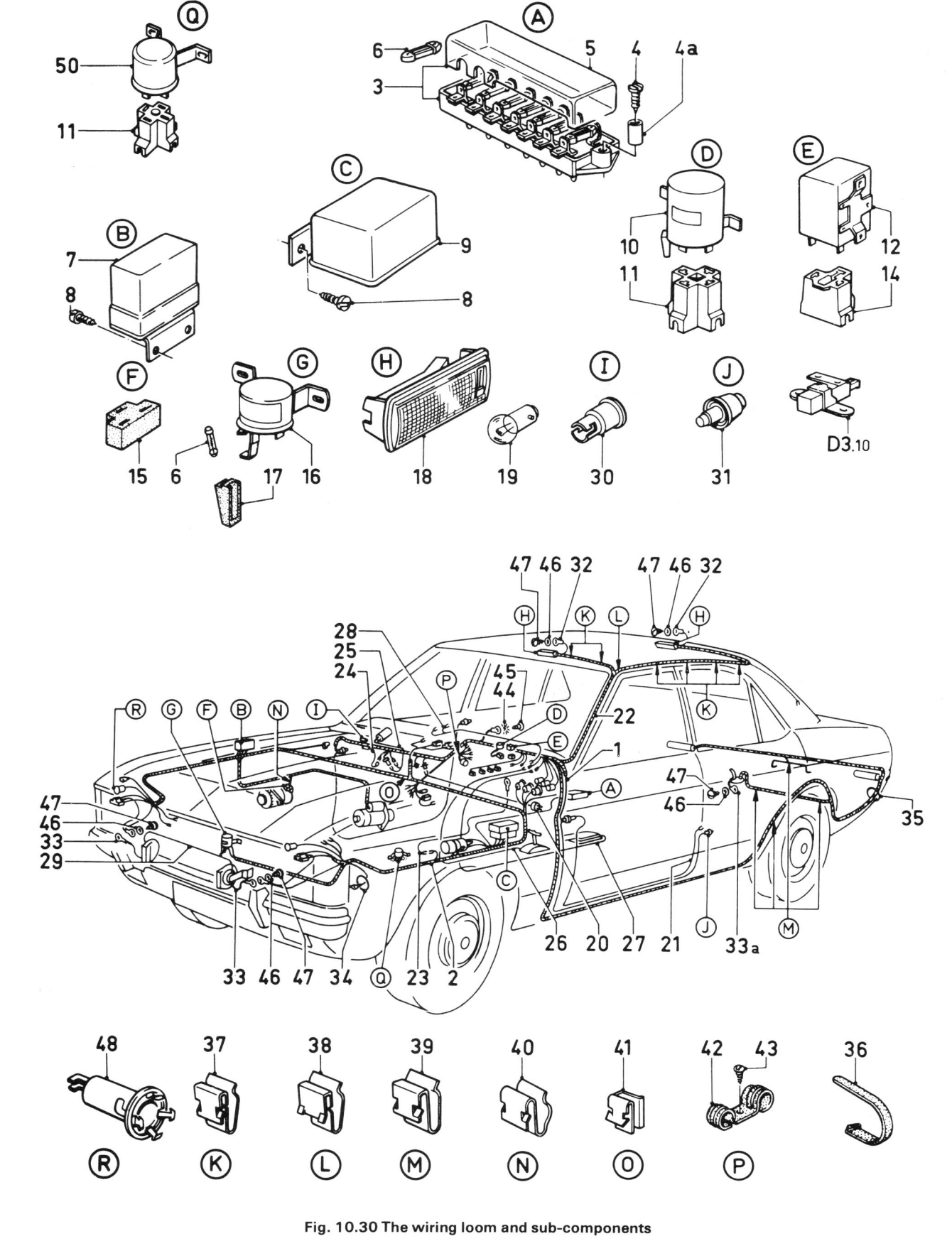

Fig. 10.30 The wiring loom and sub-components

Key to Fig. 10.30 Wiring loom and sub-components

1	Main harness	17	Cover	34	Grommet
2	Engine compartment loom	18	Interior light	35	Grommet
3	Fuse box	19	Bulb	36	Strap
4	Screw	20	Reverse light switch wiring loom	37	Clip
5	Fuse box cover	21	Rear door switch	38	Clip
5a	Cap	22	Front interior light	39	Clip
6	Fuses	23	Resistor	40	Clip
7	Voltage regulator	24	Glove compartment light	41	Clip
8	Screw	25	Clock	42	Clip
9	Headlight relay	26	Selector dial lighting	43	Screw
10	Heated rear window relay and bracket	27	Handbrake warning light	44	Lockwasher
11	4 way connector	28	Brake low pressure warning indicator	45	Screw and washer
12	Flasher unit	29	Twin horn	46	Lockwasher
13	Flasher unit bracket	30	Socket	47	Screw
14	3 way connector	31	Interior light door switch	48	Light socket
15	3 way connector housing	32	Earth cable	50	Starter motor relay
16	Horn relay	33	Earth cable		

Note: Letters indicate position of components on outline of car

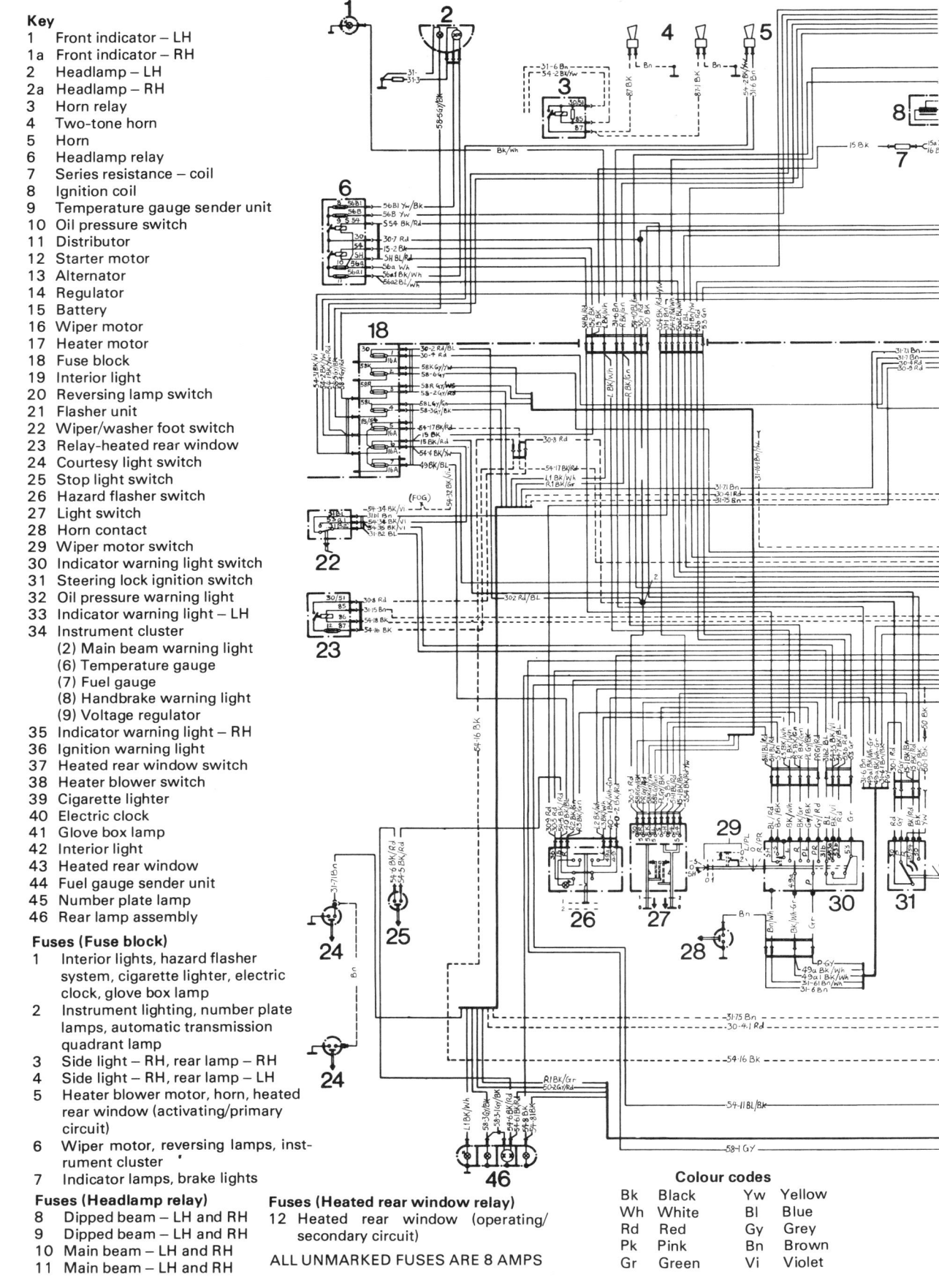

Key

1 Front indicator – LH
1a Front indicator – RH
2 Headlamp – LH
2a Headlamp – RH
3 Horn relay
4 Two-tone horn
5 Horn
6 Headlamp relay
7 Series resistance – coil
8 Ignition coil
9 Temperature gauge sender unit
10 Oil pressure switch
11 Distributor
12 Starter motor
13 Alternator
14 Regulator
15 Battery
16 Wiper motor
17 Heater motor
18 Fuse block
19 Interior light
20 Reversing lamp switch
21 Flasher unit
22 Wiper/washer foot switch
23 Relay-heated rear window
24 Courtesy light switch
25 Stop light switch
26 Hazard flasher switch
27 Light switch
28 Horn contact
29 Wiper motor switch
30 Indicator warning light switch
31 Steering lock ignition switch
32 Oil pressure warning light
33 Indicator warning light – LH
34 Instrument cluster
  (2) Main beam warning light
  (6) Temperature gauge
  (7) Fuel gauge
  (8) Handbrake warning light
  (9) Voltage regulator
35 Indicator warning light – RH
36 Ignition warning light
37 Heated rear window switch
38 Heater blower switch
39 Cigarette lighter
40 Electric clock
41 Glove box lamp
42 Interior light
43 Heated rear window
44 Fuel gauge sender unit
45 Number plate lamp
46 Rear lamp assembly

Fuses (Fuse block)

1 Interior lights, hazard flasher system, cigarette lighter, electric clock, glove box lamp
2 Instrument lighting, number plate lamps, automatic transmission quadrant lamp
3 Side light – RH, rear lamp – RH
4 Side light – RH, rear lamp – LH
5 Heater blower motor, horn, heated rear window (activating/primary circuit)
6 Wiper motor, reversing lamps, instrument cluster
7 Indicator lamps, brake lights

Fuses (Headlamp relay)

8 Dipped beam – LH and RH
9 Dipped beam – LH and RH
10 Main beam – LH and RH
11 Main beam – LH and RH

Fuses (Heated rear window relay)

12 Heated rear window (operating/secondary circuit)

ALL UNMARKED FUSES ARE 8 AMPS

Colour codes

Bk	Black	Yw	Yellow
Wh	White	Bl	Blue
Rd	Red	Gy	Grey
Pk	Pink	Bn	Brown
Gr	Green	Vi	Violet

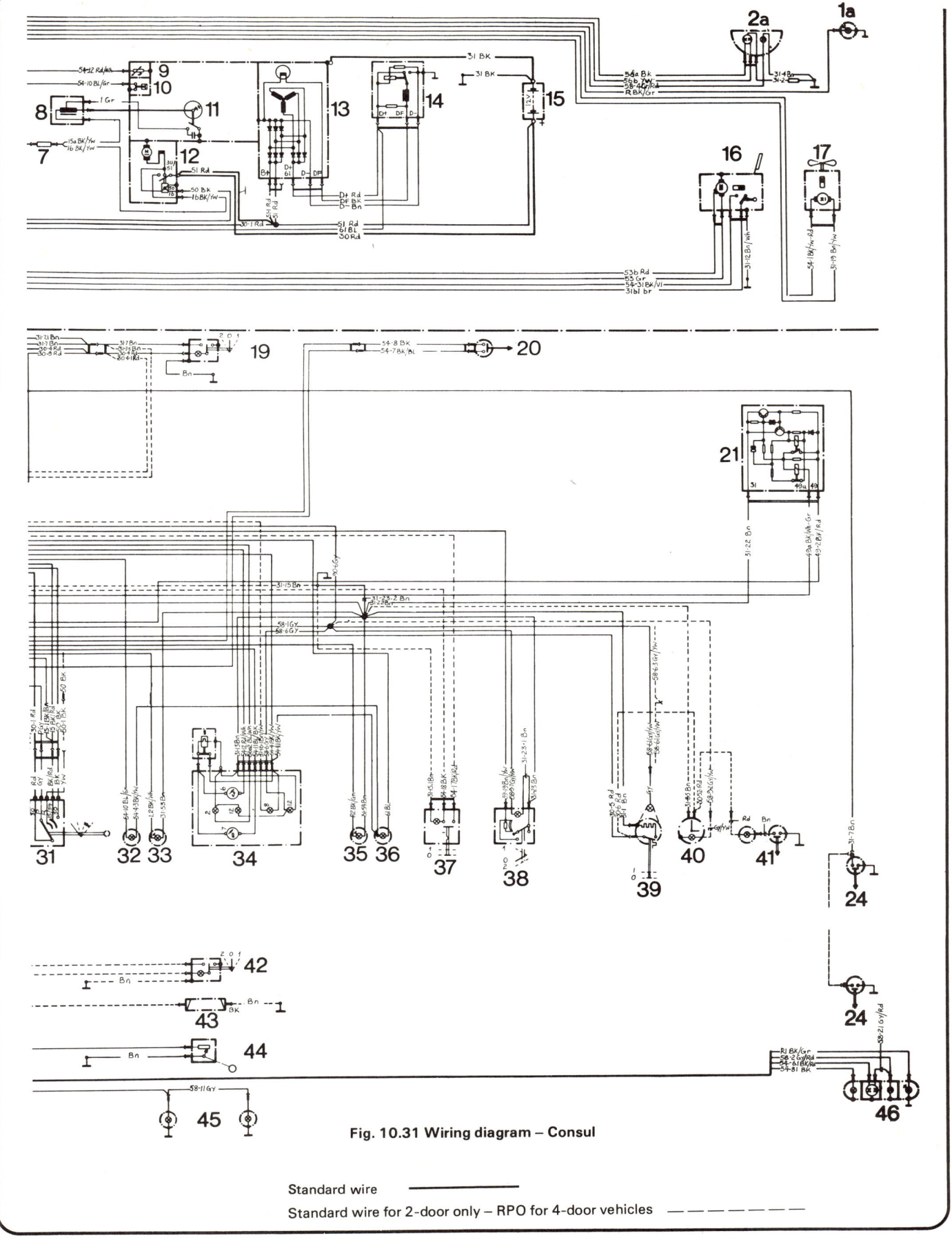

Fig. 10.31 Wiring diagram – Consul

Standard wire ————
Standard wire for 2-door only – RPO for 4-door vehicles ----

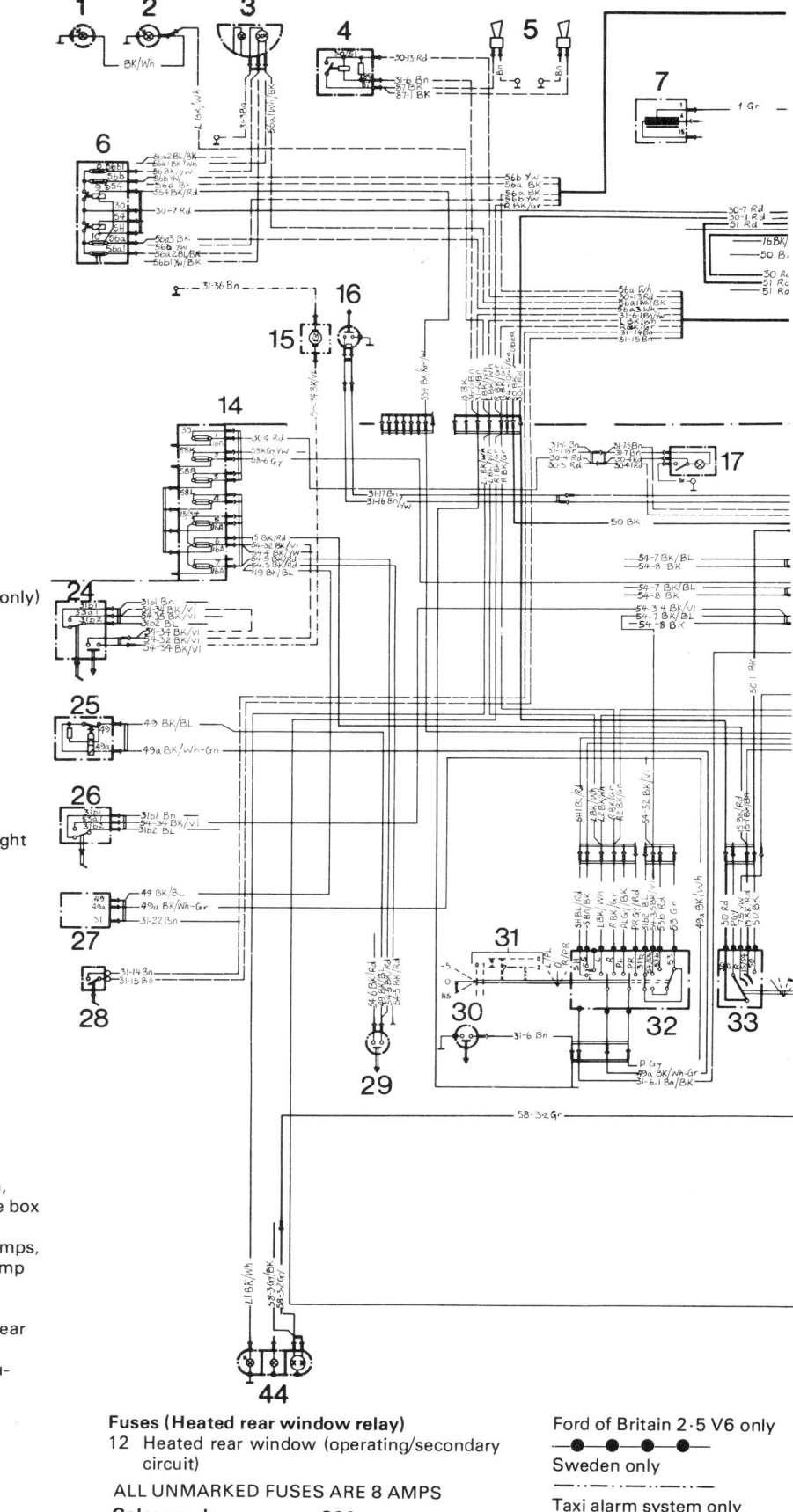

Key
- 1 Front side repeater lamp – LH
- 1a Front side repeater lamp – RH
- 2 Front indicator – LH
- 2a Front indicator – RH
- 3 Headlamp – LH
- 3a Headlamp – RH
- 4 Horn relay
- 5 Two-tone horn
- 6 Headlamp relay
- 7 Ignition coil
- 8 Temperature gauge sender unit
- 9 Oil pressure sender unit
- 10 Distributor
- 11 Starter motor
- 12 Alternator
- 13 Battery
- 14 Fuse block
- 15 Windshield washer motor
- 16 Dual braking system warning light
- 17 Interior light
- 18 Starter solenoid
- 19 Starter motor (FOB)
- 20 Inhibitor switch (auto trans)
- 21 Reversing lamp switch
- 22 Alarm stop switch (Taxi RPO)
- 23 Alarm relay (Taxi RPO)
- 24 Wiper/washer foot switch (Sweden only)
- 25 Flasher unit (FOB)
- 26 Wiper/washer foot switch (FOB)
- 27 Flasher unit
- 28 Alarm switch (Taxi RPO)
- 29 Stop light switch
- 30 Horn contact
- 31 Wiper motor switch
- 32 Direction indicator lamp switch
- 33 Steering lock/ignition switch
- 34 Light switch
- 35 Instrument cluster
    - (2) Headlamp main beam warning light
    - (6) Temperature gauge
    - (7) Fuel gauge
    - (8) Handbrake warning light
    - (9) Voltage regulator
    - (12) Instrument lights
- 36 Map reading light switch
- 37 Brake warning light switch
- 38 Estate car load floor lamp
- 39 Quadrant lamp (auto trans)
- 40 Map reading light
- 41 Side marker lamps
- 42 Radio
- 43 Number plate lamp
- 44 Rear lamp assembly

Fuses (Fuse block)
1. Interior lights, hazard flasher system, cigarette lighter, electric clock, glove box lamp
2. Instrument lighting, number plate lamps, Automatic transmission quadrant lamp
3. Side light – RH, rear lamp – RH
4. Side light – LH, rear lamp – LH
5. Heater blower motor, horn, heated rear window (activating/primary circuit)
6. Wiper motor, reversing lamps, instrument cluster
7. Indicator lamps, brake lights

Fuses (Headlamp relay)
8. Dipped beam – LH and RH
9. Dipped beam – LH and RH
10. Main beam – LH and RH
11. Main beam – LH and RH

Fuses (Heated rear window relay)
12. Heated rear window (operating/secondary circuit)

ALL UNMARKED FUSES ARE 8 AMPS
Colour code – see page 206

Ford of Britain 2·5 V6 only
●-●-●-●
Sweden only
Taxi alarm system only
Italy only

Standard wire ─────

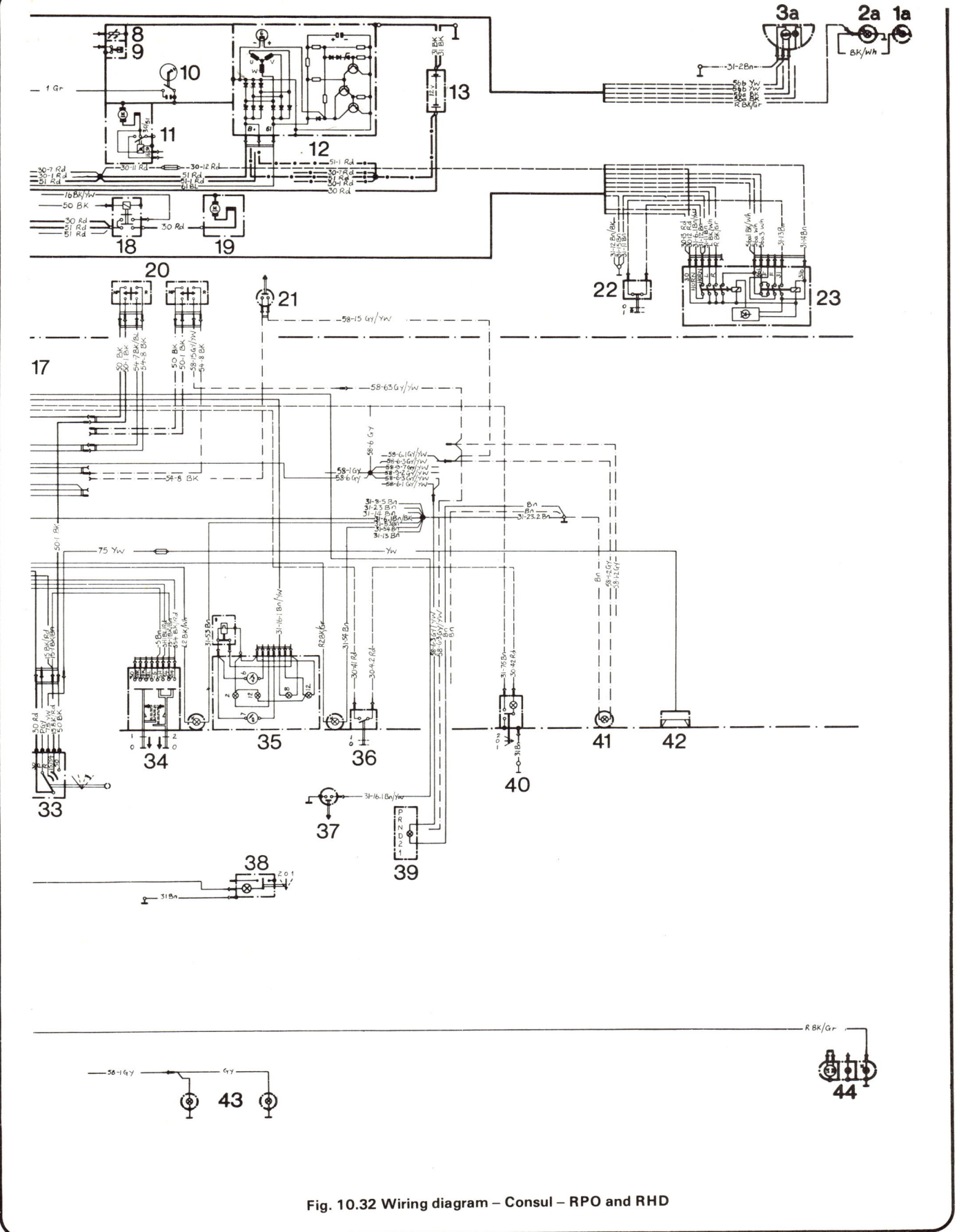

Fig. 10.32 Wiring diagram – Consul – RPO and RHD

Key

1 Front indicator – LH
1a Front indicator – RH
2 Headlamp – LH
2a Headlamp – RH
3 Fog lamp – LH
3a Fog lamp – RH
4 Two-tone horn
5 Headlamp relay
6 Horn relay
7 Ignition coil
8 Temperature gauge sender unit
9 Distributor
10 Alternator
11 Regulator
12 Battery
13 Series resistance – ignition coil
14 Starter motor
15 Wiper motor
16 Heater blower motor
17 Fuse block
18 Dual braking system warning light
19 Inhibitor switch (auto trans)
20 Reversing lamp switch
21 Interior light
22 Flasher unit
23 Wiper/washer foot switch
24 Heated rear window relay
25 Brake light switch
26 Radio fuse (2 amp)
27 Courtesy light switch
28 Hazard light switch
29 Light switch
30 Horn contact
31 Direction indicator lamp switch
32 Wiper motor switch
33 Steering lock/ignition switch
34 Interior light
35 Instrument light switch
36 Instrument cluster
 (1) Indicator warning light
 (2) Main beam warning light
 (3) Ignition warning light
 (6) Temperature gauge
 (7) Fuel gauge
 (8) Brake warning light
 (9) Voltage regulator
 (10) Ammeter
 (11) Tachometer
 (12) Instrument lights
37 Heated rear window switch
38 Fog lamp switch
39 Heater motor switch
40 Radio
41 Cigarette lighter
42 Clock
43 Glove compartment lamp switch
44 Glove compartment lamp
45 Heated rear window
46 Handbrake warning light switch
47 Quadrant lamp (auto trans)
48 Temperature gauge sender unit
49 Number plate lamp
50 Rear lamp assembly

Fuses (Fuse block)

1 Interior lights, hazard flasher system, cigarette lighter, electric clock, glove box lamp
2 Instrument lighting, number plate lamps, automatic transmission quadrant lamp
3 Side light – RH, rear lamp – RH
4 Side light – LH, rear lamp – LH
5 Heater blower motor, horn, heated rear window (activating/primary circuit)
6 Wiper motor, reversing lamps, instrument cluster
7 Indicator lamps, brake lights

Fuses (Headlamp relay)

8 Dipped beam – LH and RH

8.1 Dipped beam – LH and RH
9 Main beam – LH and RH
9.1 Main beam – LH and RH

Fuses (Heated rear window relay)

10 Heated rear window (operating/ secondary circuit)

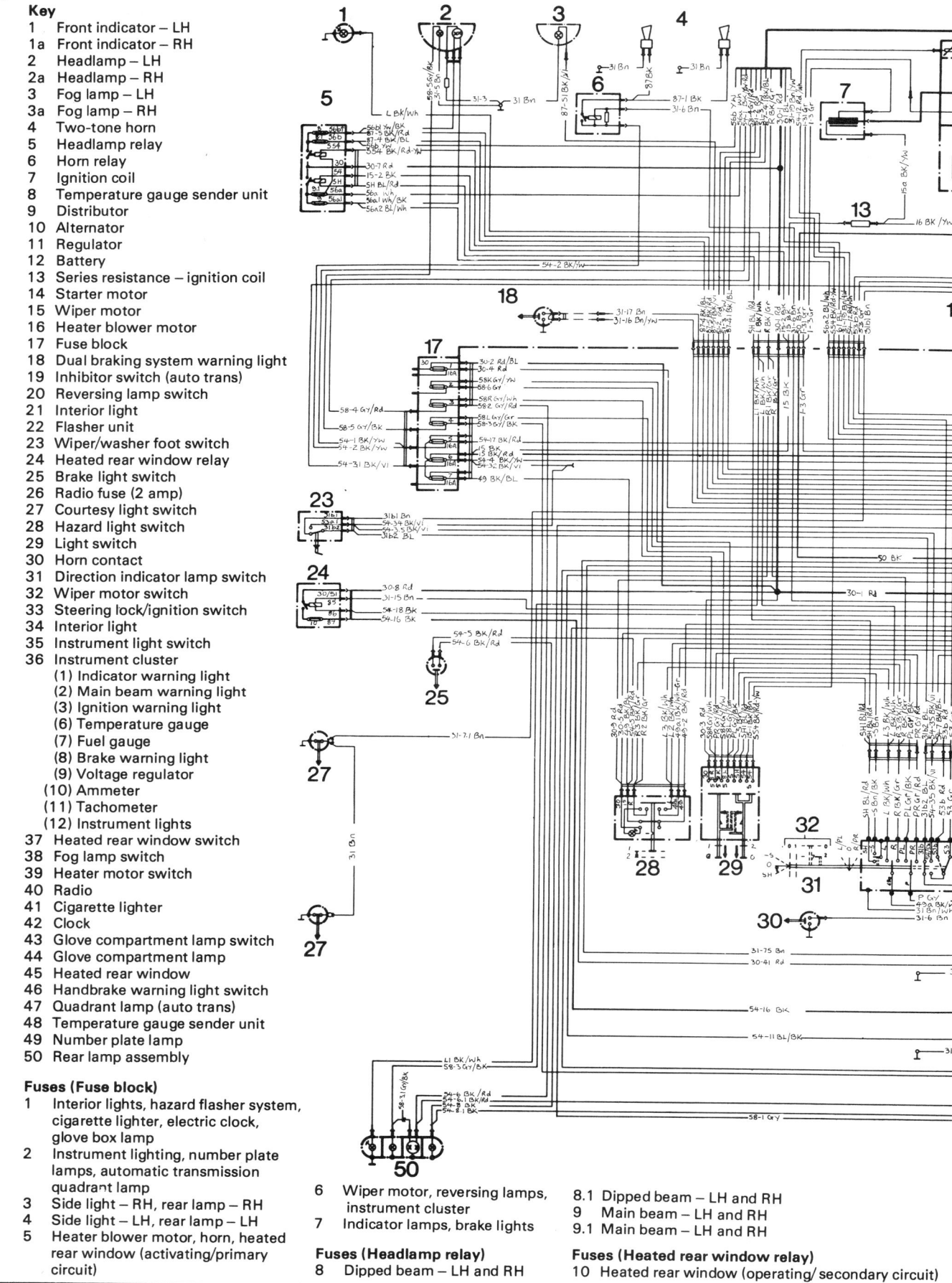

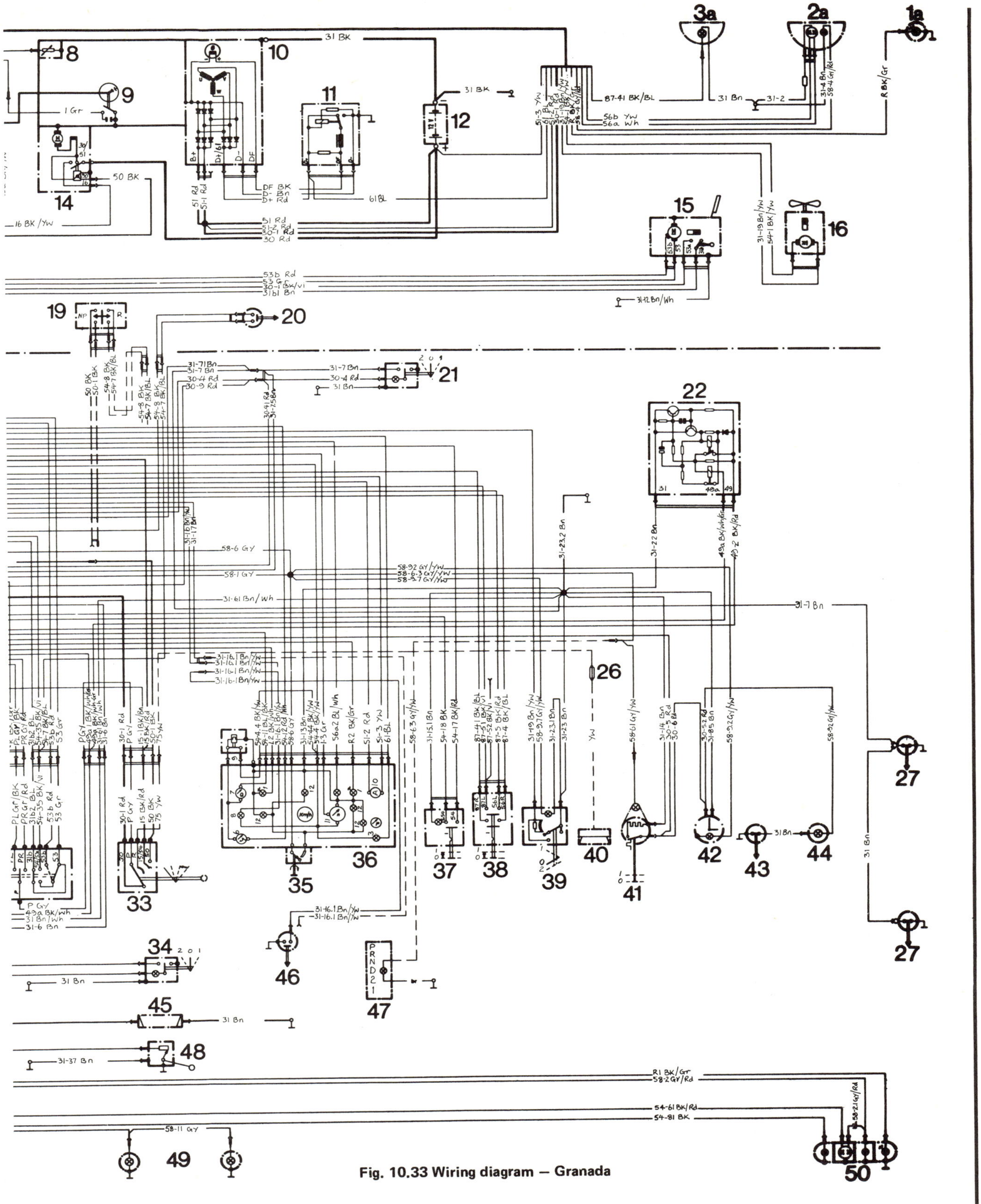

Fig. 10.33 Wiring diagram – Granada

ALL UNMARKED FUSES ARE 8 AMPS

Colour code – see page 206

Standard wire ———

Standard wire for GXL only — — —

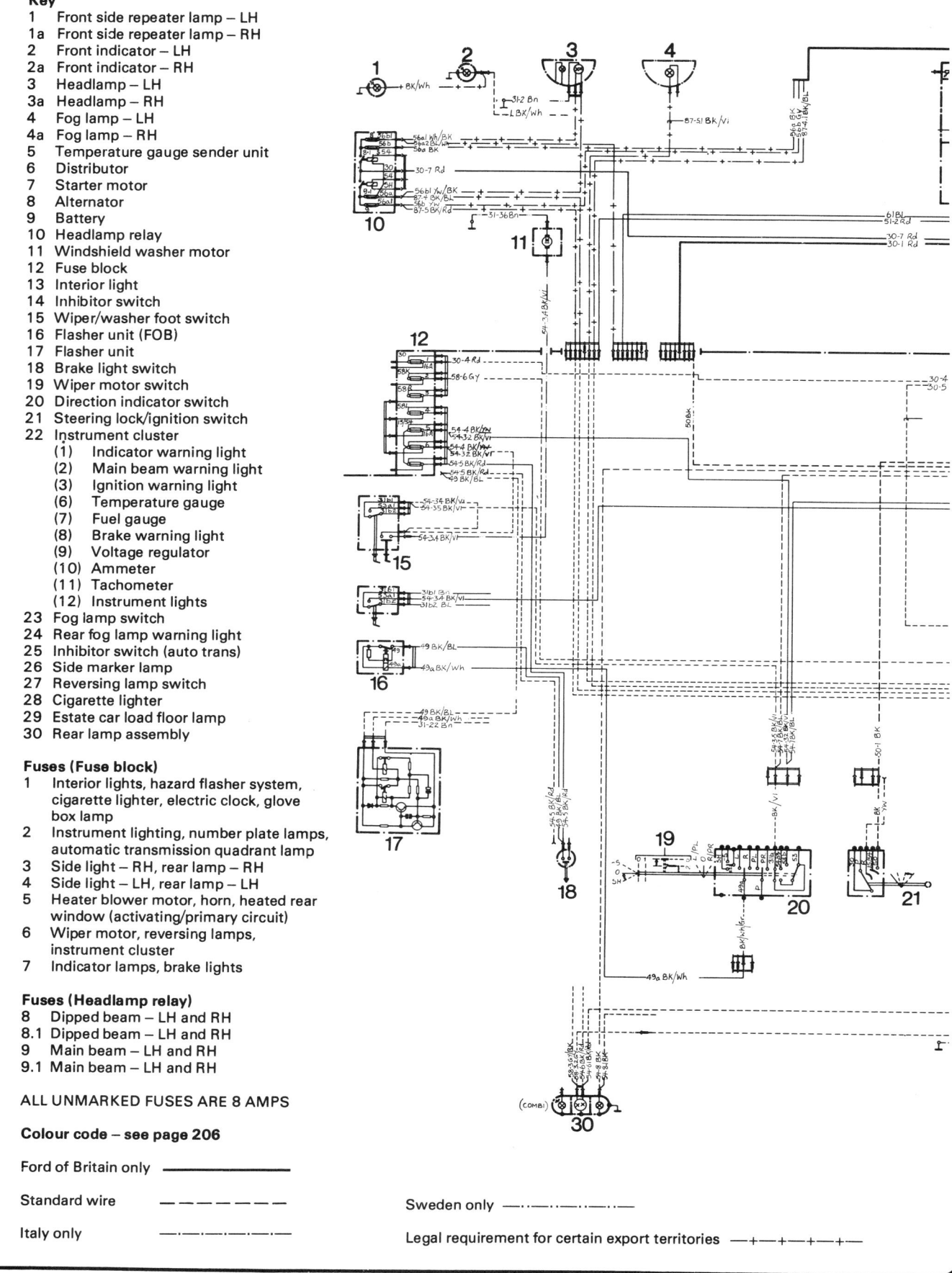

Key

1. Front side repeater lamp – LH
1a. Front side repeater lamp – RH
2. Front indicator – LH
2a. Front indicator – RH
3. Headlamp – LH
3a. Headlamp – RH
4. Fog lamp – LH
4a. Fog lamp – RH
5. Temperature gauge sender unit
6. Distributor
7. Starter motor
8. Alternator
9. Battery
10. Headlamp relay
11. Windshield washer motor
12. Fuse block
13. Interior light
14. Inhibitor switch
15. Wiper/washer foot switch
16. Flasher unit (FOB)
17. Flasher unit
18. Brake light switch
19. Wiper motor switch
20. Direction indicator switch
21. Steering lock/ignition switch
22. Instrument cluster
  (1) Indicator warning light
  (2) Main beam warning light
  (3) Ignition warning light
  (6) Temperature gauge
  (7) Fuel gauge
  (8) Brake warning light
  (9) Voltage regulator
  (10) Ammeter
  (11) Tachometer
  (12) Instrument lights
23. Fog lamp switch
24. Rear fog lamp warning light
25. Inhibitor switch (auto trans)
26. Side marker lamp
27. Reversing lamp switch
28. Cigarette lighter
29. Estate car load floor lamp
30. Rear lamp assembly

Fuses (Fuse block)

1. Interior lights, hazard flasher system, cigarette lighter, electric clock, glove box lamp
2. Instrument lighting, number plate lamps, automatic transmission quadrant lamp
3. Side light – RH, rear lamp – RH
4. Side light – LH, rear lamp – LH
5. Heater blower motor, horn, heated rear window (activating/primary circuit)
6. Wiper motor, reversing lamps, instrument cluster
7. Indicator lamps, brake lights

Fuses (Headlamp relay)

8. Dipped beam – LH and RH
8.1. Dipped beam – LH and RH
9. Main beam – LH and RH
9.1. Main beam – LH and RH

ALL UNMARKED FUSES ARE 8 AMPS

Colour code – see page 206

Ford of Britain only ——————

Standard wire — — — — —

Italy only —··—··—··—

Sweden only —·—·—·—

Legal requirement for certain export territories —+—+—+—

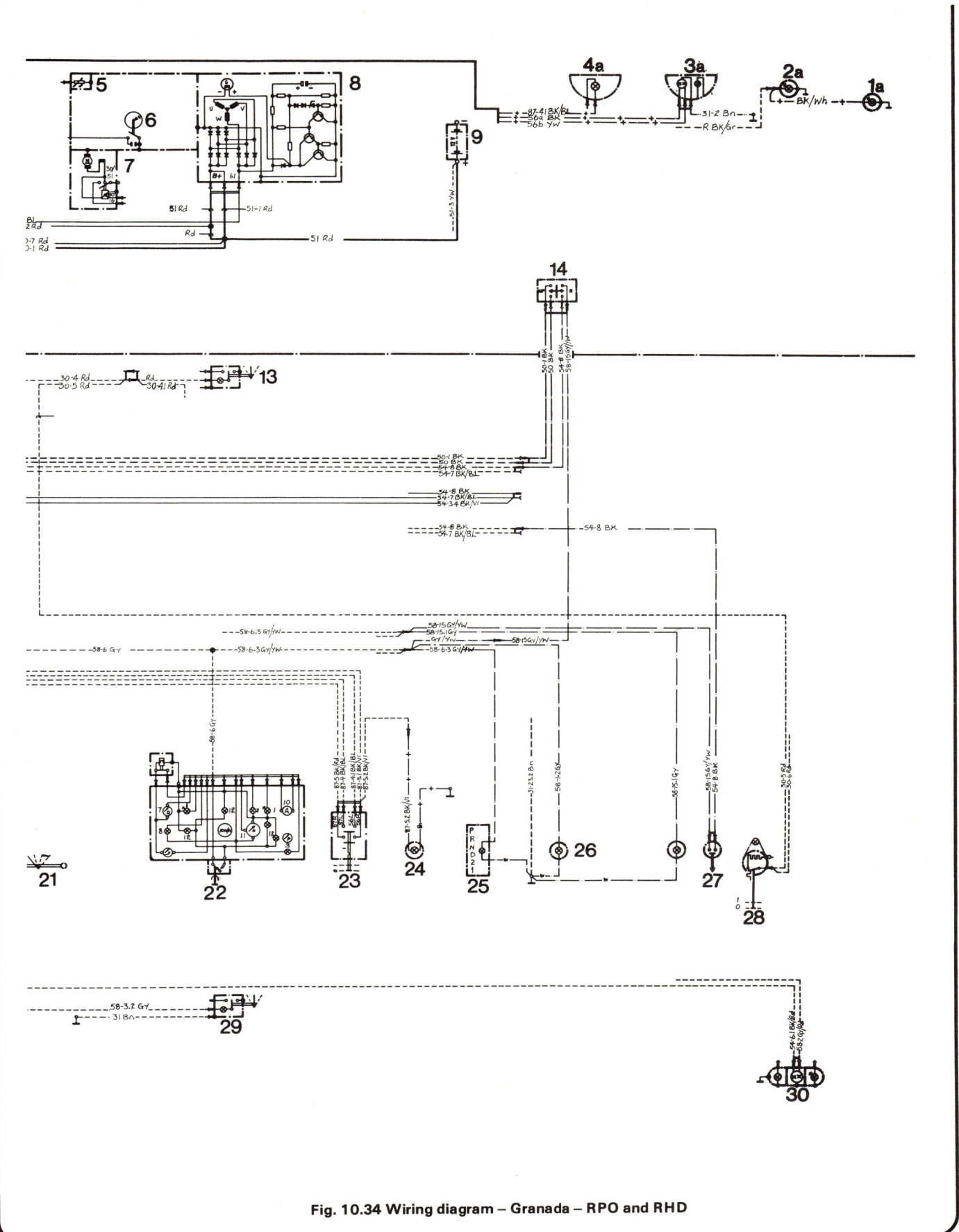

Fig. 10.34 Wiring diagram – Granada – RPO and RHD

214

Key

1. Front indicator – LH
1a. Front indicator – RH
2. Headlamp – LH
2a. Headlamp – RH
3. Auxiliary lamp – LH
3a. Auxiliary lamp – RH
4. Headlamp relay
5. Horn relay
6. Two-tone horn
7. Ignition coil
8. Series resistance – coil
9. Temperature gauge sender unit
10. Distributor
11. Starter motor
12. Alternator
13. Regulator
14. Battery
15. Wiper motor
16. Heater motor
17. Fuse block
18. Handbrake warning light switch
19. Interior light
20. Flasher unit
21. Wiper/washer foot switch
22. Heated rear window relay
23. Courtesy light switch
24. Brake light switch
25. Hazard light switch
26. Light switch
27. Wiper motor switch
28. Horn contact
29. Direction indicator switch
30. Steering lock/ignition switch
31. Instrument cluster
    (1) Indicator warning light
    (2) Main beam warning light
    (3) Ignition warning light
    (6) Temperature gauge
    (7) Fuel gauge
    (8) Brake warning light
    (9) Voltage regulator
    (10) Ammeter
    (11) Tachometer
    (12) Instrument lights
32. Heated rear window switch
33. Heater motor switch
34. Reversing light switch
35. Cigarette light
36. Clock
37. Glove compartment lamp
38. Glove compartment lamp switch
39. Interior light
40. Heated rear window
41. Temperature gauge sender unit
42. Number plate lamp
43. Rear lamp assembly

Fuses (Fuse block)

1. Interior lights, hazard flasher system, cigarette lighter, electric clock, glove box lamp
2. Instrument lighting, number plate lamps, automatic transmission quadrant lamp
3. Side light – RH, rear lamp – RH
4. Side light – LH, rear lamp – LH
5. Heater blower motor, horn, heated rear window (activating/primary circuit)
6. Wiper motor, reversing lamps, instrument cluster
7. Indicator lamps, brake lights

Fuses (Headlamp relay)

8. Dipped beam – LH
9. Dipped beam – RH
10. Main beam – RH and auxiliary lamp – LH
11. Main beam – LH and auxiliary lamp – RH

Fuses (Heated rear window relay)

12. Heated rear window (operating/secondary circuit)

ALL UNMARKED FUSES ARE 8 AMPS

Colour code – see page 206

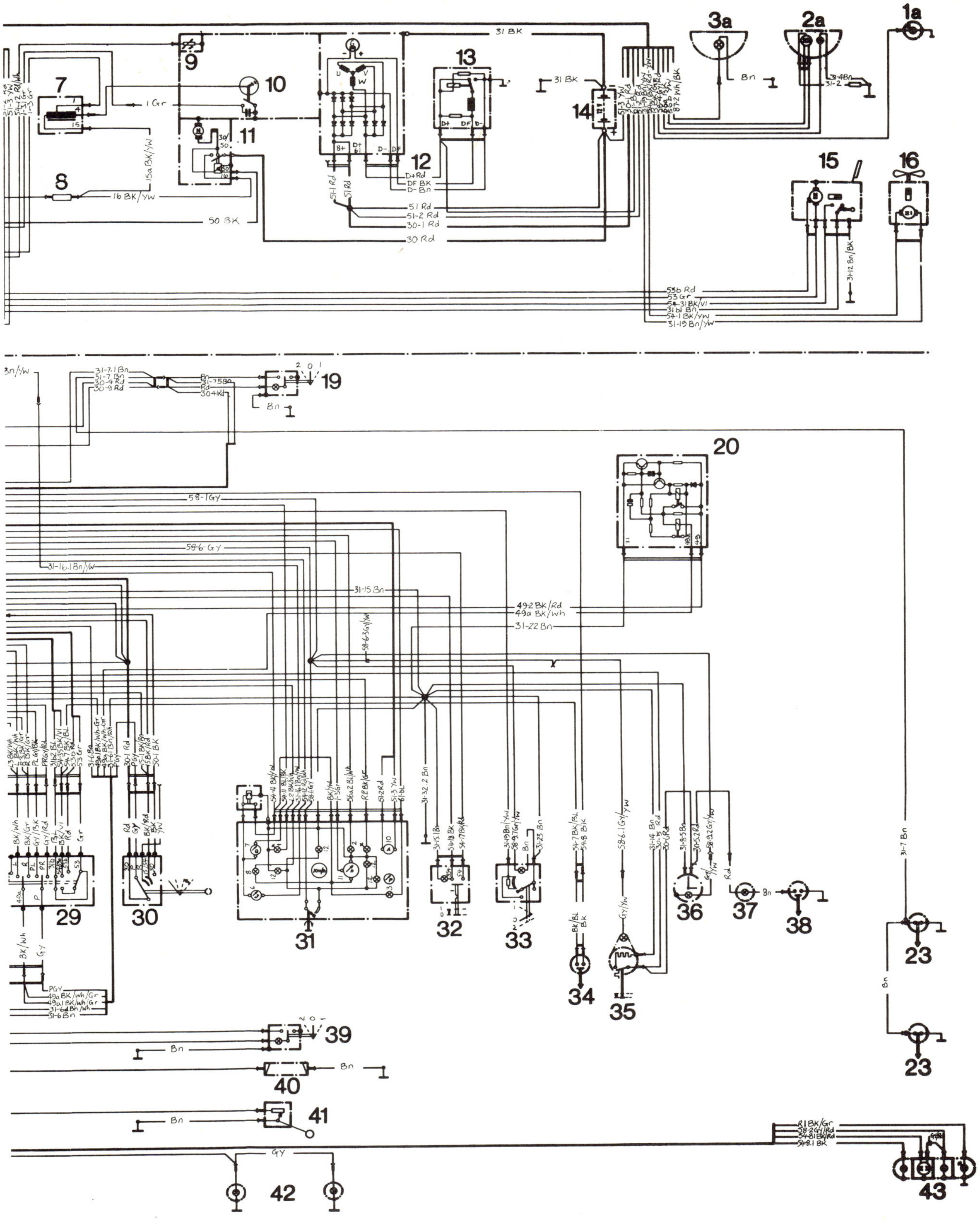

Fig. 10.35 Wiring diagram – Consul GT

Key

1. Front side repeater lamp – LH
1a. Front side repeater lamp – RH
2. Indicator lamp front – LH
2a. Indicator lamp front – RH
3. Headlamp – LH
3a. Headlamp – RH
4. Auxiliary lamp – LH
4a. Auxiliary lamp – RH
5. Headlamp relay
6. Windscreen washer motor
7. Temperature gauge sender unit
8. Distributor
9. Starter motor
10. Alternator
11. Battery
12. Fuse block
13. Handbrake warning light switch
14. Dual braking system warning light switch
15. Interior light
16. Inhibitor switch (auto trans)
17. Flasher unit
18. Wiper/washer foot switch
19. Flasher unit (FOB)
20. Brake light switch
21. Wiper motor switch
22. Direction indicator switch
23. Steering lock/ignition switch
24. Radio fuse (2 amp)
25. Radio
26. Auxiliary lamp switch
27. Instrument cluster
    (1) Indicator warning lamp
    (2) Main beam warning lamp
    (3) Ignition warning lamp
    (6) Temperature gauge
    (7) Fuel gauge
    (8) Brake warning light
    (9) Voltage regulator
    (10) Ammeter
    (11) Tachometer
    (12) Instrument lights
28. Quadrant lamp (auto trans)
29. Side marker lamp
30. Reversing lamp switch
31. Cigarette lighter
32. Rear lamp assembly

Fuses (Fuse block)

1. Interior lights, hazard flasher system, cigarette lighter, electric clock, glove box lamp
2. Instrument lighting, number plate lamps, automatic transmission quadrant lamp
3. Side light RH, rear lamp RH
4. Side light LH, rear lamp LH
5. Heater blower motor, horn, heated rear window (activating/primary circuit)
6. Wiper motor, reversing lamps, instrument cluster
7. Indicator lamps, brake lights

Fuses (Headlamp relay)

8. Dipped beam LH
9. Dipped beam RH
10. Main beam RH and auxiliary lamp LH
11. Main beam LH and auxiliary lamp RH

ALL UNMARKED FUSES ARE 8 AMPS

Colour code – see page 206

Ford of Britain only ————

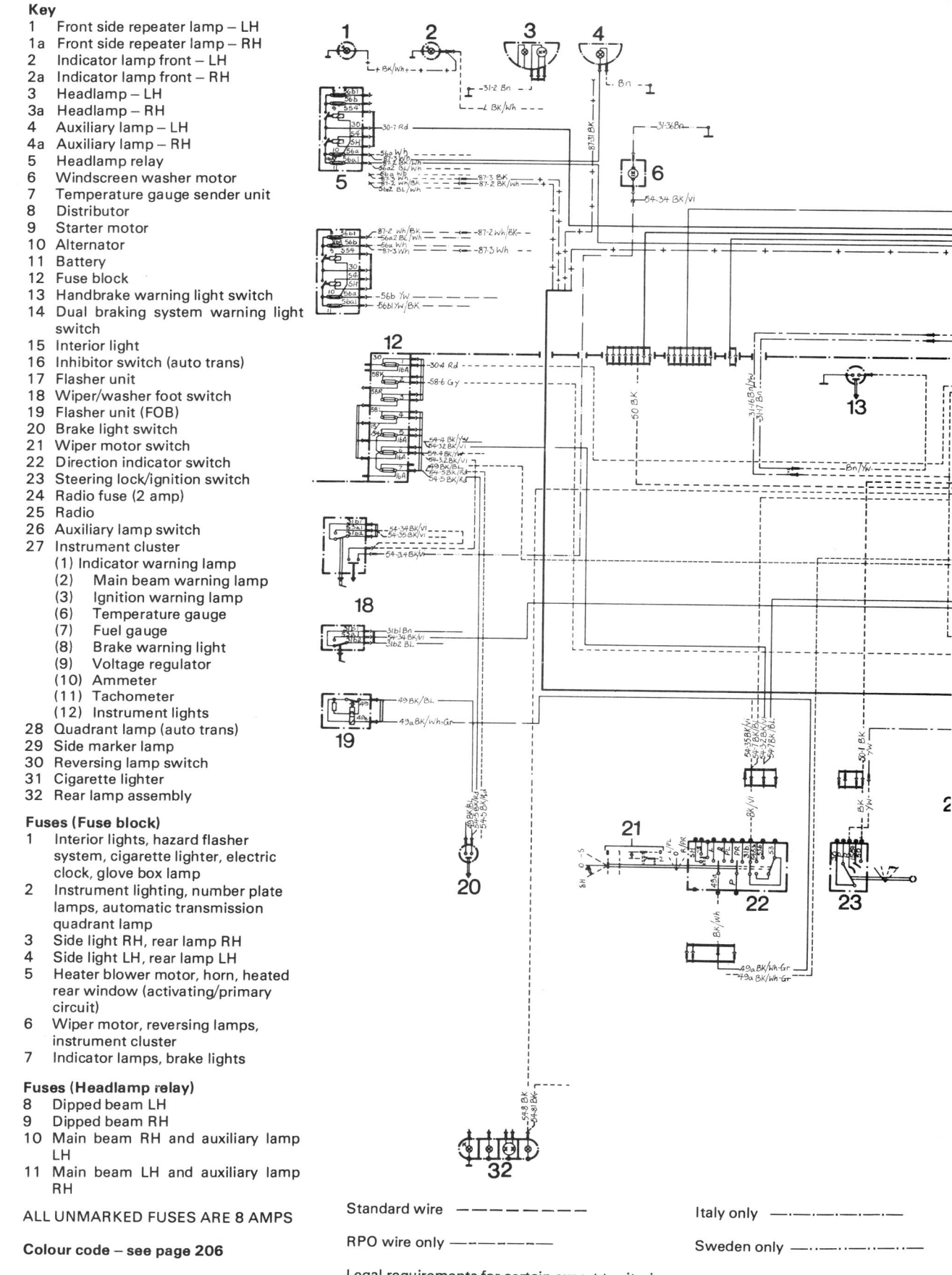

Standard wire ————
RPO wire only — — — —
Italy only — · — · —
Sweden only — · · — · · —
Legal requirements for certain export territories —+—+—+—

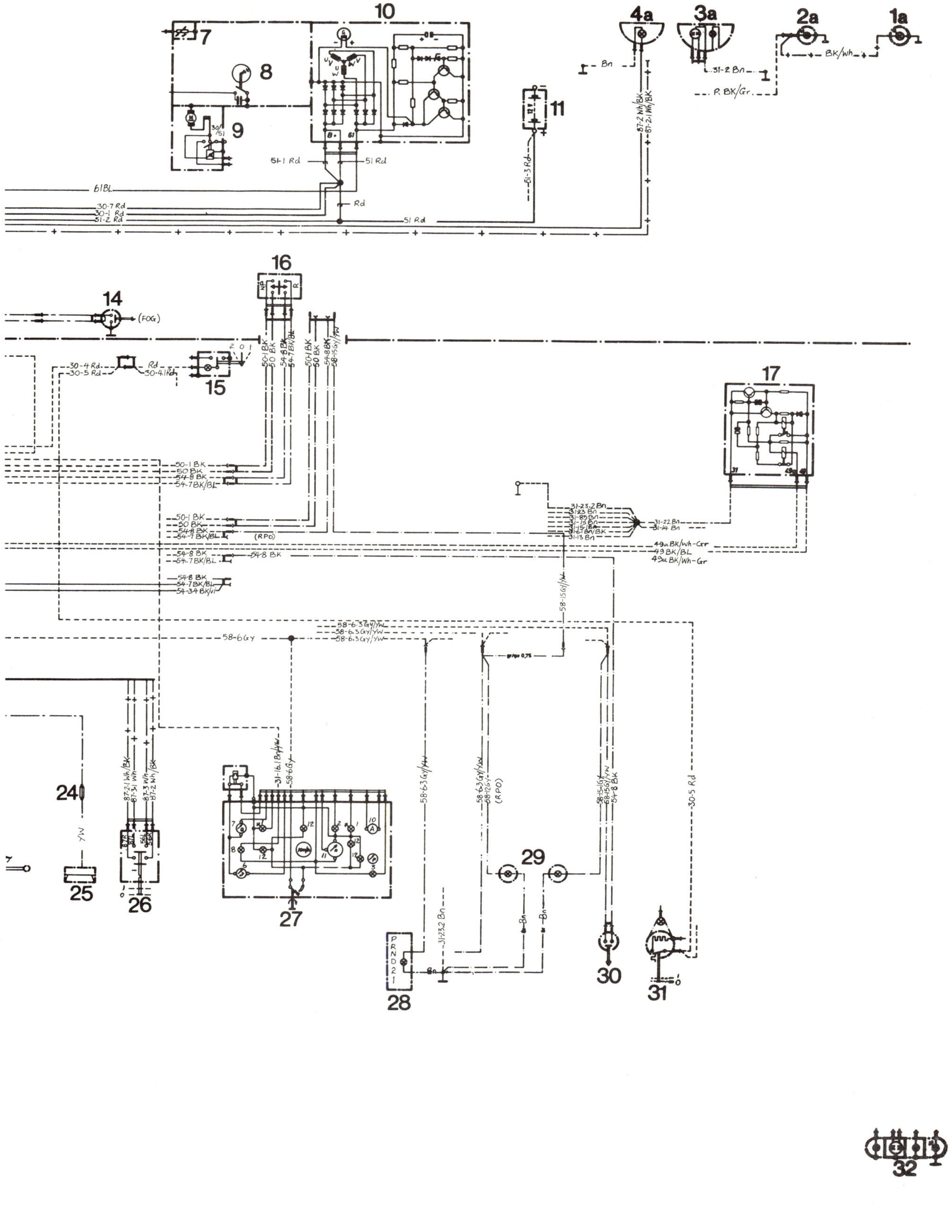

Fig. 10.36 Wiring diagram – Consul GT – RPO, RHD and Export

Chapter 11 Suspension and steering

Contents

Fault diagnosis – suspension and steering	43
Front axle assembly – overhaul	6
Front axle assembly – removal and refitting	5
Front axle mounting bushes – removal and refitting	7
Front hub bearings – adjustment	3
Front hub bearings – removal and refitting	2
Front hub – removal and refitting	4
Front shock absorbers – removal and refitting	13
Front wheel – alignment	26
General description	1
Lower suspension arm – removal and refitting	9
Power assisted steering – general	37
Power assisted steering – hydraulic fluid	38
Power assisted steering – pump drive belt adjustment	39
Power assisted steering rack and pinion – removal and refitting	41
Power assisted steering – system bleeding	42
Power assisted steering – system testing	40
Rack and pinion steering gear – adjustments	33
Rack and pinion steering gear – dismantling and reassembly	34
Rack and pinion steering gear – removal and refitting	32
Rear axle and suspension – removal and refitting	15
Rear axle half shaft – removal, overhaul and refitting	24
Rear shock absorber – removal and refitting	17
Rear suspension bump rubber – removal and refitting	21
Rear suspension coil spring – removal and refitting	16
Rear suspension front rubber insulator – removal and refitting	19
Rear suspension lower arm – removal and refitting	18
Rear suspension rear rubber insulator – removal and refitting	20
Rear suspension stub axle bearing and seals – removal and refitting	23
Rear suspension stub axle – removal and refitting	22
Stabilizer bar connecting link bush – removal and refitting	12
Stabilizer bar mounting bushes – removal and refitting	11
Stabilizer bar – removal and refitting	10
Steering column assembly – removal and refitting	28
Steering column flexible coupling assembly – removal and refitting	31
Steering column flexible coupling and universal joint assembly – removal and refitting	30
Steering column shaft – removal and refitting	29
Steering – lubrication	25
Steering rack rubber gaiter – removal and refitting	35
Steering wheel – removal and refitting	27
Stub axle – removal and refitting	8
Tie bar – removal and refitting	14
Track rod end – removal and refitting	36

Specifications

Front suspension
Independent, coil spring long and short swinging arms. Double acting, hydraulic telescopic shock absorbers

Toe-in .... 0·00 to 0·25 in (0·00 to 3·9 mm)
Castor* .... 1·46' ± 45'
Camber .... 0·20' ± 30'
*Difference between each side to be no greater than 0·45'
Coil spring specification .... Due to 13 different specifications quoted by manufacturers always refer to Ford garage for latest information. Always quote car commission number and engine specification

Rear suspension
Semi trailing arms, coil springs.
Double acting hydraulic telescopic shock absorbers

Toe-in .... 0·00 to 0·085 in (0 to 2·15 mm)
Camber .... + 0·20' ± 0·45'

Wheels and tyres
Wheel size
 Standard .... 5½J X 14
 Optional .... 6J X 14
Tyre size .... Numerous options are available as standard fitment to the Consul/Granada series
Tyre pressures .... Refer to the individual tyre manufacturer's recommendations. This is most important.

Steering
Manual:
 Type .... Rack and pinion
 Steering gear adjustment .... Shims
 Turning circle .... 34 ft 5 in (10·5 m)
 Maximum turning angle – outer wheel ... 37·51'
 Lubricant capacity (dry) .... 0·35 pint (0·20 litre)

Chapter 11 Suspension and steering

Power assisted:
   Type .... Rack and pinion Servo assisted
   Hydraulic fluid capacity .... 3·87 pints (2·2 litres) or 2·58 pints (1·47 litres)*
   Fluid type .... SQ-M2C-9007-AA, ESW-M2C-33-E or F*
   pump belt tension .... 0·5 in (12 mm)

*Specification according to model. See your local Ford dealer

Torque wrench settings

	lbf ft	kgf m
Front suspension		
Wheel bearing adjustment nut	27	3·7
Tie bar to lower arm	42 – 50	5·8 – 6·9
Lower arm pivot bolt	36 – 40	5·0 – 5·5
Upper arm pivot	36 – 40	5·0 – 5·5
Rack clamp bolts	21 – 25	2·9 – 3·5
Lower arm balljoint:		
1st pass	30 – 45	4·1 – 6·2
2nd pass	42 – 66	5·8 – 9·2
Rear suspension		
Shock absorber to suspension arm	29 – 37	4·1 – 5·1
Shock absorber to underbody:		
Saloon	29 – 37	4·1 – 5·1
Estate	51 – 66	7·1 – 9·2
Crossmember centre bolt to underbody	51 – 66	7·1 – 9·2
Hanger bracket to underbody bolt	131 – 164	182 – 22·8
Suspension arm to crossmember bolt	51 – 66	7·1 – 9·2
Crossmember bracket to underbody bolt	29 – 37	4·1 – 5·1
Extension housing to crossmember bolt	51 – 66	7·1 – 9·2
Wheel bearing carrier to suspension arm bolt	29 – 37	4·1 – 5·1
Half shaft to backplate	184 – 198	25·5 – 27·5
Rear hub assembly centre nut	180 – 200	24·9 – 27·6
Steering		
Spindle to track control arm balljoint	29 – 44	4·1 – 6·2
Track rod ends to track rod locknuts	41 – 49	5·8 – 6·9
Track control arm to crossmember:		
Lower	46 – 54	6·5 – 7·5
Upper	50 – 57	7·0 – 8·0
Crossmember to chassis mounting bush	57 – 72	8·0 – 10·0
Shock absorber to lower arm	4 – 8	0·62 – 0·9
Shock absorber upper mounting	28 – 34	3·9 – 4·8
Stabiliser to track control arm link	7 – 9	1·0 – 1·25
Stabiliser to crossmember	12 – 18	1·7 – 2·4
Rack and pinion cover plate and yoke cover	12 – 18	1·7 – 2·4
Coupling to pinion spline	12 – 15	1·7 – 2·1
Steering wheel to steering shaft	25 – 29	3·5 – 4·1
Wheel nuts/bolts		
Conical face	63 – 85	8·7 – 1·7
Flat face	85 – 103	11.7 – 14.2

1 General description

The independent front suspension comprises short and long swinging arms with coil springs and hydraulic acting shock absorbers which operate on the lower swinging arms. The main suspension framework is located on the underbody side members and acts as a mounting point for the wishbone type upper and lower single swinging arms. Attached to the upper frame are rubber bump stops to absorb excessive swinging arm movement. The suspension arms are mounted on rubber bushes and carry the stub axle ball joints at their outer ends.

Located on each axle stub are two taper roller bearings and these run in cups which are pressed into the wheel hub. To keep the grease in the hub is a spring located neoprene seal located in the inner end of the hub. The wheel studs are splined and pressed into the hub flange.

Bolted to the lower arms are rubber mounted tie-bars which control the suspension castor angle. The tie bars are linked to a stabiliser bar via a bolt and spacer and bushed at its connecting points. The stabiliser bar is mounted in split bushes which are clamped to the brackets which are bolted to the front suspension assembly crossmember frame.

Besides providing a platform for the front suspension the crossmember assembly also supports the front of the engine and the rack and pinion steering gear.

The independent rear suspension is of a new design to provide good car handling and a comfortable ride. The system is of the semi-trailing arm type with coil springs. To reduce noise and vibration, the two half shafts incorporate new constant velocity sliding joints, while the whole suspension is fitted to the body on low-rate bonded rubber insulators, producing the best possible combination of axle unit location, low noise and refined handling. This independent rear suspension assembly layout eliminates the need for sliding splines and the complete suspension action helps to keep the tyre treads flat on the road surface under all motoring conditions.

There is an inbuilt adjustment device for rear wheel toe-in and this comprises a cam plate on each inner pivot bolt of the suspension arms. The rear suspension system utilises coil springs with internally mounted telescopic double acting shock absorbers and progressive rubber bump stops.

The steering gear is rack and pinion and is located on the front crossmember by two 'U' shaped clamps. The pinion is connected to the steering column by a flexible coupling. Above the flexible coupling the steering column is split by a universal joint designed to collapse on impact, thus minimizing injury to the driver in the event of an accident. Additionally the steering column incorporates a convoluted tube type of impact absorber forming the outer jacket of the column assembly. The lower end of this assembly is supported by a steel plate and a grommet fitted to the body dash lower panel. The top end is welded to the column support bracket which is bolted to the pedal bracket by three Deirin filled retainers which shear in collision, allowing the convoluted tube to absorb the impact energy. The telescopic steering shaft assembly has a tubular lower part and a solid shaft top

Chapter 11 Suspension and steering

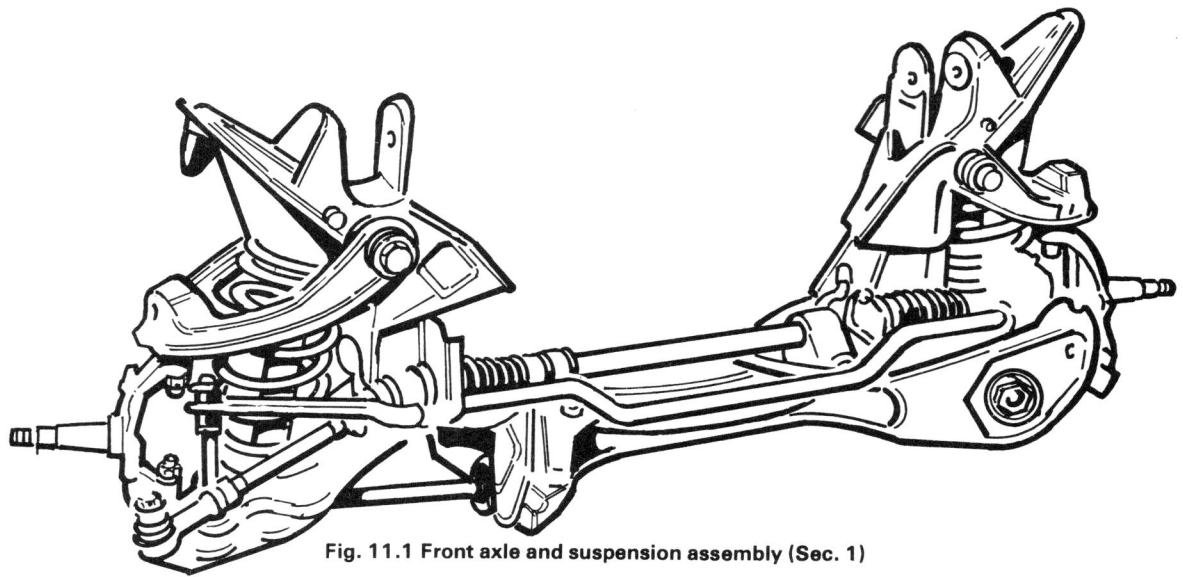

Fig. 11.1 Front axle and suspension assembly (Sec. 1)

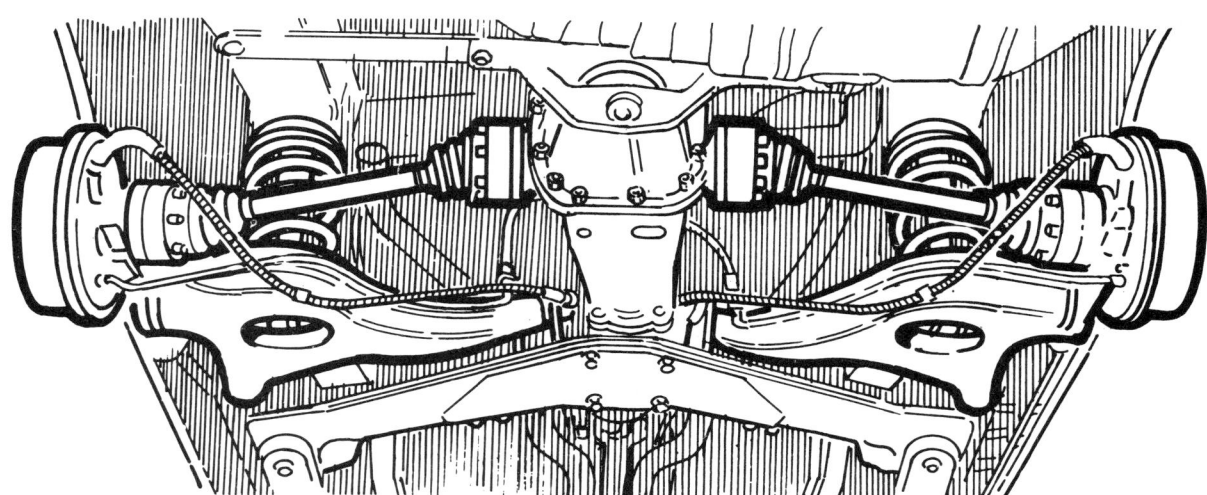

Fig. 11.2 Rear suspension and halfshafts (Sec. 1)

part joined by Deirin filling, which also shears under impact.

Turning the steering wheel causes the rack to move in a lateral direction and the track rods attached to either end of the rack pass this movement to the steering arms on the stub axle assemblies thereby moving the road wheels.

Two adjustments are possible on the steering gear, namely rack slipper bearing adjustment and pinion bearing pre-load adjustment, but the steering gear must be removed from the car to carry out these adjustments which are made by varying the thickness of the shim packs.

The two track rods are adjustable in length to allow adjustment of the toe-in setting, and make sure the wheel lock angles are correct. Lock stops in to the steering gear and are not adjustable.

Where power assisted steering is fitted steering effort is reduced by using pressure on a ram. This will provide good road feel under all motoring conditions. The steering rack is enclosed by a tube acting as the power cylinder and the rack incorporates a double acting piston, which is energised by fluid fed to either side by tubes from a spool valve. This valve, which is located in the pinion housing, is operated by helical grooves in the pinion assembly, which also includes a torsion bar to give graduated power assistance and good steering feel.

In the event of failure of the hydraulic system the steering can still be operated but more effort will be required.

A tongue in slot type steering lock is fitted to the right-hand side of the steering column and is operated by the ignition switch key.

2 Front hub bearings – removal and refitting

1 Refer to Chapter 9 and remove the disc brake caliper.
2 By judicious tapping and levering remove the dust cap from the centre of the hub.
3 Remove the split pin from the nut retainer and lift away the adjusting nut retainer.
4 Unscrew the adjusting nut and lift away the thrust washer and outer tapered bearing.
5 Pull off the complete hub and disc assembly from the stub axle.
6 From the back of the hub assembly carefully prise out the grease seal noting which way round it is fitted as shown in Fig. 11.3. Lift away the inner tapered bearing.
7 Carefully clean out the hub and wash the bearings with petrol, making sure that no oil or grease is allowed to get onto the brake disc.
8 Using a soft metal drift carefully remove the inner and outer bearing cups.
9 To fit new cups make sure that they are the right way round and using metal tubes of suitable diameter drift them into position.
10 Pack the cone and roller assembly with the recommended grease working the grease well into the cage and rollers. **NOTE**: *Leave the*

Chapter 11 Suspension and steering

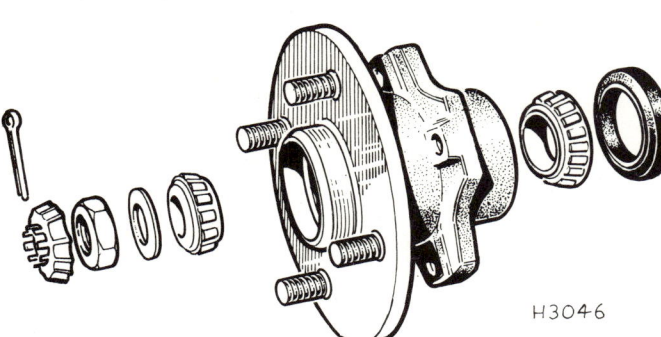

Fig. 11.3 Front hub and bearings (Sec. 2)

3.1 Check the wheel bearings for excessive play

3.3 Showing split pin and nut retainer in position with hub cap removed

12 Refit the hub and disc assembly on the stub axle and slide on the outer bearing and thrust washer.
13 Refit the adjusting nut and tighten it to the torque wrench setting given in the Specifications whilst rotating the hub and disc to ensure free movement and centralisation of the bearing. Slacken the nut back 90° which will give the required endfloat of 0.001 - 0.005 inch (0.03 - 0.13 mm). Fit the nut retainer and new split pin. Bend over the ears of the split pin.
14 Refit the dust cap to the cente of the hub.
15 Refit the caliper as described in Chapter 9.

3 Front hub bearings – adjustment

1 To check the condition of the hub bearings, jack up the front of the car and support on firmly based stands. Grasp the road wheel at two opposite points to check for any rocking movement in the wheel hub. Watch carefully for any movement in the steering gear which can easily be mistaken for hub movement (photo).
2 If a front wheel hub has excessive movement, this is adjusted by removing the hub cap and then tapping and levering the dust cap from the centre of the hub.
3 Remove the split pin from the nut retainer and lift away the adjusting nut retainer (photo).
4 If a torque wrench is available tighten the centre adjusting nut to the torque wrench setting given in the Specifications and then slacken the nut back until an endfloat of 0.001 - 0.005 inch (0.03 - 0.13 mm) is obtained. Refit the nut retainer, and lock with a new split pin.
5 Assuming a torque wrench is not available, tighten the centre adjusting nut until a slight drag is felt on rotating the wheel. Then loosen the nut very slowly until the wheel turns freely again and there is just a perceptible endfloat. Refit the nut retainer and lock with a new split pin.
6 Refit the dust cap to the centre of the hub.

4 Front hub – removal and refitting

1 Follow the instructions given in Section 2 up to and including paragraph 5.
2 Bend back the locking tab and undo the four bolts holding the hub to the brake disc.
3 If a new hub assembly is being fitted it is supplied complete with new cups and bearings. The bearing cups will already be fitted in the hub. It is essential to check that the cups and bearings are of the same manufacture, this can be done by reading the name on the bearings and by looking at the initial letter stamped on the hub, 'T' stands for Timken and 'S' for Skefco.
4 Clean with scrupulous care the mating surfaces of the hub and check for blemishes or damage. Any dirt or blemishes will almost certainly give rise to disc run-out. Using new locking tabs bolt the disc and hub together and tighten the bolts to a torque wrench setting of 30 - 34 lbf ft (4.15 - 4.70 kgf m).
5 To grease and reassemble the hub assembly follow the instructions given in Section 2 paragraph 10 onward.

5 Front axle assembly – removal and refitting

1 Chock the rear wheels, jack up the vehicle and support the body on firmly based axle-stands. Remove the front wheels.
2 Using a garage crane or overhead hoist support the weight of the engine.
3 Wipe the top of the brake master cylinder reservoir and unscrew the cap. Place a piece of polythene sheet over the top of the reservoir and refit the cap. This is to stop hydraulic fluid syphoning out during subsequent operations.
4 Wipe the area around the three way union on the axle frame and detach the main feed pipe to the union. Place some tape over the end of the pipe and open union to stop dirt ingress.
5 Bend back the lock tabs and undo and remove the two bolts securing the universal coupling from the steering column shaft.
6 Undo and remove the engine mounting securing nuts at the underside of the mounting. There is one to each mounting as shown in Fig.11.4.
7 Using a garage hydraulic jack or blocks support the weight of the

hub and grease seal empty to allow for subsequent expansion of the grease.
11 To reassemble the hub, first fit the inner bearings and then gently tap the grease seal back into the hub. A new seal must always be fitted as during removal it was probably damaged. The lip must face inwards to the hub.

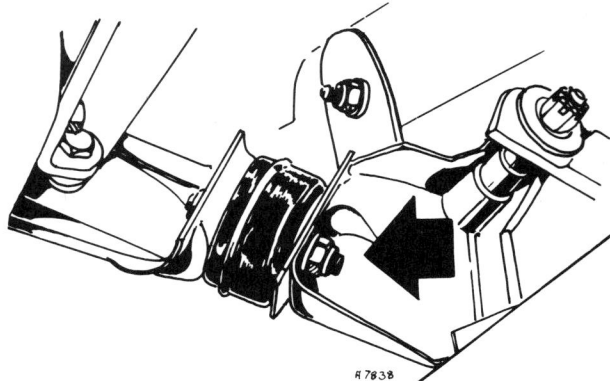

Fig. 11.4 Engine mounting securing nut (Sec. 5)

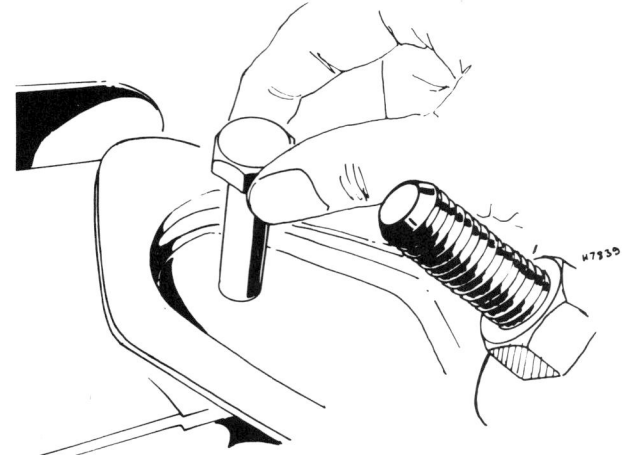

Fig. 11.5 Front axle securing bolts to body side member (Sec. 5)

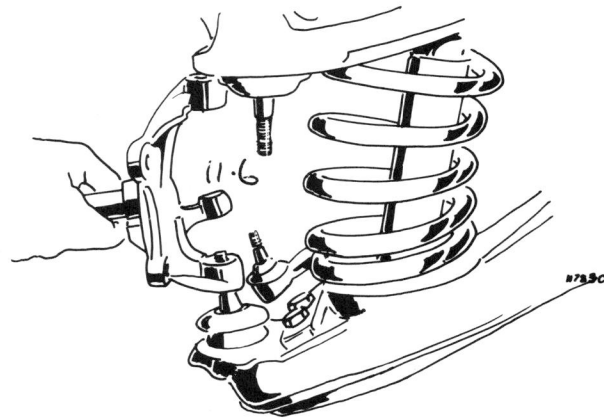

Fig. 11.6 Removal of stub axle assembly (Sec. 6)

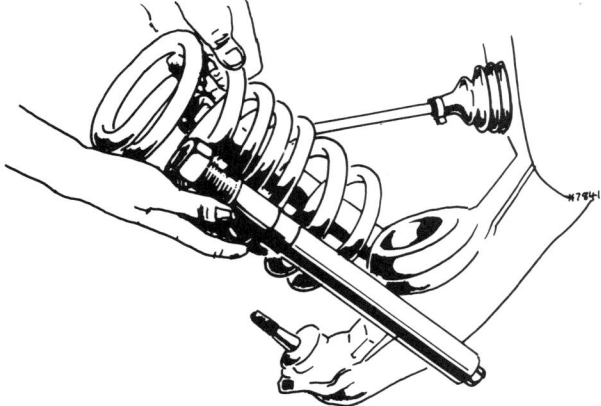

Fig. 11.7 Front coil spring with compressor fitted (Sec. 6)

front axle assembly.

8 When power assisted steering is fitted place a container under one of the reservoir hoses and detach. Allow as much hydraulic fluid to drain out as possible. Disconnect the feed and return pipe from the control valve. Plug the pipe ends to stop dirt ingress.

9 Undo and remove the frame to side member retaining nuts and bolts from both sides.

10 Undo and remove the upper suspension frame to side member retaining nut and bolts from either side. (Fig. 11.5). Carefully lower the complete assembly and draw forward from under the front of the vehicle.

11 Refitting the front axle assembly is the reverse sequence to removal.

The following additional points should be noted:

(a) Refer to Chapter 9 and bleed the brake hydraulic system.
(b) Check and adjust the front wheel toe-in. Further information will be found in Section 26.
(c) Where power assisted steering is fitted it will be necessary to bleed the system as described in Section 41.
(d) Do not tighten the universal coupling clamp bolts until the weight of the car is on the wheels.

6 Front axle assembly – overhaul

After high mileages it may be considered necessary to overhaul the complete front axle assembly. It is far better to remove the complete unit as described in Section 5 and dismantle it rather than to work on it still mounted on the car. Then proceed as follows.

1 Refer to Chapter 9 and remove the caliper.

2 Prise off the hub dust cap and withdraw the split pin and nut retainer. Undo and remove the nut.

3 Carefully pull the hub and disc assembly from the axle stub.

4 Undo and remove the ball stud securing nuts and then, using a universal ball joint separator, release the ball joint taper pins from their axle stub locations.

5 Next remove the track rod ends from their locations on the axle stubs and remove the stub axle assemblies as shown in Fig. 11.6.

6 Withdraw the long bolt that secures the upper arm to the axle frame and lift away the upper arm.

7 It is necessary to compress the spring. For this either make up a spring compressor tool comprising two parts as shown in Fig. 11.7 or borrow this from the local Ford garage quoting tool number P 4045. Do not attempt to use any makeshift tools as this can be very dangerous.

8 Using the compressors, contract the springs by at least 2 inches (50.8 mm).

9 Undo and remove the upper and lower shock absorber retaining nuts (lower fixing) and bolt (upper fixing). The shock absorbers may now be lifted away through the coil spring and lower arm aperture.

10 Undo and remove the bolts securing the tie bar to the lower arm. The lower arm should now be pulled down until there is sufficient clearance for the coil spring to be lifted away.

11 Bend back the lock tabs and unscrew and remove the four bolts that secure the steering 'U' shaped rack brackets to the front axle frame. Lift away the steering rack assembly.

12 Undo and remove the nut and bolt holding the lower arm to the front axle frame. Lift away the lower arm.

13 Using a suitable diameter drift or long bolt, piece of metal tube, packing washers and nut, remove the lower arm bush.

14 The operations described in paragraphs 1 - 13 should now be repeated for the second front suspension assembly. It will be necessary to release the coil spring compressor.

15 Undo and remove the nuts holding the tie bars to the axle frame. Lift away the connecting link, tie bar and stabilizer bar assembly.

Chapter 11 Suspension and steering

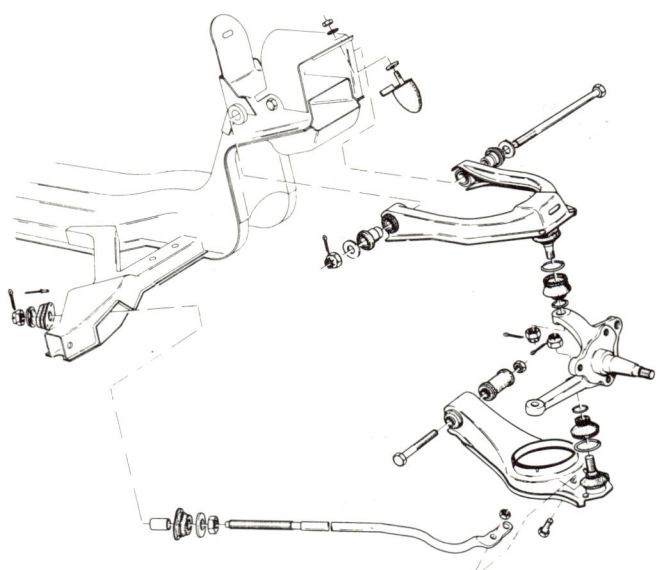

Fig. 11.8 Front suspension arms – component parts (Sec. 6)

16 Undo and remove the nuts and washers from each of the connecting links and part the stabilizer bar from the tie bars.
17 It is now beneficial to cut away the bushes in the tie bar and stabilizer which will make removal far easier.
18 Pull out the two bump stop rubbers from the axle frame.
19 Undo and remove the three way union retaining nut, release the brake pipe from its mounting clip and lift away the complete brake pipe assembly.
20 Dismantling is now complete. Wash all parts and wipe dry ready for inspection. Inspect all bushes for signs of wear and all parts for damage or excessive corrosion and, if evident, new parts must be obtained. If one coil spring requires renewal the second one must also be renewed as it will have settled over a period of time. If the brake pipe has corroded now is the time to obtain a new one.
21 During reassembly it is important that none of the rubber mounted bolts are fully tightened until the weight of the vehicle is taken on the front wheels.
22 Position the three way union and brake pipe on the front axle frame and secure in position with the nut and clips.
23 Refit the rubber bump stops. If they are difficult to insert in their locations smear with a little washing-up liquid. It may be found that the bump stops are retained with a nut and washers. If this is the case refit the nut and washers and fully tighten.
24 Fit new end bushes to the stabilizer and tie bar and then locate the connecting links in the stabilizer.
25 Next locate the connecting links in the tie bar and stabilizer bar bushes. Secure with nuts and washers.
26 Screw the nuts on the tie bar ends and follow with the washer together with the bush. Locate the tie bars in their respective positions on the frame and loosely refit the spacer, bush, nut and washer.
27 Using a bench vice and suitable diameter tube fit a new bush to the lower arm.
28 Locate the lower arm in the frame and line up the holes with a screwdriver. Refit the pivot bolt and washers making sure the bolt head is towards the front of the axle frame.
29 Refit the tie bar to the lower suspension arm and retain with the two nuts and bolts.
30 Place the coil spring between the frame and lower arm. Insert the shock absorbers through the lower arm and spring and secure the shock absorber in position with the bolt (upper fixing) and nuts (lower fixing).
31 Unscrew the spring compressor and repeat the operations in paragraphs 24 to 30 for the second front suspension assembly.
32 Check the condition of the steering rack mounting rubbers and obtain new if necessary. Position the steering rack on the axle frame and secure to the mounting brackets with the 'U' clamps. Always use a new locking plate under the bolt heads. Tighten the bolts to a torque wrench setting of 15 - 18 lbf ft (2.1 - 2.4 kgf m), and bend up the locking plate.
33 Place the upper suspension arm on the axle frame, insert the pivot bolt through the arm and frame holes so that the head is toward the front of the axle frame. Secure with the washer and nut. Repeat this operation for the second upper suspension arm.
34 Connect the stub axle assembly to the suspension arm ball joints, locate the track rod ends in the stub axle and tighten all the nuts. The track rod to steering arm nuts should be tightened to a torque wrench setting of 18 - 22 lbf ft (2.5 - 3.0 kgf m).
35 Refer to Section 4 and refit the hub and disc assemblies.
36 Refer to Chapter 9 and refit the caliper.
37 The complete front axle assembly may now be refitted to the car as described in Section 5.

7 Front axle mounting bushes – removal and refitting

1 Refer to Section 5 and remove the front axle assembly.
2 Using a piece of tube about 4 inches (102 mm) long and suitable diameter, a long bolt and packing washers, draw the bushes from the side member.
3 New bushes may now be fitted using the reverse procedure for removal. It is important that the insulator is positioned with the arrow on the flange pointing at the dimple in the side member.
4 Refit the front assembly as described in Section 5.

8 Stub axle – removal and refitting

1 Refer to Section 2 and remove the front hub and disc assembly.
2 Undo and remove the three bolts and spring washers that secure the brake disc splash shield to the stub axle.
3 Extract the split pins and then undo and remove the castellated nuts securing the three ball joints to the stub axle.
4 Using a universal ball joint separator, separate the ball joint pins from the stub axle. Lift away the stub axle.
5 Refitting the stub axle is the reverse sequence to removal. The track rod end to steering arm retaining nut must be tightened to a torque wrench setting of 18 - 22 lbf ft (2.5 - 3.0 kgf m).
6 If a new stub axle has been fitted it is recommended that the steering geometry and front wheel toe-in be checked. Further information may be found in Section 26.

9 Lower suspension arm – removal and refitting

1 Chock the rear wheels, jack up the front of the car and place on firmly based axle stands. Remove the road wheel.
2 Undo and remove the bolt fixing the brake pipe bracket and carefully push the pipes to one side.
3 It is now necessary to compress the spring. For this either make up a spring compressor comprising two parts or borrow this from the local Ford garage quoting tool number P 4045. Do not attempt to use any makeshift tools as this can be very dangerous.
4 Using the spring compressor, contract the spring by at least 2 inches (51 mm).
5 Undo and remove the upper and lower shock absorber retaining nuts (lower fixing) and bolt (upper fixing). The shock absorber may now be lifted through the coil spring and lower arm aperture.
6 Withdraw the split pin, undo and remove the castellated nut that secures the lower wishbone ball joint pin to the stub axle. Using a universal ball joint separator, separate the ball joint pin from the stub axle.
7 The lower suspension arm may now be parted and the coil spring removed.
8 Undo the tie bar locknut and remove the two bolts and nuts holding the tie bar to the lower arm.
9 Undo and remove the bolt that secures the lower arm to the front axle frame. The lower suspension arm can now be lifted rearward and downward from the front axle frame.
10 To fit a new bush first remove the old bush by using a piece of tube about 4 inches (102 mm) long and suitable diameter, a long bolt and nut and packing washer, draw the bush from the lower suspension arm. Fitting a new bush is the reverse sequence to removal.
11 Refitting the lower suspension arm is the reverse sequence to removal. The lower arm retaining bolts must be tightened once the car

has been lowered to the ground.
12 If a new lower steering arm has been fitted it is recommended that the steering geometry and front wheel toe-in be checked. Further information may be found in Section 26.

10 Stabilizer bar – removal and refitting

1 Undo and remove the bolt securing each stabilizer bar mounting bush clip to the stabilizer bar mounting bracket.
2 Release the clips and then undo and remove the three bolts and spring washer fixing each mounting bracket to the body side member.
3 Undo and remove the two nuts, dished washer and upper bushes and detach the connecting links from their locations in the stabilizer bar. The stabilizer bar may now be lifted away from the underside of the car.
4 Refitting the stabilizer bar is the reverse sequence to removal.

11 Stabilizer bar mounting bushes – removal and refitting

1 Undo and remove the bolt that secures each stabilizer bar mounting bush clip to the stabilizer bar mounting brackets.
2 Using a metal bar such as a tyre lever, carefully ease the stabilizer bar downward and push the split mounting bushes clear of their locations.
3 Push the new bushes onto the bar in their approximate positions and then align the bushes with the stabilizer bar mounting brackets and refit the retaining clips and bolts.

12 Stabilizer bar connecting link bush – removal and refitting

1 Refer to Section 10 and remove the stabilizer bar.
2 Using a sharp knife or hacksaw blade, cut the cone ends off the connecting link bushes and discard the bushes.
3 Using a bench vice, a piece of tube of suitable diameter and a socket, fit the new connecting link bushes.
4 Refit the stabilizer bar as described in Section 10.

13 Front shock absorbers – removal and refitting

1 Chock the rear wheels, jack up the front of the car and place on firmly based stands. Remove the road wheel.
2 Locate a small jack under the lower suspension arm and partially compress the coil spring.
3 Undo and remove the shock absorber top mounting bolt.
4 Undo and remove the two nuts that secure the shock absorber lower mounting. The shock absorber may now be lifted away through the coil spring and lower arm aperture.
5 Examine the shock absorber for signs of damage to the body, distorted piston rod, loose mounting or hydraulic fluid leakage. If evident a new unit should be fitted.
6 To test for damping efficiency hold the unit in the vertical position and gradually extend and contract it between its maximum and minimum limits ten times. It should be apparent that there is equal resistance on both directions of movement. If this is not apparent a new unit should be fitted - always renew shock absorbers in pairs.
7 Refitting the shock absorbers is the reverse sequence to removal.

14 Tie bar – removal and refitting

1 Chock the rear wheels, jack up the front of the car and place on firmly based axle-stands. Remove the road wheel.
2 Undo and remove the bolts fixing the tie bar to the lower suspension arm.
3 Extract the split pin from the end of the bar. Undo and remove the forward of the two nuts that secure the tie bar to the chassis frame member.
4 Where fitted, disconnect the stabilizer bar connecting link.
5 Remove the bush and spacer assembly from the threaded end of the tie bar. Lift away the tie bar.
6 If it is necessary to fit new bushes use a sharp knife or hacksaw

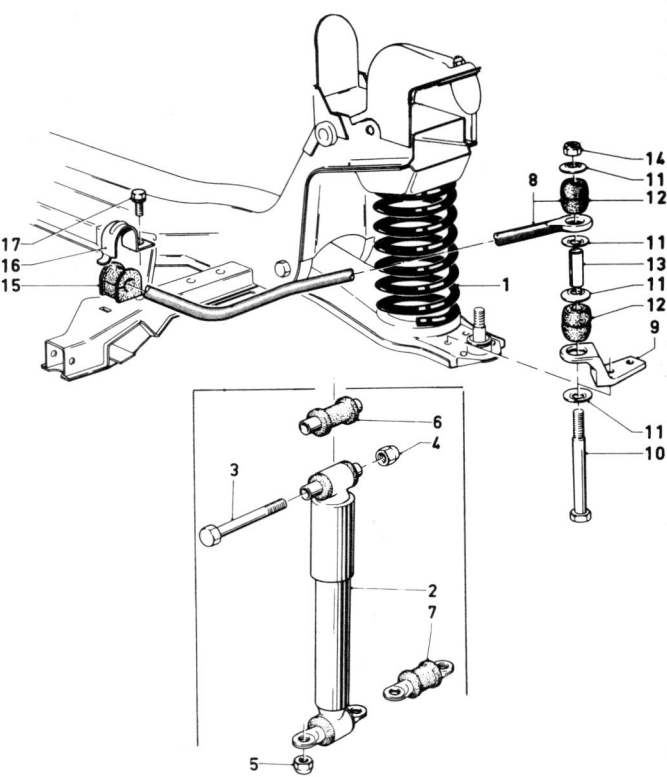

Fig. 11.9 Front suspension, stabilizer bar and shock absorber – component parts (Sec. 11)

1	Spring	10	Screw
2	Shock absorber	11	Washer
3	Bolt	12	Insulator
4	Nut	13	Spacer
5	Locknut	14	Locknut
6	Upper bush	15	Bush
7	Lower bush	16	Clamp
8	Stabilizer bar	17	Bolt and washer
9	Bracket		

blade and cut the cone ends of the tie bar bush. Discard the old bushes.
7 Using a tube of suitable diameter, a socket and bench vice, fit a new tie bar end bush.
8 Refitting the tie bar is the reverse sequence to removal. It is recommended that the steering geometry and front wheel toe-in be checked. Further information will be found in Section 26.

15 Rear axle and suspension – removal and refitting

1 Chock the front wheels, jack up the car and support on firmly based axle-stands. Remove the road wheels.
2 Disconnect the propeller shaft from the final drive unit as described in Chapter 7.
3 In a similar manner disconnect each half shaft from the stub axles.
4 Release the handbrake and remove the speed nuts retaining the brake drums. Withdraw the brake drums.
5 Refer to Chapter 9 and detach the handbrake cables from the brake shoes and arms.
6 Wipe the top of the brake master cylinder reservoir and unscrew the cap. Place a piece of polythene sheet over the top of the reservoir and refit the cap. This is to stop hydraulic fluid syphoning out during subsequent operations.
7 Disconnect the brake line at the junction and tape the open ends to stop dirt ingress. Detach the brake line junction from the underside of the floor.
8 Detach the exhaust pipe supports from the crossmember.

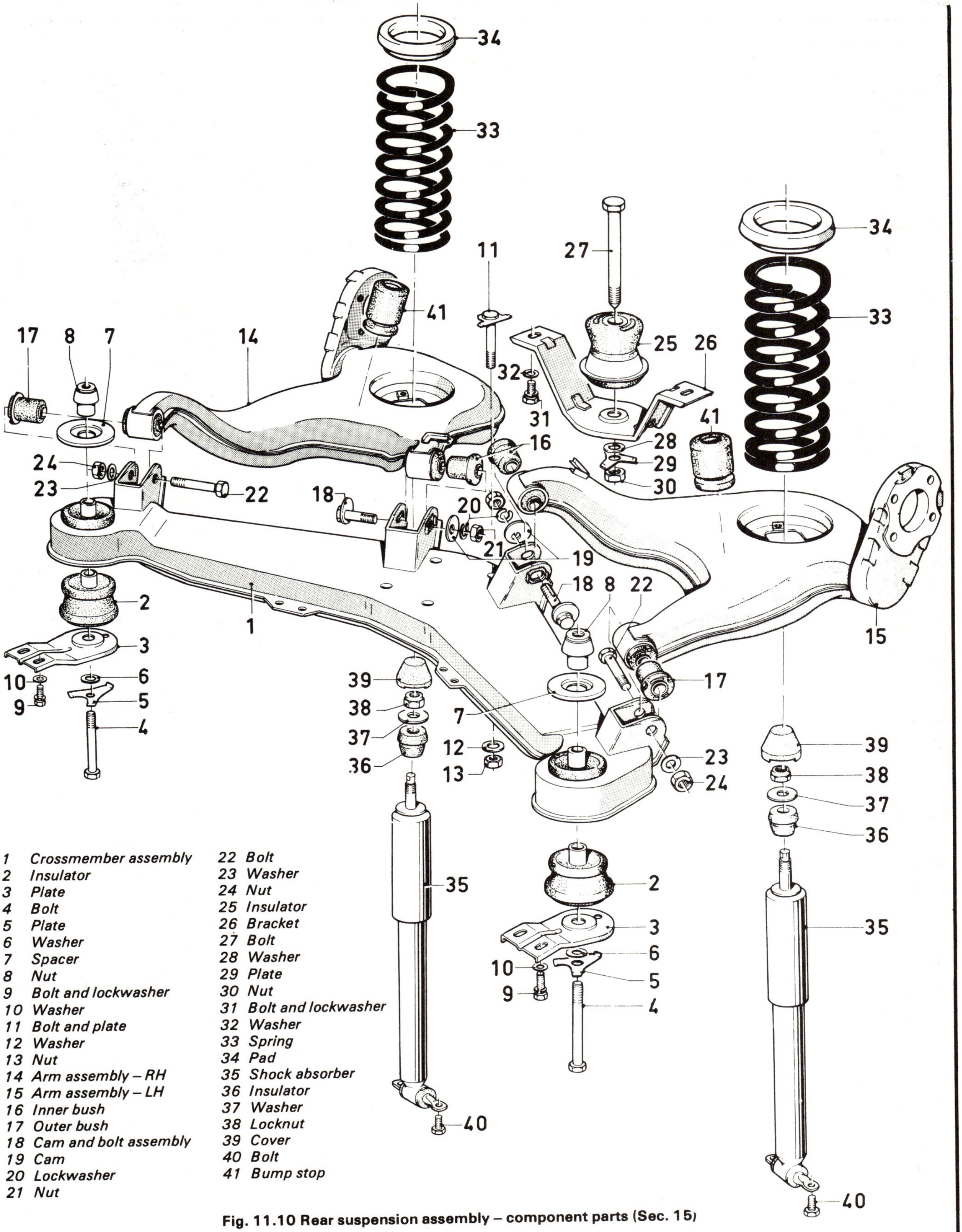

225

1 Crossmember assembly	22 Bolt
2 Insulator	23 Washer
3 Plate	24 Nut
4 Bolt	25 Insulator
5 Plate	26 Bracket
6 Washer	27 Bolt
7 Spacer	28 Washer
8 Nut	29 Plate
9 Bolt and lockwasher	30 Nut
10 Washer	31 Bolt and lockwasher
11 Bolt and plate	32 Washer
12 Washer	33 Spring
13 Nut	34 Pad
14 Arm assembly – RH	35 Shock absorber
15 Arm assembly – LH	36 Insulator
16 Inner bush	37 Washer
17 Outer bush	38 Locknut
18 Cam and bolt assembly	39 Cover
19 Cam	40 Bolt
20 Lockwasher	41 Bump stop
21 Nut	

Fig. 11.10 Rear suspension assembly – component parts (Sec. 15)

9 Using a small jack raise each suspension arm in turn and disconnect the upper shock absorber attachment from inside the boot.
10 Carefully lower each suspension arm and lift away the coil springs and seats. Unless the springs are to be renewed mark the springs so that they may be refitted in their original positions.
11 Position a garage hydraulic jack under the centre of the final drive housing. Support its weight.
12 Bend back the lock tab and then unscrew and remove the centre nut. It will be necessary to hold the bolt from inside the luggage compartment. Lift away the bolt.
13 Undo and remove the longer bracket retaining bolts and lift away the hanger bracket.
14 Bend back both locking tabs of both crossmember retaining brackets and then undo and remove the centre bolt and washers.
15 Undo and remove the two bolts, spring and plain washers securing the retaining bracket to the floor.
16 The complete final drive and suspension assembly may now be lowered and drawn rearward from the car.
17 Refitting the complete assembly is the reverse sequence to removal. It will be necessary to bleed the brake hydraulic system as described in Chapter 9 and have the geometry checked by your local Ford garage.

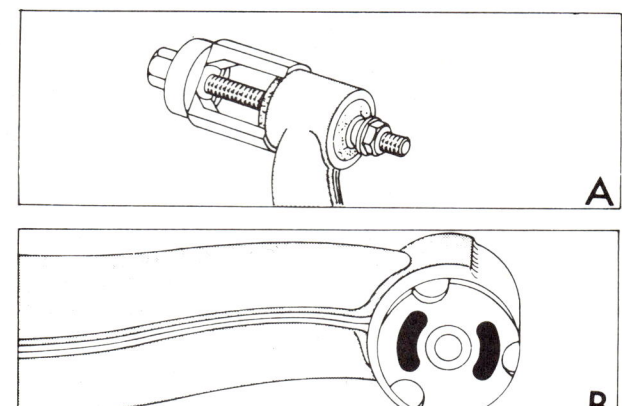

Fig. 11.11 Removal of front rubber insulator (Sec. 18)

A Removing old insulator   B Correctly fitted new insulator

16 Rear suspension coil spring – removal and refitting

1 Chock the front wheels, jack up the rear of the car and support on firmly based stands. Remove the rear wheels.
2 Undo and remove the six screws securing the half shaft to the stub axle. Using a piece of wire looped through the hole at the bottom of the wing panel support the weight of the half shaft.
3 Locate a jack under the suspension arm and raise the arm sufficiently to release the spring load from the shock absorber.
4 Working inside the luggage compartment remove the shock absorber mounting cap and then unscrew and remove the shock absorber securing nut. Lift away the retainer. On estate models access is gained once the cover plate, retained by three self tapping screws, has been removed.
5 Undo and remove the two shock absorber lower mounting bolts and washers. Carefully lower and withdraw the shock absorber.
6 The jack should now be lowered until it is possible to lift away the coil spring. Do not lower too far otherwise the brake flexible hose will be strained.
7 Lift away the coil spring and recover the upper rubber ring.
8 Check the coil spring for signs of excessive corrosion, fracture or loss of tension. If any of these conditions exist, a pair of new springs should be fitted.
9 Inspect the upper rubber ring and if damaged or perished a new ring should be obtained.
10 Refitting the rear coil spring is the reverse sequence to removal. It is recommended that the rear suspension geometry is checked by your local Ford garage.

17 Rear shock absorber – removal and refitting

1 *Estate cars only:* Working inside the luggage compartment undo and remove the three self tapping screws securing the shock absorber cover plate to the floor. Lift away the cover plate.
2 Undo and remove the nut and washer securing the shock absorber upper mounting.
3 Chock the front wheels, jack up the rear of the car and support on firmly based stands.
4 Undo and remove the two bolts and spring washers securing the shock absorber to the lower arm. Withdraw the shock absorber downwards through the spring and aperture in the lower arm.
5 Examine the shock absorber for signs of damage to the body, distorted piston rod of hydraulic leakage. If evident, a new unit should be obtained.
6 To test for damping efficiency hold the unit in the vertical position and gradually extend and contract it between its maximum and minimum limits ten times. It should be apparent that there is equal resistance on both directions of movement. If this is not apparent a new unit should be fitted - always renew shock absorbers in pairs.
7 Refitting the shock absorber is the reverse sequence to removal.

18 Rear suspension lower arm – removal and refitting

1 Refer to Section 15 and remove the rear axle and suspension assembly.
2 Undo and remove the hub nut and washer.
3 Release the brake drum retaining speed nut and withdraw the brake drum.
4 It is now necessary to draw off the hub flange. If the flange is an easy fit it may be removed with a large three leg universal puller. Otherwise the special Ford tool P 1039-A will have to be borrowed from the local Ford garage and used for this operation.
5 With the hub flange released the stub axle may now be withdrawn from the rear of the backplate and lower arm. Take care that the bearing seal is not damaged.
6 Wipe the area of the brake pipe unions on the slave cylinders and unscrew the unions. Tape the open ends to stop dirt ingress.
7 Detach the brake pipe from the lower suspension arm clips.
8 Undo and remove the four bolts retaining the hub and brake backplate. Now separate the bearing carrier.
9 Undo and remove the two bolts securing the rear shock absorber to the lower suspension arm.
10 Undo and remove the nuts and bolts attaching the lower suspension arm to the crossmember. Lift away the crossmember.
11 Inspect the suspension arm for signs of damage or excessive rust. Renew if these are evident.
12 Should it be necessary to renew the insulators, the old ones should be removed using a piece of suitable diameter tube, bolt, nut and washers.
13 Fitting the new insulators is the reverse sequence to removal. It is important that the insulators are located as shown in Fig.11.11.
14 Refitting the lower suspension arm is the reverse sequence to removal. It will be found beneficial if the hub is finally tightened when the axle and suspension assembly have been refitted.

19 Rear suspension front rubber insulator – removal and refitting

1 Chock the front wheels, jack up the rear of the car and support on firmly based stands. Remove the road wheel.
2 Undo and remove the nuts and washers securing the extension housing to the crossmember.
3 Using jacks or suitable blocks support the propeller shaft and crossmember.
4 Detach the exhaust pipe from the crossmember.
5 Bend back the lock tab and unscrew the crossmember to mounting bracket securing bolt.
6 Undo and remove the two bolts, spring and plain washers securing the mounting bracket to the floor panel. Lift away the mounting bracket.
7 Lower the jacks or blocks supporting the crossmember so as to give a minimum clearance of 6 inches between the crossmember and

Chapter 11 Suspension and steering

underside of the body. Ensure that the brake flexible pipe is not strained and the handbrake cable does not foul the axle casing.
8   The insulator may be drawn out of its location using a large diameter tube, nut, bolt and packing washers.
9   Fitting the new insulator is the reverse sequence to removal. Use a little glycerine or washing-up liquid on the outer surface.
10 Reassembly is now the reverse sequence to detachment from the underbody. It is recommended that the rear suspension geometry be checked by your local Ford garage.

20 Rear suspension rear rubber insulator – removal and refitting

1   Chock the front wheels, jack up the rear of the car and support on firmly based axle-stands. Remove the road wheels to give better access.
2   Support the final drive housing with a jack.
3   Bend back the lock tab and unscrew the nut from the hanger bracket centre bolt. It will be found beneficial to hold the centre bolt from inside the luggage compartment. Withdraw the centre bolt.
4   Undo and remove the two bolts, spring and plain washers securing the hanger bracket to the underbody.
5   Lift away the hanger bracket.
6   Place a container under the rear of the final drive unit and then wipe the area around the cover plate to stop dirt ingress.
7   Undo and remove the bolt and spring washers securing the cover plate to the rear of the final drive housing. Lift away the cover plate and recover the gasket.
8   The insulator may be drawn out of the casting using a tube of suitable diamter, nut, bolt and packing washer.
9   To fit a new insulator lubricate the outer surface with a little glycerine or washing-up liquid and pull into position using the same tube, nut, bolt and packing washers required for removal.
10 When the insulator is fitted to the cover plate, the two protrusions of the insulator should point downward and be parallel to the mating face of the cover plate.
11 Reassembly is now the reverse sequence to removal. Make sure the cover plate and final drive unit mating faces are cleaned and if possible use a new gasket. Do not forget to refill with 3.5 pints (1.8 litres) of recommended grade oil.

21 Rear suspension bump rubber – removal and refitting

Removal of a bump rubber is simply a matter of pulling it downward from its location. Before refitting apply some glycerine or washing-up liquid to the inner surface to facilitate fitting.

22 Rear suspension stub axle – removal and refitting

1   Chock the front wheels, remove the rear wheel trim and slacken the wheel and hub nuts. Jack up the rear of the car and support on firmly based stands. Remove the road wheel.
2   Remove the speed nut from the brake drum and with the handbrake released withdraw the brake drum.
3   Undo and remove the six screws securing the half shaft flange to the stub axle. Support the weight of the half shaft with wire or string.
4   It is now necessary to draw off the hub flange. If the flange is an easy fit it may be removed with a large three leg universal puller. Otherwise special Ford tool P 1039 - A will have to be borrowed from the local Ford garage and used for this operation.
5   Remove the hub nut and washer and with the hub flange released the stub axle may now be withdrawn from the rear of the backplate and lower arm.
6   Refitting the stub axle is the reverse sequence to removal. It will be found beneficial if the hub nut if finally tightened when the road wheel has been refitted and the rear of the car lowered to the ground.

23 Rear suspension stub axle bearing and seals – removal and refitting

1   Refer to Section 22 and remove the stub axle.
2   Undo and remove the four bolts retaining the hub and brake backplate. Wipe the area around the rear of the wheel cylinder and unscrew

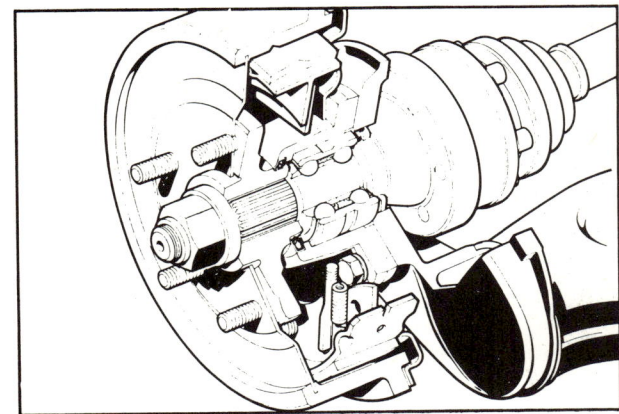

Fig. 11.12 Cross section of rear hub showing stub axle (Sec. 22)

Fig. 11.13 Use of special tool to draw off hub flange (Sec. 22)

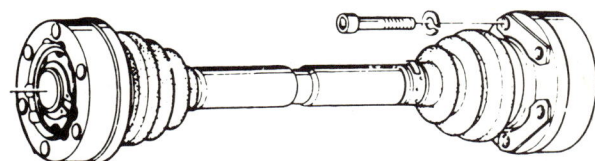

Fig. 11.14 Half shaft assembly (Sec. 24)

the pipe union. Tape the open ends to stop dirt ingress. Lift away the hub assembly.
3   Using a screwdriver carefully remove the outer grease seal.
4   The bearing assembly and second seal may now be pressed out using a tube of suitable diameter and a large bench vice.
5   Carefully clean the bearing and grease seal seats to remove any burrs.
6   Fit a new bearing using the same tube used to remove the old bearing until it abuts against the stop.
7   Fit the two grease seals with the lips facing inward using a suitable diameter tube and lightly lubricate the lip.
8   Refit the hub assembly and stub axle, this is the reverse sequence to removal.

24 Rear axle half shaft – removal, overhaul and refitting

1   Chock the front wheels, jack up the rear of the car and support on firmly based stands. Remove the road wheel to give better access.
2   Clean the area around the joints and mark the mating flanges to ensure correct alignment upon refitting.
3   Undo and remove the six screws securing each of the half shaft flanges and lift away the half shaft assembly.
4   It should be noted that two types of half shaft are fitted to vehicles covered by this manual. They are identical in appearance but the

difference lies in the diameter of the constant velocity joint.

5 To dismantle the constant velocity joint first remove the outer circlip and withdraw the constant velocity joint from the shaft (Fig. 11.15).

6 Remove the dished washers noting which way round they are fitted and then remove the inner circlips.

7 Slacken the gaiter clamps and then remove the cover and rubber sleeves.

8 Thoroughly clean all parts and inspect for wear or damage to the gaiter. Obtain new parts as necessary.

9 To reassemble first fit the gaiters and covers and secure with the gaiter clamps ensuring that the end of the outer clamps are between the bolt holes.

10 Insert the inner circlips and then fit the dished washers with the small diameter towards the half shaft and constant velocity joint. The identification groove must be away from the half shaft.

11 Refit the outer circlip.

12 Apply grease to the constant velocity joints in the following amounts.

   2 litre engine models   2 oz (55 gms)
   2.5 and 3 litre engine models 3 oz (85 gms)

13 Refitting the half shaft is the reverse sequence to removal. Make sure that the mating faces of the half shaft, final drive and stub axle are clean.

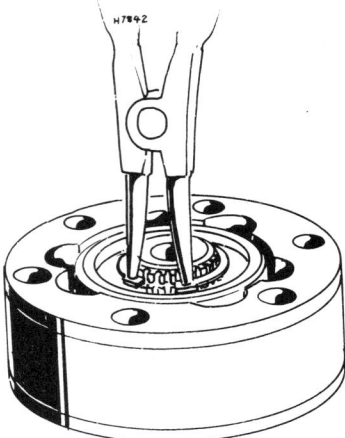

Fig. 11.15 Removal of constant velocity joint retaining circlip (Sec. 24)

25 Steering – lubrication

Lubrication of the rack and pinion during normal service operation it not necessary as the lubricant is contained on the assembly by rubber gaiters. However, should a loss occur due to a leak from the rack housing or rubber gaiters then the correct amount of oil should be inserted using an oil can. Obviously before replenishment is carried out the cause of leak must be found and rectified.

To top up the oil in the rack and pinion assembly, remove the clip from the rubber gaiter on the right-hand end of the steering rack housing and rotate the steering wheel until the rack is in the normal straight ahead position. Allow any remaining oil to seep out so that it is not overfilled. Using an oil can filled with Castrol Hypoy 90 insert the nozzle into the end of the rack housing and refill with not more than 0.25 pint (0.14 litre) of oil.

Reposition the gaiter and tighten the clip quickly to ensure minimum oil loss and then move the steering wheel from lock to lock very slowly to distribute the oil in the housing.

Important: *if at any time the car is raised from the ground and the front wheels are clear and suspended, do not use any excessive force or rapid movement when moving the wheels, especially from one lock to the other, otherwise damage could occur to the steering mechanism.*

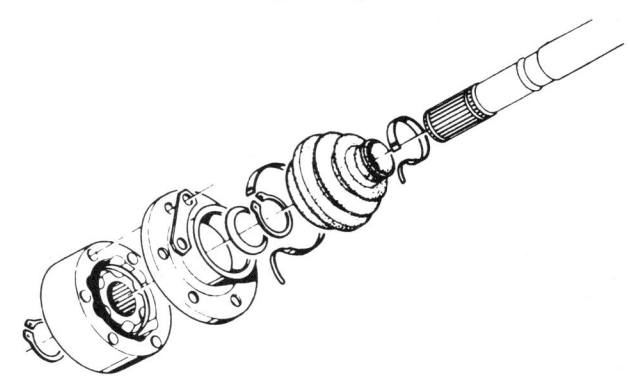

Fig. 11.16 Constant velocity joint end of the half shaft (Sec. 24)

the steering wheel hub. Lift away the inner embellishment.

3 With the front wheels in the straight ahead position note the position of the spokes of the steering wheel and mark the hub of the steering wheel and inner shaft to ensure correct positioning upon refitting.

4 Using a socket or box spanner of correct size slacken and remove the steering wheel nut. Remove the wheel by thumping the rear of the rim adjustment to the spokes with the palms of the hands which

26 Front wheel – alignment

The front wheels are correctly aligned when they are turning in at the front 0.000 - 0.16 inch (0.000 - 0.39 mm). It is important that this measurement is taken on a centre line drawn horizontally and parallel with the ground through the centre line of the hub. The exact point should be in the centre of the side wall of the tyre and not on the wheel rim which could be distorted and so give inaccurate readings.

The adjustment is effected by loosening the lock nut on each tie rod ball joint and slackening the rubber gaiter clip holding it to the tie rod, both tie rods are then turned equally until the adjustment is correct.

Measurement of the steering angles as well as the toe-in requires the use of special equipment and the job is best left to your local Ford garage. If the wheels are not in alignment or the steering angles incorrect, tyre wear will be very heavy and uneven, and the steering will be stiff and unresponsive.

27 Steering wheel – removal and refitting

1 Undo and remove the crosshead screws that secure the steering wheel embellishment to the spokes, (underside of spokes – photo).

2 Undo and remove the screws securing the inner embellishment to

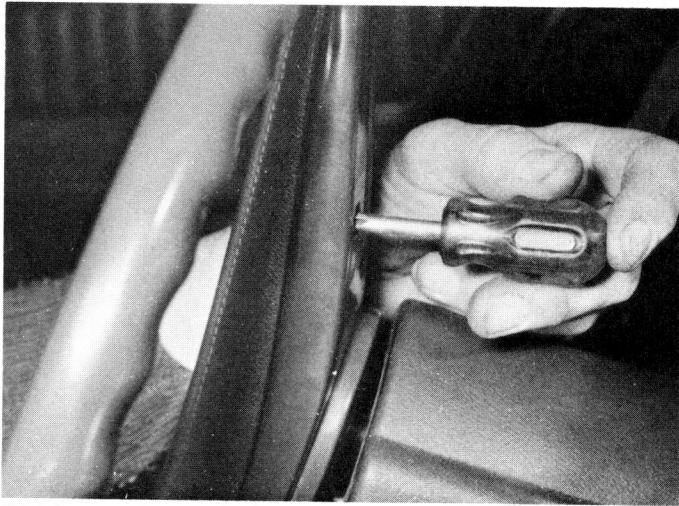

27.1 Remove the embellishment retaining screws

Chapter 11 Suspension and steering

should loosen the hub splines from the steering shaft splines. Lift away the steering wheel.
5   Refitting is the reverse procedure to removal. Carefully align the two marks previously made to ensure correct positioning of the spokes. Do not thump the steering wheel as it could cause the inner shaft to collapse. Refit the nut and tighten to the torque wrench setting given in the Specifications.

28 Steering column assembly – removal and refitting

1   Bend back the lock washer tabs, undo and remove the two bolts that secure the clamp bar to the upper universal joint assembly. Lift away the lockwasher and clamp bar (Fig. 11.17).
2   For safety reasons disconnect the battery.
3   Undo and remove the screws that hold the two halves of the column shroud together. Using a knife separate the two halves.
4   Refer to Chapter 10 and remove the instrument panel lower assembly.
5   Refer to Section 27 and remove the steering wheel.
6   Remove the direction indicator switch from the column. Further information will be found in Chapter 10.
7   Disconnect the ignition switch wires from the lock barrel assemblies. For this two crosshead screws will have to be removed.
8   When a manual choke is fitted slacken off the nut and disconnect the choke control cable from the column bracket.
9   Undo and remove the two bolts and one nut securing the upper bracket and then draw the column upward through the lower dash panel grommet. Lift the column away.
10 To refit the column first slide it through the lower dash panel grommet. Take extreme care not to cause the inner shaft to collapse by excessive end load.
11 Secure the upper bracket with the one nut and two bolts.
12 Refitting is now the reverse sequence to removal. However, do not tighten the steering column to universal coupling until the full weight of the car is on the road wheels.

29 Steering column shaft – removal and refitting

1   Refer to Section 28 and remove the column assembly from the car.
2   Remove the inner shaft retaining circlip and plain washer from its location in the direction indicator mounting casing.
3   Carefully prise open the staking on the end of the column and remove the lower bush seal.
4   Remove the upper bearing top retaining circlip using a pair of circlip pliers.
5   Using a soft faced hammer carefully tap the shaft down through the outer tube and then remove the top bearing together with its cover.
6   The shaft may now be completely removed from the outer tube. Finally remove the upper bearing lower retaining circlip.
7   Inspect the shaft for signs of collapse. The total length of the shaft must be 31.12 ± 0.02 in (790.5 ± 0.5 mm) and if it is shorter it may be carefully pulled back to the optimum length. Grasp both ends and try twisting. If backlash is evident a new shaft must be obtained. Check that the steering wheel location splines are in good order and not worn.
8   To reassemble, first fit a new upper bearing lower retainer circlip. Insert the shaft into the outer tube and slide the upper bearing onto the shaft until it locates on the splines in front of the circlip.
9   Fit the upper bearing cover and push the shaft into its final fitted position in the outer tube. Locate and fit a new upper bearing top retaining circlip.
10 Next fit the plain washer and secure the assembly with a new shaft retaining circlip.
11 Fit a new lower bearing and secure it in position by staking it in the place provided. Refit the lower bearing cover.

30 Steering column flexible coupling and universal joint assembly – removal and refitting

1   Undo and remove the nut, clamp bolt and spring washer that secures the flexible coupling bottom half to the pinion shaft (photo).

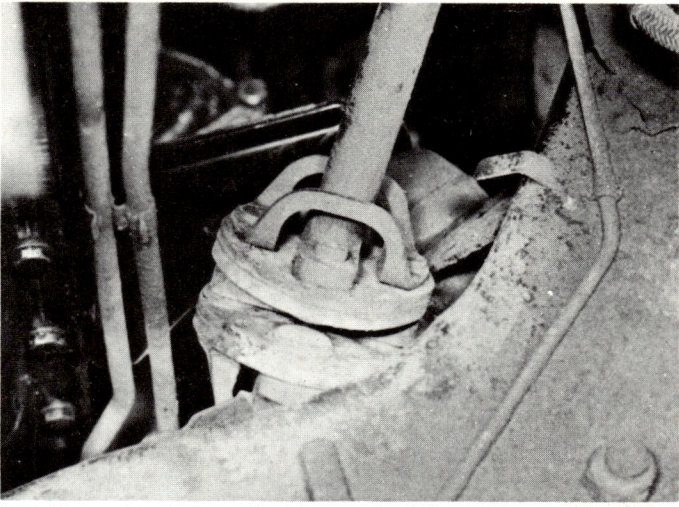
30.1 The steering column flexible coupling (viewed from underneath)

2   Bend back the lock tabs and undo and remove the two bolts securing the universal joint lock bar to the lower steering shaft. Lift away the tab washer and lock bar (Fig. 11.18).
3   The lower steering shaft may now be lifted away.
4   To refit place the lower steering shaft in its approximate fitted position and align the master splines on the shaft and pinion. Connect the shaft to the pinion.
5   Position the triangular clamp on the bottom of the steering column and secure with the clamp bar bolts and tab washer. Tighten the bolts fully and lock by bending up the tabs.
6   Refit the flexible coupling bottom half clamp bolt spring washer and nut. Tighten to the torque wrench setting given in the Specifications.

31 Steering column flexible coupling assembly – removal and refitting

1   Working under the bonnet bend back the lock tabs and then undo and remove the two bolts.
2   Disconnect the universal coupling from the steering column shaft.
3   Undo and remove the nut and bolt from the flexible coupling. The coupling assembly may now be lifted away.
4   To refit the flexible coupling assembly align the master splines on the coupling shaft and pinion.
5   Reconnect the coupling to the pinion shaft and secure the flexible coupling with the nut and bolt.
6   Reconnect the universal coupling to the steering column shaft and secure with the two bolts and lock tabs.

32 Rack and pinion steering gear – removal and refitting

1   Before starting this sequence set the steering wheel to the straight ahead position.
2   Jack up the front of the car and place blocks under the wheels. Lower the car slightly so that the track rods are in a near horizontal position.
3   Undo and remove the nut, bolt and spring washer that secures the flexible coupling bottom half clamp to the pinion shaft.
4   Bend back the lock tabs and then undo and remove the bolts securing the steering gear assembly to the mountings on the front axle frame. Lift away the bolts, lock washers and 'U' shaped clamps.
5   Withdraw the split pins and undo and remove the castellated nuts from the ends of each track rod where they join the steering arms. Using a universal ball joint separator, separate the track rod ball pins from the steering arms and lower the steering gear assembly downwards out of the car.
6   Before refitting the steering gear assembly make sure the wheels have remained in the straight ahead position. Also check the condition

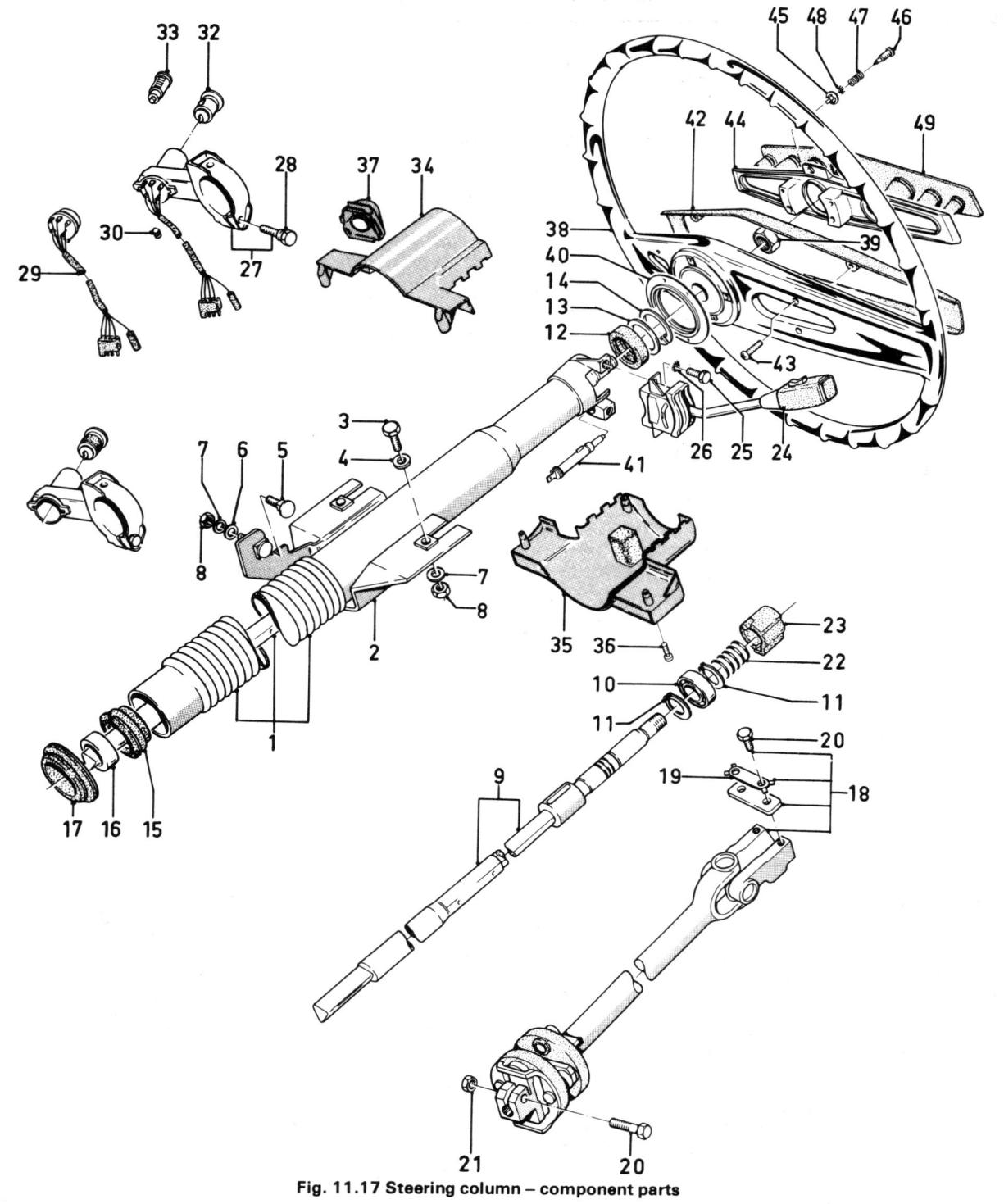

Fig. 11.17 Steering column – component parts

1	Steering column assembly	14	Circlip	26	Lockwasher	38	Steering wheel
2	Tube assembly	15	Lower bearing	27	Lock assembly	39	Nut
3	Bolt	16	Seal	28	Bolt	40	Horn brush ring
4	Washer	17	Seal	29	Ignition switch	41	Contact assembly
5	Bolt	18	Coupling and universal joint assembly	30	Stud	42	Upper pad assembly
6	Washer			31	Switch and bracket assembly	43	Screw
7	Washer	19	Plate	32	Cylinder and housing assembly	44	Horn contact bar
8	Nut	20	Bolt	33	Cylinder assembly	45	Spacer
9	Shaft	21	Nut	34	Upper shroud	46	Bolt
10	Upper bearing	22	Spring	35	Lower shroud	47	Spring
11	Circlip	23	Cam	36	Bolt	48	Lockwasher
12	Sleeve	24	Switch	37	Cover	49	Steering wheel insert
13	Washer	25	Screw				

Chapter 11 Suspension and steering

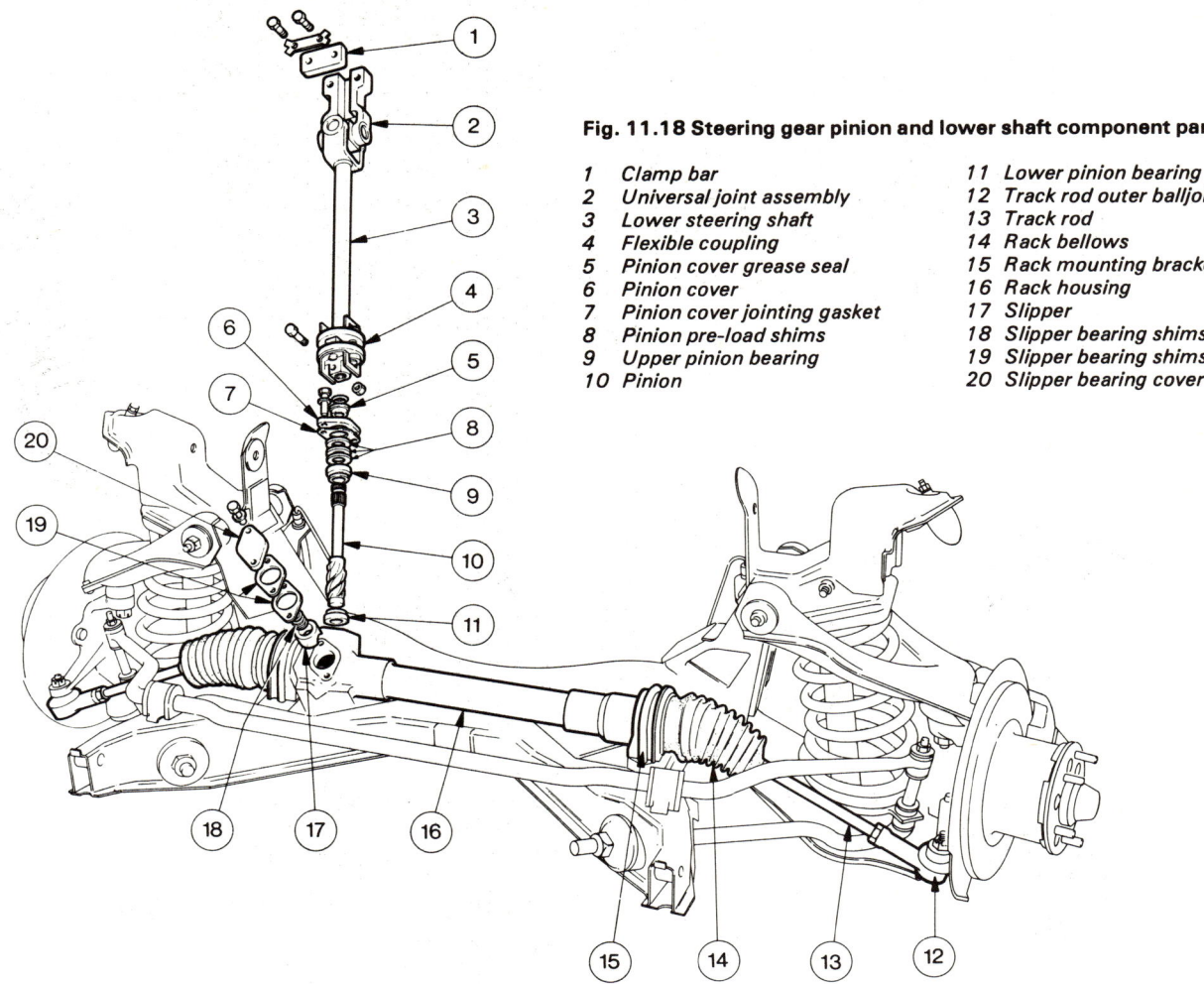

Fig. 11.18 Steering gear pinion and lower shaft component parts

1 Clamp bar
2 Universal joint assembly
3 Lower steering shaft
4 Flexible coupling
5 Pinion cover grease seal
6 Pinion cover
7 Pinion cover jointing gasket
8 Pinion pre-load shims
9 Upper pinion bearing
10 Pinion
11 Lower pinion bearing
12 Track rod outer balljoint
13 Track rod
14 Rack bellows
15 Rack mounting bracket
16 Rack housing
17 Slipper
18 Slipper bearing shims
19 Slipper bearing shims
20 Slipper bearing cover

of the mounting rubbers round the housing and if they appear worn or damaged they must be renewed.

7 Check that the steering rack is in the straight ahead position. This can be done by ensuring that the distances between the ends of both track rods and the rack housing on both sides are the same.
8 Place the steering assembly in its location on the front axle frame and at the same time mate up the splines on the pinion shaft with the splines in the clamp on the steering column flexible coupling. There is a master spline so make sure these are in line.
9 Refit the two 'U' shaped clamps using new locking tabs under the nuts, tighten the nuts to a torque wrench setting of 12 - 15 lbf ft (1.7 - 2.1 kgf m). Bend up the locking tabs.
10 Refit the track rod ends into the steering arms, refit the castellated nuts and tighten them to a torque wrench setting of 18 - 22 lbf ft (2.5 - 3.0 kgf m). Use new split pins to lock the nuts.
11 Tighten the clamp bolts on the steering column flexible coupling to the torque wrench setting given in the Specifications, having first double checked that the pinion is correctly located on the splines.
12 Jack up the car, remove the blocks from under the wheels and lower the car to the ground. The toe-in must now be checked and further information will be found in Section 26.

33 Rack and pinion steering gear – adjustments

1 For the steering gear to function correctly, two adjustments are necessary. These are pinion bearing pre-load and rack damper adjustment.
2 To carry out these adjustments, remove the steering gear from the car as described in Section 32, then mount the steering gear assembly in a soft jawed vice so that the pinion is in a horizontal position and the rack damper cover plate to the top.
3 Remove the rack damper cover plate by undoing and removing the two retaining bolts and spring washers. Lift away the cover plate, gasket and shims. Also remove the small spring and the recessed yoke, which bears onto the rack. These parts are shown in Fig. 11.19.
4 Now remove the pinion bearing pre-load cover plate from the base of the pinion, by undoing and removing the two bolts and spring washers. Lift away the cover plate, gasket and shims.
5 To set the pinion bearing pre-load correctly, refit the cover plate with the shim pack - 0.093 inch (2.35 mm) uppermost - and tighten down the bolts evenly. Note that the plain gasket has been left out at this stage.
6 Slacken off the cover bolts until the plate is only just contacting the shim pack and, using feeler gauges, measure the gap between the cover plate and the pinion housing. This should be 0.011 - 0.013 inch (0.28 - 0.33 mm). Take readings adjacent to each bolt to ensure that the inner plate is parallel. Reset the cover plate if different readings are obtained. Note the final reading.
7 Build up a shim pack to the required thickness. It is important that the shim pack contains at least two shims in addition to the 0.093 inch (2.35 mm) shim which must always be fitted next to the cover. Shim thicknesses available are listed below:

Part No.	Material	Thickness
72 BB - 3K544 - AA	Steel	0.005 in (0.13 mm)
72 BB - 3K544 - BA	Steel	0.007 in (0.19 mm)
72 BB - 3K544 - CA	Steel	0.010 in (0.25 mm)
72 BB - 3K544 - DA	Steel	0.092 in (2.35 mm)
72 BB - 3K544 - LA	Steel	0.002 in (0.05 mm)
72 BB - 3581 - AA	Buna coated flexoid	0.01 in (0.254 mm)

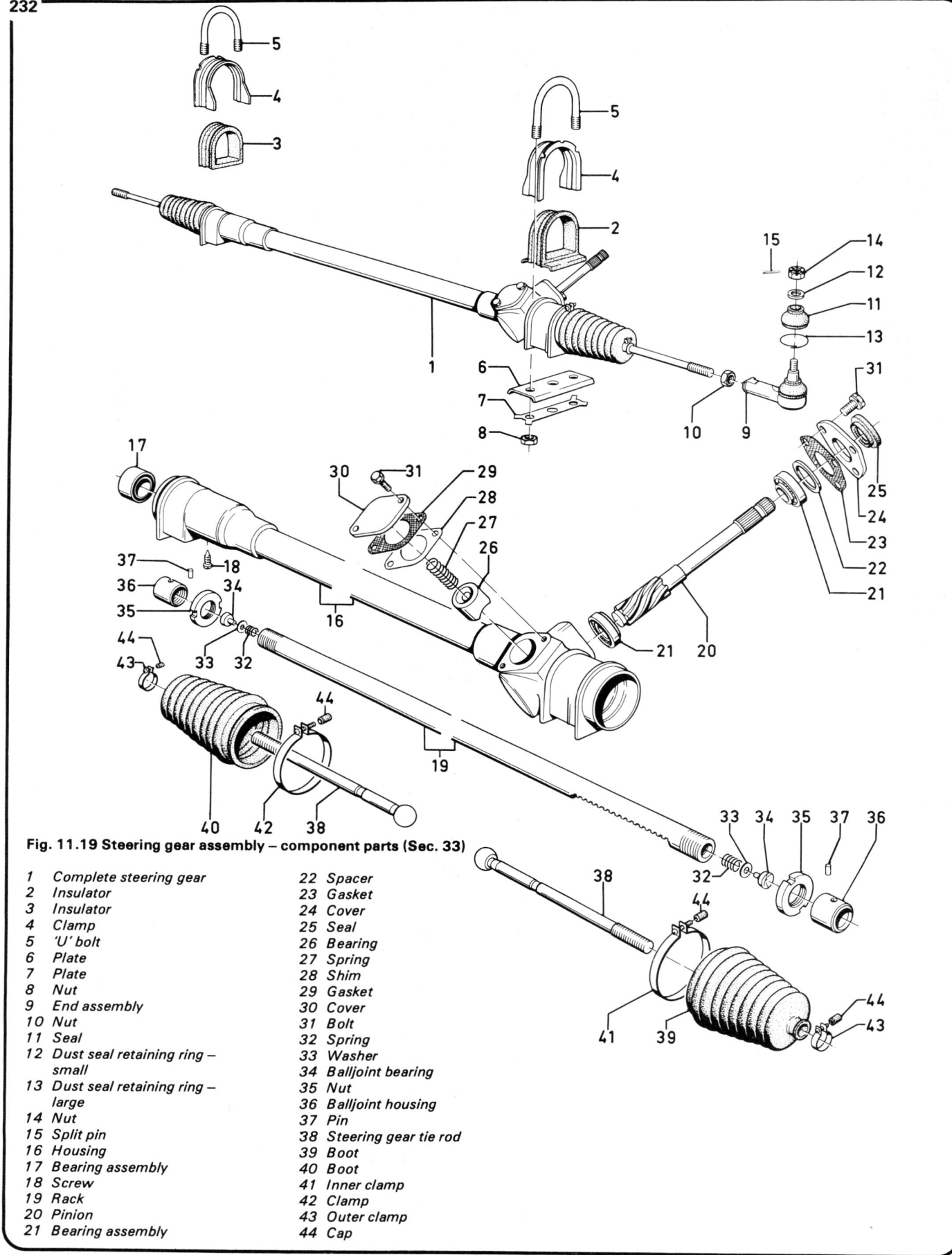

Fig. 11.19 Steering gear assembly – component parts (Sec. 33)

1 Complete steering gear
2 Insulator
3 Insulator
4 Clamp
5 'U' bolt
6 Plate
7 Plate
8 Nut
9 End assembly
10 Nut
11 Seal
12 Dust seal retaining ring – small
13 Dust seal retaining ring – large
14 Nut
15 Split pin
16 Housing
17 Bearing assembly
18 Screw
19 Rack
20 Pinion
21 Bearing assembly
22 Spacer
23 Gasket
24 Cover
25 Seal
26 Bearing
27 Spring
28 Shim
29 Gasket
30 Cover
31 Bolt
32 Spring
33 Washer
34 Balljoint bearing
35 Nut
36 Balljoint housing
37 Pin
38 Steering gear tie rod
39 Boot
40 Boot
41 Inner clamp
42 Clamp
43 Outer clamp
44 Cap

Chapter 11 Suspension and steering

8 With the cover plate removed, make sure that the pinion grease seal is packed with Castrol LM Grease. Smear jointing compound onto the cover plate mating face and refit the cover plate.
9 Smear a little Loctite or similar sealer on the threads of the bolts and tighten them down to a torque wrench setting of 6 - 8 lbf ft (0.9 - 1.1 kgf m).
10 To reset the rack damper adjustment, refit the yoke in its location on the rack and make sure it is fully home. Using a straight edge and feeler gauges, measure the distance between the top of the slipper and the surface of the pinion housing. Make a note of this dimension.
11 Assemble a shim pack including the gasket whose thickness is greater than the measurement obtained in paragraph 10, by between 0.006 – 0.0005 in (0.152 – 0.013 mm). Shim thicknesses available are listed below:

Part No.	Material	Thickness
72 BB - 3N597 - AA	Steel	0.005 in (0.127 mm)
72 BB - 3N597 - BA	Steel	0.007 in (0.19 mm)
72 BB - 3N597 - CA	Steel	0.010 in (0.25 mm)
72 BB - 3N597 - DA	Steel	0.015 in (0.38 mm)
72 BB - 3N597 - EA	Steel	0.020 in (0.50 mm)
72 BB - 3N597 - FA	Steel	0.060 in (1.5 mm)
72 BB - 3N598 - AA	Buna coated flexoid	0.010 in (0.25 mm)

12 Fit the spring into the recess in the yoke. Place the shim pack so that the gasket will be next to the cover plate and refit the cover plate. Apply a little Loctite or similar sealing compound to the bolt threads. Tighten down the bolts to a torque wrench setting of 6 - 8 lbf ft (0.9 - 1.1 kgf m).

34 Rack and pinion steering gear – dismantling and reassembly

1 Remove the steering gear assembly from the car as described in Section 32.
2 Undo the track rod ball joint locknuts and unscrew the ball joints. Lift away the plain washer and remove the locknut. To assist in obtaining an approximate correct setting for track rod adjustment mark the threads or count the number of turns required to undo the ball joint.
3 Slacken off the clips securing the rubber gaiter to each track rod and rack housing. Carefully pull off the gaiters. Have a quantity of rag handy to catch the oil which will escape when the gaiters are moved.
Note: *On some steering assemblies soft iron wire is used instead of clips. Always secure the gaiter with clips.*
4 To dismantle the steering gear assembly it is only necessary to remove the track rod which is furthest away from the pinion.
5 To remove the track rod place the steering gear assembly in a soft jawed vice. Working on the track rod ball joint carefully drill out the pin that locks the ball housing to the locknut. Great care must be taken not to drill too deeply or the rack will be irreparably damaged. The hole should be about 0.375 in (9.525 mm) deep.
6 Hold the locknut with a spanner, then grip the ball housing with a mole wrench and undo it from the threads on the rack.
7 Take out the spring and ball seat from the recess in the end of the rack and then unscrew the locknut from the threads on the rack. The spring and ball seat must be renewed during reassembly.
8 Carefully prise out the pinion dust seal and then withdraw the pinion together with the bearing assembly nearest the flexible coupling. As the bearings utilise bearing tracks and loose balls (14 in each bearing) care must be taken not to lose any of the balls or drop them into the steering gear on reassembly.
9 Undo and remove the two bolts and spring washers that secure the rack damper cover. Lift away the cover gasket shims, springs and yoke.
10 With the pinion removed, withdraw the complete rack assembly with one track rod still attached from the pinion end of the casing.
11 The remaining pinion bearing assembly may now be removed from the rack housing.
12 It is always advisable to withdraw the rack from the pinion end of the rack housing. This avoids passing the rack teeth through the bush at the other end of the casing and causing possible damage.
13 Carefully examine all parts for signs of wear and damage. Check the condition of the rack support bush at the opposite end of the casing from the pinion. If this is worn renew it. If the rack or pinion teeth are in any way damaged a new rack and pinion will have to be obtained.
14 Take the pinion seal off the top of the casing and replace it with a new seal.
15 To commence reassembly fit the lower pinion bearing and thrust washer into their recess in the casing. The loose balls can be held in place by a small amount of grease.
16 Refit the rack in the housing from the pinion end and position it in the straight ahead position by equalising the amount it protrudes at either end of the casing.
17 Refit the remaining pinion bearing and thrust washer onto the pinion and fit the pinion into its housing so that the larger masterspline on the pinion shaft is parallel to the rack and on the right-hand side of the pinion.
18 Refit the rack damper yoke, springs, shims, gasket and cover plate.
19 To refit the track rod which has been removed, start by fitting a new spring and ball seat to the recess in the end of the rack shaft and refit the locknut onto the threads of the rack.
20 Lubricate the ball, ball seat and ball housing with a small amount of Castrol Hypoy 90. Then slide the ball housing over the track rod and screw the housing onto the rack threads keeping the track rod in the horizontal position until the track rod starts to become stiff to move.
21 Using a normal spring balance hook it round the track rod 0.5 in (12.70 mm) from the end and check the effort required to move it from the horizontal position.
22 By adjusting the tightness of the ball housing on the rack threads the effort required to move the track rod must be set at 5 lb (2.8 kg).
23 Tighten the locknut up to the housing and then recheck that the effort required to move the track rod is still correct at 5 lb (2.8 kg).
24 On the line where the locknut and ball housing met, drill a 0.125 in (3.175 mm) diameter hole which must be 0.375 in (0.525 mm) deep. Even if the two halves of the old hole previously drilled out align, a new hole must be drilled.
25 Tap a new retaining pin into the hole and peen the end over to secure it.
26 Refit the rubber gaiters and track rods ensuring that they are refitted in exactly the same position from which they were removed.
27 Remove the rack damper cover plate and pour in 0.25 pint (0.15 litre) of Castrol Hypoy 90. Then carry out both steering gear adjustments as described in Section 33.
28 After the steering gear has been refitted to the car the toe-in must be checked. Further information will be found in Section 26.

35 Steering rack rubber gaiter – removal and refitting

1 Jack up the front of the car and place blocks under the wheels. Lower the car slightly so that the track rods are in a near horizontal position.
2 Withdraw the split pin and undo the castellated nut holding the ball joint taper pin to the steering arm. Using a universal ball joint separator part the taper pin from the steering arm.
3 Undo the track rod ball joint locknut and unscrew the ball joint. To assist in obtaining an approximate correct setting for track rod adjustment mark the threads or count the number of turns required to undo the ball joint.
4 Slacken off the clips securing the rubber gaiter to the track rod and rack housing end. Carefully pull off the gaiter. Have a quantity of rag handy to catch the oil which will escape when the gaiter is removed.
Note: *On some steering gear assemblies soft iron wire is used instead. Always secure the gaiter with clips.*
5 Fitting a new rubber gaiter is now the reverse sequence to removal. It will be necessary to refill the steering gear assembly with Castrol Hypoy 90. Full information will be found in Section 25.

36 Track rod end – removal and refitting

Full information will be found in Section 35, omitting paragraphs 4 and 5.

37 Power assisted steering – general

The power assisted steering system comprises a pulley driven roller pump with separate reservoir and a servo assisted rack and

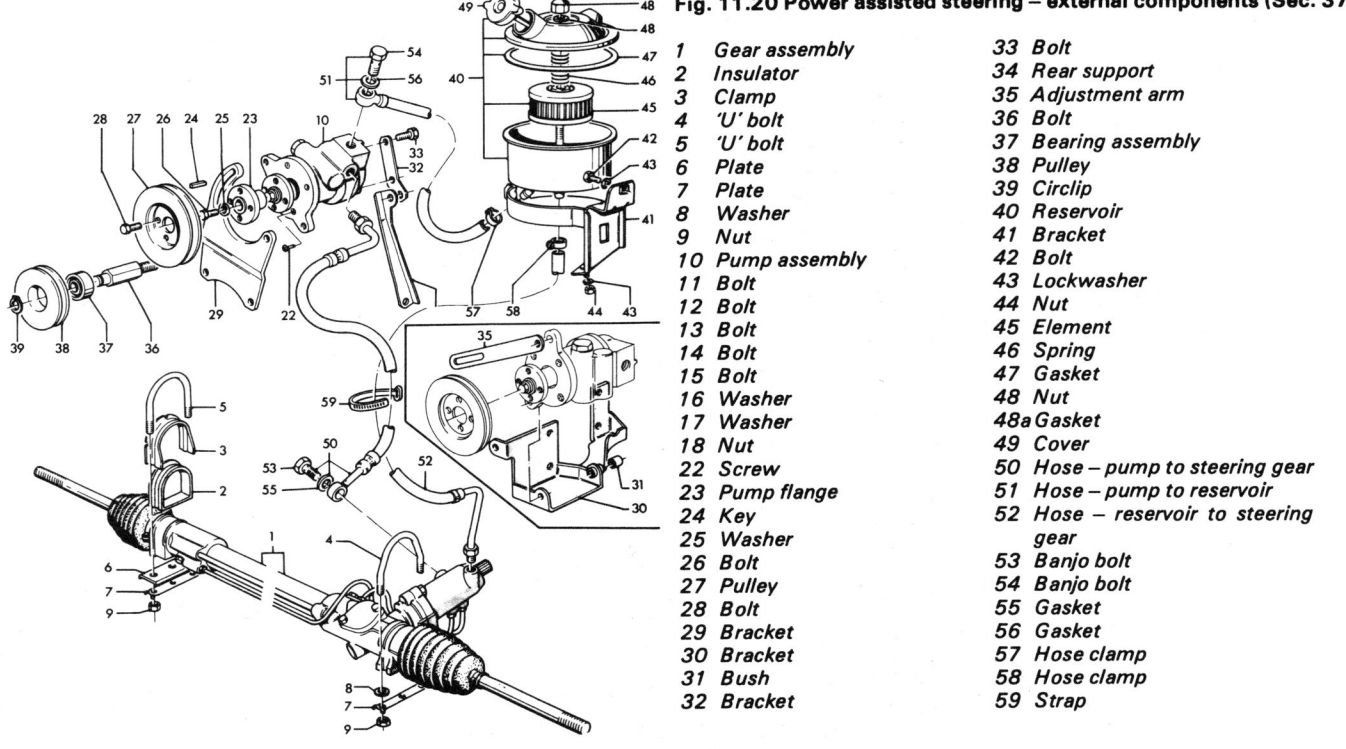

Fig. 11.20 Power assisted steering – external components (Sec. 37)

1	Gear assembly	33	Bolt
2	Insulator	34	Rear support
3	Clamp	35	Adjustment arm
4	'U' bolt	36	Bolt
5	'U' bolt	37	Bearing assembly
6	Plate	38	Pulley
7	Plate	39	Circlip
8	Washer	40	Reservoir
9	Nut	41	Bracket
10	Pump assembly	42	Bolt
11	Bolt	43	Lockwasher
12	Bolt	44	Nut
13	Bolt	45	Element
14	Bolt	46	Spring
15	Bolt	47	Gasket
16	Washer	48	Nut
17	Washer	48a	Gasket
18	Nut	49	Cover
22	Screw	50	Hose – pump to steering gear
23	Pump flange	51	Hose – pump to reservoir
24	Key	52	Hose – reservoir to steering gear
25	Washer		
26	Bolt	53	Banjo bolt
27	Pulley	54	Banjo bolt
28	Bolt	55	Gasket
29	Bracket	56	Gasket
30	Bracket	57	Hose clamp
31	Bush	58	Hose clamp
32	Bracket	59	Strap

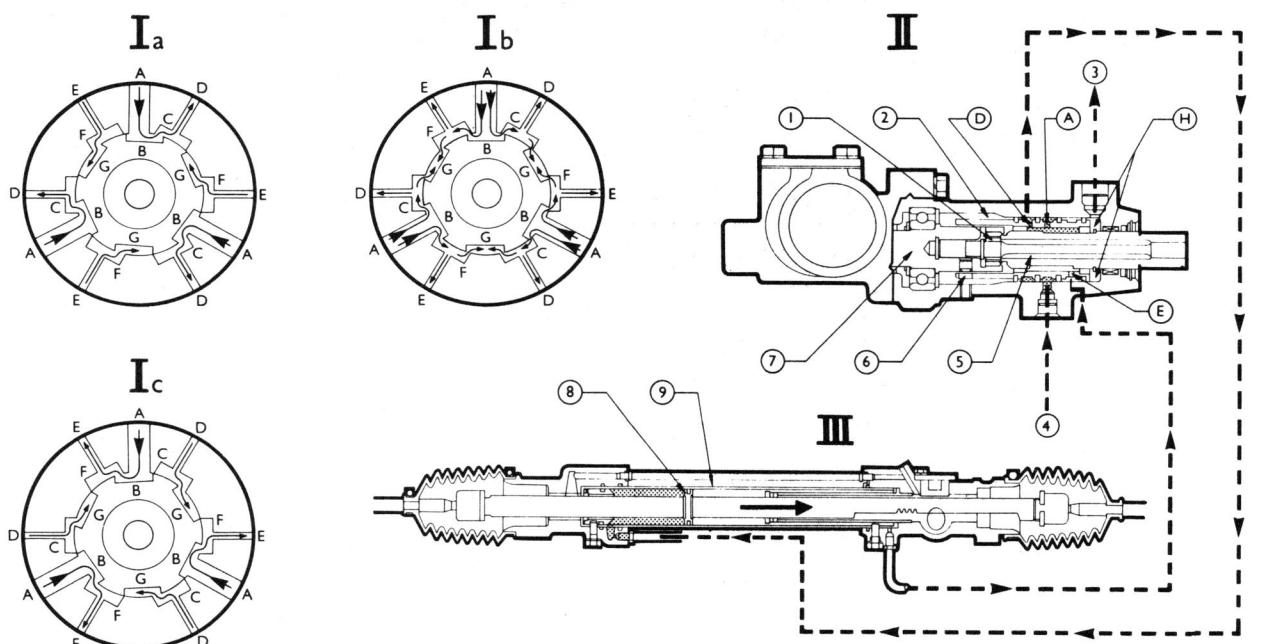

Fig. 11.21 Hydraulic circuit for power assisted steering (Sec. 37)

I Schematic cross section through valve
   a) Rack movement from left to right b) Centralised position (no rack movement) c) Rack movement from right to left

II Section through valve assembly (Rack movement from left to right)

III Section through rack assembly (Rack movement from left to right)

1	Spline connection (rotor to pinion)	2	Sleeve	4	From pump
		3	To reservoir	5	Torsion bar
6	Port	7	Pinion shaft	8	Servo piston
				9	Rack cylinder

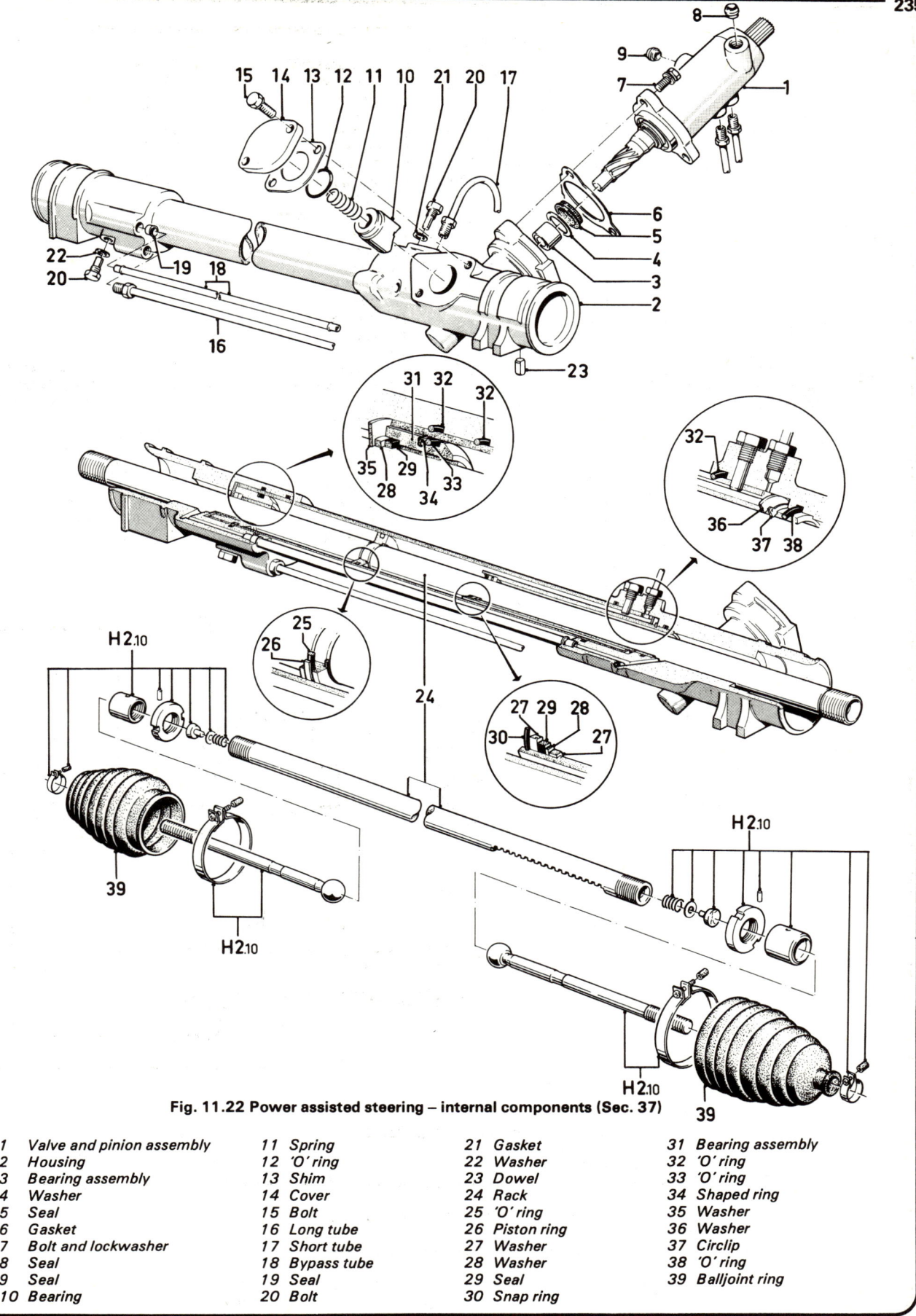

Fig. 11.22 Power assisted steering – internal components (Sec. 37)

1 Valve and pinion assembly	11 Spring	21 Gasket	31 Bearing assembly
2 Housing	12 'O' ring	22 Washer	32 'O' ring
3 Bearing assembly	13 Shim	23 Dowel	33 'O' ring
4 Washer	14 Cover	24 Rack	34 Shaped ring
5 Seal	15 Bolt	25 'O' ring	35 Washer
6 Gasket	16 Long tube	26 Piston ring	36 Washer
7 Bolt and lockwasher	17 Short tube	27 Washer	37 Circlip
8 Seal	18 Bypass tube	28 Washer	38 'O' ring
9 Seal	19 Seal	29 Seal	39 Balljoint ring
10 Bearing	20 Bolt	30 Snap ring	

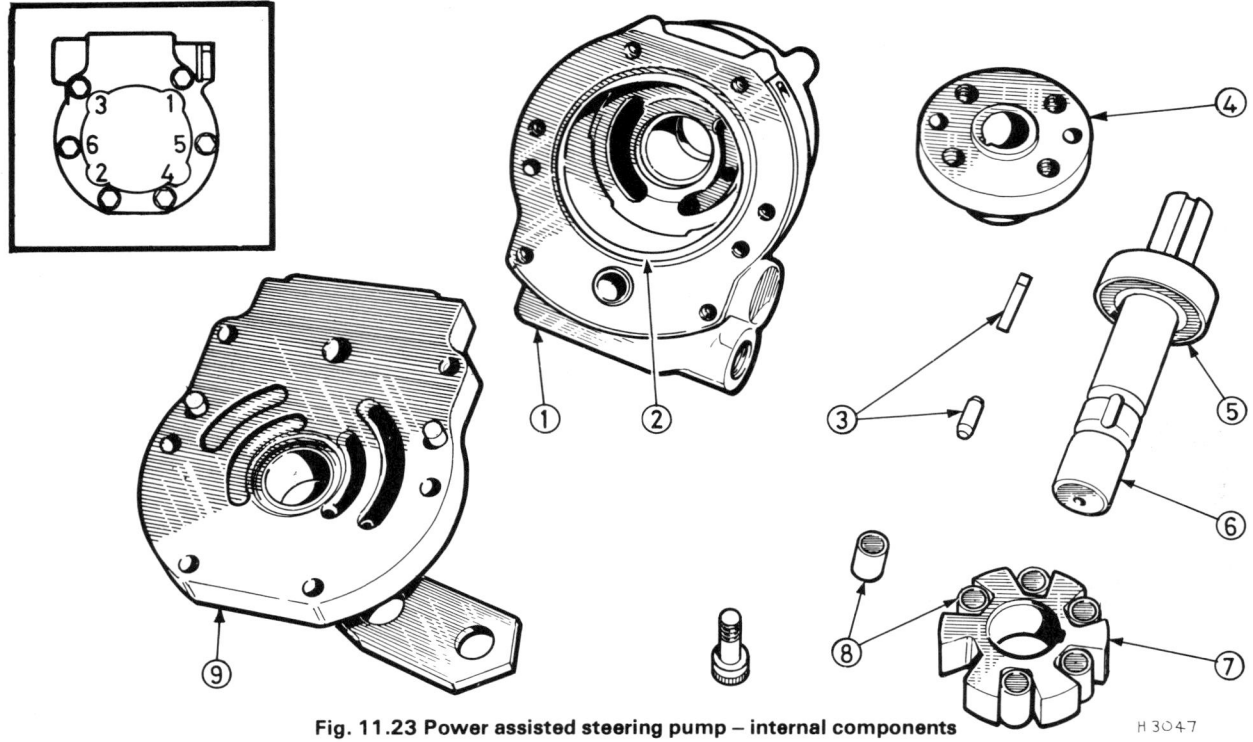

Fig. 11.23 Power assisted steering pump – internal components

1 Pump body
2 Drive gear housing
3 Pulley and drive gear keys
4 Pulley hub
5 Shaft bearing
6 Shaft
7 Drive gear
8 Rollers
9 Pump end cover

pinion assembly (Fig. 11.20 and 11.22).

The pump delivers hydraulic fluid to a flow control valve where the amount of fluid passing through is controlled to a rate of 12.0 - 13.5 pints/minute (6.4 - 7.7 litres/minute) and a pressure of 850 lbf/in^2 (59.7 kgf/cm^2). The hydraulic fluid is then passed onto the servo assisted rack and pinion assembly.

The assistance is obtained by means of a piston mounted on the rack which runs in the rack tube. This also acts as the cylinders. The degree of assistance is controlled by a rotary valve mounted co-axially with the pinion shaft.

With the engine running and the pump being driven, hydraulic fluid passes through the inlet port to the centre annular groove of the sleeves and filling the short slots B (Fig.11.21) in the rotor via holes A in the sleeve. When the input rotor is turned clockwise the fluid will flow across to the three alternate slots C in the sleeve, through holes D to the bottom annular groove, thus pressurising the left-hand side of the servo piston and moving the rack to the right.

Displaced fluid from the opposite side of the piston returns to the top annular groove, passes down holes E via the three slots in the sleeve, into the three longer slots G in the rotor, and out through the space H which is between the top end of the sleeve and input rotor end of the housing to the reservoir.

Should no further movement of the rotor take place or if the steering wheel is released the valve will be centralised by the movement of the rack turning the pinion or by the torsion bar turning the rotor. With the valve in the centralised condition hydraulic fluid passes from the rotor slots B across to the sleeves slots C - F and then back to the reservoir.

Because the top and bottom annular grooves in the sleeve are subjected to the same pressure the two sides of the servo piston will remain unaffected. The pattern of fluid flows is reversed with anti-clockwise movement of the rotor with the fluid flowing from the pump to the top annular groove in the sleeve and displaced fluid returning to the reservoir via the bottom annular groove.

Should power assistance cease the system should be tested as described in Section 40 and if the cause is not found the car should be taken to your local Ford garage for further investigation. Because of

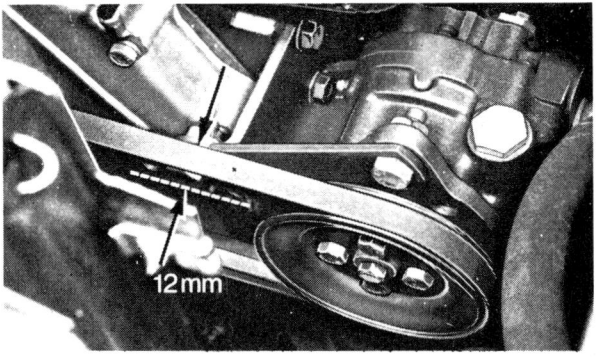

Fig. 11.24 Correct power steering pump belt tension (Sec. 39)

the necessity to use special tools and sometimes the difficulty in obtaining spare parts details of overhauling the steering assembly and pump are omitted.

38 Power assisted steering – hydraulic fluid

It is important that the level of hydraulic fluid is maintained at the correct level. Always use fluid which complies with the Ford specification to top up to the FULL mark on the dipstick.

39 Power assisted steering – pump drive belt adjustment

1 Slacken the pump mounting bolts and the bolt that clamps the pump to the adjustment arm.

Chapter 11 Suspension and steering

2   Move the pump until there is a belt of free movement of 0.5 inch (12.7 mm) midway between the crankshaft pulley and the pump pulley.
3   Tighten all the bolts and recheck the belt tension.
4   When adjusting the drivebelt only lever against the pump body, never against the reservoir or fluid inlet.

40 Power assisted steering – system testing

1   Refer to Section 38 and check the hydraulic fluid in the reservoir.
2   Refer to Section 39 and check the pump drive belt tension.
3   Check the tyre pressures and adjust as necessary.
4   Apply the handbrake and run the engine at idle speed until it has reached normal operating temperature.
5   Set the engine speed to 1,500 rpm and turn the steering between the full lock positions for 3 - 5 times. Do NOT exceed this figure otherwise flats will develop on the tyre treads.
6   Hold the steering on one full lock for 5 seconds and then return the steering wheel to the straight ahead position and attach a spring balance to the rim of the steering wheel.
7   With the engine still running determine the effort required to turn the steering wheel which should not exceed 10 lb (4.535 kg). Should this figure be exceeded it will be necessary to have the system checked by the local Ford garage.

41 Power assisted steering rack and pinion – removal and refitting

1   Chock the rear wheels, apply the handbrake, jack up the front of the car and support on firmly based stands. Remove the road wheels.
2   Place a container under one of the reservoir hoses and detach. Allow as much hydraulic fluid to drain out as possible.
3   Refer to Section 31 and remove the flexible coupling from the steering column and pinion shaft.
4   Remove the split pins and undo the castellated nuts securing the track rod ends to the steering arms. Using a universal ball joint separator detach the ball pins from the steering arms.
5   Disconnect the feed and return pipes from the control valve. Plug the pipe to stop dirt ingress.
6   Support the weight of the engine on a jack or overhead hoist and remove the engine mounting located above the control valve.
7   Detach the stabiliser to tie bolt and then disconnect the stabiliser bar on the control valve side of the car.
8   Bend back the lock tabs and remove the four nuts and clamp plates. Remove the rack 'U' clamps.
9   The steering gear may now be removed from the car on the control valve side.
10 Refitting the power assisted rack and pinion assembly is the reverse sequence to removal, but the following additional points should be noted:

(a) Do not tighten the universal coupling clamp bolts until the weight of the car is on the wheels.
(b) Check and adjust the front wheel toe-in. Further information will be found in Section 26.
(c) Bleed the steering hydraulic system as described in Section 42.

42 Power assisted steering – system bleeding

1   Make sure that all hose connections are tight and then fill the reservoir with fresh or clean hydraulic fluid, complying with the Ford specification.
2   Remove the HT lead from the centre of the ignition coil and operate the starter. Continually top up the reservoir fluid level until the level remains constant and no bubbles are seen.
3   Refit the HT lead and start the engine. Allow to idle and then turn the steering wheel between full locks three times. Return the steering wheel to the straight ahead position and recheck the reservoir hydraulic fluid level.

43 Fault diagnosis – suspension and steering

Symptom	Reason/s	Remedy
Steering feels vague, car wanders and floats at speed	Tyre pressures uneven	Check pressures and adjust as necessary
	Dampers worn	Test, and renew if worn
	Spring broken	Renew spring
	Steering gear ball joints badly worn	Fit new ball joints
	Suspension geometry incorrect	Check and rectify
	Steering mechanism free play excessive	Adjust or overhaul steering mechanism
	Front or rear suspension mounting pick-up points out of alignment	Normally caused by poor repair work after a serious accident. Extensive rebuilding necessary
Stiff and heavy steering	Tyre pressures too low	Check pressures and inflate tyres
	No grease in swivel pins	Grease thoroughly
	No oil in steering gear	Top up steering gear
	No grease in steering and suspension ball joints	Grease thoroughly
	Front wheel toe-in incorrect	Check and reset toe-in
	Suspension geometry incorrect	Check and rectify
	Steering gear incorrectly adjusted too tightly	Check and re-adjust steering gear
	Steering column badly misaligned	Determine cause and rectify (usually due to bad repair after severe accident damage and difficult to correct)
	Worn universal joints	Fit new joints
Wheel wobble and vibration	Wheel nuts loose	Check and tighten as necessary
	Front wheels and tyres out of balance	Balance wheels and tyres and add weights as necessary
	Steering ball joints badly worn	Renew steering gear ball joints
	Hub bearings badly worn	Remove and fit new hub bearings
	Steering gear free play excessive	Adjust and overhaul steering gear
	Front springs weak or broken	Inspect and overhaul as necessary

Power assisted steering – see Section 40.

Chapter 12 Bodywork and fittings

Contents

Boot lid lock – removal and refitting	20
Boot lid lock striker plate – removal and refitting	21
Boot lid – removal and refitting	19
Bonnet lock – adjustment	17
Bonnet lock – removal and refitting	16
Bonnet release cable – removal, refitting and adjustment	18
Centre console – removal and refitting	34
Door glass and regulator – removal and refitting	14
Door lock assembly – removal and refitting	13
Door outer belt weatherstrip – removal and refitting	15
Door rattles – tracing and rectification	9
Door striker plate – removal, refitting and adjustment	11
Door trim – removal and refitting	12
Facia crash panel – removal and refitting	30
Front and rear doors – removal and refitting	10
General description	1
Heater assembly – dismantling and reassembly	33
Heater assembly – removal and refitting	32
Load space trim panel – removal and refitting	31
Maintenance – bodywork and underframe	2
Maintenance – hinges and locks	7
Maintenance – PVC external roof coverings	6
Maintenance – upholstery and carpets	3
Major body damage – repair	5
Minor body damage – repair	4
Radiator grille – removal and refitting	28
Rear quarter window glass – removal and refitting	25
Rear window glass – removal and refitting	26
Sliding roof – overhaul	29
Tailgate assembly – removal and refitting	22
Tailgate lock – removal and refitting	23
Tailgate lock striker plate – removal and refitting	24
Tailgate window glass – removal and refitting	27
Windscreen glass – removal and refitting	8

1 General description

The combined body and underframe is of all steel welded construction. This makes a very strong and torsionally rigid shell.

The windscreen is slightly curved and is zone toughened for additional driver and passenger safety. In the event of windscreen shattering this 'zone' breaks into much larger pieces than the rest of the screen thus giving the driver much better vision than would otherwise be possible.

The heating system is air controlled which gives a quicker and steadier temperature control. The heater housing is easily accessible in the engine compartment and this reduces noise in the passenger compartment. Adjustable face level vents are located at each end of the dashboard to supply either cold or warm air or a combination as selected on the heater control. Air flow can be directed to the side windows as described. On Granada models hot or cold air is supplied separately to the rear passenger compartment through foot level ducts located at the rear end of the console. The air flow is controlled by a lever operated by the rear passengers.

The instrument panel is bolted on and is preassembled with all instruments. The safety crash pad covers the whole panel and projects well above the instrument surface to give maximum protection.

The seating is of a new design giving good support without being bulky or wasting passenger space. The seat springing is designed to harmonise with the whole suspension system.

For safety, single handed operation seat belts are fitted to all models. The door release levers of the pull out type are safely recessed behind the door handles.

A sliding roof which is fitted to some models provides for greatly increased ventilation. It is of a new design so that the roof can be opened a few inches considerably cutting down wind noise whilst the rear end can be tilted upward by some two inches, by operating a little lever incorporated in the winding handle housing.

Turning to the exterior the door handles are flush with the bodywork surface. On Granada models protective body side mouldings incorporate PVC strips which run the length of the car. To combat corrosion the body panels are designed to withstand 240 hours against attack by salt at 320°C!

The saloon luggage compartment has a large capacity of 13.5 cu ft whilst the estate has 41.7 cu ft with the rear seat and 77.0 cu ft with the rear seat down.

2 Maintenance — bodywork and underframe

1 The general condition of a vehicle's bodywork is the one thing that significantly affects its value. Maintenance is easy but needs to be regular and particular. Neglect, particularly after minor damage, can lead quickly to further deterioration and costly repair bills. It is important also to keep watch on those parts of the vehicle not immediately visible, for instance the underside, inside all the wheel arches and the lower part of the engine compartment.

2 The basic maintenance routine for the bodywork is washing - preferably with a lot of water from a hose. This will remove all the loose solids which may have stuck to the vehicle. It is important to flush these off in such a way as to prevent grit from scratching the finish. The wheel arches and underbody need washing in the same way to remove any accumulated mud which will retain moisture and tend to encourage rust. Paradoxically enough, the best time to clean the underbody and wheel arches is in wet weather when the mud is thoroughly wet and soft. In very wet weather the underbody is usually cleaned of large accumulations automatically and this is a good time for inspection.

3 Periodically it is a good idea to have the whole of the underside of the vehicle steam cleaned, engine compartment included, so that a thorough inspection can be carried out to see what minor repairs and renovations are necessary. Steam cleaning is available at many garages and is necessary for removal of the accumulation of oily grime which sometimes is allowed to cake thick in certain areas near the engine, gearbox and back axle. If steam facilities are not available, there are one or two excellent grease solvents available which can be brush applied. The dirt can then be simply hosed off.

4 After washing paintwork, wipe off with a chamois leather to give an unspotted clear finish. A coat of clear protective wax polish will give added protection against chemical pollutants in the air. If the paintwork sheen has dulled or oxidised, use a cleaner/polisher combination to restore the brilliance of the shine. This requires a little effort, but is usually caused because regular washing has been neglected. Always check that the door and ventilator opening drain holes and pipes are completely clear so that the water can be drained out (photos). Bright work should be treated the same way as paintwork. Windscreens and windows can be kept clear of the smeary film which often appears if a little ammonia is added to the water. If they are scratched, a good rub with a proprietary metal polish will often clear them. Never use any form of wax or other body or chromium polish on glass.

Chapter 12 Bodywork and fittings

2.4a Clean and keep the body sill drain apertures clear

2.4b Clean and keep the drain channels clear in the bottom of the doors

3 Maintenance - upholstery and carpets

1   Mats and carpets should be brushed or vacuum cleaned regularly to keep them free of grit. If they are badly stained remove them from the vehicle for scrubbing or sponging and make quite sure they are dry before refitting. Seats and interior trim panels can be kept clean by a wipe over with a damp cloth. If they do become stained (which can be more apparent on light coloured upholstery) use a little liquid detergent and a soft nail brush to scour the grime out of the grain of the material. Do not forget to keep the head lining clean in the same way as the upholstery. When using liquid cleaners inside the car do not over-wet the surfaces being cleaned. Excessive damp could get into the seams and padded interior causing stains, offensive odours or even rot. If the inside of the vehicle gets wet accidentally it is worthwhile taking some trouble to dry it out properly particularly where carpets are involved. *Do not leave oil or electric heaters inside the car for this purpose.*

4 Minor body damage - repair

The photographic sequence on pages 246 and 247, illustrates the operations detailed in the following sub-Sections.

Repair of minor scratches in the car's bodywork

If the scratch is very superficial, and does not penetrate to the metal of the bodywork, repair is very simple. Lightly rub the area of the scratch with a paintwork renovator or a very fine cutting paste, to remove the loose paint from the scratch and to clear the surrounding bodywork of wax polish. Rinse the area with clean water.

Apply touch-up paint to the scratch using a thin paint brush; continue to apply thin layers of paint until the surface of the paint in the scratch is level with the surrounding paintwork. Allow the new paint at least two weeks to harden, then, blend it into the surrounding paintwork by rubbing the paintwork in the scratch area with a paintwork renovator, or a very fine cutting paste. Finally apply wax polish.

An alternative to painting over the scratch is to use a paint transfer. Use the same preparation for the affected area, then, simply, pick a patch of a suitable size to cover the scratch completely. Hold the patch against the scratch and burnish its backing paper; the paper will adhere to the paintwork, freeing itself from the backing paper at the same time. Polish the affected area to blend the patch into the surrounding paintwork. Where the scratch has penetrated right through to the metal of the bodywork, causing the metal to rust, a different repair technique is required. Remove any loose rust from the bottom of the scratch with a penknife; then apply rust inhibiting paint to prevent the formation of rust in the future. Using a rubber or nylon applicator, fill the scratch with bodystopper paste. If required, this paste can be mixed with cellulose thinners to provide a very thin paste which is ideal for filling narrow scratches. Before the stopper paste in the scratch hardens, wrap a piece of smooth cotton rag around the top of a finger. Dip the finger in cellulose thinners and then quickly sweep it across the surface of the stopper-paste in the scratch; this will ensure that the surface of the stopper-paste is slightly hollowed. The scratch can now be painted over as described earlier in this Section.

Repair of dents in the car's bodywork

When deep denting of the vehicle's bodywork has taken place the first task is to pull the dent out, until the affected bodywork almost attains its original shape. There is little point in trying to restore the original shape completely, as the metal in the damaged area will have stretched on impact and cannot be reshaped fully to its original contour. It is better to bring the level of the dent up to a point which is about 1/8 inch (3 mm) below the level of the surrounding bodywork. In cases where the dent is very shallow anyway, it is not worth trying to pull it all out. If the underside of the dent is accessible, it can be hammered out gently from behind, using a mallet with a wooden or plastic head. Whilst doing this, hold a suitable block of wood firmly against the outside of the dent. This block will absorb the impact from the hammer blows and thus prevent a large area of bodywork from being 'belled-out'.

Should the dent be in a section of the bodywork which has a double skin or some other factor making it inaccessible from behind, a different technique is called for. Drill several small holes through the metal inside the dent area - particularly in the deeper sections. Then screw long self-tapping screws into the holes just sufficiently for them to gain a good purchase in the metal. Now the dent can be pulled out by pulling on the protruding heads of the screws with a pair of pliers.

The next stage of the repair is the removal of the paint from the damaged area, and from an inch or so of the surrounding 'sound' bodywork. This is accomplised more easily by using a wire brush or abrasive pad on a power drill, although it can be done just as effectively by hand using sheets of abrasive paper. To complete the preparations for filling, score the surface of the bare metal with a screwdriver or the tang of a file, or alternatively, drill small holes in the affected area. This will provide a really good 'key' for the filler paste.

To complete the repair see the Section on filling and re-spraying.

Repair of rust holes or gashes in the car's bodywork

Remove all paint from the affected area and from an inch or so of the surrounding 'sound' bodywork, using an abrasive pad or a wire brush on a power drill. If these are not available a few sheets of abrasive paper will do the job just as effectively. With the paint removed you will be able to gauge the severity of the corrosion and therefore decide whether to renew the whole panel (if this is possible) or to repair the affected area. New body panels are not as expensive as most people think and it is often quicker and more satisfactory to fit a new panel than to attempt to repair large areas of corrosion.

Remove all fittings from the affected area except those which will act as a guide to the original shape of the damaged bodywork (eg. headlamp shells etc). Then, using tin snips or a hacksaw blade, remove all loose metal and any other metal badly affected by corrosion. Hammer the edges of the hole inwards in order to create a slight depression for the filler paste.

Wire brush the affected area to remove the powdery rust from the surface of the remaining metal. Paint the affected area with rust inhibiting paint; if the back of the rusted area is accessible treat this also.

Before filling can take place it will be necessary to block the hole in some way. This can be achieved by the use of one of the following materials: Zinc gauze, Aluminium tape or Polyurethane foam.

Zinc gauze is probably the best material to use for a large hole. Cut a piece to the appropriate size and shape of the hole to be filled. then position it in the hole so that its edges are below the level of the surrounding bodywork. It can be retained in position by several blobs of filler paste around its periphery.

Aluminium tape should be used for small or very narrow holes. Pull a piece off the roll and trim it to the approximate size and shape required, then pull off the backing paper (if used) and stick the tape over the hole; it can be overlapped if the thickness of one piece is insufficient. Burnish down the edges of the tape with the handle of a screwdriver, or similar, to ensure that the tape is securely attached to the metal underneath.

Polyurethane foam is best used where the hole is situated in a section of bodywork of complex shape, backed by a small box section (eg. where the rocker panel meets the rear wheel arch - most cars). The usual mixing procedure for this foam is as follows: Put equal amounts of fluid from each of the two cans provided in the kit, into one container. Stir until the mixture begins to thicken, then quickly pour this mixture into the hole, and hold a piece of cardboard over the larger apertures. Almost immediately the polyurethane will begin to expand, gushing frantically out of any small holes left unblocked. When the foam hardens it can be cut back to just below the level of the surrounding bodywork with a hacksaw blade.

Bodywork repairs - filling and re-spraying

Before using this Section, see Sections on dent, deep scratch, rust hole and gash repairs.

Many types of bodyfiller are available, but generally speaking those proprietary kits which contain a tin of filler paste and a tube of resin hardener are best for this type of repair. A wide, flexible plastic or nylon applicator will be found invaluable for imparting a smooth and well contoured finish to the surface of the filler.

Mix up a little filler on a clean piece of card or board - use the hardener sparingly (follow the maker's instructions on the packet otherwise the filler will set very rapidly).

Using the applicator, apply the filler paste to the prepared area; draw the applicator across the surface of the filler to achieve the correct contour and to level the filler surface. As soon as a contour that approximates the correct one is achieved, stop working the paste - if you carry on too long the paste will become sticky and begin to "pick-up' on the applicator. Continue to add thin layers of filler paste at twenty-minute intervals until the level of the filler is just 'proud' of the surrounding bodywork.

Once the filler has hardened, excess can be removed using a plane or file. From then on, progressively finer grades of abrasive paper should be used, starting with a 40 grade production paper and finishing with 400 grade 'wet or dry' paper. Always wrap the abrasive paper around a flat rubber cork or wooden block - otherwise the surface of the filler will not be completely flat. During the smoothing of the filler surface the 'wet or dry' paper should be periodically rinsed in water - this will ensure that a very smooth finish is imparted to the filler at the final stage.

At this stage the 'dent' should be surrounded by a ring of bare metal, which in turn should be encircled by the finely 'feathered' edge of the good paintwork. Rinse the repair area with clean water, until all of the dust produced by the rubbing-down operation is gone.

Spray the whole repair area with a light coat of grey primer; this will show up any imperfections in the surface of the filler. Repair these imperfections with fresh filler paste or bodystopper, and once more smooth the surface with abrasive paper. If bodystopper is used, it can be mixed with cellulose thinners to form a really thin paste which is ideal for filling small holes. Repeat this spray and repair procedure until you are satisfied that the surface of the filler, and the feathered edge of the paintwork are perfect. Clean the repair area with clean water and allow to dry fully.

The repair area is now ready for spraying. Paint spraying must be carried out in a warm, dry, windless and dust free atmosphere. This condition can be created artificially if you have access to a large indoor working area, but if you are forced to work in the open, you will have to pick your day very carefully. If you are working indoors, dousing the floor in the work area with water will 'lay' the dust which would otherwise be in the atmosphere. If the repair area is confined to one body panel, mask off the surrounding panels; this will help to minimise the effects of a slight mis-matching in paint colours. Bodywork fittings (eg chrome strips, door handles etc) will also need to be masked off. Use genuine masking tape and several thicknesses of newspapers for the masking operation.

Before commencing to spray, agitate the aerosol can thoroughly, then spray a test area (an old tin, or similar) until the technique is mastered. Cover the repair area with a thick coat of primer; the thickness should be built up using several thin layers of paint rather than one thick one. Using 400 grade 'wet or dry' paper, rub down the surface of the primer until it is really smooth. While doing this, the work area should be thoroughly doused with water. Allow to dry before spraying on more paint.

Spray on the top coat, again building up the thickness by using several thin layers of paint. Start spraying in the centre of the repair area and then using a circular motion, work outwards until the whole repair area and about 2 inches of the surrounding original paintwork is covered. Remove all masking material 10 to 15 minutes after spraying on the final coat of paint. Allow the new paint at least two weeks to harden fully; then, using a paintwork renovator or a very fine cutting paste, blend the edges of the new paint into the existing paintwork. Finally, apply wax polish.

5 Major body damage — repair

Where serious damage has occurred or large areas need renewal due to neglect, it means certainly that completely new sections or panels will need welding in and this is best left to professionals. If the damage is due to impact it will also be necessary to completely check the alignment of the bodyshell structure. Due to the principle of construction the strength and shape of the whole can be affected by damage to a part. In such instances the services of a Ford agent with specialist checking jigs are essential. If a body is left misaligned it is first of all dangerous as the car will not handle properly and secondly, uneven stresses will be imposed on the steering, engine and transmission, causing abnormal wear or complete failure. Tyre wear may also be excessive.

6 Maintenance – PVC external roof covering

Under no circumstances try to clean any external PVC roof covering with detergents, caustic soaps or spirit cleaners. Plain soap and water is all that is required, with a soft brush to clean dirt that may be ingrained. Wash the covering as frequently as the rest of the car.

7 Maintenance – hinges and locks

Once every 3000 miles (5000 km) or 3 months, the door, bonnet and boot or tailgate hinges and locks should be given a few drops of oil from an oil can. The door striker plates can be given a thin smear of grease to reduce wear and to ensure free movement.

8 Windscreen glass – removal and renewal

1 If you are unfortunate enough to have a windscreen shatter, or should you wish to renew your present windscreen, fitting a new screen is one of the few jobs which the average owner is advised to leave to a professional. For the owner who wishes to attempt the job himself the following instructions are given.
2 Cover the bonnet with a blanket or cloth to prevent accidental damage and remove the windscreen wiper blades and arms as detailed in Chapter 10.
3 Put on a pair of lightweight shoes and get onto one of the front

Chapter 12 Bodywork and fittings

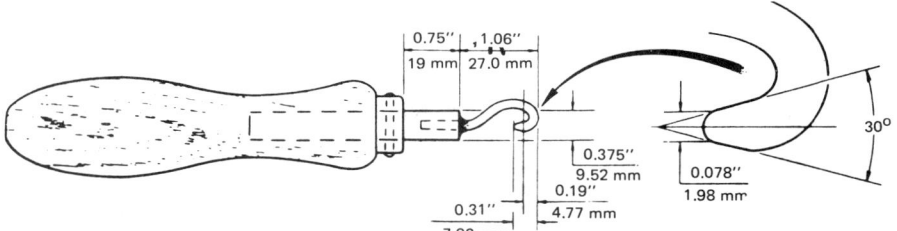

Fig. 12.1 Special tool for inserting chrome moulding (Sec. 8)

seats. An assistant should be ready to catch the glass as it is released from the body aperture.
4 Place a piece of soft cloth between the soles of your shoes and the windscreen glass and with both feet on one top corner of the windscreen push firmly.
5 When the weatherstrip has freed itself from the body aperture flange in that area repeat the process at frequent intervals along the top edge of the windscreen until from outside the car the glass and weatherstrip can be removed together.
6 If you are having to renew your windscreen due to a shattered screen, remove all traces of sealing compound from the weatherstrip and body flange.
7 Now is the time to remove all pieces of glass if the screen has shattered. Use a vacuum cleaner to extract as much as possible. Switch on the heater boost motor and adjust the screen controls to 'screen defrost' but watch out for flying pieces of glass which might be blown out of the ducting.
8 Carefully inspect the rubber moulding for signs of splitting or deterioration.
9 To refit the glass, first fit the weatherstrip onto the glass with the joint at the lower edge.
10 Insert a piece of thick cord into the channel of the weatherstrip with the two ends protruding by at least 12 inches (300 mm) at the top centre of the weatherstrip.
11 Mix a concentrated soap and water solution and apply to the flange of the windscreen aperture.
12 Offer the screen up to the aperture and with an assistant to press the rubber surround hard against one end of the cord moving round the windscreen and so drawing the lip over the windscreen flange of the body. Keep the draw cord parallel to the windscreen. Using the palms of the hands, thump on the glass from the outside to assist the lip in passing over the flange and to seat the screen correctly into the aperture.
13 To ensure a good watertight joint apply some Seelastik SR51 between the weatherstrip and the body and press the weatherstrip against the body to give a good seal.
14 Any excess Seelastik may be removed with a petrol moistened cloth.
15 A special shaped tool is now required to insert the finisher and full details of this are given in Fig. 12.1. A handyman should be able to make up an equivalent using netting wire and a wooden file handle.
16 Fit the eye of the tool into the groove and feed in the finisher strip.
17 Push the tool around the complete length of the moulding, feeding the finisher into the channel as the eyelet opens it.
18 Refit the wiper arms and blades and do not forget the Tax disc.

9 Door rattles – tracing and rectification

1 The most common cause of door rattle is a misaligned, loose or worn striker plate; however other causes may be:

   a) Loose door or window winder handles;
   b) Loose or misaligned door lock components;
   c) Loose or worn remote control mechanism.

2 It is quite possible for door rattles to be the result of a combination of the above faults so a careful examination should be made to determine their exact cause.
3 If striker plate wear or misalignment is the cause, the plate should be renewed or adjusted as necessary. The procedure is detailed in Section 11.
4 Should the window winder handle rattle, this can be easily rectified by inserting a rubber washer between the escutcheon and door trim panel.

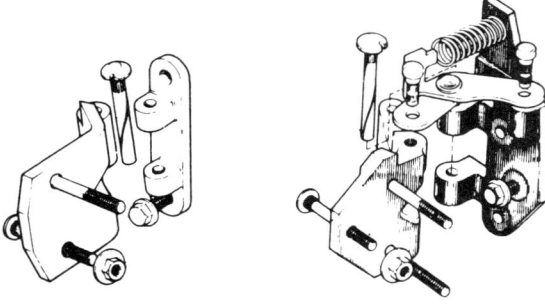

Fig. 12.2 The front and rear hinges (Sec. 10)

5 If the rattle is found to be emanating from the door lock it will in all probability mean that the lock is worn and therefore should be replaced with a new lock unit as described in Section 13.
6 Lastly if it is worn hinge pins causing rattles they should be renewed.

10 Front and rear doors – removal and refitting

1 Using a pencil, accurately mark the outline of the hinge relative to the door once the hinges have been released. Remove the two bolts that secure each hinge to the pillar and lift away the complete door.
2 For storage it is best to stand the door on an old blanket and allow it to lean against a wall also suitably padded at the top to stop scratching.
3 Refitting the door is the reverse sequence to removal. If, after refitting, adjustment is necessary, it should be done at the hinges to give correct alignment, or the striker reset if the door either moves up or down on final closing.

11 Door striker plate – removal, refitting and adjustment

1 If it is wished to renew a worn striker plate, mark its position on the door pillar so a new plate can be fitted in the same position.
2 To remove the plate simply undo and remove the crosshead screws which hold the plate in position. Lift away the plate (photo).
3 Refitting of the door striker plate is the reverse sequence to removal.
4 To adjust the door striker plate slacken the four crosshead screws and move the striker plate in or out as necessary. Make sure that the lock engages fully when the door is flush with the body exterior line. It is very important that the door is not adjusted to be flush with the body in the safety catch position. When the correct position has been found tighten the four crosshead screws firmly.

12 Door trim – removal and refitting

1 Using a knife or thin wide blade screwdriver carefully prise the plastic trim from its recesses in the window winder handle. This will expose the handle retaining screw (photo).
2 Unscrew and remove the lock button (photo).
3 Wind up the window and note the position of the handle. Undo and remove the crosshead retaining screw and lift away the handle.

11.2 The door striker plate

12.1 Prise back the handle insert sufficiently to gain access to the retaining screw

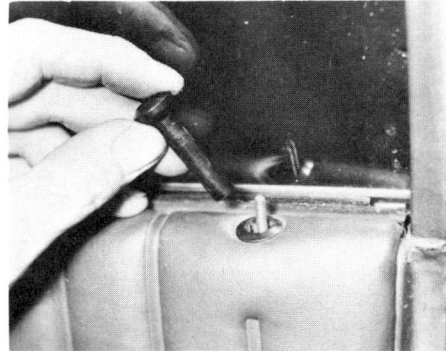
12.2 Remove the lock button

12.4 Remove the door pull/arm rest

12.5 Remove the housing bezel

12.7 Remove the panel and plastic sheeting from the inner door panel

4   Undo and remove the two crosshead screws securing the door arm rest. Lift away the door arm rest (photo).
5   Using a screwdriver carefully remove the door lock remote control housing bezel by sliding the bezel towards the hinge end of the door. Lift away the bezel (photo).
6   Insert a thin strip of metal with all the sharp edges removed, or a thick knife blade, between the door and the trim panel. This will release one or two of the trim panel retaining clips without damaging the trim. The panel can now be gently eased off by hand.
7   Carefully remove the plastic weatherproof sheeting. Removal is now complete. Check drain holes are clear (photo).
8   Refitting is generally a reversal of the removal procedure. **Note:** When refitting the panel ensure that each of the trim panel retaining clips is firmly located in its hole by sharply striking the panel in the approximate area of each clip with the palm of the hand. This will make sure the trim is seated fully (Figs. 12.3 and 12.4).

13 Door lock assembly – removal and refitting

1   Refer to Section 12 and remove the door interior trim.
2   Carefully ease out the door lock remote control housing assembly clear of its location in the door inner panel. Unhook the remote control rod and remove the remote control unit (Figs. 12.5 and 12.6).
3   Working inside the door shell carefully prise the two control rods clear of their locations in the lock assembly (photo).
4   Undo and remove the two bolts that secure the door exterior handle to the door outer panel. The exterior handle assembly complete with controls rods can now be removed.
5   Undo and remove the three crosshead screws and cup shaped shakeproof washers fixing the lock assembly to the door shell. The lock assembly may now be lifted away from inside the door.
6   Refitting the door lock assembly is the reverse sequence to removal. Lubricate all moving parts with a little grease.

14 Door glass and regulator – removal and refitting

1   Using a screwdriver carefully ease out the door inner and outer weatherstrips from their retaining clips on the door panel.
2   Undo and remove the two bolts holding the door glass to the window regulator. Tilt the glass and carefully remove it upward.
3   Undo and remove the bolts that secure the window regulator to the door inner panel and lift away the regulator mechanism through the large aperture in the bottom inner panel (photo).
4   Should it be necessary to remove the glass run channel, start at the front lower frame end and carefully ease the glass run channel from its location in the door frame.
5   Refitting the door glass and regulator is the reverse sequence to removal. Lubricate all moving parts with a little grease. Before refitting the trim panel check the operation and alignment of the glass and regulator and adjust if necessary. When all is correct fully tighten all securing bolts.

15 Door outer belt weatherstrip – removal and refitting

1   Wind the window down to its fullest extent. Carefully prise its weatherstrip out of the groove in the door outer bright metal finish moulding.
2   To refit correctly position the weatherstrip over its groove and using the thumbs carefully press the strip fully into the groove.
3   Wind the window up and check that the weatherstrip is correctly fitted.

16 Bonnet lock – removal and refitting

1   Open the bonnet and support it open using the bonnet stay. To act as a datum for refitting, mark the position of the hinges relative to the

Chapter 12 Bodywork and fittings

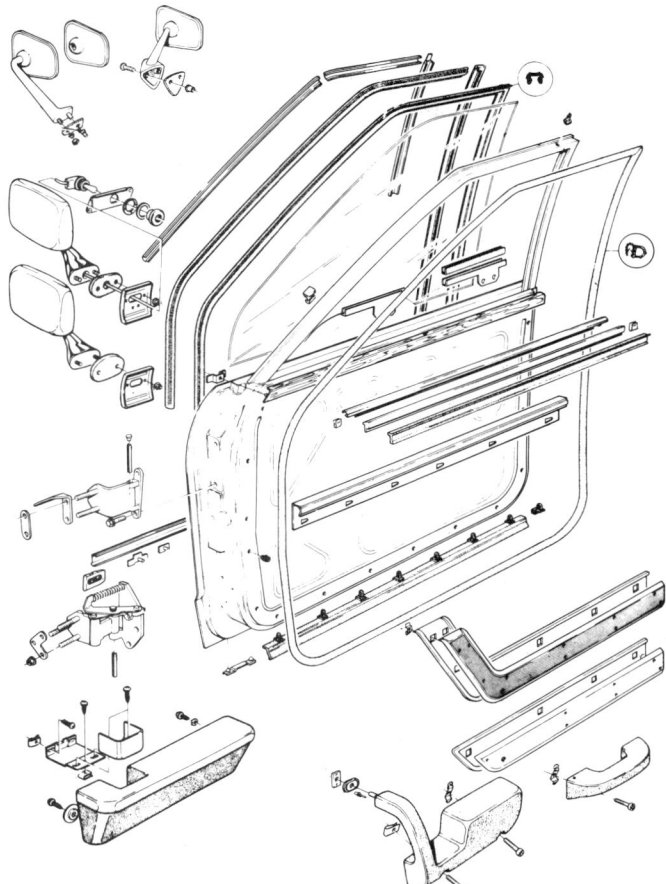

Fig. 12.3 The front door glass and trim (Sec. 12)

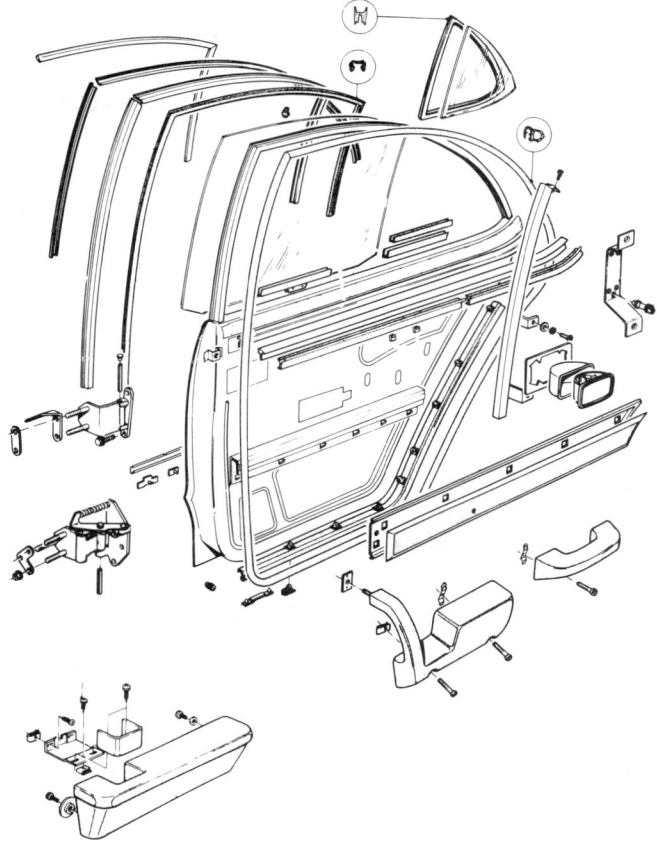

Fig. 12.4 The rear door glass and trim (Sec. 12)

13.3 The door lock showing the two control rods

14.3 The regulator and retaining bolts

bonnet inner panel.
2 With the assistance of a second person hold the bonnet in the open position and release the stay.
3 Undo and remove the two bolts, spring and plain washers that secure each hinge to the bonnet, and lift away the bonnet taking care not to scratch the top of the wings.
4 Lean the bonnet up against a wall, suitably padded to prevent scratching the paint.

5 Refitting the bonnet is the reverse sequence to removal. Any adjustment necessary can be made either at the hinges or the bonnet catch.

17 Bonnet lock – adjustment

1 Should it be necessary to adjust the bonnet catch first slacken the

Chapter 12 Bodywork and fittings

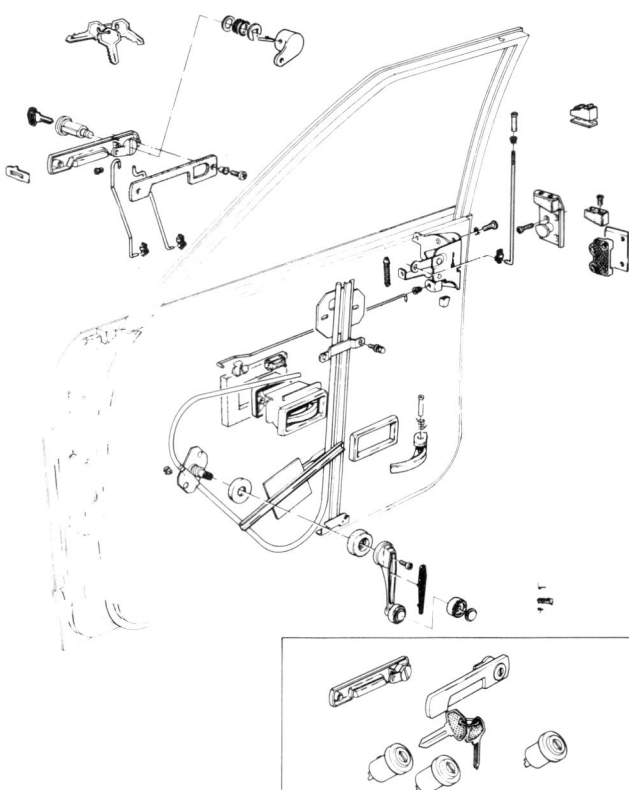

Fig. 12.5 Front door lock and window regulator components (Sec. 13)

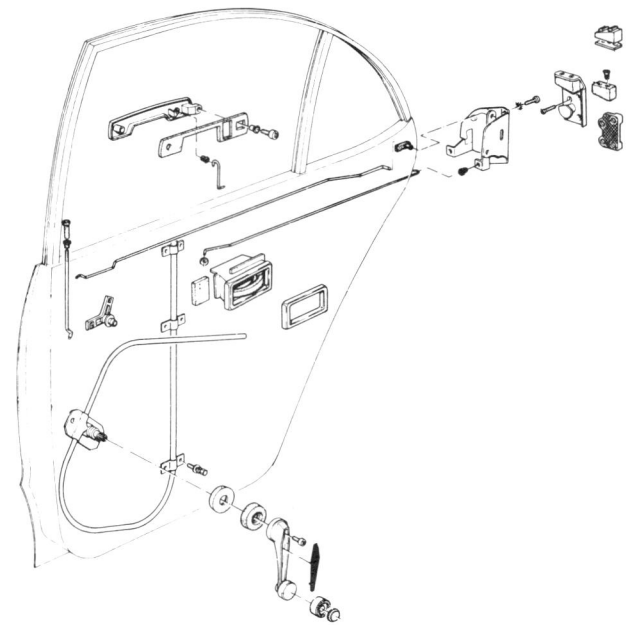

Fig. 12.6 Rear door lock and window regulator components (Sec. 13)

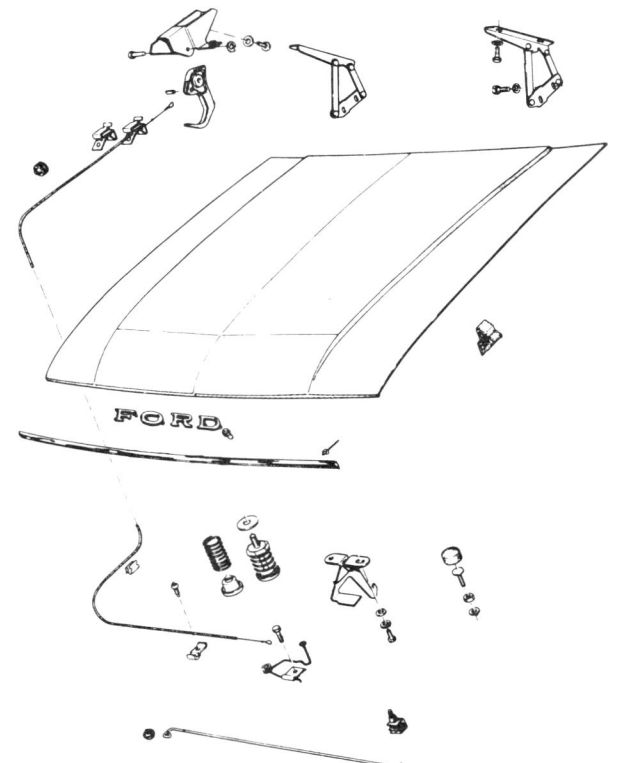

Fig. 12.7 Bonnet and lock components (Sec. 18)

locknut securing the shaft in position.
2 Using a wide bladed screwdriver, screw the shaft in or out as necessary until the correct bonnet front height is obtained. Tighten the locknut.

18 Bonnet release cable – removal, refitting and adjustment

1 Detach the operating cable from the bonnet lock spring and then undo and remove the bolt and clamp holding the outer cable to the front panel (Fig. 12.7).
2 Working under the dashboard remove the spring clip securing the inner cable clevis pin. Withdraw the clevis pin. It may be found easier if the two bonnet release bracket retaining screws are removed before the clevis pin is withdrawn to give better access.
3 Release the outer cable from its spring clips and withdraw it from the grommet in the bulkhead.
4 Well lubricate the inner and outer cable and then refit which is the reverse sequence to removal.
5 To adjust the cable slacken the bolt that secures the cable clip nearest to the lock assembly. Push or pull the outer cable as necessary to adjust the inner cable tension and secure in its new position by tightening the clamp bolt.

19 Boot lid – removal and refitting

1 Open the boot lid to its fullest extent. To act as a datum for refitting, mark the position of the hinge relative to the lid inner panel.
2 With the assistance of a second person hold the boot in the open position and then undo and remove the two bolts, spring and plain washers fixing each hinge to the boot lid. Lift away the boot lid taking care not to scratch the top of the rear wings.
3 Lean the boot lid up against a wall, suitably padded to prevent scratching the paint.
4 Refitting the boot lid is the reverse sequence to removal. Any adjustment necessary can be made at the hinge.

20 Boot lid lock – removal and refitting

1 Open the boot lid and carefully withdraw the spring clip located at the end of the lock spindle.
2 Undo and remove the three bolts and spring washers that secure the lock to the boot lid (Fig. 12.8). Lift away the lock assembly.
3 Refitting the lock assembly is the reverse sequence to removal.

Chapter 12 Bodywork and fittings

2 Undo and remove the two bolts with spring and plain washers securing the striker plate. Lift away the striker plate.
3 Refitting the striker plate is the reverse sequence to removal. Line up the striker plate with the previously made marks and tighten the securing bolts.

22 Tailgate assembly – removal and refitting

1 Open the tailgate and with a pencil mark the outline of the hinges relative to the inner panel.
2 With the assistance of a second person hold the tailgate in position and then undo and remove the bolts, spring and plain washers that secure each hinge to the tailgate. Detach the tailgate stays. Lift away the tailgate taking care not to scratch the side panels.
3 Refitting the tailgate is the reverse sequence to removal. Any adjustment may be made at the hinges.

23 Tailgate lock – removal and refitting

1 Use a wide bladed screwdriver or a thick knife blade between the tailgate and the trim panel. Progressively release the trim panel retaining clips without damaging the trim. The panel can now be gently eased out by hand.
2 Undo and remove the large hexagonal nut that retains the lock cylinder. Lift away the lock cylinder (Fig. 12.9).
3 Undo and remove the lock securing bolts and spring washers and lift away the lock and operating rod assembly.
4 Undo and remove the two nuts, spring and plain washers that secure the tailgate handle. Lift away the tailgate handle and its gasket.

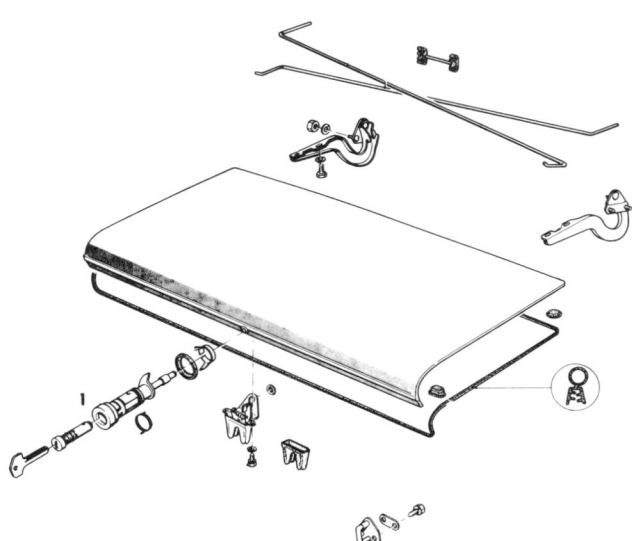

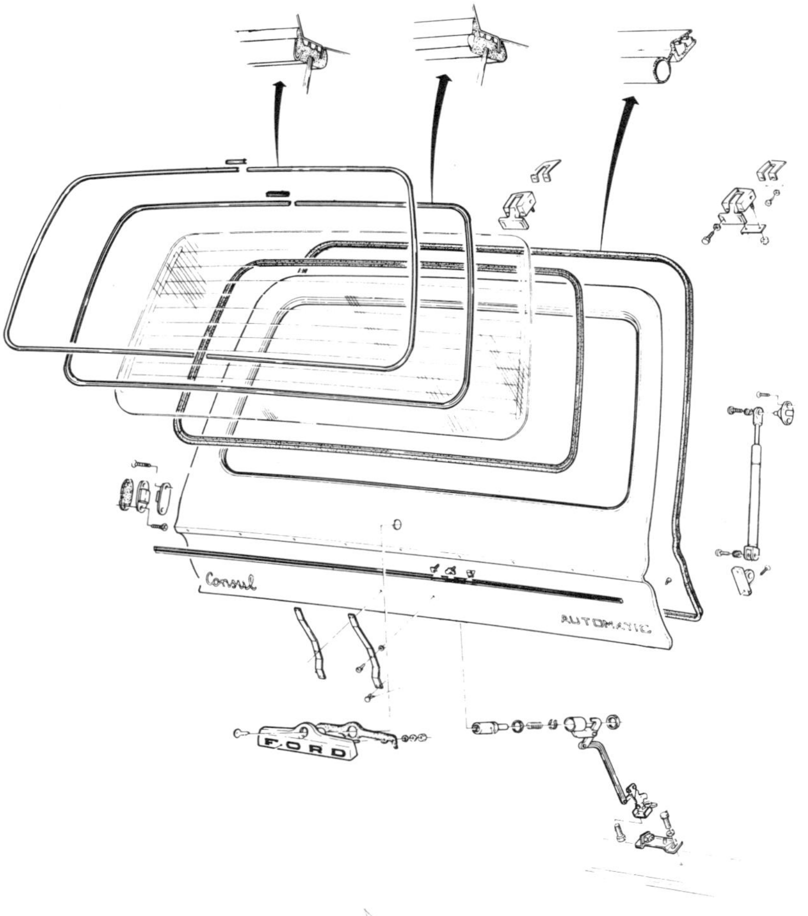

Fig. 12.8 Boot lid and attachments (Saloon models) (Sec. 20)

21 Boot lid lock striker plate – removal and refitting

1 Open the boot lid and with a pencil mark the outline of the striker plate relative to the inner rear panel to act as a datum for refitting.

Fig. 12.9 Tailgate assembly (Estate models) (Sec. 23)

This sequence of photographs deals with the repair of the dent and scratch (above rear lamp) shown in this photo. The procedure will be similar for the repair of a hole. It should be noted that the procedures given here are simplified - more explicit instructions will be found in the text

In the case of a dent the first job - after removing surrounding trim - is to hammer out the dent where access is possible. This will minimise filling. Here, the large dent having been hammered out, the damaged area is being made slightly concave

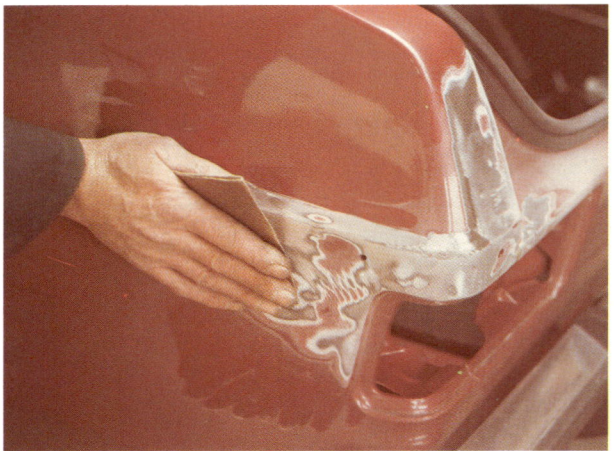

Now all paint must be removed from the damaged area, by rubbing with coarse abrasive paper. Alternatively, a wire brush or abrasive pad can be used in a power drill. Where the repair area meets good paintwork, the edge pf the paintwork should be 'feathered', using a finer grade of abrasive paper

In the case of a hole caused by rusting, all damaged sheet-metal should be cut away before proceeding to this stage. Here, the damaged area is being treated with rust remover and inhibitor before being filled

Mix the body filler according to its manufacturer's instructions. In the case of corrosion damage, it will be necessary to block off any large holes before filling - this can be done with zinc gauze or aluminium tape. Make sure the area is absolutely clean before ...

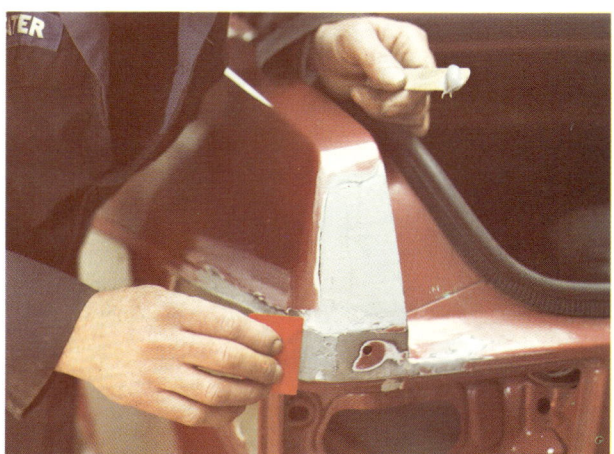

... applying the filler. Filler should be applied with a flexible applicator, as shown, for best results: the wooden spatula being used for confined areas. Apply thin layers of filler at 20-minute intervals, until the surface of the filler is slightly proud of the surrounding bodywork

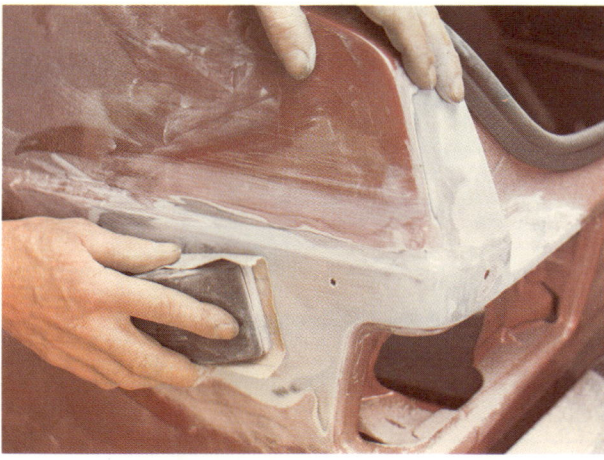

Initial shaping can be done with a Surform plane or Dreadnought file. Then, using progressively finer grades of wet-and-dry paper, wrapped around a sanding block, and copious amounts of clean water, rub-down the filler until really smooth and flat. Again, feather the edges of adjoining paintwork

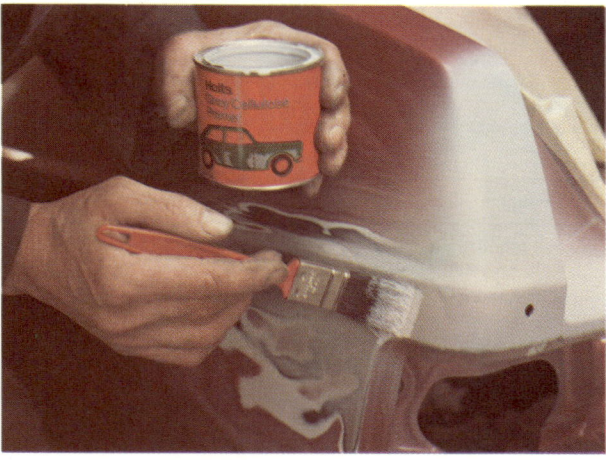

The whole repair area can now be sprayed or brush-painted with primer. If spraying, ensure adjoining areas are protected from over-spray. Note that at least one-inch of the surrounding sound paintwork should be coated with primer. Primer has a 'thick' consistency, so will fill small imperfections

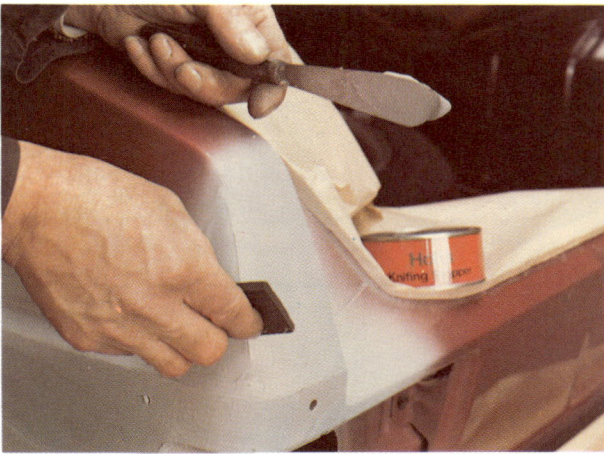

Again, using plenty of water, rub down the primer with a fine grade of wet-and-dry paper (400 grade is probably best) until it is really smooth and well blended into the surrounding paintwork. Any remaining imperfections can now be filled by carefully applied knifing stopper paste

When the stopper has hardened, rub-down the repair area again before applying the final coat of primer. Before rubbing-down this last coat of primer, ensure the repair area is blemish-free - use more stopper if necessary. To ensure that the surface of the primer is really smooth use some finishing compound

The top coat can now be applied. When working out of doors, pick a dry, warm and wind-free day. Ensure surrounding areas are protected from over-spray. Agitate the aerosol thoroughly, then spray the centre of the repair area, working outwards with a circular motion. Apply the paint as several thin coats.

After a period of about two-weeks, which the paint needs to harden fully, the surface of the repaired area can be 'cut' with a mild cutting compound prior to wax polishing. When carrying out bodywork repairs, remember that the quality of the finished job is proportional to the time and effort expended

5 To refit the lock assembly is the reverse sequence to removal. Do not tighten the lock and operating rod assembly bolts until the lock cylinder has been refitted and the cylinder keyways connected to the operating rod assembly.

24 Tailgate lock striker plate – removal and refitting

1 Open the tailgate and with a pencil mark the outline of the striker plate relative to the luggage compartment floor.
2 Undo and remove the bolts, spring and plain washers which hold the striker plate and lift away the striker plate.
3 Refitting the striker plate is the reverse sequence to removal. Line up the striker plate with the previously made mark and tighten the securing bolts.

25 Rear quarter window glass – removal and refitting

Fixed quarter glass (saloon)
1 Using a blunt screwdriver carefully ease the moulding from the weatherstrip.
2 An assistant should now be ready to catch the glass as it is released from the body aperture. Working inside the car push on the glass next to the weatherstrip so releasing it from the aperture flange. Lift away the glass and weatherstrip.
3 Remove the weatherstrip and clean off all traces of sealer. Inspect the weatherstrip for signs of splitting or deterioration and, if evident; a new weatherstrip must be obtained.
4 To refit the glass assembly first fit the moulding to its groove in the weatherstrip and apply a little sealer to the groove in which the glass seats. Fit the glass to the weatherstrip.
5 Fit a draw cord in the weatherstrip to body groove and position the glass to the aperture. Working inside the car, pull on the draw cord whilst the assistant pushes on the glass so drawing the lip over the flange.
6 Apply a little sealer to the weatherstrip to aperture flange. Clean off surplus sealer with a petrol moistened cloth.

Hinged quarter glass (Coupe)
7 Carefully prise the trim back to gain access to the hinge and lever attachment screws (Fig. 12.10).
8 Open the quarter glass and supporting the glass remove the securing screws from the hinge and lever, then carefully remove the glass complete with lever unit.
9 To dismantle the lever unit, carefully drive out the hinge roll pins using a suitable drift and supporting the window if still attached.
10 Reassembly is the reverse of removal.

26 Rear window glass – removal and refitting

1 Undo and remove the self tapping screws securing the front edge of the rear seat cushion to the heel plate. Lift out the cushion taking care not to damage the upholstery or headlining.
2 Open the boot lid and undo and remove the screws which fix the top of the rear seat backrest to the body. Carefully lift away the backrest.
3 Remove the retainers and bend back the lock tabs securing the rear parcel shelf. Lift away the parcel shelf.
4 Place a blanket over the boot lid so that it is not accidently scratched and remove the rear window glass using the same procedure as for the front windscreen. Further information will be found in Section 8 paragraphs 3 to 5 inclusive. Take extreme care if a heated rear window glass is fitted. Disconnect the terminal connectors.
5 Refitting the rear window glass is similar to the refitting of the front windscreen. Refer to Section 8, paragraphs 8 to 17 inclusive.

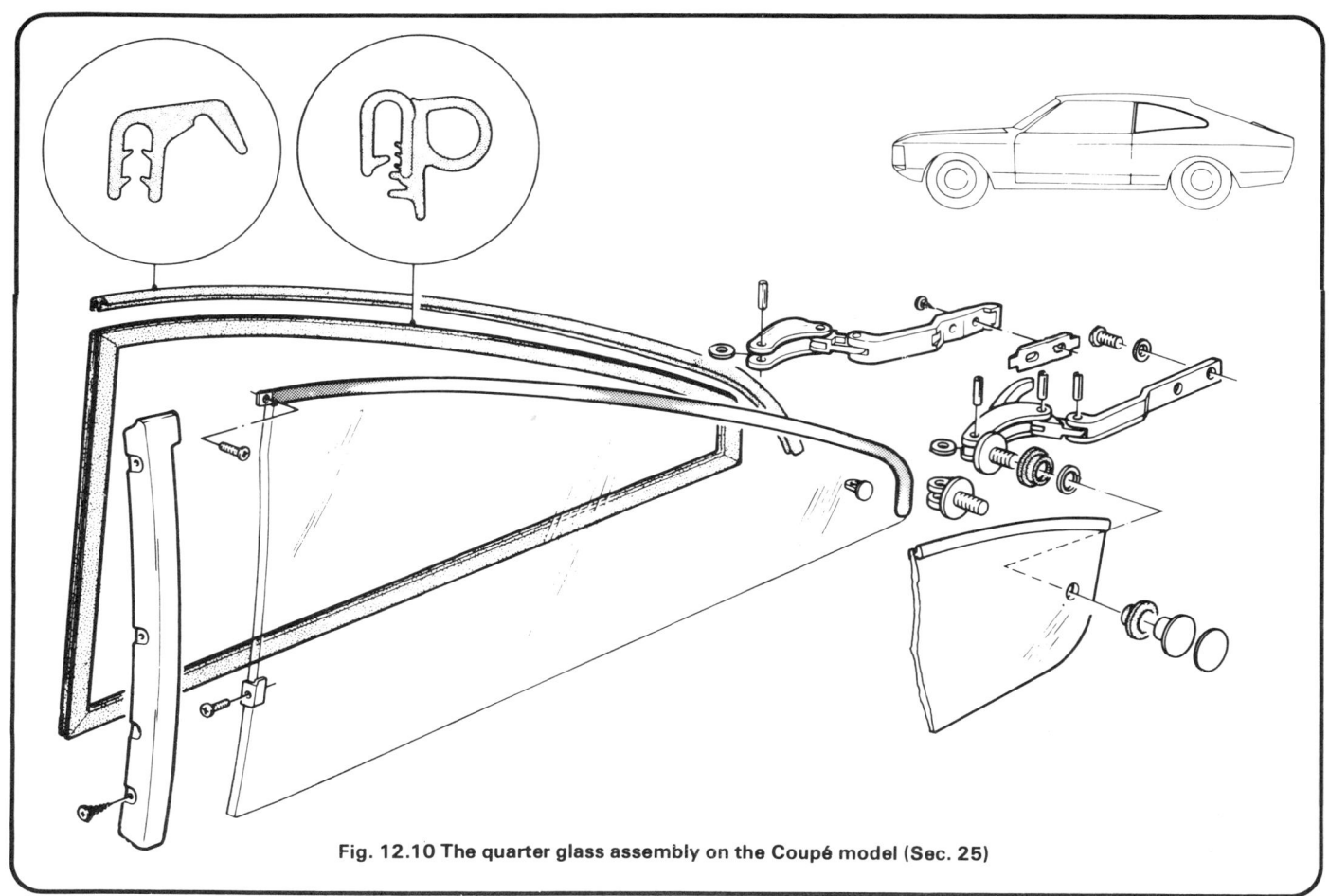

Fig. 12.10 The quarter glass assembly on the Coupé model (Sec. 25)

Chapter 12 Bodywork and fittings

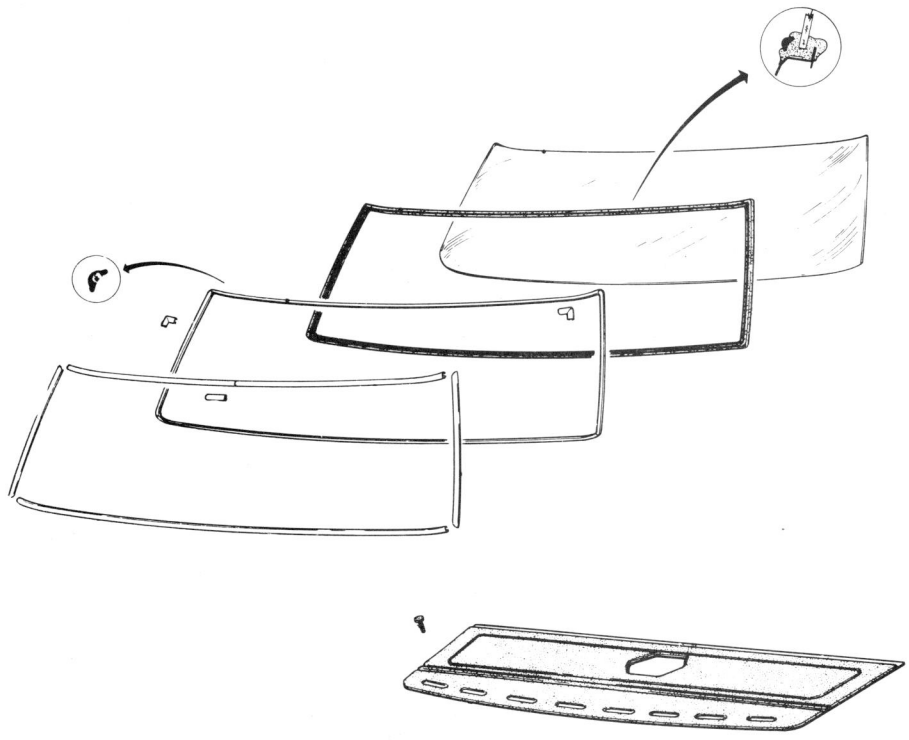

Fig. 12.11 Rear window and parcel shelf trim attachments (Sec. 26)

27 Tailgate window glass – removal and refitting

The procedures for removing and refitting the tailgate window glass is basically identical to that for the rear window glass. Refer to Section 26, paragraphs 4 and 5 for full information.

28 Radiator grille – removal and refitting

Open the bonnet and support in the open position. Undo and remove the crosshead screws that secure the radiator grille to the front body panels. Lift away the radiator grille. Refitting is the reverse

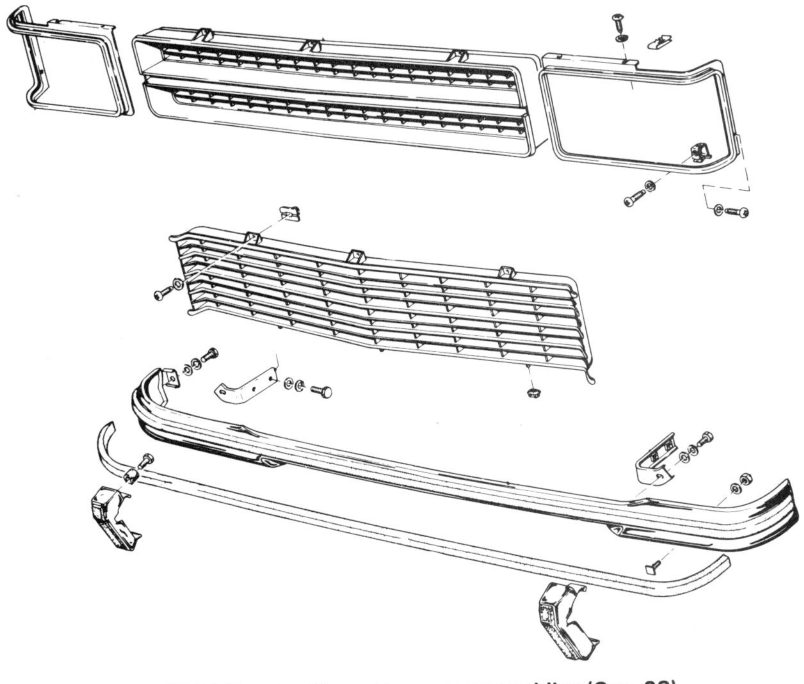

Fig. 12.12 Front grille and bumper assemblies (Sec. 28)

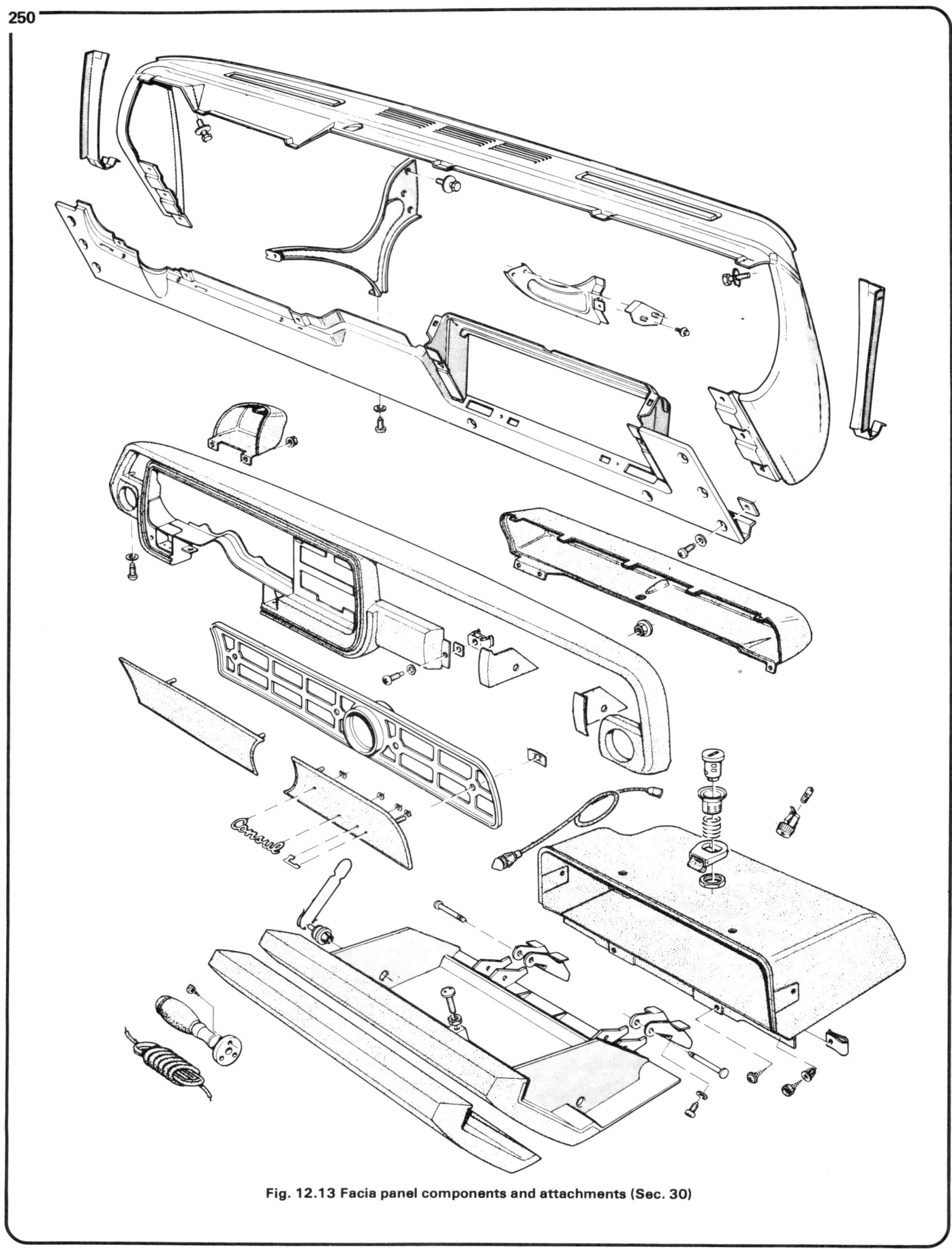

Fig. 12.13 Facia panel components and attachments (Sec. 30)

Chapter 12 Bodywork and fittings

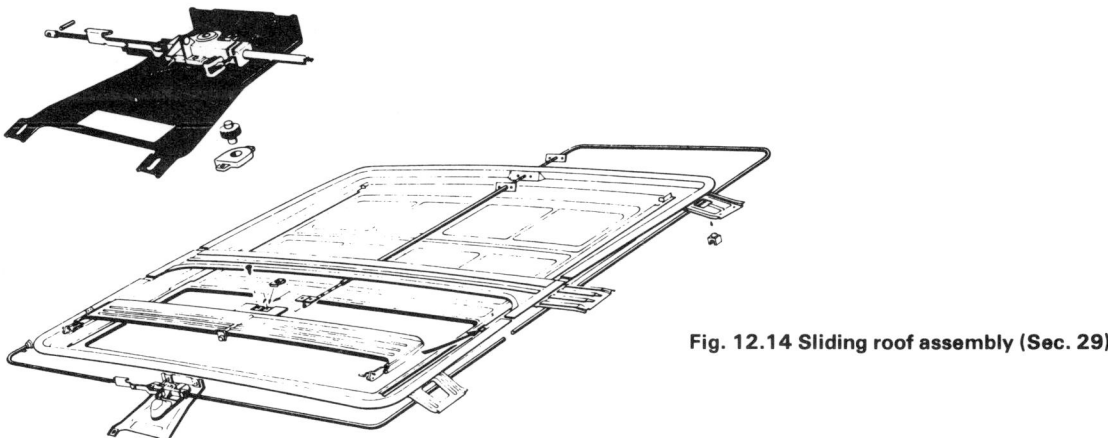

Fig. 12.14 Sliding roof assembly (Sec. 29)

sequence to removal but take care to locate the grille tabs in their respective slots in the front lower panel.

29 Sliding roof – overhaul

It is strongly recommended that, if any service attention is required on the sliding roof assembly, this be left to the specialist due to knowledge and experience necessary to effect a satisfactory repair.

30 Facia crash pad – removal and refitting

1   Refer to Chapter 10 and remove the instrument cluster.
2   Undo and remove the two bolts that secure the heater control panel and push the panel to one side.
3   Remove the radio set attachments. The method will depend on the type of radio fitted. Refer to Chapter 10 Fig. 10.29 which shows the factory fitted type.
4   Undo and remove the four screws that secure the two halves of the steering column shroud and detach the shroud.
5   Open the glove compartment lid and remove the glove box lid lock. This is secured by one nut.
6   Undo and remove the six crosshead screws fixing the crash pad to the belt rail.
7   Undo and remove the four screws securing the crash pad to the instrument lower panel (photo).
8   Release the glove box lid supports and remove the clips on which they run. This is done by pushing the centre pin through and carefully pulling out the clip. New clips will be required on reassembly.
9   The glove box side covers should next be removed. Disengage the locating tangs so as to expose the two crosshead screws that secure the crash pad to the instrument lower panel. Undo and remove these screws.
10 Carefully ease the crash pad forward to expose the rear of the asssembly.
11 Detach the face level vent supply pipes.
12 Disconnect the multi pin connectors to the push switches and the wiring loom connections to the clock. The crash pad may now be lifted away from the car.
13 Refitting the crash pad assembly is the reverse sequence to removal.

31 Load space trim panel – removal and refitting

1   This section is only applicable to estate cars.
2   Open the tailgate and lower the rear seat.
3   Using a wide bladed screwdriver or knife carefully prise the 8 panel clips from their holes along the upper edge of the panel location.
4   Lift the panel up and away from the inside of the car.
5   Refitting the load space trim panel is the reverse sequence to removal.

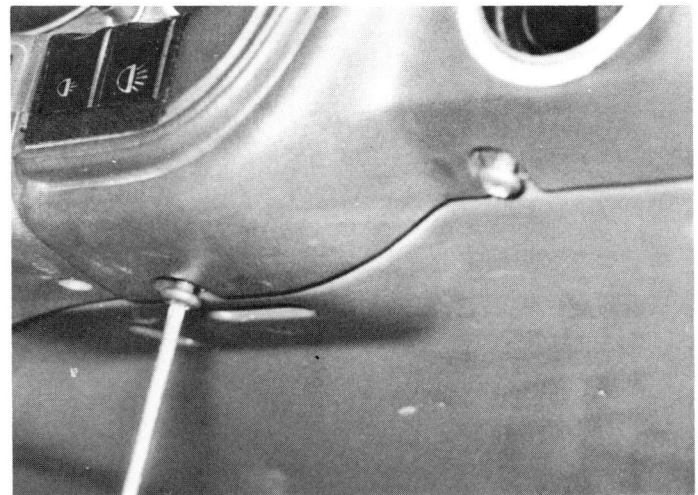

30.7 The lower crash pad retaining screws

32 Heater assembly – removal and refitting

1   Refer to Chapter 2 and drain the cooling system.
2   Locate the multi-pin connector for the heater unit blower motor and detach the plug from the socket.
3   Remove the water drain pipe from the air inlet chamber.
4   Slacken the clips that secure the heater water pipes to the heater unit. Note which way round the pipes are fitted and carefully withdraw the two pipes.
5   Undo and remove the self tapping screws fixing the heater unit to the bulkhead. Detach the heater control flap operating lever and draw the heater away from the bulkhead.
6   Note that there are three gaskets located between the heater housing flange and if these are damaged they must be renewed.
7   To refit the heater assembly, stick on three new gaskets to the heater joint face. If the original gaskets are to be retained apply some sealer to the free face of the gasket pack.
8   Move the flap located in the centre of the heater housing and the control lever inside the car to either the 'cold' or 'hot' position.
9   Fit the heater to the bulkhead and connect the quadrant of the control valve pivot. Secure the heater with the self tapping screws.
10 Refit the water drain pipe and reconnect the multi-pin plug to the blower motor.
11 Reconnect the two hoses to the heater unit and secure with the clips.
12 Refill the cooling system as described in Chapter 2.

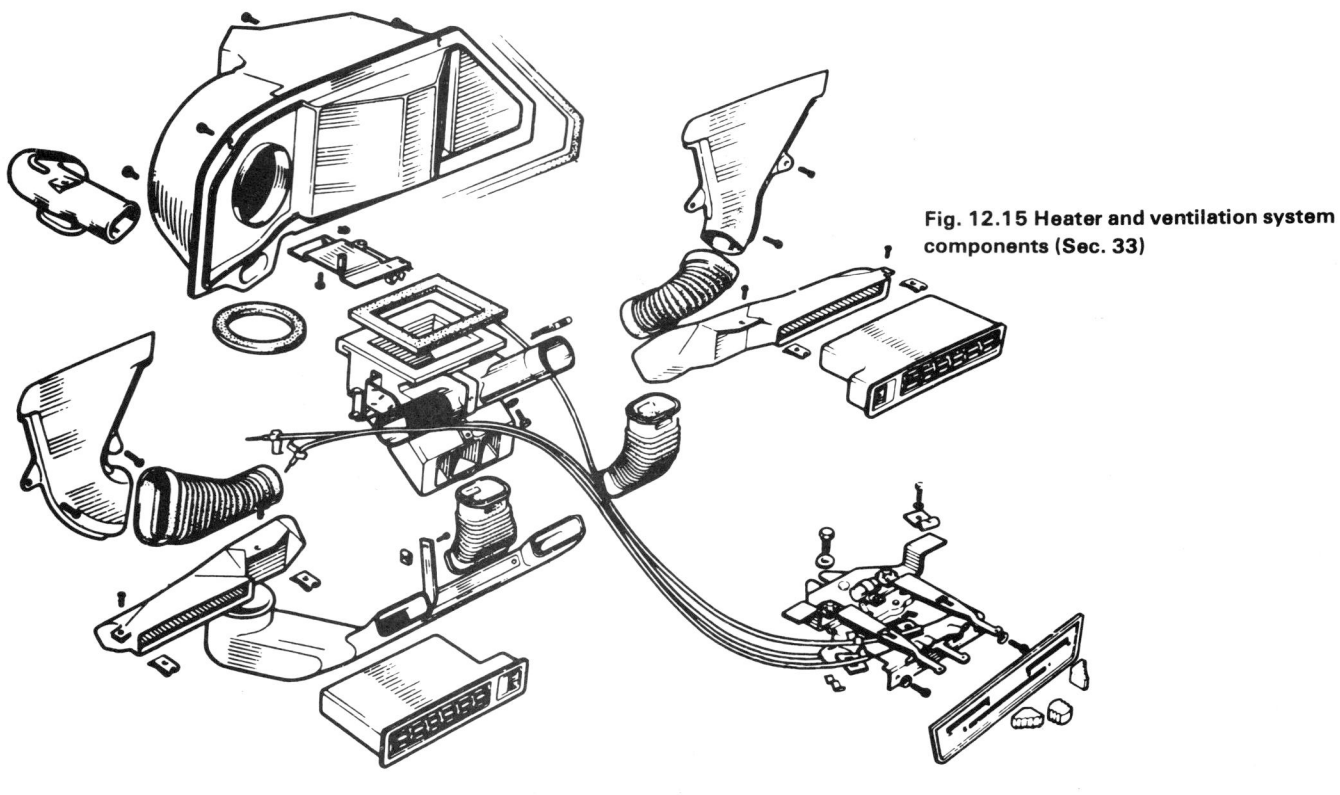

Fig. 12.15 Heater and ventilation system components (Sec. 33)

33 Heater assembly – dismantling and reassembly

1 Refer to Section 32 and remove the heater assembly.
2 Undo and remove the self tapping screws that secure the heater radiator lower panel to the main casing. Lift away the lower panel (Fig. 12.15).
3 Carefully slide out the heater radiator together with its foam rubber packing.
4 Undo and remove the three bolts that secure the blower motor base plate and lift away the blower motor assembly (Fig. 12.16).
5 Inspect the heater radiator for signs of leaks which, if evident, may be repaired in a similar manner used for the engine cooling system radiator as described in Chapter 2. It is a good policy to reverse flush the heater radiator to remove any sediment.
6 Reassembling the heater assembly is the reverse sequence to removal.
7 It is possible to remove the heater radiator and the blower motor whilst the heater assembly is still fitted in the car.

34 Centre console – removal and refitting

1 Three types of centre console have been fitted as shown in Fig. 12.17 but the removal/refitting procedure is basically the same for each type.

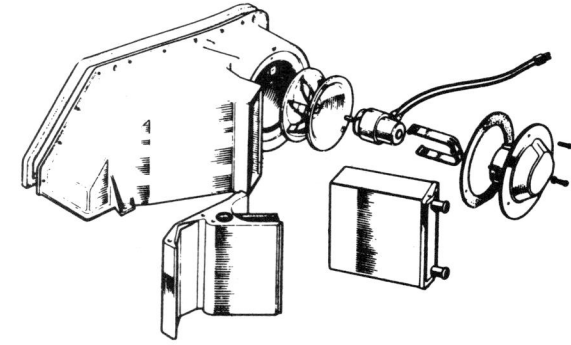

Fig. 12.16 Heater unit blower motor and radiator (Sec 33)

2 Detach the battery terminals.
3 Slide the seats back to gain access to the rearmost console retaining screws on each side. Unscrew and remove each of the screws.
4 Lift the console carefully, sufficient to disconnect the wires to the cigarette lighter and/or clock. Detach the wire retaining clips and lift the console clear.
5 Refit in the reverse order of removal.

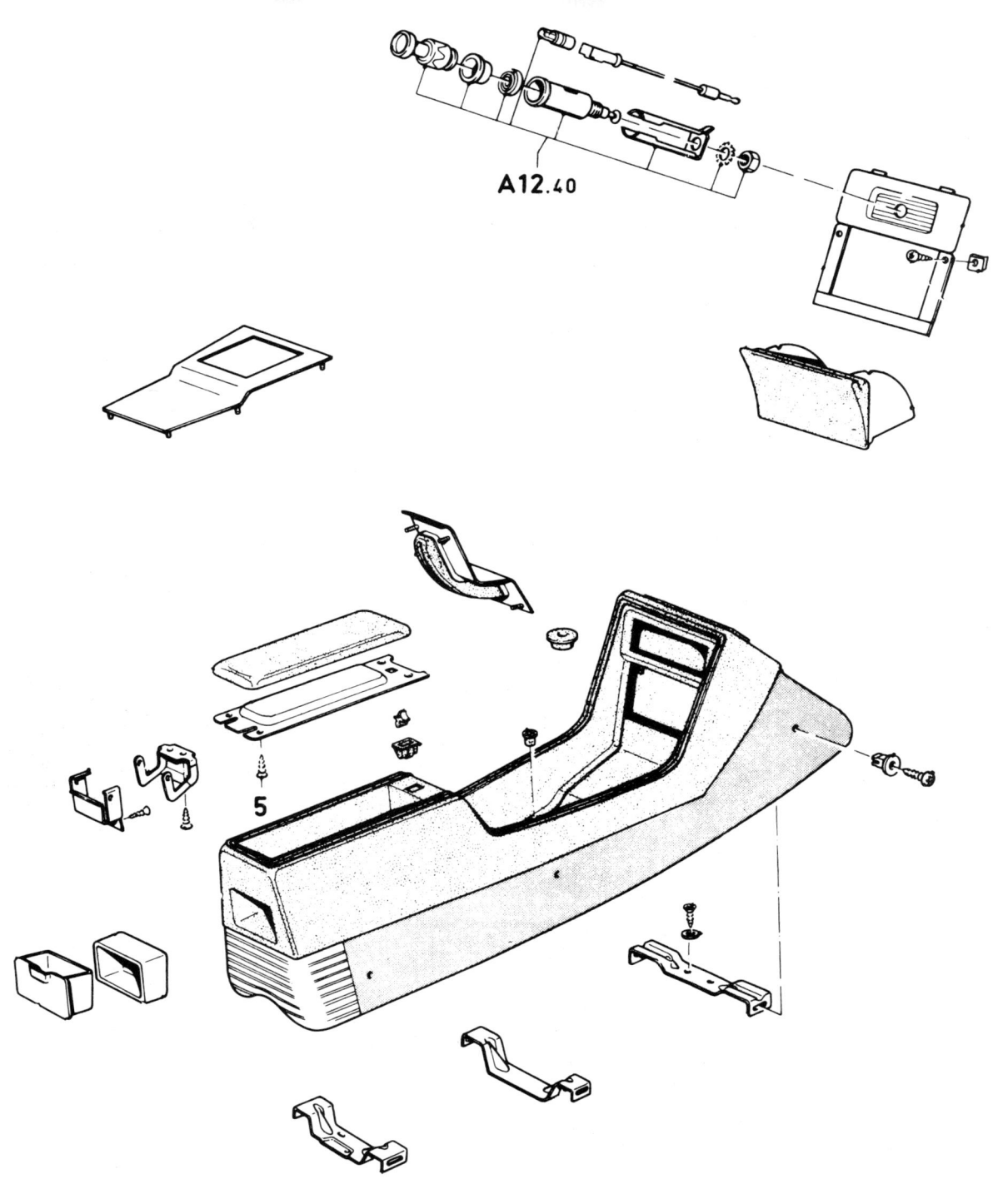

Fig. 12.17a Centre console showing the attachments (see pages 254 and 255 for alternative types) (Sec. 34)

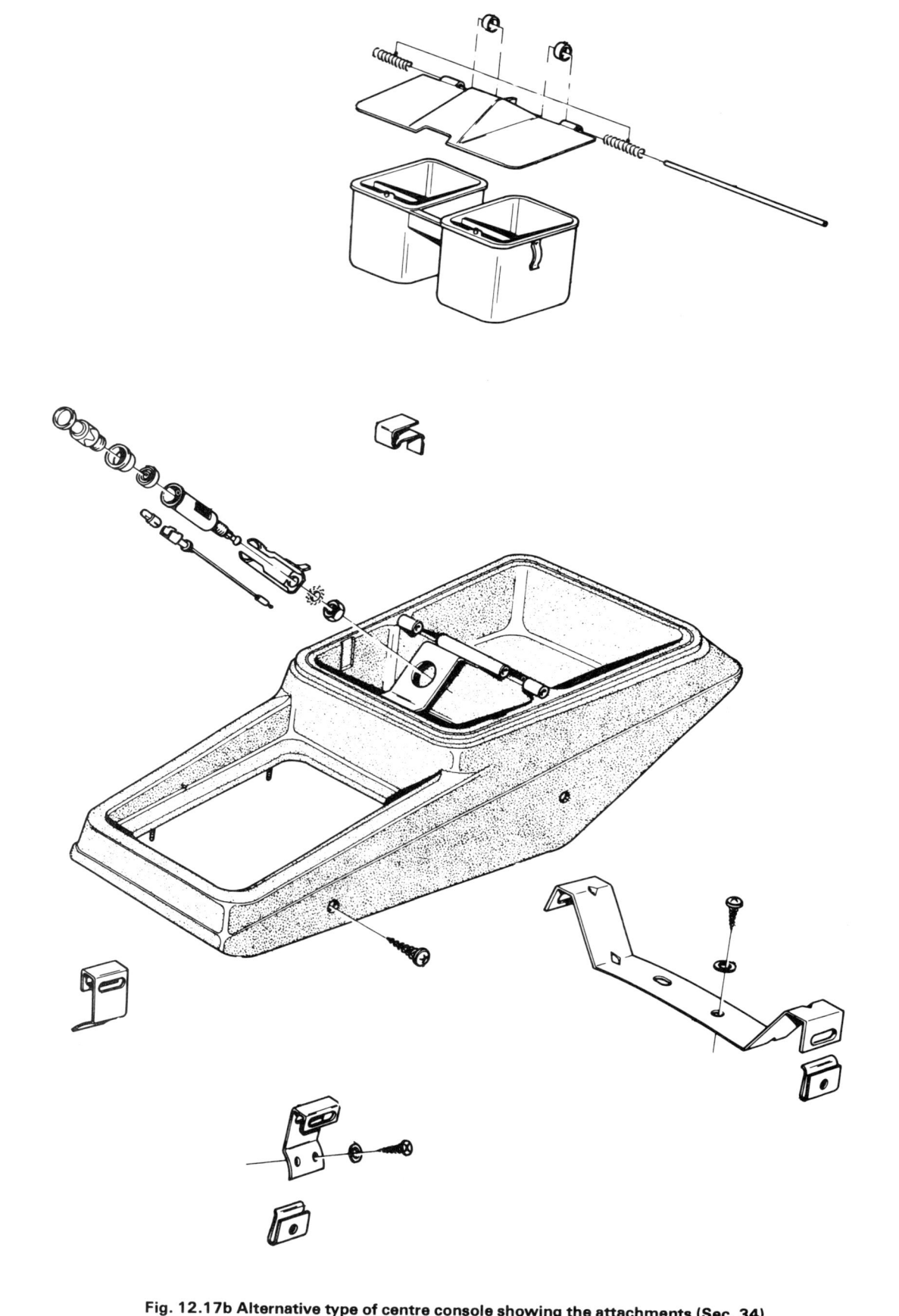

Fig. 12.17b Alternative type of centre console showing the attachments (Sec. 34)

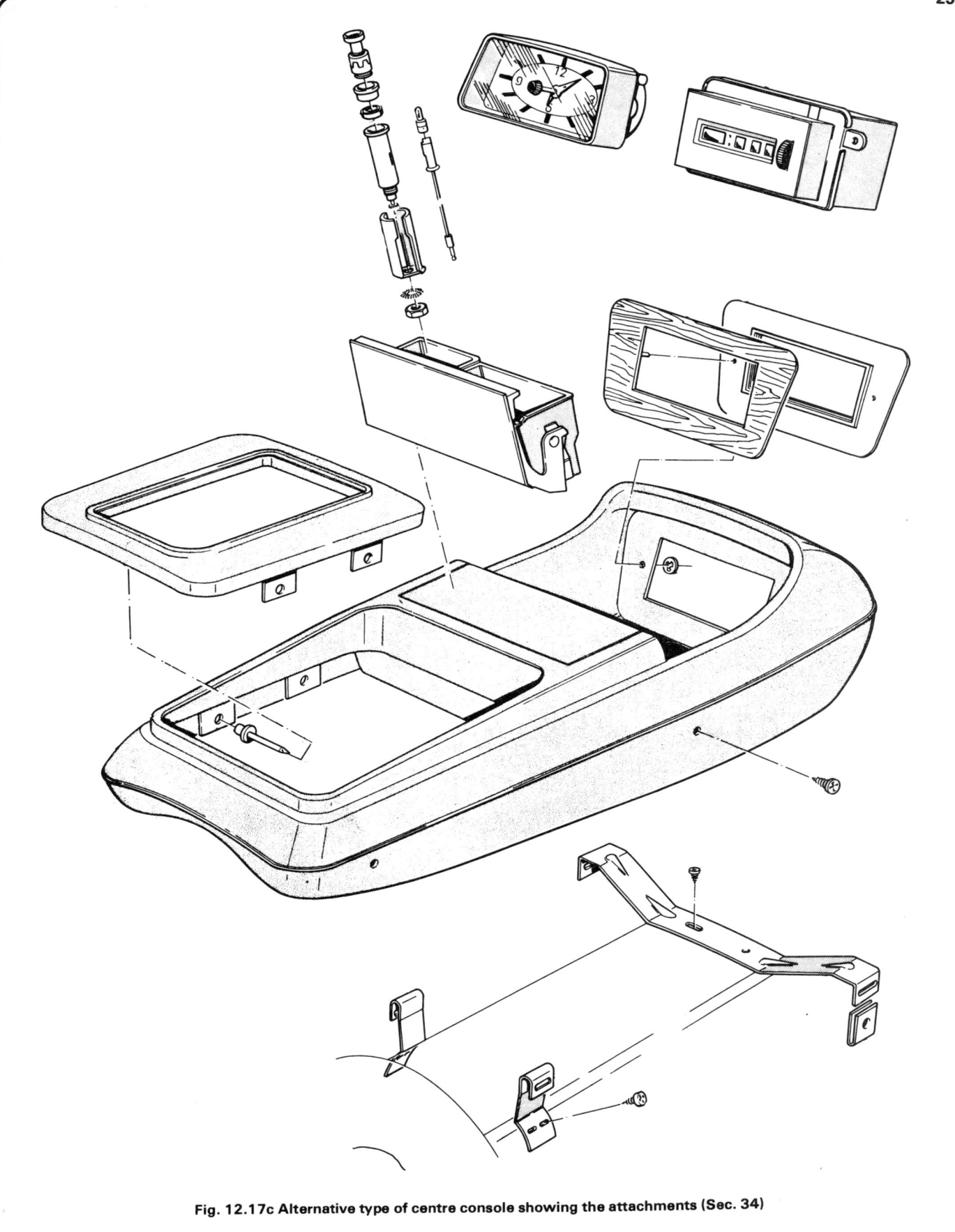

Fig. 12.17c Alternative type of centre console showing the attachments (Sec. 34)

Chapter 13 Supplement

Contents

Introduction	1
Specifications	2
Engine	3
2.0 litre in-line ohc economy engine package	
Carburation	4
Economy carburettor	
Ignition system	5
Static ignition timing – V4 and V6 models	
Propeller shaft	6
Modified centre bearing and revised driveline angle	
Braking system	7
Hydraulic system – bleeding	
Electrical system	8
Headlamp washer system	
Suspension and steering	9
Suspension upper and lower balljoints – renewal	
Tyre sizes and pressures	
Wheel alignment changes	
Front wheel bearings – revised adjustment procedure	
Power steering system – modified type	
Bodywork	10
Rear door lock reinforcement plate	

1 Introduction

The information included in this Chapter became available too late for inclusion in the main body of the manual, which had gone to press. Owners are requested to read through this Chapter, and to note any modifications and revisions which may affect the particular operations or adjustments which they are carrying out, before referring to the relevant text in earlier Chapters.

2 Specifications

Engine

2.0 litre in-line ohc economy engine
Cam lift (inlet and exhaust) .... 0.235 in (5.964 mm)

Carburation

Weber carburettor
(Fitted to 1974 Consul with 2.0 litre in-line ohc engine)
Carburettor numbers .... 71HF9510ED and 71HF9510DD
Throttle barrel diameter 32/36
Venturi diameter 26/27
Main jet 140/140
Idling speed .... 680 to 720 rpm
Float level:
    metal float .... 1.61 ± 0.01 in (41 ± 0.25 mm)
    plastic float .... 1.38 ± 0.01 in (35 ± 0.25 mm)
Float stroke .... 0.49 ± 0.06 in (12.5 ± 1.5 mm)
Choke plate pull down .... 0.26 ± 0.01 in (6.5 ± 0.25 mm)
De-choke setting .... 0.07 ± 0.01 in (1.75 ± 0.25 mm)

Motorcraft carburettor
(Fitted to 2.0 litre in-line ohc economy engine with manual transmission)
Carburettor number 76HF9510KAA
Throttle barrel diameter 34
Venturi diameter 25
Main jet 130
Automatic choke pull down .... 0.16 in (4.0 mm)
De-choke setting .... 0.21 in (5.3 mm)
V-mark setting .... 0.20 in (5.0 mm)
Fast idle speed .... 2000 rpm
Vacuum piston link hole .... Outer
Thermostatic spring slot .... Centre
Accelerator pump stroke .... 0.11 in (2.8 mm)
Slow running (idle) speed .... 800 rpm
CO percentage 1.5
Float level setting .... 1.14 in (29.0 mm)

Chapter 13 Supplement

Ignition system

2.0 litre in-line ohc economy engine
Spark plug type .... Motorcraft BRF42

Rear axle
(Used in conjunction with 2.0 litre in-line ohc engine)

Final drive ratio .... 3.64 : 1

Suspension and steering

Front suspension
Castor .... 1° 01' to 2° 46'
Camber .... -0° 25' to 1° 05'
Variation between left-hand and right-hand sides (maximum permissible):
    Castor .... 0.45'
    Camber .... 1° 00'
Front wheel alignment (total toe-in) .... 0.16 in (4.0 mm)

Rear suspension
Toe-in (per wheel) .... 0 to 0.10 in (0 to 2.5 mm)
Camber .... varies according to ride height – see text
Maximum permissible variation left-hand to right-hand sides .... 1° 00'

Tyre sizes and pressures*

Tyre size	Engine size (litres)	Front lbf/in²	Front kgf/cm²	Rear lbf/in²	Rear kgf/cm²
6.45 x 14 PR	V4 2.0	21	1.5	23	1.6
6.95S x 14 4PR	2.0 ohc	23	1.6	24	1.7
	V6 2.5	27	1.9	27	1.9
175SR - 14	V4 2.0	23	1.6	23	1.6
	2.0 ohc	23	1.6	23	1.6
	V6 2.5	24	1.7	24	1.7
	V6 3.0 (auto)	26	1.8	26	1.8
175HR - 14	V6 3.0 (man)	26	1.8	26	1.8
185SR - 14	V4 2.0	21	1.5	21	1.5
	2.0 ohc	21	1.5	21	1.5
	V6 2.5	23	1.6	23	1.6
	V6 3.0 (auto)	24	1.7	24	1.7
185HR - 14	V6 3.0 (man)	24	1.7	24	1.7
195/70HR - 14	V6 3.0	24	1.7	24	1.7

* These pressures are for normal usage (two passengers and luggage) and normal road speeds. Pressures should be increased for fully laden operation and sustained high cruising speeds.

Torque wrench settings
	lbf ft	kgf m
Swivel joint to stub axle	40	5.5
Swivel joint to suspension arm bolts	24	3.3
Tie-rod to suspension arm	50	6.9
Stabiliser bar to suspension arm	50	6.9

3 Engine

2.0 litre in-line ohc economy engine package

1 As from February 1976, an economy version of the 2.0 litre in-line ohc engine became available for the Granada.
2 Engines of this type can be identified by the code letters KAA stamped on the float chamber of the carburettor which is of Motorcraft type.
3 The engine number plate carries the identification letters NS.
4 With this type of engine, other modifications have also been carried out and these include:

    a) Inlet manifold modified for new carburettor.
    b) Changed valve lift details on camshaft.
    c) Modified rear axle ratio.
    d) Revised ignition advance curves (static advance remains unchanged)

5 Procedures relating to this particular engine remain as detailed in Chapter 1 Part B.

4 Carburation

Economy carburettor

The servicing operations for this type of carburettor are identical to those described for the Ford carburettor in Chapter 3, but reference must be made to the Specification at the beginning of this Chapter for details of calibration and setting.

5 Ignition system

Static ignition timing – V4 and V6 models

The timing mark representation for V4 and V6 models is as shown

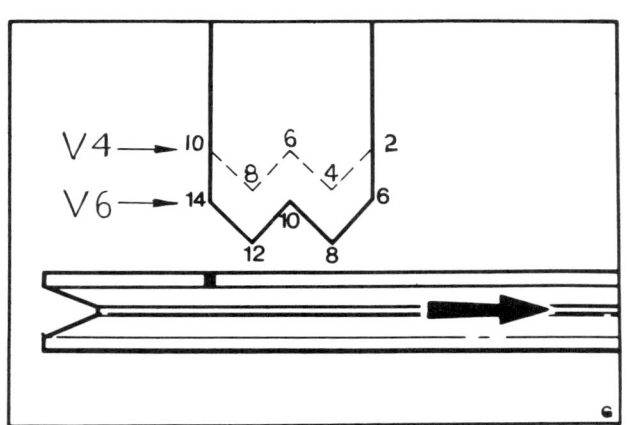

Fig. 13.1 Ignition timing pointer showing location of 14° BTDC mark (V6) or 10° BTDC (V4) (Sec. 5)

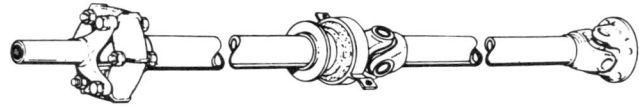

Fig. 13.2 Propeller shaft without handbrake cable guides on centre bearing housing (Sec. 6)

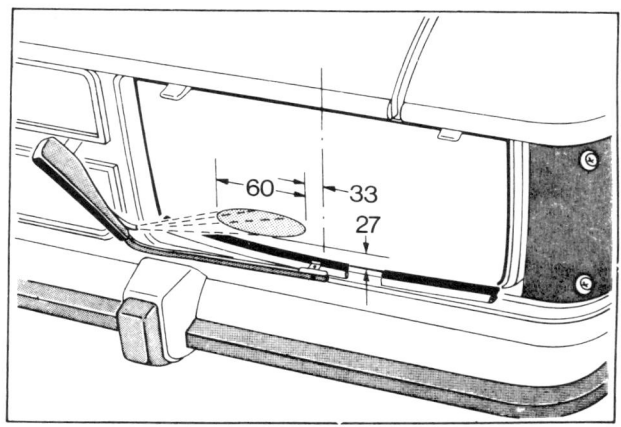

Fig. 13.3 Driveline angles (propeller shaft without handbrake cable guides) (Sec. 6)

Angle B must be greater than angle A by 1° 15' ± 0° 30'

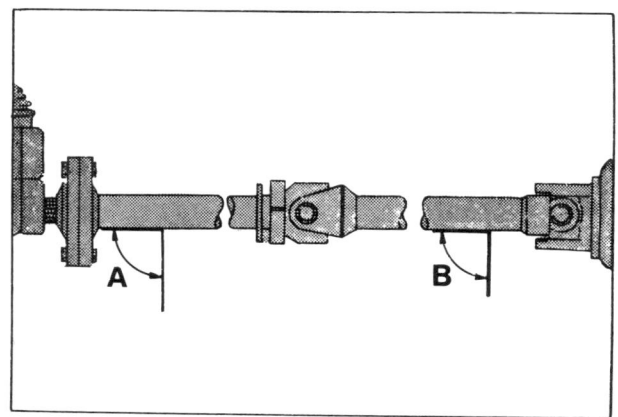

Fig. 13.4 Washer jet pattern – headlamp lower park wiper arm (dimensions in mm) (Sec. 8)

Chapter 13 Supplement

in Fig. 13.1. Note that the representation is different for each engine type.

6 Propeller shaft

Modified centre bearing and revised driveline angle

1 Commencing February 1975, vehicles fitted with a front flexible coupling on the propeller shaft no longer have the handbrake cable guides incorporated in the centre bearing housing. These guides are now moved to the underside of the floor.
2 With this type of propeller shaft, the rear angle of the shaft must be greater than the one at the front as shown in Fig. 13.3. Adjustment of the driveline angle is carried out by varying the shims at the centre bearing housing, but as these angles are difficult to measure accurately, it is recommended that the job is left to your Ford dealer who has the necessary setting gauges.

7 Braking system

Hydraulic system – bleeding

1 It is possible that due to the inclined attitude of the rear wheel cylinders, some air may be trapped above the bleed nipple and be very difficult to remove.
2 In cases where a satisfactory brake pedal cannot be obtained, even after following the description given in Chapter 9, Section 2, repeat the bleeding sequence on the rear brakes but kick the brake pedal down vigorously once the bleed nipple has been opened. Tighten the nipple with the pedal held in the fully depressed position.

8 Electrical system

Headlamp washer system

1 Commencing with 1974 models, certain vehicle specifications include a headlamp washer system.
2 The system includes an independent wiper motor, arm/blade assembly and a foot operated switch. Removal and refitting is carried out as follows.
3 Withdraw the multi-pin plug from the wiper motor and then detach the link which connects the wiper motor to the arm/pivot shaft.
4 Remove the wiper motor with bracket.
5 Disconnect the hoses from the nozzles on the arms. Remove the arms.
6 Remove the radiator grille.
7 Detach the link from both arm and pivot shaft assemblies and remove it.
8 Remove the arm/pivot shaft assemblies and their brackets and

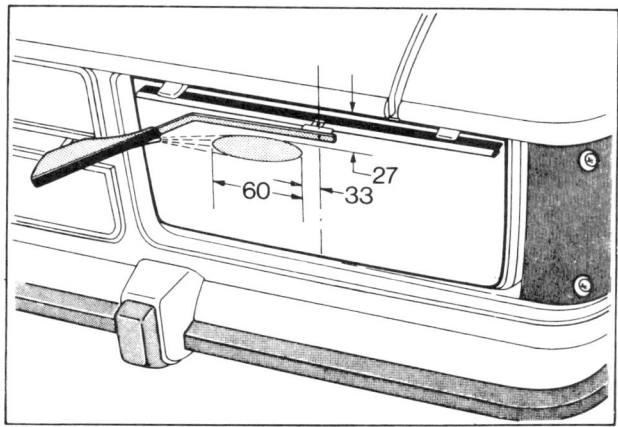

Fig. 13.5 Washer jet pattern – headlamp upper park wiper arm (dimensions in mm) (Sec. 8)

separate the components.
9 Refitting is a reverse of the removal procedure.
10 After installing the washer components, the spray nozzles should be adjusted. On some models, the wiper blades park at the bottom of the headlamp glass, on others at the top.
11 Adjust the nozzles by careful bending so that the water jet strikes the glass as shown in Fig. 13.4 or Fig. 13.5 according to the type of installation.

9 Suspension and steering

Suspension upper and lower balljoints – renewal

1 Repair kits are now available to enable the suspension balljoints to be renewed in situ. Previously, wear in the balljoints could only be rectified by renewal of the complete suspension arm.
2 Raise the front of the vehicle and fit axle stands.
3 Remove the roadwheel and support the suspension lower arm by placing a jack under it.
4 Cut off the heads of the three rivets which hold the upper balljoint assembly to the suspension arm. Take care not to damage the suspension arm. Drill the head partially out if necessary and then use a sharp cold chisel as shown in Fig. 13.6.
5 Unscrew the nut from the ballstud and, using a suitable tool, separate the balljoint from the eye of the stub axle and discard it.
6 Install the new balljoint so that the fixing bolts supplied have their heads below the suspension arm as shown in Fig.13.7.
7 Tighten the self-locking nuts to the specified torque.
8 Reconnect the balljoint to the stub axle and tighten the nut to the specified torque. If the split pin hole is not aligned with the slots in the nut, tighten the nut further, do not unscrew it. Fit a new split pin.
9 Removal of the lower balljoint is carried out in a similar way, first chiselling off the heads of the two securing rivets as shown in Fig. 13.8.
10 Unscrew and remove the two nuts and bolts which hold the tie bar and stabiliser bar to the lower suspension arm.
11 Using the extractor, separate the balljoint from the eye of the stub axle.
12 Install the new balljoint using the two bolts and self-locking nuts supplied and making sure that the bolt heads are located on the top surface of the suspension arm as shown in Fig. 13.9. Tighten the nuts to the specified torque.
13 Connect the balljoint to the stub axle and fit the nut, tighten to the specified torque and slightly more if necessary to be able to insert a new split pin.
14 Connect the tie bar and the stabiliser bar to the suspension arm and tighten the bolts to the specified torque.
15 Refit the roadwheel and lower the vehicle to the ground.

Tyre sizes and pressures

16 Some instances have arisen of heavy steering being encountered, possibly due to the fitting of unsuitable tyres or maintaining the pressures at too low a level.
17 The tyres and pressures listed in the Specifications Section of this Chapter should be used as the most suitable recommendations.

Wheel alignment changes
Front suspension
18 As from March 1976, the steering and front wheel alignment angles have been modified to improve the steering and roadholding and to reduce tyre wear. Refer to the Specifications Section at the beginning of this Chapter.

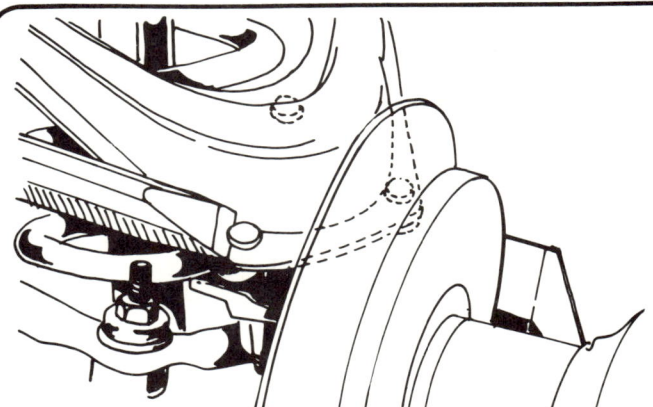

Fig. 13.6 Cutting off upper swivel balljoint rivet on front suspension (Sec. 9)

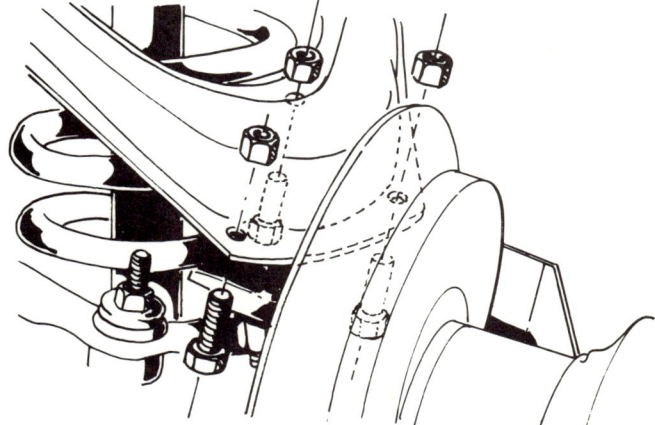

Fig. 13.7 Upper swivel balljoint kit bolts and nuts (Sec. 9)

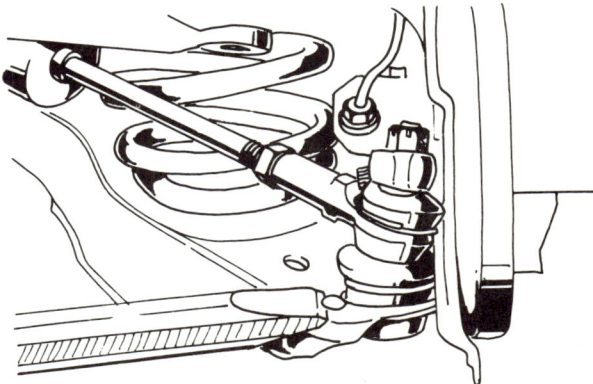

Fig. 13.8 Cutting off lower swivel balljoint rivet on front suspension (Sec. 9)

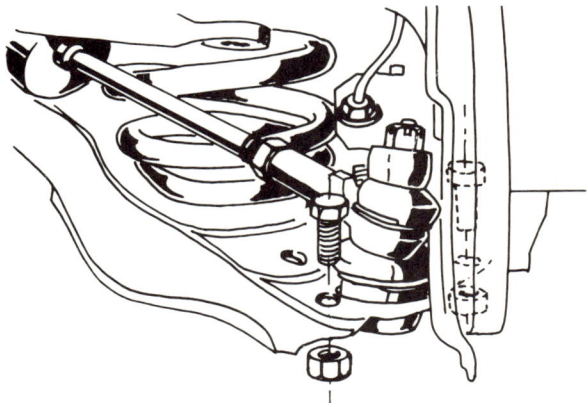

Fig. 13.9 Lower swivel balljoint kit bolts and nuts (Sec. 9)

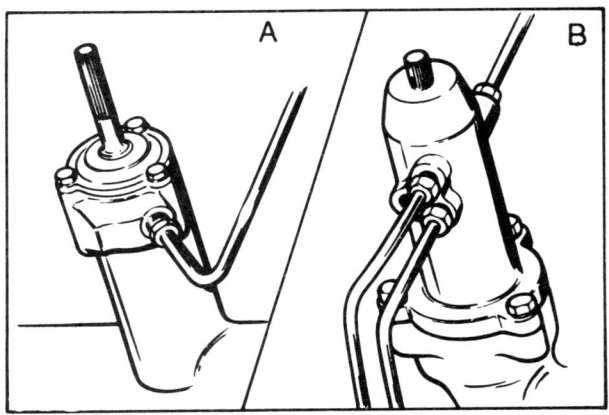

Fig. 13.10 Power steering gear identification (Sec. 9)

A – Axial valve type   B – Rotary valve type

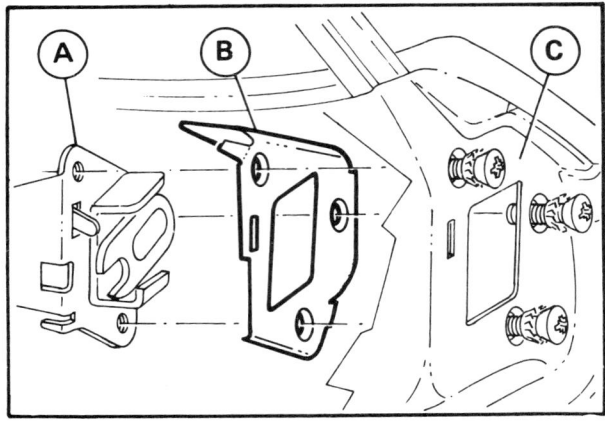

Fig. 13.11 Door lock reinforcement plate (February 1976 on) (Sec. 10)

A – Lock   B – Reinforcement plate   C – Door panel

Rear suspension

19 Revised camber angles are specified for later models, and these are dependent on the measured ride height of the car and on the type of bolts used to hold the rear axle pinion extension housing to the subframe. If for any reason the rear wheel geometry needs checking or adjusting in any way, it is recommended that this work is entrusted to a local Ford dealer, who will have the equipment necessary for this to be done accurately.

Front wheel bearings – revised adjustment procedure

20 A simpler adjustment procedure is now recommended for owners who do not have the facilities for accurately measuring front hub endfloat (refer to Chapter 11, Section 3).
21 Raise the front of the vehicle and remove the hub cap.
22 Prise off the dust cap and extract the split pin and nut retainer.
23 Slacken the hub retaining nut and, while rotating the hub, tighten the nut to a torque of 27 lbf ft. (3.7 kgfm).
24 Now unscrew the nut through 120° (two flats), fit the nut retainer, a new split pin and the dust cap.
25 Refit the hub cap and lower the vehicle to the ground.

Power steering system – modified type

26 Granada vehicles equipped with power steering and built after January 1976 are fitted with an axial valve type assembly instead of the previously fitted rotary valve type.
27 Dismantling and adjustment are best left to your Ford dealer due to the need for special tools and equipment but the difference in appearance of the two types of power steering assembly is shown for information purposes in Fig. 13.10.

10 Bodywork

Rear door lock reinforcement plate

As from February 1976, the rear door locks of four-door model Granada vehicles are fitted with a modified reinforcement plate which is located between the lock and panel (See Fig 13.11). It is held in position by the lock screws instead of being welded to the door panel as was the case with earlier vehicles.

Metric conversion tables

Inches	Decimals	Millimetres	Millimetres to Inches		Inches to Millimetres	
			mm	Inches	Inches	mm
1/64	0.015625	0.3969	0.01	0.00039	0.001	0.0254
1/32	0.03125	0.7937	0.02	0.00079	0.002	0.0508
3/64	0.046875	1.1906	0.03	0.00118	0.003	0.0762
1/16	0.0625	1.5875	0.04	0.00157	0.004	0.1016
5/64	0.078125	1.9844	0.05	0.00197	0.005	0.1270
3/32	0.09375	2.3812	0.06	0.00236	0.006	0.1524
7/64	0.109375	2.7781	0.07	0.00276	0.007	0.1778
1/8	0.125	3.1750	0.08	0.00315	0.008	0.2032
9/64	0.140625	3.5719	0.09	0.00354	0.009	0.2286
5/32	0.15625	3.9687	0.1	0.00394	0.01	0.254
11/64	0.171875	4.3656	0.2	0.00787	0.02	0.508
3/16	0.1875	4.7625	0.3	0.01181	0.03	0.762
13/64	0.203125	5.1594	0.4	0.01575	0.04	1.016
7/32	0.21875	5.5562	0.5	0.01969	0.05	1.270
15/64	0.234375	5.9531	0.6	0.02362	0.06	1.524
1/4	0.25	6.3500	0.7	0.02756	0.07	1.778
17/64	0.265625	6.7469	0.8	0.03150	0.08	2.032
9/32	0.28125	7.1437	0.9	0.03543	0.09	2.286
19/64	0.296875	7.5406	1	0.03937	0.1	2.54
5/16	0.3125	7.9375	2	0.07874	0.2	5.08
21/64	0.328125	8.3344	3	0.11811	0.3	7.62
11/32	0.34375	8.7312	4	0.15748	0.4	10.16
23/64	0.359375	9.1281	5	0.19685	0.5	12.70
3/8	0.375	9.5250	6	0.23622	0.6	15.24
25/64	0.390625	9.9219	7	0.27559	0.7	17.78
13/32	0.40625	10.3187	8	0.31496	0.8	20.32
27/64	0.421875	10.7156	9	0.35433	0.9	22.86
7/16	0.4375	11.1125	10	0.39370	1	25.4
29/64	0.453125	11.5094	11	0.43307	2	50.8
15/32	0.46875	11.9062	12	0.47244	3	76.2
31/64	0.48375	12.3031	13	0.51181	4	101.6
1/2	0.5	12.7000	14	0.55118	5	127.0
33/64	0.515625	13.0969	15	0.59055	6	152.4
17/32	0.53125	13.4937	16	0.62992	7	177.8
35/64	0.546875	13.8906	17	0.66929	8	203.2
9/16	0.5625	14.2875	18	0.70866	9	228.6
37/64	0.578125	14.6844	19	0.74803	10	254.0
19/32	0.59375	15.0812	20	0.78740	11	279.4
39/64	0.609375	15.4781	21	0.82677	12	304.8
5/8	0.625	15.8750	22	0.86614	13	330.2
41/64	0.640625	16.2719	23	0.90551	14	355.6
21/32	0.65625	16.6687	24	0.94488	15	381.0
43/64	0.671875	17.0656	25	0.98425	16	406.4
11/16	0.6875	17.4625	26	1.02362	17	431.8
45/64	0.703125	17.8594	27	1.06299	18	457.2
23/32	0.71875	18.2562	28	1.10236	19	482.6
47/64	0.734375	18.6531	29	1.14173	20	508.0
3/4	0.75	19.0500	30	1.18110	21	533.4
49/64	0.765625	19.4469	31	1.22047	22	558.8
25/32	0.78125	19.8437	32	1.25984	23	584.2
51/64	0.796875	20.2406	33	1.29921	24	609.6
13/16	0.8125	20.6375	34	1.33858	25	635.0
53/64	0.828125	21.0344	35	1.37795	26	660.4
27/32	0.84375	21.4312	36	1.41732	27	685.8
55/64	0.859375	21.8281	37	1.4567	28	711.2
7/8	0.875	22.2250	38	1.4961	29	736.6
57/64	0.890625	22.6219	39	1.5354	30	762.0
29/32	0.90625	23.0187	40	1.5748	31	787.4
59/64	0.921875	23.4156	41	1.6142	32	812.8
15/16	0.9375	23.8125	42	1.6535	33	838.2
61/64	0.953125	24.2094	43	1.6929	34	863.6
31/32	0.96875	24.6062	44	1.7323	35	889.0
63/64	0.984375	25.0031	45	1.7717	36	914.4

Metric Conversion Tables

1 Imperial gallon = 8 Imp pints = 1.20 US gallons = 277.42 cu in = 4.54 litres

1 US gallon = 4 US quarts = 0.83 Imp gallon = 231 cu in = 3.78 litres

1 Litre = 0.21 Imp gallon = 0.26 US gallon = 61.02 cu in = 1000 cc

Miles to Kilometres		Kilometres to Miles	
1	1.61	1	0.62
2	3.22	2	1.24
3	4.83	3	1.86
4	6.44	4	2.49
5	8.05	5	3.11
6	9.66	6	3.73
7	11.27	7	4.35
8	12.88	8	4.97
9	14.48	9	5.59
10	16.09	10	6.21
20	32.19	20	12.43
30	48.28	30	18.64
40	64.37	40	24.85
50	80.47	50	31.07
60	96.56	60	37.28
70	112.65	70	43.50
80	128.75	80	49.71
90	144.84	90	55.92
100	160.93	100	62.14

lbf ft to kgf m		kgf m to lbf ft		lbf/in^2 to kgf/cm^2		kgf/cm^2 to lbf/in^2	
1	0.138	1	7.233	1	0.07	1	14.22
2	0.276	2	14.466	2	0.14	2	28.50
3	0.414	3	21.699	3	0.21	3	42.67
4	0.553	4	28.932	4	0.28	4	56.89
5	0.691	5	36.165	5	0.35	5	71.12
6	0.829	6	43.398	6	0.42	6	85.34
7	0.967	7	50.631	7	0.49	7	99.56
8	1.106	8	57.864	8	0.56	8	113.79
9	1.244	9	65.097	9	0.63	9	128.00
10	1.382	10	72.330	10	0.70	10	142.23
20	2.765	20	144.660	20	1.41	20	284.47
30	4.147	30	216.990	30	2.11	30	426.70

Index

A

Accelerator – 103
Air cleaner – 99
Alternator
    brushes – 183
    description – 181
    fault finding – 183
    maintenance – 181
    removal and refitting – 183
    special procedures – 183
Antifreeze mixture – 94
Automatic transmission
    description – 145
    downshift cable – 148
    fault finding – 150
    fluid level – 145
    intermediate band – 149
    low and reverse band – 150
    maintenance – 145
    removal and refitting – 145
    selector cable – 148
    selector lever assembly – 147, 148
    selector rod – 148
    specifications – 128
    starter inhibitor switch – 148
    torque wrench settings – 129
Auxiliary shaft (4 cyl in-line)
    refitting – 77
    removal – 62
    sprocket refitting – 79

B

Balance shaft (V4)
    reassembly – 35
    removal – 30
Battery
    charging – 181
    electrolyte replenishment – 181
    maintenance – 180
    removal and refitting – 180
Big-end bearings
    reassembly (V4) – 37
    reassembly (V6) – 44
    removal (4 cyl in-line) – 65
    removal (V4 and V6) – 29
    renovation (4 cyl in-line) – 32, 71
    renovation (V4 and V6) – 32

Bodywork
    centre console – 252
    description – 238
    hinges – 240
    load space trim panel – 251
    locks – 240, 242, 243, 244, 245
    maintenance – 238, 239, 240
    repair, major damage – 240
    repair, minor damage – 239
    sliding roof – 251
Bonnet – 242, 243, 244
Boot – 244, 245
Braking system
    bleeding hydraulic system – 164, 258
    description – 164
    differential valve assembly – 174, 176
    drum brake backplate – 170
    drum brake shoes – 167
    drum brake wheel cylinder – 169
    fault diagnosis – 177
    flexible hose – 164
    front brake caliper – 165
    front brake disc and hub – 166
    front brake pads – 164
    handbrake – 170, 172
    hydraulic pipes and hoses – 174
    master cylinder – 171
    pedal – 172
    specifications – 163
    torque wrench settings – 163
    vacuum servo unit – 172, 173

C

Cam followers (4 cyl in-line)
    refitting – 81
    renovation – 71
Camshaft
    drivebelt refitting (4 cyl in-line) – 83
    drivebelt tensioner refitting (4 cyl in-line) – 83
    reassembly (V4) – 35
    reassembly (V6) – 47
    refitting (4 cyl in-line) – 81
    removal (4 cyl in-line) – 67
    removal (V4 and V6) – 28
    renovation (4 cyl in-line) – 71
    renovation (V4 and V6) – 33

Index

Carburettor dismantling and reassembly – 103, 106, 110
Carburettor (Ford)
    accelerator pump adjustment – 109
    choke and fast idle adjustment – 109
    description – 103
    dismantling and reassembly – 106
    economy – 257
    float level height adjustment – 110
    removal and refitting – 106
    slow running adjustment – 109
Carburettor (Weber)
    description – 104
    dismantling and reassembly – 110
    economy – 257
    float level height adjustment – 112
    removal and refitting – 110
    slow running adjustment – 112
Carpets – 239
Cigarette lighter – 197, 200
Clock, electric – 197
Clutch
    adjustment – 124
    cable – 127
    description – 124
    dismantling – 125
    faults – 127
    pedal – 127
    refitting – 126
    refitting (4cyl in-line) – 79
    release bearing – 127
    removal – 124
    specifications – 124
    torque wrench settings – 124
Condenser – 116
Connecting rods
    reassembly (4 cyl in-line) – 75
    reassembly (V4) – 37
    reassembly (V6) – 44
    reassembly to crankshaft (4 cyl in-line) – 77
    removal (4 cyl in-line) – 65
    removal (V4 and V6) – 29
    renovation – 32, 71
Contact breaker points – 116
Cooling system
    description – 86
    draining – 88
    fault diagnosis – 95
    filling – 89
    flushing – 88
    specifications – 86
    torque wrench settings – 86
Crankcase ventilation system (4 cyl in-line) – 69
Crankcase ventilation system (V4 and V6) – 30
Crankshaft
    reassembly (V4) – 35
    reassembly (V6) – 44
    refitting (4 cyl in-line) – 74
    removal (4 cyl in-line) – 66
    removal (V4 and V6) – 29
    renovation – 31, 71
Crankshaft drivebelt removal – engine in car (4 cyl in-line) – 67
Crankshaft oil seals – reassembly (V6) – 47
Crankshaft pulley
    reassembly (V4) – 41
    reassembly (V6) – 47
    refitting (4 cyl in-line) – 79
    removal (4 cyl in-line) – 65
    removal (V4 and V6) – 28
Crankshaft rear oil seal
    refitting (4 cyl in-line) – 77
    removal (V4 and V6) – 29
Crankshaft sprocket
    refitting (4 cyl in-line) – 79
    removal (4 cyl in-line) – 65
Cylinder bores renovation – 32, 71

Cylinder head
    refitting (4 cyl in-line) – 81
    removal – engine in car (4 cyl in-line) – 62
    removal – engine on bench (4 cyl in-line) – 62
Cylinder heads
    decarbonisation – 34, 71
    dismantling (V4 and V6) – 27
    reassembly (V4) – 41
    reassembly (V6) – 49
    removal (V4 and V6) – 27

D

Decarbonisation – 34, 71
Distributor
    dismantling (Ford) – 117
    dismantling (Bosch) – 118
    lubrication – 117
    reassembly (Ford) – 120
    reassembly (Bosch) – 120
    removal and refitting – 117
    repair – 120
Doors
    front – 241
    glass and regulator – 242
    lock – 242, 260
    outer belt weatherstrip – 242
    rattles – 241
    rear – 241
    striker plate – 241
    trim – 241

E

Electrical system
    clock – 197
    description – 180
    fault diagnosis – 202
    flasher circuit – 186
    specifications – 178
    torque wrench settings – 179
    voltage regulator – 196
    wiring diagrams – 206—217
    wiring loom – 204
Engine (4 cyl in-line)
    components examination for wear – 31, 71
    description – 58
    dismantling – 62
    economy engine package – 257
    fault diagnosis – 52, 85
    operations requiring engine removal – 60
    operations with engine in place – 60
    reassembly – 74
    removal method – 60
    removal without transmission – 60
    removal with transmission – 62
    specifications – 55, 256
Engine (V4 and V6)
    ancillary components reassembly (V6) – 50
    components examination for wear – 31
    description – 20
    dismantling – 26
    end plate reassembly (V4) – 37
    end plate reassembly (V6) – 47
    fault diagnosis – 52
    front cover reassembly (V4) – 37
    front cover reassembly (V6) – 47
    operations requiring engine removal – 22
    operations with engine in place – 22
    rear cover reassembly (V6) – 47
    rear plate reassembly (V4) – 41
    reassembly, general – 34
    reassembly (V4) – 35
    reassembly (V6) – 44

Index

refitting without transmission (V6) – 50
refitting with transmission (V6) – 51
removal (automatic transmission) – 26
removal methods – 22
removal with manual gearbox – 24
removal without transmission – 22
specifications – 15
start-up after overhaul – 52
torque wrench settings – 20
Exhaust emission control description – 99
Exhaust system – 113

F

Facia crash pad – 251
Fan
　belt – 93
　overhaul – 93
Fault diagnosis
　automatic transmission – 150
　braking system – 177
　clutch – 127
　cooling system – 95
　electrical system – 202
　engine – 52, 85
　fuel system – 114
　gearbox (manual) – 150
　ignition system – 122
　propeller shaft – 154
　rear axle – 162
　steering – 237
　suspension – 237
Flywheel
　reassembly (V4) – 41
　reassembly (V6) – 47
　refitting (4 cyl in-line) – 79
　removal (4 cyl in-line) – 65
　removal (V4 and V6) – 28
　ring gear renovation – 34, 71
Fuel gauge – 196, 200
Fuel gauge sender unit – 102
Fuel line filter – 103
Fuel pump
　description – 100
　overhaul – 102
　removal and refitting – 100
　servicing – 100
　testing – 101
Fuel system
　description – 99
　fault diagnosis – 114
　specifications – 96, 256
　torque wrench settings – 98
Fuel tank – 102
Fuses – 200

G

Gearbox (manual)
　description – 129
　dismantling – 131
　inspection – 139
　reassembly – 139
　removal and refitting – 129
　specifications – 128
　torque wrench settings – 128
Gudgeon pins
　removal (4 cyl in-line) – 67
　removal (V4 and V6) – 29
　renovation – 32, 71

H

Heater – 251, 252

Headlamp washer system – 258
Horn – 190
Hub, front – 221, 260
Hub bearings, front – 220, 221

I

Ignition switch – 198
Ignition system
　description – 116
　fault finding – 122
　specifications – 115, 257
　timing – 122, 257
Instrument cluster – 196, 198, 200
Instruments – 195
Intermediate plate (V4 and V6) –
　removal – 28

J

Jacking – 10

L

Lights
　auxiliary – 193, 194
　fog – 192, 193
　front direction indicator – 192
　front side – 192
　headlamps – 190, 191
　interior – 195
　number plate – 195
　rear – 194, 195
Lubricants, recommended – 14
Lubrication chart – 14
Lubrication system (4 cyl in-line) – 69
Lubrication system (V4 and V6) – 30

M

Main bearings
　reassembly (V4) – 35
　reassembly (V6) – 44
　removal (4 cyl in-line) – 66
　removal (V4 and V6) – 29
　renovation (4 cyl in-line) – 32, 71
　renovation (V4 and V6) – 32
Maintenance, routine – 8
Manifold, inlet
　reassembly (V4) – 41
　reassembly (V6) – 49
Manual gearbox – see 'Gearbox (manual)'

O

Oil filter
　removal and refitting (4 cyl in-line) – 31, 71
　removal and refitting (V4 and V6) – 31
Oil pressure gauge – 196
Oil pump
　dismantling and reassembly (4 cyl in-line) – 69
　overhaul (V4 and V6) – 30
　reassembly (V4) – 35
　reassembly (V6) – 47
　refitting (4 cyl in-line) – 77
　removal (4 cyl in-line) – 65
　removal (V4 and V6) – 29

P

Piston rings
    reassembly (V4) – 37
    reassembly (V6) – 44
    refitting (4 cyl in-line) – 75
    removal (4 cyl in-line) – 69
    removal (V4 and V6) – 29
    renovation (4 cyl in-line) – 32, 71
    renovation (V4 and V6) – 32

Pistons
    reassembly (4 cyl in-line) – 75
    reassembly (V4) – 37
    reassembly (V6) – 44
    refitting (4 cyl in-line) – 76
    removal (4 cyl in-line) – 65
    removal (V4 and V6) – 29
    renovation (4 cyl in-line) – 32, 71
    renovation (V4 and V6) – 32

Propeller shaft
    centre bearing – 152, 258
    description – 151
    fault diagnosis – 154
    Hardy flexible disc – 153
    modified – 258
    removal and refitting – 151
    specifications – 151
    torque wrench settings – 151
    universal joints – 154

R

Radiator – 89
Radiator grille – 249
Rear axle
    description – 155
    fault diagnosis – 162
    final drive, overhaul – 157
    final drive, removal and refitting – 155
    specifications – 155, 257
    torque wrench settings – 155

Rocker gear (V4 and V6)
    dismantling – 27
    renovation – 34

Routine maintenance – 8

S

Spare parts, buying – 5
Spark plugs – 122
Speedometer – 196, 200
Starter motor
    description – 183
    M35J – 185
    2M100 – 185, 186

Steering
    column – 229
    description – 219
    fault diagnosis – 237
    front wheel alignment – 228, 259
    gear, rack and pinion – 229, 231, 233
    lubrication – 228
    power assisted – 233, 236, 237, 260
    rack rubber gaiter – 233
    specifications – 218
    torque wrench settings – 219
    track rod end – 233
    wheel – 228

Sump
    inspection (4 cyl in-line) – 71
    reassembly (V4) – 41
    reassembly (V6) – 47
    refitting (4 cyl in-line) – 79

    removal (4 cyl in-line) – 65
    removal (V4 and V6) – 28

Suspension
    axle (front) – 221, 222, 223
    axle half shaft (rear) – 227
    axle (rear) – 224
    balljoints renewal – 259
    bump rubber (rear) – 227
    coil spring (rear) – 226
    description – 219
    fault diagnosis – 237
    front rubber insulator (rear) – 226
    lower arm (front) – 223
    lower arm (rear) – 226
    rear – 224, 260
    rear rubber insulator – 227
    shock absorbers (front) – 224
    shock absorbers (rear) – 226
    specifications – 218, 257
    stabilizer bar – 224
    stub axle (front) – 223
    stub axle (rear) – 227
    tie bar – 224
    torque wrench settings – 219, 257

Switches – 198, 200

T

Tailgate – 245, 248
Tappets (V4 and V6)
    removal – 28
    renovation – 33

Temperature gauge – 94
Thermostat
    housing, refitting (4 cyl in-line) – 83
    housing, removal (4 cyl in-line) – 67
    removal, testing and refitting – 90

Timing cover (4 cyl in-line)
    refitting – 77
    removal – 65

Timing gear and cover (V4 and V6), removal – 28
Timing gears
    reassembly (V4) – 37
    reassembly (V6) – 47
    renovation (4 cyl in-line) – 71
    renovation (V4 and V6) – 34

Tools – 11
Towing – 10
Tyre pressures – 257
Tyre sizes – 257

U

Universal joints – 154
Upholstery – 239

V

Valve clearances (4 cyl in-line) checking and adjustment – 84
Valve guides (4 cyl in-line) inspection – 71
Valve rocker clearances
    adjustment (V4) – 43
    adjustment (V6) – 49

Valves
    dismantling (V4 and V6) – 27
    reassembly (V4) – 41
    reassembly (V6) – 49
    refitting (4 cyl in-line) – 81
    removal (4 cyl in-line) – 67
    renovation – 33, 71

Vehicle identification numbers – 5

W

Water pump
   overhaul – 91
   refitting (4 cyl in-line) – 79, 90
   removal and refitting – 90
Windows
   rear – 248
   rear quarter – 248
   tailgate – 249
Windscreen glass – 240
Windscreen washer – 189
Windscreen wiper – 186, 187, 188
Windscreen wiper (rear) – 189
Wiring diagrams – 206—217
Wiring loom – 204

Printed by
Haynes Publishing Group
Sparkford Yeovil Somerset
England